Digital Health: Telemedicine and Beyond

Digital Health

Telemedicine and Beyond

Edited by

Dipu Patel
Department of PA Studies, University of Pittsburgh,
Pittsburgh, United States

ELSEVIER

ACADEMIC PRESS
An imprint of Elsevier

Academic Press is an imprint of Elsevier
125 London Wall, London EC2Y 5AS, United Kingdom
525 B Street, Suite 1650, San Diego, CA 92101, United States
50 Hampshire Street, 5th Floor, Cambridge, MA 02139, United States

ISBN: 978-0-443-23901-4

For information on all Academic Press publications visit our website at https://www.elsevier.com/books-and-journals

Publisher: Stacy Masucci
Acquisitions Editor: Linda Buschman
Editorial Project Manager: Sam Young
Production Project Manager: Gomathi Sugumar
Cover Designer: Christian Bilbow

Typeset by TNQ Technologies

Dedication

To my Rebel Alliance—Anya and Bodhi

Contents

Contributors

Mercedes Dodge ReDirect Wellness, PLLC, Austin, TX, United States; Orion Behavioral Health Network, Eagle River, AK, United States

Dua Abbas School of Medicine, Yale Univeristy, New Haven, CT, United States

Muhiyadin Aden Augsburg University, Department of PA Studies, Minneapolis, MN, United States

Chelsea Backer Access Sports Medicine and Orthopaedics, Concussion Management, Exeter, NH, United States

Allison Bakowicz University of Pittsburgh, Department of PA Studies, Pittsburgh, PA, United States

Arta Bakshandeh Alignment Health, Orange, CA, United States; USC Keck School of Medicine, Los Angeles, CA, United States; Global Physicians Corps, CA, United States

David Beck School of Health and Rehabilitation Sciences (SHRS), Department of PA Studies, University of Pittsburgh, Pittsburgh, PA, United States

Vanessa Bester Augsburg University, Department of PA Studies, Minneapolis, MN, United States

Sarah Bolander Department of Physician Assistant Studies, Northern Arizona University, Phoenix, AZ, United States

Josh Borgstadt Mesa, AZ, United States

Amy Brown Department of Physician Assistant Studies, University of Pittsburgh, Pittsburgh, PA, United States

Stefan Buttigieg Faculty of Health Sciences, University of Malta, Msida, Malta

Harvey Castro Helpp ai, Chief Medical Intelligence Officer, Dallas, TX, United States

Rachel Irene Cole School of Medical Sciences, Harrogate, TN, United States

Agnes Marcia Compagnone School of Medical Sciences, Harrogate, TN, United States

Jeffrey C. Cooper University of Pittsburgh, Pittsburgh, PA, United States

Christina Davis Department of PA Studies, University of Pittsburgh, Pittsburgh, PA, United States

Amit Kumar Dey Department of Diabetology, Apollo Sugar Clinics, Kolkata, India

Mark DiMauro Multimedia and Digital Culture, University of Pittsburgh-Johnstown, Johnstown, PA, United States

Megan Gallagher University of Pittsburgh, Department of PA Studies, Pittsburgh, PA, United States

Sara Gallo Clinical Insighters Consulting, Health Equity & Transformation Consultant, Denver, CO, United States

Jessica Grasso Department of Surgery, Massachusetts General Hospital, Boston, MA, United States

Carlos Gutierrez Department of Physician Assistant Studies, University of Pittsburgh, Pittsburgh, PA, United States; InclusiCare Medical, Phoenix, AZ, United States; A.T. Still University, Kirksville, MO, United States

Amy Haller University of Pittsburgh, Department of PA Studies, Pittsburgh, PA, United States

Eric Van Hecke Concordia University, Department of PA Studies, St. Paul, MN, United States

Stephanie Jalaba Department of PA Medicine, Michigan State University, East Lansing, MI, United States

Amy Joseph Orrick, Herrington & Sutcliffe LLP, Boston, MA, United States

Aditi U. Joshi Nagamed Digital Consulting, Paris, France

Samarth Kashyap DS Digital Consulting, Digital Evolution and Implementation, Delhi, India

Caitlin Kelley Kelley Medical Consultants LLC/RAIsonance Group, Springfield, TN, United States

Mona Kelley Kelley Medical Consultants LLC/RAIsonance Group, Springfield, TN, United States

Ryan Kingsley Mayo Clinic College of Medicine and Science, Hospital Internal Medicine, Rochester, MN, United States

Derek Leben Tepper School of Business, Carnegie Mellon University, Pittsburgh, PA, United States

Emily Lewis CCRP, CHES, Castle Rock, CO, United States; Digital Care Transformation, UCB Pharma, Smyrna, GA, United States

Hina Mazharuddin PAVMT, Houston, TX, United States

Susan McDiarmid Westfield State University PA Program, Westfield, MA, United States

Thomas Micklewright ORCHA Health, Daresbury, United Kingdom

Nathan Miracle Department of Physician Assistant Studies, University of Pittsburgh, Pittsburgh, PA, United States

Sonia V. Otte California State University - San Bernardino, San Bernardino, CA, United States

Dipu Patel Department of PA Studies, University of Pittsburgh, Pittsburgh, PA, United States

Kathryn Reed Department of Physician Assistant Studies, University of Pittsburgh, Pittsburgh, PA, United States

Ben Reynolds UPMC, Pittsburgh, PA, United States

Christine Rodgers Department of Physician Assistant Studies, University of Pittsburgh, Pittsburgh, PA, United States

Danny Van Roijen EU, Brussels, Belgium

Marty Rosenheck Cognitive Advisors, Evanston, IL, United States

Debra Maria Ruh Ruh Global IMPACT, Rockville, VA, United States

Jeremy Sherer Orrick, Herrington & Sutcliffe LLP, Boston, MA, United States

Lisa Shock Independent Healthcare Consultant

Shambhavi Singh DS Digital Consulting, Digital Health and Research, Mumbai, Maharashtra, India

Michael Robert Smith Chobanian and Avedisian School of Medicine, Boston University, Boston, MA, United States

Whitney Kay Stewart Independant author

Kathryn Werner White Pine Mental Health & Wellness, Prattville, AL, United States; Johnson & Johnson, New Brunswick, NJ, United States

Foreword

A transformative era in medicine—The cognitive age

John Nosta

We are at a unique time in human history. While this notion has become commonplace as a mantra for innovation and transformation, today represents a divergence from even this expression. Across the span of human civilization, there are epochs that redefine the contours of life, marking not just the passage of time, but also the evolution of thought itself. In medicine, this story is particularly profound, chronicling humanity's unending quest to understand and heal the human body. Our journey from the shamanistic rituals of ancient times to the evidence-based practices of today is nothing short of miraculous, a testament to our relentless pursuit of knowledge and the application of this wisdom to those who are ill and injured. Now, as we stand at the threshold of a new age, we are witnessing a transformation that promises to be as significant as any that has come before—an era where the boundaries between artificial intelligence, digital technology, and human expertise are blurring, heralding a new era in healthcare.

The historical canvas of medicine

While some may feel that this "technological inflection point" is singularly disruptive, this new chapter in the annals of medical history is not an isolated phenomenon but the culmination of a continuous process of its own clinical evolution. The story of medicine is rich and diverse, stretching from the herbal remedies of ancient civilizations to the sophisticated genomic therapies of the modern era. Each stage in this journey has been marked by discoveries that have expanded our understanding of the human body and its ailments. The invention of antibiotics brought about a revolution in treating infectious diseases, while the completion of the Human Genome Project ushered in an era where treatments could be tailored to the genetic makeup of the individual. Today, as we embark on this new era, we are witnessing the convergence of different streams of knowledge and technology, creating a synergy that promises to redefine our approach to health and disease.

AI and the transformation of medical practice

The integration of artificial intelligence into the fabric of medical practice is perhaps the most significant hallmark of this new era. AI, with its ability to process and analyze vast amounts of data, is not just augmenting medical practice; it is reshaping it. Technologies like generative pretrained transformers (GPTs) are at the forefront of this revolution. By enhancing diagnostic accuracy, informing treatment plans, and augmenting patient care, these technologies are creating a new paradigm in medicine—a synergy of human expertise and machine intelligence that promises to enhance patient outcomes.

The impact of AI in medicine is profound and multifaceted. It challenges our traditional notions of medical expertise, redefining the role of physicians in the digital age. The physician, once the sole custodian of medical knowledge, is now a part of a broader ecosystem where machine learning models and algorithms play an increasingly significant role. This shift is not about replacing physicians but enhancing their capabilities, enabling them to provide better care by leveraging the power of AI.

The legal and ethical implications of AI in medicine

As AI becomes more embedded in healthcare, it brings with it a host of legal and ethical challenges. The traditional "standards of care," defined by the medical community's collective knowledge and experience, are being reevaluated in the light of these technological advancements. The integration of AI in diagnostics and treatment planning raises critical questions about the liability and definition of malpractice in the age of machine learning. These questions are not just academic; they have real-world implications for how healthcare is delivered and how practitioners are held accountable for the care they provide.

The evolution of AI in healthcare necessitates a reexamination of our legal and ethical frameworks. As machine learning models become more sophisticated, they challenge our conventional understanding of decision-making in healthcare. This evolution calls for a reassessment of how we define the "standard of care" and the responsibilities of healthcare providers in the digital age.

AI and the patient journey

The transformation brought about by AI is perhaps the most evident in the patient journey. From the initial diagnosis to the final stages of recovery, AI is redefining how care is delivered. In the realm of diagnostics, AI algorithms are providing insights that were previously beyond the reach of human practitioners. These tools can analyze medical images, patient histories, and genetic data, offering diagnoses that are faster and often more accurate than those made by humans alone.

In the realm of treatment planning, AI is enabling a level of personalization that was once the stuff of science fiction. By analyzing vast amounts of data, AI can help practitioners develop treatment plans that are tailored to the individual needs of each patient. This personalization extends to the management of chronic diseases, where AI can monitor patient data in real time, adjusting treatment plans as needed to ensure the best possible outcomes.

The recovery phase of the patient journey is also being transformed by AI. In rehabilitation, AI algorithms can analyze patient progress, adapting exercises and therapies in real time to suit the changing needs of the patient. This level of adaptive care ensures that patients receive the most effective treatment at every stage of their recovery.

Finally, and perhaps most importantly, AI is building a relationship with patients and caregivers that uniquely tailors solutions that are aligned with their needs—from language to clinical nuances.

The future of diagnosis—The promise of disease stage zero

Advancing diagnostics serves as a prime example of how AI is reshaping medical specialties. For example, the introduction of AI algorithms in radiology has revolutionized diagnostic processes, enhancing the accuracy and efficiency of imaging studies—letting us see what is unseen or unnoticed. Furthermore, the advancements of early disease detection in laboratory science and pathology are leading indicators of this transformation. This shift is a harbinger of the changes that are coming to other areas of medicine. As AI continues to advance, it will transform not just diagnostics, but every aspect of healthcare delivery.

Furthermore, in an interesting twist, the emergence of earlier diagnoses will be a critical path on the journey to disease prevention. As imaging and diagnostic technology reveals disease pathology at subclinical stages, we functionally share a border with prevention and address disease at stage zero and establish interventions that are likely suggested as having optimal outcomes.

The human element in the age of AI

Despite the advancements in AI, the human element remains central to healthcare. The empathy, understanding, and connection that physicians provide are irreplaceable, and the goal of AI integration is not to supplant these human qualities, but to enhance them. AI can relieve physicians of routine tasks, freeing them to focus on the aspects of care that require a human touch. In this new era, the role of the physician will evolve, but their importance will remain undiminished.

Customizing patient education with AI

In patient education, AI offers a significant departure from the one-size-fits-all approach. AI can tailor educational materials to individual patients, ensuring that they are both understandable and relevant. This personalization extends beyond just the content of the materials; AI can adapt the delivery of information to suit the learning style and preferences of each patient. This approach ensures that patients are not just passive recipients of information but active participants in their care.

The role of AI in primary care

The decline in primary care physicians presents a significant challenge, but AI offers a potential solution. AI can augment the capabilities of primary care providers, enhancing their reach and efficiency. In preventive care, AI can analyze patient data to identify trends and risks, enabling early intervention and reducing the incidence of preventable illnesses. In diagnosis, AI-powered virtual assistants can provide quick and accurate assessments of common conditions, reducing the need for in-person visits and allowing primary care providers to focus on more complex cases.

The intersection of joy and purpose in medicine

In the Cognitive Age, as we experience the seamless integration of technology and medicine, an unexpected but crucial aspect emerges: the rediscovery of joy in the practice of healthcare. This phenomenon can be framed within the context of Maslow's hierarchy of needs, where the fulfillment derived from technological integration in medicine addresses not just the basic and psychological needs of efficiency and proficiency, but also ascends to the level of self-actualization.

In the realm of healthcare, AI technologies like GPT are evolving beyond just being tools of mere convenience. They are becoming the instruments of intellectual and creative expression, transforming mundane tasks into opportunities for deeper engagement and satisfaction. This shift elevates the practice of medicine, aligning it with the higher tiers of Maslow's hierarchy. The joy derived from these technological interactions is not superficial; it stems from a deeper sense of fulfillment, a feeling that one is not just performing a task, but engaging in meaningful work that resonates with their core values and professional aspirations.

For clinicians, the adoption of AI in tasks, such as navigating electronic health records or formulating differential diagnoses, transcends operational efficiency. It fulfills a more profound need for intellectual stimulation and creative problem solving, which are the key elements of self-actualization. The transformation of routine administrative work into intellectually enriching activities aligns with Maslow's concept of peak experiences—moments where individuals feel a heightened sense of purpose and fulfillment.

This new era in medicine, therefore, is not just about leveraging technology for enhanced productivity. It's about how these technological advancements align with the intrinsic needs and aspirations of medical professionals, enabling them to find greater joy and fulfillment in their work. In this light, the Cognitive Age in healthcare can be seen as a journey toward self-actualization, where the integration of AI and digital technologies enriches the professional lives of clinicians, allowing them to reach their fullest potential, both as individuals and as healthcare providers.

The promise and challenges of AI in healthcare

As we look to the future, the promise of AI in healthcare is clear. AI has the potential to transform every aspect of healthcare delivery, from prevention to recovery. However, this transformation is not without its challenges. The integration of AI into healthcare raises complex questions about ethics, liability, and the role of the physician. As we navigate this new landscape, we must be mindful of these challenges, ensuring that the integration of AI into healthcare enhances, rather than diminishes, the quality of care we provide.

Embracing the new era of medicine

As we embark on this new era of medicine, we do so with a sense of excitement and responsibility. The integration of AI and digital technology into healthcare offers tremendous opportunities for improving patient outcomes and enhancing the efficiency of care. However, it also presents challenges that must be addressed with care and thoughtfulness. As we traverse this new landscape, our goal is not just to embrace the potential of technology, but also to ensure that it is used in a way that enhances the human element of healthcare. In this new era, our challenge is to harness the power of AI and digital technology to improve healthcare delivery, enhance patient outcomes, and redefine what it means to provide exceptional medical care.

Furthermore, at the heart of this transformation—or should I say brain—is the central idea of cognition. The advances in AI and technology, in general, offer the clinician new tools to stay ahead of the clinical curve and assimilate data and insights that today are often viewed as insurmountable. It's been said, "As I think, so I act. As I act, so I become." Never before has this been more true that in today's Cognitive Age where thought—a tool for care and compassion—is at the very edge of our transformative journey.

Preface

As we stand at the precipice of a new era, the healthcare landscape is at an inflection point of transformation. What was once theoretical and thought to be in the distant future is now core to our medical ecosystem and is redefining the contours of medical innovation, practice, and education. This book aims to highlight the facets of digital health as a spectrum of possibilities for the future of care delivery. Wires, waves, and signals are as crucial to the delivery of care as compassion, heart, and hugs. Digital health is important today because it will shape our thinking, care delivery, ecosystem, policies, and education for decades to come. It collectively represents a seismic shift from the stethoscope to the smartphone, from the physical exam to the digital interface. This book is for healthcare providers, educators, students, tech entrepreneurs, scientists, researchers, and patients, and anyone who is touched by healthcare.

For healthcare providers, this book is a way to empower healthcare delivery by leveraging wireless networks, digital tools, and big data to remove the barriers to access and care. It is a fresh lens to the true meaning of bedside to webside care. Healthcare providers will find this book to be a compass for navigating the digital health terrain and how to harness digital tools to improve patient outcomes while staying true to the Hippocratic Oath.

Tech entrepreneurs will be able to glean insights into the pressing needs of the healthcare community. As architects of ecosystems that support life and wellness, this book aims to provide a roadmap for innovation, scalability, and growth, keeping in mind the challenges faced by healthcare providers.

Educators and students of healthcare will find new ways to improve, adapt, and enhance curricula for the digital age, learning not just how to use the technology, but also how to permeate it with the values of medicine and academics. This book will serve as a cornerstone for a fresh pedagogical approach to healthcare education, marrying tradition with technology, creativity with practicality.

Scientists and researchers will find this book a valuable resource in navigating digital health landscape and the data it generates. This book addresses privacy and security issues and how to harness big data, artificial intelligence (AI), and machine learning (ML) to uncover insights for improved patient care, how clinical trials will be impacted, and how to unlock the potential for new discoveries in biomedicine.

By providing a comprehensive understanding of the digital health landscape and its potential for evolution, this book empowers each reader to be an agent of change. Whether this be through improving patient outcomes, drafting new policies, developing innovative solutions to complex problems, or educating the next generation of healthcare professionals.

This book is divided into six parts. Although each chapter can stand alone, the themes of digital health, patient care, and education are woven throughout this book.

Part 1, *Introduction*, begins with a brief history and overview of digital health and then dives into the foundational aspects of AI in healthcare and medical education.

Part 2, *Digital Medicine in Practice*, focuses on all the aspects of digital health through the lens of clinical practice, from the use of apps and remote patient monitoring to digital therapeutics and robotic-assisted surgery. It further discusses the future of electronic health records, primary care, and precision medicine from a systems-level viewpoint.

Part 3, *Billing and Coding*, discusses telehealth coding guidelines and expands the discussion globally, comparing and contrasting ICD-10 and SNOMED CT codes.

Part 4, *Legal and Ethical Issues*, is a thought-provoking collection of chapters focused on ethics in AI, medicolegal issues in digital health, and health policy. These chapters grapple with current issues and lay the foundation of how these issues will impact future laws and policies.

Part 5, *Research*, examines how the research landscape will be impacted in the digital era. This includes a fresh take on the IRB processes and functions, consent, and clinical trials.

Part 6, *Where to Now?* looks toward the future. These chapters delve into battling misinformation in the digital age and how to adapt teaching and learning medicine in the digital era to better prepare the next generation of healthcare professionals. The final chapters provide several compelling viewpoints and perspectives from students, patients, and healthcare organizations.

When I first came up with the idea of writing this book, generative AI was not a term known to most. Although many aspects of digital health were already in use in various forms and systems, generative AI had not made its foray into the mainstream. In 1 year, the tectonic structure of the how, when, and where healthcare could, would, and should be delivered has shifted. The exponential pace at which technology is evolving requires all healthcare stakeholders to elevate their thinking to deliver care in a new age. My hope is that this book does just that. I hope this book serves as a platform for all to embrace the inevitable change, to innovate with purpose, and to reinforce the fact that the deployment of technology should always be augmented with a human touch.

Dipu Patel

Acknowledgments

First and foremost, my gratitude to my children, Anya and Bodhi, who have been my unwavering source of inspiration and joy. Your curiosity in life and learning and embrace of technology (gaming) are a reminder to never stop learning and the importance of innovation. You teach me to see the world through fresh eyes, and your resilience and adaptability inspire me to do better, and be better, every day in every aspect of my life.

To my family, who have provided me with the foundation upon which my life's work is built. You have been my cheerleaders in moments of triumph, celebrated my successes, and stood by me while I worked through the challenges of life. Your encouragement and support have guided me through the rigors of the writing process and allowed me to stand up again.

My friends, my tribe! You know who you are! You have been the sounding board for ideas, big and small, during long walks and plane rides. You have shared your perspectives and heartfelt discussions both professionally and personally, over wine, bourbon, popcorn, and sushi, and for that, I will always be thankful. You have lent your ears, shoulders, and voices to elevate my spirit and resolve to complete this project. For the laughter, the debates, and the camaraderie, I am eternally grateful.

I owe a debt of gratitude to my brilliant colleagues, contributors, and reviewers for their dedication to healthcare. The expertise in clinical, academic, and professional practice that you have shared in this book has informed my learning journey and impacted my understanding of digital health. This book has been enriched by your collective knowledge and experiences. A special thank you to all my colleagues at the University of Pittsburgh, Department of PA Studies, who believed in me and supported me throughout this journey.

To my mentors, the giants upon whose shoulders I stand, thank you for your wisdom and guidance. Your mentorship has been invaluable in this journey, and I am indebted to you.

To all of you, I owe you my deepest appreciation. Without you, your experiences, and your support, this book would not exist. Thank you for being a part of my journey.

—Dipu

Reviewers

Reviewer	Affiliation
Mary Allias, EdD, MPAS, PA-C, DFAAPA	Associate Professor, Director of the Doctor of PA Studies Program, University of Pittsburgh Department of PA Studies
Vanessa Bester, EdD, PA-C	Augsburg University, Director of the School of Health, Associate Professor, Minneapolis, MN
Sarah Bolander, DMSc, MMS, PA-C, DFAAPA	Northern Arizona University, Department of PA Studies
Jeff Cooper, PhD, MBA	Adjunct Assistant Professor, University of Pittsburgh Department of PA Studies
Mark DiMauro, PhD	Assistant Professor of Digital Humanities, University of Pittsburgh—Johnstown
Julia Dubis, MPAS, PA-C	Assistant Professor, Director of Simulation, University of Pittsburgh Department of PA Studies
Rosa Fannie, DPAS, MPA, PA-C	Assistant Professor, Associate Program Director, Director of Clinical Education, University of Pittsburgh Department of PA Studies
Carl Garrubba, DMSc, PA-C, DFAAPA, CPA	Vice-Provost, School of Health Sciences, Samuel Merritt University
Tonya C. George, PA-C, MSHS, MSPH, PhD, DFAAPA	Adjunct Assistant Professor, University of Pittsburgh Department of PA Studies
Susan Graff, EdD, MS, PA-C	Assistant Professor, Director of PA Studies Residential Program, University of Pittsburgh Department of PA Studies
Toni Higgins, BSN, RN, OCN	Clinical Informatics Nurse
M. Janie McDaniel, MS, MLS(ASCP)SC	Assistant Professor Adjunct, Director of Alumni Affairs, Emeritus Chair of Admissions, Yale School of Medicine Physician Assistant Online Program
Jessica Oest, MA	University of Pittsburgh School of Health and Rehabilitation Sciences; NeverTechLate
Dipu Patel, DMSc, MPAS, ABAIM, PA-C	Professor, Vice Chair of Innovation, University of Pittsburgh Department of PA Studies
Sally Russick, BBA, MA	Instructional Designer, University of Pittsburgh Office of Online Learning, School of Health and Rehabilitation Sciences
Kevin Schuer, DrPH, PA-C	Program Director, Associate Professor, University of Kentucky, Department of PA Studies
Carla Shamblen, DMSc, PA-C, DFAAPA	Professor, Clinical Faculty, Franklin Pierce University MPAS Program, Arizona
Monique J. Williams, PhD, MSPA	Authentic Wellness LLC, Eastvale, CA

CHAPTER 1

Digital health: Ancient wisdom, modern medicine

Dipu Patel
Department of PA Studies, University of Pittsburgh, Pittsburgh, PA, United States

> *Mitigating the risk of extinction from AI should be a global priority alongside other societal scale risks such as pandemics and nuclear war.*
>
> ***Ref. [1].***

Introduction

Do no harm. Spoken many millennia ago and practiced to this day, these three words are the heart of medicine. Every healthcare provider swears an oath to uphold them above all else in their practice. The practice of medicine has evolved, but the oath remains. It is foundational to the patient-provider relationship. It drives decisions of care, consideration of ethics, and the pursuit of better health outcomes.

In this era of the fourth industrial revolution, technological advancement within digital health has emerged as a transformative force, seamlessly blending the art and science of healing with the power of innovation and ingenuity [2]. From telemedicine consultations that bridge the distances between patients and providers to artificial intelligence(AI)-driven data mining and diagnostics that unlock unprecedented insights, the realm of digital health holds immense promise to truly democratize healthcare for the betterment of humanity.

The world of digital health has been expanding into paradigm shifts in patient care, healthcare accessibility, and knowledge acquisition. As this landscape continues to take shape, we as stewards of medicine and patient care must navigate these new frontiers, guided by our enduring principles, starting with, "do no harm."

Significance of digital health in modern healthcare

Digital health (DH) is a multidisciplinary approach to care that encompasses the intersection of healthcare and digital technologies, aiming to improve care delivery and

Digital Health. https://doi.org/10.1016/B978-0-443-23901-4.00001-5

outcomes of healthcare services. It involves the use of various technologies such as artificial intelligence (AI), the Internet of Things (IoT), telemedicine, wearables, electronic health records (EHRs), and mobile health applications. These are just a few categories, and the list is growing. Digital health has become increasingly significant in modern healthcare because of its potential to enhance patient care, improve access to healthcare services, and optimize healthcare workflows and clinical processes. By leveraging digital tools and data analytics, healthcare providers can gain insights into patient health trends, facilitate personalized medicine, and enable remote patient monitoring. Furthermore, digital health empowers individuals to take an active role in managing their health through self-monitoring, access to health information, and telehealth services.

Furthermore, shared objective data promotes a cultural shift: from a hierarchical or authoritarian (doctor to patient) approach to a democratic (shared decision-making) approach [3]. This embrace of new technology shifts care from the hospital to the patient's home, and the patient's role from being a passive receiver of care and information to a shared responsibility in care. Digital health has the potential to revolutionize healthcare delivery and transform the patient-provider relationship.

Importance of digital health for both professionals and individuals

Technology has become ubiquitous in our lives. And as technology evolves, healthcare providers must continually remain knowledgeable of how digital health tools inform their practice and how to leverage them to provide safe, high-quality, and outcome-driven care. Clinicians should equip themselves to harness digital health to make clinical decisions that are directed through comprehensive patient data mining and seamlessly communicate and collaborate with patients and colleagues. By integrating digital health solutions into their workflows, professionals can streamline various administrative tasks, enhance diagnostic accuracy, and optimize treatment plans that can be personalized to the patient. Furthermore, a deeper understanding of digital health can aid in improving patient outcomes and increase productivity and efficiency while providing patient-centered care. For example, a facility with telemedicine can increase access to care to underserved populations or those who may be home-bound due to chronic conditions. Improvements in access to care can lead to a decrease in complications from chronic conditions by increasing screenings and other preventive care measures. This, in turn, can lead to a decrease in the economic costs of providing care.

Learning to embrace this paradigm shift in healthcare brings to the forefront issues of digital health literacy, geographical and technological barriers, and privacy and consent concerns.

Digital health literacy is defined as the skills needed to navigate, access, and use technological and electronic tools to engage and participate in their care journey [4]. Digital health literacy allows patients to access care and resources online, and that can lead to informed decision-making with regards to health and wellbeing [5]. For example, mobile health applications and wearable devices have improved patient's ability to track and monitor health conditions, engage in preventive measures, and manage chronic conditions more effectively [6]. From the perspective of the clinician, digital health has helped facilitate telemedicine care, remote patient monitoring of acute and chronic diseases, and improved patient-provider communication while overcoming geographical barriers. This aspect of digital health also has the potential to impact social determinants of health and bridge the gap of care outside the walls of the clinic. Furthermore, by understanding digital health, patients can more nimbly navigate privacy and security considerations related to the use of health technologies, ensuring the protection of their personal health information.

As we begin to embrace the transformative potential of digital health, it is crucial for both patients and providers to understand how it will impact care and its delivery. Clinical workflows will shift to include sensors and IoT; clinical operations will be informed by connectivity and access; and clinical decisions will be untethered from the walls of a clinic or hospital. Clinicians who embrace digital health will be able to enhance their practice while providing patient-centered care, and patients who have an understanding of digital health literacy will be able to actively engage in their own healthcare, make informed decisions, access resources, and utilize technologies to allow them to monitor and manage their health from anywhere. The patient-provider relationship will truly become a partnership that will foster a more proactive and empowered approach to health, leading to improved health outcomes and a more efficient and patient-centric healthcare system overall.

Evolution of health and care: From traditional to digital

Historical perspective on traditional healthcare delivery methods

For many centuries, healthcare was delivered in the home. Doctors, religious leaders, and elder tribesmen were often called to provide care in the comfort of the patient's own home or to contain the spread of disease. The shift to hospital care is a relatively modern notion that was driven by industrialization, the improvement of medical technology and principles, and the professionalization of healthcare practice [7]. With the increased use of digital technology, we are returning to care at home. The historical perspective of medical care allows us to appreciate the foundation on which modern medicine was built and informs us on how future policy should be written and implemented. Although not without its challenges, digital health is bringing healthcare delivery full circle.

Emergence and impact of digital technologies in healthcare

Digital technology and healthcare have intersected for decades; the first EHR was developed in the 1960s, and telemedicine has been in use in some form since the 1970s [8]. However, it wasn't until the 2000s, due to smartphones and the increasing availability of broadband internet, that digital health really made its mark. The integration of technology into healthcare systems has allowed patients to access their health records, improved efficiency and accuracy of documentation, and facilitated seamless coordination of care.

Partly due to the COVID-19 pandemic, telemedicine has emerged as a force multiplier in driving access to care while breaking down geographical barriers to care. Globally, telemedicine has empowered women to take charge of their own and their families' health, increased health education, and increased vaccination rates [9]. The downstream impact of this relatively small change in care delivery has been immense.

By leveraging digital health tools and services, individuals can take ownership of their well-being, access healthcare remotely, and collaborate with healthcare providers as partners in their care.

Key technologies driving digital health

Major technologies shaping digital health

Digital health is now a rapidly growing field. There are now billions of mobile health apps available, and EHRs are used by millions of healthcare providers. Digital health is also being used to improve public health, track chronic diseases, and manage patient care through the use of wearables, IoT, and big data analytics: a true shift to healthcare everywhere.

Artificial intelligence (AI) and Machine Learning (ML) in healthcare

Artificial Intelligence (AI) and Machine Learning (ML) have become ubiquitous in our lives. From detecting traffic patterns to improve our driving experience to face recognition to unlock our smartphones, AI and ML have made our evermore complex and connected lives easier to manage. Similarly, AI and ML are helping healthcare providers make better-informed decisions about patient care by summarizing vast amounts of data, detecting diseases earlier for improved outcomes, and personalizing treatment recommendations based on risk assessments. AI and ML have evolved over the past few decades, yet their impact is just now being felt. Emerging subfields of generative AI are revolutionizing how we document, connect, and educate. Future generations of healthcare providers and patients will no doubt benefit from being better informed about their care. Although still in the nascent stages of development and use, generative AI models will continue to impact all areas of care. There remains a lot to be learned about how these models will evolve and how we can harness their application to combat not only diseases but also bias in care.

Internet of things (IoT) and its applications in healthcare

IoT devices have changed the way we navigate healthcare. IoT connectivity enables patients to monitor vital signs, get medication reminders, and track adherence. This enables clinicians to review data that is gathered in the patient's daily life and to make healthcare decisions on how best to personalize care. IoT has not only improved patient care and safety but also allows proactive management of chronic diseases, early detection of abnormalities, and efficient resource allocation.

Big data and analytics in improving patient outcomes

When the term big data was first coined, it was used as a term of convenience [10]. Since its first use, it has evolved to mean the datasets used in the application and research of various fields of science. Today, big data is being leveraged to gain insights into population health trends, treatment effectiveness, and global disease patterns. Advanced analytic algorithmic models have been able to uncover correlations that would have taken decades and predict disease progression, thereby allowing for personalized interventions based on evidence.

Big data has played a crucial role in public health [11]. It has accelerated research, driven information sharing and gathering, while improving public health outcomes on many fronts. Big data has made collating, analyzing, and sharing of data globally feasible, which has led to improved responses to public health crises [11]. Some recent examples include Zika, Ebola, COVID-19, and Avian flu.

Telemedicine and remote patient monitoring (RPM)

Telemedicine and remote patient monitoring (RPM) gained traction during the COVID-19 pandemic. During the pandemic, patients were able to access care without risking the spread of infection, and clinicians were able to provide care in a safe and effective manner. Although telemedicine and the technology to enable it have been around for decades, the pandemic highlighted not only that it could be done, but also that it could be done at scale with the ability to serve remote areas and connect caregivers and patients to timely care.

Remote patient monitoring has facilitated real-time data collection that has allowed clinicians to make clinical decisions and develop treatment plans quickly and shift plans if needed. Remote patient monitoring has also reduced numbers and lengths of hospital visits, improved patient outcomes, and empowered the patient to be engaged in their healthcare [12,13].

Both telemedicine and remote patient monitoring have proven to be game-changers in the delivery of safe care without the restriction of walls, cost-effectiveness, and patient satisfaction. While the policies on these two modes of care delivery are still in flux, consumers are demanding solutions as providers embrace this new method of care delivery.

Wearable devices and mobile health (mHealth) applications

Just as telemedicine and RPM have helped improve the delivery of care, wearables and mobile health (mHealth) have revolutionized personal health monitoring and management. Wearables have changed both the health and fitness industries. Although there is a long way to go in the management of chronic diseases that are caused by poor diet and exercise, wearables continue to be game-changing in many patients' lives. Up to 62% of consumers agree that wearables will put people in control of their health, and 60% agree that wearables will lead to healthier lifestyles. And a whopping 90% would be willing to share personal data from a wearable or an app with a provider. According to a report by IQVIA, "Health-related mobile applications available to consumers on top app stores worldwide now surpass 350,000, with more than 90,000 digital health apps added in 2020 — an average of more than 250 apps per day." [14] While the majority of these apps are in the fitness (55%) category, many offer health engagement at various levels for multiple diseases. The mix of apps has shifted since 2015, with 47% of apps now focused on health condition management, up from 27% in 2015, and wellness management (especially exercise and fitness apps) declining in relative representation [14]. This is indicative of growth not only in technology but cultural acceptance of digital health.

Personalized medicine and precision healthcare

Precision medicine has had several breakthroughs over the past few decades. Starting with the full sequencing of the human genome, precision medicine has become more clinically relevant and applicable. Advances in genomic profiling, immunotherapies, targeted biologics, and liquid biopsies are bringing precision medicine to the clinical setting. Strides are being made not only in cancer diagnostics and care but also in Alzheimer's and Parkinson's disease [15–17]. Precision medicine's full potential is just coming to life and will benefit all patients.

Revolutionizing healthcare professionals and workforce

As patients and consumers demand a digital-first experience with regard to their healthcare, healthcare organizations will need to rise to the occasion to meet this demand [18]. Healthcare systems need to prepare for digital transformation by planning and including a culture of communication, transparency, and a digital-first approach. Furthermore, healthcare provider education and training will be crucial for the success of any digital transformation within a healthcare system [19]. Although an upfront investment is needed in developing a digital ecosystem, healthcare leadership should consider the return on investment and align their business strategies to include the support systems and infrastructure needed to provide care in the next century. Those who fail to plan or adapt to this new landscape will fail to be successful.

Ethical, legal, and regulatory considerations in digital health

Medical, legal, ethical, and regulatory concerns emerge at the forefront of global discussions as digital health evolves. From a patient perspective, issues of informed consent remain a point of discussion. From provider and health organization perspectives, issues of medical malpractice, cognitive biases, and automation of diagnostic algorithms all pose legal and ethical risks; all are areas of active debate.

The European Union (EU) and the United States (US) have very different regulatory frameworks with regard to what type of information is protected, how the data is de-identified, and who has access to the data [20]. Working within HIPAA to protect personal health information is becoming increasingly complex in the digital world for several reasons, including complicated informed consent forms [20]. As Grande et al. noted, there are "five medical legal and ethical issues regarding personal data processing: invisibility (patients don't know their data are processed), inaccuracy of the data collected, immortality (no timeline for the data storage), marketability, and identifiability (even when the data are anonymized, it is often possible to reidentify the patient)." [21].

As we continue to use AI to perform clerical office tasks, informed consent becomes more critical. Patients should know when they are communicating with an AI model versus a human. However, not all patients or providers are fully educated and understand the complexity of this issue [20]. No matter how well-intentioned, algorithmically sound, or medically accurate, AI-generated advice could potentially put the provider's license at risk if there is a misunderstanding in the communication between the bot and the human. The issue is further complicated when minors are involved.

The GDPR aims primarily to give control back to citizens and residents over their personal data and to simplify the regulatory environment for international business by unifying the regulation within the EU. Although the EU's General Data Protection Regulation (GDPR) does not specifically address AI, provisions relevant to AI in healthcare include the following [22,23].

Articles 13 and 14 GDPR, *The right to be informed*: Individuals have the right to be informed about how their personal data is being collected and used. This includes the right to know the purpose of the processing, the categories of personal data being processed, and the recipients of the personal data.

Article 15 GDPR, *The right to access*: Individuals have the right to access their personal data and request that it be corrected if it is inaccurate.

Article 17 GDPR, *The right to erasure*: Individuals have the right to request that their personal data be erased if it is no longer necessary for the purpose for which it was collected.

Article 18 GDPR, *The right to restrict processing*: Individuals have the right to restrict the processing of their personal data in certain circumstances, such as if they believe that the data is inaccurate or that the processing is unlawful.

Article 19 GDPR, *The right to data portability*: Individuals have the right to receive their personal data in a structured, commonly used, and machine-readable format. This allows individuals to transfer their data to another organization if they wish.

The GDPR applies to all organizations that process the personal data of individuals in the EU, regardless of whether the organization is located in the EU or not. This means that any organization that uses AI in healthcare to process the personal data of EU citizens must comply with the GDPR. These regulations will continue to evolve as the digital health landscape changes.

Benefits, opportunities, and challenges in digital health

In 2020, the World Health Organization (WHO) put forth a global strategy on digital health. It stated, in part, "Digital health should be an integral part of health priorities and benefit people in a way that is ethical, safe, secure, reliable, equitable, and sustainable [24]. It should be developed with principles of transparency, accessibility, scalability, replicability, interoperability, privacy, security, and confidentiality." [24].

The WHO puts forth four strategic objectives [24]

1. Promote global collaboration and advance the transfer of knowledge on digital health
2. Advance the implementation of national digital health strategies
3. Strengthen governance for digital health at global, regional, and national levels
4. Advocate people-centered health systems that are enabled by digital health

Through these objectives, the WHO calls on all health sectors to "enhance and complement the work of existing and newly created."

The many benefits to adopting and using digital health technology include improved patient care, reduced cost of care delivery and diagnostics, and improved population health. Digital health can help patients manage their health more effectively, communicate with their healthcare providers more easily, and access care more quickly. It can also help reduce healthcare costs by improving efficiency and reducing the need for unnecessary tests and procedures. From a public health lens, it can help track diseases, identify and risk stratify populations, and promote healthy behaviors.

Furthermore, digital health tools can aid in improving social determinants of health and digital determinants of health [25,26]. These tools could be used to improve access to care or improve medication compliance by sending reminders, or help in connecting patients to community resources.

The challenges of implementing digital health involve multiple factors. The lack of interoperability standards makes it difficult to communicate across health organizations and specialties. Imperfect adoption of digital health by providers and patients can slow or negate change implemented by organizations. Finally but of most paramount concern are issues of data security, privacy, and consent. As noted by Dal Mas et al., "external healthcare stakeholders, such as suppliers, technology providers, and third-party organizations, must develop capabilities and skills useful to implement data-driven approaches to offer additional smart and personalized services to healthcare management (e.g., smart and virtual hospitals, hospital management). To date, practitioners have paid the most attention to clinical and organizational processes, such as the adoption of digital technologies in hospitals or the measurement of care efficiency for patients. Managers of healthcare organizations may also wish to consider how patient data might benefit national social security systems and mechanisms of payment and reimbursement." [27].

Digital health technology is becoming more affordable, accessible, and user-friendly. As this technology continues to develop, it will have an even greater impact on all aspects of healthcare. As consumers become comfortable with the use of wearables and other monitoring devices, they will demand the use of the data collected through these devices to be part of their health decisions. Although the questions of consent, marketing, and secondary research remain unanswered at this time, these issues will also evolve as driven by patients and policymakers. AI and ML will continue to harness the power of algorithms to diagnose, treat, and personalize care. The various realities (VR, AR, MR) will continue to develop, improve, and eventually be used not only to train providers but also to treat, deliver care to, and educate patients.

Conclusion

Digital health is a rapidly growing field that has the potential to revolutionize healthcare. This technology is already having a major impact on the way healthcare is delivered, managed, and financed. As digital health continues to develop, it will have an even greater impact on the future of healthcare. As we embrace new horizons, we should keep at the forefront our ideals that are rooted in the "do not harm" principle and strive for improving healthcare for all of humanity.

Digital health has represented a transformative change in practice and care delivery thus far. No doubt this will continue. As we continue to learn about this evolving ecosystem, consider the following facts and statistics through the lens of implications to patient care, provider education and training, healthcare systems, climate change, policy, medicolegal, ethical, and regulatory landscape. It behooves us to plan for these inevitabilities to remain successful as a species.

1. The global population is expected to reach 8.6 billion by 2030 and 9.8 billion by 2050 [28].
2. The WHO projects a shortage of 15 million healthcare workers by 2030 [29].
3. "By 2025, global healthcare data is predicted to exceed 10 zettabytes, which equals 10 trillion gigabytes." Secondary data mining and analytics will aid in improving research [30,31].
4. In 5 years, healthcare team roles that exist today will be replaced by ones that don't exist today [32].
5. Interprofessional healthcare teams will expand to include data scientists, computer scientists, and technologists.
6. By 2026, Precision Medicine will improve personalized care through AI-powered diagnostics of early detection and treatment of disease and wellbeing all from the comfort of your home [33].
7. By 2026, Artificial Intelligence and AI assistants will bring smart living to life through personalized lifestyle recommendations, home care, and education [33].
8. According to the World Economic Forum, "Six in 10 workers will require training before 2027, but only half of the workers are seen to have access to adequate training opportunities today." [34].
9. AR/VR/XR and the Metaverse will become commonplace in the use of mental health treatments as well as other diseases [35].
10. Digital health tools will impact climate change for the better [36].

References

[1] Abrahams B. Experts issue a dire warning about AI and encourage limits be imposed. NPR; May 31, 2023. Published, https://www.npr.org/2023/05/31/1179030677/experts-issue-a-dire-warning-about-ai-and-encourage-limits-be-imposed.

[2] What are industry 4.0, the fourth industrial revolution, and 4IR? McKinsey & Company; July 15, 2022. https://www.mckinsey.com/featured-insights/mckinsey-explainers/what-are-industry-4-0-the-fourth-industrial-revolution-and-4ir.

[3] Meskó B, Drobni Z, Bényei É, Gergely B, Győrffy Z. Digital health is a cultural transformation of traditional healthcare. Mhealth 2017;3:38. https://doi.org/10.21037/mhealth.2017.08.07.

[4] Improving digital health literacy - RHIhub health literacy toolkit. Ruralhealthinfo.org; 2022. https://www.ruralhealthinfo.org/toolkits/health-literacy/2/digital-literacy#:~:text=Digital%20health%20literacy%20describes%20the,health%20information%20and%20patient%20resources.

[5] Koutsouleris N, Hauser T, Skvortsova V, Choudhury MDe. From promise to practice: towards the realisation of AI-informed mental health care. The Lancet 2022;4(11):e829–40. https://doi.org/10.1016/s2589-7500(22)00153-4.

[6] Ferguson T, Olds T, Curtis R, et al. Effectiveness of wearable activity trackers to increase physical activity and improve health: a systematic review of systematic reviews and meta-analyses. The Lancet 2022;4(8):e615–26. https://doi.org/10.1016/s2589-7500(22)00111-x.

[7] bioMerieux Connection. In: From homes for the ill to institutions of science and technology: the evolution of American hospitals - bioMérieux connection. bioMérieux Connection; May 14, 2020. https://www.biomerieuxconnection.com/2020/05/14/from-homes-for-the-ill-to-institutions-of-science-and-technology-the-evolution-of-american-hospitals/#:~:text=In%20the%201700s%20and%20much,part%20of%20their%20civic%20duty.

[8] Scott Evans R. Electronic health records: then, now, and in the future. Yearbook of Medical Informatics 2016;25(S 01):S48–61. https://doi.org/10.15265/iys-2016-s006.

[9] World. WHO supports COVID-19 vaccine rollout, highlights women in health and boosts telemedicine during the pandemic thanks to donors. Who.int; March 23, 2021. https://www.who.int/news-room/feature-stories/detail/who-supports-covid-19-vaccine-rollout-highlights-women-in-health-and-boosts-telemedicine-during-the-pandemic-thanks-to-donors.

[10] Press G. A very short history of big data. Forbes; July 17, 2019. https://www.forbes.com/sites/gilpress/2013/05/09/a-very-short-history-of-big-data/?sh=43c9ee8165a1.

[11] Dolley S. Big data's role in precision public health. Frontiers in Public Health 2018;6(68). https://doi.org/10.3389/fpubh.2018.00068.

[12] De KR, Snoswell CL, Taylor M, Gray LC, Caffery LJ. Economic evaluations of remote patient monitoring for chronic disease: a systematic review. Value in Health 2022;25(6):897–913. https://doi.org/10.1016/j.jval.2021.12.001.

[13] Mosnaim G, Greiwe J, Jariwala S, Pleasants RA, Merchant R. Digital inhalers and remote patient monitoring for asthma. Journal of Allergy and Clinical Immunology: In Practice 2022;10(10):2525–33. https://doi.org/10.1016/j.jaip.2022.06.026.

[14] IQVIA. Digital health trends 2021. July 2021. www.iqvia.com. https://www.iqvia.com/-/media/iqvia/pdfs/institute-reports/digital-health-trends-2021/iqvia-institute-digital-health-trends-2021.pdf?_=1628089218603%20(for%20350K%20stat%20and%20disease%20charts).

[15] Behl T, Kaur I, Sehgal A, et al. The road to precision medicine: eliminating the "One Size Fits All" approach in Alzheimer's disease. Biomedicine & Pharmacotherapy 2022;153:113337. https://doi.org/10.1016/j.biopha.2022.113337.

[16] Sahu M, Gupta R, Ambasta RK, Kumar P. Artificial intelligence and machine learning in precision medicine: a paradigm shift in big data analysis. Progress in Molecular Biology and Translational Science 2022;190(1):57–100. https://doi.org/10.1016/bs.pmbts.2022.03.002.

[17] Ann-Kathrin S, Rahman N, Monzón-Sandoval J, Sandor C. Deep phenotyping for precision medicine in Parkinson's disease. Disease Models and Mechanisms 2022;15(6). https://doi.org/10.1242/dmm.049376.

[18] Murphy H. Clinics tap GPT-4 to ease charting burden, improve patient care. Health Exec; June 9, 2023. https://healthexec.com/topics/health-it/medical-records/clinics-tap-gpt-4-ease-charting-burden.

[19] Shudes C, Shukla M, Chang C, Appleby C, Hendricks J, Wurz J. Digital transformation. Deloitte Insights; October 26, 2021. https://www2.deloitte.com/us/en/insights/industry/health-care/digital-transformation-in-healthcare.html.

[20] Oliva A, Grassi S, Vetrugno G, et al. Management of medico-legal risks in digital health era: a scoping review. Frontier Medicine 2022;8. https://doi.org/10.3389/fmed.2021.821756.

[21] Grande D, Luna Marti X, Feuerstein-Simon R, et al. Health policy and privacy challenges associated with digital technology. JAMA Network Open 2020;3(7):e208285. https://doi.org/10.1001/jamanetworkopen.2020.8285.

[22] European Parliment. The impact of the general data protection regulation (GDPR) on artificial intelligence. 2020. https://www.europarl.europa.eu/RegData/etudes/STUD/2020/641530/EPRS_STU(2020)641530_EN.pdf.
[23] General Data Protection Regulation GDPR. Final text neatly arranged. General data protection regulation (GDPR). October 6, 2016. https://gdpr-info.eu/art-14-gdpr/.
[24] WHO. Draft global strategy on digital health 2020- 2025 global strategy on digital health _ 1. 2021. https://www.who.int/docs/default-source/documents/gs4dhdaa2a9f352b0445bafbc79ca799dce4d.pdf.
[25] Pickar Abernethy A, Adams L, Barrett MA, et al. The promise of digital health: then, now, and the future. NAM Prespectives 2022;6(22). https://doi.org/10.31478/202206e.
[26] Sieck CJ, Sheon AR, Ancker JS, Castek J, Callahan B, Siefer A. Digital inclusion as a social determinant of health. Npj Digit Med 2021;4(1). https://doi.org/10.1038/s41746-021-00413-8.
[27] Francesca DM, Massaro M, Rippa P, Secundo G. The challenges of digital transformation in healthcare: an interdisciplinary literature review, framework, and future research Agenda. Technovation 2023;123:102716. https://doi.org/10.1016/j.technovation.2023.102716.
[28] Nations U. World population projected to reach 9.8 billion in 2050, and 11.2 billion in 2100. United Nations. United Nations; 2021. https://www.un.org/en/desa/world-population-projected-reach-98-billion-2050-and-112-billion-2100#: ~ :text=The%20current%20world%20population%20of,Nations%20report%20being%20launched%20today.
[29] Digital health market size, share & trends report Grandviewresearch.com; 2023. https://www.grandviewresearch.com/industry-analysis/digital-health-market.
[30] Scaling smart solutions with AI in health: unlocking impact on high-potential use cases. https://www3.weforum.org/docs/WEF_Scaling_Smart_Solutions_with_AI_in_Health_Unlocking_Impact_on_High_Potential_Use_Cases.pdf.
[31] Wu W, Li YJ, Feng A, et al. Data mining in clinical big data: the frequently used databases, steps, and methodological models. Military Medical Research 2021;8(1). https://doi.org/10.1186/s40779-021-00338-z.
[32] O'Connor M. 7 Jobs that don't exist today but will in the next 5 years because of A.I. Inc.com. May 13, 2023. https://www.inc.com/megan-oconnor/7-jobs-that-dont-exist-today-but-will-in-next-5-years-because-of-ai.html.
[33] Dock C. The future of generative AI. 2023. https://assets.website-files.com/632b0bdc16573f0b323fc7b1/647f5c96b15cb4f1d22931e9_CD_AI_REPORT.pdf.
[34] World Economic Forum. The future of jobs report 2023. World Economic Forum; 2023. https://www.weforum.org/reports/the-future-of-jobs-report-2023/digest.
[35] World Economic Forum. Top 10 emerging technologies of 2023 flagship report. World Economic Forum; 2023. https://www3.weforum.org/docs/WEF_Top_10_Emerging_Technologies_of_2023.pdf.
[36] How could digital health fight against the climate Catastrophe? - the medical futurist. The Medical Futurist; July 11, 2019. https://medicalfuturist.com/digital-health-and-the-climate-catastrophe/.

Further reading

[1] Roser M. Technology over the long run: zoom out to see how dramatically the world can change within a lifetime. Our World in Data; February 22, 2023. https://ourworldindata.org/technology-long-run.
[2] Liang W, Yuksekgonul M, Mao Y, Wu E, Zou J. GPT detectors are biased against non-native English writers. https://arxiv.org/pdf/2304.02819.pdf.
[3] Artificial intelligence in medicine and public health: prospects and challenges beyond the pandemic | blogs | CDC. Cdc.gov. March 2022. https://blogs.cdc.gov/genomics/2022/03/01/artificial-intelligence-2/.
[4] Zahir K, Crowe B, Rodman A. Accuracy of a generative artificial intelligence model in a complex diagnostic challenge. Research Letter 2023;330(1):78. https://doi.org/10.1001/jama.2023.8288.
[5] Jiang LY, Liu XC, Pour Nejatian N, et al. Health system-scale language models are all-purpose prediction engines. Nature 2023;619(7969):357–62. https://doi.org/10.1038/s41586-023-06160-y.

[6] Chenais G, Lagarde E, Gil-Jardiné C. Artificial intelligence in emergency medicine: a viewpoint of current applications, foreseeable opportunities and challenges. June 2, 2022. https://doi.org/10.2196/40031.
[7] The shaky foundations of foundation models in healthcare. Stanford HAI; Published 2023. https://hai.stanford.edu/news/shaky-foundations-foundation-models-healthcare.
[8] Brown TMH, Bewick M. Digital health education: the need for a digitally ready workforce. Archives of Disease in Childhood - education and Practice. June 13, 2022. https://doi.org/10.1136/archdischild-2021-322022.
[9] Striving to become more patient-centric in life sciences. Deloitte Insights; 2023. https://www2.deloitte.com/us/en/insights/industry/life-sciences/patient-centricity.html.
[10] Act A. EU AI Act: first regulation on artificial intelligence | News. European Parliament. Europa.eu; August 6, 2023. https://www.europarl.europa.eu/news/en/headlines/society/20230601STO93804/eu-ai-act-first-regulation-on-artificial-intelligence?xtor=AD-78-[Social_share_buttons]-[linkedin]-[en]-[news]-[society]-[ai-risks]&.
[11] Birkner C. AMA to develop guidelines to combat AI inaccuracies in healthcare. McKnight's Senior Living; June 14, 2023. https://www.mcknightsseniorliving.com/home/news/tech-daily-news/ama-to-develop-guidelines-to-combat-ai-inaccuracies-in-healthcare/.

CHAPTER 2

Diagnosing the future: The role of artificial intelligence in the forthcoming medical epoch

Mark DiMauro
Multimedia and Digital Culture, University of Pittsburgh-Johnstown, Johnstown, PA, United States

Introduction

There is scarcely an industry that, by this point, has not been influenced either directly or tangentially by the rapidly expanding reach of artificial intelligence (AI). The adoption of this novel technology has reshaped the conventional, and conventional wisdom, within everything from ethics to operations to logistics and beyond. As this text goes to print, there is even a likelihood, perhaps an inevitability, that some of the technology or applications discussed herein have not already been usurped by newer, more advanced versions or ideas. Seemingly every day, the media is abuzz with articles referencing ideation regarding AI application within medicine: can it help us diagnose malignant cells? Can it assist with the creation of new pharmaceuticals? Can it be relied upon during a crisis? Can it substitute for a physician or a physician's judgment? Sam Altman, CEO of OpenAI (the company behind ChatGPT) insists that "If we went back 500 years and said 'People's lives were OK, but I can't believe they lived without modern medicine,' that's what people are going to say about (modern society) and (AI) in 50 years" [1]. We will, without doubt, answer some of these burning inquiries in the months and perhaps years to come, and perhaps even prove Altman correct. For the moment, however, it is important to recognize that AI, once stripped of its perhaps hyperbolic hype or portents of the end of human employment, is but another invaluable tool in the arsenal of the caregiver, one that can assist in the bleakest of scenarios with unflinching objectivity, and, when properly steered by a trained physician, arm everyone from the diagnostician to the pharmacologist with the information required to make informed medical recommendations.

This chapter will not go into detail regarding the inner workings of AI and the technology that powers its rise and success; such a discussion is beyond our scope. What *is* important

Digital Health. https://doi.org/10.1016/B978-0-443-23901-4.00002-7

to note, however, is that all AI is the product of a large-scale algorithm, a recombination of data (whether text, image, or fragment) guided into an understandable and recognizable output by a technology called a neural net (NN). What we are then left with is an incredibly powerful information sorting algorithm, one that can identify patterns that may escape the layperson, and certainly would escape anyone that hasn't devoted significant time and resources to studying said source data. Everything from cipher character information (CryptoCrack) to language (ChatGPT) to mRNA (Baidu Research) can be encoded within these structures, the analysis of which may be done at an incredible speed and at scale, enabling a boost in efficiency once deemed unpragmatic at best, absolutely impossible at worst. By reframing our own conceptions of this data, for example, reimagining the various structures of language, like sentence structure, vocabulary choice, diction, audience consideration, etc., as data points, we can then train an AI agent on this information and analyze it at incredible speed with a relatively high degree of accuracy. Note that this chapter uses the term *agent* rather than *bot* to describe vocationally tuned AI systems. This nomenclature is relevant when examining the MDAP (Metadata-Defined Agent Persona) prompt engineering methodology, which will be disseminated later in the chapter, and helps us differentiate between AI for entertainment and distraction, as is often the type found within social media (for example), and instead for trained, directed, private models associated with particular vocational uses, like medicine.

Inevitable hesitancy

Please note the presence of the conditional in the previous paragraph: "relatively." Herein lies the largest and most prescient issue with AI adoption within the medical community: *is it trustworthy*? Can the data we give it (patient information especially, which must of course be secured according to HIPPA guidelines) be kept private? Are we to agree that the conclusions it generates are accurate? Furthermore, if we cannot trust the system with absolute certainty, why are we utilizing it? After all, even Steven Wolfram (physicist and director of the *Wolfram Physics Project* and co-creator of the Wolfram Alpha mathematical AI) concedes that we can't mathematically determine how the neural network makes distinctions within data [2]. Speaking specifically about the capabilities of neural nets and AI to process image recognition, he quite literally states that it is "just doing what the neural net does" [2] and that "… it turns out that [it] normally seems to agree fairly well with the distinctions we humans make" (30) [2].

This, perhaps, goes a long way in outlining why many within the medical industry have expressed hesitation at the idea of utilizing AI within either their own practice specifically or within the discipline generally. A 2020 survey conducted by Health Education England, for example (note: this survey was conducted before the worldwide release of ChatGPT, arguably the most famous AI software available, in any industry), noted: " … that a substantial majority of [those surveyed] had minimal to zero exposure or understanding of the unfolding narrative around AI and automation" [3], thus demonstrating that, until very recently, most practitioners hadn't even considered AI to be a relevant or perhaps even worthwhile investment within medicine, despite its near 50-year existence. The advent of Deep Learning in the mid 2010s, for example, did not sway opinions; why would the next iteration, the Large Language Model (LLM, of which ChatGPT is the industry for example)? Varlamov et al. noted in a 2019 overview of AI in medicine that "Human—human interpersonal communications should resist AI" [4], and later that "Doctor—AI—patient" [4] must be examined. This study concluded that despite ongoing improvements to AI structures, a foundational, perhaps even uncrossable chasm existed within systems of trust among both practitioners and patients. This unwillingness to trust the AI output pervades the common mentality within the industry, and, in truth, many industries; education, law, and art/design have all had recent, well-publicized examples of systemic overtrust. Perhaps the most famous topical example involves Kevin P. Castel, a federal judge, fining two lawyers from the firm Levidow, Levidow, and Oberman for their case brief, written entirely by ChatGPT, which included fictitious legal precedent fabricated by the LLM. The lingering question is readily obvious and must be addressed before delving further into the role of AI in healthcare: how can we trust medical decision-making to a system that may be fallacious?

A partial answer to this conundrum, where the promise of AI dangles the carrot of hyper-fast, ultra-efficient, and eminently capable communication within the shadow of the stick of misinformation or outright fabrication, comes to us via the work of Pavel Hamet and Johanne Tremblay. Hamet and Trembley argue in "Artificial Intelligence in medicine" that two distinct spheres of AI should be employed when considering the application of such technology in the industry [5]. They make the case that these spheres should be comprised of "virtual and physical" [5] domains, where, ostensibly, the "virtual" domain is AI-safe, and the "physical" domain should be met with more caution [5]. The flagrant objection—that an AI system is ill-equipped to diagnose a patient, and what the disastrous consequences might be if a practitioner were to trust that system's potentially fallacious guidance—falls squarely into the "physical" domain, one our authors argue should require more caution on our part. It must be noted here that the physical domain they outline is typically where the primary controversy within AI lies, and also where the headlines are typically made. The rhetorical questions earlier addressed—everything from mRNA vaccines to pharmacological interventions to control systems for remote surgical robots—all lie in the physical domain. Caution should be exercised when allowing AI to permeate this sphere of healthcare Hamet and Trembley argue [5]; such an intrusion cannot be taken lightly, as the ramifications for error are, quite literally in many cases, a question of life and death. Their sentiment is echoed by Amisha et al. in a 2019 metanalysis, which identifies this bifurcated structure within AI applications. In truth, each source is engaging in a form of risk assessment, and correctly identifying physical interventions as the most potentially damaging should AI go awry, or, more precisely, *fail to be properly employed*, a key distinction we will touch upon later.

Rather, each source identifies Hamet and Trembley's "virtual" sphere, the tangential healthcare application, including everything from patient notes to charting to instructions to medical and pharmaceutical advertising and beyond, as a suitable application space for AI. Indeed, many of these perhaps healthcare-tangential spaces are already highly populated with AI models, including but not limited to healthcare education, healthcare advertising, healthcare management, and healthcare record keeping, to say nothing of even further tangential spaces which are all but overtaken by AI, including insurance and law.

These various healthcare verticals remind us of a key fact, one which seems all too easily overlooked in the hyperbolic rush to press we often see in our 24 h news cycle, a key fact that seems equal parts obvious and immutable: *the closer to patient care we get, the more AI is found distasteful*. This is the observation Varlamov et al. ascertain [5], and the point is just as prescient when they made it in 2019 as it is in today's post-ChatGPT AI-assisted vocational marketplace. The flow of information and care once marked by "Doctor—Patient" [5], as they state, must now necessarily be "Doctor—AI—Patient" [5], and the role of the healthcare scholar in this domain has now become a determination not of *where* or *if* AI fits into this process but rather *how*. The question of *if*, they assert, is one suited for the philosopher (a squaring of the role of artificiality with that of the Hippocratic Oath, for example). I tend to disagree with this assessment, not because I do not exalt the potential role of AI and its value in improving patient care and ultimately outcomes but rather to assume that AI necessarily *requires* or even *deserves* a role in patient care is to take agency away from physician and patient, itself an unethical act. In conjecture, this may perhaps be the root of some of the concern regarding AI within healthcare's physical sphere; it is a loosening of the reins of control, a removal of human agency from within the confines of provided care that many find distasteful at best and unethical and unsafe at worst.

I would be remiss here not to point out that such technology, trusted or not, has been at the forefront of medical care for almost centuries. Many of the systems found within the other pages of this text, for example, while not necessarily driven by, informed by, or designed alongside AI are nonetheless trusted systems for patient care, but that trust must of course be earned. This process of earned trust within the new system takes place gradually, as Rogers argues, occasionally assisted by a generational swap of practitioners or a wave of early adopters [6]. Given the novelty of AI, not to mention the misleading nomenclature of "artificial *Intelligence*" asserting a cognitive process akin to humanity is the root of the system's decision-making, such caution is both understandable and perhaps wise, so long as the potential power and efficiency of AI is not collateral damage to this caution.

Wendell Wallach, author of both *Moral Machines* [7] and *A Dangerous Master* [8], one of the preeminent thinkers in the world of AI Ethics and algorithmic morality, makes the case quite clearly. He states, much like John Searle asserts in the famous "Chinese Room Experiment" [9] that "Hard AI" (or, as Wallach calls it, "General Artificial Intelligence" [11], the same system referred to by Altman as AGI [1]) does not yet exist, and is far from being on the horizon. In an interview with podcaster and author Andrew Klavan, Wallach notes that the primary function of AI is to break apart the various underpinnings of human intelligence such that we can successfully and artificially mimic them, whether they be creation, intuition, or memory [11]. He further notes that perhaps because of "Hollywood's 3 decade treatment of AI," we've come to be conditioned to automatically mistrust it, and he states that if empathy is a core component of human intelligence, we've yet to design a system that can either successfully imitate it or at least imitate its outcomes [11]. Considering the importance of empathy within the world of medicine, especially within Hamet and Tremblay's "physical" domain [5], Wallach's assertions go a long way to explaining the hesitation among practitioners to adopt such advancements, despite it swirling about them in everyday headlines and promising ever-greater patient outcomes at ever-greater speed, with ever-greater efficiency and ever-greater cost savings for institutions which employ such technology.

Specifically within the medical industry, British statistician David Spiegelhalter argues that there is a multilayered and highly complex interplay between the mental states we typically label "trust" and "confidence" [13]. As outlined by both Spiegelhalter and the NHS AI guidelines, the potential efficiency of AI tools remains *necessarily* grounded by human oversight and, potentially, validation. This fail-safe mechanism, in addition to the pragmatic concerns of ensuring editorial control and agency, remains with the individuals most affected by the decision: physician and patient. Simultaneously, and one might argue paradoxically, this practice of grounding places a limit on the efficiency AI might bring to bear. Ultimately, I speculate that in the near future—perhaps within 20, or even 10 years—a model will emerge which places the AI system, whatever form it takes, as trusted assistant to the physician, where Varlamov's model would not be the outlier but rather the norm, much in the same way a diagnosis becomes more accurate with the assistance of modern medical imaging like MRI. In fact, such a set up was posited in medicine all the way back in 1982, a date most associate as decades before the AI systems of which they are currently aware, by Peter Szolovitz, who argued in *Artificial Intelligence in Medicine* that, ultimately, only three matrices of decision-making are necessary, whether they are AI or grounded in human agency: Databases, Flowcharts, and Decision Theory (5–10). He argues that "Encoding human expertise in the computer is amazingly difficult … the problems of acquiring, organizing, retrieving, and applying the large amount of knowledge we now believe necessary are part of the *knowledge based systems* research in AI" [14]. Although we must acknowledge that Szolovitz was writing in a time when the systems he references could certainly not achieve the same levels of mimicry in the human decision-making process of which our current systems are capable, the theory and thought-process that undergirds his conclusions remains valid: trust and validation are prerequisite for proper institution of (any) technology, and the requirement for Spiegelhalter's labels of "trust" and "confidence" are higher the more advanced the technology becomes. Systems that assist the physician, continuing to allow the practitioner to exercise agency rather than the technology, are consistently viewed in a far more positive light than those that surrender utter control to Szolovitz's decision theory. In sum, patients would be just as likely to reject a diagnosis from a flow chart as they would from an AI, no matter how complex a flowchart the AI mimics. Far fewer patients and practitioners would object to a physician using such a chart within the diagnostic process, rather than acting as ultimate arbiter.

Speculation asserts that this might simply be a generational gap, and once a new crop of physicians trained within the appropriate application of AI software completes residency and emerges to their own practices, such distrust might retreat, but this speculation relies on a previously discussed notion: that AI's accuracy increases when properly employed.

From AI-adjacent to AI-empowered

This datum should come as no surprise to anyone; the more practiced one is with any new technological process or equipment, the more efficient and accurate that equipment and its subsequent use cases become. Practice, as humanity has long accurately professed, makes perfect. AI, interestingly, seems to occupy a different viewpoint in the collective consciousness, within both the medical field and otherwise. The power and promise of AI is such that when it is exposed to be fallacious (as in the case of Kevin P. Castel) that mistrust increases all the more. The new AI tech is viewed as equal parts incredible (by advocates) and untrustworthy at best, and dangerous at worst (by detractors). Both sides, however, fall victim to believing the tech is both impenetrable and incomprehensible, an arcane existence more similar to magic than technology, perfectly embodying the sentiment expressed by Arthur C. Clarke that "There is no sufficiently advanced technology which is indistinguishable from magic."

We are therefore left in a situation where, within medicine, many of AI's advocates claim it should be used everywhere at all times for any reason, while the detractors argue precisely the opposite. The advocates call the detractors luddite, the detractors call the advocates heartless and short-sighted, and nothing of value gets accomplished. This is true, incidentally, of every field struggling to adapt to the new augmented workforce promised by AI. Hamet and Trembley's model offers a potential solution: virtual medical space for the AI and physical medical space for the human, but this, I postulate, is too heavy-handed an approach. Much like a carpenter or contractor carefully selects the tool for the job, the physician, the X-ray technician, and the pharmacologist et al. must also ask on a case-by-case and patient-by-patient basis whether or not AI diagnostics or AI charting is applicable. To this end, AI is, and should be viewed as, another potential tool at the disposal of the practitioner, with whom ultimate decision-making lies. The reason earlier in the chapter it was necessary to clarify "go awry" with "failure to direct" implies a problem with the tool rather than the operator. When a hammer hits a nail, everything goes as expected. When a hammer hits a hole in the wall, the problem isn't necessarily with the hammer. AI education is, therefore, an inevitable and important aspect of its adoption into medical practice, and should be treated as such. If we reposition our own interpretation of AI as *high-quality software* rather than *dangerous supertechnology*, we are far more likely to engage with it and its potential improvements to patient care and outcomes. For more information on how to change this perspective, a further discussion of AI within medical education can be found in Chapter 3 of this book. With this in mind, let us now turn to a brief illustration of some of the ways in which prompt engineering techniques benefit the LLM operator, as these techniques will, in all likelihood, become commonplace within the instanced and directed systems employed by various healthcare providers.

Outside of the context of this chapter, I have developed a set of prompt engineering principles for LLM application, which have been used to create everything from adaptive agents that assist with marketing to virtual patients who respond to queries from the practitioner or educator. These techniques are capable of aligning with given datasets, responding within parameters set by the designer, and are wholly customizable, as they were developed for the business sector but are fully capable of being modified for the healthcare vertical. They require no computer science experience to create and improve ease of use and efficiency of LLM and AI art models by an almost unmappable factor. Two primary examples of these techniques I developed include MDAP (Metadata-Defined Agent Persona) and MPE (Multiple Persona Embodiment). These are far from the only methodologies which are rapidly springing into use, however. Yao et al. developed the "Tree of Thoughts" model in May of 2023, itself utilizing and employing the "Chain of Thoughts" methodology from earlier that same year. Other agent designs are no doubt coming, and when bolstered by datasets and training data that are associated with modern medical care, are only bound to become stronger, faster, more efficient, and, ultimately, more accurate. There is perhaps the potential for individual hospitals to create their own instanced AI agents, as is already being done at the enterprise level of Fortune 500 institutions. Or, perhaps, this methodology might be constructed and sold as a textbook, a "How to Prompt for Medical Accuracy" which becomes as common as the PDR in hospital reference sections. I tend to speculate that the former is more likely, owing to a common and oft-overlooked aspect of LLM application: HIPAA and patient privacy.

Health Insurance Portability and Accountability Act (HIPAA) standards are quite strict in the United States, and of course guide most medical record-keeping practices. The UK NHS (United Kingdom's National Health Service) employs a similar methodology, as do most organized healthcare structures worldwide. What is far less regulated, however, is the servers of AI companies which necessarily must capture user input to pass into the corresponding LLM. Sending a query to ChatGPT, for example, BARD (Google's LLM offering) or LLAMA (Meta's) involves the neural network present on those servers analyzing the information from the prompt and then, necessarily, generating a response from the training data set, guided by the algorithm designed by the neural network programmers. You may have undoubtedly already spotted the flaw: patient information—any identifiable characteristic, including vital data, diagnosis, medical history, family history, or, most especially, name—has now been transmitted to a non-HIPAA compliant server. What happens to that data? Where does it go? Is there a record of it? One of the hallmarks of LLMs is their ability to engage in Machine Learning (that is, to record previous aspects of conversations and build them into future responses, improving accuracy). This is, not coincidentally, why repeated iteration of LLM prompts is such an effective tool for the prompt designer. Nevertheless, in order for machine learning to occur, the system must have access to that data, and that data must necessarily be stored somewhere. Until a HIPAA-compliant server or system exists, each and every such LLM application represents a potential data breach and certainly a violation of federal statute.

This concern is relevant to Hamet and Tremblay's "virtual" domain of medical practice, affecting everything from patient charting to release instructions. Anything that includes specifically tailored information for the patient, anything which is not a stock document like a template or a form letter (which do not require AI in the first place) ultimately becomes a potential violation. Would practitioners take that chance? Would attorneys or insurance companies? Ultimately, with the aid of some speculation, I believe the answer is *yes*; the allure and power promised by AI will prove more powerful than HIPAA; not in the sense that flagrant violations will occur, but only such that cybersecurity experts are likely about to be called on to readily update LLMs to be HIPAA compliant. It is likely that HIPAA-compliant versions of LLMs are instanced for medical providers, for example. An instanced LLM, or any instanced software, is a version of that software that is accessible only to the users of that client-side software while still utilizing the same common data center, in this case the neural network which defines and drives the AI.

Diagnosing the future

We have thus far spent a good deal of time examining the potential drawbacks and objections to AI in medicine, as well as its overall role. To reiterate, it is my position that such technology has outstanding potential to transform patient care and outcomes, and it behooves us to examine a few of the ways it might do so. Please note that many of these applications are, at the time of this printing, purely theoretical, though some steps have been taken in a positive direction. Let us first return to a previous point made early in the chapter when we discussed the structure of AI as an algorithm that examines data. Large Language Models analyze text as data, or message or communication as such. Art generating programs (DALLE-2, Midjourney, Stable Diffusion) analyze art and pictures as data, specifically, as pixel-by-pixel constructions. One of the strengths of AI within the medical field is its ability to analyze human conditions in much the same way.

Given the appropriate factors, factors which are normally examined by a physician, like family history, patient history, drug and alcohol use, current diagnosis, vitals, and so on, an AI assistant can potentially define an individual's treatment plan (again, when properly guided) in a fraction of the time a physician might. Even better, it might generate a list of potential symptoms or conditions that may not have occurred to even the most thorough physician upon routine examination, allowing for less opportunity for diagnoses to slip through the cracks. Let us outline an example:

Imagine a patient presents with generalized anxiety. Given the Occam's Razor approach of "Think Horses, not Zebras," a physician might at first suspect a neurological condition, heart disease, stress, or withdrawal, once other factors like family medical history are considered. However, an AI assistant might analyze that data and present four other potential diagnoses (something like hyperthyroidism or irritable bowel syndrome (IBS)), which can also present the same way [10]. This is not to say that every diagnosis must follow these guidelines—the "horses not zebras" mantra exists for a reason—but rather to illustrate that a practitioner, overworked in a hospital setting, might benefit from a second opinion, even one created by AI. That practitioner could, furthermore, create a "custom algorithm," based on one, or multiple, of the prompt engineering methodologies discussed previously, and create a diagnostic assistant which examines issues in a more reliable, trustworthy, and ultimately familiar manner. Multiple Persona Embodiment (MPE, a type of prompt engineering methodology), for example, can be designed such that it embodies a series of expert physicians capable of differential diagnosis given a series of symptomatic and patient history input. It can do so in seconds, with access to more medical information than any human can read and absorb in a lifetime, and its recommendation, once affirmed or rejected by the attending, potentially save a life or even a lengthy and expensive hospital stay.

The nurse, overwhelmed by patient load and recovering from an emergency situation in another room, could type patient name and vague incident details into an LLM, which would complete the chart for her, avoiding the painstaking process of accurate notes which, when small pieces get overlooked, can cause major issues (drug interactions, for example, in a patient taking an unknown medication).

The researcher, whose AI datapoints are not patients and symptoms but rather molecular data or DNA markers, can use AI to create new drugs by exploiting patterns the system discovers, speeding the process of new pharmaceutical creation while simultaneously lowering the cost of research and development for new drugs. The hospital administrator or independent medical contractor can use AI within marketing data or advertising to get novel technology or methodology to where it is most needed. Outreach programs can employ AI to analyze trends in behavior to better locate or reach individuals in need of help, or identify latent conditions that may be hiding under obvious ones (mental illness invisible because of substance abuse, for example). The medical educator can embody virtual patients or design realistic, responsive scenarios within which students can train, like responsive surgical models or diagnostic training scenarios. The hospital manager can use AI to most effectively deploy resources, leveraging available manpower or mitigating risk during a triage situation, all with the capabilities of an instant and objective logistics expert.

In an example already within practice, imaging technicians can get a secondary viewpoint on documents like MRIs, X-rays, or ultrasounds by employing one of the most common and stable applications of AI to date, image recognition, the same technology employed by facial recognition software. Although going into extensive details about the inner operations of various neural network models is beyond the scope of this chapter, it is important to note that Convolutional Neural Nets (CNNs) are better suited to problem-solving and spatial data analysis, which is why they are employed for image recognition tasks, while Recurrent Neural Networks (RNNs) are more suited to sequential data like temporal event recognition or language. Each has a specific application, and the 2020 study by Banjeree et al. illustrates that *both* have potential within medical applications, whether that is using CNN systems as Wolfram outlines (for image recognition within medical imaging tech like MRI), a "second set of eyes," or as a data-processing and trend-locating RNN which can combine and organize various datapoints from hundreds or even thousands of training examples to promote accuracy:

> To identify imaging studies that are positive for (pulmonary embolism), like many other radiology diagnoses, information extraction from the free-text radiology reports is needed in order to perform large-scale analyses. If the hospital was able to leverage the computerized tools, it would be possible to rapidly and accurately account for the percentage of positive and negative studies, per provider/service/specialty, and use that data over time to identify opportunities for implementing or reeducating ordering providers about decision support tools for PE evaluation and reduce the number of negative examinations in a targeted approach [12].

Whether using the image recognition capabilities of AI as discussed by Wolfram or the textual pattern analytics described by Banjeree et al., this application of AI within medicine is already a reality and will only expand in use and accuracy as further advancements are made and processing power and neural network size and reliability increase.

The possibilities are almost endless because the power of AI resides within its ability to discern, analyze, and discuss data within patterns. Humans are, by all accounts, fairly adept at discovering and exploiting patterns, but AI's power takes that advantage to 11. Anywhere patterns of data exist, or even might be expected to exist, AI can be leveraged toward a better outcome, and the creativity on the part of the medical professional is only discovering a method through which various "non-data points," like human behavior or tendencies, may be identified as such. Once the cybersecurity to protect that data reaches a trustworthy point, and once patients and physicians turn the corner from "trust" to "confidence," as Spiegelhalter asserts, the shackles come off and AI can truly shine in medical service. So long as human agency is not removed from the decision-making process, an ethical guarantee that should be part of *any* AI integration, not simply those within the medical field, then the sky truly becomes the limit.

Such a day is likely in the not-too-distant future, and there is much excitement to see what it brings when it arrives. I can't wait to see what you create when empowered with AI.

Discussion questions

1. What do you believe the healthcare industry will look like in 5 years? 10 years? 50 years? Will we see automation on the scale of that found in the automotive industry, for example, or will the pushback on the part of practitioners and patients prevent this from happening?
2. Acceptance of AI within the medical space is much like acceptance of any new technology, often a question of generational exposure. Younger generations, which have more exposure to such tech (and at an earlier age), are often more likely to accept it as part of the established order. Do you believe the sea-change of AI acceptance will come with generational shift? Or do you believe hesitation will remain? Why or why not?
3. If you could identify one particular medical field within which you believe the use of AI should be strictly prohibited, or at the very least counter-productive as opposed to effective, what would it be and why?
4. Imagine a spectrum of AI integration in healthcare, as I've laid out in the chapter. At the most extreme left end is a position of "I am willing to do anything and everything to assist patient care and improve outcomes," while on the other extreme is a position of "Healthcare cannot, should not, and will not ever be a domain for automated

systems. The human cannot be replaced and we should not try." Where do you imagine yourself on that spectrum, and why?

5. What AI advancement in medicine are you most excited for, and which, if any, gives you the most apprehension?

References

[1] Rogan J. Sam Altman. The Joe Rogan Experience 2023;2044.

[2] Wolfram S. What is ChatGPT doing … and why does it work? Stephen Wolfram writings RSS. February 14, 2023. https://writings.stephenwolfram.com/2023/02/what-is-chatgpt-doing-and-why-does-it-work/.

[3] National Data Guardian ICO. Artificial intelligence: NHS transformation directorate. NHS choices; 2023. https://transform.england.nhs.uk/information-governance/guidance/artificial-intelligence/.

[4] Varlamov OO, Chuvikov DA, Adamova LE, Petrov MA, Zabolotskaya IK, Logical ZTN. Philosophical and ethical aspects of AI in medicine. International Journal of Machine Learning and Computing December 2019;9(6). https://pdfs.semanticscholar.org/5825/c38124a45dc34cffd1b82593aacb35baa6b6.pdf.

[5] Hamet P, Tremblay J. Artificial intelligence in medicine. Metabolism: Clinical and Experimental 2017. https://pubmed.ncbi.nlm.nih.gov/28126242/.

[6] Rogers E. Diffusion of innovations. 5th ed. Free Press: Simon and Schuster; 2003.

[7] Wallach W, Allen C. Moral machines: teaching robots right from wrong. Oxford University Press; 2010.

[8] Wallach W. A dangerous master: how to keep technology from slipping beyond our control. Basic; 2015.

[9] Searle J. The Chinese room argument. Minds, Brains, and Programs. 1980. https://rintintin.colorado.edu/∼vancecd/phil201/Searle.pdf.

[10] Mayo Clinic. Generalized anxiety disorder. Mayo Clinic; October 13, 2017. https://www.mayoclinic.org/diseases-conditions/generalized-anxiety-disorder/symptoms-causes/syc-20360803.

[11] Klavan A, Wallach W. What does the future of artificial intelligence look like? The Daily Wire 2023.

[12] Banerjee I, Ling Y, Chen MC, et al. Comparative effectiveness of convolutional neural network (CNN) and recurrent neural network (RNN) architectures for radiology text report classification. Artificial Intelligence in Medicine June 2019. https://www.ncbi.nlm.nih.gov/pmc/articles/PMC6533167/.

[13] Spiegelhalter D. Should we trust algorithms? Harvard Data Science Review 2020;2(1).

[14] Szolovitz P. Artificial intelligence in medicine. Routledge; 2018.

Further reading

[1] Yoav M, Ronit B. Introduction to artificial intelligence in medicine. Minimally Invasive Therapy & Allied Technologies 2019;28(2):73−81. https://www.tandfonline.com/doi/abs/10.1080/13645706.2019.1575882.

[2] Kaul V, Enslin S, Gross S. History of artificial intelligence in medicine. Gastrointestinal Endoscopy 2020;92(4):807−12. https://www.sciencedirect.com/science/article/pii/S0016510720344667.

[3] Haleem A, Mohd J, Khan IH. Current status and applications of artificial intelligence (AI) in medical field: an overview. Current Medicine Research and Practice 2019;9(6):231−7. https://www.sciencedirect.com/science/article/abs/pii/S235208171930193X.

[4] Varun HB, Irfan A, Maruthappu M. Artificial intelligence in medicine: current trends and future possibilities. British Journal of General Practice 2018;68(668):143−4. https://bjgp.org/content/68/668/143.short.

[5] King M. The future of AI in medicine: a perspective from a chatbot. Annals of Biomedical Engineering 2022;51:291−5. https://link.springer.com/article/10.1007/s10439-022-03121-w.

CHAPTER 3

AI in medical education: Challenges and opportunities

Marty Rosenheck
Cognitive Advisors, Evanston, IL, United States

> *We're at the cusp of using AI for probably the biggest positive transformation that education has ever seen.*
>
> **Kahn [1].**

> *Educators must act now to incorporate training in AI across health professions or risk creating a health workforce unprepared to leverage the promise of AI or navigate its potential perils.*
>
> **Lomis et al. [2].**

The artificial intelligence (AI) revolution is changing everything. The influence of artificial intelligence will likely be equivalent to, or perhaps even greater than, that of the invention of the printing press, the steam engine, or the Internet. Machine learning and, more recently, generative AI have already begun to permeate various areas of knowledge creation and dissemination, to say nothing of the way work is both conceptualized and ultimately performed. This trend is expected to not only continue but accelerate, and healthcare and clinical practice are no exceptions to this AI-focused future. Given the tremendous opportunities and significant risks of the AI revolution, it is imperative that healthcare educators move quickly and thoughtfully to prepare healthcare professionals to intelligently incorporate AI into their learning and their practice.

AI will play an increasingly pivotal role in the education and continual professional development of healthcare providers [3]. At every stage of their careers, healthcare professionals will need to learn *about* AI. Healthcare providers will need to understand what it is, how to use it effectively and ethically, evaluate it, interpret its results, and explain how it is used in their clinical practice. In addition, healthcare trainees will need to learn *with* AI tools for adaptive learning and assessment, simulation, and knowledge retrieval. To optimize learning and enhance patient care, healthcare trainees, professionals,

Digital Health. https://doi.org/10.1016/B978-0-443-23901-4.00003-9

and institutions should embrace an adaptive systems perspective, follow an evidence-based integration approach, and maintain a human-centered, ethical orientation when using AI. This adaptivity and discernment are critical to ethical and effective use of AI, especially in light of the rapidly accelerating pace of technological advancement.

While AI adoption in healthcare and medical practice is slower than in some other fields, such as marketing, financial services, and transportation, the rate of adoption is beginning to accelerate. Despite this increasing speed, however, the implementation of AI into medical, nursing, and allied health *schools* has been much slower [4], even though many medical educators and students recognize the growing importance and desirability of AI education in both learning and practice [5].

The slow adoption of AI in medical education may be due to a number of barriers as enumerated by Otles et al [6]. One significant hurdle is resistance to change, as some educators and institutions are hesitant to embrace new technologies, teaching methods, and content [7]. This is similar to what happened during early attempts to introduce evidence-based medicine into medical school curricula in the 1990s. Additionally, many faculty and administrators feel they don't have the time to develop their understanding of AI and keep up with this rapidly evolving field. Another factor is the difficulty of finding room for AI in an already overcrowded curriculum, especially given the lack of research and documented best practices for incorporating AI into curricula. Further barriers include the cost of AI systems and tools and lack of resources necessary to maintain them, which present obstacles particularly for underfunded institutions. The use of AI also raises ethical concerns, such as ensuring data privacy, assuring accuracy, intellectual property rights, and accountability for AI decision-making in clinical scenarios.

There is a major benefit to overcoming these barriers because AI has the potential to mitigate, if not solve, some of the longstanding challenges in medical education [8,9] including:

- The ever-growing body of medical knowledge and resulting "information overload" [10].
- The high cost [8] and long duration [11] of medical education
- The lack of diversity and equity in the medical profession [12].
- The emphasis on test-taking and memorization
- The lack of sufficient early clinical practice and experience
- The stress of medical school

These formidable challenges require innovative solutions in curriculum content and structure, learning methods, infrastructure, and administration [13]. AI holds great promise as a toolset to address these challenges in clinical education.

This chapter will explore the potential opportunities and considerations for successfully implementing AI in healthcare education at every stage of healthcare professionals' development, from undergraduate medical education to graduate training and ongoing professional development in the workplace and through professional associations.

Design and implementation principles

The effective design and implementation of AI in healthcare education require a principled approach. This section introduces six key principles for consideration:

- Adaptive Systems Thinking
- Ethical Compass
- Evidence-Based Learning
- Human-Centered Design
- Integrative Approach
- Change Leadership

Taken together, these mutually supportive and overlapping principles provide useful guidance for taking healthcare education into the next stage in its evolution.

Adaptive systems thinking

Successful integration of this transformative new technology into medical education systems is a complex endeavor. The emerging field of complex adaptive system (CAS) has become an increasingly dominant lens for understanding natural and social sciences. It is also a fruitful approach for understanding and designing human organizations, including healthcare education systems, within the broader context of healthcare systems. These complex organizations are analogous to biological organisms with multiple subsystems that continuously adapt and coevolve with the changing ecosystem of which they are a part. With a complex adaptive systems mindset, we view medical education as a dynamic system made up of interconnected parts, such as students, teachers, patients, institutions, medical knowledge, technology, and the healthcare delivery systems, each of which is constantly evolving (both independently and, often, interconnectedly) and adapting to new challenges and opportunities [14,15].

The key characteristics of a CAS are:

- **Nonlinearity**: The behavior of a CAS is not always predictable from the behavior of its individual parts and small changes in one part of the system can have large and unpredictable effects on other parts of the system. Colloquially, the *Butterfly Effect.*

- **Emergence**: CASs exhibit emergent properties, which are properties that arise from the interactions of the individual parts but are not present in the parts themselves. Colloquially, the principle that states that *the whole is greater than the sum of the parts.*
- **Self-organization**: CASs are able to organize themselves without the need for central control.
- **Adaptation**: CASs are able to learn and adapt to their environment, allowing them to survive and thrive in changing conditions.

Systems thinking with a CAS approach can provide valuable guidance for the successful integration of AI technologies into medical education. For instance, this approach underscores that decision-making would be largely ineffective if it remains primarily a top-down process. Instead, it promotes the involvement of cross-functional teams, which should include administrators, faculty, students, and members of various departments and disciplines (e.g., data science, informatics, and/or curriculum designers). Furthermore, it encourages the perspective of viewing the medical or nursing school as part of the larger system of undergraduate and postgraduate medical education, healthcare systems, and professional organizations.

It also means that leaders must avoid falling into the trap of creating a top-down, detailed plan that will never be implemented. Instead, they can adopt an adaptive approach, by establishing clearly defined goals and principles, and then gradually taking small steps, conducting experiments, assessing effectiveness, and making adjustments. This "Crawl-Walk-Run" approach as proposed by Paul and Tanniru [16,17] aligns well with the rapidly changing AI and technology landscape. Further, it allows for continuous iteration and adaption based on outcome feedback and in response to the incorporation of new medical knowledge and technologies (at this stage, Paul and Tanniru's "Crawl"). The next stage entails the expansion of initiatives that have proven successful ("Walk"), followed by systemwide implementation ("Run"), all while maintaining a constant focus on sensing feedback and adapting to emerging challenges and changes.

The importance of the ethical compass

It is crucial to develop an ethical compass that guides the design and implementation of medical education curricula, methods, and assessments. There is a growing body of work in ethical guidelines for AI in medicine and clinical education [18]. The six core principles for ethical AI in healthcare identified by the World Health Organization (WHO) can serve as an excellent starting point for developing an ethical compass: (1) protect autonomy; (2) promote human well-being, human safety, and the public interest; (3) ensure transparency, explainability, and intelligibility; (4) foster responsibility and accountability; (5) ensure inclusiveness and equity; (6) promote AI that is responsive and sustainable [19].

Evidence-based learning

Just as evidence-based medicine has been nearly universally embraced in the field of medicine and medical education, there is an opportunity to integrate evidence-based *learning* methods into medical education. Although there is a wealth of research and best practices on learning and cognition currently available, its adoption has been slow in higher education as a whole and in healthcare education specifically. Some of the most promising evidence-based educational practices include:

- *Competency-Based Medical Education* – An outcomes-focused approach that emphasizes demonstrated proficiency in applying essential skills and knowledge to medical practice, rather than time spent in training [20].
- *Deliberate Practice* – Focused, extensive, purposeful practice with coaching and feedback with the goal of developing adaptive expertize [21].
- *On-Demand Knowledge* – the ability to quickly access and apply relevant medical knowledge when and where it is needed [22].
- *Personalized Adaptive Learning* – Learning paths and experiences that are dynamically tailored to the individual needs and interests of the learner [23].
- *Feedback and Coaching* – The provision of personalized guidance and support to help learners improve their performance [24].
- *Applied/Situated Learning* – Learning that is embedded in real-world (or simulated) contexts and activities [25].
- Spiral Curriculum – Learning that is designed to periodically circle back to build on prior knowledge and skills in a gradual and supportive way [26].

Part of the challenge in implementing these and other evidence-based practices parallels the challenges faced when adopting evidence-based medicine: individuals often teach in the manner they were taught. There is a crucial need to distill and disseminate this extensive body of learning science research for practical use by medical educators and curriculum developers, as well as to conduct practical research on the implementation, effectiveness, and evaluation of these and other learning methods in healthcare education.

While these methods can be highly effective, they can also be challenging time-consuming and resource-intensive to implement. However, AI tools that are currently in development have the potential to make it much easier and cost-effective to incorporate these learning methods.

Human-centered design

Human-Centered Design, a subset of Design Thinking, emphasizes a people-centered approach to guide the development of educational solutions that prioritize the genuine needs and perspectives of healthcare students, faculty, and ultimately, patients. These design methods can significantly enhance the design and implementation of AI in medical education.

Donald Norman [27] outlined the four principles of human-centered design:

1. *People-centered:* Focus design on all the impacted people and their context, including students, instructors, practitioners, and administrators, instead of focusing on technology.
2. *Solve the core problems:* Understand and solve the right problems and their root causes, not the symptoms.
3. *Systems approach:* Focus on the system of interconnected parts, not only individual components.
4. *Rapid prototyping:* Begin with small, simple interventions, test them, learn from them, and refine to ensure that solutions truly meet the needs of your constituents.

An integrative approach

Given the complex systems nature of healthcare education organizations, it is unlikely that one-off solutions, such as adding a single course on AI or an AI-based virtual patient in a lab somewhere will suffice. Instead, AI must be thoughtfully integrated into the very fabric of curricula and processes. I have a cautionary tale that illustrates this point. Many years ago, I led a team that developed a simulation for teaching immunology to first-year medical students. This simulation provided short immunology tutorials in the context of assessing a simulated patient. During an early trial, students found it engaging and effective. However, when we introduced it into 10 top medical schools, it turned out to be an abject failure. We discovered that the reason for this was that the simulator was not integrated into the faculty's courses; rather, it was tucked away in a lab as an optional activity, resulting in both minimal use and minimal impact.

Change leadership

AI is a disruptive technology that will necessitate change in most if not all fields. It behooves healthcare education institutions and leaders to engage in an intentional change management process such as Kotter's Leading Change [28], or Prosci's ADKAR model [29] to foster participation, buy-in, and acceptance of change by all constituents.

Karl Luke [30] proposed 12 tips for managing change in medical education. These tips are:

1. Consider individual change
2. Anticipate resistance to change
3. Ensure adequate change management resources

4. Establish active and visible sponsorship
5. Create "desire" to engage in the change
6. Manage change with effective training and coaching
7. Develop effective communication plans
8. Engage in constructive dialog
9. Create opportunities for codesign
10. Reinforce the change and celebrate successes
11. Begin the change process early
12. Use ADKAR to develop a change management plan

With these six key principles of design and implementation in mind, the next section explores considerations for learning *about* and *with* AI tools.

Learning about *AI*

Given the inexorable rise of AI in all fields, including healthcare, students and practitioners need to be aware of the current state of AI in the healthcare professions, and more importantly, they must develop the skills to research, evaluate, and skillfully use new tools as they emerge in the future. This must be done while confronting and navigating ethical considerations, potential biases, and privacy issues. Key skills such as discernment and the ability to separate hype from facts are also essential as they continuously research and evaluate the utility of emerging AI tools and technologies.

Clinical education about AI must go beyond learning about specific AI tools, which will likely become obsolete within years, if not months. It needs to focus on the development of core skills and competencies that will serve students as they become practitioners in this rapidly changing field. Russell and her collaborators [31] identified six competencies and 25 subcompetencies for AI in medical education.

Competencies for AI in Medical Education:

1. Understand the basics of AI and its applications in healthcare.
2. Comprehend the social and ethical implications of AI.
3. Integrate AI-enhanced clinical encounters to create patient-centered care plans.
4. Evaluate AI-based tools and their underlying data sets in patient care.
5. Analyze and adapt to changes in teams, roles, responsibilities, workflows from AI-based tools.
6. Engage in continuing professional development and practice-based learning related to AI in healthcare.

From another perspective, Wartman and Combs [10] recommend major features that curricula must address in order to respond to the challenges of AI.

Key Areas to be Addressed in AI Curricula:

1. Knowledge capture, not knowledge retention
2. Collaboration with and management of AI applications
3. A better understanding of probabilities and how to apply them meaningfully in clinical decision-making with patients and families
4. The cultivation of empathy and compassion.

Similar competencies can apply to faculty and administrators as well. There are a growing number of courses and curricula on the basics of AI in healthcare available from AMA, MIT, Stanford, Coursera, and others, so educators do not have to start from scratch.

Incorporating AI competencies into the curriculum is a complex task. A group of physicians and educators from the University of Michigan and the AMA [4,32] advocate for teaching AI as a "fundamental toolset of medicine," not just as an add-on course. They recommend a spiral curriculum, suggesting that fundamental knowledge about AI in medicine should be introduced early, then revisited throughout the course of medical training as the students learn more specialized skills. AI tools and assistants can be incorporated into case studies and situations so that students learn how to use (and how not to use) these tools in working with patients and solving problems. They can learn, in context, how to interpret and evaluate these AI applications in terms of accuracy and ethics, to provide quality healthcare to their patients.

Healthcare professionals will benefit from seeing AI differently than other "dumb" tools, instead considering AI to be a partner in practice—part of the patient—clinician—AI triad [33,34]. The emerging agency of AI enables it to serve as an invaluable assistant, offering focused expertise, similar to consulting with a colleague. However, they must learn to evaluate, select, and make wise and ethical use of these AI tools. "Trust and verify" should be a guiding principle. Clinicians must remember to validate results and not become complacent, as they remain ultimately responsible for patient care, much like pilots are responsible for passenger safety, even when flying with autopilot.

The imperative to incorporate learning about AI into the curriculum runs into the aforementioned challenges regarding the already overcrowded curriculum and the time, resources, and effort it takes to implement. Fortunately, AI can also be used to support learning, while reducing instructional and administrative time.

Learning with *AI*

AI has the potential to enhance, even revolutionize, the healthcare educational and learning process itself. Indeed, AI, used in a principled way, can solve, or at least mitigate many of the challenges that medical education is facing. This section will focus on some of the most promising ways of learning with AI tools and "partners."

Knowledge on demand

The explosion of medical knowledge has created an overwhelming challenge for healthcare students and practitioners. The current information-based focus is leading to information overload, becoming increasingly untenable and stressful for students. There's a growing recognition of the need to shift from memorization and didactic learning approaches to a greater emphasis on the application of evidence-based medical knowledge.

AI tools are rapidly emerging that can swiftly search, synthesize, and summarize medical information, reducing the need for memorization. AI can serve as a "partner" to faculty, clinicians, and students, aiding in the distillation of knowledge into targeted, useful, and digestible forms. AI tools are already simplifying the process of unearthing and summarizing relevant content from the vast body of medical research and knowledge. Specialized AI medical tools such as the one under development by the American Medical Association and Massachusetts Institute of Technology [35] can ingest and analyze a patient's medical records to quickly gather pertinent research and knowledge for that individual, facilitating optimal clinical decision-making. Similar tools can be used to enhance and focus learning from clinical case studies and simulations in clinical education by providing the relevant information at "the teachable moment."

Despite these promising developments, there are caveats regarding accuracy, "hallucinations," and bias in AI-provided information. These issues are rapidly being addressed through the introduction of large language models trained on verified medical sources (e.g., Med-PaLM 2, BioGPT, and ClinicalBERT) and fine-tuning through reinforcement learning from human feedback (RLHF) to improve accuracy and reduce bias. Nevertheless, clinical professionals need to learn how to discern and evaluate the output to ensure reliable and unbiased results.

AI powered simulations

AI-based simulation platforms can address the need for increased early clinical practice and experience in assessment, diagnosis, and communication. They are beginning to offer cost-effective and diverse opportunities for the extensive deliberate practice. As elaborated by K. Anders Ericsson et al. [21], such deliberate practice is essential for the development of clinical expertise by automating the provision of numerous challenging tasks, providing feedback, coaching, and opportunities for reflection.

AI-powered virtual patients [36] are now available through chatbot conversational platforms delivered on a phone, tablet, or personal computer. More sophisticated systems are also emerging, providing realistic AI video renderings of simulated patients with voice recognition and speech generation to provide robust simulations. These can be implemented on a computer screen, embedded within virtual reality (VR) systems, and even incorporated into physical manikins.

These AI simulation technologies go beyond static "canned" patient responses or a human "puppeteer" with limited conversational and feedback options. They create dynamically generated dialog and responses with virtual patients. These interactions can be assessed in real time by AI "coaches" to provide tailored scaffolding and feedback. Performance tracking protocols, such as Experience API, can be embedded to automatically analyze data generated in simulations to personalize feedback and recommendations for the optimal next learning experience. They can support Competency-Based Medical Education (CBME) with simulations designed to develop and assess key competencies.

There are many applications of these tools across the spectrum of clinical training for medical, nursing, and allied health students and practitioners. AI simulators offer active learning opportunities to practice applying medical knowledge to realistic assessment, diagnosis, and treatment planning. They extend beyond medical aspects of interactions to incorporate communication practice, with virtual patient responses that include verbal reactions, and even facial expressions and body language. Soft skills, such as active, empathic listening and clear, respectful communication in culturally sensitive ways, can be practiced in simulated interactions with diverse patient populations to reduce bias. Virtual reality simulations and AI-powdered robotics are used for training surgeons in selecting and implementation surgical techniques. They can even be used for practicing counseling, patient education, and consultation skills. AI simulations also enhance interpersonal communication and collaboration with interdisciplinary teams, colleagues, and other professionals.

While AI simulators offer great potential for these use cases, they must be well-designed and validated to provide accurate information, relevant responses, and avoid introducing bias. Effort and cost associated with producing robust simulations can be prohibitive, but development of AI simulators aims to streamline the process and make it more cost-effective than traditional methods.

Adaptive learning and assessment

AI-driven adaptive learning and assessment platforms are being developed and used to create personalized learning. M*acroadaptive* learning customizes learning paths and delivers learning experiences based on dynamic assessments of learner knowledge and skills. *Microadaptive* learning tools, often called intelligent tutoring systems, provide targeted feedback and coaching based on continuous assessment of the gaps between students' current performance and desired outcomes. These tools, when used appropriately, can streamline the learning process, reduce learner overwhelm, and expedite time to proficiency by tailoring learning to the individual needs of each student, regardless of their educational and cultural background.

Competency-Based Medical Education (CBME), which is being adopted by an increasing number of medical institutions, coupled with AI, presents a solution to many challenges in medical education. CBME offers a systematic, personalized path for developing the knowledge, skills, and behaviors necessary for learners to become proficient healthcare practitioners [37]. When effectively implemented, CBME can make the growing body of medical knowledge more manageable by focusing on the essential knowledge required for competency. The personalized and practical approach of CBME can reduce the time and cost of medical education, alleviate stress, and boost student motivation. Additionally, it can ensure that the challenges in medical education, such as understanding social determinants of health, honing communication skills, and AI education, are effectively addressed.

AI can aid in overcoming the significant curricular and institutional challenges in implementing CBME by assisting in the development and updating of competency models, making educational processes more efficient and effective. The Medbiquitous [38] consortium, sponsored by AAMC, provides machine readable competency models for various clinical specialties that can be easily be used by AI systems. AI can automate personalization of competency-based learning plans for students by analyzing their individual capabilities and learning preferences, thus minimizing the manual work for faculty. It can also be used for assessing individual learner performance, providing real-time targeted feedback rather than lump-sum grading based on standard criteria.

Conclusion

The AMA has identified a set of desired aims of AI in healthcare education, including enhancing the learner's experience, improving learning outcomes, enhancing educators' work life, reducing costs, and improving educational equity [18].

Healthcare education can be transformed to achieve these aims by incorporating AI into the curriculum and leveraging AI for enhanced knowledge retrieval, simulations, and personalized learning. Although transitioning to AI may present challenges and even disruptions, it simultaneously offers an opportunity to overcome many challenges in healthcare education. By embarking on this transformation using the six principles of AI design and implementation, these aims are well within reach.

AI disclosure

During the preparation of this work the author used generative AI for initial research, brainstorming, and ideation support. It was not used for writing the final draft. After using this tool/service, the author reviewed and edited the content as needed and takes full responsibility for the content of the publication.

References

[1] Kahn S. TED Talk: AI in the classroom can transform education. 2023. https://blog.khanacademy.org/sal-khans-2023-ted-talk-ai-in-the-classroom-can-transform-education/. [Accessed 1 May 2023].

[2] Lomis K, Jeffries P, Palatta A, Sage M, Sheikh J, Sheperis C, Whelan A. Artificial intelligence for health professions educators. NAM Perspectives 2021. https://doi.org/10.31478/202109a.

[3] Nagi F, Salih R, Alzubaidi M, Shah H, Alam T, Shah Z, Househ M. Applications of artificial intelligence (AI) in medical education: a scoping review. Studies in Health Technology and Informatics 2023;305:648−51. https://doi.org/10.3233/SHTI230581.

[4] Grunhut J, Marques O, Wyatt ATM. Needs, challenges, and applications of artificial intelligence in medical education curriculum. JMIR Medical Education 2022;8(2). https://doi.org/10.2196/35587.

[5] Mousavi Baigi SF, Sarbaz M, Ghaddaripouri K, Ghaddaripouri M, Mousavi AS, Kimiafar K. Attitudes, knowledge, and skills towards artificial intelligence among healthcare students: a systematic review. Health Science Reports 2023;6(3). https://doi.org/10.1002/hsr2.1138.

[6] Ötleş E, James CA, Lomis KD, Woolliscroft JO. Teaching artificial intelligence as a fundamental toolset of medicine. Cell Reports Medicine 2022;3(12):100824. https://doi.org/10.1016/j.xcrm.2022.100824.

[7] James CA, Wheelock KM, Woolliscroft JO. Machine learning: the next paradigm shift in medical education. Academic Medicine 2021;96(7):954−7. https://doi.org/10.1097/ACM.0000000000003943.

[8] Pierson L. Medical schools need to do more to reduce students' debt. Harvard Law Bill of Health 2021. https://blog.petrieflom.law.harvard.edu/2021/12/13/medical-schools-need-to-do-more-to-reduce-students-debt/. [Accessed 29 November 2023].

[9] Majumder MAA, Haque M, Razzaque MS. Editorial: trends and challenges of medical education in the changing academic and public health environment of the 21st century. Frontiers in Communication 2023;8. https://doi.org/10.3389/fcomm.2023.1153764.

[10] Wartman SA, Combs CD. Reimagining medical education in the age of AI. AMA Journal of Ethics 2019;21(2):146−52. https://doi.org/10.1001/amajethics.2019.146.

[11] Grady D. The drawn-out medical degree. The New York Times; 2014. https://www.nytimes.com/2014/08/03/education/edlife/the-drawn-out-medical-degree.html.

[12] Rosenkranz KM, Arora, Termuhlen, Stain SC, Misra, Dent D, Nfonsam, Diversity. Equity and inclusion in medicine: why it matters and how do we achieve it. Journal of Surgical Education 2021;78.

[13] Densen P. Challenges and opportunities facing medical education. Transactions of the American Clinical and Climatological Association 2011;122:48−58 [undefined].

[14] Kiviliene J, Blazeviciene A. Review of complex adaptive systems in nursing practice. Journal of Complexity in Health Sciences 2019;2(2):46−50. https://doi.org/10.21595/chs.2019.21169.

[15] Wilson T, Holt T, Greenhalgh T. Complexity science: complexity and clinical care. BMJ 2001;323(7314):685−8. https://doi.org/10.1136/bmj.323.7314.685.

[16] Paul C. The crawl, walk, run progression for strategic communication. In: 7th international conference on information warfare and security, ICIW 2012; 2012. p. 379−86.

[17] Tanniru MR, Xi Y, Sandhu K. Leadership to advance innovation for digital healthcare transformation. 2020. p. 1−24. https://doi.org/10.4018/978-1-7998-2799-3.ch001.

[18] Advancing AI in medical education through ethics, evidence and equity. American Medical Association; 2023. https://www.ama-assn.org/practice-management/digital/advancing-ai-medical-education-through-ethics-evidence-and-equity. [Accessed 30 November 2023].

[19] Ethics and governance of artificial intelligence for health: WHO guidance. Geneva: World Health Organization. World Heath Organization; 2021.

[20] Carraccio C, Englander R, Van Melle E, Ten Cate O, Lockyer J, Chan MK, Frank JR, Snell LS. Advancing competency-based medical education: a charter for clinician-educators. Academic Medicine 2016;91(5):645–9. https://doi.org/10.1097/ACM.0000000000001048.

[21] Ericsson KA. Deliberate practice and the acquisition and maintenance of expert performance in medicine and related domains. Academic Medicine 2004;79(10):S70–81. https://doi.org/10.1097/00001888-200410001-00022.

[22] Gottfredson C, Stroud C, Jackson M, Stevenson RL, Archer J. Optimizing learning in healthcare: how Island Health is evolving to learn at the speed of change. Healthcare Quarterly 2014;17(4):46–51. https://doi.org/10.12927/hcq.2015.24117.

[23] Fontaine G, Cossette S, Maheu-Cadotte M-A, Mailhot T, Deschênes M-F, Mathieu-Dupuis G, Côté J, Gagnon M-P, Dubé V. Efficacy of adaptive e-learning for health professionals and students: a systematic review and meta-analysis. BMJ Open 2019;9(8):e025252. https://doi.org/10.1136/bmjopen-2018-025252.

[24] Kappy B, Herrmann LE, Schumacher DJ, Statile AM. Building a doctor, one skill at a time: rethinking clinical training through a new skills-based feedback modality. Perspectives on Medical Education 2021;10(5):304–11. https://doi.org/10.1007/s40037-021-00666-9.

[25] Brown JS, Collins A, Duguid P. Situated cognition and the culture of learning. Educational Researcher 1989;18(1):32–42. https://doi.org/10.3102/0013189x018001032.

[26] Harden RM, Stamper N. What is a spiral curriculum? Medical Teacher 1999;21(2):141–3. https://doi.org/10.1080/01421599979752.

[27] What is human-centered design? Interaction design foundation - IxDF. Interaction Design Foundation - IxDF; 2021. https://www.interaction-design.org/literature/topics/human-centered-design. [Accessed 30 November 2023].

[28] Kotter J. Leading change. Harvard Business School Press; 1996.

[29] Hiatt JM, Creasey TJ. Change management: the people side of change. Prosci Inc; 2012.

[30] Luke K. Twelve tips for managing change in medical education. Meded Publish 2021;10(1). https://doi.org/10.15694/mep.2021.000053.1.

[31] Russell RG, Lovett Novak L, Patel M, Garvey KV, Craig KJT, Jackson GP, Moore D, Miller BM. Competencies for the use of artificial intelligence–based tools by health care professionals. Academic Medicine 2023;98(3):348–56. https://doi.org/10.1097/acm.0000000000004963.

[32] Grunhut J, Wyatt ATM, Marques O. Educating future physicians in artificial intelligence (AI): an integrative review and proposed changes. Journal of Medical Education and Curricular Development 2021;8. https://doi.org/10.1177/23821205211036836. 238212052110368.

[33] James CA, Singh K, Valley TS, Wiens J. The patient-clinician-artificial intelligence triad. Content last reviewed July 2023. In: Agency for healthcare research and quality. Publication No. 23-0040-4-EF. Agency for healthcare research and quality: Rockville, MD; 2023.

[34] Lorenzini G, Arbelaez Ossa L, Shaw DM, Elger BS. Artificial intelligence and the doctor–patient relationship expanding the paradigm of shared decision making. Bioethics 2023;37(5):424–9. https://doi.org/10.1111/bioe.13158.

[35] Marks JW, Pickhardt D, Gee WP, Brown ARA, Soares LdeF, Nuyts RC. U.S. Patent application No. 16/900,751. Medical literature recommender based on patient health information and user feedback. 2021. https://patents.justia.com/patent/20210391075. [Accessed 30 November 2023].

[36] Mergen M, Junga A, Risse B, Valkov D, Graf N, Marschall B. Immersive training of clinical decision making with AI driven virtual patients – a new VR platform called medical tr.AI.ning. GMS Journal for Medical Education 2023;40(2). https://doi.org/10.3205/zma001600.

[37] Hamza DM, Hauer KE, Oswald A, van Melle E, Ladak Z, Zuna I, Assefa ME, Pelletier GN, Sebastianski M, Keto-Lambert D, Ross S. Making sense of competency-based medical education (CBME) literary conversations: a BEME scoping review: BEME Guide No. 78. Medical Teacher 2023;45(8):802–15. https://doi.org/10.1080/0142159X.2023.2168525.
[38] MedBiquitous: the standards development program of the AAMC. 2023.

CHAPTER 4

Telemedicine: History, foundation, and clinical implementation

Mercedes Dodge[1,2] and Kathryn Werner[3,4]
[1]ReDirect Wellness, PLLC, Austin, TX, United States; [2]Orion Behavioral Health Network, Eagle River, AK, United States; [3]White Pine Mental Health & Wellness, Prattville, AL, United States; [4]Johnson & Johnson, New Brunswick, NJ, United States

History of telemedicine

Introduction

The American Telemedicine Association (ATA) defines telemedicine as "the use of medical information exchanged from one site to another via electronic communications to improve a patient's clinical health status" [1]. This definition makes it easy to consider telemedicine a modern phenomenon. However, if we consider a broader definition of telemedicine to be "distant medicine," then the trajectory of telemedicine mirrors that of medicine with slow progress for the bulk of human history and more rapid growth over the last century (Fig. 4.1).

Early concepts and precursors (prior to 1960s)

- African villagers may have used smoke signals and drumlines to warn others in times of illness [2].
- During the Bubonic Plague, Europeans may have transmitted information through heliographs, a messaging system of mirrors and light [2].
- Telegraphs were used during the American Civil War to transmit information for the treatment of soldiers, coordination of supplies, and reporting of casualties [2].

By the turn of the 20th century, radio and telephone brought about the expansion of early telemedicine. Notable events included:

- 1905: Willem Einthoven used the phone to transmit the first teleelectrocardiogram from his lab to his home [3].
- 1948: radiographic and fluoroscopic images were transmitted through telephone [4,5].

Digital Health. https://doi.org/10.1016/B978-0-443-23901-4.00004-0

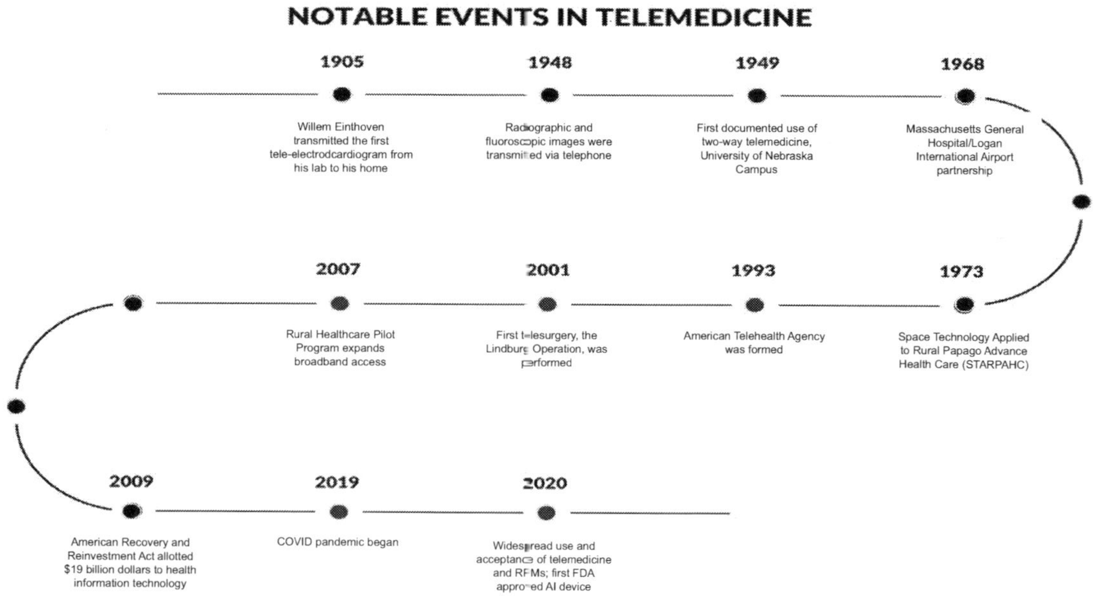

Figure 4.1

Notable events in telemedicine the milestones in history of telemedicine.

- 1949: first documented use of two-way telemedicine transmitted neurological exams across the University of Nebraska campus [6].
- 1950s: closed-circuit television transmits inpatient psychiatric consultations between the University of Nebraska and the University of Norfolk [7].

Emergence and development (1960–1980s)

The 1960s saw the growth of wireless transmission through radio, microwave, and satellite technologies. Removing the barrier of wired infrastructure allowed for improved accessibility and connectivity.

During the 1970s, the US Department of Health, Education, and Welfare (now the Department of Health & Human Services) and the National Aeronautics and Space Administration (NASA) partnered to provide care for the Papago Indians of Arizona in a program called Space Technology Applied to Rural Papago Advanced Health Care (STARPAHC). NASA tested telemedicine through satellite for manned spaceflight missions while DHHS was able to explore care in remote areas [8].

In 1968, Massachusetts General Hospital (MGH) connected hospital nurses to Boston's Logan International Airport through microwave relay to provide medical services [9]. This program expanded to psychiatric services at the Bedford, Massachusetts Veterans

Administration Hospital from the 1970s into the 1980s [10]. Similar programs were implemented nationwide [11].

Recognition and integration (1990–2010s)

In the 1990s, telemedicine was becoming more viable in expanding access and care, but the technology was only accessible by large health systems due to cost and lack of consistency across networks. Government and large health systems utilized government funding or grants from telecommunications companies to invest in "hub and spoke" setups linking larger medical systems to smaller facilities in rural areas. In 1993, the American Telemedicine Association was created to advance telemedicine, and subsequently, there were several pieces of legislation passed advancing telemedicine regulation. Numerous states, the Veteran's Administration (VA), and other health organizations began utilizing telemedicine more regularly [2].

The early 2000s saw a great expansion in telemedicine. The first telesurgery, known as the Lindberg Operation, was performed in 2001. A surgical team in New York led by Professor Jacques Marescaux controlled the arms of a robot in France to perform a minimally invasive total colectomy. The patient then went on to have an uncomplicated recovery [12]. In 2007, The Federal Communications Commission (FCC) initiated the Rural Health Care Pilot Program to expand broadband access to rural areas, and The American Recovery and Reinvestment Act of 2009 allotted $19 billion dollars to health information technology including telemedicine [13]. This increased funding and access to the Internet coupled with a better understanding of telemedicine allowed telemedicine to expand into almost every area of medicine and achieve increased recognition [14].

Current landscape

Currently, 99% of Americans have access to internet speeds and devices that support telemedicine. This level of access coupled with the COVID-19 pandemic has resulted in the global expansion of telemedicine. Due to safety concerns during the pandemic, the number of patient telehealth visits increased dramatically. The CDC reported a 154% increase in video visits for a large hospital system during March 2020 over March 2019 [15]. A single academic center in New York City showed over 8000% increase in the same period [16].

During this time, telemedicine was implemented to decrease the exposure to Coronavirus and much of the public encountered telemedicine for the first time despite their reservations. This exposure greatly changed the public perception of telehealth. Before the COVID-19 pandemic, 65% of patients doubted that telehealth would provide quality healthcare. After the pandemic, a survey of over 1000 patients reported that 91% were satisfied with video visits and 86% with audio only [17]. Many countries adopted laws and regulations to allow for easier access, insurance companies implemented telemedicine reimbursement, and patients and providers have become familiar with and accepting of telemedicine. Data indicate widespread use and acceptance of telemedicine even after the pandemic, which indicates that telemedicine will continue to be a part of the healthcare landscape of the future [18].

Future of telemedicine

As we consider telemedicine to be an ongoing means of care, technological, organizational, and legislative developments will likely continue to evolve to better integrate telehealth into our existing system of medical care.

The current Health Insurance Portability and Accountability Act (HIPAA) does not explicitly address current apps and telehealth platforms and leaves some ambiguity that could jeopardize patient information security. Additionally, current medical licensing is state-specific. This type of legislation does not adequately represent our current reality where telecommunication and patient mobility are not limited by geographical boundaries. The Interstate Licensing Compact by the Federation of State Medical Boards aims to ease the burdens of multistate licensing and has expanded to selected medical professionals, but has only been adopted by select states and for select medical professions. Modernization of HIPAA and medical licensing practices could greatly impact the future of telemedicine and expand patient access to care.

Technological advances will also continue to shape telemedicine. Both remote patient monitoring (RPM) and artificial intelligence (AI) are becoming increasingly sophisticated and prevalent. Their application and utilization will likely provide obvious benefits such as improved specificity of patient data, standardization of care, and increased access. However, there will also likely be unintended consequences including an overwhelming amount of data for providers, security and privacy issues, as well as ethical concerns [19].

Telemedicine basics

Types

Synchronous versus asynchronous

A telemedicine visit, commonly referred to as a televisit, can occur through various methods, enabled by advanced technology communication. Patients now have the option to use audio, electronic, and video platforms to engage with clinicians, both asynchronously and synchronously (Fig. 4.2 Types of Telehealth Encounters). This flexibility extends to hybrid and fully remote models. Regardless of the delivery method, the standard-of-care requirements remain consistent with in-person care standards.

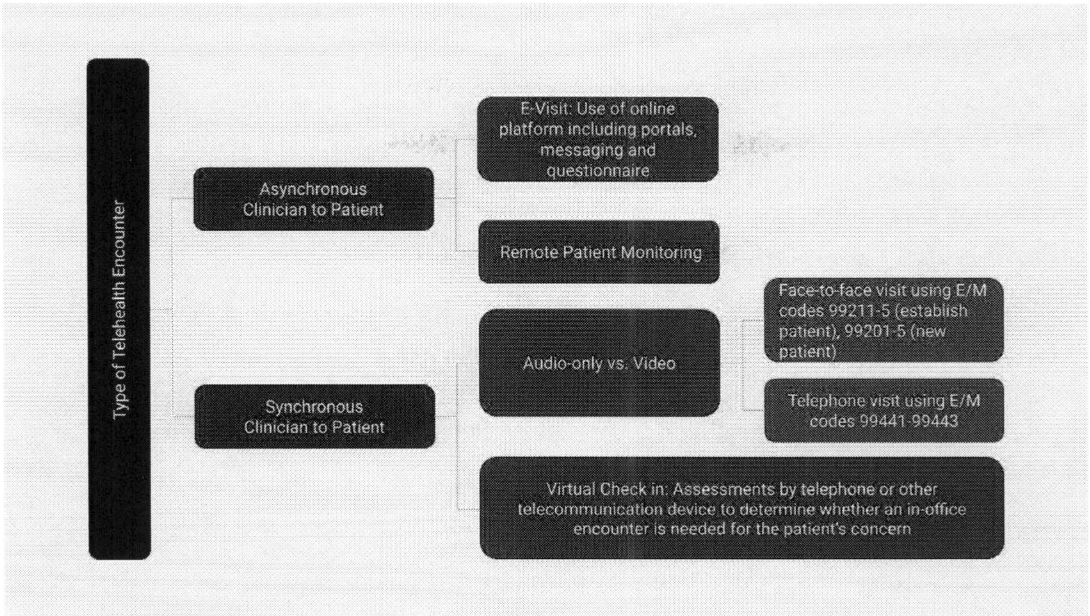

Figure 4.2
Types of telehealth encounters reviews the types of televisits.

Asynchronous communication involves patients sharing information with providers for later review [20]. Such interactions encompass messages, questionnaires, laboratory results, images, or other data exchanged between the medical team and patients, commonly known as "store and forward." This approach finds frequent use in specialties such as pathology, dermatology, radiology, and ophthalmology due to the ability to use image-based triage, and the ability to review relevant data remotely without real-time connection [21]. While clinical protocols may differ, the clinical data collected are customized to facilitate diagnostic and treatment decisions.

Conversely, synchronous televisits, also known as virtual visits, occur in real-time between clinicians and patients utilizing audio or video communications [21]. These visits are particularly relevant when immediate provider-to-patient interaction is needed such as in primary care and mental health.

Audio only versus audio—video

Telehealth visits can be audio only or a combination of audio and video. While audio—video visits provide an experience that is more comparable with an in-person visit, audio-only visits allow for care in situations where video may not be available or necessary. While audio-only visits may provide sufficient information for some patient concerns, it is not sufficient for others. Providers must be careful to select the appropriate mode of communication and make arrangements for alternative care if the available means are not appropriate.

Some insurances do not reimburse for audio-only care. Providers are responsible not only for providing the appropriate Current Procedural Terminology (CPT) modifier for the type of visit but also for complying with insurance requirements.

Technology and video platforms

While the origins of telemedicine predate that of modern technology, technological advances in communication have been pivotal in the expansion of telemedicine. Advances in technology have provided the ability to transmit EKGs, share imaging, transmit live video, and even control surgical equipment, all of which have contributed to the current widespread use of telemedicine.

Video platforms

Two-way live video transmission is the cornerstone of telemedicine. Not only does it allow a physical exam to be performed, but it also enhances the patient–provider relationship through nonverbal communication. During the COVID-19 Public Health Emergency, the requirement for an HIPAA-compliant telecommunication provider was waived. However, at present, it is required to use an HIPAA video communication service that offers end-to-end encryption where only the visit participants are able to join or observe the visit [22,23].

Remote patient monitoring

Remote patient monitoring (RPM) is the use of technology to send patient data. Scales, blood glucometers, blood pressure cuffs, pulse oximeters, fetal monitors, and other specialized devices can be used to monitor conditions such as diabetes, hypertension, asthma, sleep apnea, and even Parkinson's disease. Benefits of RPM include fewer emergency room visits, shorter hospitalizations, improved patient outcomes, and reduced risk of illness for caregivers [24].

Backup plans

While technology is increasingly more dependable, there are still lapses in connectivity. Planning for such disruptions can minimize disturbance. For video visits, having a second video platform available is preferable, but if the video is not available, converting the video visit to an audio-only visit is permissible as long as all necessary patient data can be obtained. If a physical exam is still needed and unable to be performed, the provider can schedule the patient back as soon as possible or refer to an alternate provider for immediate care.

Practice license considerations

While telemedicine predates the 2020 COVID pandemic, its widespread adoption has led to revisions in Federal and State laws. Providers and healthcare organizations must remain familiar with evolving regulations. Refer to the following resources: The National Consortium of Telehealth Resource Centers includes the Center for Connected Health Policy (CCHP), a federally funded program under the Department of Health and Human Services, and the American Telemedicine Association (ATA), a nonprofit organization that facilitates medical care access through telecommunications technology.

Key telemedicine practice and licensure considerations

- Prescribing regulations vary by state [25]. For Example: Does your state require prior in-person visits before prescribing? Does your state require electronic prescriptions?
- Controlled substance prescribing has both state and federal restrictions.
- DEA specifies telemedicine-controlled substance regulations.
- Post-COVID modifications. For Example: Is an in-person medical evaluation visit required beyond the public health emergency (PHE) exception?
- The interstate license allows cross-state patient care if the recipient state recognizes the compact.
  - Some states offer interstate compact licenses for specific medical professionals including: MDs, Nurses, Advanced Practice Nurses, Emergency Medical Technicians, Physical Therapist, Psychologists, Audiology & Speech Language Therapist, Occupational Therapist, and Licensed Professional Counselors (LPCs).
  - Physician Assistant (PA) Licensure Compact was created in collaboration with the *Council of State Governments* (CSG) and the Federation of State Medical Boards (FSMB) and is currently being evaluated at the state legislative level.
  - FSMB provides further information online.
- Instead of interstate licenses, some states, such as Florida and Arizona, offer out-of-state telehealth provider registration.

Settings

Currently, telemedicine is being used in almost every medical specialty and setting of medicine with innovative uses and platforms expected to expand. Traditional telemedicine occurs when a patient physically presents at a medical facility (the "origination site") and interacts with a provider at a distant site. This can be useful if the patient lacks the technology or ability to connect independently or when additional resources such as personnel, equipment, or medication are needed. Direct-to-consumer telemedicine refers to the delivery of telehealth while the patient is at their preferred location instead of a medical facility [26]. Direct-to-consumer telehealth offers convenience for the patient.

Outpatient

Numerous studies across multiple specialties have demonstrated the effectiveness of telemedicine in outpatient care. Notably, a cohort study of 526,874 patients demonstrated significantly better patient outcomes related to testing and screening in 13 of 16 measures with only insignificant benefits of in-office care in three of five measures related to medication use [27]. A 2020 study of 99 patients showed hypertension management by telehealth resulted in improved blood pressure control [27a]. Another study showed no significant difference in in-person versus telehealth diagnosis and treatment of upper respiratory complaints [27b].

Rural and underserved areas

In total, 15%–20% of Americans live in rural areas with limited healthcare access and poorer health outcomes [27c]. Ideally, telehealth would increase the number of individuals with access to care, decrease wait times for care, improve access to specialty care, and ultimately improve patient outcomes. However, as of 2016, 39% of rural Americans lacked access to high-speed broadband, which significantly limits telehealth capabilities [13].

Emergency department (ED)

Telehealth offers numerous solutions to problems frequently faced in the emergency department. Using telehealth to staff emergency departments allows for the rapid adjustment of personnel based on need and can decrease the rate of transfers from rural to urban EDs. Additionally, telemedicine provides the ability to connect EDs to specialty care. Teleneurology use in the ED can increase the rate of patients receiving appropriate stroke care by up to 50% [28]. Telepsychiatry in the ED decreased admission rates, length of stay, and cost of care while increasing patient satisfaction [29]. Both of these findings demonstrate that telemedicine can improve patient care and decrease the systemic cost of care.

Operating room

Since the first telesurgery in 2001, telesurgery has continued to evolve alongside technology. Benefits include providing surgical care to underserved or inaccessible areas, decreasing travel risk and cost, and allowing real-time collaboration between surgeons at different locations. Additionally, telehealth can be utilized for pre- and postoperative appointments. However, there continues to be a lack of clarity around billing, licensing, and general procedures for telesurgery [30].

Global health and disaster response

Telemedicine has been used in numerous instances across the globe to provide global disaster relief. Additionally, telemedicine could be particularly useful to improve access and decrease costs in rural areas where health education, disease prevention and surveillance, and access to care are severely limited. However, widespread utility is limited by infrastructure, especially in the areas where resources are most limited. Currently, 98% of the world's population has access to broadband internet, but coverage is widely variable by region. In 2021, only 70% of individuals in rural Africa and 75% of individuals in rural North and South America can access the Internet [31].

Mental healthcare

Because the traditional in-person mental healthcare visit can be largely reproduced during a telehealth visit and because of the shortage of mental healthcare providers, psychiatry and therapy are areas where telehealth is increasingly being utilized. In 2021, 40% of psychiatry visits were conducted virtually [32]. While data are still lacking, there seems to be no difference in the quality of care but increased patient satisfaction and decreased cost of care when telemedicine is used in comparison to in-person care [33].

Other

In addition to these broader categories, telehealth is used in almost every setting where healthcare is needed, including correctional facilities, nursing facilities, home health, military installations, student health centers, health education, and even the International Space Station. While the early 21st century has seen exponential growth in telemedicine, ongoing education and training for healthcare providers, evolving legislation and policy, and improved technological infrastructure are needed to realize telehealth's full potential.

Barriers

Barriers known to exist for telemedicine require innovative design processes and implementation that meet the needs of the patients while taking into account limiting factors. There has been a learning curve in telehealth adoption at the level of patients/consumers, providers, payers, and policymakers. Per the 2020 Telehealth Impact Study: Physician Study by the COVID-19 Healthcare Coalition, the foremost obstacle to maintaining telehealth services is reimbursement challenges, followed by technology challenges for patients [34].

First, consumer access to high-speed broadband internet is crucial for seamless telehealth interactions. The digital divide can hinder access to healthcare for populations in remote regions, such as rural and underserved areas, preventing them from benefiting from telemedicine services. To better advance the use of telehealth globally, the World Health Organization launched a Global Strategy on Digital Health 2020–25 calling for member states to evaluate and advance policies and infrastructure to support telehealth [35]. Thus, continued efforts to policymakers both at the federal and state levels are still required to increase broadband and connectivity.

Second, successful telemedicine interactions necessitate a level of comfort and proficiency with technology. Some patients, particularly elderly individuals or those with limited exposure to technology, may lack the technology and digital literacy to navigate virtual platforms effectively. This can lead to frustration, miscommunication, and reduced patient engagement, ultimately hindering the potential benefits of telemedicine. Potential options for solutions include creating a culturally competent digital literacy toolbox for patients and their caregivers, and also the ability to use audio only, email, text, and other tools to connect patients with technology should be used. Selecting a platform that provides clear navigation and connectivity will support both providers and patients and improve patient experience.

Certain medical conditions require in-person assessments that involve hands-on examinations, palpation, and auscultation. Therefore, it is important to align the needs of the patient and medical appropriateness for telemedicine visits. For example, certain medical specialties and conditions require specialized equipment for diagnosis and treatment. An opportunity for improvement here is to support hybrid models, to enlist care coordinators, and to ensure a seamless transition process from a telemedicine encounter to an in-person visit when required.

Benefits

Telemedicine provides numerous benefits for patients, providers, health systems, and communities.

Patients

Patient outcomes in telemedicine have been studied extensively with outcomes that are equal to or better than in-person care for a variety of measures and disease states including blood glucose goals, hypertension management, stroke management, pain control, mental health support, glaucoma detection, and preterm labor prevention [36]. These improved outcomes may be related to increased follow-up rates, improved patient satisfaction, and increased access to specialists.

Patient satisfaction with telemedicine is generally high due to comfort, convenience, and cost savings with a 95%–100% acceptance rate [37]. However, there is some nuance depending on the presenting complaint, previous relationship with the provider, technology used, and patient demographics [37]. A 2020 patient survey of over 4000 consumers reported that patient convenience, faster access to care, and ease of access to medical information are the top three reasons patients choose telehealth. Other areas of potential benefit from telemedicine include decreased patient risk from infectious disease and improved patient comfort possibly leading to increased disclosure when they are seen in a familiar environment.

Providers

A recent survey of physicians by the AMA showed that physicians felt telemedicine increased their work satisfaction by 54.2% and 44% of physicians reported decreased cost of care. More importantly, 75% of clinicians reported improved patient care [34]. Other theorized benefits of telemedicine would be decreased patient–provider violence, decreased risk of infection, and improved efficiency.

Other stakeholders

While patients and providers are most directly influenced by telemedicine, there are impacts on other stakeholders including hospital systems, employers, and communities. Decreased visit and commute time, a healthier workforce, and decreased healthcare costs should equate to higher productivity and profitability for employers. This is an area for future study.

For example, reviewing the benefit of using telemedicine in reducing time and expenses for caregivers needing to take family members to visits.

Conducting a telemedicine visit

Previsit preparation

Similar to in-person visits, previsit preparation is essential to ensure safe and effective virtual patient encounters. The workflow for traditional visits is well-established for both providers and patients. Thoughtful preparation and communication for telehealth visits can increase the likelihood of a successful visit.

Technological readiness

Both provider and patient should have access to appropriate devices, stable Internet connections, and a Health Insurance Portability and Accountability Act of 1996 (HIPAA) compliant telecommunication platform.

It can be helpful to provide the patient with written instructions at the time of scheduling and also allow additional time in the visit to troubleshoot any technological issues. In telemedicine, the patient experience is influenced by the ease of using the technology. For example, in cancer center delivery, a retrospective study revealed that heightened patient satisfaction was linked to comprehensive support for both patients and clinicians in preparing for telehealth visits [38].

Additional consideration should be given to lighting, background noise, and privacy. Providers regularly engaging in telemedicine may consider using a wired internet connection for stability and security as well as investing in a simple ring light, microphone, or headset for better sound and visual quality.

Patient education and consent

Each state has different requirements for patient education and consent around telehealth (which can be found at The National Consortium of Telehealth Resource Centers website). Some states allow verbal consent while others require signed, written consent. Be aware that some states require consent prior to each visit, and others require consent only at the beginning of care. Consent should explain telehealth, potential risks, potential benefits, and security measures. If consent is oral, it should be documented in the visit note [39].

Patients should also be educated about the structure of the visit including how to connect for their visit, who should be present during the visit, requirements around the physical location of the patient during the visit, the importance of safety during the visit, and the importance of limiting distractions. It may also be useful to educate the patient on what to do if telecommunication is disconnected and provide a backup method of communication [40].

Safety planning

Since telehealth involves meeting a patient outside the physical proximity of the provider, it is necessary to create a plan for safety specific to the patient's location. At the beginning of the visit, document the patient's exact location, the phone number of a local emergency medical provider, and the phone number of a local emergency contact. Discuss with the patient the circumstances that would lead to utilizing the safety plan, verbalize their understanding, and document appropriately [41].

Webside manner

The initial, fleeting moments lay the foundation for lasting perception. A 10th of a second exposure is sufficient for patients to make specific trait inferences from a facial experience [42]. Some ways to provide an optimal experience include:

- Ensuring a visually pleasant space that mirrors the professionalism of a medical setting
- Positioning the camera and any on-screen software in a way that allows the provider a natural and engaging gaze

- Orienting patients to the virtual experience and addressing potential technology-related issues
- Moving hand gestures into the field of view of the camera
- Narrating why you are looking away—at a different screen to review labs, for example
- Expanding treatment plans to encompass logistics, such as how to obtain vital signs
- Using screen share to show any visuals or drawings that would be helpful
- Sending educational materials electronically

Visit structure

The telehealth visit structure varies depending on which service model and setup have been created for the patient experience. In asynchronous virtual visits, patients are asked to complete a list of questions regarding their chief complaint. In a synchronous visit, where the patient is located at a clinical site while the provider is working remotely, the medical assistant, nurse, or clinical support staff may prepare the visit with preliminary questions, obtain vitals, and ensure proper paperwork is obtained. In the virtual encounter where both provider and patient are remotely logging in to the HIPAA-compliant video platform, the provider will most times manage the visit from beginning to end.

Interview

The Telehealth interview mirrors the standard outline of an in-person medical visit, covering the Chief complaint, History of Present Illness (HPI), Past Medical and Social History, Family History, Allergies, Medications, Assessment, Diagnoses, and Follow-up Plan. In a prospective study, a group of internists determined the final diagnosis in 76% of patients by obtaining the relevant diagnostic information through medical history alone [43]. This is consistent with other studies that report that most diagnoses are made from the medical history [44,45].

Examination

The physical examination is an important part of the tele-visit still and involves adapting clinical assessment skills and referring to in-person exams when necessary. Patients, parents, or on-site medical staff can assist when feasible.

Following are some guidelines for a telemedicine physical examination, which can be modified depending on the chief complaint and history collected Table 4.1.

Advancements in digital tools, such as medical digital otoscopes for viewing the outer and inner ear and interactive digital/electronic stethoscopes for lung and cardiac auscultations, aid healthcare providers.

Table 4.1: Examination tips and pearls.

	Tips and pearls

General appearance > including vitals	• General description of appearance, alertness, and orientation (AO)
	• Obtain patient-assisted recording of respirations and pulse (can be collected during visit or prior to encounter by a medical assistant).
	  • For pulse, the patient is asked to take 2 fingers (middle and index finger) from one hand and place them on the base of the thumb of the other hand. The provider will ask the patient to find the pulse and then count aloud each beat they feel while the provider times 15 s then multiply by 4. The patient can also comment on the regularity of the pulse.
	  • For respirations, the patient is asked to cross their arms and place them on the opposite shoulder. The provider will ask the patient to relax and the rate will be counted visually by the provider for 15 s and multiplied by 4.
	• If available also from home monitoring devices:
	  • Digital upper-arm BP cuff to provide BP and pulse
	  • Smartwatch to provide pulse
	  • Thermometer for temperature, document type of thermometer used-oral, tympanic, temporal artery (scans the surface of the forehead).
	  • Electronic scale for weight
	  • Pulse oximeter for oxygen level [46]
	  • Peak flow meter
	• Vital signs may also be documented from recent clinic visits
	• Check skin turgor dehydration by asking the patient to pinch skin over the back of the hand, or the abdomen, or chest under the collarbone

Dermatology complaint	• Obtain patient-assisted reports and visualization of new bruises, rashes, swelling • Expose skin areas on patients as much as possible when appropriate. • Use a coin placed by the patient alongside the rash or lesion to provide a size comparison. • Use a transparent cup or bottle to press against the skin to check for blanching. • Use an alcohol swab (if available) to check for terra firme forme dermatosis

Head, Eyes, Ears, Nose, Throat (HEENT) complaint	• Instruct patient to use their phone flashlight, or additional light source to assist with examination as needed
	• Head: document if normocephalic, atraumatic
	• Eyes:
	  • Document findings or absence of sclera injection, discharge, allergic shiners, cobblestoning, lid swelling, EOM (extraocular movement) intact, PERRL (pupils, equal, round, reactive, light, accommodation)
	  • Instruct patient to close eyes for examination for xanthelasma [46]
	• Ears: Document findings or absence of ear canal discharge, pain to palpation of pinna/tragus, mastoid tenderness
	• Nose: Sinus tenderness, nasal deformity, nasal discharge
	• Throat: Pharynx edema/exudates/drainage, tonsillar enlargement, mucous membrane, oral lesions, dental caries
	• Modified centor criteria for assessment of sore throat

Table 4.1: Examination tips and pearls.—cont'd

	Tips and pearls
Hematological/ lymphocytic complaint Pulmonology complaint	• Instruct patient how to feel for enlarged or tender cervical lymph nodes or axillary lymph nodes, as appropriate for the chief complaint • Document if the patient able to speak full sentences and if with normal effort • Request the patient to deeply inhale and hold for 10 s • Request to deeply inhale and exhale through open mouth • Document and observe for abnormal changes in respiratory rate, increased respiratory distress, coughing, wheezing, tachypnea

Cardiology complaint	• Document general appearance, distress level, and signs of cyanosis such as blue lips or facial pallor.
	• Document if the patient is dizzy when standing from a sitting position
	• Patient-assisted check on capillary refill
	• Neck:
	  • Document findings or absence of jugular venous distention, Corrigan's pulse.
	  • Instruct the patient to turn their head to their left while the provider observes any neck vein distention that would be above the clavicle. Ask the patient to inhale, and if there is consistent swelling this is consistent with Kussmaul's sign.
	• Extremity:
	  • Assess for color and skin changes
	  • Ask the patient to press their thumb into the pretibial area to assess for edema

Abdominal complaint	• Patient-assisted, ask the patient to lay down in a supine position with the camera angled onto the abdomen, ask the patient
	  • To palpate to assess if soft or firm, nontender or tender, and normal in size or distended [46]
	  • To point to the area of pain location
	  • To describe any changes in color
	  • To describe how any scars were obtained
	• Observe and document if facial grimacing is noted during the self-palpation of the exam to document guarding or rebound tenderness
	• Instruct patient to jump up and down to assess for guarding
	• If needed, instruct the patient to tap over the costovertebral angle (CVA) for tenderness

Psychiatric complaint	• Document the following mental status exam components
	  • General Appearance, hygiene, grooming, and eye contact level.
	  • Attitude - how does the patient relate to the provider and to the encounter
	  • Mood indicated in the patient's own words. Describe facial expression whether full range, reactive, dull, or blunted, for example. Document Affect and if congruent or appropriate to the complaint.
	  • Speech - describe rate, rhythm, volume - as if normal or pressured, for example.
	  • Thought process/association such as organized, goal-oriented, circumstantial, tangential.

Table 4.1: Examination tips and pearls.—cont'd

	Tips and pearls
	• Thought content including hallucinations, delusions, suicidal ideation, self-harm and homicidal ideation • Cognition is determined by the level of alertness and orientation. If concerned then consider mini Cog, or expand to a mini Mental Status Exam. • Insight/Judgment assessed as poor, fair, good. • Reliability is determined if the information provided is consistent with other resources • Abnormal Involuntary movement Scale (AIMS) can be completed by carefully positioning the camera
Musculoskeletal complaint	• Expose joint areas on patients as much as possible when appropriate. For example, wear a tank top for a shoulder exam. Assess for swelling, deformity, and ROM (range of movement). • Document cervical spine FROM (full range of motion) by asking the patient to look over the right shoulder and then the left shoulder to touch their chin, extend their neck, and rotate laterally [46]. • Visualize for erythema during the exam, and ask the patient to express if any warmth or tenderness was noted during the exam

Neurological complaint	• Describe speech and cadence
	• Modified neurological examination of Cranial Nerves III, IV, VI, the motor of V, VII, IX, X, and XII to include
	  • Assess EOM/PERRL/ptosis for III, IV, VI
	  • Patient-assisted touch to both sides of the face for equal sensation and if noted facial muscle weakness for V
	  • Patient instructed to blink, frown, smile, puff out cheeks for VII
	  • Check the presence of nystagmus for VIII
	  • Instruct patient to open mouth and say "AHH" for IX, X
	  • Instruct patient to move cervical neck to check for ROM, and then shrug shoulder for XI
	  • Ask the patient to extend the tongue for XII
	• For cerebellar assessment use the rapid alternating movement activity of finger-nose-finger. Also can use heel-to-shin. Assess for seated pronator drift by asking the patient to hold arms out with straight elbows, spreading fingers, then turning palms facing upward (supinated)
	• Glasgow Coma Scale
	• Face symmetry and if equal
	• Describe gait and test for Romberg. Ask the patient to rise up from a seated position with their arms folded across the chest [46]

Extremity complaint	• Document perceived temperature by the patient - hands or feet colder than usual, and whether it is isolated to just fingertips and toes [40] • Use thumb to press on the pretibial area to assess for pitting edema [40] • Instruct patient to put hands around claves to determine if swelling more than the other calf • Patient-assisted palpation over the foot to examine isolated tenderness or pain over anatomical locations

The telehealth examination can provide providers with clinical signs and indicators that the patient might benefit from an in-person examination [40]. It's crucial to ensure patient education and follow-up plans clearly communicate when more severe symptoms warrant an in-person or emergency visit.

Documentation

Documentation for telehealth visits serves the same purposes as documentation for in-person visits—to accurately capture the care provided for continuity of care, medicolegal protection, and billing. Similar to in-person visits, patient identification, date of service, relevant consents, the contents of clinical discussion, physical exam findings, diagnosis, treatment plan, risks and benefits of treatment, and relevant billing codes should be documented.

However, there is some additional information that must be captured for telehealth including:

- The specific location of the patient (originating site)
- Location of the provider and their state licensure
- The method of communication (audiovisual, audio only, asynchronous, the platform used)
- The patient's phone number
- A safety plan
- Telemedicine consent (verbal and/or written consent to discuss health information through telehealth technology)
- The appropriate CPT modifiers for telehealth (different payers require different modifiers, which change periodically; staying informed is crucial for appropriate coding)
- Any assistance provided by the patient, family member, or onsite medical staff
- Any limitations or constraints affecting the examination, such as poor lighting, technical disruptions, limitations due to video quality, or inability to perform certain examinations.

Resources

- PAs in Virtual Medicine and Telemedicine (PAVMT), www.pavmt.org
- The National Consortium of Telehealth Resource Centers, https://www.telehealthresourcecenter.org/
- Practice Guidelines: American Telehealth Association, https://www.americantelemed.org/resources/atas-practice-guidelines/

Assessments and questions

Assessment 1

Case study: Telemedicine in primary care

Background: You are a Physician Associate (PA) working in a primary care clinic that has recently adopted telemedicine. You have a scheduled telemedicine visit with a patient named Sarah, a 40-year-old woman who has been experiencing persistent allergy symptoms. This is your first telemedicine visit with Sarah.

Scenario: During the telemedicine visit, Sarah describes her symptoms, including sneezing, runny nose, and itchy eyes. She mentions that these symptoms have been affecting her daily activities and sleep. You conduct a virtual examination by asking about her medical history, allergies, and current medications. You recommend over-the-counter antihistamines and advise her to monitor her symptoms. Sarah agrees with your recommendations and asks about possible side effects of the medication.

Follow-Up Questions.

- How did prepare the patient for the telehealth visit?
- What steps did you take to ensure a professional and appropriate virtual environment for the visit?
- What information should you document in Sarah's electronic health record?
- How did you ensure effective communication and active listening during the telemedicine visit?
- What physical exam was performed and how did you modify those for telehealth?
- Identify any potential barriers that could have affected the quality of the telemedicine visit and explain how you addressed them.
- How does telemedicine contribute to positive outcomes in primary care, considering Sarah's case?

Assessment 2

Case study: Examination and documentation

A 7-year-old boy joins his mother in a virtual home visit, complaining of abdominal pain that has been troubling him for the past 5 days. He describes the pain as affecting his entire abdomen and mentions that it comes and goes throughout the day. There are moments when he seems completely fine, with regular eating and normal play, but he also experiences times when he interrupts his activities to express intense belly pain. He has had a few instances of loose stools on and off this week and has even returned from school with soiled underwear at times. This morning, he conveyed feelings of nausea and reluctance to attend school. His mother is unsure whether his desire to stay home is due to potential embarrassment or an emerging illness, prompting her to keep him home for observation.

What is the most appropriate physical examination approach in a telemedicine visit?

1. Palpate the abdomen with the mother's assistance
2. Assess the patient's coordination and balance
3. Observe the patient's behavior while eating during the visit
4. Request the patient to display a sample of stool on camera
5. Utilize the Bristol stool scale for the patient to describe stool characteristics

Correct answer: The patient's abdominal examination with palpation is the most appropriate next step to determine location, tenderness, and absence or presence of guarding. These examination findings along with additional history will help obtain a differential, for example, epigastric pain suggests GERD, gallbladder, or pancreatitis, while Left Lower Quadrant (LLQ) abdominal pain can suggest constipation, diverticulitis, or Inflammatory Bowel Disease (IBD). In this case, the patient demonstrates chronic constipation resulting in overflow fecal incontinence (diarrhea), and through additional history, no behavioral or psychological concerns were revealed. The Bristol stool scale is a diagnostic pictorial aid designed to classify stool into seven categories. Although it may help gather information on the severity of constipation, it is most sensitive in monitoring the effectiveness of treatments for various diseases of the bowel.

What would be a physical exam finding document for the above case?

Example:

Constitutional: Well appearing, no apparent distress. A&O.

Eyes: Conjunctiva clear without icterus, pallor, or injection.

ENT: Nose without external redness or drainage. Mouth with normal dentition; moist mucous membranes.

CV: No lower extremity peripheral edema or signs of cyanosis.

Respiratory: Breathing comfortably and speaking in full sentences without evident tachypnea or signs of respiratory distress.

GI: Abdomen is nondistended. Tender to palpation throughout LLQ, performed by mother. Skin No visible rashes.

Psychological: Appropriate affect. Intact thought and speech.

Neurological: Alert and oriented. Moving upper extremities appropriately.

AI disclosure

During the preparation of this work, the author(s) used ChatGPT in order to for purpose of improving readability and language for the reader. After using this tool/service, the author(s) reviewed and edited the content as needed and take(s) full responsibility for the content of the publication.

References

[1] Telehealth. American medical association. 2023.

[2] Bashshur, Shannon GW. History of technological foundations of telemedicine. In: history of telemedicine: evolution, context, and transformation. Mary Ann Liebert, Inc; 2009. p. 25–76.

[3] Barold SS. Willem Einthoven and the birth of clinical electrocardiography a hundred years ago. Cardiac Electrophysiology Review 2003;7(1):99–104. https://doi.org/10.1023/A:1023667812925.

[4] Gershon-Cohen J, Cooley AG. Telognosis. Radiology 1950;55(4):582–7. https://doi.org/10.1148/55.4.582.

[5] Jutras A. Teleroentgen diagnosis by means of video-tape recording. American Journal of Roentgenology, Radium Therapy and Nuclear Medicine 1959;82:1099–102.

[6] Wittson CL, Benschoter R. Two-way television: helping the Medical Center reach out. American Journal of Psychiatry 1972;129(5):624–7. https://doi.org/10.1176/ajp.129.5.624.

[7] The role of telehealth in an evolving health care environment: workshop summary. vol. 3. National Academies Press; 2012.

[8] Telemedicine: a guide to assessing telecommunications in health care. National Academy Press; 1996.

[9] Murphy RL, Bird KT. Telediagnosis: a new community health resource. Observations on the feasibility of telediagnosis based on 1000 patient transactions. American Journal of Public Health 1974;64(2):113–9. https://doi.org/10.2105/AJPH.64.2.113.

[10] Crump WJ, Pfeil T. A telemedicine primer: an introduction to the technology and an overview of the literature. Archives of Family Medicine 1995;4(9):796–803. https://doi.org/10.1001/archfami.4.9.796.

[11] Scannell KM, Perednia DA, Kissman HM. Telemedicine: past, present, future. 1995. 1995.

[12] Telesurgery - an efficient interdisciplinary approach used to improve the health care system. Journal of Medical Life 2014;7:137–41.

[13] Federal communications commission. The FCC's rural health care Pilot program: consumer guide. 2016. 2016.

[14] Kelch D. Staying connected – a progress report: reimbursement under the telemedicine development Act of 1996, center for connected health policy. 2010. 2010.

[15] Koonin LM, Hoots B, Tsang CA, Leroy Z, Farris K, Jolly B, Antall P, McCabe B, Zelis CBR, Tong I, Harris AM. Trends in the use of telehealth during the emergence of the COVID-19 pandemic - United States, January-March 2020. Morbidity and Mortality Weekly Report 2020;69(43):1595–9. https://doi.org/10.15585/MMWR.MM6943A3.

[16] Ramaswamy A, Yu M, Drangsholt S, Ng E, Culligan PJ, Schlegel PN, Hu JC. Patient satisfaction with telemedicine during the COVID-19 pandemic: retrospective cohort study. Journal of Medical Internet Research 2020;22(9). https://doi.org/10.2196/20786.

[17] Imlach F, McKinlay E, Middleton L. Telehealth consultations in general practice during a pandemic lockdown: survey and interviews on patient experiences and preferences. BMC Family Practice 2020;21(1):269. https://doi.org/10.1186/s12875-020-01336-1.

[18] Omboni S, Padwal RS, Alessa T, Benczúr B, Green BB, Hubbard I, Kario K, Khan NA, Konradi A, Logan AG, Lu Y, Mars M, McManus RJ, Melville S, Neumann CL, Parati G, Renna NF, Ryvlin P, Saner H, Schutte AE, Wang J. The worldwide impact of telemedicine during COVID-19: current evidence and recommendations for the future. Connected Health 2022. https://doi.org/10.20517/ch.2021.03.

[19] Jin MX, Kim SY, Miller LJ, Behari G, Correa R. Telemedicine: current impact on the future. Cureus 2020. https://doi.org/10.7759/cureus.9891.
[20] Asynchronous direct-to-consumer telehealth. telehealth.hhs.gov. Published October 28, 2022. https://telehealth.hhs.gov/providers/best-practices-guides/direct-to-consumer/asynchronous-direct-to-consumer-telehealth.
[21] Caffery LJ, Farjian M, Smith AC. Telehealth interventions for reducing waiting lists and waiting times for specialist outpatient services: a scoping review. Journal of Telemedicine and Telecare 2016;22(8):504–12. https://doi.org/10.1177/1357633X16670495.
[22] HHS office for Civil rights announces the expiration of COVID-19 public health emergency HIPAA notifications of enforcement discretion. 2023. https://www.hhs.gov/about/news/2023/04/11/hhs-office-for-civil-rights-announces-expiration-covid-19-public-health-emergency-hipaa-notifications-enforcement-discretion.html. [Accessed 15 September 2023].
[23] Epalm. Data privacy and telehealth: protect the data, protect the patient. 2021. 2021.
[24] Telehealth and remote patient monitoring | Telehealth. hhs.gov. 2023.
[25] Drug Enforcement Administration. Electronic prescriptions for controlled substances (EPCS) Q&A.
[26] Telehealth for direct-to-consumer care (no date) Introduction to direct-to-consumer telehealth | Telehealth. HHS.gov. 2023 [Available].
[27] Baughman DJ, Jabbarpour Y, Westfall JM, Jetty A, Zain A, Baughman K, Pollak B, Waheed A. Comparison of quality performance measures for patients receiving in-person vs telemedicine primary care in a large integrated health system. JAMA Network Open 2022;5(9). https://doi.org/10.1001/jamanetworkopen.2022.33267.
[27a] Yatabe J, Yatabe MS, Okada R, Ichihara A. Efficacy of telemedicine in hypertension care through home blood pressure monitoring and videoconferencing: randomized controlled trial. JMIR Cardio 2021;5(2):e27347. https://doi.org/10.2196/27347.
[27b] Accorsi TAD, Moreira FT, Pedrotti CHS, et al. Telemedicine diagnosis of acute respiratory tract infection patients is not inferior to face-to-face consultation: a randomized trial. Einstein (Sao Paulo) 2022;20:eAO6800. https://doi.org/10.31744/einstein_journal/2022AO6800.
[27c] Warshaw R. Health disparities affect millions in rural U.S. communities. AAMC. 2017 https://www.aamc.org/news-insights/health-disparities-affect-millions-rural-us-communities.
[28] Totten AM, Womack DM, Griffin JC, McDonagh MS, Davis-O'Reilly C, Blazina I, Grusing S, Elder N. Telehealth-guided provider-to-provider communication to improve rural health: a systematic review. Journal of Telemedicine and Telecare 2022. https://doi.org/10.1177/1357633X221139892.
[29] Reinhardt I, Gouzoulis-Mayfrank E, Zielasek J. Use of telepsychiatry in emergency and crisis intervention: current evidence. Current Psychiatry Reports 2019;21(63). https://doi.org/10.1007/s11920-019-1054-8.
[30] Choi PJ, Oskouian RJ, Tubbs RS. Telesurgery: past, present, and future. Cureus 2018. https://doi.org/10.7759/cureus.2716.
[31] Facts and figures 2021. 2021. 2021.
[32] Zhu JM, Myers R, McConnell KJ, Levander X, Lin SC. Trends in outpatient mental health services use before and during the COVID-19 pandemic. Health Affairs 2022;41(4):573–80. https://doi.org/10.1377/hlthaff.2021.01297.
[33] Langarizadeh M, Tabatabaei MS, Tavakol K, Naghipour M, Rostami A, Moghbeli F. Telemental health care, an effective alternative to conventional mental care: a systematic review. Acta Informatica Medica 2017;25(4):240–6. https://doi.org/10.5455/aim.2017.25.240-246.
[34] Telehealth impact study: physician survey, COVID-19 healthcare coalition. 2020. 2020.
[35] Global strategy on digital health 2020-2025. World Health Organization; 2021. https://apps.who.int/iris/handle/10665/344249. [Accessed 15 September 2023].
[36] Snoswell CL, Chelberg G, De Guzman KR, Haydon HH, Thomas EE, Caffery LJ, Smith AC. The clinical effectiveness of telehealth: a systematic review of meta-analyses from 2010 to 2019. Journal of Telemedicine and Telecare 2021. https://doi.org/10.1177/1357633x211022907.

[37] Nguyen M, Waller M, Pandya A, Portnoy J. A review of patient and provider satisfaction with telemedicine. Current Allergy and Asthma Reports 2020;20(11). https://doi.org/10.1007/s11882-020-00969-7.

[38] Patel KB, Alishahi Tabriz A, Turner K, Gonzalez BD, Oswald LB, Jim HSL, Nguyen OT, Hong Y-R, Aldawoodi N, Cao B, Wang X, Rollison DE, Robinson EJ, Naso C, Spiess PE. Telemedicine adoption in an NCI-designated cancer center during the CCVID-19 pandemic: a report on patient experience of care. Journal of the National Comprehensive Cancer Network 2023;21(5):496–502. https://doi.org/10.6004/jnccn.2023.7008.

[39] Center for Connected Health Policy. Telehealth policy 101 - CCHP. 2022. https://www.cchpca.org/policy-101/?category=informed-consent. [Accessed 15 September 2023].

[40] Helping patients prepare for their telehealth appointment | Telehealth. 2023.

[41] Creating an emergency plan | Telehealth. 2023.

[42] Willis J, Todorov A. First impressions: making up your mind after a 100-ms exposure to a face. Psychological Science 2006;17(7):592–8. https://doi.org/10.1111/j.1467-9280.2006.01750.x.

[43] Peterson MC, Holbrook JH, Von Hales D, Smith NL, Staker LV. Contributions of the history, physical examination, and laboratory investigation in making medical diagnoses. Western Journal of Medicine 1992;156(2):163–5.

[44] Roshan M, Rao AP. A study on relative contributions of the history, physical examination and investigations in making medical diagnosis. Journal of the Association of Physicians of India 2000;48(8):771–5.

[45] Hampton JR, Harrison MJ, Mitchell JR, Prichard JS, Seymour C. Relative contributions of history-taking, physical examination, and laboratory investigation to diagnosis and management of medical outpatients. BMJ 1975;2(5969):486–9. https://doi.org/10.1136/bmj.2.5969.486.

[46] Benziger CP, Huffman MD, Sweis RN, Stone NJ. The telehealth ten: a guide for a patient-assisted virtual physical examination. The American Journal of Medicine 2021;134(1):48–51. https://doi.org/10.1016/j.amjmed.2020.06.015.

CHAPTER 5

Beyond the wrist: Wearables in healthcare

Hina Mazharuddin
PAVMT, Houston, TX, United States

Introduction

Wearable devices refer to electronics that can be worn on the body, most commonly seen as accessories or clothes. Popular examples of wearables include smart watches, fitness trackers, smart glasses, and smart clothing. Wearables gather data through sensors that can be used to monitor health, fitness metrics, provide notifications or alerts, and integrate into larger systems. These data can be used for historical tracking, real-time tracking, and predictive future analysis [1].

Background

The foundation of wearable computers can be linked back to the 16th century with women's wristwatches. Traditionally, men used pocket watches, and the idea of using a wristwatch was once viewed as feminine. It took a war to change that notion. Toward the end of the 19th century, military men started to adopt the use of wristwatches as a discreet wearable device to synchronize maneuvers without disclosing themselves to the enemy [2].

Edward O. Thorp, a mathematics professor at the Massachusetts Institute of Technology, and Claude Shannon conceived the first wearable computer to predict the roulette wheel in the 1960s [3]. Since then, wearable technology has flourished and cross-pollinated in different fields such as healthcare, education, culture, social networking, and the military [1].

Types of wearable devices

Smartwatches

One of the most widely used wearable devices are smart watches, which have the computational ability and sensors of a miniature computer blending fashion and functionality. Smartwatches provide the user with a hands-free approach to a multitude of

Digital Health. https://doi.org/10.1016/B978-0-443-23901-4.00005-2

features including fitness tracking, heart rate monitoring, notifications for calls, messages, music control, and a digital wallet. In addition to the ease it provides, the data collected can enable self-monitoring, pattern analysis and have the ability to be shared with others. These data can be shared through smartphones, interactions with apps, and uploaded to electronic medical records empowering families and medical teams.

"Smartwatches have the potential to transform healthcare by supporting and evaluating health in everyday living because they [1]: are familiar to most people [2]; are increasingly available as a consumer device [3]; enable near-real-time continuous monitoring of physical activity and physiological measures [4]; support tailored messaging and reminders [5]; enable communication between patients, family members, and healthcare providers; and [6] allow for in situ, mini-surveys and behavior verification based on sensor-based measures." [4].

Smartwatches can also be used as specialty devices for activities such as hiking, diving, and flying. These specialized devices can use a Global Positioning System (GPS), monitor basic vitals, forecast weather, calculate dive times, flight logging, and provide barometric data, and more!

Fitness trackers

Fitness trackers, often integrated into smartwatches and other wearable devices, are an easy way to track physical activity, steps, and calories burned. Fitness trackers can monitor heart rate, heart rate variability, body composition, and sleep tracking. "Wearable activity trackers have been shown to be associated with improved physiological outcomes, such as reduced BMI, reduced blood pressure, and increased aerobic capacity which might occur via increases in physical activity." [5] Wearable activity trackers can also potentially improve psychosocial outcomes such as anxiety and depression. Physical activity has been shown to have antidepressant and anxiolytic effects. Fitness trackers can also allow for goal setting, self-monitoring, and gamification encouraging users to make educated positive decisions.

Smart glasses

Smart glasses are another wearable device that blends technology with eyewear. These glasses allow for the ability to display information directly in the consumer's field of vision, changing the way we perceive and interact with our surroundings. Smart glasses allow for an overlay of augmented reality to the real world with built-in cameras, speakers, microphones, and videos working together for an immersive experience. Smart glasses can be utilized in multiple areas such as entertainment, gaming, and redesigning workspaces for multiple fields.

For gaming and entertainment, smart glasses create experiences where gamers can be visually transported into the game. Coupled with augmented reality, smart glasses can allow users to interact with their surroundings during gameplay.

Smart glasses could also be utilized by emergency medical services and first responders to improve their workflow given the "hands-free nature and capability of processing and capturing various patient data" [6] Imagine a first responder, such as a firefighter, who may have access to smart glasses, which could provide a hands-free, real-time access to information and resources. Smart glasses could also serve to enhance situational awareness, decision-making, and response capabilities by providing a visual with an overlay of maps, building infrastructure, and information that can help a first responder navigate unfamiliar locations and avoid potential hazards. Glasses can provide eye protection without obstructing vision. In emergent situations, smart glasses allow for an added bonus of enhanced vision with more information in the user's visual field for better-informed decisions. Smart glasses also allow for a hands-free ability to collaborate. Smart glasses are revolutionizing the way we perceive and engage with our surroundings.

Smart clothing

Smart clothing is wearable textiles that can assist us by enhancing our daily lives. By combining fashion and functionality, these garments are embedded with sensors, microprocessors, and wireless connectivity turning them into intelligent devices that can monitor health, regulate body temperature, and even generate energy. Such textiles allow for seamless integration into clothing, making wearables more comfortable and discreet. Combining LED displays and haptic feedback systems allows for an interactive experience with smart clothing.

Smart textiles can be used for healthcare, fitness, health, and safety. Performance-enhancing smart clothing can analyze biomechanics and can be used to optimize athletic training and medical rehabilitation. In addition, smart clothing can incorporate safety through visibility enhancements, emergency alerts, and GPS. Smart clothing can also integrate with mobile apps or other devices to share data with loved ones or other teams such as medical providers. A study using smart clothes assistance yielded positive results by offering supplementary support to family caregivers by providing interactions in real time to help manage medical conditions. Wearable garments that also provided data helped enhance the predictability of the care recipient's behaviors and provided emotional support [7,8].

Health monitoring devices

Currently, the majority of our healthcare system has become a "sick care" system where we wait for people to become ill before we introduce medical interventions. Wearable devices allow us to not only monitor those with medical conditions but also monitor our wellness *before* we develop any illness.

Wearable medical devices can also allow for the monitoring of chronic conditions such as diabetes, cardiovascular disease, hypertension, chronic obstructive pulmonary disease, and polycystic ovarian syndrome, to name a few. Managing chronic conditions requires constant monitoring of key indicators. Traditional measurements often include blood sugar, heart rate, blood pressure, pulse oximetry, and temperature. Wearables can also obtain noninvasive measurements from biofluids such as sweat, tears, saliva, and interstitial fluids. Wearables can also utilize electrochemical, optical sensors, metabolites, bacteria, and hormones to capture data and thus make predictive outcomes for the future [9,10]. With wearable medical devices, timely interventions may be easily accessible to prevent complications and improve quality of life.

Continuous glucose monitoring (CGM) systems were initially created for monitoring diabetes in patients. CGM allows for real-time insights for better glycemic control. A small sensor is typically inserted under the skin to measure glucose levels in the interstitial fluid. These readings are then transmitted to a receiver or smartphone. However, CGMs can also benefit healthy adults in healthcare, wellness, and sports. Beyond their traditional use, CGMs can provide valuable insight into the body's response to nutrition, activities, and stressors to optimize health. In sports, athletes can use such feedback to modify their training, nutrition, and recovery with glucose levels. In healthcare, CGMs can also provide feedback on sleep quality, diet, exercise, and glucose regulation. This personalization can lead to accountability and self-modification for desired outcomes [11,12]. Wearables give us the ability to change the healthcare system from reactive to proactive and the potential to be predictive.

Remote patient monitoring devices

Remote patient monitoring (RPM) allows for the monitoring of chronic health conditions such as diabetes regardless of location. With distance not being a factor, healthcare providers can detect changes or abnormalities and intervene promptly. RPM allows medical providers to monitor an aspect of patient health such as glucose levels remotely eliminating the need for frequent in-person visits, reducing hospitalizations due to complications from poorly managed blood sugars, and giving patients the ability to manage conditions from their homes. RPM can be conducted through telemonitoring, home health, mobile phone–based, and videoconferencing.

RPMs can be used to help monitor acute, chronic, and complex conditions. A study used RPMs for heart failure noted "Telemonitoring and home telehealth appear generally effective in reducing heart failure rehospitalization and mortality." [13] Heart failure clinical outcomes are correlated with how well a person can manage their condition between office visits with their healthcare provider. When patients with heart failure are not well managed, studies show that patients have higher readmission to hospitals. To avoid exacerbations and rehospitalizations, patients are encouraged to monitor and modify their lifestyles and symptoms. By using remote patient monitoring, patients can participate in the monitoring and management of their disease progression [13,14].

Digital tattoos

Among the various different types of wearables, "digital tattoos" stand out as a novel tool. These tattoos are technologically advanced electronic devices that can temporarily be worn on the skin. These devices are often made of ultrathin electronics and sensors and have connectivity features allowing them to collect and connect to transmit data to a sensor or a smartphone app. These tattoos can be made from flexible electronic circuits, conductive ink patterns, or temporary adhesive patches.

In healthcare, these can be used for tracking data such as vitals, glucose, or early detection of disease states. Since digital tattoos are directly on the skin, they can enhance human–computer interaction by enabling gesture recognition, touch-sensitive controls, and display information through electronic ink or microdisplays. Uses of digital tattoos can include monitoring alcohol levels through sweat analysis, changes of color in a tattoo in response to fluctuating glucose levels, and UV radiation exposure. While the future with wearable biosensors holds great potential, a better understanding of how to use biofluids is needed to improve reliability. Larger studies will be needed to validate biosensor performance for greater clinical acceptance [9].

Benefits and applications

There are many benefits and applications of wearable devices. In the area of health and fitness, wearables can provide improved tracking of physical activity and workouts, motivation and goal setting for a healthier lifestyle, and early detection of health issues through continuous monitoring.

Productivity and convenience can be easily obtained with notifications and quick access to information. Hands-free voice command options make wearables easily integrated into our lives. The ability to integrate with other smart devices can allow for a seamless user experience.

Safety features can also be addressed with wearable devices. Wearables such as watches have built-in safety and emergency assistance with fall detection and emergency alerts. Global positioning service tracking allows for personal safety and medical alert functions for immediate assistance in times of need [15,16].

Wearables can also have specialized applications such as virtual reality (VR) headsets that can be used in gaming, entertainment, and healthcare. Studies use beneficial outcomes when using VR with pediatric patients who undergo procedures from vaccines and intravenous injections to laceration repair and wound care. Immersive VR can cause adequate distraction and attention diversion leading to a slower response to incoming pain signals. "Preliminary results have shown that VR is effective, either alone or in combination with standard care, in reducing the pain and anxiety patients experience compared with standard care or other distraction methods" [17].

Wearable technology has been shown to be useful in sports for performance optimization, injury prevention, rehabilitation, and tracking mental performance. For performance optimization, wearables can help track and analyze movement patterns providing athletes with data such as speed, acceleration, and agility. This information can help coaches and trainers focus on areas for improvement and help design training programs to optimize an athlete's performance. Injury prevention can also be addressed by using wearables to monitor factors such as impact forces or joint movements. Such personalized data can be used to identify an athlete's movement or prevent imbalances or injuries. Wearables can also aid in rehabilitation by tracking progress, measuring range of motion, and providing feedback on proper form during exercises. While sports may highlight the physical aspects of an athlete, mental performance is also important. Some wearables can use sensors to track brain activity to provide insight into things such as focus, endurance, and stress levels. Wearable technology continues to evolve expanding its reach and ability to provide a comprehensive approach to caring for athletes and users alike [18].

Wearables with their advanced sensors, data analytics, and user-friendly interfaces show the potential to serve as assisted devices for people with disabilities. "Wearables, such as Apple Watch, Android Wear, and specialized monitoring devices, represent another useful source of data that users are increasingly adopting. One of the advantages of these wearable devices is that they can easily become an intrinsic and inseparable part of people with disabilities. Another consideration is the unobtrusive nature of these wearables, which can stream data without hindering the everyday activities of the people with disabilities" [19]. Wearable exoskeletons and robotic prosthetics can aid those with limb loss or paralysis to regain mobility and independence. Wearables that use gesture recognition and haptic feedback can be useful for those with visual impairments or hearing disabilities by providing navigation assistance and support. Haptic feedback stimulates the somatosensory system and provides the ability to use touch as a means of communication. Using this kind of somatosensory feedback can be beneficial by providing another way of communication for those who may need it. The integration of wearable technology can empower humans with disabilities promoting inclusivity, autonomy, and better quality of life [20].

Challenges and considerations

With the widespread adoption of wearable tech, there are also significant concerns about privacy. One concern is the data collection. Wearable devices are like telemetry—constantly gathering and storing data from biometrics, user location, and even preferences and habits. If these sensitive data are breached or mishandled, it can lead to identity theft or other malicious activities.

Unauthorized access to data stored on the wearable device or interception when it synchronizes to cloud services during transmission is a concern. Wearables that integrate with third-party applications or services may increase the risk of potentially compromised data. Wearable devices used at workplaces or public spaces may have some privacy concerns related to surveillance and consent. Similarly, the use of wearable cameras, such as smart glasses in public spaces, can infringe upon privacy. Regulatory entities have struggled to keep up with the growth and advancements of wearables leading to privacy concerns. Companies will need to show transparency about data collection and how it is being used and retained. Users should have clear consent options and control over data enabling them to opt out of certain data collections if desired.

Despite these concerns, wearable technology also offers opportunities for privacy-enhancing features. Manufacturers can implement privacy-by-design principles, ensuring that privacy is a central consideration during the development process. For example, data anonymization techniques can be employed to protect user identities while still providing valuable insights for research and product improvement. While wearables can provide benefits and convenience, one must remain vigilant about protecting personal data and ensuring that the right to privacy is respected in this rapidly evolving digital landscape.

Wearables user experience (UX) and design play a pivotal role in determining the success and adoption of these devices. UX can make wearable experiences intuitive, engaging, and seamlessly integrated into users' lives, whereas a poorly designed one can lead to frustration and abandonment. The best wearables are mindful of comfort, aesthetics, and customization to enhance a user's experience. The use of discrete sensors, such as in a fitness tracker, can automatically detect when the user is exercising and provide real-time workout statistics. This data can be proactive in meeting the user's needs and enhancing their overall experience.

Long battery life is essential for wearables, reducing the need for frequent charging. Using energy-efficient displays and low-energy sensors can impact user satisfaction.

Designers must consider accessibility and inclusivity when creating wearable technology. Features such as adjustable straps, text-to-speech capabilities, and user-friendly interfaces for people with disabilities can broaden the device's user base and make it more accommodating to a diverse audience.

The landscape of wearables is forever changing and being updated as new tools and technology emerge. Designs must adopt an iterative approach to continue improving by implementing user feedback and data analytics to remain relevant.

Software updates are essential in addressing issues, adding new features, and keeping the wearable relevant [21].

Future trends and innovations

The future of wearable technology is poised to be exciting with a multitude of trends and innovations on the horizon. As technology advances, we expect developments in health monitoring, medical applications, smart fabrics and e-textiles, augmented reality glasses, wearable robotics, neural interfaces, mental health, energy harvesting, environmental sensing, security advancements, haptic feedback, and collaboration with artificial intelligence (AI).

In the health and medical field, it is expected that wearables will continue to evolve tracking various biometric indicators with greater accuracy and reliability. Future wearables might include features such as continuous glucose monitoring, advanced sleep tracking, blood pressure monitoring, and early detection of health conditions through data analysis and AI-powered algorithms.

Wearable devices may have a new look with integration into clothing and textiles. Smart fabrics and e-textiles can embed sensors enabling unobtrusive monitoring and seamless integration of wearables into everyday apparel to gather data.

Augmented reality (AR) wearables are expected to become more sophisticated, providing immersive and interactive experiences. AR wearables could enhance productivity, navigation, gaming, and entertainment, blending digital content seamlessly into the real world. With the use of haptic feedback, wearables can provide a richer tactile experience for users for a more immersive experience. Wearables will increasingly collaborate with AI and the Internet of Things (IoT) to provide more personalized and context-aware experiences. Wearables could provide data for AI algorithms for better insight and predictive suggestions.

Wearable exoskeletons could revolutionize industries such as healthcare, manufacturing, and construction by providing physical assistance and reducing the risk of injuries for workers. Wearable exoskeletons can also play a role in first responders or military personnel, keeping them safe by enhancing strength, endurance, load-carrying capacity, and improving ergonomics. In addition, wearable exoskeletons can augment physical activity and provide safety by reducing physical injury with repetitive tasks, loads, or motions. Additionally, exoskeletons may have applications in rehabilitation and mobility support for those with mobility impairments.

Advancements in brain–computer interfaces (BCIs) could lead to wearable devices that communicate directly with the brain allowing users to control technology with their thoughts. This could open possibilities for enhanced communication and accessibility for those with disabilities. Wearables may employ advanced sensors and AI algorithms to detect emotions and monitor mental health. This technology could offer valuable insights into stress levels, emotional well-being, and potential mental health conditions.

Future wearables may incorporate energy-harvesting technologies to generate power from ambient sources such as body heat, motion, or sunlight. The ability to harvest energy with wearables could be used to auto-power devices extending battery life or becoming self-sustaining. Wearables can be integrated into environmental sectors by using sensors to monitor air quality, ultraviolet exposure, and other measurable factors enabling users with real-time and safety data.

As wearable technology becomes more mainstream, clothing designers and textile manufacturers can focus on creating stylish and customizable wearables that appeal to broader audiences. Customization of wearables will allow for more inclusivity and diverse options for all.

Overall, the future of wearable technology is full of possibilities. As these innovations continue to develop, they have the potential to transform various aspects of our lives, from health and productivity to communication and entertainment. It will be fascinating to witness how these trends shape the wearable technology landscape in the years to come [22–25].

Conclusion

Wearable technology that started with a simple wristwatch has now become cutting-edge augmented reality glasses and smart fabrics woven into our futures seamlessly integrating into our daily routines. Wearables empower us to be more connected, informed, and efficient.

Wearable technology has found applications in diverse industries, from manufacturing and transportation to healthcare, education, and entertainment industries. The convergence of technologies such as AI, IoT, and wearable devices has expanded a world of possibilities for creating smarter, more intuitive, and context-aware devices. Wearables must continue to embrace innovation, collaboration, and user-centric design.

On an individual user level, wearables may provide convenience, empowerment, and improved well-being. For researchers, developers, and businesses, wearables allow for cross-disciplinary collaborations. This cross-pollination opens a potential for vast growth as wearables intersect with fields such as healthcare, fashion, engineering, and beyond. By investing in research and development, wearables will be more sophisticated, secure, and privacy-centric.

It is important to address the challenges that come with wearable technology. Ensuring robust security measures, protecting user privacy and data, and addressing ethical considerations are critical steps to building trust and fostering widespread adoption.

In conclusion, wearable technology represents a pivotal moment in the ever-evolving landscape of human−computer interaction highlighting our ability to innovate, adapt, and leverage technology to enhance our lives. The future of wearables will allow enhancement of our daily experiences and lead us toward a more connected, informed, and empowered world.

AI disclosure

During the preparation of this work the author(s) used ChatGPT in order to help draft outline. After using this tool/service, the author(s) reviewed and edited the content as needed and take(s) full responsibility for the content of the publication.

References

[1] Lu L, Zhang J, Xie Y, et al. Wearable health devices in healthcare: narrative systematic review. JMIR Mhealth Uhealth 2020;8(11):e18907. https://doi.org/10.2196/18907.
[2] Changed Status of the Wrist Watch. New York Times. https://www.ablogtowatch.com/wp-content/uploads/2015/11/New-York-Times-1916-Wrist-Watch-Article.pdf. (Accessed 1 August 2023).
[3] Amft O, Lukowicz P. From backpacks to smartphones: past, present, and future of wearable computers. Pervasive computing. IEEE 2009;8:8−13. https://doi.org/10.1109/MPRV.2009.44.
[4] Reeder B, David A. Health at hand: a systematic review of smart watch uses for health and wellness. Journal of Biomedical Informatics 2016;63:269−76. https://doi.org/10.1016/j.jbi.2016.09.001.
[5] Ferguson T, Olds T, Curtis R, et al. Effectiveness of wearable activity trackers to increase physical activity and improve health: a systematic review of systematic reviews and meta-analyses. Lancet Digit Health 2022;4(8):e615−26. https://doi.org/10.1016/S2589-7500(22)00111-X.
[6] Zhang Z, Ramiya Ramesh Babu NA, Adelgais K, Ozkaynak M. Designing and implementing smart glass technology for emergency medical services: a sociotechnical perspective. JAMIA Open 2022;5(4):ooac113. https://doi.org/10.1093/jamiaopen/ooac113.
[7] Hou YJ, Zeng SY, Lin CC, et al. Smart clothes-assisted home-nursing care program for family caregivers of older persons with dementia and hip fracture: a mixed-methods study. BMC Geriatrics 2022;22(1):104. https://doi.org/10.1186/s12877-022-02789-y.
[8] Sung YL, Huang HL, Lin CC, et al. Experiences of family caregivers of persons living with dementia with and without a smart- clothes assisted home nursing program during the heightened COVID-19 alert. BMC Geriatrics 2022;22(1):697. https://doi.org/10.1186/s12877-022-03379-8.
[9] Kim J, Campbell AS, de Ávila BE, Wang J. Wearable biosensors for healthcare monitoring. Nature Biotechnology 2019;37(4):389−406. https://doi.org/10.1038/s41587-019-0045-y.
[10] Sharma A, Badea M, Tiwari S, Marty JL. Wearable biosensors: an alternative and practical approach in healthcare and disease monitoring. Molecules 2021;26(3):748. https://doi.org/10.3390/molecules26030748.
[11] Holzer R, Bloch W, Brinkmann C. Continuous glucose monitoring in healthy adults-possible applications in healthcare, wellness, and sports. Sensors 2022;22(5):2030. https://doi.org/10.3390/s22052030.

[12] Vettoretti M, Cappon G, Acciaroli G, Facchinetti A, Sparacino G. Continuous glucose monitoring: current use in diabetes management and possible future applications. Journal of Diabetes Science and Technology 2018;12(5):1064–71. https://doi.org/10.1177/1932296818774078.

[13] Bashi N, Karunanithi M, Fatehi F, Ding H, Walters D. Remote monitoring of patients with heart failure: an overview of systematic reviews. Journal of Medical Internet Research 2017;19(1):e18. https://doi.org/10.2196/jmir.6571.

[14] Majumder S, Mondal T, Deen MJ. Wearable sensors for remote health monitoring. Sensors 2017;17(1):130. https://doi.org/10.3390/s17010130.

[15] Jung S, Hong S, Kim J, et al. Wearable fall detector using integrated sensors and energy devices. Scientific Reports 2015;5:17081. https://doi.org/10.1038/srep17081.

[16] Pannurat N, Thiemjarus S, Nantajeewarawat E. Automatic fall monitoring: a review. Sensors 2014;14(7):12900–36. https://doi.org/10.3390/s140712900.

[17] Arane K, Behboudi A, Goldman RD. Virtual reality for pain and anxiety management in children. Canadian Family Physician 2017;63(12):932–4.

[18] Aroganam G, Manivannan N, Harrison D. Review on wearable technology sensors used in consumer sport applications. Sensors 2019;19(9):1983. https://doi.org/10.3390/s19091983.

[19] Moon NW, Baker PM, Goughnour K. Designing wearable technologies for users with disabilities: accessibility, usability, and connectivity factors. Journal of Rehabilitation and Assistive Technologies Engineering 2019;6. https://doi.org/10.1177/2055668319862137.

[20] Yetisen AK, Martinez-Hurtado JL, Ünal B, Khademhosseini A, Butt H. Wearables in medicine. Advanced Materials 2018;30(33):e1706910. https://doi.org/10.1002/adma.201706910.

[21] Loncar-Turukalo T, Zdravevski E, Machado da Silva J, Chouvarda I, Trajkovik V. Literature on wearable technology for connected health: scoping review of research trends, advances, and barriers. Journal of Medical Internet Research 2019;21(9):e14017. https://doi.org/10.2196/14017.

[22] Dunn J, Runge R, Snyder M. Wearables and the medical revolution. Personalized Medicine 2018;15(5):429–48. https://doi.org/10.2217/pme-2018-0044.

[23] Smith B, Sverdlov A. Digital technology: the future is bright. Clinical Pharmacology & Therapeutics 2018;104(1):9–11. https://doi.org/10.1002/cpt.1092.

[24] Stavropoulos TG, Papastergiou A, Mpaltadoros L, Nikolopoulos S, Kompatsiaris I. IoT wearable sensors and devices in elderly care: a literature review. Sensors 2020;20(10):2826. https://doi.org/10.3390/s20102826.

[25] Mridha MF, Das SC, Kabir MM, Lima AA, Islam MR, Watanobe Y. Brain-computer interface: advancement and challenges. Sensors 2021;21(17):5746. https://doi.org/10.3390/s21175746.

CHAPTER 6

mHealth - a pocket-sized revolution

Stefan Buttigieg
Faculty of Health Sciences, University of Malta, Msida, Malta

Introduction

A brief overview of mHealth

The convergence of mobile technology and healthcare has catalyzed the birth of a new dynamic domain known as mobile health, commonly referred to as mHealth. mHealth is a rapidly emerging discipline with the potential to revolutionize the delivery and accessibility of healthcare services. It extends the reach of healthcare beyond traditional boundaries and offers an innovative solution to some of the most pressing challenges in modern healthcare. The essence of mHealth is rooted in the use of mobile and wireless technologies to support the achievement of health objectives.

Tracing its origin, the advent of mHealth has been largely tied to the proliferation of mobile technology. The evolution of mobile devices from mere communication tools to sophisticated, multipurpose gadgets has been a pivotal factor in the development of mHealth. With over 4 billion people worldwide owning a mobile device, healthcare services are now potentially within the reach of almost everyone, regardless of their geographical location [1].

As the digital age unfolds, the importance of mHealth in telemedicine has become increasingly apparent. By enhancing communication between healthcare providers and patients, mHealth has enabled remote patient monitoring, teleconsultations, and access to health information for millions. Moreover, its role in disease surveillance, health promotion, and emergency response is becoming increasingly vital.

This chapter aims to explore the role and relevance of mHealth in the broader landscape of telemedicine, delving into its technological aspects, clinical applications, regulatory issues, and future potential. This is an attempt to understand mHealth as a robust and versatile tool that redefines how healthcare is delivered and accessed in the digital age.

Digital Health. https://doi.org/10.1016/B978-0-443-23901-4.00006-4

Historical development and importance of mHealth

Early beginnings of mHealth (1990–2000s)

The emergence of mHealth can be traced back to the late 1990s and early 2000s when mobile technologies began to be used for healthcare applications. During this period, mobile phones were utilized to send health alerts and reminders, which represented the initial foray into the potential of mobile devices in healthcare. One notable milestone during this era was the implementation of SMS (short message service) for healthcare communication [2].

Rapid growth and adoption (2005–present)

With the advent of smartphones and improved connectivity, mHealth began to experience rapid growth. By 2010, thousands of mHealth apps were available, enabling various functions from fitness tracking to chronic disease management. This proliferation of applications was driven by advancements in smartphone technology, which allowed for the development of more sophisticated health-related apps and the integration of various sensors and functionalities [3].

The use of mobile applications for chronic disease management in particular gained particular momentum to such an extent that it has garnered fine-tuned and specific research interest in the topic. A specific disease that has garnered significant attention is diabetes, and there is dedicated research on the role of apps for self-management [4].

Integration with telemedicine

mHealth's integration with telemedicine marked a significant milestone. Telehealth platforms began to leverage mobile devices for remote consultations, patient monitoring, and data collection, making healthcare more accessible and convenient. The COVID-19 pandemic further accelerated this trend, as healthcare providers and patients sought alternatives to in-person visits, leading to a surge in telehealth services that integrated seamlessly with mobile technology.

Global initiatives and collaborations

Recognizing the potential of mHealth to address healthcare disparities, global health organizations initiated programs and collaborations aimed at expanding its reach. The World Health Organization (WHO), for instance, launched the mHealth program to combat noncommunicable diseases (NCDs) in low- and middle-income countries [2]. Collaborations between governments, NGOs, and private sectors facilitated the implementation of mHealth solutions in underserved regions.

One noteworthy example of such collaboration is the Mobile Alliance for Maternal Action (MAMA) [5], which partners with governments, nonprofits, and mobile operators to deliver vital maternal and child health information to women in resource-limited settings through mobile phones. Social enterprises also play a role in this global effort, companies such as "Universal Doctor" have tackled a number of specific case scenarios through mHealth Solutions focusing on Maternal Health such as "Zero Mothers Die" and even Migration Health in collaboration with the International Organization for Migration (IOM) [6]. These global efforts have demonstrated the potential of mHealth in improving healthcare access and outcomes on a global, regional, and local scale.

Importance in modern healthcare

mHealth has become vital in modern healthcare, playing a key role in patient engagement, chronic disease management, healthcare accessibility, and emergency response. Its significance is underscored by its ability to empower patients with tools for self-management, provide healthcare access to remote populations, and enhance the overall quality of care.

Moreover, mHealth has proven to be a valuable tool in emergency response scenarios, allowing for rapid communication and coordination among healthcare providers and first responders during natural disasters or public health emergencies.

The historical development of mHealth, from its early beginnings as a simple SMS-based service to its integration with advanced telemedicine and its adoption on a global scale, highlights its transformative impact on healthcare. As mHealth continues to evolve and innovate, its importance in modern healthcare is poised to grow, offering unprecedented opportunities to improve health outcomes and healthcare delivery.

Understanding mHealth

Definition and explanation of mHealth

Mobile Health, or mHealth, refers to the practice of medicine and public health supported by mobile devices. It involves the use of mobile technologies such as smartphones, tablets, patient monitoring devices, personal digital assistants (PDAs), and other wireless devices to deliver healthcare services. mHealth forms a subset of eHealth, the application of information and communication technologies (ICT) in health, and serves as a fundamental component of telemedicine [7].

This mobile health strategy leverages the ubiquity and connectivity of mobile devices to collect health data, provide healthcare information, deliver healthcare services, monitor patient vital signs, and offer personalized health interventions, among others [8]. Through such capabilities, mHealth is gradually transforming the traditional patient—caregiver interaction, creating an environment that fosters proactive and informed health decisions.

The role of smartphones and wearable devices in mHealth

The exponential rise of smartphones and wearable devices has significantly influenced the growth of mHealth. As of 2024, smartphone adoption continues to surge globally, penetrating even in low- and middle-income countries [1]. These portable devices, equipped with powerful processors, sensors, and internet connectivity, serve as an ideal platform for various mHealth applications.

Healthcare apps are perhaps the most visible aspect of mHealth, providing services ranging from health education and reminders to teleconsultations and remote patient monitoring. In addition, wearable technology, including fitness trackers and smartwatches, is gaining traction for its ability to continuously monitor health parameters such as heart rate, oxygen saturation, sleep patterns, activity levels, and more, offering valuable inputs for preventive care and disease management.

Key components of mHealth

The field of mHealth comprises several key components that collectively contribute to the healthcare delivery process.

1. Health Apps: Mobile applications provide a range of services such as disease education, medication reminders, virtual consultations, self-monitoring, and more.
2. Teleconsultation: It allows healthcare professionals and patients to connect remotely, facilitating consultations, follow-ups, and medical advice [9].
3. Remote Patient Monitoring (RPM): With the help of connected medical devices, the health parameters of patients can be continuously monitored remotely, aiding in chronic disease management and posthospitalization care [10].
4. Health Data Collection: mHealth technologies assist in collecting health data on a large scale, supporting public health initiatives, research, and surveillance. Tools such as Magpi take into consideration multiple use cases and different technology and networking infrastructures [11].

By understanding the breadth and depth of mHealth, it becomes clear that its potential is vast and continues to expand as technology evolves. In the next section, we will delve deeper into the intersection of mHealth and telemedicine, illustrating how these two innovative health strategies complement and enhance each other.

Technological innovations in mHealth

Recent advancements in mHealth technology

In the past decade, the field of mHealth has experienced a remarkable pace of innovation, significantly transforming healthcare delivery and management. Recent breakthroughs in this area include.

1. Smart Wearables and Internet of Things (IoT): The emergence of smart wearables, such as fitness bands and smartwatches, has enabled continuous health monitoring. These devices, connected through IoT, can track various health parameters, including heart rate, sleep patterns, and activity levels, contributing to preventive care and wellness [3].
2. Augmented Reality (AR) and Virtual Reality (VR): AR and VR are being employed in mHealth for diverse purposes, such as medical training, patient education, and therapeutic applications, including pain management and mental health treatment. The field has evolved to such an extent that there are dedicated organizations and academic journals specifically dedicated to Medical Extended Reality [12].
3. Biosensors and Medical Devices: Advancements in biosensor technology have led to the development of sophisticated medical devices that can monitor various physiological parameters, aiding in the effective management of conditions such as diabetes [10], hypertension, and cardiovascular diseases.

The impact of artificial intelligence (AI) and machine learning (ML) on mHealth

Artificial Intelligence (AI) and Machine Learning (ML) have been game-changers in the mHealth landscape. They are used in various capacities, including.

1. Predictive Analytics: AI algorithms can analyze extensive health data to predict health risks and outcomes, enabling proactive care.
2. Personalized Health Recommendations: Machine learning algorithms can provide personalized health recommendations based on individual health data, promoting more personalized care.
3. Natural Language Processing: AI-powered chatbots and virtual health assistants use natural language processing (NLP) to interact with patients, provide health information, and even support mental health.

Future trends in mHealth technology

As we look to the future, several exciting trends could further shape the mHealth landscape:

1. Integration of Distributed Ledger Technologies (DLT): DLT could enhance data security, patient privacy, and interoperability in mHealth, providing a reliable and secure platform for health data exchange and transactions. Transactional technology can potentially play a bigger role in mHealth through implementations such as Non-Fungible Tokens (NFTs) and Smart Contracts.
2. Adoption of 5G: The global rollout of 5G could significantly improve the speed and reliability of mHealth services, especially in remote patient monitoring and telehealth consultations.
3. Expansion of Remote Patient Monitoring: As wearable and at-home medical devices become more advanced and affordable, remote patient monitoring will likely become more widespread, changing how chronic diseases are managed.
4. Precision Medicine: With the capability to analyze massive amounts of health data, mHealth will play a crucial role in the emergence of precision medicine, providing customized healthcare based on individual multiomic data, environment, and lifestyle [13].

In the subsequent sections, we will delve into the clinical applications of mHealth, exploring how these technological innovations are being employed in real-world healthcare scenarios.

Clinical applications of mHealth

Chronic disease management

mHealth offers robust tools for individuals with chronic diseases. Apps and devices help in the continuous monitoring of vital parameters such as blood pressure, glucose levels, and heart rate. They also aid in tracking symptoms, offering medication reminders, and providing disease-specific guidance, enhancing self-management and health outcomes. Diabetes [14], cardiovascular diseases, and COPD [15] are a few of the conditions where mHealth has shown significant positive impacts.

Mental health services

Mobile health technologies have emerged as a pivotal ally in mental health services. Apps offering cognitive-behavioral therapy, stress relief exercises, counseling services, and meditation have gained traction. They've shown promise in managing conditions such as depression [28], anxiety, and stress, providing users with immediate access to therapeutic tools and resources.

Emergency medicine

In acute care settings, mHealth can be a lifesaver. Apps can quickly locate the nearest medical facilities, provide real-time advice for first aid, or allow virtual consultations in critical situations. Some platforms also enable emergency medical responders to access vital patient information en route, ensuring timely and tailored medical intervention [16].

Public health

At the community and population levels, mHealth plays a significant role in health promotion, disease surveillance, and outbreak tracking. Mobile platforms can facilitate the delivery of health education, promote vaccination campaigns, and monitor the spread of infectious diseases, helping public health agencies in decision-making and intervention planning. The COVID-19 Pandemic was the classic example of how mHealth can be deployed in a Public Health setting through apps such as proximity tracing applications and vaccine certification apps. The European Commission and the World Health Organization have played a significant role in creating technical frameworks that can be sustained for a longer term basis through the Global Digital Health Certification Network [17].

Design frameworks and software development kits in mHealth

Design frameworks in mHealth

As mHealth continues to establish itself as an integral part of healthcare delivery and management, the underlying technologies that power these mobile health solutions become paramount. These are often facilitated through design frameworks—software development kits (SDKs) and tools provided by technology giants, tailored specifically for health applications. These frameworks not only simplify the development process but also ensure that mHealth apps meet the requisite standards for privacy, security, and functionality.

Apple HealthKit and ResearchKit

Recognizing the potential of mHealth in both personal health management and research, Apple introduced two distinct but complementary frameworks: HealthKit and ResearchKit.

HealthKit functions as a repository for health and fitness data on iPhone and Apple Watch, allowing apps to access and share this data with permission. By centralizing health data from various third-party apps and devices, HealthKit provides a comprehensive view of an individual's health metrics. For developers, HealthKit offers an integrated way to utilize these metrics within their apps, ensuring a seamless user experience [18].

ResearchKit, on the other hand, aims to revolutionize medical research. By turning iPhones into powerful diagnostic tools, ResearchKit allows researchers to gather more frequent and accurate data from participants anywhere in the world. Apps developed with ResearchKit have been employed in studies ranging from asthma and Parkinson's disease to heart health, illustrating the framework's versatility [19].

Android—Google Health Connect

The Google Health Connect SDK [20] serves as Google's counterpoint to Apple's HealthKit, tailored for the Android ecosystem. This has been migrated from the Google Fit SDK [21] with a cut-off date of 30th June 2025. It provides developers with a robust set of APIs to build health and wellness applications that can read and write to Google Health Connect's centralized store of fitness data. Designed for Android devices and wearables, Google Health Connect assists in collecting information from various sensors and apps, such as step count, calories burned, and sleep patterns. By offering real-time access to this data, the SDK allows for the creation of more personalized and dynamic mHealth applications. Its focus on user privacy and data security makes it a reliable choice for developers aiming to deliver a seamless and trustworthy health management experience.

Open health stack and Android FHIR SDK

Google's Open Health Stack and Android FHIR SDK are a testament to the open-source ethos, offering developers a flexible and customizable framework for health app development. Catering to Android's vast ecosystem, this stack provides essential tools to capture, store, and process health data, ensuring that they are aligned with global health standards [22].

Samsung

With its prominent footprint in the global smartphone market, Samsung ventured into mHealth with its Samsung Health SDK. This framework integrates seamlessly with Samsung's suite of wearables and smartphones, providing developers with tools to build apps that track, manage, and analyze health data.

The Samsung Health SDK stands out by offering a myriad of trackers, including those for heart rate, oxygen saturation, and stress levels, presenting a holistic approach to health monitoring [23].

Other mobile vendors

Beyond the big players, several smartphone vendors have recognized the importance of mHealth and have launched their SDKs. These frameworks, while not as widely adopted as the ones from Google, Apple, or Samsung, provide vital tools and integrations for niche markets or specific regional needs. They underline the universal acknowledgment of mHealth's significance in today's digital health landscape.

Behavioral design thinking for mHealth

Behavioral Design Thinking, when applied to mHealth, encapsulates a holistic approach that marries user-centered design principles with behavior change theories to create impactful digital health solutions. A clear example of this has been elucidated in the development of a family-oriented, healthy eating app, showcasing a systematic process grounded in theory and evidence while being finely attuned to the users' preferences and needs. It underscores the importance of understanding the problem at hand and the target user's preferences at the outset. By leveraging frameworks such as the Transtheoretical Model and Intervention Mapping, it provides a blueprint for designers and developers to iteratively create, test, and refine mHealth solutions. The process includes stages of problem understanding, ideation, and intervention development, underlined by a continuous feedback loop with the target user population to ensure that the final app is both engaging and effective in promoting healthy behavior change [24].

Regulatory and ethical considerations in mHealth

Data privacy and security issues in mHealth

With the increasing adoption of mHealth technologies, concerns surrounding data privacy and security have emerged. Health data are highly sensitive, and the risk of data breaches can have serious implications. Providers need to ensure encryption, secure data storage, and safe transmission channels to prevent unauthorized access to patient information. Additionally, users must be educated on maintaining their privacy and security while using these technologies.

Regulatory frameworks for mHealth

In navigating the vast and evolving terrain of mHealth, adherence to regulatory frameworks is indispensable. These frameworks ensure the safety, efficacy, and data privacy associated with mHealth applications. In the United Kingdom, the Medicines and Healthcare products Regulatory Agency (MHRA) oversees the regulation of mHealth applications, ensuring that they meet the requisite standards for medical devices. These efforts in the UK are also further enhanced by the guidelines published via the NHS Digital Technology Assessment Criteria (DTAC) [25]. Germany's Digital Healthcare Act (DVG) encompasses regulations for mHealth applications and aims to enhance the digital infrastructure of the healthcare system. It facilitates the integration of health apps into the nation's health insurance coverage. Similarly, in France, the Haute Autorité de Santé (HAS) establishes guidelines for mHealth apps ensuring that they adhere to a high standard of quality and safety.

The regulatory landscape in China is managed by the National Medical Products Administration (NMPA), which sets the standards for mHealth applications ensuring that they comply with the country's stringent requirements concerning medical devices. In the United States, the Food and Drug Administration (FDA) oversees the regulation of mHealth and coordinates with multiple entities including the Federal Trade Commission, providing developers with guidance on the development of mobile health apps [26]. The overlap between mHealth, Digital Medical Devices (DMDs) and Digital Therapeutics (DTx) is significant, as they all utilize digital platforms to deliver health solutions. Consequently, regulatory frameworks governing mHealth often extend to digital therapeutics and digital medical devices. These frameworks play a crucial role in the evolving narrative of digital health, bridging the gap between technological innovation and regulatory compliance, thus fostering a conducive environment for the growth and acceptance of mHealth, digital therapeutics and digital medical devices.

Ethical dilemmas and considerations in mHealth

Several ethical issues emerge with the use of mHealth. The digital divide may lead to health inequities, as not everyone has equal access to mobile technologies. Also, ensuring informed consent in the digital age poses challenges, given the complexity of mHealth technologies. There are also concerns about the quality and reliability of health information and interventions provided through mHealth, as well as the risk of overreliance on technology at the expense of human interaction in healthcare.

Challenges and limitations of mHealth

Technological challenges

Despite its immense potential, mHealth faces several technological challenges. These include issues of connectivity, especially in rural and remote areas; interoperability of various systems and devices; and the usability and accessibility of mHealth technologies, particularly for elderly populations or those with limited digital literacy.

Societal challenges

Societal challenges include addressing the digital divide that may leave certain populations unable to take advantage of mHealth technologies. Digital literacy and health literacy also play a significant role in how effectively individuals can use and benefit from mHealth.

Health system challenges

Within the health system, challenges such as integration of mHealth into traditional healthcare, legal and liability issues, and reimbursement for mHealth services need to be addressed. The rapid pace of technological innovation also poses challenges for regulation, as regulatory bodies struggle to keep up with the evolving landscape of mHealth.

Despite these challenges, the potential of mHealth is significant, and continued innovation and thoughtful implementation strategies can help in addressing these barriers. The upcoming section will take a look at what the future might hold for mHealth in the realm of telemedicine.

The future of mHealth

Emerging opportunities in mHealth

The dynamic and rapidly evolving nature of mHealth offers several opportunities for growth and advancement. The integration of emerging technologies such as AI, blockchain, and IoT will continue to enhance the capabilities of mHealth, providing a more personalized, efficient, and proactive approach to healthcare. For instance, the increased use of AI in health apps can provide personalized health tips, predict diseases, and help with mental health support.

Moreover, the future holds the promise of more integrated care, where mHealth devices seamlessly connect with the broader digital health ecosystem, improving communication and cooperation among healthcare providers and resulting in better patient care.

EU projects—Label2Enable

The Label2Enable project is an initiative funded by the European Union. Its primary objective is to promote the adoption of CEN-ISO/TS 82304-2 and its quality label for health and wellness apps. The project aims to create a digital single market where quality health apps are used at scale in prevention, health care, and self-care.

The project consists of seven Work Packages (WPs) and is built on three pillars: Trust, Use, and Adoption. It started on June 1, 2022, under the Horizon Europe project. Fourteen organizations from seven countries (Belgium, Croatia, Germany, Italy, Lithuania, the Netherlands, and Spain) have joined forces for 2 years to promote the ISO/TS 82304-2 health app assessment framework and label in Europe.

The Label2Enable project is a significant step toward ensuring the quality and reliability of health and wellness apps across Europe [27].

Future challenges and how to overcome them

The future of mHealth is not without challenges. Ensuring equitable access to mHealth technologies, particularly in low-income regions, is a significant hurdle that must be addressed. Investments in infrastructure, affordable technologies, and digital literacy programs can help overcome this challenge.

Data privacy and security will continue to be of paramount importance, requiring robust frameworks and constant vigilance. Leveraging technologies such as blockchain can help create a secure environment for data exchange in mHealth.

Additionally, regulatory frameworks will need to adapt rapidly to keep pace with technological advancements in mHealth. Collaboration among technologists, healthcare professionals, policymakers, and patients will be essential to develop regulations that protect users without inhibiting innovation.

Envisioning mHealth's role in the future of healthcare

As the world moves deeper into the digital age, the role of mHealth in reshaping healthcare becomes increasingly important. It offers a new way of delivering healthcare that is patient-centered, data-driven, and widely accessible, overcoming the geographical, economic, and temporal barriers of traditional healthcare.

By harnessing the power of mobile technologies, mHealth has the potential to make healthcare more proactive, preventive, personalized, and participatory. While there are challenges to be addressed, the potential benefits of mHealth for patients, healthcare providers, and societies are immense. The journey ahead is promising, and with thoughtful design, effective regulation, and inclusive implementation, mHealth can contribute significantly to the future of healthcare in the digital age.

Conclusion

In this digital age, mHealth is rapidly emerging as a transformative force in healthcare, offering a novel approach to address some of the most pressing challenges of traditional healthcare systems. Through the application of mobile technologies, mHealth has the power to revolutionize healthcare by making it more accessible, personalized, efficient, and patient-centered.

As a crucial component of telemedicine, mHealth extends healthcare beyond the conventional boundaries, making it a reality for patients to receive care whenever they need it and wherever they are. From health apps and teleconsultations to remote patient monitoring and health data collection, mHealth has opened up new frontiers in healthcare delivery and management.

In the face of rapid technological advancements, mHealth continues to evolve, bringing in its fold exciting possibilities such as AI, IoT, VR, and blockchain. However, along with these promising opportunities come challenges that need to be addressed—including data security, regulatory compliance, and ensuring equal access.

The future of mHealth is undeniably bright, but it requires a collaborative, conscientious effort from all stakeholders—technology providers, healthcare professionals, regulators, and patients themselves. Together, they can shape a future where mHealth not only complements traditional healthcare but also drives a new wave of patient-centered, data-driven, and accessible healthcare.

In essence, mHealth stands at the intersection of healthcare, technology, and human potential, offering a vision of healthcare that aligns with the realities and expectations of the digital age. As we navigate this exciting journey, one thing is clear—mHealth will play a pivotal role in shaping the future of healthcare and telemedicine, forever transforming our understanding and experience of care.

AI disclosure

During the preparation of this work, the author(s) used ChatGPT in order to assist the author with establishing an initial outline on which to build a very early draft and outline. At later stages, the chapter evolved into a draft that the author heavily contributed to. After using this tool/service, the author(s) reviewed and edited the content as needed and take(s) full responsibility for the content of the publication.

References

[1] GSMA. Smartphone owners are now the global majority, new GSMA report reveals. 2023. https://www.gsma.com/newsroom/press-release/smartphone-owners-are-now-the-global-majority-new-gsma-report-reveals/#:~:text=SMARTPHONE%20OWNERS%20ARE%20NOW%20THE%20GLOBAL%20MAJORITY%2C%20NEW%20GSMA%20REPORT%20REVEALS,-Like%20what%20you&text=11th%20October%202023%2C%20London,2023%20(SOMIC)%20published%20today. [Accessed 11 October 2023].

[2] World Health Organization. Be He@lthy, Be Mobile (BHBM). 2020. https://www.who.int/activities/Addressing-mobile-health. [Accessed 20 August 2023].

[3] Adibi S. Mobile health A technology road map. Springer series in bio-/neuroinformatics. 1. Springer International Publishing; 2015. https://link.springer.com/book/10.1007/978-3-319-12817-7.

[4] Brew-Sam N. App use and patient empowerment in diabetes self-management. 1. Springer Wiesbaden; 2020. https://doi.org/10.1007/978-3-658-29357-4.

[5] Coleman J, Eriksen J, Black V, Thorson A, Hatcher A. The mobile alliance for maternal action text message-based mHealth intervention for maternal care in South Africa: qualitative user study. JMIR Human Factors 2020;7(2):e14078. https://doi.org/10.2196/14078.

[6] Universal Doctor. Universal doctor. 2023. https://www.universaldoctor.com/. [Accessed 19 September 2023].

[7] International Telecommunication Union. What is mHealth, what does it do and how does it benefit countries? 2023. [Accessed 19 September 2023].

[8] Hausman V, Miller R, Qiang Z, Yamamichi M. Mobile applications for the health sector. World Bank; 2012. Accessed 17, 9, https://documents.worldbank.org/en/publication/documents-reports/documentdetail/751411468157784302/Mobile-applications-for-the-health-sector.
[9] Fast N, van Kessel R, Humphreys K, Ward NF, Roman-Urrestarazu A. The evolution of telepsychiatry for substance use disorders during COVID-19: a narrative review. Current Addiction Reports 2023;10(2):187–97. https://doi.org/10.1007/s40429-023-00480-9.
[10] NHS. Continuous glucose monitoring (CGM) and flash. 2023. https://www.nhs.uk/conditions/type-1-diabetes/managing-blood-glucose-levels/continuous-glucose-monitoring-cgm-and-flash/. [Accessed 19 September 2023].
[11] Magpi. Magpi. 2023. https://www.magpi.com/. [Accessed 25 August 2023].
[12] American Medical Extended Reality Association. Journal of medical extended reality. 2023. https://home.liebertpub.com/publications/journal-of-medical-extended-reality/680. [Accessed 19 September 2023].
[13] Acosta JN, Falcone GJ, Rajpurkar P, Topol EJ. Multimodal biomedical AI. Nature Medicine 2022;28(9):1773–84. https://doi.org/10.1038/s41591-022-01981-2.
[14] Sherazi BA, Stephanie L, Svea K, Armin D, Sabina S, Emina O. Functions of mHealth diabetes apps that enable the provision of pharmaceutical care: criteria development and evaluation of popular apps. International Journal of Environment Research and Public Health 2022;20(1):64. https://doi.org/10.3390/ijerph20010064. In press, https://www.mdpi.com/1660-4601/20/1/64.
[15] Davies H, et al. myCOPD app for managing chronic obstructive pulmonary disease: a NICE medical technology guidance for a digital health technology. Applied Health Economics and Health Policy 2023;21. https://doi.org/10.1007/s40258-023-00811-x. In press, https://link.springer.com/article/10.1007/s40258-023-00811-x; 2023. [Accessed 19 August 2024].
[16] Niyonsaba, et al. Challenges and opportunities to improve efficiency and quality of prehospital emergency care using an mHealth platform: Qualitative study in Rwanda. https://www.sciencedirect.com/science/article/pii/S2211419X2300037X?via%3Dihub. [Accessed 19 August 2024].
[17] World Health Organization. Global Digital Health Certification Network. https://www.who.int/initiatives/global-digital-health-certification-network. [Accessed 19 August 2024].
[18] Apple. Apple HealthKit developer documentation. 2023. https://developer.apple.com/documentation/healthkit. [Accessed 29 September 2023].
[19] Apple. Apple research kit. 2023. https://developer.apple.com/researchkit/. [Accessed 29 September 2023].
[20] Google. Google Health Connect. https://health.google/health-connect-android/. [Accessed 19 August 2024].
[21] Google Fit. 2023. https://developers.google.com/fit/. [Accessed 29 September 2023].
[22] Open Health Stack. https://developers.google.com/open-health-stack. [Accessed 29 September 2023].
[23] Samsung. Samsung health SDKs. 2023. https://developer.samsung.com/health. [Accessed 19 September 2023].
[24] Curtis KE, Lahiri S, Brown KE. Targeting parents for childhood weight management: development of a theory-driven and user-centered healthy eating app. JMIR mHealth and uHealth 2015;3(2). https://doi.org/10.2196/mhealth.3857.
[25] NHS England. Digital Technology Assessment Criteria. https://transform.england.nhs.uk/key-tools-and-info/digital-technology-assessment-criteria-dtac/. [Accessed 19 August 2024].
[26] Federal Trade Commission. Mobile health app interactive tool. 2023. http://ttps://www.ftc.gov/business-guidance/resources/mobile-health-apps-interactive-tool. [Accessed 25 September 2023].
[27] Label2Enable project. 2023. https://label2enable.eu/. [Accessed 29 September 2023].
[28] Duarte-Díaz A. Efficacy, safety, and evaluation criteria of mHealth interventions for depression: systematic review. JMIR Mental Health 2023;10. https://doi.org/10.2196/46877. https://mental.jmir.org/2023/1/e46877; 2023.

CHAPTER 7

Looking ahead: The future of electronic health records

Emily Lewis[1,2]
[1]CCRP, CHES, Castle Rock, CO, United States; [2]Digital Care Transformation, UCB Pharma, Smyrna, GA, United States

Introduction

The electronic health record (EHR) has been one of the most significant advancements in healthcare, offering a myriad of benefits to both healthcare providers and patients. EHRs have revolutionized the way health information is stored, accessed, and utilized, significantly improving the efficiency and quality of healthcare delivery. However, as we stand on the cusp of a new era defined by digital transformation, EHRs are poised for another dramatic evolution, promising to further redefine healthcare dynamics.

Digital transformation—the integration of digital technology into all aspects of a business or system—is not a new phenomenon. Yet, its impact and potential in healthcare, particularly in the context of EHRs, are an area of growing interest. With the ability to enhance accessibility, interoperability, and real-time data exchange, digital transformation promises to address some of the key challenges faced by the current EHR systems, thereby driving improved outcomes in care delivery. Digital transformation in EHRs has shifted EHRs from simply digitizing paper medical records to creating comprehensive, dynamic, and interactive health data ecosystems.

Complementing this transition is the sophistication of artificial intelligence (AI), which brings forth opportunities to further leverage the wealth of data within EHRs. AI can help analyze complex data, generate insights, predict patient outcomes, and assist in decision-making. In a healthcare landscape that is increasingly data-driven, the integration of AI and EHRs can lead to a transformation of care models, ensuring more personalized, efficient, and effective patient care. This chapter aims to explore the potential impact of digital transformation on EHRs, shedding light on the opportunities, challenges, and future trajectories of this exciting intersection of healthcare and technology.

Digital Health. https://doi.org/10.1016/B978-0-443-23901-4.00007-6

An overview of EHRs

EHRs began as digital versions of a patient's paper medical chart. They have become a real-time, patient-centered record that makes information available instantly and securely to authorized healthcare providers. They contain a patient's medical history, diagnoses, medications, treatment plans, immunization dates, allergies, radiology images, and laboratory test results.

What are the benefits of EHRs?

EHRs bring numerous benefits to healthcare providers, patients, and the overall healthcare system. These advantages span several areas, from improved efficiency and accuracy to patient care and cost savings. They make patient information accessible in real time, allowing healthcare providers to improve the quality of patient care by allowing them to make better-informed decisions and facilitate more preventative care by reminding them about patient screenings and checkups. They also streamline administrative tasks, reduce duplication of tests, and facilitate communication and sharing of information between different healthcare providers. This can improve the coordination of care, especially for patients with complex conditions requiring care from multiple providers.

From another angle, EHRs can provide valuable data for health research and quality improvement initiatives. They can be used to monitor trends, track the effectiveness of interventions, and identify potential areas for improvement in healthcare delivery. They can also help reduce medical errors by improving the legibility and completeness of medical records, as well as provide clinical decision support with features such as drug–drug interaction checks and allergy alerts.

Beyond healthcare providers, EHRs can also allow patients to access their own medical records, lab results, and treatment plans through a patient portal. These portals are secure online websites that give patients convenient, 24-hour access to personal health information from anywhere with an Internet connection. Beyond displaying medical information, they can also provide appointment schedules, billing information, and secure messaging with the patient's healthcare providers for nonurgent questions, prescription refill requests, specialty referral requests, and other health maintenance-related alerts and tools to help patients manage their health. These features can help to increase patient engagement and participation in their own healthcare.

On a more macroscale, the use of EHRs can lead to cost savings by reducing overall paperwork, avoiding the duplication of tests, and improving health through better preventative care. Furthermore, in case of disasters, having EHRs means that patient medical histories can be accessed when paper records are destroyed or inaccessible, ensuring continuity of care.

What are the challenges of EHRs?

The implementation and use of EHRs are not without challenges. Issues remain related to cost, interoperability, workflow, and data security. The associated cost not only includes the initial cost of purchasing EHR software but also the ongoing costs of training, system maintenance, and updates. Smaller practices or those in low-resource settings may find these costs prohibitive. Additionally, achieving a return on investment often takes time, and the financial benefits may not be immediately realized. Cost-related challenges extend beyond financial resources, with time being another substantial investment factor. The time required for training staff, transitioning existing records, and adapting to new workflows can be considerable, leading to initial productivity losses. As workflows are not always aligned with standards of care, but built for billing efficiency, this can also be a source of lost productivity.

Interoperability, or the ability of different EHR systems to communicate and exchange data with each other, is another critical challenge. Despite progress in health information exchange standards, many EHR systems still struggle to share data effectively. This leads to fragmentation of patient records across different systems and can hinder coordinated care, particularly for patients who see multiple providers. It also poses challenges for public health data aggregation and analysis.

In addition to all these challenges, the issue of data privacy and security is paramount. EHRs contain sensitive health information, making them potential targets for data breaches. Healthcare providers must ensure they have robust security measures in place to protect these data, which can be complex and costly. Moreover, there are legal and ethical considerations associated with data storage and sharing, and healthcare providers must navigate these considerations while ensuring compliance with laws such as the Health Insurance Portability and Accountability Act (HIPAA). These challenges underscore the need for thoughtful, strategic approaches to EHR implementation and use.

How EHRs have evolved

Over the last 15 years, EHRs have undergone significant evolution and transformation already, revolutionizing the way healthcare data are captured, stored, and accessed. Initially, the focus was on digitizing patient records and transitioning from paper-based systems to electronic formats. This shift eliminated the challenges associated with managing physical records, such as storage limitations and manual retrieval. With the widespread adoption of EHRs, healthcare providers gained the ability to access patient information instantly, enhancing efficiency and enabling better coordination of care across different settings. Government initiatives, such as the Health Information Technology for Economic and Clinical Health (HITECH) Act in the United States, have played a crucial role in promoting EHR adoption.

As EHR adoption grew, so did the emphasis on interoperability. In the early stages, EHR systems operated in silos, making it difficult to exchange patient data between different providers and healthcare organizations. However, significant strides have been made in developing standardized protocols and frameworks for data sharing, enabling the exchange of patient data between healthcare organizations and systems. Standards, such as Health Level 7 (HL7) and Fast Healthcare Interoperability Resources (FHIR), have been developed to facilitate data sharing and integration across disparate EHR platforms. This interoperability has greatly improved care coordination, allowing healthcare professionals to access comprehensive patient information regardless of the system or organization where it originated (e.g., laboratories, specialists, medical imaging facilities, pharmacies, emergency facilities, and school and workplace clinics). This has led to safer and more efficient care.

In the United States, the Centers for Medicare and Medicaid Services (CMS) implemented the Meaningful Use program, which incentivized healthcare providers to adopt EHRs and demonstrate their meaningful use. The program emphasized the use of EHRs for improving patient care, clinical outcomes, and data exchange.

With the proliferation of smartphones and tablets, EHR systems have become increasingly accessible through mobile devices. Mobile EHR applications allow healthcare professionals to access patient information, view test results, and perform various clinical tasks on the go, enhancing productivity. Also, the adoption of cloud computing technology has revolutionized EHR systems to offer scalability, flexibility, and cost-effectiveness, as they eliminate the need for on-premises infrastructure and allow seamless data access from multiple locations.

The COVID-19 pandemic accelerated the adoption of telehealth and virtual care solutions. EHRs have been integrated with telemedicine platforms, allowing healthcare providers to conduct remote consultations. Virtual care has only provided access to healthcare services but also enabled the seamless flow of information between patients, providers, and EHR systems, ensuring next-level continuity of care.

The current state of EHRs

Modern EHR systems offer enhanced functionality and features, such as clinical decision support tools, computerized physician order entry (CPOE), e-prescribing, and integration with medical devices. These capabilities aim to improve patient safety, better streamline workflows, reduce medication errors, and support evidence-based care.

EHRs now incorporate more robust data analytics capabilities, allowing healthcare organizations to derive insights from large datasets. By analyzing aggregate patient data, EHRs contribute to population health management and identify trends and patterns that help in disease prevention, early intervention, and resource allocation.

Given the sensitive nature of health data, there has been increased focus on privacy and security measures to safeguard EHRs. Encryption, access, controls, audit trails, and adherence to regulations such as HIPAA are critical components of modern EHR systems.

The future of EHRs

Digital transformation has brought a focus on improving the user experience and usability of EHR systems. Human-centered design principles are being applied to EHR interfaces, making them more intuitive, user-friendly, and tailored to the specific needs of healthcare professionals. Enhanced user experience not only improves efficiency but also reduces cognitive burden and enhances the overall satisfaction of users.

Overall, digital transformation is reshaping EHRs by leveraging technologies such as AI, the Internet of things (IoT), cloud computing, and blockchain to enhance data analysis, interoperability, patient engagement, and the overall quality of care. These advancements have the potential to significantly improve healthcare outcomes, reduce costs, and empower both patients and healthcare providers in the management and delivery of healthcare services.

Emerging technologies influencing the future of EHRs

Artificial intelligence and machine learning

The integration of AI and machine learning (ML) technologies is already beginning to revolutionize EHRs. Natural language processing (NLP) algorithms can extract valuable information from unstructured clinical notes, make connections between different parts of a patient's chart, and facilitate accurate coding and data analysis. More broadly, AI-powered algorithms can analyze vast amounts of patient data, identify patterns, and extract valuable insights to support clinical decision-making. ML algorithms can assist in tasks such as risk prediction, early disease detection, and personalized treatment recommendations, enhancing the accuracy and efficiency of healthcare delivery.

AI algorithms can analyze vast amounts of patient data, research papers, and medical literature to provide clinicians with real-time clinical decision support based upon the latest scientific evidence. AI-powered remote monitoring systems can collect and analyze patient data in real time allowing healthcare professionals to monitor patients remotely and intervene proactively when necessary. AI algorithms can detect derivations from normal health parameters and alert healthcare providers for timely interventions.

While many EHRs already include clinical decision support in terms of alerts and reminders in relation to drug–drug interactions and contraindications, we will see more order sets, which are predefined sets of orders based on current clinical guidelines. We will also see libraries of care plans, personalized algorithms, an integration of care team decision support [1]. More important than merely saving time, they will ensure that healthcare providers are following the most up-to-date evidence-based guidelines. In practice, we will also see EHRs incorporate clinical pathways, which are step-by-step protocols for treating a specific condition. This can help healthcare providers ensure that they are providing the best possible care by making more informed decisions, which reduce the likelihood for errors. By recruiting AI to increase the intelligence of clinical information systems, relevant information can be synthesized and contextualized for each member of a patient care team by area of interest, enabling a version of "care traffic control" [2].

AI can also facilitate the implementation of personalized medicine approaches by analyzing patient data, genetic profiles, and clinical research to tailor treatments to individual patients. AI algorithms will predict patient responses to specific therapies, identify optimal dosages, and suggest personalized treatment plans based on a patient's unique characteristics. This can optimize treatment outcomes, minimize adverse events, and improve patient satisfaction.

Internet of medical things (IoMT), wearable devices, and 5G/6G

The proliferation of IoMT devices and wearable technologies has enabled the collection of real-time patient data, which can be seamlessly integrated with EHRs. Vital signs, fitness tracking, and other health-related information from wearables can be directly transmitted to EHRs, providing a more comprehensive and up-to-date view of the patient's health status. This integration facilitates remote patient monitoring, early intervention, and personalized care management.

Voice assistants will enable healthcare professionals by retrieving patient data from EHRs, summarizing visit conduct and automating the transcription of structured clinical notes captured in the EHR, and providing relevant information during consultations. Healthcare professionals will use voice commands to update patient records, dictate clinical notes, and create prescriptions and referrals. This hands-free and natural language interaction with the EHR systems will allow the optimization of clinical workflows. This chapter in the evolution of EHRs recently started with Epic integrating Suki's voice assistant into its EHR [3].We have also seen Augmedix announce a partnership with HCA Healthcare to accelerate the development of AI-enabled ambient documentation as well as Northwell Health strike a partnership with AllScripts to pursue voice recognition AI in EHR platforms [4]. As the automated data capture market expands, the industry will rely more on robotic process automation (RPA) to ensure fix flaws and ensure accuracy.

As there are privacy concerns with voice assistants in a clinical setting due to their ambient listening abilities, patients and healthcare professionals should have clear visibility and control over the data collected and shared by voice assistants. Transparency in data usage and obtaining explicit consent for data collection will be critical in ensuring privacy preferences align with individual needs and HIPAA compliance requirements.

Wearable devices, or wearables, are devices that have sensors, which measure biometric data such as activity levels, steps walked, and other environmental factors. Oftentimes, the data from the device are paired with mobile apps on the user's smartphone. In the coming years, we will see the optionality for patients to share this data, and its insights, directly with the EHR system for remote monitoring around the clock. The following startup organizations have already been identified to be developing wearable health technology with EHR integration for health systems: Overlap, Royal Phillps, Vivify Health, Validic, Doximity Dialer, Xealth, Redox, Conversa, Human API, and Glooko [5].

As the IoMT will require the exchange of huge amounts of data, the availability of 5G will be critical to ensuring that Internet speeds are sufficient for devices to upload data at speed. What's more, transmission bandwidth is set to increase with the advent of 6G in 2024, allowing even greater capacity for rapid IoMT data exchange [6].

Cloud computing and big data analytics

In the next decade, we will see EHRs collect health data from a greater variety of sources, including patients, healthcare providers, and medical devices. We will see patients collect self-reported symptoms, lifestyle habits, and medication adherence information through both wellness and software as a medical device application. EHRs will function more as a platform providing an ecosystem, which allows the integration of more seamlessly with wearable devices, such as fitness trackers and smartwatches, to collect data on physical activity, heart rate, sleep, and vital signs.

Beyond commercially available devices, EHRs will also connect more directly with medical devices, such as continuous glucose monitors and blood pressure cuffs, allowing healthcare providers to have a more comprehensive view of a patient's health and well-being. To this end, the next generation of EHRs will move toward cloud-based storage, which allows for more efficient and flexible data storage with greater scalability and accessibility. This will enable healthcare organizations to store and process large volumes of data efficiently.

Cloud infrastructure provides the foundation for advanced analytics, allowing healthcare providers to leverage big data analytics tools and techniques to derive meaningful insights from EHRs. The cloud will allow for data layering and learning loops, which will enable "right data, right time" or just-in-time insights. Data analytics will identify trends, predict outcomes, optimize treatments, and support population health management initiatives. Google's Care Studio product applies Google's data-gathering and data-presentation strengths to improve clinical workflows by pooling pertinent data for easy review and analysis [7].

EHR systems will become more sophisticated, offering advanced features such as predictive analytics capabilities that can help healthcare providers improve patient care and outcomes. Analyzing vast amounts of patient data to identify patterns and trends that may be missed by human analysis alone, AI algorithms can learn from past patient data to predict future outcomes and offer suggestions for more personalized treatment plans. Predictions may include identifying high-risk patients (more likely to develop adverse events or complications), predicting medication efficacy, or predicting hospital readmission rates. Knowing which individuals are at risk can then allow providers to intervene earlier and work toward prevention.

Blockchain technology

Blockchain technology will increasingly be used to improve data security, interoperability, patient control, and privacy. Patient health information stored on a blockchain will be encrypted, time-stamped, and distributed across multiple nodes, making it difficult for unauthorized access and tampering. The decentralized storage of data will also help prevent data breaches. Blockchain technology will authenticate users, manage consent, and enforce fine-grained access controls, ensuring that patient data are only accessed by authorized parties.

The immutability of blockchain will ensure the integrity and auditability of EHR data. Once recorded on the blockchain, health records will not be able to be altered or deleted without consensus among network participants. This feature will ensure the long-term preservation and accuracy of patient data, mitigating the risk of fraudulent activities. Healthcare organizations will rely on blockchain-based EHRs for auditing, compliance, and regulatory purposes, reducing the burden of record-keeping, preserving data provenance, enabling secure data sharing (e.g., with healthcare providers, researchers, etc.), and enhancing traceability and transparency.

The use of EHRs to improve population health

Next-generation EHRs have the potential to significantly improve population health by facilitating comprehensive data analysis, promoting evidence-based care, and supporting population-level interventions. Aggregated patient data analyzed at the population level can help us to enable risk stratification (e.g., enable the identification of subpopulations with specific health needs or high healthcare utilization), understand the prevalence of diseases, identify high-risk populations, and design targeted population health management interventions to improve health outcomes. These interventions could be disease management programs, health education campaigns, and proactive outreach efforts to address the specific needs of different population segments.

Leveraging advanced analytics, EHRs can aid in the early detection and prevention of diseases and identify individuals who may be at a higher risk for certain diseases or conditions based on their medical history, family history, or demographic factors. This enables healthcare providers to implement proactive measures such as targeted screenings, preventive interventions, and health promotion initiatives to mitigate risks and prevent the onset or progression of diseases.

Ultimately, EHRs will play a vital role in population health surveillance and reporting. By integrating EHR systems with public health databases, healthcare organizations will report notifiable diseases, track outbreaks, and monitor population-level health indicators. Timely and accurate data sharing will occur between EHRs and public health agencies to facilitate early detection of infectious diseases, enabling targeted interventions and more effective public health responses.

The impact of EHRs on the healthcare workforce

The aforementioned technologies will reshape the roles and responsibilities of healthcare professionals by automating routine tasks (e.g., data entry, documentation) and freeing up time to focus on more complex and critical activities such as patient care, decision-making, and having more meaningful interactions with patients. It will, in essence, augment and enhance the healthcare workforce, not replace it. As different EHR systems will communicate and share data with one another, regardless of the specific platform or vendor. Improved interoperability will make it easier for healthcare providers to access patient information across different care settings, leading to more coordinated and efficient care.

These new technologies will also require healthcare professionals to develop new skill sets. It will be important for healthcare workers to acquire knowledge in data analytics, AI, and digital technologies to effectively collaborate with more sophisticated computer systems. Healthcare providers will need to understand the limitations and capabilities of these tools, interpret their insights, and make informed decisions in conjunction with AI-based recommendations. Continuous professional development and training will be essential to ensure that healthcare providers are equipped to leverage the technology safely and effectively in practice.

Needless to say, the human touch, empathy, and expertise of healthcare workers remain critical in providing compassionate care and making complex healthcare decisions. The successful integration of these technologies in healthcare will require a collaborative approach that leverages the strengths of both the technology and healthcare professionals to achieve optimal patient outcomes.

The role of policy and regulatory changes

Policy and regulatory changes will play a pivotal role in shaping the continued digital transformation of EHRs by providing an ongoing framework for standardization, interoperability, data privacy, and security. Governments and regulatory bodies need to continue to establish guidelines and requirements that promote the adoption and effective use of EHRs across healthcare systems. Policy changes should create a secure environment for the digital storage, transmission, and management of EHRs, instilling trust among patients and healthcare providers alike. As EHRs evolve, they will likely incorporate more robust encryption technologies and data anonymization techniques. Concepts such as "privacy by design" will be integral, meaning privacy assurance and user control of personal information will be embedded into EHR systems from the outset.

Moreover, policy changes incentivize the adoption and meaningful use of EHRs, further driving their digital transformation. Governments and regulatory bodies often provide financial incentives and define criteria for demonstrating the meaningful use of EHR systems. These incentives will encourage healthcare providers to effectively utilize EHRs, resulting in improved patient care, clinical outcomes, and data exchange. Future policy frameworks will also support the integration of emerging technologies by adapting regulations to accommodate new care delivery models and technologies.

The way ahead

The digital transformation of EHRs is a complex and challenging process, but by overcoming the challenges and seizing the opportunities, we can create a healthcare system that is more patient-centered, efficient, and effective. The EHR industry continues to be ripe for disruption and improvement. The future of EHRs is likely to involve many recent advancements in technology. As a whole, these systems will become more user-friendly, allowing for easier input and retrieval of patient information. EHRs are now moving beyond the standard clinical data collected in a provider's office to be more inclusive of a broader view of a patient's overall health.

The next generation of EHRs have the potential to make healthcare more patient-centered, efficient, and effective. AI technologies are just now being integrated into EHR systems to automate tasks, assist with advanced clinical decision-making, and enable predictive analytics. The recent partnership between Epic and Microsoft was truly groundbreaking in setting the stage for what's to come. Press releases mentioned natural language queries and interactive data analysis abilities, which will help healthcare providers explore data in a conversational and intuitive way [8].

EHRs are poised to play a critical role in the evolution to learning health systems (LHS); a concept centered on continuous learning from healthcare data to improve patient outcomes, enhance efficiency, and reduce costs. The LHS era promises a more responsive healthcare delivery system by continuously learning from the care it delivers by utilizing data and feedback loops. The core idea is to create a dynamic, knowledge-driven system where scientific discovery and real-world care delivery continuously learn from each other, thereby accelerating the application of new insights into clinical practice. In addition to facilitating the rapid translation of research findings into practice, they can highlight gaps in knowledge that require further research [9].

The need for continuous research and development

EHRs will provide a rich source of data for research and evidence-based care. With proper data anonymization and patient consent processes in place, EHRs will contribute to population-based studies, comparative effectiveness research, and the development of clinical guidelines. By leveraging aggregated EHR data, researchers can generate insights, identify best practices, and drive evidence-based care delivery to improve population health outcomes.

Future outlook

There are still many ethical implications associated with these technological advancements, including data privacy, exacerbation of the "digital divide," and the need for standardized regulations and policies. The evolution of EHRs, while exciting, must be navigated with care to temper innovative practices with ethical responsibility and an eye toward ensuring health equity. Although controversial, there is a push for next-generation EHRs to gather more information on social determinants of health to help identify and address health disparities and identify biases in care to promote equitable treatment.

As EHRs are currently regulated by a patchwork of state and federal laws in the United States, it can be difficult for healthcare providers to comply with all of the regulations, and it can also make it difficult for patients to understand their rights. Flexible policymaking is needed within the United States and beyond to navigate this challenge in a way that respects patient rights.

In looking toward addressing these concerns, the goal will be to create EHR systems that not only support the needs of healthcare providers but also patients and caregivers alike. This will be a complex task requiring multidisciplinary collaboration, including input from healthcare professionals, technologists, ethicists, and policymakers. It will also likely involve international collaborations and consensus-building efforts to develop harmonized global standards. Without a doubt, constant vigilance and proactive strategies will be needed to ensure that all stakeholders are continuously engaged in what will surely be perpetual considerations of design, ethics, and proper governance and oversight.

AI disclosure

During the preparation of this work the author used ChatGPT in order to brainstorm, ideate, and generate initial drafts. After using this tool, the author reviewed and edited the content to ensure content tone and accuracy.

References

[1] Preparing for the next generation of electronic health records. 2022. https://www2.deloitte.com/us/en/insights/industry/health-care/ehr-systems-the-future-of-electronic-health-records.html. Accessed 18, 5, 2023.

[2] Jeter Hansen A. ScopeA roadmap for the future of electronic health records—scope. 2018. https://scopeblog.stanford.edu/2018/09/18/a-roadmap-for-the-future-of-electronic-health-records/. Accessed 5, 2023.

[3] Adams K. MedCity NewsEpic integrates Suki's voice assistant into its EHR. 2023. https://medcitynews.com/2023/05/epic-ehr-burnout-ai-dication-healthcare/. Accessed 5, 2023.

[4] Inc A. Augmedix announces partnership with HCA healthcare to accelerate the development of AI-enabled ambient documentation. GlobeNewswire News Room; 2023. https://www.globenewswire.com/en/news-release/2023/04/20/2650798/0/en/Augmedix-Announces-Partnership-with-HCA-Healthcare-to-Accelerate-the-Development-of-AI-enabled-Ambient-Documentation.html. Accessed 5, 2023.

[5] Dinh-Le C, Chuang R, Chokshi S, Mann D. Wearable health technology and electronic health record integration: scoping review and future directions. JMIR mHealth and uHealth 2019;7(9):e12861. https://doi.org/10.2196/12861.

[6] Dugar D. Future of electronic medical records | EMR trends for 2020. selecthub.com. 2019.

[7] Bryan RG. InsideSourcesGoogle, MEDITECH and the future of electronic health records. 2022. https://insidesources.com/google-meditech-and-the-future-of-electronic-health-records/. Accessed 5, 2023.

[8] Microsoft and Epic expand strategic collaboration with integration of Azure OpenAI Service. 2023, 4, 17. Stories, https://news.microsoft.com/2023/04/17/microsoft-and-epic-expand-strategic-collaboration-with-integration-of-azure-openai-service/. Accessed 5, 2023.

[9] Evans RS. Electronic health records: then, now, and in the future. Yearbook of Medical Informatics 2016:S48–61. https://doi.org/10.15265/IYS-2016-s006.

CHAPTER 8

Bridging the gap: Empowering patients with health apps

Thomas Micklewright
ORCHA Health, Daresbury, United Kingdom

Introduction

Traditional models of healthcare are represented by discreet interactions between patients and healthcare providers. Patients will meet with their healthcare provider to seek advice, undergo investigation, receive treatment, and review their progress. Between these touchpoints, however, patients must process information, weigh up their choices, adhere to management plans, or adapt them where necessary, with little support until their next appointment. Health apps provide an opportunity to fill this gap.

A health app is a software application or computer program, designed with an interactive user interface that supports health and/or healthcare delivery. Health apps can exist as downloadable products, to be run from a smartphone, tablet, smartwatch, or other mobile device. They may also exist as web apps; these are computer programs that are accessed through a web browser, with more interactivity than traditional websites.

Health apps very seldom require training to use or expensive hardware, utilizing the mobile devices that over 86% of the US population already own [1]. They can help to empower citizens to become active players in their health, instead of passive recipients and ensure that healthcare no longer ends when a patient leaves the clinic. However, for all of the opportunities, health apps also pose unique challenges that must be considered before their use becomes part of routine clinical practice.

This chapter will therefore provide an overview of health apps and their use as well as a discussion about their current use and some of the barriers to their adoption. We'll then explore the role that assurance frameworks play in helping to regulate the use of health apps before considering the practical elements of deploying them within a healthcare setting.

Digital Health. https://doi.org/10.1016/B978-0-443-23901-4.00008-8

An overview of the health app market

The health app market is expanding rapidly. In 2022, the global market was valued at $211bn and is anticipated to grow at a rate of 18.6% from 2023 to 2030 [2]. In the USA, most health apps used are exercise and fitness apps, such as step counters or heart rate monitors. Yet, 36% of US adults also use a blood pressure application, 23% use a health app to support their mental health, and 17% use one for managing their diabetes [3].

The modern health app market caters to a range of audiences, languages, and illnesses. It is as easy to find health apps to support a child with anxiety as it is to find one to support an elderly person at risk of falls. Furthermore, a breadth of funding models (free, free with in app purchases, or paid) and accessibility options that support text-to-speech and adjustable displays means that health apps are more inclusive than ever before.

Market drivers

A significant driver of this widespread adoption of health apps was the COVID-19 pandemic. The first COVID-19 lockdown in the United Kingdom saw a 343% increase in searches for health apps, particularly in the initial 2 months of the lockdown [4]. These increased search volumes were sustained for several months after the lockdowns were introduced, with the greatest increases seen in apps to support musculoskeletal illness (2036%), allergy (1253%), and general healthy living apps (1051%) [4].

In the United Kingdom, the increased interest in health apps may in part be explained by the launch of the NHS App. This app enables healthcare users to access a range of national health services in England, such as appointment booking and prescription ordering, and became the national vehicle for disseminating COVID-19 vaccination certificates, a prerequisite for traveling overseas at the time. As of July 2023, almost 40 million patients in England have downloaded the NHS App [5], marking a societal shift toward accessing healthcare through one's mobile phone. Indeed, this pattern has played out globally, as major healthcare providers, such as the Mayo Clinic [6], Kaiser Permanente [7], and Helsinki University Hospital [8] have made app-based care routines and introduced patients to the health app market.

Gaps in the market

Notwithstanding this interest, gaps in the current healthcare market remain. Having assessed over 20,000 health apps [9], ORCHA, the Organization for the Review of Care and Health Apps, has reported that there are over 18 times as many mental health apps as there are apps for gastrointestinal disease or skin complaints [10]. Many health apps collect, share, or provide health information, whereas only a minority will provide treatment or attempt to change health behavior. And health apps specifically designed for children or older adults remain scarce.

Current patterns of use

A 2023 poll of US residents found that most people (79%) believed health apps should be considered when looking at new ways to manage our health [11]. What's more, 76% of people have used a health app already; in the USA, that represents 252 million people [11]. The spread of health app adoption is not equitable, however. Health app usage dropped beyond middle age, despite this age group continuing to advocate for digital health usage in general [11]. The poll also demonstrated that people were more likely to use a health app in the Northeast and Midwest (84% and 80%) than in the South (77%) or the West (66%) [11].

While the support for health apps among citizens is encouraging, this comes with an important public health warning: almost half of people will choose a health app without consulting with a healthcare professional [11]. In fact, US users were as likely to choose their health apps based on a recommendation of a friend or family member, as they were to base it upon a clinical recommendation Fig. 8.1. In the United Kingdom, the situation is worse, with users more likely to do their own research than to seek the advice of a doctor when it comes to their health apps [11].

Patients as consumers

This result is not surprising. The public availability of health apps on app stores is no different from other e-commerce markets. If I do not need to consult with a store clerk to buy my clothes online, why should I speak with a clinician to buy a health app? This consumerist approach would be reasonable if it were easy for consumers to make informed decisions about health apps based on their safety and quality, but this is far from the case. Among those that have used health apps in the past, 60% based their decision on customer reviews and 53% on the number of downloads the app had received [11], despite these being poor indicators of an app's clinical effectiveness or safety [12]. Only a minority of users report checking an app's HIPAA compliance or whether any healthcare professionals were involved in the development of the app [11]. This means that without clinical direction, patients may be choosing health apps based on their popularity or their marketing capital, rather than their appropriateness, efficacy, or safety.

Although efforts abound to better regulate products on the app stores and to enforce these regulations, it will be hard to reverse the open market that has emerged for health apps. Instead, we can seek to leverage the powerful relationships that patients have with their healthcare teams to have informed discussions with patients about health apps. Many

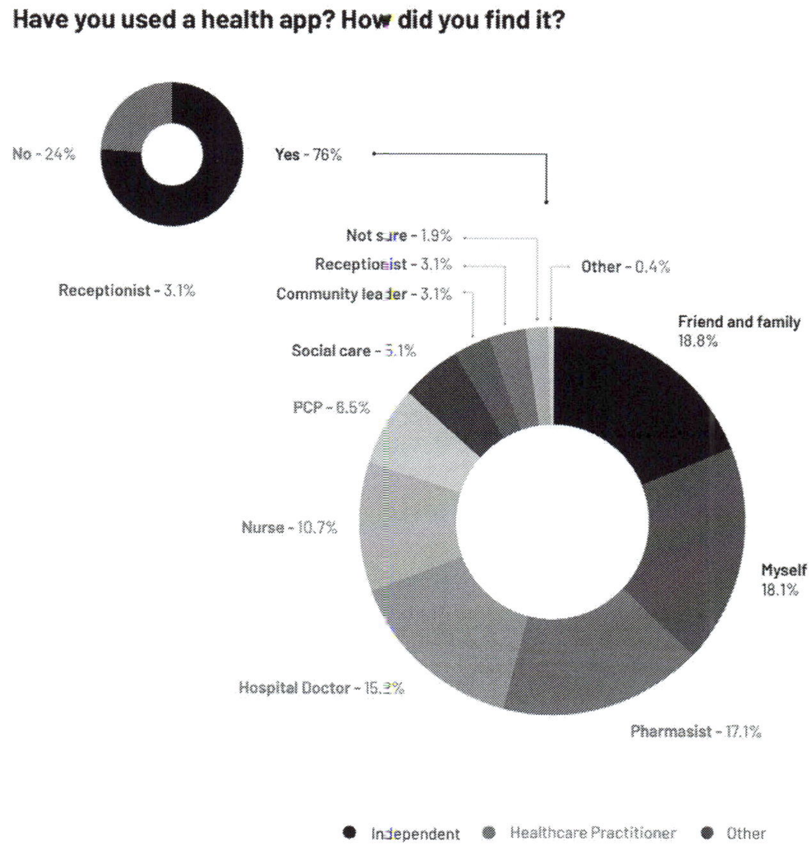

Figure 8.1
Sources of health app recommendations. In the USA, app users are more likely to search for health apps themselves or take the recommendation of a friend or family member, than to be directed to one by a doctor, nurse, or pharmacist. *From ORCHA. Public attitudes to digital health across the US. Published May 30, 2023. Accessed September 26, 2023. https://info.orchahealth.com/digital-health-attitudes-behavior-2023-report-us.*

healthcare professionals will feel unprepared for these conversations and avoid them altogether, but with training, the provision of resources, and the development of new care pathways that embed digital options, the clinical workforce can be better prepared for the future.

Opportunities for apps in healthcare

Although not yet mainstream, health apps are playing a larger role in clinical practice. Health apps have been used to change health behaviors [13], support patient health education [14], enable patient-centered care [15], and create peer support networks [16]. When surveyed, the majority of primary care physicians reported benefits to health apps, particularly in medicine management, disease prevention, and healthy lifestyle support [17]. Health apps, such as clinical calculators and guideline apps, can also be used by healthcare professionals themselves to improve the safety and quality of care they deliver [18].

Health apps, however, become increasingly important when considered among the wider health-economic context. By 2050, it is estimated that the world's population of people aged over 60 will double, and numbers aged over 80 will triple, both compared with 2020 levels [19]. This will bring increasing demand on healthcare services from multimorbidity and frailty, at a time when the cost of healthcare is already rising, from new drug developments, personalized care, genomics, and increasing technological advancement. Yet, exacerbating these challenges are significant workforce shortages, especially in frontline clinical roles [20]. Against a backdrop of increasing demand and reduced capacity, digital health, and health apps, in particular, are a critical part of the solution (Fig. 8.2).

For instance, health apps can improve self-management and control of long-term conditions such as type 2 diabetes mellitus [21] and COPD [22], which are known to cause longer-term complications and emergency admissions if poorly controlled. Triaging and signposting apps have led to better use of healthcare resources by directing patients to the right services for their needs and releasing cost savings simultaneously [23]. Remote monitoring apps used to support virtual wards and home-based care have been shown to have half the number of telephone consultations that patients require [24]. And apps that automate elements of a patient's operative journey have been shown to significantly reduce the need for pre- and postoperative appointments [25,26].

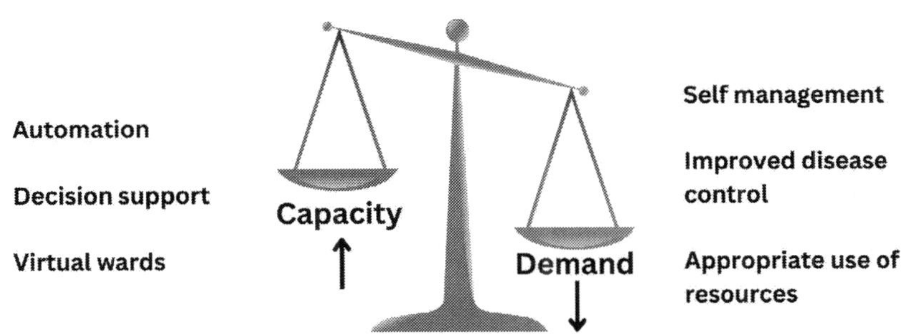

Figure 8.2
The impact of digital health on health service pressures health apps have the potential to both reduce demand on healthcare services and to increase the capacity of healthcare providers to deliver care.

Aggregated benefits

These examples typically use health apps as a single-point solution; one app to solve one particular problem, such as blood glucose monitoring in a patient with diabetes. As the evidence in favor of digital health continues to consolidate though, we will begin to see an aggregated deployment of health apps across patient care pathways and patient groups. Already, we are seeing this pattern emerge. In England, the National Health Service is compiling case studies where digital tools have been aligned to various care pathways, including in Oncology [27], and ORCHA is working with Integrated Care Boards to integrate health apps specifically into care pathways [28]. Similarly, HUS Helsinki University Hospital, in Finland, has developed a myriad of web-app services to support patients at different stages of their healthcare journey [29]. There is still research to be done to support this multipoint deployment of health apps, but the opportunity to personalize health app recommendations to meet the specific needs of patients at specific points in time is without doubt gaining interest.

Risks and barriers to using apps in healthcare

While the opportunities for health apps are exciting, it would be wrong to assume that all health apps are ready for these opportunities. In 2022, the internet research nonprofit Mozilla revealed that only 10% of the most popular pregnancy and period tracking apps had safe data and privacy features [30]. This took on new meaning following Roe v Wade earlier that year, in which private health messages were extracted from social media to prosecute a woman who terminated her pregnancy.

Clinical risks

ORCHA has assessed over 20,000 health apps across clinical safety, evidence, usability, and data security and reports that only 20% meet their minimum quality thresholds [11]. For an app that has a diagnostic or therapeutic function, such as a diabetes app for calculating insulin dosing, the consequences of an error could be life-threatening. Health apps that carry the highest risks, including those with diagnostic or therapeutic functions, are often categorized as medical devices and face additional regulatory requirements before being able to enter the market. This provides some safeguards, but relies on a self-selecting sample of developers submitting their products for regulatory approval. Apps that qualify as medical devices continue to enter the App and Play stores without appropriate certification, and even after they are certified, the speed with which digital products update and evolve makes it exceptionally difficult for regulators to keep their assessments up-to-date.

Even among those apps not considered to be medical devices, inherent design flaws may have safety implications for users. Apps designed to educate and direct patients to appropriate services must be kept up-to-date, with controls in place to ensure the accuracy of their content. Where apps integrate with other solutions, such as electronic health records, patient data must transfer seamlessly, or risk important medical information, such as drug allergies, being lost. Apps that support online, peer-support networks must ensure all safeguards are in place to protect patients.

Barriers among patents and clinicians

In addition to the risks associated with health apps, a number of other barriers exist among patient and clinician populations. Patient time and effort required to learn how to use an app are an identified barrier to adoption, which highlights the importance of user testing in app design. What's more, digital literacy and awareness of suitable apps also influence adoption [31]. This suggests not only that there is a need to educate the general public about health apps but also that patients need to be guided toward health apps that match their needs; a function that could be fulfilled by clinicians in the future.

Clinicians may face similar barriers in terms of digital literacy and awareness, but their primary concern is trust. In a discreet choice experiment with 222 clinicians in the UK NHS, health apps were most likely to be recommended to patients if they were approved by the NHS or had been recommended by a clinical colleague [32]. This effect was more pronounced than the cost of the technology or even a published study demonstrating safety and effectiveness [32]. Therefore, while education and guidance are needed to overcome some of the patient barriers to health app adoption, demonstrating assurance and endorsement may be more powerful for clinical adoption (Fig. 8.3).

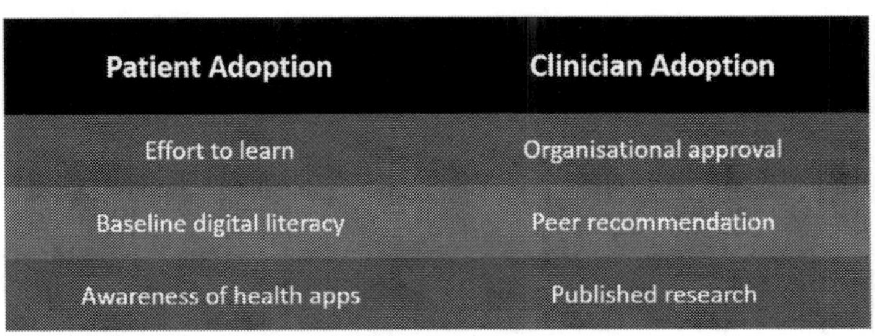

Figure 8.3
Factors affecting health app adoption different factors influence the use of health apps by patients and clinicians. Patients are influenced by usability and ease of access, whereas clinicians seek professional assurances before using health apps.

Assuring apps in healthcare

To mitigate these risks, a standardized approach to assuring the quality of health apps is needed. Numerous assessment frameworks have now been developed or are in development across the world, led by academic institutions, private organizations, and some third-sector groups. Some of these frameworks focus on a specific domain, such as data security, and some will focus on specific types of health apps, such as mental health apps. Among those that are non-domain-specific, however, the domains with the greatest commonality include data privacy, clinical effectiveness, and design and usability [33].

Data privacy

Data privacy domains pertain to the data that the app collects, whether or not it is sensitive or personally identifiable, how these data are used and stored, and whether there is compliance against national data standards, such as the Health Insurance Portability and Accountability Act (HIPPA) in the USA or The General Data Protection Regulation (GDPR) in the EU. If the app interacts with third-party software or devices, the sharing of data and whether the user can opt in or out may also be considered here.

Design and usability

Design and usability domains typically examine the design of the app and in particular, the user interface. Design standards, such as WC3 for web design, Web Content Accessibility Guidelines (WCAG), or ISO 9241 should ideally be adhered to. Assessments will also often look for evidence of user testing or involvement and whether or not adjustments can be made to the user interface to allow users with sensory impairments to use the app. Apps should have clear navigational aids to assist usability by those with low digital literacy, and it should be easy for users to access support or to report problems that they encounter.

Clinical effectiveness

Clinical effectiveness domains describe the validity of the content of the app, its agreement with best practice or published clinical guidelines, and its safety profile. The majority of assessment frameworks will also examine the availability of clinical evidence of effectiveness and whether or not this is sufficient given the functionality of the app [33]. This issue of proportionality of evidence is an important consideration. Within the pharmaceutical industry, products usually progress through three phases of clinical trials prior to licensing, at which point they enter Phase IV, collecting longer-term safety data [34]. This life cycle can take 10–20 years to complete with significant financial investment. Compared with the life sciences industry, however, the digital health industry is smaller, with a larger number of startup companies seeking to introduce innovative solutions to the market. What's more, the functional breadth of health apps is vast with significant differences in clinical risk between products. Requiring apps that only digitize patient information leaflets, or that support fitness and wellness behaviors, to adhere to the same regulatory and research lifecycle as pharmaceuticals would be disproportionate and block many of these innovations from the market altogether.

One approach used to address this issue of proportionality is evidence standard frameworks. These frameworks, such as that produced by The National Institute for Health and Care Excellence (NICE) in England [35], allow digital health products to be categorized based on their functions. Each category has different evidence requirements, with lower-risk apps, such as a staff rostering app, requiring a lower level of evidence than higher-risk apps, such as a diagnostic app for atrial fibrillation.

Evidence can also be provided as part of this domain to satisfy users of an app's safety, not just its effectiveness. Some assurance frameworks, such as the Digital Health Assessment Framework [36] in the USA or the Digital Technology Assessment Criteria (DTAC) in England [37], will take a detailed interest in how risk management practices have been applied to the development of an app. This may include considering whether a risk management plan is in place, how safety incidents are managed, and whether or not a clinician has been involved in the development of the app.

Progress in medical AI

Although not the focus of this chapter, a brief mention of AI, in relation to its safe use in health apps, is important here. AI in health apps is vulnerable to the same risks as AI elsewhere, including poor or biased training data, poor generalizability of the data model, and lack of transparent decision-making. At the time of writing, a number of organizations, including the Food and Drug Administration [38], The American Medical Association [39], and the NHS AI and Digital Regulations Service [40] are developing approaches for the safe regulation of AI, but it remains unclear whether this will include the use of AI in health apps.

Deploying health apps in practice

While medicine has developed rapidly in recent years, the fundamental components of good clinical practice, and the structure of a consultation, have largely remained the same. The introduction of digital, consumer health products into routine healthcare, however, risks disrupting these traditions. We have already explored the technical, procedural, and human factors that affect the adoption of health apps. This section shall consider the

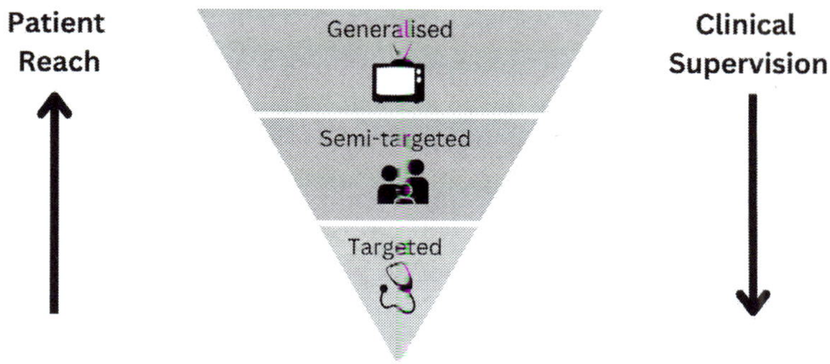

Figure 8.4

Different approaches to health app deployment there are three approaches to deploying health apps, with increasing patient reach often coming at the expense of clinical supervision and support.

practicalities of embedding health apps into existing workstreams and the different deployment routes available.

The pharmaceutical industry is a valuable analogy when analyzing digital health technologies. Once a new medicine has received regulatory approval to enter the market, companies have three routes by which to get their product into the hands of a user (Fig. 8.4). These are.

- Direct-to-consumer advertising for over-the-counter products—this represents *a generalized approach.*
- Nationally sponsored public health campaigns (e.g., vaccination products)—dependent on the cohort targeted, this can be a *semitargeted approach.*
- Prescriptions from a healthcare professional—this is the most *targeted approach.*

Generalized and semitargeted approaches

The experience of many professionals working in digital transformation is that generalized approaches are easiest to implement as they are more direct and do not require clinician engagement. Generalized approaches leverage existing health communication channels, such as mainstream media, social media, print media, batch SMS messaging and others. Opportunities also exist to segment patient populations and to take a semitargeted approach, for instance, recommending dieting and weight loss apps to all patients enrolled in a diabetes prevention program [41], or smoking cessation apps to patients with COPD. Population Health data will make it increasingly easy to identify at-risk cohorts and offer a mix of *generalized* and *semitargeted approaches* to health app deployment.

However, there are two main drawbacks to this strategy. First, there is a loss of clinical supervision. Without a healthcare professional to guide the patient, the *generalized approach* assumes that the patient has the knowledge and health literacy to determine their suitability for a particular health app themselves. There is a risk that patients may download the wrong app in error or an app that is unsuitable for their specific needs. This risk is higher with apps that have a diagnostic or therapeutic function and might be better held behind the wall of a professional recommendation, akin to higher-risk drugs requiring a doctor's prescription.

The second drawback is that a direct-to-consumer method creates a blind spot for healthcare teams, who otherwise could draw insight from their patients' use of digital technologies. Knowing whether a patient is using a health app might influence other elements of their care plan and, in the future, have implications for medical coding and reimbursement.

These drawbacks can be mitigated by directing patients to safe sources of preselected health apps rather than to the apps or app stores themselves. Curated health app libraries and formularies, where criteria such as evidence base, data security, and interoperability have led to a short list of approved apps, allow healthcare providers and payers to guide patients to the most suitable apps [42]. Such formularies can also provide data on app downloads and support pricing workflows [42].

Targeted approaches

The *targeted approach* can also overcome these drawbacks, so long as the healthcare professional feels qualified to make a digital health recommendation. To this end, online formularies of approved health apps can also empower clinicians to make such recommendations, and their use can be seen in health systems across the USA and the United Kingdom [43,44]. What's more, when healthcare professionals make a targeted health app recommendation, download rates from patients are high. Unpublished data from the UK Company ORCHA showed a 90% download rate in health apps that were recommended to patients by a mental health professional [45].

However, a targeted approach can be challenging. Setup, training, feedback, and workflow integration are resource-intensive activities, and considerable effort will be needed upfront to gain support from those professionals who will be recommending health apps to patients. Giving healthcare professionals the autonomy to choose how to integrate health apps into their practice and the time to cocreate new workflows is critical in order to scale any healthcare innovation [46]), including health apps.

Further reading and next steps

We suggest that you read about the US Digital Health Assessment Framework (DHAF) here: https://dhealthframework.org/.

The DHAF was developed in collaboration between The American College of Physicians, The American Telemedicine Association, and The Organization for the Review of Care and Health Apps, to help assess the quality of digital health apps.

In addition to this, you may wish to consider the following projects within your own organization, to help embed some of the learning from this chapter.

- Conduct an audit of the current use of health apps in your organization. In particular, strive to understand the breadth of what is being used and/or recommended to patients; how staff are selecting apps and recommending them; and how are the outcomes from these apps are measured. Is this in line with any existing organizational policy about digital health use?
- Identify a problem within a care pathway that you work with, for which there may be a digital solution. Conduct a horizon scan of apps that could help, searching online search browsers and academic literature, and screen apps using the DHAF or a similar framework. Alternatively, if you have access to an organization-approved health app library, identify one or two apps using your library and redesign your care pathway to include these apps.
- Develop a teaching session for your peers about health apps, being sure to highlight both the opportunities and the important considerations to their use in healthcare.

References

[1] Mobile fact sheet. Pew Research Center. Published April 7, 2021. Accessed October 10, 2023. https://www.pewresearch.org/internet/fact-sheet/mobile/

[2] Digital health market size, share & trends analysis report by technology (Healthcare Analytics, mHealth, Tele-healthcare, Digital Health Systems), By Component (Software, Hardware, Services), By Region, And Segment Forecasts, 2023–2030. Grand View Research. Published November 15, 2022. Accessed September 20, 2023. https://www.grandviewresearch.com/industry-analysis/digital-health-market.

[3] Zipp, R. The public's use of health apps and wearables has increased in recent years. But digital health still has room to grow. Morning Consult. Published February 21, 2023. Accessed September 20, 2023. https://pro.morningconsult.com/trend-setters/use-of-digital-health-apps-wearables-growing.

[4] Leigh S, Daly R, Stevens S, et al. Web-based internet searches for digital health products in the United Kingdom before and during the COVID-19 pandemic: a time-series analysis using app libraries from the Organisation for the Review of Care and Health Applications (ORCHA). BMJ Open 2021;11:e053891. https://doi.org/10.1136/bmjopen-2021-053891.

[5] NHS App Reporting Dashboard. NHS England. Updated September, 2023. Accessed September 26, 2023. https://tabanalytics.data.england.nhs.uk/#/views/NHSAppReportingDashboard-Uptake/Summary?

[6] Mayo clinic [mobile application]. Version 10.8. Rochester, MN: Mayo Clinic; 2012.

[7] Kaiser Permanente [mobile application]. Version 5.18.0. Oakland, CA: Kaiser Permanente; 2012.
[8] Helsinki University Hospital (HUS). Health Village Story. Digital Health Village. Published: Date Unknown. Accessed September 26, 2023. https://www.digitalhealthvillage.com/en/health-village-story.
[9] Market facts and figures. ORCHA. Published December 20, 2022. Accessed October 5, 2023. https://orchahealth.com/market-facts-and-figures/.
[10] ORCHA. Reviews by category. Assessment dashboard. Updated October 5, 2023. Accessed October 5, 2023. [Data on file at ORCHA, please ask for access].
[11] ORCHA. Public attitudes to digital health across the US. Published May 30, 2023. Accessed September 26, 2023. https://info.orchahealth.com/digital-health-attitudes-behavior-2023-report-us.
[12] Leigh S, Ouyang J, Mimnagh C. Effective? Engaging? Secure? Applying the ORCHA-24 framework to evaluate apps for chronic insomnia disorder. Evidence-Based Mental Health 2017;20(4):e20. https://doi.org/10.1136/eb-2017-102751.
[13] Milne-Ives M, Lam C, De Cock C, van Velthoven MH, Meinert E. Mobile apps for health behavior change in physical activity, diet, drug and alcohol use, and mental health: systematic review. JMIR Mhealth and Uhealth 2020;8(3):e17046. https://doi.org/10.2196/17046.
[14] Blythin AM, Elkes J, van Lindholm T, et al. Can digital health apps provide patients with support to promote structured diabetes education and ongoing self-management? A real-world evaluation of myDiabetes usage. Digital Health 2023;9. https://doi.org/10.1177/20552076221147109.
[15] Finkelstein J, Knight A, Marinopoulos S, et al. Enabling patient-centered care through health information technology. Evidence Report—Technology Assessment 2012;(206):1−1531.
[16] Moorhead SA, Hazlett DE, Harrison L, Carroll JK, Irwin A, Hoving C. A new dimension of health care: systematic review of the uses, benefits, and limitations of social media for health communication. Journal of Medical Internet Research 2013;15(4):e85. https://doi.org/10.2196/jmir.1933.
[17] Wangler J, Jansky M. The use of health apps in primary care-results from a survey amongst general practitioners in Germany. Wiener Medizinische Wochenschrift 2021;171(7−8):148−56. https://doi.org/10.1007/s10354-021-00814-0.
[18] Mayer MA, Rodríguez Blanco O, Torrejon A. Use of health apps by nurses for professional purposes: web-based survey study. JMIR Mhealth and Uhealth 2019;7(11):e15195. https://doi.org/10.2196/15195.
[19] Steverson, M. Ageing and Health. World Health Organization. Published October 1, 2022. Accessed August 10, 2023. https://www.who.int/news-room/fact-sheets/detail/ageing-and-health.
[20] Medlock, M., Radis, E., Abrams, K., Bhatt, J., Elsner, N. and Malhotra, R. Addressing health care's talent emergency. Deloitte Insights. Published November 15, 2022. Accessed August 10, 2023. https://www2.deloitte.com/us/en/insights/industry/health-care/healthcare-workforce-shortage-solutions.html.
[21] Stevens S, Gallagher S, Andrews T, Ashall-Payne L, Humphreys L, Leigh S. The effectiveness of digital health technologies for patients with diabetes mellitus: a systematic review. Frontiers in Clinical Diabetes and Healthcare 2022;3:936752. https://doi.org/10.3389/fcdhc.2022.936752.
[22] McLaughlin, K. and Skinner, E. A real-world service evaluation of myCOPD. My mHealth. Published Dec 14, 2020. Accessed August 10, 2023. https://mymhealth.com/studies/real-world-service-evaluation-mycopd-mmh-e04.
[23] Hanlon, J. and Varghese, A. YHEC economic benefit study. Accessed August 10, 2023. Published January 2023. https://info.klinikhealthcaresolutions.com/yhec-case-study?_gl=1*1a4sult*_ga*Mjk1NDE0MDYuMTY5NDAxMjU0Mg..*_ga_WSTZT27YG3*MTY5NjUxNzIzOC4yLjEuMTY5NjUxNzM5NC4yNC4wLjA.*_ga_H2N4WFVJ1W*MTY5NjUxNzM1OC4yLjAuMTY5NjUxNzM1OC42MC4wLjA.*_gcl_au*MTE4MjQyMzUxOS4xNjk0MDEyNTQ0&_ga=2.21776187.1202846l1.1696517238-29541406.1694012542.
[24] Shah SS, Gvozdanovic A, Knight M, Gagnon J. Mobile app-based remote patient monitoring in acute medical conditions: prospective feasibility study exploring digital health solutions on clinical workload during the COVID crisis. JMIR Formative Research 2021;5(1):e23190. https://doi.org/10.2196/23190.
[25] NHS Lanarkshire's electronic pre-operative assessment process optimises patient flow and helps fill surgical slots. Buddy Healthcare. Published: Date Unknown. Accessed August 10, 2023. https://www.buddyhealthcare.com/en/customers-stories/nhs-lanarkshire-case-study?hsCtaTracking=27e5cc68-0c8c-41e4-b61b-20b79ca6da28%7C6903d0bc-f36f-4e56-bc2d-0d0b8cfe5cbd.

[26] How Orton hospital reduced its orthopaedic patients's post-operative vists by 20% with the BuddyCare Platform. Buddy Healthcare. Published: Date Unknown. Accessed August 10, 2023. https://www.buddyhealthcare.com/en/customers-stories/orthopedic-case-study?hsCtaTracking=53d6c861-c231-4bfd-9b83-df42a888fcbf%7C65ed3c1c-1172-422e-bcd9-6fe1ef6db3ff.
[27] Cancer Pathway. NHS england transformation directorate. Updated 2023. Accessed August 16, 2023. https://transform.england.nhs.uk/key-tools-and-info/digital-playbooks/cancer-digital-playbook/cancer-pathway/.
[28] Case study: ORCHA. Growth platform. Published May 18, 2022. Accessed October 5, 2023. https://growthplatform.org/news/2022/05/case-study-orcha/.
[29] Digital health village: How Helsinki empowers healthcare professionals to improve care. Health Capital Helsinki. Published August 9, 2023. Accessed August 16, 2023. https://growthplatform.org/news/2022/05/case-study-orcha/.
[30] In post Roe v Wade era, Mozilla labels 18 of 25 popular period and pregnancy tracking tech with *privacy not included warning. Mozilla. Published August 17. 2022. Accessed October 5, 2023. https://foundation.mozilla.org/en/blog/in-post-roe-v-wade-era-mozilla-labels-18-of-25-popular-period-and-pregnancy-tracking-tech-with-privacy-not-included-warning/.
[31] Peng W, Kanthawala S, Yuan S, Hussain SA. A qualitative study of user perceptions of mobile health apps. BMC Public Health 2016;16(1):1158. https://doi.org/10.1186/s12889-016-3808-0.
[32] Leigh S, Ashall-Payne L, Andrews T. Barriers and facilitators to the adoption of mobile health among health care professionals from the United Kingdom: discrete choice experiment. JMIR Mhealth and Uhealth 2020;8(7):e17704. https://doi.org/10.2196/17704.
[33] Frey, A., Phillips, B., Baines, R., McCabe, A., Weston, P., Andrews, T. and Leigh, S. Domain coverage and criteria convergence among digital health technology assessment frameworks: a systematic review. Submitted, awaiting acceptance.
[34] Medicine Lifecycle. ABPI. Updated September 20, 2023. Accessed October 5, 2023. https://www.abpi.org.uk/value-and-access/uk-medicine-pricing/medicine-lifecycle/.
[35] Evidence standards framework for digital health technologies. National Institute for Health and Care Excellence (NICE). Updated August 9, 2022. Accessed October 3, 2023. https://www.nice.org.uk/corporate/ecd7.
[36] Digital Health Assessment Framework. Digital Health Assessment Framework. Published May 2, 2022. Accessed October 5, 2023. https://dhealthframework.org/about-the-framework/.
[37] Digital technology assessment criteria for health and social care (DTAC). NHSX. Updated April 16, 2021. Accessed October 3, 2023. https://transform.england.nhs.uk/documents/60/DTAC_version_1.0_FINAL_updated_16.04.odt.
[38] FDA releases artificial intelligence/machine learning action plan. Food and Drug Adminstration (FDA). Published January 12, 2021. Accessed October 5, 2023. https://www.fda.gov/news-events/press-announcements/fda-releases-artificial-intelligencemachine-learning-action-plan.
[39] Advancing health care AI through ethics, evidence and equity. American Medical Association. Published January, 2022. Accessed October 5, 2023. https://www.ama-assn.org/practice-management/digital/advancing-health-care-ai-through-ethics-evidence-and-equity.
[40] Understanding regulations of AI and digital technology in health and social care. NHS England. Published August 2, 2023. Accessed October 5, 2023. https://www.digitalregulations.innovation.nhs.uk/.
[41] Jeans, A. NHS diabetes prevention programme includes ORCHA. Published February 19, 2019. Accessed October 5, 2023. https://orchahealth.com/nhs-diabetes-prevention-programme-includes-orcha/#:~:text=%E2%80%98Healthier%20You%E2%80%99%20is%20a%2040-week%20support%20programme%20which,people%20are%20given%20a%20Health%20and%20Wellbeing%20Coach.
[42] Gordon WJ, Landman A, Zhang H, Bates DW. Beyond validation: getting health apps into clinical practice. NPJ Digital Medicine 2020;3:14. https://doi.org/10.1038/s41746-019-0212-z.
[43] Lydon, C. ORCHA creates UK's first digital health formulary. Published March 23, 2023. Accessed July 11, 2023. https://www.digitalhealth.net/2023/03/orcha-creates-uks-first-digital-health-formulary/.

[44] Soch, H. The digital health formulary: An idea whose time has come. Talking Healthcare Technology. Published August 4, 2021. Accessed October 5, 2023. https://www.digitalhealth.net/2023/03/orcha-creates-uks-first-digital-health-formulary/.

[45] Micklewright, T. How can digital support healthcare pressures? PowerPoint presented at: digital health assessment assembly; May 11 2023; Daresbury, UK.

[46] Horton, T., Illingworth, J. and Warburton, W. The spread challenge. Published September, 2018. Accessed October 5, 2023. https://www.health.org.uk/sites/default/files/upload/publications/2018/The-spread-challenge.pdf.

CHAPTER 9

Remote patient monitoring

Lisa Shock
Independent Healthcare Consultant

Remote patient monitoring continues to develop with expanded adoption globally. New studies show promise for health outcomes, and future innovations will expand the capabilities of chronic disease management.

While telehealth is a broad term that defines the industry and technology that enables healthcare to be delivered through smartphone applications or video platforms, remote patient monitoring (RPM) specifically uses digital devices to promote and facilitate clinical interactions in the home. Telehealth visits typically occur through a video call on a tablet, smartphone, or computer. RPM uses devices such as a scale, blood pressure monitor, or blood glucose meter to gather patient information and vital signs in order to communicate that information electronically back to a healthcare provider for medical management.

Remote patient monitoring complements telehealth care delivery when patients need ongoing medical monitoring for chronic conditions. Many symptoms and health conditions can be addressed and proactively monitored using RPM. Several of these include: hypertension, diabetes, congestive heart failure (CHF), chronic obstructive pulmonary disease (COPD), sleep apnea, and asthma [1].

Monitoring of chronic conditions has often been done using wearable devices. The American Heart Association supports initiatives that increase access to and incentivizes the use of RPM in disease management [2]. The timely transfer of patient-generated data from the patient to the care team and back to the patient is one primary goal of RPM. To capture data, RPM can employ wired or wireless peripheral measurement devices such as biosensors, blood pressure cuffs, glucometers, and pulse oximetry, in addition to sensors that collect data passively (e.g., motion sensors in a home that can transmit data on movement and specific activity/inactivity) [2]. RPM has proven useful in improving transitions from the postdischarge setting or between routine office visits.

Digital Health. https://doi.org/10.1016/B978-0-443-23901-4.00009-X

Use of RPM equipment has several benefits including: extending the reach of providers and physicians, enabling a constant relationship connection between patients and caregivers, and offering real-time health data exchange [3]. Data exchange has evolved, and now RPM devices can transmit user-entered data, store the data in secure records systems accessible to clinicians or care monitors, flag abnormal readings or responses, and alert clinicians/caregivers to abnormalities through email or text messages [2].

By creating a bidirectional exchange between patient and clinician, it is possible to monitor changes in clinical condition in real time. Abnormal vital signs such as weight gain in a patient with congestive heart failure or a decreased oxygen level in a patient with chronic obstructive pulmonary disease can allow for emergent interventions that could, in some cases, prevent hospitalization. In response to these alerts, clinicians can log into the system dashboard, review real-time data, follow up with patients, and facilitate other appropriate interventions, such as a home visit.

Some systems have the capacity to connect patients with additional resources such as patient health records (PHRs) or electronic medical records (EMRs), targeted educational materials, interactive self-care tools, and medication optimization technologies [2]. Integration of RPM devices into the electronic medical record helps to facilitate care management efforts and is also a requirement for Medicare reimbursement to show utilization of the device [4]. These integration solutions are beneficial and becoming even more critical to improving patient health outcomes. Clinicians can make more informed decisions and reduce the incidence of medical errors by integrating EMRs with patient monitoring devices [5].

Most RPM technologies allow patients to generate and contribute their own data. Patient-generated health data (PGHD) are data created, recorded, or gathered by or from patients (or family members or other caregivers) to support their health and well-being. These data may include variables related to health history, biometric data, symptoms, and lifestyle information. Advances in RPM have the potential to allow patients and their caregivers to independently and seamlessly capture and share their health data electronically with clinicians from any location [2].

The significant increase in wearables has supported RPM efforts. Some estimate that 70.6 million US patients, or 26.2% of the population, will use RPM tools by 2025 [6]. Individuals of any age who use a wired or wireless device to remotely track or collect data have significantly increased since 2020, and this upward trend is predicted to continue [6].

When EMR integration solutions are combined with an RPM program, including wearables, it can provide decision support to caregivers and clinicians while elevating patient care to a new, proactive level. This bidirectional data exchange makes it easier to document and bill for patient care while reducing additional workload for the clinical teams [5].

Remote patient monitoring helps clinical teams have a more robust picture of a patient's clinical health. RPM can allow interprofessional teams to be more efficient and collaborative by sharing data in real time. Use of technology in the form of remote patient monitoring must include adaptations that integrate mobile and wearable technologies into clinical workflows and the virtual office. There must be an incorporation of real-time data collection that facilitates decision-making [7]. Enhanced clinical decision-making using RPM requires process flexibility, between visit data exchange, and review and supervision for both trainees and team members [7].

Within healthcare ecosystems, incorporation of new technology through RPM requires clinical, technical, policy, and administrative workflows to comply with legal and ethical mandates as well as reimbursement requirements and regulations. In order to create adequate and efficient processes, technological factors related to the use of equipment and the ease of its use are directly correlated to patient literacy and skill [7]. Some RPM tools offer new approaches to an otherwise in-person task or function such as vital sign intake or an assessment of emotional well-being, i.e., a depression screen. Newer and more sophisticated technologies may require additional skills, such as an application that uses speech recognition or natural language processing [7].

Chronic diseases are often associated with increased emergency room utilization, recurrent hospitalizations, and decreased quality of life [8]. RPM has the potential to reduce unnecessary utilization and improve overall chronic disease management efforts. Cost and outcome evidence for RPM in a systematic review by De Guzman et al. indicated that RPM was cost-effective for hypertension management [8]. The cost and outcome evidence for chronic obstructive pulmonary disease (COPD) and heart failure (CHF) differed due to the heterogeneity of study populations, and there were limited economic evaluations of RPM for diabetes management (DM) within their analysis [8].

In an effort to assess return on investment, De Guzman states that capital costs may be recuperated after initial investment if RPM prevents future high-cost health events [8]. This review further demonstrated that RPM investment costs may reduce over time because of technological innovation and less costly equipment, which was also supported by other studies that highlighted how the development of more affordable and accessible information and communication technology systems can reduce RPM capital costs [8].

Patient experience metrics for patients with chronic disease showed increases in disease-specific knowledge, triggered earlier clinical assessment and treatment, and improved self-management and shared decision-making using remote patient monitoring (RPM) [9]. Use of RPM also supported patient self-management and shared decision-making with their clinical care team. Remote monitoring helped to promote patient confidence to self-manage their condition, including independently making changes to medication regimens [9]. This was supported within several studies and particularly noted in patients with heart failure who were encouraged to adjust fluid management medications based on daily data such as weight [9]. Patients also felt more empowered and a more equal partner in their care, allowing them to be "better equipped to engage with health care services" when they were able to discuss their monitoring data [9].

Slow adopters of RPM have concerns related to trust and safety. The systematic review by Walker et al. that examined patient expectations and experiences found that some patients were apprehensive about using technology because they felt unfamiliar with it and doubted its reliability [9]. Additional patient concerns also included fears that their healthcare would become more focused on clinical data rather than personal interaction, and this might lead to fewer face-to-face consultations with clinicians [9]. In addition, some patients also anticipated an increased personal burden and challenge of having to input data and manage the technology [9].

In order to address health outcomes more definitively attributed to RPM, a systematic literature review of PubMed, Embase, and CINAHL electronic databases was undertaken in July 2019 and updated in October 2020 for studies published from January 2015 to October 2020 reporting RPM and through its use, effect on hospitalizations, length of stay, or emergency department presentations for all populations and disease conditions [10]. Within this comprehensive review, RPM for all disease conditions was reported to have reduced admissions, length of stay, and ED presentations in 49% (n = 44 of 90), 49% (n = 23 of 47), and 41% (n = 13 of32) of studies, respectively, for studies that reported each measure of acute care use [10]. The remaining studies largely reported no change in acute care use for remotely monitored patients. It has also been hypothesized that patients may have enhanced self-management through the use of RPM technology, facilitating more collaboration around chronic disease management and care [11,12].

Recent years have seen a dramatic increase in the use of RPM technology, and the recent pandemic has further promoted the growth and utilization of digital solutions. The global market for RPM devices is expected to register double-digit growth in 2023 [3]. RPM technology continues to grow significantly from a total market value of $1.18 billion in 2022, to $1.34 billion in 2023 and $2.14 billion by 2027 [3]. The largest global markets for remote patient monitoring technologies will continue to be Asia—Pacific and North America [3]. The push for the rapid demand in the RPM device market is thought to be directly related to the increased shortages of qualified health professionals and the resulting limitations to healthcare operations resulting from burnout and staff attrition [3].

Remote patient monitoring is pushing the boundaries of data collection and biofeedback. Advances in Bluetooth technology may further enhance asthma and chronic obstructive pulmonary disease medication management through the use of sensors within the dose inhalers [13]. The sensor will then alert when the correct dose of medication is not administered [13]. Digital tools continue to be enhanced within smartwatch technology to monitor motor functioning in patients with Parkinson's disease, and a remote system using scalp electrodes is being trialed for paralyzed patients to assist with driving their wheelchairs [13].

The prevalence of chronic disease is continuing to increase, and these chronic diseases are responsible for more than two-thirds of all deaths worldwide [14]. While the rapid growth of digital health companies during the pandemic offers potential, many haven't yet definitively demonstrated a significant impact on disease burden or cost savings within the healthcare system [15]. As the postpandemic period sees health systems, payers, and purchasers reevaluating their contracts and investments, it will be critical that chosen digital health solutions are both clinically robust and economically sustainable and equitable for population health. The next decade will showcase innovation, refining the digital health landscape, and a strong emphasis must also be placed on validating claims for positive health outcomes as well as ensuring patient safety [15].

Assessment (case examples, discussion questions, etc.)

Use Case Examples for Remote Patient Monitoring:

1. An accountable care organization would like to address prevalent hospital admissions for congestive heart failure. A care program was initiated and each patient enrolled in the program received a Bluetooth-enabled scale to monitor daily weights at home. Patients were advised to weigh first thing every morning, and the results were sent back through Bluetooth to the provider's office. A nurse reviewed the results on a daily basis, and any elevation of weight greater than 5 pounds prompted a phone call to ensure that symptoms were not worsening and medications could be adjusted if needed.
2. Patients with poorly controlled diabetes were given a Bluetooth-enabled glucometer for home use across a physician practice group. Instructions were given to check morning sugars as well as after meals and at bedtime. Results were wirelessly communicated using Wi-Fi back to the clinician's practice to be included in the electronic health record. Obtaining a variety of values both fasting and after meals allows the provider to more accurately adjust medications and potentially prevent drops in blood sugar levels.

Future directions—assessment of patient preference and incorporation of feedback

How would the incorporation of patient preference research help inform the design of future RPM technologies?

Remote monitoring devices may benefit from a user-centered design approach that takes into account patient preferences, requirements, and needs [9]. Enhancing patient and provider team communication through an RPM messaging system may provide additional support, access, and reassurance to patients that they are being closely monitored for changes in clinical status [9]. Increasing the number of randomized controlled clinical trials to evaluate the acceptability and usability of RPM technology in diverse patient populations, including assessments of literacy, connectivity, and accessibility, may help remote monitoring meet the needs of multiple types of patients [9].

AI disclosure

All opinions stated within this work are the author's own, and this work is an independent work product, done outside of her regular job responsibilities. This content was not developed using artificial intelligence.

References

[1] Telehealth and remote patient monitoring | Telehealth.HHS.gov. https://telehealth.hhs.gov/providers/preparing-patients-for-telehealth/telehealth-and-remote-patient-monitoring. Accessed August 19, 2023.
[2] Using remote patient monitoring technologies for better cardiovascular disease outcomes guidance.
[3] Remote patient monitoring trends and health devices in 2023. https://www.insiderintelligence.com/insights/remote-patient-monitoring-industry-explained/. Accessed May 12, 2023.
[4] How Telehealth, RPM Interoperability with EHR Systems Boosts Care. https://ehrintelligence.com/news/how-telehealth-rpm-interoperability-with-ehr-systems-boosts-care. Accessed August 20, 2023.
[5] EMR integrations that can transform healthcare systems. https://www.osplabs.com/insights/emr-integrations-that-can-transform-healthcare-systems/. Accessed August 20, 2023.
[6] The technology, devices, and benefits of remote patient monitoring in the healthcare industry. https://www.insiderintelligence.com/insights/remote-patient-monitoring-industry-explained/.
[7] Hilty DM, Armstrong CM, Edwards-Stewart A, et al. Sensor, wearable, and remote patient monitoring competencies for clinical care and training: Scoping Review. https://doi.org/10.1007/s41347-020-00190-3.
[8] De Guzman KR, Snoswell CL, Taylor ML, Gray LC, Caffery LJ. Economic evaluations of remote patient monitoring for chronic disease: a systematic review. Value in Health 2022;25(6):897−913. https://doi.org/10.1016/J.JVAL.2021.12.001.
[9] Walker RC, Tong A, Howard K, Palmer SC. Patient expectations and experiences of remote monitoring for chronic diseases: systematic review and thematic synthesis of qualitative studies. International Journal of Medical Informatics 2019;124:78−85. https://doi.org/10.1016/J.IJMEDINF.2019.01.013.
[10] Taylor ML, Thomas EE, Snoswell CL, Smith AC, Caffery LJ. Does remote patient monitoring reduce acute care use? A systematic review. BMJ Open 2021;11(3). https://doi.org/10.1136/BMJOPEN-2020-040232.
[11] Jordan RE, Majothi S, Heneghan NR, et al. Supported self-management for patients with moderate to severe chronic obstructive pulmonary disease (COPD): an evidence synthesis and economic analysis. Health Technology Assessment 2015;19(36):1−515. https://doi.org/10.3310/HTA19360.
[12] Barlow J, Wright C, Sheasby J, Turner A, Hainsworth J. Self-management approaches for people with chronic conditions: a review. Patient Education and Counselling 2002;48(2):177−87.
[13] The future belongs to remote patient monitoring—Mayo Clinic platform. https://www.mayoclinicplatform.org/2023/02/27/the-future-belongs-to-remote-patient-monitoring/. Accessed September 5, 2023.

[14] El-Rashidy N, El-Sappagh S, Riazul Islam SM, El-Bakry HM, Abdelrazek S. Mobile health in remote patient monitoring for chronic diseases: principles, trends, and challenges. Diagnostics 2021;11(4). https://doi.org/10.3390/diagnostics11040607.

[15] Dashevsky J. The wild west of digital health. https://workweek.com/2023/08/19/the-wild-west-of-digital-health/?utm_source=Sailthru&utm_medium=email&utm_campaign=Healthcare%20Huddle%20–%208/20/23&utm_term=Healthcare%20Huddle. https://workweek.com/2023/08/19/the-wild-west-of-digital-health/?utm_source=Sailthru&utm_medium=email&utm_campaign=Healthcare Huddle – 8/20/23&utm_term=Healthcare Huddle. Published August. Accessed August 20, 2023.

CHAPTER 10

From data to diagnosis: The power of precision medicine in digital health

Dipu Patel[1] and Josh Borgstadt[2]

[1]Department of PA Studies, University of Pittsburgh, Pittsburgh, PA, United States; [2]Mesa, AZ, United States

Imagine Sam, a 45-year-old woman, who has been feeling fatigued and generally "rundown" for several months. Sam goes to see her primary care provider, who runs some tests that reveal that she has breast cancer. Her primary care provider refers Sam to a precision medicine clinic, where she meets with a team of experts who run more tests to map her genetic information. They use this genetic information to develop a personalized treatment plan that is unique to Sam.

Working with her oncology team, the experts at the precision medicine clinic used Sam's genetic information to identify targeted therapies that were most likely to be effective for her. They also use her genetic information to identify potential side effects of these therapies, the severity of the adverse effects, and to develop a plan to manage those side effects preemptively. Because this information is specific to Sam and her particular type of cancer, she is able to receive treatment in a timely manner that allows her to manage her overall health the way she wants.

Sam's story is an example of how precision medicine (PM) can be used to improve the diagnosis and treatment of breast cancer or any cancer or disease. Paired with genetic testing, targeted therapies can improve patient outcomes and quality of life. Precision medicine is a rapidly evolving field, and there is great potential for this technology to improve the lives of patients with a variety of diseases including Parkinson's disease, diabetes, and cardiovascular diseases.

What is precision medicine?

Precision medicine (PM), also known as personalized medicine, is defined as using a person's genomic and biomarker data to provide individualized care that is tailored to the individual's needs, this includes genetics, lifestyle, and cultural background. Precision medicine aims to optimize patient outcomes, minimize adverse events, and improve healthcare delivery.

Digital Health. https://doi.org/10.1016/B978-0-443-23901-4.00010-6

In a way, we have always strived for the practice of PM. Long before the National Health System of the United Kingdom outlined the four “P’s” of PM in their work and the four genetic bases (A, C, T, G) were discovered, Hippocrates used the four “humors” to diagnose and treat diseases [1,2]. Since the completion of the sequencing of the human genome in 2003, there have been exponential strides made in every aspect of genomics, from agriculture and microbiome to pharmaceuticals and rare diseases [3]. Precision medicine has impacted every aspect of humanity and its success [4].

Historically, medications have had a one-size-fits-all approach; one pill tested among all patients for its efficacy and effectiveness. Personalized medicine focuses on efficacy for the individualized patient based on their genetics, background, and lifestyle. Although we are biologically similar, the manifestation of diseases is unique in each of us, necessitating the need for individualized treatment. Personalized medicine aims to provide patient-centered care and can aid in providing individualized care with regard to preventive medicine, diagnosis, diagnostics, and treatment of disease. While genetics and biomarkers are one aspect of PM, several areas of digital health inform individualized care [5].

At the core of personalized medicine is the foundational approach that each patient is unique based on their biological makeup. This unique biological makeup allows providers to provide a tailored approach to patient care, everything from drugs to preventive counseling. One area where personalized medicine is used currently is in the treatment of cancer [6]. As no two cancers are alike, genetic sequencing allows oncologists to individualize therapy based on genetic markers. Although this has become more commonplace, use of biologics and immunotherapy drugs is truly making a mark on personalized medicine.

Other areas where personalized medicine can be applied include cardiovascular disease treatment, treatment of HIV, treatment of Parkinson’s and Alzheimer’s as well as stroke patients [7,8]. This chapter explores PM, its underlying principles, and advancements and utility within healthcare.

As the field of PM continues to evolve, four aspects of PM will shape the speed of implementation and adoption: genomics, diagnostics, big data, and artificial intelligence (AI)/machine learning (ML) (Fig. 10.1).

Big data analytics can be used to analyze large datasets of biomedical data to identify new biomarkers for disease, develop personalized treatment plans, predict patient outcomes, and monitor patient progress [9]. This information can then be used to develop new diagnostic tests and targeted therapies and to guide clinical decision-making.

Here are some specific examples of how big data analytics is being used in precision medicine today.

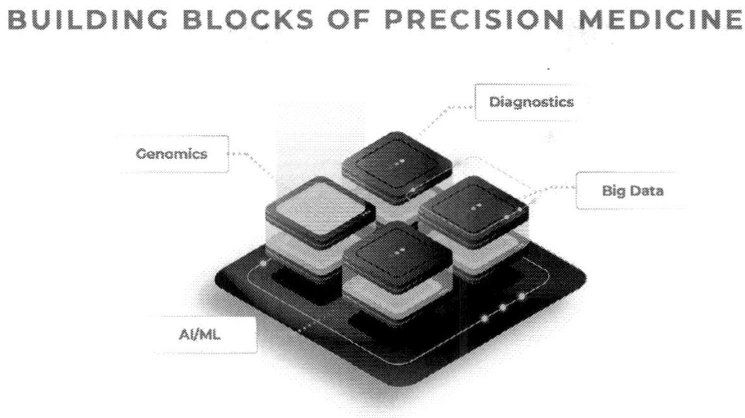

Figure 10.1
Building blocks of precision medicine. *Dipu Patel.*

- Cancer research: Big data analytics is being used to identify new cancer genes and develop targeted therapies against them. For example, researchers have used big data analytics to identify a new gene that is associated with breast cancer. This gene could be used to develop a new targeted therapy for breast cancer.
- Cardiology research: Big data analytics is being used to identify new risk factors for heart disease and develop personalized prevention strategies. For example, researchers have used big data analytics to identify a new genetic variant that is associated with an increased risk of heart disease. This information could be used to develop a new personalized prevention strategy for patients with this genetic variant.
- Public health research: Big data analytics is being used to track the spread of infectious diseases and develop public health interventions. For example, researchers have used big data analytics to track the spread of the Zika virus and develop interventions to prevent its spread.

One of the key challenges in precision medicine is the complexity of biomedical data. These data are often high-dimensional and heterogeneous, making it difficult to analyze using traditional methods. Big data analytics can help to overcome this challenge by providing new tools and techniques for processing and analyzing large datasets.

Another challenge in precision medicine is the need to develop new machine learning algorithms that can handle the scale and complexity of biomedical data. Machine learning algorithms can be used to identify patterns in data that are too complex for humans to detect. This information can then be used to develop new diagnostic tests and targeted therapies and to guide clinical decision-making.

History of precision medicine

The concept of personalized medicine dates back to ancient times [2]. The ancient Greeks were informed by ancient Egyptian notions of personalized medicine [2]. "The adaptation of that ancient "Egyptian medicine" to an individual's health status was further elucidated in the Classical period from Herodotus when the practice of medicine was divided into categories and every doctor was a specialist for one disease, one body part." [2] Hippocrates hypothesized that "that every human is distinct, and this affects both the disease prediction and the treatment." [2].

The evolution of PM had been slow; however, in the past two centuries, there has been an exponential pace of growth within the field. One of the reasons for this growth is the discovery of DNA and its implications and, in more recent decades, mapping of the human genome. The Human Genome Project is probably one of the most significant steps toward the realization of personalized medicine. The mapping of the human genome has allowed clinicians and scientists to identify thousands of genetic variations and has allowed for research to grow and flourish. Establishment of the Precision Medicine Initiative in 2015, by President Barack Obama, was followed by the development of Clustered Regularly Interspaced Short Palindromic Repeats (CRISPR) technology and the FDA's approval of the liquid biopsy.

What took decades to develop, is now taking months to years and shifting the PM landscape. The bench-to-bedside timeline has decreased significantly with the help of technology and research.

Timeline of precision medicine (Figs. 10.2 and 10.3)

1550 BCE: Egyptian concept of PM ("personalized medicine")

400–500BCE: Hippocratic concept of PM ("personalized medicine")

1862: Mendel presented his methodical hypothesis; the testing and careful application of mathematical models to the study of biological inheritance [10].

1909: Archibald Garrod is best known for his book Inborn Errors of Metabolism (1909), in which he argued that four diseases were inherited as Mendelian autosomal recessive traits—alkaptonuria, albinism, cystinuria, and pentosuria [11].

1944: Oswald Avery, Colin MacLeod, and Maclyn McCarty showed that DNA (not proteins) can transform the properties of cells, clarifying the chemical nature of genes. Avery, MacLeod, and McCarty identified DNA as the "transforming principle" while studying Streptococcus pneumoniae, bacteria that can cause pneumonia [12].

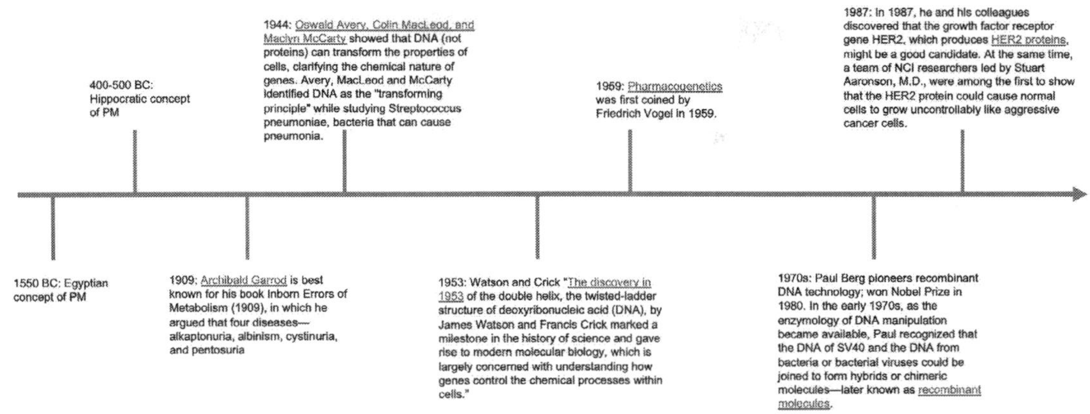

Figure 10.2
Timeline 1 timeline of PM. *Dipu Patel.*

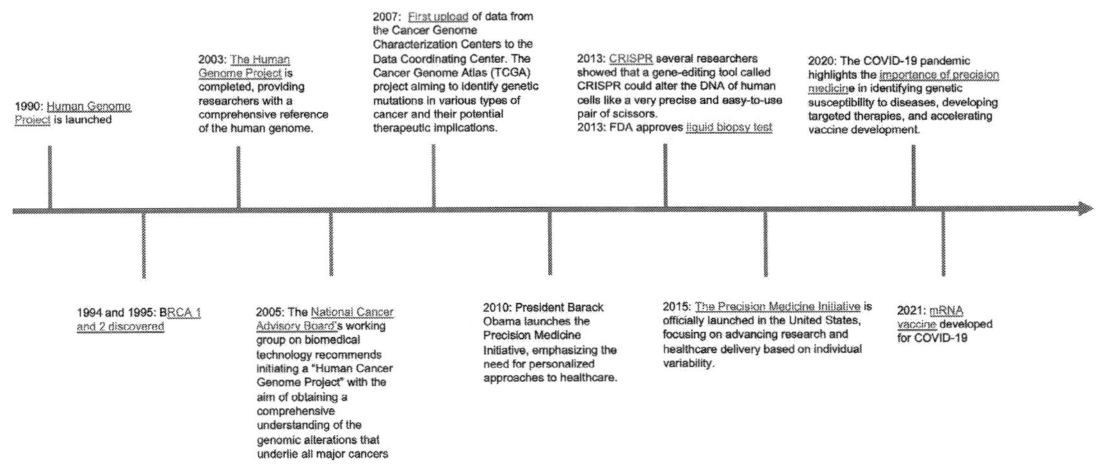

Figure 10.3
Timeline 2 timeline of PM. *Dipu Patel.*

1953: Watson and Crick discovered the double helix, the twisted-ladder structure of deoxyribonucleic acid (DNA) [13].

1959: Pharmacogenetics was first coined by Friedrich Vogel in 1959 [14].

1970s: Paul Berg pioneered recombinant DNA technology; won Nobel Prize in 1980. In the early 1970s, as the enzymology of DNA manipulation became available, Berg recognized that the DNA of SV40 and the DNA from bacteria or bacterial viruses could be joined to form hybrids or chimeric molecules—later known as recombinant molecules [15].

1987: In 1987, Dennis Slamon, M.D. and his colleagues discovered that the growth factor receptor gene HER2, which produces HER2 proteins, might be a good candidate. At the same time, a team of NCI researchers led by Stuart Aaronson, M.D., was among the first to show that the HER2 protein could cause normal cells to grow uncontrollably like aggressive cancer cells [16].

1990: The Human Genome Project was launched [17].

1994 and 1995: BRCA 1 and 2 gene mutations discovered [18].

2003: The Human Genome Project was completed, providing researchers with a comprehensive reference of the human genome [17].

2005: The National Cancer Advisory Board's working group on biomedical technology recommends initiating a "Human Cancer Genome Project" with the aim of obtaining a comprehensive understanding of the genomic alterations that underlie all major cancers [19].

2007: First upload of data from the Cancer Genome Characterization Centers to the Data Coordinating Center. The Cancer Genome Atlas (TCGA) project aims to identify genetic mutations in various types of cancer and their potential therapeutic implications [19].

2010: President Barack Obama launched the Precision Medicine Initiative, emphasizing the need for personalized approaches to healthcare.

2013: CRISPR Several researchers showed that a gene-editing tool called CRISPR could alter the DNA of human cells like a very precise and easy-to-use pair of scissors [20].

2013: FDA approved liquid biopsy test [21].

2015: The Precision Medicine Initiative was officially launched in the United States, focusing on advancing research and healthcare delivery based on individual variability [22].

2020: The COVID-19 pandemic highlighted the importance of precision medicine in identifying genetic susceptibility to diseases, developing targeted therapies, and accelerating vaccine development [23].

2021: mRNA vaccine developed for COVID-19 [24].

Precision medicine in practice

Precision medicine (PM) is revolutionizing patient care in fields with multiple care pathways such as oncology. The ability to provide the right care at the right time is a hallmark of PM. This will help to limit treatments that might not be as useful or efficient and ensure that patients are receiving timely care that is targeted at their specific disease presentation. Genetics plays an important role in the treatment of many cancers, and the field of oncology has certainly benefited from the advancement in technology that has enabled PM to develop and flourish. Several fields in medicine also look to benefit from the techniques being developed. The process is iterative and will continue to evolve as technology advances and utilization increases.

Looking at the care pathway for treating Sam's breast cancer, multiple imaging modalities, appointments, and treatment sessions were generated to provide care. Utilizing PM techniques, artificial intelligence and genomics are combined to provide the best individualized treatment plan. This includes the right choice in chemotherapy agents, use of radiation, timing, and use of surgery.

The pursuit of precision medicine by providers and health systems creates the opportunity to greatly reduce medical error, adverse effects, and treatment nonadherence, individualizing therapy based on data from the human genome, biomedical sciences, and the environment. Multiple fields in medicine are looking to adopt tenets of PM. Oncology is currently the specialty most entrenched in utilizing PM techniques in daily practice.

Large amounts of data are being collected on individuals on a regular basis from areas such as wearables, social and behavioral determinants, environmental, and lifestyle considerations. These data, in combination with genomic data, are being analyzed and synthesized, using artificial intelligence (AI) algorithms, to help create the individualized care pathways of PM [25]. The successful adoption of AI into healthcare requires initial thought and continual monitoring of data and security, analytics and insight, and provider expertise. The combination of AI, genomics, social determinants, and lifestyle data, with a medical provider's expertise and insight, is the recipe for a successful PM project (Fig. 10.2) [26].

The amount of data being generated is an inevitable reality when the percentage of day-to-day data points is compared with that of electronic medical record data that are captured by a health system. Looking through the lens of overall health data, 60% incorporates social determinants and lifestyle data, 30% is genomics, and 10% is data from the health record [26]. This further highlights the need for a broad look across multiple data points, utilizing AI for analytics, to help create meaningful clinical PM care pathways (Fig. 10.4).

Augmented intelligence, introduced by W.R. Ashby in the 1950s, describes the intersection between the data described earlier, computational analysis, and synthesis of data utilizing artificial intelligence and machine learning techniques, with the medical provider's expertise [26]. This is a picture of PM and allows individual trends to appear within data to tailor treatment plans accordingly (Fig. 10.2).

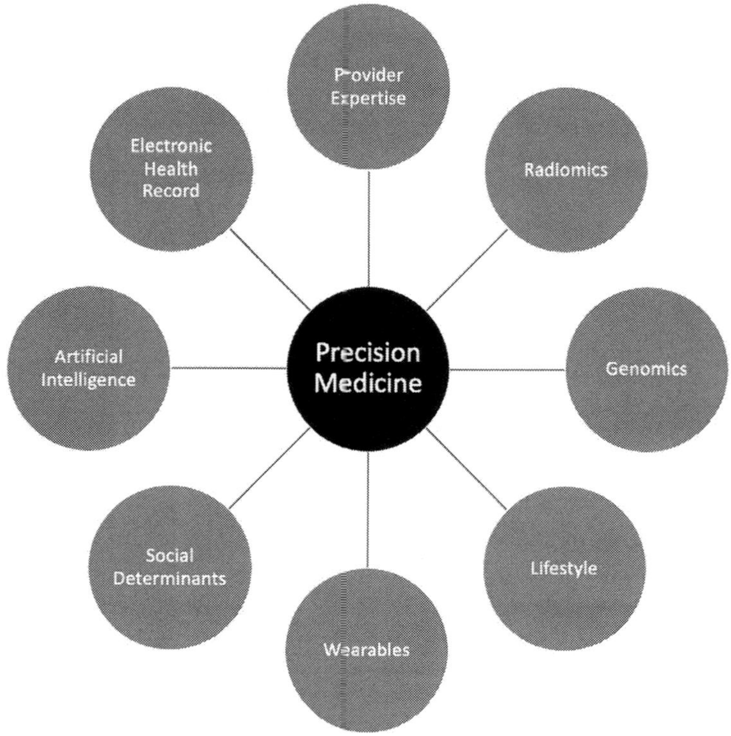

Figure 10.4
Components of PM care pathway. *Josh Borgstadt.*

Artificial intelligence and machine learning utilize large datasets to provide predictions based on analytics. In PM, the use of AI allows a variety of datasets to be analyzed looking for trends and correlations to provide individualized care. These algorithms require a large amount of heterogeneous data to ensure accuracy [26].

It can be helpful to understand big data through the five V's: volume, velocity, variety, veracity, and value [2] (Fig. 10.5). Value refers to the synthesis of data into actionable considerations in respective business or areas of study. The volume, veracity, velocity, and variety of data further emphasize the need for analytics, using AI, to understand insights in the data [26]. Data are vital to the creation of a meaningful algorithm. Aspects of the data are considered and evaluated such as the logistics of storing large amounts of data, the speed of said data, the varying avenues of which data are obtained such as structured and unstructured, and the relevance of the data for the project at hand [26].

In clinical practice, in combination with medical providers, AI is being utilized for clinical decision support, as a prediction tool for both disease states and adverse outcomes, and process improvement for clinical support and back office functions [26]. An AI-assisted breast cancer predicting tool, trained on 38,444 mammograms from 9611 women,

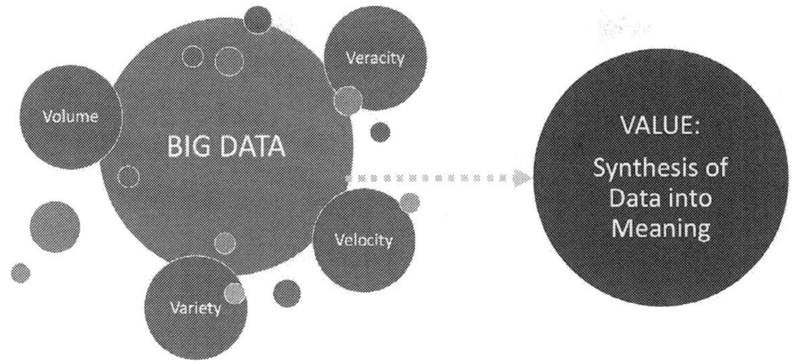

Figure 10.5
Five V's of big data. *Josh Borgstadt.*

combines data from images as well as electronic health data to provide an accurate prediction of breast cancer comparable with radiologists [26]. This tool could be used to help accurately validate diagnoses and decrease errors in missed diagnoses.

An example of precision medicine technique in clinical practice is an individualized and tailored treatment plan through genotype-guided therapy with AI. Data scientists have created algorithms that may not have clinical applications. While these algorithms help to further the technology in pursuit of precision medicine, some applications may not find widespread use. Clinicians utilize a guideline for genotype-based drug recommendations published by the Clinical Pharmacogenetics Implementation Consortium [26]. Information from this guideline has helped determine the accurate dosing of warfarin [27]. Providers, using genomic data for tumor profiling, utilize targeted therapies for breast and lung cancer patients. The combination of genomics and radiomics with AI has great potential to provide precision medicine for breast cancer patients including individualized therapy for triple-negative disease [27].

Genomic profiling of tumors is one way that PM can tailor therapy to the individual with the end goal of improving outcomes. Taking mutations and molecular target agents into account, PM techniques are using gene panels to develop targeted therapy [27]. Precision medicine, in conjunction with computational analytics through AI, can improve safety and efficiency of care pathways, find novel treatments, and ensure accurate diagnosis for patients utilizing data from the human genome, imaging studies, social determinants, and lifestyle considerations, as well as data from the health record [27,28].

In considering the oncology and surgical team's role in PM, it would be helpful to take another look at Sam's care pathway. The oncology and surgical team utilized Sam's genomic information, coupled with imaging, social determinants, and lifestyle to form an individualized treatment plan. The plan included a decision on the exact chemotherapeutic agents, dosing, and duration of treatment. This tailored approach to therapy will help to minimize side effects, improve adherence and efficacy of drugs, with the end goal of improving outcomes. Utilizing AI, the team was able to decide on tailored surgical intervention as well as targeted radiation to tissue based on analysis of tumor cells.

PM care pathways are being considered in other areas of medicine such as primary care. According to an article from the University of California San Francisco, a platform called Bridge has been created to incorporate computational analysis across all phases of the clinic creating a user-friendly interface to help foster personalized care [29].

Digital twins is another concept that is captivating thought leaders and has the potential to change the future of healthcare. Utilizing genomic data and AI-driven modeling, data scientists are looking to create digital copies of persons, processes, and organizations with the purpose of testing changes before implementing in real time [30].

This concept has use in the public, private, and education arenas. Examples of this concept include digital twins being considered for meaningful models in health education, a HeartModel, created by Siemens, that cardiologists and cardiothoracic surgeons can utilize to predict outcomes for interventions. Data privacy and cost are two big concerns that need to be addressed [30].

Precision medicine in clinical practice has the potential to improve efficiency, decrease error, and improve outcomes across the spectrum of healthcare. Barriers to PM are cost, lack of resources, lack of heterogeneous datasets to train algorithms, and lack of infrastructure to support computational analysis. Ethical issues surrounding the use of genomic data, AI, and privacy of health data are a concern that leaders and scientists continue to discuss. Genomics and the use of digital twins are a new area of study in medicine. More research and real-world study are needed to understand and address the major ethical ideals involved. Medicine lags behind other industries regarding the ability to institute computational analysis across multiple datasets. The infrastructure of data in EHR is there. More research and advocacy for meaningful interoperability are needed to realize precision medicine on a large scale.

Implications of precision medicine to social determinants of health

Health equity is an important consideration when analyzing a health system or clinic's pursuit of precision medicine. Social determinants of health (SDOH) are well known and studied, and data are still lacking [31]. The SDOH comprise the underlying effects of daily living on an individual's health as well as the health of the total population in small communities, nation, and the world. Economic factors, education, transportation, food disparity, environment, and overall health all play a role when looking at the determinants that influence a person's ability to pursue and achieve health goals. Digital disparity is an important factor to evaluate in the age of precision medicine. If an individual or community lacks the knowledge or infrastructure to adequately engage in technology, then a health divide will develop, and inequities become apparent in certain populations [31].

Before engaging a patient population with new technology to enhance the healthcare experience, it is important to understand the digital health literacy of said population. Evaluating and improving the digital literacy of a population can be accomplished through surveys, community events, free educational events, and easy-to-follow educational literature [31,32]. Health leaders must keep SDOH, especially digital literacy, in mind when considering development and deployment of new technology for patient engagement and care.

When looking at population health, the evaluation of SDOH plays a vital role in determining a baseline for patient's and the population to engage with healthcare services in a meaningful way. AI and ML algorithms are used to help analyze data and create possible action points to improve the environment for care by health systems, communities, and individuals. Deciphering these data can be tricky due to the lack of complete SDOH datasets [32]. Aspects of SDOH are personal and often not shared. This was apparent in the recently completed All of Us campaign looking at SDOH among the general population in the United States [32]. It will be important to continue to evaluate these data for trends as the dataset continues to become more robust.

Another consideration for the use of SDOH in precision medicine is the lack of consistency for which determinants are assessed in the clinic and addressed in treatment plans [31]. With the use of AI/ML and large language models, data can be analyzed, and treatment options are assessed in real time [26,31]. This has the potential to have a meaningful impact on patients' ability to meet basic needs to reach a baseline to engage in health for themselves and those close to them. Engaging the population over SDOH, with the use of AI/ML, will help to limit health disparity over emerging trends in health technology.

Key issues involving ethical use of health data, privacy, and bias must be considered by leaders and developers during strategic analysis, development, and deployment of any AI/ML tool in medicine [26]. The use of personal health information is an important aspect to consider as these data are vital to the creation of useful algorithms in medicine. Consent for the use of data, data privacy, and diversity of persons in said datasets are all areas to be mindful of when pursuing AI projects [26].

Precision medicine has made significant strides in various medical fields. In the realm of oncology, it has revolutionized lung cancer treatment by pinpointing specific genetic mutations that drive tumor growth. Patients with these mutations benefit from targeted therapies such as estimated glomerular filtration rate (EGFR) inhibitors, which not only improve survival rates but also enhance their quality of life compared with traditional chemotherapy [33]. Another domain where precision medicine shines is pharmacogenomics [34]. This approach tailors drug treatments to an individual's genetic makeup [35]. Take the anticoagulant drug Warfarin, for instance, where genetic markers guide healthcare providers in prescribing the most effective and safe dose, reducing the risk of adverse events [36]. Furthermore, precision medicine is advancing our understanding and treatment of neurodegenerative diseases such as Alzheimer's and Parkinson's by utilizing genetic and biomarker data to identify early disease markers, predict progression, and develop personalized treatment plans [37,38].

The future of clinical practice will no doubt be impacted by the research of precision medicine. It will be used in daily practice in the management of acute diseases but also for chronic conditions. For example, for a patient diagnosed with high blood pressure, there may be a number of medication options that would be under consideration. Currently, we make these decisions based on the patient's age, race, gender, and other comorbid conditions. Oftentimes, patients are asked to follow up in 4–6 weeks to see if the medication is working. If it's not working, we may switch them to another medication either in the same class or a different class altogether. This sort of trial-and-error approach has been shown to lead to poor clinical outcomes, expense to the healthcare system, and patient dissatisfaction. Through the use of personalized medicine, we can streamline the medications we would recommend by either assessing certain biomarkers or genetic testing and based on that patient's biological profile, provide treatment options to the patient. The conversation with the patient in selecting the best medication will include a discussion on the likelihood of responding to medication X or less likely to have an adverse reaction to medication Y [39]. This allows not only for personalized medical care but also patient engagement, allowing for patient-centered care and share decision-making to be part of the process. Similar work in diabetes management is underway [40].

Benefits and challenges of precision medicine

The advantages of PM are substantial. Precision medicine can significantly enhance treatment efficacy by allowing healthcare providers to choose treatments based on a patient's genetic and molecular profile, thus reducing adverse effects [39]. Patients also receive personalized care, taking into account their unique genetic makeup, lifestyle, and cultural background, which promotes patient-centered care and shared decision-making. Furthermore, precision medicine can lead to reduced healthcare costs by avoiding ineffective treatments and costly adverse events. Early disease detection through genetic testing and biomarker analysis is another key benefit, enabling more effective interventions and better outcomes. Additionally, precision medicine contributes to advancements in research by deepening our understanding of diseases at the molecular level, fueling innovation in treatments and potential cures.

Despite its promise, PM faces challenges that need attention. Data privacy and security are paramount, as precision medicine relies heavily on sensitive patient data, including genetic information [41]. Ensuring the protection of these data from breaches is crucial. Access and equity are also concerns, as there is a risk that only certain populations may benefit, potentially leading to healthcare disparities. Cost and affordability pose another challenge, given the expenses associated with developing and implementing precision medicine technologies, which could limit widespread adoption. Regulatory and ethical issues, including data use, informed consent, and genetic discrimination, must be carefully addressed. Moreover, interpreting genetic and molecular data is intricate and demands specialized expertise, highlighting a shortage of healthcare professionals with the necessary genomics training.

Finally, one of the most formidable obstacles lies in the intricacy of biomedical data and its conversion to clinical use and implementation. Because data exhibit high-dimensional and heterogeneous attributes, rendering conventional analytical approaches inadequate for thorough examination that makes the need for clean and useful data paramount [9]. Fortunately, the advent of big data analytics has emerged as a powerful solution, offering a repertoire of novel tools and methodologies tailored for processing and deciphering extensive datasets.

One such example is the recent publication of the prediction of ischemic heart disease using the Cleveland IHD dataset [42]. This study showed that by incorporating clinical (human) expertise into the machine learning(ML) process, the method outperformed conventional data-driven models, boasting an accuracy rate of 94.4% [42]. The study emphasizes the importance of feature selection, underscoring its role in augmenting model accuracy. Furthermore, meticulous data preprocessing techniques expedite model training, fostering an ecosystem for scalable ML models. The significance of this work is underscored by the reduction in clinical recording requirements by 63%, making it a promising avenue for practical clinical application [43]. This study highlights the importance of human-in-the-loop (HITL) training of algorithms.

As the landscape of machine learning algorithms evolves and becomes capable of discerning intricate patterns within data that surpass human perceptual capabilities, the potential to unlock valuable insights is slowly becoming a reality. These insights, in turn, can facilitate the creation of innovative diagnostic protocols, the formulation of precision-targeted therapies, and the augmentation of informed clinical decision-making processes.

Future of precision medicine

Education and clinical training

Precision medicine's successful implementation hinges on educating healthcare professionals to harness its full potential [43–45]. Training programs must be designed to equip clinicians with the knowledge and skills required for interpreting genetic and molecular data, understanding the complexities of precision treatments, and making informed decisions. Additionally, curricula should emphasize the ethical considerations surrounding the use of patient genetic information and ensure that healthcare providers prioritize patient privacy and consent. Bridging this knowledge gap may require collaborations between medical schools, genetic counselors, and institutions specializing in genomics education.

Interdisciplinary approach

Precision medicine thrives on interdisciplinary collaboration, necessitating the integration of genomics and molecular biology into medical education. This extends beyond traditional medical schools to encompass a broader spectrum of healthcare professionals, including physician assistants, nurse practitioners, nurses, pharmacists, genetic counselors, and health science programs [46]. Interdisciplinary training programs enable healthcare teams to work cohesively, ensuring seamless integration of precision medicine into patient care. These programs should emphasize the importance of multidisciplinary case discussions, where specialists from various fields collectively analyze patient data to develop comprehensive treatment plans. By fostering an environment of continuous learning and collaboration, precision medicine can become an integral part of healthcare delivery.

Conclusion

In summary, precision medicine stands as a transformative approach to healthcare, offering individualized care through genetic and molecular information. It has already showcased its potential in various fields, including oncology, pharmacogenomics, and neurodegenerative diseases. The future of precision medicine promises further advancements with the integration of artificial intelligence and machine learning to enhance data analysis and treatment recommendations. However, to fully realize its potential, precision medicine must confront challenges such as data privacy, equitable access, cost considerations, regulatory complexities, and the need for specialized expertise. Through continued research, investment, and a commitment to equitable access, precision medicine has the potential to revolutionize healthcare, improve patient outcomes, and ultimately save lives.

Assignment options

Assignment 1:

Students will watch this video and choose a specific disease or condition and research how precision medicine is currently being used to diagnose, treat, or prevent it. Write a short report (3–5 pages) or create a presentation summarizing their findings. The report or presentation should include the following information.

- A brief overview of the disease or condition
- How precision medicine is being used to diagnose, treat, or prevent it
- The benefits and challenges of using precision medicine for this disease or condition
- A discussion of the future of precision medicine for this disease or condition.

Assignment 2:

Students will work in groups to develop a personalized medicine plan for a specific patient. The patient will be a fictional character with a complex medical history and multiple comorbidities. The students will need to research the patient's medical history, identify any relevant genetic or biomarker data, and develop a treatment plan that is tailored to the patient's individual needs. The students will present their treatment plan to the class and explain their rationale for each decision.

Assignment 3:

Students will create a public service announcement (PSA) about precision medicine. The PSA should be designed to educate the public about precision medicine and its potential benefits. The PSA can be in any format, such as a video, poster, or social media post. The PSA should be creative and engaging, and it should accurately convey the key messages about precision medicine.

References

[1] England N. NHS England» Personalised medicine. England.nhs.uk. Published 2023. Accessed September 16, 2023. https://www.england.nhs.uk/healthcare-science/personalisedmedicine/.

[2] Visvikis-Siest S, Theodoridou D, Kontoe M-S, Kumar S, Marschler M. Milestones in personalized medicine: from the ancient time to nowadays—the provocation of COVID-19. Frontiers in Genetics 2020;11. https://doi.org/10.3389/fgene.2020.569175.

[3] Human genome project timeline. Genome.gov. Published 2019. Accessed September 16, 2023. https://www.genome.gov/human-genome-project/timeline.

[4] 15 ways genomics influences our world. Genome.gov. Published 2019. Accessed September 16, 2023. https://www.genome.gov/dna-day/15-ways.

[5] Eirini P, Pepe G, Konitsiotis S, et al. The evolution of comprehensive genetic analysis in neurology: implications for precision medicine. Journal of the Neurological Sciences 2023;447. https://doi.org/10.1016/j.jns.2023.120609. 120609-120609.

[6] Schwaller F. How personalized medicine is transforming healthcare. Drug Discovery from Technology Networks. Published April 5, 2022. Accessed September 16, 2023. https://www.technologynetworks.com/drug-discovery/articles/how-personalized-medicine-is-transforming-healthcare-359684.

[7] O'Bryant S, Petersen M, Zhang F, Johnson L, Mason DC, Hall J. Analysis of a precision medicine approach to treating Parkinson's disease: analysis of the DATATOP study. Parkinsonism and Related Disorders 2022;94:15–21. https://doi.org/10.1016/j.parkreldis.2021.11.027.

[8] Gomes P, Tzouanou F, Skolariki K, et al. Extracellular vesicles and Alzheimer's disease in the novel era of Precision Medicine: implications for disease progression, diagnosis and treatment. Experimental Neurology 2022;358. https://doi.org/10.1016/j.expneurol.2022.114183. 114183-114183.

[9] Cirillo D, Valencia A. Big data analytics for personalized medicine. Current Opinion in Biotechnology 2019;58:161–7. https://doi.org/10.1016/j.copbio.2019.03.004.

[10] Gregor Mendel and the principles of inheritance | Learn science at Scitable. Nature.com. Published 2014. Accessed September 16, 2023. https://www.nature.com/scitable/topicpage/gregor-mendel-and-the-principles-of-inheritance-593/.

[11] Perlman RL, Govindaraju DR. Archibald E. Garrod: the father of precision medicine. Genetics in Medicine 2016;18(11):1088–9. https://doi.org/10.1038/gim.2016.5.

[12] 1944: DNA is "Transforming principle". Genome.gov. Published 2013. Accessed September 16, 2023. https://www.genome.gov/25520250/online-education-kit-1944-dna-is-transforming-principle.

[13] The discovery of the double Helix, 1951–1953. Francis Crick—Profiles in science. Published March 12, 2019. Accessed September 16, 2023. https://profiles.nlm.nih.gov/spotlight/sc/feature/doublehelix.

[14] Müller DJ, Rizhanovsky Z. From the origins of pharmacogenetics to first applications in psychiatry. Pharmacopsychiatry 2019;53(04):155–61. https://doi.org/10.1055/a-0979-2322.

[15] Paul Berg (1926–2023). Science. Published 2023. Accessed September 16, 2023. https://www.science.org/doi/10.1126/science.adh2943.

[16] HER2 genetic link to breast cancer. National Cancer Institute. Published April 11, 2018. Accessed September 16, 2023. https://www.cancer.gov/research/progress/discovery/her2.

[17] The Human Genome Project. Genome.gov. Published 2023. Accessed September 16, 2023. https://www.genome.gov/human-genome-project.

[18] The BRCA2 team: Researchers behind the breast cancer gene discovery. Icr.ac.uk. Published 2022. Accessed September 16, 2023. https://www.icr.ac.uk/news-features/latest-features/the-brca2-team-the-scientists-behind-the-breast-cancer-gene-discovery.

[19] TCGA timeline and milestones. ccg - National Cancer Institute. Published 2013. Accessed September 16, 2023. https://www.cancer.gov/ccg/research/genome-sequencing/tcga/history/timeline-milestones.

[20] How CRISPR is changing cancer research and treatment. National Cancer Institute. Published July 27, 2020. Accessed September 16, 2023. https://www.cancer.gov/news-events/cancer-currents-blog/2020/crispr-cancer-research-treatment.

[21] The evolution of liquid biopsy in cancer care—The ASCO post. Ascopost.com. Published 2023. Accessed September 16, 2023. https://ascopost.com/issues/october-10-2021/the-evolution-of-liquid-biopsy-in-cancer-care/.

[22] White House Precision Medicine Initiative. The White house. Published 2015. Accessed September 16, 2023. https://obamawhitehouse.archives.gov/precision-medicine.

[23] Pereira NL, Ahmad F, Byku M, et al. COVID-19: understanding inter-individual variability and implications for precision medicine. Mayo Clinic Proceedings 2021;96(2):446–63. https://doi.org/10.1016/j.mayocp.2020.11.024.

[24] Fang E, Liu X, Li M, et al. Advances in COVID-19 mRNA vaccine development. Signal Transduction and Targeted Therapy 2022;7(1). https://doi.org/10.1038/s41392-022-00950-y.

[25] Denny JC, Collins FS. Precision medicine in 2030—seven ways to transform healthcare. Cell 2021;184(6):1415–9. https://doi.org/10.1016/j.cell.2021.01.015.

[26] Johnson KB, Wei WQ, Weeraratne D, et al. Precision medicine, AI, and the future of personalized health care. Clinical and Translational Science 2020;14(1):86–93. https://doi.org/10.1111/cts.12884.

[27] Subhan A, Parveen F, Shah H, Siva S, Ataide JA, Torchilin V. Recent advances with precision medicine treatment for breast cancer including triple-negative sub-type. Cancers 2023;15(8). https://doi.org/10.3390/cancers15082204. 2204-2204.
[28] Saxena S, Jena B, Gupta N, et al. Role of artificial intelligence in radiogenomics for cancers in the era of precision medicine. Cancers 2022;14(12). https://doi.org/10.3390/cancers14122860. 2860−N.PAG.
[29] Bove R, Schleimer E, Sukhanov P, et al. Building a precision medicine delivery platform for clinics: the university of California, San Francisco, BRIDGE experience. Journal of Medical Internet Research 2022;24(2). https://doi.org/10.2196/34560. e34560-e34560.
[30] Huang PH, Kim KH, Schermer M. Mapping the ethical issues of digital twins for personalised healthcare service (preprint). ResearchGate. Published August 23, 2021. Accessed September 19, 2023. https://www.researchgate.net/publication/354182673_Mapping_the_Ethical_Issues_of_Digital_Twins_for_Personalised_Healthcare_Service_Preprint.
[31] Kwon IWG, Sung HK, Martin D. Integrating social determinants of health to precision medicine through digital transformation: an exploratory roadmap. International Journal of Environmental Research and Public Health 2021;18(9). https://doi.org/10.3390/ijerph18095018. 5018-5018.
[32] Bhavnani SK, Zhang WB, Bao D, et al. Subtyping social determinants of health in all of us: network analysis and visualization approach. medRxiv. Published online January 28, 2023. https://doi.org/10.1101/2023.01.27.23285125.
[33] Yang SR, Schultheis AM, Yu HA, Mandelker D, Ladanyi M, Büttner R. Precision medicine in non-small cell lung cancer: current applications and future directions. Seminars in Cancer Biology 2022;84:184−98. https://doi.org/10.1016/j.semcancer.2020.07.009.
[34] Hockings JK, Pasternak AL, Erwin AL, Mason NT, Eng C, Hicks JK. Pharmacogenomics: an evolving clinical tool for precision medicine. Cleveland Clinic Journal of Medicine 2020;87(2):91−9. https://doi.org/10.3949/ccjm.87a.19073.
[35] Muyambo S, Ndadza A, Soko ND, et al. Warfarin pharmacogenomics for precision medicine in real-life clinical practice in Southern Africa: harnessing 73 variants in 29 pharmacogenes. OMICS 2022;26(1):35−50. https://doi.org/10.1089/omi.2021.0199.
[36] Mohamed Fahmi A, Elewa H, Eljilany I. Warfarin dosing strategies evolution and its progress in the era of precision medicine, a narrative review. International Journal of Clinical Pharmacy 2022;44(3):599−607. https://doi.org/10.1007/s11096-022-01386-8.
[37] Azher A, Khatoon S, Rasool I, et al. The future of precision medicine in the cure of Alzheimer's disease. Biomedicines 2023;11(2). https://doi.org/10.3390/biomedicines11020335. 335-335.
[38] Frasier M, Fiske B, Sherer T. Precision medicine for Parkinson's disease: the subtyping challenge. Frontiers in Aging Neuroscience 2022;14. https://doi.org/10.3389/fnagi.2022.1064057.
[39] Center. Personalized medicine: A biological approach to patient treatment. U.S. Food and Drug Administration. Published 2019. Accessed September 16, 2023. https://www.fda.gov/drugs/news-events-human-drugs/personalized-medicine-biological-approach-patient-treatment.
[40] Nolan JJ, Kahkoska AR, Semnani-Azad Z, et al. ADA/EASD precision medicine in diabetes initiative: an international perspective and future vision for precision medicine in diabetes. Diabetes Care 2022;45(2):261−6. https://doi.org/10.2337/dc21-2216.
[41] Hassan M, Faryal MA, Naz A, et al. Innovations in genomics and big data analytics for personalized medicine and health care: a review. International Journal of Molecular Sciences 2022;23(9). https://doi.org/10.3390/ijms23094645. 4645-4645.
[42] Meng J, Xing R. Inside the "black box": embedding clinical knowledge in data-driven machine learning for heart disease diagnosis. Cardiovascular Digital Health Journal 2022;3(6):276−88. https://doi.org/10.1016/j.cvdhj.2022.10.005.
[43] Gammal RS, Yee ML, Petry N, et al. Pharmacists leading the way to precision medicine: updates to the core pharmacist competencies in genomics. American Journal of Pharmaceutical Education 2022;86(4). https://doi.org/10.5688/ajpe8634. 8634-8634.

[44] Schaibley VM, Ramos IN, Woosley RL, Curry SC, Hays SM, Ramos KS. Limited genomics training among physicians remains a barrier to genomics-based implementation of precision medicine. Frontiers of Medicine 2022;9. https://doi.org/10.3389/fmed.2022.757212.

[45] Khoury MJ, Bowen S, David Dotson W, et al. Health equity in the implementation of genomics and precision medicine: a public health imperative. Genetics in Medicine 2022;24(8):1630−9. https://doi.org/10.1016/j.gim.2022.04.009.

[46] Mitchell S, Jaccard E, Schmitz F, et al. Investigating acceptability of a training programme in precision medicine for frontline healthcare professionals: a mixed methods study. BMC Medical Education 2022;22(1). https://doi.org/10.1186/s12909-022-03613-2.

Further reading

[1] Bierzynska A, McCarthy H, Soderquest K, et al. Genomic and clinical profiling of a national nephrotic syndrome cohort advocates a precision medicine approach to disease management. Kidney International 2017;91(4):937−47. https://doi.org/10.1016/j.kint.2016.10.013.

[2] Manchia M, Pisanu CP, Squassina A, Carpiniello B. Challenges and Future Prospects of Precision Medicine in Psychiatry. Pharmacogenomics and Personalized Medicine. Published 2020. Accessed September 16, 2023. https://www.tandfonline.com/doi/full/10.2147/PGPM.S198225.

[3] Fagherazzi G. Deep digital phenotyping and digital twins for precision health: time to dig deeper. Journal of Medical Internet Research 2020;22(3). https://doi.org/10.2196/16770. e16770-e16770.

[4] Primorac D, Bach-Rojecky L, Vađunec D, et al. Pharmacogenomics at the center of precision medicine: challenges and perspective in an era of Big Data | Pharmacogenomics. Pharmacogenomics. Published 2020. Accessed September 16, 2023. https://www.futuremedicine.com/doi/10.2217/pgs-2019-0134.

[5] Goetz LH, Schork NJ. Personalized medicine: motivation, challenges, and progress. Fertility and Sterility 2018;109(6):952−63. https://doi.org/10.1016/j.fertnstert.2018.05.006.

[6] Personalized medicine at FDA. https://www.personalizedmedicinecoalition.org/Userfiles/PMC-Corporate/file/report.pdf.

[7] Davis SM. siRNAs—a new class of medicines. JAMA 2023;329(24). https://doi.org/10.1001/jama.2023.4570. 2185-2185.

[8] Murthy P, Muggia F. Women's cancers: how the discovery of BRCA genes is driving current concepts of cancer biology and therapeutics. Ecancermedicalscience 2019;13. https://doi.org/10.3332/ecancer.2019.904.

[9] Gemmati D, Varani K, Bramanti B, et al. "Bridging the gap" everything that could have been avoided if we had applied gender medicine, pharmacogenetics and personalized medicine in the gender-omics and sex-omics era. International Journal of Molecular Sciences 2019;21(1). https://doi.org/10.3390/ijms21010296. 296-296.

CHAPTER 11

Hospital to home: Bridging the gap with personalized medicine

Dipu Patel[1] and Harvey Castro[2]
[1]Department of PA Studies, University of Pittsburgh, Pittsburgh, PA, United States; [2]Helpp ai, Chief Medical Intelligence Officer, Dallas, TX, United States

Introduction

What do you imagine the future of care will look like? Do you think it will be better, worse, or about the same? How will it be better, worse, or the same? These are some of the questions being actively discussed in forums, board posts, and conferences. Let us share what we think the future of care could look like.

Taylor's story

Imagine you have a 70-year-old patient, Taylor, who lives alone. Taylor has lived in this home for over 40 years. Recently, his wife passed away after having a stroke. He has three kids. His kids live far enough away not to visit regularly, but one does live within driving distance and tries to stay every few weeks. Since the passing of his wife, Taylor has been dealing with prolonged grief and is having difficulty adjusting to being alone. He has friends, but they all have difficulty getting around and cannot meet regularly in a central location. Taylor also has hypertension, Parkinson's disease, and osteoarthritis. While he can complete most activities of daily living without assistance, he is now realizing how much his wife assisted with cooking meals and cleaning.

This scenario is not uncommon. In fact, with growing life expectancy, this scenario is becoming the norm. The population of 65 and above is expected to grow from 10% in 2022 to 16% by 2050 [1].

In our current healthcare system, Taylor must make appointments with his primary care provider, cardiologist, rheumatologist, and neurologist separately. He would have to drive himself or find a mode of transportation to go to the appointments and get to the pharmacy to pick up medications. Taylor is also lonely and most likely has a diagnosis of depression for which he would have to seek a therapist. The cost and level of care coordination

Digital Health. https://doi.org/10.1016/B978-0-443-23901-4.00011-8

require savviness, dedication, and knowledge to navigate an extremely complex system. And we haven't even talked about health insurance yet. All these services would have to be covered for Taylor to afford the care he needs.

The Future State: A Systems Approach Now imagine a future systems approach. A system where many of these services are brought to Taylor, and his providers have the information they need to make real-time decisions about his care. Taylor wore various devices connected to all his providers, and communication was sent in real-time to the providers. Information includes distance walking within the home, balance, and gait data, blood pressure, renal function, and cardiac output. Additionally, his house would have sensors within various rooms and furniture: rugs with sensors to monitor gait and assess fall risk, a kitchen with smart utensils to detect how much and often Taylor was eating, beds with sensors to detect how long he was spending in bed and what his routine was. This information would help providers make informed decisions on how to best provide care for Taylor, personalized to him and his needs. His providers could provide care through televisit through the smart television, avoiding the need for Taylor to drive and improving compliance with appointments, medications, and care plans.

Additionally, his kids could join the telehealth visit and be involved in Taylor's care. This future system is not too far in the future. It will be the reality within the next 5–10 years.

This chapter discusses personalized medicine and how digital tools better inform the care we deliver at home. We begin with discussing the cost, ethical, and systems considerations that will no doubt impact the rate of adoption of smart technologies and devices. The future of healthcare is shifting from being delivered within the four walls of a clinic or hospital to being delivered at home. In a way, we have come full circle; we are returning to an earlier era when the doctor would visit your home to see you if you were ill. The same will be true in the future, except now, healthcare providers will be armed with personalized data through digital health tools.

Ethical considerations

The integration of digital health tools into our daily lives brings forth a myriad of ethical dilemmas. At the forefront is the issue of data privacy. With continuous monitoring and data transmission, how do we ensure that Taylor's, and millions like him, personal and health data remain confidential? There's also the risk of data breaches, where sensitive information could fall into the wrong hands, leading to potential misuse or even identity theft.

Moreover, there's the question of control and consent. While Taylor might be comfortable with 24/7 monitoring, others might find it intrusive. Thus, it is essential to ensure that individuals are informed about what data is being collected, how it will be used, and have the autonomy to opt-out.

Furthermore, the potential for bias in digital health tools is a significant concern that cannot be overlooked. If these tools are designed based on data from a limited demographic, they may not be as effective or accurate for diverse populations, thereby exacerbating health disparities. Achieving inclusivity in the design and testing of these technologies is paramount to ensure equitable access to healthcare benefits for all individuals.

The integration of digital health tools brings not only promises of improved healthcare but also a range of ethical considerations that demand rigorous attention. Balancing the potential benefits with the need to safeguard data privacy, respect individual autonomy, and mitigate biases is essential in the responsible development and deployment of these technologies in the healthcare landscape.

Cost implications

While the initial investment in smart health tools and home modifications might be substantial, the potential for long-term savings is significant. Fewer physical consultations mean reduced transportation costs for patients like Taylor and less time off work for younger individuals. Additionally, proactive interventions could lead to early diagnosis and treatment, potentially reducing expensive hospital stays or advanced treatments.

However, the onus is on manufacturers, healthcare providers, and policymakers to ensure these technologies are affordable and accessible. As noted by Basarir-Ozel, Turker, and Nasir, "Parallel to the literature, relative advantage, image, enjoyment, design, and technology innovativeness are identified as facilitators. In contrast, high cost, lack of compatibility, lack of trialability, lack of observability, lack of a trusted brand, lack of facilitating conditions and support services, complexity, and technology anxiety are the obstacles to Smart Home Technology (SHT) adoption." Potential strategies could include tiered pricing models, subsidies for low-income individuals, or partnerships with insurance providers to cover some or all costs.

Integration with existing healthcare systems

The seamless integration of smart health tools with existing healthcare systems is a logistical challenge. Healthcare providers must be trained to interpret real-time data and integrate it with traditional medical records. There is also the interoperability challenge—ensuring that different digital tools and platforms can communicate effectively.

Moreover, there's the potential for information overload. Healthcare providers could be inundated with data, making it challenging to discern what's relevant. Implementing Artificial Intelligence (AI)-driven analytics tools could help sift through the data, highlighting anomalies or critical changes that require attention.

The evolution of healthcare, driven by digital health tools, promises a future where care is more personalized, proactive, and patient-centric. However, this journey is fraught with ethical, financial, and logistical challenges. As we stand at this crossroads, it is essential to navigate these challenges with foresight, ensuring that the benefits of digital health are realized without compromising individual rights, equity, or the quality of care.

Smart home

Smart home technology, also known as home automation or "domotics" from the Latin 'domus' meaning home, refers to devices that provide some digitally connected, automated, or enhanced services to building occupants [2,3]. According to one report in 2022, the global smart home market was valued at $80.2 billion [4]. This is projected to grow to $338.28 billion by 2030 [4]. The COVID-19 pandemic has highlighted the need for care outside hospital and clinic walls. Consumers are demanding respect that is convenient, safe, and cost-effective. The technology to deliver such care has been available for many decades. However, in recent years, we have seen adoption and demand for these services and care delivery methods rise. With an aging population and a shrinking healthcare workforce, the smart home and personalized care can aid in improving access while providing care in the comfort of the patient's home. Whether the care is urgent, chronic, or palliative, smart homes and devices leverage technology to bring care where needed.

Smart home hubs and voice assistants

Smart home hubs (SHHs) and voice assistants, such as Google's Home and Amazon's Echo, have become the foundation of many homes. Due to the ease of use, the adoption of these assistants has been rapid. Smart home hubs can control various smart home devices, such as lights, thermostats, and locks. They have quickly advanced to personalized care through accessing health and wellness data, such as heart rate, blood pressure, and glucose levels.

The integration of smart home technologies into the existing healthcare system is a multifaceted endeavor that requires collaboration, innovation, and adaptation. Several factors need thoughtful consideration:

Interoperability: One of the primary challenges is ensuring that smart home devices can seamlessly communicate with existing electronic health record (EHR) systems. This would allow healthcare providers to access real-time data from patients' homes, enabling more proactive and informed care decisions.

Data Privacy and Security: With the increasing connectivity of devices, there's a heightened risk of data breaches. The healthcare system must ensure that data transmitted from smart homes is encrypted and stored securely, adhering to regulations such as the Health Insurance Portability and Accountability Act (HIPAA).

Training and Education: Healthcare professionals must be trained to interpret and act upon the data from smart home devices. This includes understanding the limitations of such devices and ensuring they don't solely rely on them for diagnostic or treatment decisions.

Cost and Reimbursement: Integrating smart home technologies into healthcare might initially increase prices due to the need for new infrastructure, training, and devices. However, in the long run, these technologies have the potential to reduce hospital readmissions and improve patient outcomes, leading to overall cost savings. Payers and insurance companies must determine reimbursement models for care delivered through these technologies.

Patient Engagement: For successful integration, patients must be willing to use these technologies and understand their benefits. This requires education and demonstrating the tangible benefits they can derive from such an integrated system.

The fusion of smart home technologies with the healthcare system represents a paradigm shift in delivering care. As we transition from reactive to proactive maintenance, the home becomes a pivotal point for health monitoring and intervention. While challenges exist, the potential benefits of improved patient outcomes, reduced healthcare costs and enhanced patient experience are immense.

The future of healthcare is not just about advanced hospitals or cutting-edge clinics; it's about turning every home into a potential point of care, ensuring that individuals receive the right care at the right time, right where they are. As technology evolves and the healthcare sector adapts to these changes, we can envision a world where healthcare is truly personalized, efficient, and accessible to all.

Smart pills

Smart pills, digital pills, or ingestible sensors represent groundbreaking advancements in medicine and health monitoring. These pills, once ingested, can transmit data to external devices, allowing for real-time monitoring of various physiological parameters. The primary components of a smart pill include a sensor, a micro battery, and a transmitter.

While the use of smart pills is an emerging area, the potential applications of smart pills are vast. A few current use examples are listed below:

Medication Adherence: One of the primary uses of smart pills is to ensure patients take their medications as prescribed. When the drug is ingested, it sends a signal to an external device, confirming that the medication has been taken. This can be particularly useful for patients with chronic conditions where medication adherence is crucial.

Gastrointestinal Monitoring: Smart pills can monitor various aspects of the gastrointestinal tract. For instance, they can measure pH levels and temperature and even capture images as they travel through the digestive system. This can aid in diagnosing conditions such as Crohn's disease, ulcers, and other gastrointestinal disorders [5].

Personalized Medicine: In the future, smart pills could be used to deliver customized doses of medication based on real-time data For instance, a smart pill could release insulin when it detects high blood sugar levels.

While the potential of smart pills is immense, there are challenges to consider, including privacy concerns, potential health risks, and the cost of development and production. However, as technology advances and these challenges are addressed, smart pills could revolutionize how we approach healthcare and medication management.

Smart appliances and utensils

Smart appliances are appliances that can be connected to the internet and controlled remotely. They have been a growing trend in the home automation market. Smart washers and dryers, smart toasters, smart ovens, smart vacuums, and smart refrigerators all make lives a little bit easier in the home. Smart appliances save money and energy, while giving peace of mind to consumers and their caregivers. While some smart appliances can be expensive, they are becoming increasingly ubiquitous in the day-to-day lives of consumers. Paired with smart home hubs, smart appliances add convenience and ease of use. For example, smart appliances can be used to control lights and thermostats through a smartphone, set timers, and monitor energy usage to aid in improving cost and energy savings. Some examples of daily-use appliances include smart water bottles, smart coffee makers, and smart air purifiers [6].

Smart utensils are utensils that can track food intake and share data with healthcare providers. Smart utensils are promising for both lifestyle and healthcare benefits [7]. They can aid in improving not only the quantity of food being consumed but the quality as well. The list of diseases, both chronic and acute, that can be impacted through diet, food, and tracking is long. Smart utensils can help in mitigating and managing heart disease, diabetes, obesity, and anorexia but also aid in lifestyle improvements in patients with Parkinson's disease [8,9]. Furthermore, smart utensils help in food waste tracking, personalized nutrition plans, and provide support and education in maintaining a healthy lifestyle. The Smart Plate is a good example; equipped with cameras and weight sensors, these plates can analyze the food you're eating, providing insights into calories, nutrients, and portion sizes [10]. While smart utensils are in the early stages of development, as technology improves, so will the adoption of these devices.

Integrating smart technology into everyday objects is not just about convenience; it's about enhancing our quality of life, making informed decisions, and promoting better health and well-being. We can expect even more innovative solutions to everyday challenges as technology evolves.

Smart thermostats

Google's Nest, Ecobee, and other smart thermostats have revolutionized home automation and become the norm in many homes [11]. Connectivity is making it easier for us to control and optimize our homes while improving efficiency, cost, and perhaps even climate change. Smart thermostats can be programmed to adjust temperature based on preferences and daily schedules. The advantages of smart thermostats allow for better insights into energy consumption and efficiency using your smartphone or other smart device. Although smart thermostats are simple to install, some do require professional installation.

The advent of smart thermostats can have potential implications for health and well-being. From a medical standpoint, maintaining an optimal indoor temperature can profoundly affect an individual's health [12].

Chronic Respiratory Conditions: Patients with asthma or chronic obstructive pulmonary disease (COPD) can benefit from a stable indoor environment. Fluctuations in temperature and humidity can trigger respiratory symptoms. Smart thermostats can be programmed to maintain conditions that minimize these triggers.

Cardiovascular Health: Extreme hot and cold temperatures can strain the cardiovascular system. Maintaining a consistent indoor temperature can be crucial for patients with heart conditions. Sudden cold snaps can increase blood pressure and the risk of heart attacks, while excessive heat can lead to dehydration and heat-related illnesses.

Sleep Quality: Sleep is a vital component of overall health. A room that's too hot or cold can disrupt the sleep cycle. Smart thermostats can be programmed to create an optimal sleep environment, adjusting the temperature to the ideal range for deep, restorative sleep [13].

Elderly and Vulnerable Populations: The elderly, infants, and those with compromised immune systems are particularly sensitive to temperature fluctuations. Smart thermostats can maintain their living environment, reducing the risk of temperature-related health issues.

Mental Health: Seasonal affective disorder (SAD) is a type of depression related to seasonal changes. While light therapy is the primary treatment, maintaining a warm indoor environment during the colder months can help alleviate symptoms.

Incorporating smart thermostats into patient care plans can be a proactive approach for healthcare providers. By recommending these devices, doctors can ensure patients have one more tool in their arsenal to maintain and improve their health. However, it's essential to weigh the benefits against the costs, as these devices, while increasingly affordable, may still be out of reach for some patients. Additionally, while many smart thermostats tout easy installation, those who are not technologically savvy or have specific home setups may require professional installation. As with any medical recommendation, it's crucial to consider each patient's individual needs and circumstances.

Smart lighting: Implications for health and well-being from a medical perspective

Smart lighting, similar to smart thermostats, plays an important role in energy management. Smart lights can be controlled through a smart device to create various moods and atmospheres while saving energy. Integrating smart lighting systems, such as Philips Hue, LIFX, and Wyze, into our homes and workplaces is not just a matter of convenience or energy efficiency. From a medical standpoint, light quality, intensity, and color can significantly impact human health [14].

Circadian Rhythm Regulation: Our body's internal clock, or circadian rhythm, is closely tied to light exposure. Smart lighting can be programmed to mimic the natural progression of daylight, gradually increasing in the morning to simulate sunrise, and decreasing in the evening to simulate sunset. This can aid in regulating sleep-wake cycles, improving sleep quality and overall well-being.

Mood and Productivity: Studies have shown that exposure to bright light during the day can boost mood and increase alertness. For patients with mood disorders, such as depression or seasonal affective disorder (SAD), smart lighting can adjunct traditional treatments, providing therapeutic light exposure when natural light is unavailable.

Eye Health: Prolonged exposure to harsh or inappropriate lighting can strain the eyes, leading to conditions such as computer vision syndrome or exacerbating existing eye conditions. Smart lighting allows for adjustments in brightness and hue, reducing glare and providing optimal lighting for reading, working, or relaxation [15].

Skin Conditions: Certain skin conditions such as psoriasis or eczema can benefit from specific light therapies. While specialized medical devices are used for targeted treatments, smart lighting can offer supplementary support, especially with UVB light functionalities [15].

Safety for the Elderly: Falls are a significant concern for the elderly. Smart lighting can be programmed to provide adequate illumination in home areas prone to accidents, such as staircases or bathrooms, reducing the risk of falls.

Migraine and Headache Management: Some individuals are particularly sensitive to specific light frequencies, which can trigger migraines or exacerbate headaches. Smart lighting systems can be adjusted to eliminate these triggers, providing a more comfortable environment for those affected.

Incorporating smart lighting recommendations into patient care can be a holistic approach for healthcare providers. By understanding the potential health benefits and tailoring lighting environments to individual needs, healthcare providers can offer patients an additional tool to enhance their health and quality of life. However, as with all interventions, it's essential to consider the individual's specific health conditions and needs. Proper guidance on the use and settings of smart lighting systems can ensure that patients reap the maximum benefits while minimizing potential risks.

Smart TVs and fall prevention: Integrating ambient intelligence for enhanced safety

In the realm of technological advancements, Smart TVs have not only transformed our entertainment experience but also hold the potential to enhance safety, especially in healthcare settings. With the integration of ambient intelligence (devices working together with people to carry out activities of daily living), as seen in platforms such as helpp.ai, Smart TVs can play a pivotal role in fall prevention [16].

Ambient Intelligence in Smart TVs for Fall Prevention:

Early Warning Systems: Just as helpp.ai provides early warnings before a patient exits their bed, Smart TVs equipped with ambient intelligence can detect unusual or sudden movements in real-time. This can trigger an alert to caregivers or medical staff, allowing for timely intervention and preventing potential falls [17].

Patient Monitoring: Smart TVs with integrated cameras and sensors can monitor patients' movements, especially those who cannot walk independently. This can be particularly beneficial when patients attempt to get out of bed, often to use the bathroom, a common scenario leading to falls.

Automated Clinical Decision Making: Another area where Smart TVs might be useful in the future will be educating patients and aiding clinicians in basic decision-making. By analyzing the data collected, Smart TVs can aid in clinical decision-making, reducing practitioner burnout. For instance, if a patient shows signs of restlessness or increased movement during the night, the system can suggest additional sedatives or interventions to ensure the patient's safety.

Activity Notifications: Smart TVs can optimize their behavior based on patient movement changes. For example, if a patient shows increased activity after rest, the system can notify caregivers to check on the patient.

Integration with Other Systems: Smart TVs can supplement clinical decision support systems by providing a computer-based understanding of physical activities in healthcare settings. This holistic approach ensures that all patient data is considered when making clinical decisions [18].

Cost Savings: Every year, patient falls cost the US Healthcare system 34 billion dollars. Integrating ambient intelligence in Smart TVs can significantly reduce these costs by preventing falls.

Integrating ambient intelligence in Smart TVs offers a promising avenue for enhancing patient safety, especially in preventing falls but also in digital health literacy. Furthermore, Smart TVs will become an additional device through which patients seek care through telemedicine and providers will utilize it for remote patient monitoring. As healthcare providers, staying updated with these technological advancements and considering their potential benefits in improving patient care and safety is essential [19].

Smart toilets

Smart toilets, such as Toto's Neorest and Kohler's Numi, have several advantages over the normal toilet [20]. Smart toilets not only save water but are self-cleaning, and can be monitored for maintenance issues and can monitor gastrointestinal health. While still early in the adoption cycle, they will have a role to play in the diagnosing of various medical conditions [21]. More recently, Casana received FDA clearance for its "heart seat," which measures pulse and oxygen saturation [22]. Smart toilets are redefining how we perceive sanitation and health. These toilets prioritize environmental sustainability by saving water and emphasizing hygiene with their self-cleaning features. However, the most groundbreaking aspect of these toilets lies in their potential to monitor gastrointestinal health. As we move forward in the era of health tech, integrating diagnostic tools in our daily utilities can be a significant step in early diagnosis and proactive patient care.

Gastrointestinal Health Monitoring: Smart toilets can analyze stool and urine samples in real-time, offering insights into hydration levels, potential infections, the presence of blood, and other vital indicators. Such immediate feedback can lead to timely medical interventions, preventing complications and aiding in the early detection of diseases [23].

U-Scan: The Future of Urinalysis: Withings' U-Scan is a testament to the potential of smart toilets in health monitoring. This hands-free connected home urine lab is designed to fit within any toilet bowl and provides an immediate snapshot of the body's balance by monitoring and detecting various biomarkers found in urine. With over 3000 metabolites, urine is a significant indicator of our health. Regular access to these metrics from the comfort of one's bathroom can revolutionize health monitoring. The U-Scan system is noninvasive, effortless, and automatic, with each cartridge designed to last 3 months. It can detect and measure parameters such as ketones for energy metabolism and vitamin C levels [24].

Cardiovascular Health Monitoring: The recent FDA clearance of Casana's "heart seat" highlights the potential of smart toilets in cardiovascular health monitoring. By measuring pulse and oxygen saturation, these toilets can provide daily data on a person's heart health, aiding in the early detection of cardiovascular issues [22].

Hygiene and Infection Control: From a medical standpoint, maintaining hygiene is crucial in preventing infections. Smart toilets, with their self-cleaning capabilities, ensure a sanitary environment, potentially reducing the risk of urinary tract infections and other hygiene-related conditions.

Smart toilets also have broader implications beyond individual health. They contribute to water conservation, which is essential for public health and ecological sustainability. Moreover, early detection of health issues can lead to cost savings in the long run by preventing complications and reducing hospital stays. With their advanced features and health monitoring capabilities, smart toilets represent a significant advancement in the intersection of technology and healthcare. As a healthcare provider, the potential for early diagnosis, continuous health monitoring, and improved patient care make smart toilets an exciting prospect in the future of healthcare and diagnostics.

Smart mirrors: A medical perspective on reflective health monitoring

In the era of smart homes and IoT (Internet of Things), the humble mirror has transformed into a "smart mirror." [25–27]. These mirrors, equipped with sensors, cameras, and displays, offer more than a reflection [28]. They can provide real-time health metrics, skincare analysis, and mental health check-ins [25–27]. From a healthcare provider's viewpoint, integrating health monitoring tools in such a daily utility can significantly advance proactive patient care and health awareness.

Skin Health Monitoring: Skin analysis is one of the primary features of many smart mirrors. These mirrors can detect changes in skin moisture, pore size, redness, and signs of aging. Early detection of skin anomalies, such as moles changing shape or size, can be crucial in diagnosing conditions such as skin cancer at an early stage.

Vital Signs Measurement: Some advanced smart mirrors are equipped with sensors that can measure vital signs such as heart rate and oxygen saturation just by a person standing before them. Regular monitoring of these vitals can help detect cardiovascular issues or respiratory diseases early [26].

Mental Health Check-ins: Mental health is as crucial as physical health. Smart mirrors with facial recognition capabilities can detect signs of stress, fatigue, or mood changes based on facial expressions. While not a replacement for professional mental health evaluations, these mirrors can serve as a daily check-in, reminding individuals to take breaks, practice mindfulness, or seek help if consistent mood changes are detected.

Medication Reminders: For patients on regular medication, adherence to the regimen is crucial. Smart mirrors can be programmed to provide daily reminders for medication, ensuring that patients don't miss their doses.

Telemedicine Integration: With built-in cameras and displays, smart mirrors can be used for telemedicine consultations. Patients can have face-to-face consultations with their healthcare providers without needing additional devices, making the process seamless and more integrated into their daily routines.

Smart mirrors can collect data over time, providing trends and insights into a person's health allowing healthcare providers to make better informed decisions. This data can be integrated with other health apps or shared with healthcare providers, providing a comprehensive view of a patient's health [27]. While the potential benefits of smart mirrors are immense, it is essential to address privacy concerns. It is crucial to ensure that the data collected is encrypted and that patients have control over who accesses their data.

Smart mirrors represent the convergence of technology and healthcare in our daily lives. They offer a unique opportunity for continuous health monitoring, early diagnosis, and patient engagement [29]. As a healthcare provider, the potential for integrating health awareness into daily routines, ensuring medication adherence, and providing a holistic view of a patient's health makes smart mirrors a promising tool in the future of healthcare.

Smart cars: A medical perspective on automotive health integration

The automotive industry has seen rapid advancements with the introduction of smart cars. These vehicles, equipped with advanced sensors, connectivity, and automation features, are not just about enhancing the driving experience but also have significant implications for health and well-being [30]. From a clinician's viewpoint, integrating health monitoring and emergency response tools in smart cars can be a transformative step in road safety and proactive health management.

Health Monitoring While Driving: Some smart cars come equipped with sensors in the steering wheel or seats that can monitor the driver's vital signs, such as heart rate, blood pressure, and stress levels. Continuous monitoring can provide real-time feedback, alerting drivers if any anomalies are detected potentially preventing medical emergencies while driving [31].

Fatigue and Drowsiness Detection: One of the leading causes of road accidents is driver fatigue. Advanced smart cars have systems that can detect signs of drowsiness or inattention, alerting the driver to take a break or even taking autonomous control to ensure safety.

Emergency Response Integration: In the event of an accident, smart cars can automatically send alerts to emergency services, providing precise location data and potentially information about the driver's medical condition. This can lead to faster response times and better-prepared medical teams [32].

Air Quality and Allergen Monitoring: The air quality inside the car can be crucial for individuals with respiratory conditions or allergies. Smart vehicles can monitor and adjust the internal air quality, filtering out pollutants and allergens ensuring a safer environment for those with health concerns.

Ergonomics and Posture: Prolonged driving can lead to musculoskeletal issues due to poor posture. Advanced seating in smart cars can adjust based on the driver's physique and driving duration, promoting better posture and reducing the risk of back and neck problems.

Mental Well-being: Features such as ambient lighting, calming music integration, and noise cancellation can contribute to a more relaxed driving environment, reducing stress and anxiety, especially during long drives or heavy traffic [33].

Telemedicine Integration: As telemedicine becomes more prevalent, future smart cars might integrate virtual health consultations. Imagine a scenario where a driver feeling unwell can instantly connect with a healthcare provider through the car's infotainment system.

While the health benefits of smart cars are promising, it's essential to address the potential concerns of data privacy. Ensuring that health data collected by the vehicle is encrypted and giving drivers control over who accesses their data is vital. Smart cars represent a significant intersection of technology and healthcare on the move. They offer the potential not only for enhanced driving safety but also for continuous health monitoring and intervention. As a healthcare provider, the prospect of integrating health awareness, emergency response, and proactive health management into daily commutes and long drives makes smart cars a valuable asset in the future of healthcare and transportation.

Smart rugs and floors: Ground-level health monitoring

Technology integration into our living spaces has reached even the ground we walk on. Smart rugs and floors, equipped with sensors and connectivity features, are emerging as valuable tools for health monitoring and safety. From a medical standpoint, these innovations can be pivotal in the early detection of falls, fall prevention, and overall well-being [33–35].

Fall Detection and Prevention: One of the most significant benefits of smart floors is their ability to detect and prevent falls, especially in older people. These floors can sense changes in weight distribution, alerting caregivers or family members if a fall is detected. Early intervention can prevent complications and ensure timely medical attention [34].

Gait Analysis: Smart rugs and floors can monitor an individual's walking pattern or gait. Changes in gait can indicate various medical conditions, from musculoskeletal issues to neurological disorders. Continuous monitoring can lead to early detection and intervention [34–36].

Weight Monitoring: Integrated scales in smart floors can provide daily weight measurements, helping track weight loss or gain. This can be particularly beneficial for patients with heart failure, where sudden weight gain can indicate fluid retention and worsening of the condition.

Temperature Sensing: Some smart floors come equipped with temperature sensors, which can detect fever or changes in body temperature, alerting individuals to potential health issues [35].

Hygiene and Infection Control: Smart floors in medical settings can be designed to detect contaminants or pathogens, ensuring a sanitary environment and reducing the risk of hospital-acquired infections.

Rehabilitation and Physical Therapy: For patients undergoing physical therapy, smart floors can track progress, monitor exercises, and provide feedback on posture and movement. This can aid in more personalized and effective rehabilitation programs [35].

Environmental Monitoring: Beyond individual health, smart floors can also monitor the environment, detecting moisture (which can lead to mold growth) or changes in room temperature, ensuring a healthy living space

Smart floors can be integrated with other smart home devices, such as lighting or alarms. For instance, lights can be automatically turned on if a fall is detected, or an alarm can be triggered. As with all smart devices, it is essential to consider the implications of data collection and privacy. Users should have control over their data, with clear encryption and sharing protocols. Smart rugs and floors represent a seamless integration of health monitoring into our daily lives. The ability of smart floors to provide continuous monitoring, early detection of health problems, and seamless integration with therapeutic interventions make them a game-changer in healthcare and home living, offering clinicians the opportunity to revolutionize patient care.

Smart locks

The advent of smart locks, which offer enhanced security features through digital mechanisms and connectivity, has transformed how we think about home and facility security. Beyond the obvious benefits of improved safety and convenience, smart locks also have potential healthcare implications [37]. From a medical standpoint, these devices can affect patient safety, medication management, and overall well-being.

Medication Security: One of the primary concerns in both home and clinical settings is the secure storage of medications, especially controlled substances. Smart locks can be used on medicine cabinets or storage units, ensuring that only authorized individuals have access. This can prevent accidental overdoses, misuse, or theft of medications.

Patient Safety in Care Facilities: In care facilities catering to patients with dementia or cognitive impairments, wandering can be a significant concern. Smart locks can be programmed to allow or restrict access based on the time of day or specific patient profiles, ensuring patient safety without compromising their autonomy.

Remote Access for Caregivers: For elderly individuals living alone or those with chronic conditions, smart locks can allow caregivers or family members remote access to the home in case of emergencies. This ensures timely intervention without the need for physical keys.

Data Logging and Monitoring: Smart locks can log access data, providing insights into patterns. For instance, if a patient accesses their medication cabinet more frequently than prescribed, it could indicate potential misuse or confusion about dosage, prompting a medical review.

Ease of Use for Individuals with Disabilities: Traditional locks can pose challenges for individuals with physical disabilities. Smart locks, with features such as voice commands or remote smartphone access, can offer a more accessible solution.

Smart locks can be integrated with other health monitoring systems. For example, if a fall detection system is triggered, the smart lock can automatically unlock the front door, allowing emergency responders to enter without delay. Furthermore, smart locks can be integrated with smart home systems to control air quality, temperature, and lighting based on the individual's health needs. Certain areas may hold sensitive patient information in medical facilities. Smart locks can ensure that only authorized personnel have access, safeguarding patient confidentiality. While smart locks offer numerous benefits, addressing potential cybersecurity risks is essential. Ensuring robust encryption and regular software updates can mitigate the risk of unauthorized access or data breaches. With their advanced security and connectivity features, smart locks represent a convergence of safety and healthcare. As a clinician, the potential for enhanced medication management, patient safety, and integration with broader health systems makes smart locks a valuable tool in the modern healthcare landscape.

Smart gardens

The concept of gardening has been redefined with the introduction of smart gardens. These technologically advanced systems, incorporating sensors, automation, and data analytics, offer a modern approach to cultivating plants, herbs, and vegetables. From a medical standpoint, smart gardens can have profound implications for therapeutic well-being, nutritional health, and overall quality of life [38].

Therapeutic Benefits: Gardening has long been recognized for its therapeutic properties, aiding in stress reduction, mental relaxation, and cognitive stimulation. Smart gardens, with their automated features, allow even those without a green thumb to experience the therapeutic benefits of gardening, making it accessible to a wider population [38].

Nutritional Health: Smart gardens enable individuals to grow herbs, vegetables, and fruits. This ensures fresh, organic produce and promotes a diet rich in essential vitamins, minerals, and antioxidants. Regular consumption of home-grown produce can aid in preventing chronic diseases, boosting immunity, and promoting overall health.

Air Quality Improvement: Plants play a crucial role in purifying air by absorbing pollutants and releasing oxygen. Smart gardens, especially those designed for indoor use, can improve indoor air quality, which benefits patients with respiratory conditions such as asthma or allergies [38].

Physical Activity: While smart gardens automate many processes, they still require some physical interaction, such as planting, pruning, or harvesting. This encourages gentle physical activity, promoting joint mobility and muscle strength, especially in the elderly.

Mental Health and Well-being: Watching plants grow and thrive can offer a sense of accomplishment and purpose. For individuals battling depression, anxiety, or other mental health conditions, this can be a source of solace and positivity [38].

Educational Value: Smart gardens often have integrated apps or platforms that provide insights into plant growth, nutritional values, and gardening tips. This educational aspect can particularly benefit children, fostering an interest in biology, nutrition, and the environment.

Future iterations of smart gardens might integrate with health monitoring apps, suggesting specific herbs or plants based on an individual's nutritional needs or health conditions. On a broader scale, promoting home-grown produce can reduce the carbon footprint of transporting food items. This has positive implications for environmental health, impacting public health [39]. One of the significant concerns with store-bought produce is the potential presence of pesticides. Smart gardens, with their controlled environment, can ensure pesticide-free growth, reducing the risk of chemical ingestion. Smart gardens represent a harmonious blend of technology and nature, offering numerous health benefits. As a healthcare provider, the potential for therapeutic engagement enhanced nutritional intake, and the promotion of mental well-being makes smart gardens a commendable addition to the modern healthcare paradigm.

Smart feeders and AI pets: Modern pet care

Smart feeders

Smart feeders have revolutionized the way pet owners manage their pets' nutrition. These devices allow for scheduled feeding, portion control, and real-time monitoring, ensuring pets receive the right amount of food even in the owner's absence [40,41].

They play a pivotal role in dietary management, a critical aspect of pet care. Overfeeding or underfeeding can lead to a myriad of health issues in pets, ranging from obesity to malnutrition. Smart feeders address this concern by ensuring the provision of consistent portion sizes meticulously tailored to the pet's specific requirements, including considerations for age, weight, and dietary needs [40,41]. Beyond portion control, these ingenious devices also facilitate medication administration, a vital aspect of pet healthcare. Some smart feeders can be programmed to dispense medications, ensuring not only timely but also consistent delivery of essential treatments, thereby aiding in the management of chronic conditions or recovery from illness.

Moreover, certain advanced smart feeders extend their functionality to monitor hydration, a critical aspect of pet health often overlooked. These feeders keep a watchful eye on water intake, which is instrumental in detecting early signs of dehydration or kidney issues, enabling pet owners to take prompt action and seek veterinary care if necessary. Additionally, these smart feeders provide invaluable nutritional insights through integrated apps. Pet owners can gain comprehensive insights into their pet's eating patterns, facilitating early detection of any deviations that may indicate underlying health issues, such as changes in appetite, which can be early indicators of various medical conditions. In this manner, smart feeders contribute significantly to improving pet health by promoting optimal nutrition, medication adherence, hydration monitoring, and early health issue detection.

AI pets

The realm of pet companionship is undergoing a profound transformation with the advent of AI-powered "animals." [42,43] These AI companions can follow their owners, recognize humans, and even adapt and learn through artificial intelligence algorithms. While they provide a novel solution to those seeking companionship, it is essential to recognize their limitations. Although AI pets can offer mental health support, they cannot replicate the rich and multidimensional experience of caring for a living animal. The realm of pet companionship is witnessing a paradigm shift with the introduction of AI-powered "animals." As highlighted in this August 2023 Fox News article [42]:

Continuous Companionship: AI pets, such as Go1, developed by Unitree Robotics, offer constant companionship without the maintenance needs of real pets. They can follow their owners, recognize humans, and even adapt and learn through AI [43].

Mental Health Support: While AI pets can offer companionship and mental health support, they cannot replicate the rich experience of caring for a real animal. Unlike real pets, AI pets don't encourage physical activities such as walking or playing [42].

Data Privacy Concerns: There are potential risks related to data privacy and an over-dependency on AI pets for companionship, which might lead to the neglect of real-life relationships.

Long-term Effects: The long-term psychological and emotional effects, especially on children, of having AI pets are yet to be fully understood. While they present a unique alternative for companionship and can play a role in improving mental health, they should be seen as a partial replacement for real pets.

In contemplating the adoption of AI pets, it is crucial to consider their long-term psychological and emotional effects, especially among children. While AI pets offer a unique alternative for companionship and can contribute positively to mental health, their role should be viewed as a complementary one, rather than a complete replacement for real pets. Continuous evaluation of the benefits and risks associated with AI pets is essential, both from a medical and psychological standpoint, to strike a balance between the convenience they offer and the irreplaceable benefits of genuine pet-human relationships.

Smart buildings: Advanced infrastructure and privacy considerations

The concept of smart buildings refers to structures that use integrated technologies, sensors, and automation to optimize building operations, energy consumption, and occupant comfort. These buildings are designed to be energy-efficient, environmentally friendly, and responsive to the needs of their occupants [44,45]. From a medical standpoint, smart buildings can significantly affect public health, safety, and well-being.

Health Monitoring: Advanced HVAC systems in smart buildings can monitor and improve indoor air quality, reducing the risk of respiratory diseases and allergies. Additionally, lighting systems can be adjusted to mimic natural light patterns, promoting better sleep and circadian rhythm regulation.

Safety and Emergency Response: In real-time, smart buildings can detect emergencies such as fires or gas leaks, ensuring timely evacuation and minimizing health risks. They can also be integrated with medical alert systems, providing immediate assistance in case of medical emergencies [45,46].

Therapeutic Environments: Smart buildings can be programmed to create therapeutic environments for patients, adjusting lighting, temperature, and sound based on individual needs. This can particularly benefit healthcare facilities, promoting faster recovery and well-being.

Accessibility: For individuals with disabilities, smart buildings offer enhanced accessibility features, from voice-activated elevators to automated doors, ensuring a safe and comfortable environment.

Privacy considerations

While smart buildings offer a multitude of advantages, they also give rise to significant concerns regarding data privacy and security that must not be overlooked [47]. One prominent issue is data collection; smart buildings continuously gather data on occupants' behaviors, preferences, and daily routines. While this data can be invaluable for optimizing building operations and enhancing user experiences, it simultaneously presents a potential vulnerability that could lead to privacy breaches if not appropriately safeguarded. Moreover, the realm of cybersecurity poses a considerable risk for smart buildings. Like all interconnected systems, these structures are susceptible to cyberattacks. Unauthorized access to a smart building's systems could not only compromise the safety and comfort of its occupants but also result in data breaches, potentially exposing sensitive information to malicious actors.

Ensuring consent and transparency is another pivotal aspect of ethical data management within smart buildings. Occupants should be fully informed about the types of data being collected, the purposes for which it is being gathered, and how it will be utilized. Obtaining informed consent from building occupants is paramount to maintaining ethical standards in data collection and utilization. Furthermore, policies regarding data storage duration and sharing protocols should be firmly established within smart building management. Data should be securely encrypted to prevent unauthorized access, and access should be restricted solely to authorized personnel who require it for legitimate purposes.

As the landscape of smart building technologies continues to evolve, there is an imperative need for the development and implementation of regulations and compliance measures that specifically address data privacy concerns. Building operators must take proactive steps to ensure that their practices align with local and international data protection laws, thus safeguarding the privacy and security of the individuals who occupy these technologically advanced structures. Balancing the numerous benefits of smart buildings with the critical imperative of data privacy and security is essential for realizing a future where these structures enhance the well-being of occupants without compromising their personal information or safety.

Smart buildings represent the future of urban living, offering enhanced comfort, safety, and health benefits. However, as a profession concerned about the health and well-being of its patients and society, it's essential to balance these advantages with the potential risks associated with data privacy. Continuous evaluation and adherence to ethical standards are crucial to ensure the well-being and trust of building occupants.

Digital tattoos

The use of digital or smart tattoos has the ability to revolutionize how we diagnose, treat, and even screen for diseases. Digital tattoos have applicability across many industries beyond healthcare; athletic training, communications, and public health just to name a few. Digital tattoos are an emerging field of increasingly precise level of information gathering and will replace many wearables that are currently in use today [48,49]. Digital tattoos, an innovative intersection of technology and medicine, are poised to redefine the landscape of health diagnostics, treatment, and screening. While their applications span various sectors, including athletic training, communications, and public health, their most profound impact is anticipated in healthcare.

Digital tattoos are temporary tattoos that are embedded with sensors that can track a variety of health data, such as heart rate, blood pressure, blood sugar levels, and various electrolyte levels. Through the use of biosensitive inks, pairing, and leveraging the properties of elements and polymers, digital tattoos can provide valuable data about body fluids and electrolytes [50–52]. The data collected by digital tattoos can be seamlessly transmitted through a smartphone or other devices to healthcare providers.

Digital tattoos have a number of advantages over traditional wearable health trackers [53]. They are more discreet and comfortable to wear, and they can be placed in areas of the

Figure 11.1
Potential uses cases of digital tattoos. *Dipu Patel.*

body that are difficult to reach with traditional wearables. Furthermore, digital tattoos can be customized to track specific health data and can be updated with new features as the technology evolves.

Some of the potential use cases for digital tattoos are included in Fig. 11.1.

- Monitoring patients with chronic diseases, such as diabetes and heart disease.
- Tracking athletes' fitness and performance
- Measuring sleep quality.
- Creating personalized medicine interventions.
- Measuring electrolyte levels.
- Tracking mental health data, such as stress levels and mood.
- Monitoring environmental factors, such as air quality and noise levels.
- Creating personalized beauty products that respond to the wearer's individual needs.
- Monitoring skin for UV absorption and other metrics

Advantages Over Traditional Wearables:

- Discreet and Comfortable: Unlike bulky wearables, digital tattoos are hidden, allowing patients to monitor their health without drawing attention.

- Customizability: They can be tailored to monitor specific health metrics, offering personalized health tracking.
- Evolution with Technology: As technology advances, digital tattoos can be updated with new features, ensuring they remain at the forefront of health monitoring.

Potential Medical Applications:

- Chronic Disease Management: They can be instrumental in monitoring patients with chronic ailments such as diabetes and heart disease.
- Athletic Performance: Athletes can use them to track their fitness levels and performance metrics.
- Sleep Quality Assessment: They can provide insights into sleep patterns and quality by monitoring vital signs.
- Personalized Medicine: They can aid in devising customized treatment plans based on real-time health data.
- Electrolyte Monitoring: Useful in tracking hydration levels and electrolyte imbalances.
- Mental Health Tracking: Can monitor stress levels, mood fluctuations, and other mental health indicators.
- Environmental Monitoring: Can track exposure to harmful environmental factors such as UV radiation, air quality, and noise levels.
- Skin Health: Monitoring skin for UV absorption and other vital metrics.

Research and development

Recent advancements have seen the development of digital tattoos that can monitor muscle performance, heart activity, and movement and even administer medicine. For instance, a glucose monitoring patch developed by a South Korean research team can track body temperature and the pH of sweat in individuals with Type 2 diabetes [54]. This data is then relayed to a smartphone app, which can administer medicine through a small needle in the patch.

Another notable development comes from the collaboration between Harvard University and the Massachusetts Institute of Technology (MIT). They introduced a color-changing e-tattoo, the Dermal Abyss, which uses sensitive inks to change colors based on body changes, providing sodium, pH, and glucose measurements. This technology holds promise for patients with diabetes, where real-time glucose monitoring can be life-saving.

Digital tattoos, though currently in their early stages of development, hold immense potential to revolutionize healthcare and various other sectors. They offer the promise of making healthcare more convenient, affordable, and less intrusive while empowering individuals with valuable real-time health data. As technology advances and research continues, it is likely that digital tattoos will become an integral part of our healthcare ecosystem, representing a remarkable advancement in personalized medicine.

Furthermore, these digital tattoos signify a beacon of hope in the realm of personalized medicine. Their continuous evolution promises to unlock innovative and useful applications beyond healthcare, potentially impacting education and various aspects of care delivery and monitoring. With each advancement in this field, we move closer to a future where digital tattoos play a pivotal role in enhancing our understanding of physiology, thus contributing to improved overall health and well-being.

Implications on care

Provider perspective

The integration of smart technologies into homes has significant implications for healthcare providers. The data from smart homes can offer real-time insights into a patient's health and well-being. For instance, the article from ScienceDirect titled "Motivations, barriers, and risks of smart home adoption: From a systematic literature review to conceptual framework" highlights that prominent technology services in smart homes are associated with healthcare, energy efficiency, and home security [55]. The primary motivations for adopting smart home technology include efficient energy management, better home-based healthcare services, potential financial savings, and enhanced quality of life. However, barriers such as distrust, limited perception of smart homes, financial concerns, privacy and security issues, and technology anxiety can hinder adoption.

From a provider's perspective, the data from smart homes can be invaluable in monitoring patients with chronic diseases, ensuring medication adherence, and even predicting potential health crises before they occur [56]. However, providers need to be trained to interpret and integrate this data into their care plans. Additionally, there are concerns about data privacy and security, which need to be addressed to gain the trust of both providers and patients.

Patient perspective

For patients, smart homes can offer a sense of security and empowerment. Managing and monitoring their health in real-time can lead to better health outcomes and increased independence, especially for older people or those with chronic conditions. The convenience of having health metrics monitored and sent directly to their healthcare providers can lead to timely interventions and better communication between patients and providers.

However, there are also concerns from the patient's perspective. The potential for data breaches and the feeling of being constantly monitored can be unsettling for some. Technology literacy is also challenged; not all patients are comfortable using or interpreting data from smart devices.

Opportunities and barriers

The future of smart homes is promising, with advancements in technology leading to more integrated and sophisticated systems [57]. The articles from digitaltrends.com and forbes.com predict innovations that will make homes more responsive to residents' needs, enhancing comfort, safety, and health monitoring [58,59].

However, barriers to widespread adoption remain. The ScienceDirect article highlights that distrust, financial concerns, and technology anxiety are significant hurdles. There's also the challenge of ensuring these technologies are accessible to all, regardless of socio-economic status.

Future smart homes

The smart home concept is evolving, with the potential to become fully integrated health hubs. The article from 7wireventures.com titled "Home is where the health is" envisions a future where homes monitor and actively improve residents' health [60]. This could be through air purification systems that reduce allergens, lighting systems that enhance mood and sleep, or even floors that can detect falls and alert healthcare providers.

In conclusion, while the potential benefits of smart homes for healthcare are immense, there are challenges to overcome. Both providers and patients need to be educated about the benefits and potential risks, and there needs to be a robust framework in place to ensure data privacy and security. With collaboration between tech developers, healthcare providers, and patients, the smart home can revolutionize healthcare delivery.

References

[1] Chen C, Ding S, Wang J. Digital health for aging populations. Nature Medicine 2023;29(7):1623−30. https://doi.org/10.1038/s41591-023-02391-8.

[2] Yasar K, Shea S. smart Home. IoT Agenda. 2023. https://www.techtarget.com/iotagenda/definition/smart-home-or-building#:~:text=A%20smart%20home%20is%20a,such%20as%20lighting%20and%20heating. [Accessed 20 September 2023].

[3] Sovacool BK, Furszyfer DD. Smart home technologies in Europe: A critical review of concepts, benefits, risks and policies. Renewable and Sustainable Energy Reviews 2020;120:109663. https://doi.org/10.1016/j.rser.2019.109663.

[4] Smart home market size, share & trends | statistics [2030]. 2023. Fortunebusinessinsights.com. [Accessed 20 September 2023]. https://www.fortunebusinessinsights.com/industry-reports/smart-home-market-101900.

[5] Cummins G. Smart pills for gastrointestinal diagnostics and therapy. Advanced Drug Delivery Reviews 2021;177:113931. 113931, https://doi.org/10.1016/j.addr.2021.113931.
[6] Ständer M, Hadjakos A, Lochschmidt N, Klos C, Renner B, Mühlhäuser M. A smart kitchen infrastructure. 2012. https://doi.org/10.1109/ism.2012.27.
[7] Huang Q, Yang Z, Zhang Q. Smart-U: smart utensils know what you eat. 2018. https://doi.org/10.1109/infocom.2018.8486266.
[8] A smart utensil for detecting food pick-up gesture and amount while eating. In: Proceedings of the 11th Augmented Human International Conference. ACM Other conferences; 2020. https://dl.acm.org/doi/10.1145/3396339.3396361. [Accessed 20 September 2023].
[9] Verily's "smart spoon" combats Parkinson's Tremors. Pharmaphorum. 2023. https://pharmaphorum.com/news/verilys-smart-spoon-combats-parkinsons-tremors. [Accessed 20 September 2023].
[10] Best Food & Diet Tracking App | Calorie Calculator App - SmartPlate®. Getsmartplate.com. Published 2022. [Accessed August 27, 2024]. https://www.getsmartplate.com/
[11] Imagining the thoughtful home: google nest and logics of domestic recording. Critical studies in media communication. 2023. https://www.tandfonline.com/doi/abs/10.1080/15295036.2022.2143838. [Accessed 20 September 2023].
[12] Oetomo A. Smart Monitoring of Population Health Risk Behaviour - Kirti Sundar Sahu, Arlene Oetomo, Plinio Morita. Proceedings of the International Symposium on Human Factors and Ergonomics in Health Care 2019. https://journals.sagepub.com/doi/abs/10.1177/2327857919081017. [Accessed 27 August 2024].
[13] Jalali N, Sahu K, Oetomo A, Morita P. Usability of smart home thermostat to evaluate the impact of weekdays and seasons on sleep patterns and indoor stay: observational Study. Jmir mhealth and uhealth 2022;10(4):e28811. https://doi.org/10.2196/28811.
[14] Moe Soheilian, Fischl G, Aries M. Smart lighting application for energy saving and user well-being in the residential environment. Sustainability 2021;13(11):6198. 6198, https://doi.org/10.3390/su13116198.
[15] Ticleanu C. Impacts of home lighting on human health. Lighting Research & Technology; 2021. Accessed August 27, 2024. https://journals.sagepub.com/doi/full/10.1177/14771535211021064
[16] helpp.ai -Ambient Intelligence. 2023. https://www.helpp.ai/. [Accessed 20 September 2023].
[17] Landi H. Samsung rolls out smart healthcare TV, digital health tools for hospitals. Fierce Healthcare 2022. https://www.fiercehealthcare.com/health-tech/himss-2022-samsung-rolls-out-smart-healthcare-tv-digital-health-tools-hospitals. [Accessed 20 September 2023].
[18] Bridging the digital divide: the smart TV as a platform for digital literacy among the elderly. Behaviour and Information Technology 2022. https://www.tandfonline.com/doi/abs/10.1080/0144929X.2021.1934732. [Accessed 20 September 2023].
[19] Will your smart tv serve as a remote care platform? The Medical Futurist; 2022. https://medicalfuturist.com/remote-care-through-smart-television/. [Accessed 20 September 2023].
[20] Cranz A. Kohler's Numi 2.0 Smart Toilet has Alexa inside and is coming soon. The Verge 2022. https://www.theverge.com/2022/12/19/23510864/kohler-numi-smart-toilet-alexa-ces-2022. [Accessed 20 September 2023].
[21] Saner E. The smart toilet era is here! Are you ready to share your analprint with big tech? The Guardian 2021. https://www.theguardian.com/lifeandstyle/2021/sep/23/the-smart-toilet-era-is-here-are-you-ready-to-share-your-analprint-with-big-tech. [Accessed 20 September 2023].
[22] FDA clears smart toilet to measure heart rate and oxygen saturation. 2023. Fdanews.com. [Accessed 20 September 2023]. https://www.fdanews.com/articles/211859-fda-clears-smart-toilet-to-measure-heart-rate-and-oxygen-saturation.
[23] Zhou J, McNabb J, Capite N De, et al. Stool image analysis for digital health monitoring by smart toilets. IEEE Internet of Things Journal 2023;10(5):3720–34. https://doi.org/10.1109/jiot.2022.3158886.
[24] Withings | U-Scan. 2022. https://www.withings.com/us/en/u-scan. [Accessed 20 September 2023].
[25] Dowthwaite L, Cruz GR, Rita Pena Ana, et al. Examining the use of autonomous systems for home health support using a smart mirror. 2023. https://doi.org/10.20944/preprints202307.0254.v1.
[26] Krishnamurthy I, Dhandayudam P, Karthika M. IoT-based smart mirror for health monitoring. 2020. https://doi.org/10.1016/b978-0-12-819779-0.00007-1.

[27] Miotto R, Matteo D, Scelza J, Kidd B, Dudley JT. Reflecting health: smart mirrors for personalized medicine. NPJ Digital Medicine 2018;1(1). https //doi.org/10.1038/s41746-018-0068-7.

[28] Mariappan R, Naga Prasanna P, Tehmeem Sulthana SK, Ramprasad A, Shalini PC. Design of smart medical mirror using Raspberry Pi. Journal of Physics 2023;2466(1). https://doi.org/10.1088/1742-6596/2466/1/012022. 012022-012022.

[29] Prajugjit N, Silapasuphakornwong P, Sookhanaphibarn K, Uehira K. Friendly chatbot with IBM Watson assistant support elderly delightful in smart mirror. In: 2022 IEEE 11th Global Conference on Consumer Electronics (GCCE); 2022. https://doi.org/10.1109/gcce56475.2022.10014288.

[30] Wang J, Warnecke J, Mostafa H, Deserno T. Unobtrusive health monitoring in private spaces: the smart vehicle. Sensors 2020;20(9):2442. 2442, https://doi.org/10.3390/s20092442.

[31] Acharya AD, Patil SN. IoT based Health Care Monitoring Kit March;1:2020;1:2020. https://doi.org/10.1109/iccmc48092.2020.iccmc-00068.

[32] Ibrahim Mamun Md, Rahman A, Abdul Khaleque Md, Mridha MF, Hamid A. Healthcare monitoring system inside self-driving smart car in 5G cellular network. 2019. https://doi.org/10.1109/indin41052.2019.8972144.

[33] Admin health, wellness and well-being features in cars to accelerate due to COVID 19. Frost & Sullivan; 2020. https://www.frost.com/frost-perspectives/health-wellness-and-well-being-features-in-cars-to-accelerate-due-to-covid-19/. [Accessed 20 September 2023].

[34] Killian L, Maitre J, Bouchard K, et al. Managing the Fall risk in smart homes using monocular cameras, ambient sensors and an interactive social robot. 2022. https://doi.org/10.1109/smartblock4health56071.2022.10034526.

[35] Monge J, Ribeiro G, Raimundo A, Octavian P, Joel. AI-based smart sensing and AR for gait rehabilitation assessment. Information 2023;14(7):355. https://doi.org/10.3390/info14070355.

[36] Joel O, Mendes D. Ambient assisted living using non-intrusive smart sensing and IoT for gait rehabilitation. In: 2022 IEEE International Conference on Metrology for Extended Reality, Artificial Intelligence and Neural Engineering (MetroXRAINE); 2022. https://doi.org/10.1109/metroxraine54828.2022.9967674.

[37] Aggarwal S, Sharma S. Voice based secured smart lock design for internet of medical things: an artificial intelligence approach. 2022. https://doi.org/10.1109/wispnet54241.2022.9767113.

[38] Thompson RCA. Gardening for health: a regular dose of gardening. Clinical Medicine 2018;18(3):201−5. https://doi.org/10.7861/clinmedicine.18-3-201.

[39] Building sustainable, resilient, and nutritionally enhanced local food systems through home gardens in developing countries. Development in Practice 2023. https://www.tandfonline.com/doi/abs/10.1080/09614524.2023.2218068. [Accessed 20 September 2023].

[40] Jain E, Badwaik S, Khirwadkar S, Thakare S, Uike M, Chandankhede PH. Design of smart pet food dispenser using embedded system. 2023. https://doi.org/10.1109/esci56872.2023.10100166.

[41] Prithviraj V, Sriharipriya KC. Smart pet feeder system based on google assistant. In: 2022 IEEE International Conference on Distributed Computing and Electrical Circuits and Electronics (ICDCECE); 2022. https://doi.org/10.1109/icdcece53908.2022.9792789.

[42] Stabile A. AI pets could replace dogs and cats, but expert warns that "long-term effects" are unknown. Fox News; 2023. https://www.foxnews.com/lifestyle/ai-pets-could-replace-dogs-cats-expert-warns-long-term-effects-unknown. [Accessed 20 September 2023].

[43] UNITREE Robotics® SHOP | Official Unitree Robot Dogs A1 Go1. Official Unitree Robot Dogs A1 Go1. 2021. https://unitreerobotics.net/. [Accessed 20 September 2023].

[44] Pinto G, Wang Z, Roy A, Hong T, Capozzoli A. Transfer learning for smart buildings: A critical review of algorithms, applications, and future perspectives. Advances in Applied Energy 2022;5:100084. https://doi.org/10.1016/j.adapen.2022.100084.

[45] Wearable technologies for improved safety and health on construction sites | blogs | CDC. 2019. https://blogs.cdc.gov/niosh-science-blog/2019/11/18/wearables-construction/. [Accessed 20 September 2023].

[46] Tripathi A, Sindhwani N, Anand R, Dahiya A. Role of IoT in smart homes and smart cities: challenges, benefits, and applications. Springer eBooks; 2022. p. 199−217. https://doi.org/10.1007/978-3-031-04524-0_12.

[47] Chinonso Ejidike C, Mewomo MC. Benefits of adopting smart building technologies in building construction of developing countries: review of literature. SN Applied Aciences 2023;5(2). https://doi.org/10.1007/s42452-022-05262-y.
[48] Long M. digital tattoos: the wearable tech of the future for health monitoring. 2020. https://www.electropages.com/blog/2020/05/get-inked-how-tattoos-are-being-used-medical-purposes. [Accessed 20 September 2023].
[49] Notman N. Smart tattoos are keeping tabs on our health. Chemistry World 2021. https://www.chemistryworld.com/features/smart-tattoos-are-keeping-tabs-on-our-health/4013366.article. [Accessed 20 September 2023].
[50] Project overview ‹ dermalabyss: possibilities of biosensors as a tattooed interface – MIT Media Lab. 2016. https://www.media.mit.edu/projects/d-Abyss/overview/. [Accessed 20 September 2023].
[51] Stewart G. Monitoring glucose levels, no needles required. 2021. https://www.psu.edu/news/research/story/monitoring-glucose-levels-no-needles-required/. [Accessed 20 September 2023].
[52] Moon M. Graphene-based patch can help monitor blood sugar levels. Engadget; 2016. https://www.engadget.com/2016-03-22-graphene-based-patch-diabetes.html. [Accessed 20 September 2023].
[53] Digital tattoos make healthcare more invisible. The Medical Futurist 2022. https://medicalfuturist.com/digital-tattoos-make-healthcare-more-invisible/. [Accessed 20 September 2023].
[54] Wearable/disposable sweat-based glucose monitoring device with multistage transdermal drug delivery module. Science Advances; 2017. [Accessed 27 August 2024]. https://www.science.org/doi/10.1126/sciadv.1601314
[55] Li W, Tan Yigitcanlar, Erol I, Liu A. Motivations, barriers and risks of smart home adoption: From systematic literature review to conceptual framework. Energy Research & Social Science 2021;80:102211. 102211, https://doi.org/10.1016/j.erss.2021.102211.
[56] Noury N, Virone G, Barralon P, Ye J, Rialle V, Demongeot J. New trends in health smart homes. 2004. https://doi.org/10.1109/health.2003.1218728.
[57] Patrick Lucas Austin. What Will Smart Homes Look Like 10 Years From Now? Time. 2019. https://time.com/5634791/smart-homes-future/. [Accessed 20 September 2023].
[58] Chang L. A single sensor could hold the key to the future of the smart home. Digital Trends 2017. [Accessed 27 August 2024]. https://www.digitaltrends.com/home/smart-home-sensor/
[59] Friedman D. Council Post: Smarter Homes: Moving From Tech For Tech's Sake To Tech With A Purpose. *Forbes*. https://www.forbes.com/councils/forbestechcouncil/2023/09/05/smarter-homes-moving-from-tech-for-techs-sake-to-tech-with-a-purpose/. August 12, 2024. [Accessed 27 August 2024].
[60] Barry J. 7wireVentures: Home is Where the Health Is - Digital Health Wire. Digital Health Wire; July 17, 2023. [Accessed 27 August 2024]. https://digitalhealthwire.com/7wireventures-home-is-where-the-health-is/

Further reading

[1] Reid L, Sisel G. Digital care at home: Exploring the role of smart consumer devices. Health and Place 2023;80:102961. https://doi.org/10.1016/j.healthplace.2022.102961.
[2] Acosta J, Falcone GJ, Rajpurkar Pranav, Topol EJ. Multimodal biomedical AI. Nature Medicine 2022;28(9):1773–84. https://doi.org/10.1038/s41591-022-01981-2.
[3] Kim MJ, Cho ME, Han JJ. Developing design solutions for smart homes through user-centered scenarios. Frontiers in Psychology 2020;11. https://doi.org/10.3389/fpsyg.2020.00335.
[4] Progress of advanced devices and internet of things systems as enabling technologies for smart homes and health care. ACS Materials Au 2022. https://pubs.acs.org/doi/full/10.1021/acsmaterialsau.2c00001. [Accessed 20 September 2023].
[5] Zhang S, Chhetry A, Abu Zahed Md, et al. On-skin ultrathin and stretchable multifunctional sensor for smart healthcare wearables. NPJ Flexible Electronics 2022;6(1). https://doi.org/10.1038/s41528-022-00140-4.

CHAPTER 12

Robot-assisted surgery: Past, present, and future

Jessica Grasso
Department of Surgery, Massachusetts General Hospital, Boston, MA, United States

Objectives

- Robot-assisted surgery has undergone significant developments since its inception in the 1960s. The original design for active robot-assisted surgery systems that work autonomously has predominately transitioned to dependent, master—slave systems that provide unique benefits over traditional open and laparoscopic surgery.
- The significant benefits of robot-assisted surgery include enhanced visualization, enhanced precision, and improved ergonomics. While there are many benefits to robot-assisted surgery, it has limitations. Limitations include the lack of or diminished haptic feedback, the high costs associated with purchasing, maintaining, and operating the systems, and the specialized training required of both the surgeon and care teams to operate these systems effectively.
- Integrating future technological advances in artificial intelligence, machine learning, virtual reality, and augmented reality into robot-assisted surgery is suspected to enhance the surgeon's decision-making and technical skills, not completely replace human surgeons. These advances will not come without a unique set of legal and ethical considerations.

Introduction

Robot-assisted surgery (RAS) has emerged as a transformative force in healthcare and demonstrates the power of digital medicine. This review delves into the remarkable journey of RAS, tracing its origins from visionary concepts in the 1960s to its present-day uses across various surgical specialties. The evolution of RAS embodies a fascinating tale of innovation, collaboration, and the relentless pursuit of precision and improved patient outcomes.

Digital Health. https://doi.org/10.1016/B978-0-443-23901-4.00012-X

As we look deeper into the world of RAS, this review explores the various levels of autonomy RAS systems are designed with, their advantages, limitations, and the dominant player, the da Vinci surgical systems. Furthermore, it examines the emergence of new players in the RAS industry, such as Medtronic's Hugo RAS system, signaling increased competition and choices in the field.

The review also considers the role of Artificial Intelligence (AI), Machine Learning (ML), Augmented Reality (AR), and Virtual Reality (VR) in shaping the future of RAS and the critical legal and ethical considerations that must be accounted for.

A look back on the development of robot-assisted surgery

The use of robots throughout the healthcare industry is widespread. However, the adaptation and integration of robots in surgery are unparalleled. The early ideas for RAS stem back to the 1960s when researchers began to investigate the concept of remotely controlled devices to perform medical procedures. The first use of a robotic system in surgery was in the 1980s, with the development of the PUMA 560 robotic system [1]. This system allowed for stereotactic brain biopsies to be performed. A needle inserted by a robot decreased the risk of error caused by even the slightest human hand tremors. This same system served as a precursor for the PROBOT system, designed for use in transurethral resections of the prostate (TURP) [1]. Integrated Surgical Systems developed ROBODOC around that same time. They became the first FDA-approved active robotic system [1]. ROBODOC was an orthopedic, image-guided system to improve the precision of prosthetic hip replacements. Around the time these procedure-specific, computer- and image-guided robotic systems were being developed, there was parallel research being undertaken by SRI International and the Defense Advanced Research Projects Agency (DARPA) to develop a multipurpose, teleoperated, robotic system that could decrease battlefield casualties [1]. These efforts led to the robotic surgical systems we are familiar with today: surgeon-controlled, multipurpose, robotic telepresence surgery systems.

It was a partnership between researchers at SRI International, who were interested in robotics and telemanipulation for dexterity enhancement, and researchers at the NASA Ames Research Center, who were working on computer-generated environments (now known as virtual reality) to create an immersive experience (telepresence), which launched the idea of a teleoperated robotic surgery system [2]. General surgeon COL Richard M. Satava, MD, at Silas B. Hayes Army Hospital, was introduced to this partnership at a conference and was invited to participate in the project. Together, they developed what became known as the Green Telepresence Surgery System. COL Satava presented a video demonstration of a bowel anastomosis being performed using the Green Telepresence Surgery System (open technique) to the Association of Military Surgeons of the United

States in 1992 [2]. It became immediately evident that this system could improve surgical care and decrease battlefield casualties. When Surgeon General Alcide LaNoue was shown the video, he assigned COL Satava to the Defense Advanced Research Projects Agency (DARPA), which conducts the military's leading-edge research [2]. The funding that came with being associated with DARPA led to rapid developments of the Green Telepresence Surgery System that could be used to provide remote surgical care on the battlefield. The surgeon console was installed in a Mobile Advanced Surgical Hospital (MASH) tent. The MASH was intended to be 10–35 km behind the active combat [2]. The surgery system was mounted in an armored vehicle known as the Medical Forward Area Surgical Team (MEDFAST), which could be driven directly into the battlefield where the soldier was injured. In 1994, the first demonstration of a remote telesurgical procedure (intestinal anastomosis on ex-vivo porcine intestine) was performed by a wireless microwave connection between the MASH tent and MEDFAST vehicle. Despite the early goal for RAS to allow for long-distance telesurgery to become widely available, there have only been a few cases where this has occurred [3]. Rather, the many other benefits of RAS, which will be discussed in this chapter, led to the increased interest and demand to develop robotic surgical systems further.

Surgeon and entrepreneur Frederic H. Moll, MD, soon after acquired the license for this telepresence surgical system to commercialize the system [2]. He created the company Intuitive Surgical. Intuitive Surgical is now the key player in the surgical arena for RAS. After he acquired the licensing, the system underwent a complete renovation. By 1997, the first telepresence surgery (cholecystectomy) was performed in Belgium [2]. This marked the start of the RAS revolution, which has since become the standard of care for many operations.

Two companies, Intuitive Surgical and Computer Motion, dominated the RAS industry for about a decade. Intuitive Surgical revamped the formerly known Green Telepresence Surgery System to develop an early version of the current da Vinci system [1]. The components of the da Vinci surgical system will be discussed later in this chapter. What set it apart from its competitors was the addition of compatible surgical instruments with articulated wrists. The main competitor of Intuitive Surgical was Computer Motion. Computer Motion developed a surgical system known as ZEUS. Using their Automated Endoscopic System for Optimal Positioning (AESOP), ZEUS allowed surgeons to control the position of a laparoscopic camera using voice controls [1].

Intuitive Surgical and Computer Motion merged in 2003. From then on, future innovations focused on improving the da Vinci platform [1]. The da Vinci system has dominated the RAS industry since then. In the past few years, other companies have developed RAS systems to create some level of competition and choice within the field [1].

Three main types of robotic surgical systems

Robotic surgical systems can be grouped into three main categories depending on their level of autonomy.

Active

Active systems are designed to work autonomously. These systems have preprogrammed tasks that work along preset coordinates to complete tasks with very little, if any, intervention from the surgeon [1]. Many of the early robotic surgical systems were designed to be active surgical systems. The ROBODOC described earlier was an example of this.

Semiactive

Semiactive systems are also designed to complete preprogrammed tasks while allowing the surgeon to complement the actions.

Dependent (master—slave)

The master—slave system is the mainstay of current robotic surgical systems, including the da Vinci platform. These systems lack autonomy, i.e., they do not contain preprogrammed tasks and are entirely controlled by the surgeon. Surgeon hand movements performed at a control console are then transmitted to laparoscopic surgical instruments at the surgical field [1].

Advantages of robot-assisted surgery

Robot-assisted surgical systems' innovation and technology lead to many unique benefits. As with general laparoscopic surgery, the patients reap the benefits of minimally invasive surgery (MIS), such as smaller incisions, reduced pain, less scarring, and quicker recovery times. Further, we discuss some significant benefits RAS can provide that other forms of MIS do not.

Enhanced visualization

Image

Many RAS systems (i.e., Intuitive Surgery da Vinci systems) provide 3D high-definition (HD) visualization to create an immersive surgical experience [4]. Bidimensional vision, which most laparoscopic endoscopes provide, results in loss of depth perception. The 3DHD views many robotic endoscopes produce provide a clear and magnified view that does not compromise depth perception. This enhanced visualization helps surgeons to distinguish tissue planes clearly and to more easily identify and navigate delicate structures [4]. The camera used with the da Vinci systems provides a view that is 10 times more magnified than what the human eye can see.

Control

In addition to the enhanced surgical view, surgeons maintain control over the camera's positioning. Unlike in laparoscopic surgery, where an assistant is often maneuvering the camera while the surgeon has an instrument in each hand, in RAS, the surgeon can easily switch between maneuvering the camera and the surgical instruments. In traditional laparoscopic surgery, the camera view is projected on a monitor that is positioned away from the surgical field. The surgeon is looking in one direction (toward the surgical display monitor), while their hands are operating in a different direction (toward the surgical field). In RAS, the surgeon is seated at the surgeon console, looking straight at the endoscopic view of the surgical field and working in the same direction.

Fluorescence capability

The da Vinci endoscope has integrated fluorescence capabilities. The surgeon can activate the endoscope to fluoresce injected dye using near-infrared technology [4]. This allows for real-time, image-guided identification of key anatomical structures, as well as tumor identification [4].

Enhanced precision

Robot-assisted surgical systems offer a high level of precision and improved control of the surgical instruments. Intuitive has patented EndoWrist instruments for use with the da Vinci surgical system [5]. EndoWrist instruments are designed with articulated wrists that allow for seven degrees of freedom, compared with the four degrees of freedom offered by conventional rigid laparoscopic instruments [1]. Additionally, built-in technology seamlessly adjusts hand-to-instrument ratios while simultaneously utilizing tremor reduction technology to enhance the precision and control of the instruments' tips [5]. These highly precise and steady movements reduce the risk of unintended damage to surrounding tissues. Articulated instruments also make it easier to work in deep or narrow areas of the body, such as the pelvis, where rigid laparoscopic instruments are difficult to operate. More recent innovations have also led to the development of fully wristed endoscopes.

Improved ergonomics

RAS allows for improved ergonomics for the surgeon while operating. This can reduce surgeon fatigue and the overall physical strain placed on surgeons throughout their careers.

RAS allows the surgeon to control the surgical instruments while seated at the console. This eliminates the need for a surgeon to be standing in fixed and often awkward long-term postures during the duration of the surgery. Each surgeon can adjust the operating consoles for height and reach to optimize comfort. Lee et al. [6] compared physical and cognitive ergonomic workloads using RAS and conventional laparoscopy to perform basic training tasks. Physical workload was assessed using EMG from back, shoulder, arms, and forearms muscles, and mental workload using NASA-TLX index [6,7]. This study demonstrated that physical and cognitive ergonomics with RAS were significantly less challenging [6,7].

Limitations of robot-assisted surgery

Haptic feedback

The major drawback for surgeons performing RAS is the current lack of, or decreased, haptic feedback the systems can provide. Systems that offer haptic feedback do not fully replicate the surgeon's sense of touch as in traditional surgery. This lack of, or decreased, haptic feedback creates a learning curve for the surgeon. Surgeons must learn to rely heavily on visual clues and how the tissue responds to gauge things they would typically evaluate by touch in an open or traditional laparoscopic surgery, such as how much pressure the instruments are applying to the tissue or trying to palpate a mass within an organ.

Cost

Robot-assisted surgical systems are expensive to acquire and maintain. These high costs can be a limiting factor for smaller hospitals to be able to purchase the systems and offer RAS. To help make access to RAS more financially obtainable, many manufacturers now offer different financing options, including usage-based models where you pay per case rather than purchasing the system in total upfront. Depending on the surgeon's experience level and the procedure, RAS may lend itself to longer operative times, another potential factor for increased costs. The instruments used with the RAS systems often come with a higher equipment cost than the typical open or laparoscopic surgery equipment.

Training

RAS requires surgeons and care teams to have specialized training on the proper usage and management of the robotic systems. Training surgeons to become proficient at RAS is a multistep process that includes an introduction to the system and technology, virtual training tasks and simulation work, hands-on tissue labs, case observations, and proctored cases. RAS companies such as Intuitive Surgical have developed structured training programs for surgeons, residents, and the OR staff. Because of the specialized skill set required by the surgeon and care teams, many hospitals in more rural areas do not have access to properly trained staff and thus cannot offer RAS. Intuitive Surgical has begun offering remote case observation and proctoring using telepresence technology to address this issue [8]. As RAS continues to grow in prevalence and RAS becomes the standard of care for some procedures, more surgeons will be proficient in RAS upon completion of their residency. As of 2022, over 210 academic medical centers in the United States had da Vinci systems [8]. As the next generation of surgeons enter practice proficient in RAS and patients continue to request it, hospitals will need to establish and/or grow their RAS programs.

Intuitive Surgical—da Vinci systems

The da Vinci surgical systems by Intuitive are the leading workhorses of robotic surgery today. The da Vinci Xi surgical system is the fourth generation of the Intuitive Surgical da Vinci system. Globally, more than 10 million cases have been performed using the da Vinci system since 2000 [9]. Utilization of the da Vinci system has continued to grow rapidly. According to the 2022 annual report put out by Intuitive Surgical, the number of da Vinci procedures performed annually grew approximately 18% compared with 2021 [10]. At the time of writing, there are currently three da Vinci systems: da Vinci X, da Vinci Xi, and da Vinci SP. These systems are currently approved for use in the following surgical specialties: cardiac, thoracic, urology, gynecology, colorectal, general, and head and neck.

Intuitive has recently conducted a large-scale metaanalysis examining outcome measures between robotic-assisted procedures using the da Vinci surgical system, laparoscopic surgery (or VATS), and open surgery. Results were based on a metaanalysis of peer-reviewed literature for robotic-assisted procedures (right colectomy, LAR/TME, prostatectomy, partial nephrectomy, lobectomy, and hysterectomy) published between 2010 and 2020 [11]. RAS was associated with lower rates of conversions to an open procedure, blood transfusions, 30-day complications, length of stay, 30-day mortality, and 30-day readmissions [11].

The system is composed of *three main components*.

1. *Patient Cart*: The patient cart is a four-armed system designed to be an extension of the surgeon's hands and eyes. Metal laparoscopic ports are inserted into the patient and serve as an attachment point for each arm of the system. One arm houses a camera with a binocular lens that allows for 3D vision. The other three arms are used to hold surgical instruments.
2. *Surgeon Console(s)*: After the patient cart is docked to the patient, the surgeon can visualize the surgical field and control the instruments from the surgeon console. The

surgeon visualizes the surgical field in 3DHD by looking through the eyepieces. Using the hand pieces, the surgeon has complete control over the surgical instruments and the camera. Built-in innovation offers tremor filtration [12]. When instruments capable of monopolar and bipolar energy are used, the surgeon can activate the energy using the foot pedals. When considering the surgeon's ergonomics, it is also important to note that the console can be adjusted in many ways to fit the surgeon's height and reach correctly. The da Vinci surgical system can have two surgeon consoles. While this enables two surgeons to control different instruments simultaneously, its predominant utility is for an attending surgeon to have a trainee (fellow or resident) with them at the other console. The attending surgeon and trainee can both visualize the field in 3DHD, and the attending surgeon can take control of the instruments the trainee is using at any point.

3. *Vision Cart*: The vision cart serves as the central hub. It allows communication between the three components and houses the advanced vision and energy technologies [12]. The energy generator is housed on the vision cart. The vision cart is also responsible for image processing and the information systems [12]. At the top of the vision cart is an HD touchscreen display that broadcasts the camera view for the other OR staff. The touchscreen display also allows the surgeon or trainee to mark and/or draw on the display, which is then visible in the surgeon console.

Other robotic surgical systems

The da Vinci surgical systems by Intuitive have led the way for robotic surgery, but the industry has more recently seen some new systems (i.e., Medtronic Hugo RAS system) enter the surgical arena, providing some degree of competition and choice. While the da Vinci surgical systems are multiuse systems, they do not currently have orthopedic surgery or neurosurgery applications. There are many uses for robotic surgery within these specialties, and recent innovations have worked to develop surgical systems that can address these needs.

Orthopedic surgery

Orthopedic surgeons utilize RAS systems to perform joint replacements and spine surgery. In hip and knee replacement surgery, RAS systems can be used to aid in operative planning, create a 3D model that replicates the patient's unique anatomy, predict implant size preoperatively, and guide the placement of implants with high precision using real-time computer navigation. Real-time computer navigation is accomplished using navigational pins inserted into the bone. The real-time intraoperative data allow continuous assessment of the patient's range of motion and ligamentous tension [13,14]. Some RAS systems are designed with haptic feedback, enabling the surgeon to remove damaged bone and cartilage and implant artificial joints [15]. This can result in better alignment and less tissue damage, potentially leading to faster recovery times [15]. While RAS has many potential benefits for joint replacements, two complications are unique to robot-assisted joint replacements. These complications are related to using navigational pins not used in conventional joint replacement surgery. Navigational pins can lead to pin-hole fractures and pin-site infections [13]. In spinal surgeries, such as spinal fusion, RAS systems can enhance the precision of screw placement and ensure the spine's stability.

Neurosurgery

One of the slowest adopters of robotic surgery has been the field of neurosurgery. The first FDA-approved neurosurgical robot was NeuroMate (Integrated Surgical Systems, Sacramento, California) in the 1990s for craniofacial and spinal stereotactic neurosurgery [16,17]. Since then, several other robotic neurosurgery systems have been developed including ROSA (Zimmer Biomet, Montpellier, France), Pathfinder (Prosurgics, High Wycombe, United Kingdom), NeuroArm (University of Calgary, Calgary, Alberta, Canada), SpineAssist (MAZOR Robotics, Caesarea, Israel), MKM (Zeiss, Oberkochen, Germany), CyberKnife (Accuray, Palo Alto, California, US), Steady Hand System (Johns Hopkins University, Baltimore, Maryland) and NeuRobot (Shinshu University, Matsumoto, Japan) [17]. Some of the uses of RAS in neurosurgery include stereotactic biopsies, depth electrode placement, drill guidance for burr hole placement, pedicle screw placement in spine surgery, microsurgical dissection, intracranial tumor resection, hematoma evacuation, deep brain stimulation implants, endoscopic third ventriculostomy, and the endoscopic placement of stents [17].

Robot-assisted flexible bronchoscopy

Robot-assisted flexible bronchoscopy improves the precision of endoscopic biopsies and expands the possibilities of what can be biopsied. Ion by Intuitive is a robot-assisted minimally invasive biopsy platform leading the way in this arena. Lung cancer is the leading cause of cancer deaths worldwide. Early detection and diagnosis of malignant lung masses can improve survival outcomes. Limiting factors for early diagnosis and, thus, intervention include the mass size and location. The mass must be large enough to locate and obtain a sufficient biopsy sample, and the mass's location must be amenable to biopsy. More than 70% of all lung cancer nodules are located in the peripheral one-third of the lung [18,19]. The narrow airways in the periphery of the lung make it challenging for a standard bronchoscope to navigate through to obtain a sufficient diagnostic sample. Using the Ion system has made it possible to sample smaller masses (earlier in the course of the disease) and masses far out into the periphery of the lung, which previously would not be possible using traditional methods [19].

Before a robot-assisted flexible bronchoscopy and biopsy, the patient's CT scan is uploaded to generate 3D airway trees [20]. From this model, a digital roadmap is created that is then used during the procedure to guide the proceduralist to the identified target [20]. Ion utilizes a 3.5 mm catheter with a 2.0 mm working channel that can articulate 180 degrees in any direction, allowing advanced maneuverability to all 18 segments of the lungs [20]. The system is also designed with shape sense technology that measures the full shape of the catheter, providing real-time precise location and shape information throughout navigation and biopsy [20]. The provider's view from Ion's vision probe is synchronized with the virtual roadmap created during the preprocedural planning to provide navigational guidance to the desired target [20]. Ion's software allows for integration with radial endobronchial ultrasound (EBUS), external cone-beam CT, and Cios Spin (Siemens Medical Solutions, Pennsylvania, US) to improve navigation to the target to account for CT-to-body divergence [20]. The catheter is locked in place once the targeted pulmonary nodule is reached [20]. This allows multiple biopsy needle passes without catheter movement. Robot-assisted minimally invasive bronchoscopy for lung biopsies, specifically with the Ion system by Intuitive, is still relatively new. However, early data from a multicenter study demonstrate a diagnostic yield of 83%, a mean lesion size of 17 mm, a sensitivity for cancer between 84% and 88%, and a 0% pneumothorax rate requiring a chest tube [21]. In addition to its use in pulmonary biopsies, the Ion system has been used intraoperatively to aid in locating masses that are too small to identify or those situated deep in the lunch parenchyma. Using the Ion system, the bronchoscope is navigated to the pulmonary nodule, and then indocyanine green is injected into the nodule. The da Vinci system is then docked, and when the fluorescence technology is activated, the indocyanine green fluoresces to identify the location of the pulmonary nodule for surgical resection.

The future of robot-assisted surgery and the role artificial intelligence, machine learning, augmented reality, and virtual reality will play

As discussed, RAS has developed and undergone many advancements relatively quickly. RAS is now used in almost every surgical subspecialty and, in some cases, has become the standard of care. As innovation continues and new technology emerges, RAS will continue to transform. From the system's design, it is expected that the systems will become more compact, allowing for a smaller overall blueprint of the system. This will help increase accessibility where smaller operating spaces are a limiting factor for offering RAS. From an accessibility standpoint, developing secure, reliable, and cost-effective infrastructure for telesurgery could vastly improve training and patient care access. A trained surgeon in one part of the world could provide advanced surgical care to a patient in another, where they otherwise may not have had access to that level of care.

Haptic feedback

The addition/improvement of haptic feedback would address a significant limitation that surgeons face with RAS. Haptics encompasses both kinesthetic (force) and cutaneous (tactile) feedback. In the context of RAS, this refers to the surgeon's sense of force feedback and touch that allows the surgeon to manipulate tissues and delicate structures safely. Many RAS systems lack haptic feedback, and those that offer some element of haptics are limited in their abilities. Diminished or absent haptic feedback can potentially lead to increased intraoperative injury. Current systems can better be defined as "haptic-enabled robotic systems." [22] These systems achieve haptic feedback through sensory substitution, such as visual excessive force alerts, vibration alerts, color marking overlay, and warning sounds [22]. The goal of haptic technology in RAS is for the surgeon to feel their hands are in contact with the patient rather than the robot instruments. To achieve haptic feedback, you need artificial haptic sensors on the patient-side robot to acquire haptic information and haptic displays to convey the information to the surgeon [23]. Reducing the latency between the surgeon's input and feedback is crucial to ensure precise control. Developing and integrating improved haptic feedback into RAS systems are critical to enhancing the surgeon's precision.

RAS has developed significantly from a technological standpoint over the past 20 years. However, we have only just begun to release its full potential. The continued integration of advances in Artificial Intelligence, Machine Learning, Augmented Reality, and Virtual Reality holds a lot of promise and potential for the future of RAS.

Artificial intelligence

Artificial Intelligence (AI) could provide real-time information for surgical planning and intraoperative decision-making guidance. Preoperatively, surgeons will use AI to risk-stratify patients. An AI-generated analysis of all preoperative mobile and clinical data could provide a more personalized risk score for operative planning and yield valuable predictors for postoperative care [24]. Preoperatively, AI could also analyze patient imaging such as CT scans and MRIs. 3D reconstructions made from the imaging can then be used in surgical planning. Overlaying these models that were created preoperatively on the surgeon's view during surgery will guide intraoperative decisions and aid in precise navigation. This will allow for better intraoperative planning as it will be able to identify critical structures, locate where a tumor is, and inform surgeons of possible anatomic anomalies that may be present.

Intraoperative monitoring of EMR data with real-time operative video, vital signs, instrument/hand tracking, and electrosurgical energy use could lead to real-time prediction and avoidance of adverse events [24]. AI can anticipate an operation's next 15–30 s based on its review of millions of surgical videos [25]. In the future, AI predictions could allow surgeons to change their course of action if necessary [25].

Postoperative data from the EMR and personal devices worn by the patient after discharge could be used to predict complications [24].

AI has the potential to augment surgical decision-making across all phases of perioperative care and to create more personalized patient-driven surgical plans based on predictive data. In addition to augmenting individual patient care, it also has the capability to enhance the sharing of knowledge to generate a database of practices and techniques that can then be applied to a multitude of patients.

Machine learning

Machine Learning (ML) enables machines to learn and make predictions by recognizing patterns [24]. As ML advances within the surgical arena, robotic surgical systems could gain some degree of autonomy. Under the surgeon's supervision, the system could perform preprogrammed simple tasks such as suturing and knot tying with little human intervention. AI and ML are positioned to augment the surgeon's decision-making and technical skills, but do not completely replace human surgeons [25]. ML could also benefit novice surgeons by analyzing their performance and then creating personalized training plans based on their strengths and weaknesses.

Augmented and virtual reality

Augmented Reality (AR) and Virtual Reality (VR) will further enhance visualization to continue to improve precision and accuracy. We have already elaborated on future uses of AR in our discussions on haptic feedback and image overlay from AI. Perhaps one of the most significant benefits of AR, VR, and AI within RAS is their use in training. The merging of VR and haptic feedback technological advances could prove invaluable for training purposes. Novice surgeons to RAS and residents will be able to practice and develop their skills on simulators that provide a realistic and immersive experience. This will enable surgeons to better understand tissue properties and practice surgical techniques and procedures to refine their skills in a risk-free environment.

The capabilities of RAS and the integration of AI, ML, AR, and VR have only just begun to be exposed. Ongoing technological advancements and innovations will transform all phases of surgical care and how the next generation of surgeons are trained. These changes will require extensive testing, validation, and regulatory approval to ensure the technology is reliable, secure, and well-integrated into the existing infrastructure to ensure patient safety and efficacy.

Legal and ethical considerations of robot-assisted surgery

The use of RAS and the integration of AI, ML, AR, and VR pose unique legal and ethical considerations to ensure patient safety and privacy.

Patient safety

Patient safety has to be at the forefront of all discussions and implementations of RAS. RAS should not compromise patient safety or increase adverse event rates. RAS systems are complex machines that rely on advanced technology and programming. Emergency mechanisms and trained personnel must be in place to deal with mechanical and technological failures that can arise during a procedure. Surgeons must be well-trained and proficient in using RAS systems to minimize the risk of errors and complications.

Informed consent

The informed consent process should remain transparent about the surgeon's intent to perform RAS. Patients must understand the risks and benefits and be educated on alternative care modalities.

Accessibility and equity

As discussed within the limitations of RAS, the cost of acquiring, maintaining, and utilizing RAS systems is currently high. Ethical considerations must be made to ensure that access to RAS is equitable and not limited to certain socioeconomic groups.

Liability and accountability

In rare cases where the RAS system may malfunction, there has been a lot of discussion regarding who should be liable for potential adverse advents. As RAS systems continue to gain some degree of autonomy, this discussion will gain increased importance and necessitate clear guidelines and ethical frameworks.

Data security and privacy

RAS and the integration of AI, ML, VR, and AR lend to collecting large amounts of patient data, including intraoperative videos. Robust security measures must be in place to maintain patient confidentiality and comply with privacy regulations.

Conclusion

RAS has emerged as a remarkable convergence of technology and medicine, revolutionizing the way surgical procedures are planned and conducted. A look back at the history of RAS has unveiled a fascinating journey from its inception in the 1960s to its present-day dominance in several surgical specialties, exemplified by the da Vinci surgical system.

RAS systems have been categorized into three types, with the master–slave configuration typified by the da Vinci system dominating the landscape. The advantages of RAS, including enhanced visualization, precision, and improved ergonomics, have been thoroughly examined. Yet, it's crucial to acknowledge the current limitations, such as the absence of haptic feedback, cost considerations, and the need for specialized training.

Looking to the future, the continued integration of AI, ML, AR, and VR into RAS holds immense promise. These technologies are poised to transform surgical planning, intraoperative decision-making, and surgical training, offering real-time insights, unparalleled precision, and immersive educational experiences.

Ethical and legal considerations have been brought to the forefront, emphasizing the paramount importance of patient safety, transparent informed consent, equitable access, clear liability frameworks, and robust data security and privacy measures.

In conclusion, robot-assisted surgery has redefined modern surgical care standards and paved the way for a future where technology and medicine harmonize to enhance patient outcomes. The legacy of RAS in digital medicine is one of ingenuity, innovation, precision, and a commitment to advancing the frontiers of healthcare.

Assessment

1. Should future advancements in robot-assisted surgery focus on enhancing the collaboration between the robotic surgical system and the surgeon or on robot autonomy?
2. How will artificial intelligence influence surgical planning and interventions in the future?
3. Who should be held liable for adverse events that occur in rare instances of RAS systems malfunctioning?
4. What would it take to make remote surgery (telesurgery) a reality? How would this expand access to healthcare?

References

[1] Lane T. A short history of robotic surgery. Annals of the Royal College of Surgeons of England 2018;100(6_sup):5–7. https://doi.org/10.1308/rcsann.supp1.5.

[2] Satava RM. Robotic surgery: from past to future—a personal journey. Surgical Clinics of North America 2003;83(6):1491–500. https://doi.org/10.1016/S0039-6109(03)00168-3.

[3] George EI, Brand TC, LaPorta A, Marescaux J, Satava RM. Origins of robotic surgery: from skepticism to standard of care. Journal of the Society of Laparoendoscopic Surgeons 2018;22(4). https://doi.org/10.4293/jsls.2018.00039.

[4] Intuitive Surgical 2023. Da Vinci learning. 2023. https://www.intuitive.com/en-us/learning. [Accessed 4 September 2023].

[5] Intuitive Surgical 2023. Why robotic bronchoscopy. 2023. https://www.intuitive.com/en-us/products-and-services/ion/why-robotic-bronchoscopy. [Accessed 13 September 2023].

[6] Lee GI, Lee MR, Clanton T, Sutton E, Park AE, Marohn MR. Comparative assessment of physical and cognitive ergonomics associated with robotic and traditional laparoscopic surgeries. Surgical Endoscopy 2014;28(2):456–65. https://doi.org/10.1007/s00464-013-3213-z.

[7] Sánchez-Margallo FM, Sánchez-Margallo JA, Arshad M. Laparoscopic surgery. In: InTech ergonomics in laparoscopic surgery; 2017. https://doi.org/10.5772/66170. 978-953-51-2963-9.

[8] Intuitive Surgical 2023. Da Vinci instruments. 2023. https://www.intuitive.com/en-us/products-and-services/da-vinci/instruments. [Accessed 4 September 2023].

[9] Intuitive Surgical 2023. Maturing clinical evidence. 2021. https://www.intuitive.com/en-us/-/media/ISI/Intuitive/Pdf/maturing-clinical-evidence-outcomes-summary.pdf.

[10] Intuitive Surgical 2022. Annual Report 2022. https://isrg.intuitive.com/static-files/0cb4f097-4e55-47b2-bfb8-dd4f9d45182b. [Accessed 29 August 2023].

[11] Intuitive Surgical 2023. Intuitive reaches 10 million procedures performed using da Vinci surgical systems. 2021. https://isrg.intuitive.com/news-releases/news-release-details/intuitive-reaches-10-million-procedures-performed-using-da-vinci/. [Accessed 6 September 2023].

[12] Intuitive Surgical 2023. Da Vinci surgical systems. 2023. https://www.intuitive.com/en-us/products-and-services/da-vinci/systems. [Accessed 2 September 2023].

[13] Nogalo C, Meena A, Abermann E, Fink C. Complications and downsides of the robotic total knee arthroplasty: a systematic review. Knee Surgery, Sports Traumatology, Arthroscopy 2023;31(3):736–50. https://doi.org/10.1007/s00167-022-07031-1.

[14] Marchand RC, Sodhi N, Bhowmik-Stoker M, Scholl L, Condrey C, Khlopas A, Sultan AA, Newman JM, Mont MA. Does the robotic arm and preoperative CT planning help with 3D intraoperative total knee arthroplasty planning? Journal of Knee Surgery 2019;32(08):742–9. https://doi.org/10.1055/s-0038-1668122.

[15] Siljander B, Vigdorchik J, Sheth NP. Robotic-assisted joint replacement. 2022. 2023, https://www.orthoinfo.org/en/robotic-assisted-joint-replacement/. [Accessed 2 September 2023].

[16] Benabid AL, Cinquin P, Lavalle S, Le Bas JF, Demongeot J, De Rougemon J. Computer-driven robot for stereotactic surgery connected to CT scan and magnetic resonance imaging: technological design and preliminary results. Applied Neurophysiology 1987;50(1–6):153–4. https://doi.org/10.1159/000100701.

[17] Ryoo J, McGuire LS, Slavin K. AANS neurosurgeon the state of robotics in neurosurgery. 2021. 2021, https://aansneurosurgeon.org/feature/the-state-of-robotics-in-neurosurgery/. [Accessed 2 September 2023].

[18] Horeweg N, van der Aalst CM, Thunnissen E, Nackaerts K, Weenink C, Groen HJM, Lammers J-WJ, Aerts JG, Scholten ET, van Rosmalen J, Mali W, Oudkerk M, de Koning HJ. Characteristics of lung cancers detected by computer tomography screening in the randomized NELSON trial. American Journal of Respiratory and Critical Care Medicine 2013;187(8):848–54. https://doi.org/10.1164/rccm.201209-1651OC.

[19] Intuitive Surgical 2023. How ion works. 2023. https://www.intuitive.com/en-us/products-and-services/ion/how-ion-works. [Accessed 13 September 2023].

[20] Intuitive Surgical 2023. Da Vinci vision. 2023. https://www.intuitive.com/en-us/products-and-services/da-vinci/vision. [Accessed 4 September 2023].

[21] Ost D, Pritchett M, Reisenauer J, Simoff M, Diaz-Mendoza J, Fernandez-Bussy S, Majid A, Casal R, Keyes C, Parikh M, Folch E. Prospective multicenter analysis of shape-sensing robotic-assisted bronchoscopy for the biopsy of pulmonary nodules: results from the PRECIsE study. Chest Journal 2021;160(4):A2531–3. https://doi.org/10.1016/j.chest.2021.08.034.

[22] Alip SL, Kim J, Rha KH, Han WK. Urologic Clinics of North America, Future Platforms of Robotic Surgery. 2021. p. 49. 2023, https://www.clinicalkey.com/#!/content/playContent/1-s2.0-S0094014321018723?scrollTo=%23hl0000181.

[23] Okamura AM. Haptic feedback in robot-assisted minimally invasive surgery. Current Opinion in Urology 2009;19(1):102–7. https://doi.org/10.1097/MOU.0b013e32831a478c.

[24] Hashimoto DA, Rosman G, Rus D, Meireles OR. Artificial intelligence in surgery: promises and perils. Annals of Surgery 2018;268(1):70–6. https://doi.org/10.1097/SLA.0000000000002693.

[25] McCartney J. ACS bulletin. 2023 ACS Bulletin 2023;108(66). 8-15 AI Is Poised to "Revolutionize" Surgery, https://www.facs.org/for-medical-professionals/news-publications/news-and-articles/bulletin/2023/june-2023-volume-108-issue-6/.

CHAPTER 13

Digital therapeutics

Agnes Marcia Compagnone and Rachel Irene Cole
School of Medical Sciences, Harrogate, TN, United States

Objectives

- There are 10 core principles that a digital product must adhere to in order to be defined as a digital therapeutic.
- The time and monetary expense to develop and bring a digital therapeutic product to market are significantly less than those of a pharmaceutical agent.
- DTx allow clinicians and healthcare teams to close several healthcare gaps while expanding their scope of services and care to patients.
- As traditional medical approaches intertwine with cutting-edge digital solutions, the need for the clinician to access accurate and reliable information becomes paramount.

Understanding digital therapeutics

Place in the digital health ecosystem

Digital health, digital medicine, and digital therapeutics are distinct yet interconnected facets of the healthcare landscape, each with its unique focus and purpose (Table 13.1). Digital health encompasses a broad spectrum of technology-driven solutions aimed at improving healthcare delivery and patient outcomes. It encompasses everything from electronic health records (EHRs) and telemedicine platforms to wearable devices and mobile health apps, all designed to enhance healthcare accessibility, efficiency, and patient engagement.

Digital health has been described as "the convergence of health care and the internet." [5] According to Ronquillo et al., "Digital health refers to the use of information and communications technologies in medicine and other health professions to manage illnesses and health risks and to promote wellness." [1] The objective of digital health is to enhance the efficiency of healthcare delivery using both hardware and software, including mobile phones and applications, wearable devices, and remote monitoring sensors [3].

Digital Health. https://doi.org/10.1016/B978-0-443-23901-4.00013-1

Table 13.1: Key chapter terms and definitions.

Key terms	Definition
Digital health	Digital health refers to the use of information and communications technologies in medicine and other health professions to manage illnesses and health risks and to promote wellness [1].
Digital medicine	A subset of digital health that specifically emphasizes the use of technology to diagnose, monitor, and treat medical conditions [2].
Digital therapeutics (DTx)	A distinct category within digital medicine, focusing primarily on software-based interventions to treat, manage, or prevent specific medical conditions [3,4].
Digital biomarker	An objective, quantifiable, physiological, and behavioral measure collected using digital devices that are portable, wearable, implantable, or digestible.
SaMD, SiMD	Software *as* a medical device, software *in* a medical device
Prescription DTx (PDTx)	A digital therapeutic product that is prescribed by a licensed healthcare practitioner.
Internet of Things (IoT)	The network of devices that contain the hardware, software, firmware, and actuators, which allow the devices to connect, interact, and freely exchange data and information.
Digital therapeutics Alliance (DTA)	A global nonprofit founded in 2017 engaged in the evidence-driven advancement of digital therapeutics.

Digital medicine, on the other hand, is a subset of digital health that specifically emphasizes the use of technology to diagnose, monitor, and treat medical conditions. It often involves the integration of advanced sensors, data analytics, and artificial intelligence into medical devices and interventions, enabling healthcare professionals to make more informed decisions and patients to manage their health more effectively, for example, an ingestible sensor [2].

Digital therapeutics (DTx) represent a distinct category within digital medicine, focusing primarily on software-based interventions to treat, manage, or prevent specific medical conditions.

Defining and differentiating digital therapeutics within the digital health space

Unlike general health apps, DTx undergo rigorous clinical testing and receive regulatory approvals, affirming their efficacy and safety. These therapeutic solutions can range from cognitive-behavioral therapy apps for mental health disorders to software programs that assist with medication adherence for chronic diseases. DTx not only extends the traditional boundaries of medicine but also offers the potential to deliver highly personalized, evidence-based treatments directly to patients, often in conjunction with or as an alternative to traditional pharmaceuticals [6]

While digital health encompasses a wide range of technology-enabled healthcare solutions, digital medicine narrows the focus to the use of technology in the diagnosis and treatment of medical conditions [2]. DTx, as a subset of digital medicine, specifically refers to software-driven interventions with proven clinical benefits, providing a promising avenue for the future of healthcare delivery and patient care. Table 13.2.

Table 13.2: Digital therapeutic product examples.

Focus areas: medical condition	DTx product website	Product overview	Clinical outcomes/impact
Psychiatry and behavioral health			
Anxiety (GAD)	Daylight® https://www.bighealth.com/daylight/	Based on proven cognitive behavioral therapy, users access a structured, responsive program, and can see improvements within a few weeks and only 10 minutes usage per day. Indicated for adults ages 18 years and older.	Helped 71% of patients achieve clinical improvement in anxiety.
Attention disorders (ADHD)	Endeavor® https://www.endeavorrx.com/	A PDT video gamification platform that improves attention function as measured by computer-based testing in children ages 8–12 years old with primarily inattentive or combined-type ADHD, who have a demonstrated attention issue.	Demonstrated improvements in ADHD impairment, with responder rates ranging 48%–50% after 1-month treatment and 68% following a second month of treatment.
Depression	SparkRx® https://www.sparkrx.com/	Delivers core components of cognitive behavioral therapy (CBT) through a patient's mobile device. Indicated for patients 13–22 years of age with depressive symptoms.	Clinically meaningful reduction in depression symptoms. 24% of participants showed a treatment response and 17% were in remission by the end of the intervention.
Posttraumatic stress disorder (PTSD) Panic disorder (PD) Panic Attacks	Freespira® https://freespira.com/for-individuals/	A digital therapeutic that incorporates a proprietary sensor, physiological feedback display, and coaching to train patients over 28-days to normalize the respiratory irregularities underlying a key physiological driver of anxiety attacks and PTSD symptoms (carbon dioxide hypersensitivity).	PTSD: At 6-month posttreatment, 89% reported significant decrease in symptom based on CAPS-5 Score (validated PTSD assessment) and 50% were in remission. Panic: 86% panic attack free immediately posttreatment; 73% panic attack free 12 months posttreatment; 94% clinically significant reduction in panic symptoms at 12 months posttreatment

Continued

Table 13.2: Digital therapeutic product examples.—cont'd

Focus areas: medical condition	DTx product website	Product overview	Clinical outcomes/impact
Alcohol use	Vorvida® https://us.vorvida.com/	An online program that can be accessed 24/7 on any device. It uses artificial intelligence to interact with live therapists, asks questions and analyzes responses to provide customized feedback and strategies to help manage drinking behaviors.	Demonstrated a statistically significant reduction in average daily alcohol consumption at 3 and 6 months when compared to care-as-usual.
Diabetes			
Diabetes (Type 2 diabetes)	d-Nav® https://d-nav.com	A PDT that combines an FDA-cleared mobile app and virtual clinical support to automatically interprets data and independently initiate management; adjusts insulin prescription directly to the patient. Patient glucose readings and insulin recommendations are available for clinicians to review via a dedicated provider portal.	Clinical trials demonstrated improved A1C without increasing the risk for hypoglycemia; 90% of patients saw lower A1C levels in 90 days; long-lasting A1C reduction sustained for over 3 years.
Diabetes (Type 1 and Type 2 diabetes)	Dario® https://mydario.com/	Dario Smart Meter and accompanying app; interaction with live coaches and real-time data analytics provide personalized support for better health. Help individuals with type 1 and type 2 diabetes perform self-testing to monitor the effectiveness of diabetes control.	People with high-risk type 2 diabetes improved their A1c by 1.4% over 12 months; 40% reduction in average high readings (>180 mg/dL); 14% reduction in glucose variability sustainable for 2 years.
Diabetes and depression	Hellobetter® depression & diabetes https://hellobetter.de/en/online-courses/diabetes-and-depression/	An online digital intervention program accessible via the web or a mobile device that treats depressive symptoms in people with type 1 and 2 diabetes; developed and evaluated by a team of scientists and psychotherapists and is based on proven cognitive behavioral therapy concepts.	Clinically proven to reduce depressive symptoms and diabetes-related emotional distress, and improve quality of life for individuals with diabetes. RCT validated, with 92% satisfaction rates saying that they would recommend the program.

Continued

Table 13.2: Digital therapeutic product examples.—cont'd

Focus areas: medical condition	DTx product website	Product overview	Clinical outcomes/impact
OTHER INDICATIONS			
Pain disorder	HelloBetter® chronic pain https://hellobetter.de/en/online-courses/chronic-pain/	A digital therapeutic program aimed at reducing the extent to which chronic pain hinders engagement with physical, cognitive, emotional, and recreational activities. This digital intervention was developed and evaluated by a team of scientists and psychotherapists and is based on the well-established methods of cognitive behavioral therapy (CBT) and acceptance and commitment therapy (ACT).	Clinically proven to reduce pain interference, increase pain acceptance and improve overall quality of life for individuals with chronic pain. Extensively studied and found to be effective in a randomized controlled trial.
Sleep health (poor Sleep and Insomnia)	Sleepio® https://www.bighealth.com/sleepio/	Intended for the improvement of poor sleep and the management of insomnia disorder in adults aged 18 years. The program accessible via a computer or mobile device. Adjunct therapy with usual medical care for insomnia or self-help tool to improve poor sleep.	Helped 76% of patients achieve clinical improvement in insomnia. Significant improvements in sleep, functional health, psychological well-being, and sleep-related quality of life.
Urinary and Fecal Incontinence	Leva® Pelvic health system https://www.levatherapy.com/	Treats female urinary and chronic fecal incontinence through rehabilitation and training of weak pelvic floor muscles. Consists of an intravaginal motion sensor and an app-based software program accessible via web or mobile device. The software program directs exercise performance and dosing, monitors symptoms and outcomes, and provides health education.	Participants using Leva report statistically and clinically significant symptom improvement as early as 4-week and continued improvement through the 8-week study period, as measured by validated outcome measures.

Digital Therapeutic Alliance-Product Library https://dtxalliance.org/understanding-dtx/product-library/

Categories

DTx can be broadly categorized into three distinct but interconnected domains: prevention, management, and treatment [4]. In the realm of prevention, DTx are designed to proactively mitigate the risk of developing specific health conditions or diseases. These interventions often leverage data analytics, predictive algorithms, and personalized guidance to help individuals adopt healthier lifestyles, make informed choices, and adhere to preventive measures [6].

DTx also excel in the management of chronic conditions. They provide tools and support systems that enable patients to monitor their health, track symptoms, and adhere to treatment plans. This category includes remote monitoring solutions for chronic diseases such as diabetes, hypertension, and asthma, which allow healthcare providers to remotely assess patient data and make timely interventions. Moreover, management-focused DTx often incorporates behavioral interventions, fostering patient engagement and improving disease management outcomes.

The treatment category of DTx represents a more advanced and specialized subset, where software-based interventions are used as primary or adjunctive treatment for specific medical conditions [6]. In summary, DTx deliver evidence-based therapeutic interventions driven by high-quality software programs to prevent, manage, or treat a medical disorder or disease [3]. In fact, the first of the 10 core principles of DTx outlines that a DTx must act within one of these categories.

Core principles

Ten core principles underpin this groundbreaking field of DTx. Each principle encapsulates a fundamental tenet, from rigorous clinical validation to patient-centered design, reflecting the ethos of an innovative industry dedicated to enhancing healthcare outcomes through the power of software and data. The core principles of DTx provide a comprehensive framework for understanding the specific characteristics a digital health product must have to be defined as a digital therapeutic per the Digital Therapeutic Alliance (DTA) [3].

The DTA outlines the foundational core principles to which all DTx products must adhere [3]

1. Prevent, manage, or treat a medical disorder or disease.
2. Produce a medical intervention that is driven by software.
3. Incorporate design, manufacture, and quality best practices.
4. Engage end users in product development and usability processes.
5. Incorporate patient privacy and security protections.
6. Apply product deployment, management, and maintenance best practices.
7. Publish trial results inclusive of clinically meaningful outcomes in peer-reviewed journals.

8. Be reviewed and cleared or certified by regulatory bodies as required to support product claims of risk, efficacy, and intended use.
9. Make claims appropriate to clinical evaluation and regulatory status.
10. Collect, analyze, and apply real-world evidence and/or product performance data.

A product cannot claim to be a digital therapeutic unless it meets ALL of these criteria [3].

Regulatory landscape

Regulatory oversight of DTx is a critical component of ensuring patient safety and the effectiveness of these innovative healthcare solutions. In the United States, the primary regulatory authority is the Center for Devices and Radiological Health (CDRH) within the U.S. Food and Drug Administration (FDA) [7]. Within the FDA, DTx are categorized as a medical device, including Software as a Medical Device (SaMD) and Software in a Medical Device (SiMD) [7].

Depending on the level of risk and intended use, DTx may require FDA clearance or approval. Lower-risk products may go through the FDA's 510(k) clearance process, which assesses whether the device is substantially equivalent to an existing legally marketed device [7]. Higher-risk products may need to undergo the more rigorous premarket approval (PMA) process, which involves extensive clinical testing to demonstrate safety and effectiveness [7]. For more details on the regulatory landscape surrounding digital therapeutics, please refer to the next chapter, Digital Therapeutics II.

Benefits, barriers, and challenges

As digital therapeutic deliverables expand, further evolve, gain momentum into routine clinical care, and become more prominent healthcare contributors, clinicians, healthcare teams, organizations, and industry stakeholders (including patients) must broaden their knowledge of the innovative benefits, barriers, and challenges digital therapeutics present. Table 13.3.

Gaining diverse viewpoints on digital therapeutic advantages, shortcomings, and difficulties will advance the future innovation, implementation, and adoption of these novel resources from global health, clinical practice, and patient perspectives.

The following readings will explore digital therapeutic benefits, barriers, and challenges to the adoption and highlight the implications these new treatments have on healthcare economics, delivery, and accessibility.

Table 13.3: Benefits and barriers.

	Benefits	Barriers
Economics	• Time to market • Development cost • 40% reduction in ED visits post AMI • 30% reduction in 30- and 90-day hospital readmission rates post AMI	• Costs of training for clinicians, healthcare team members, patients, caregivers • Financial burden of supporting technological architecture
Clinicians/ Clinical Setting	• Decreases fiscal, time, and QoL burdens of chronic disease by improving patient monitoring • Enable clinician monitoring of patient disease metrics • Increased focus and time-efficiency of visits	• Training and integration into clinical workflows • Patient buy-in • Added cybersecurity and IT measures to be obtained
Patients	• No drug toxicity, medication side effects • Promotion of healthy behaviors to prevent poor outcomes • Empowers patients with self-specific information driving more active role in self-care • Increases access to care	• Access to digital devices • Broadband internet availability • Digital hardware costs • Low technology literacy • Fears of compromised health data • Low cognitive ability • Lack of patient education

Benefits

Digital therapeutics benefits are reshaping how the world interfaces with healthcare. These innovative approaches are transforming health system operations, healthcare delivery, clinical team practices, patient accessibility, and impacting health outcomes.

Economic: Therapeutic development costs, time to market, and means of distribution have significant financial implications, collectively influencing healthcare at all levels. The time to develop and bring a digital therapeutic product to market is significantly less than that of a pharmaceutical agent because it requires fewer clinical trials and mandated regulations to get regulatory approval. According to Van Dorman, the development period for a DTx averages 3–7 years. Whereas traditional (nonpandemic) pharmaceutical agents take an average of 12 years [8–10]. Furthermore, pharmaceutical development costs are estimated to be 1.8 billion, and DTx are considerably lower, resulting in substantial financial savings and time efficiencies compared with traditional pharmacotherapies.

Research evaluating DTx in the form of digital care and disease management solutions has demonstrated substantial reductions in hospital readmission and emergency room visit rates. In a study conducted by Mayo Clinic and Healarium, involving post acute myocardial infarction (AMI) patients, digital integration of tracking measures, reminders, health status, goals, and education elements successfully decreased 3 month readmission and emergency department visits for 40% of the post an acute myocardial infarction (AMI) patients [11,12]. Reductions in hospitalizations and emergency room visits produce sizable cost savings globally, for healthcare systems, clinical practices, and individual patients.

Clinicians and Clinical Settings: Digital therapeutics can complement pharmacotherapies, existing medical modalities, clinical interventions, and disease management practices. These novel technological tools provide healthcare teams and clinicians boundless possibilities, including providing personalized treatment plans and interventions to influence patient health outcomes positively [9,11]. With multiple patient information touchpoints, clinicians and healthcare teams can effectively monitor patients' medication adherence, behavior changes, and personal data, decreasing fiscal, time, and quality of life burdens of chronic diseases [11].

A patient's adherence to a prescribed medication regimen is instrumental in clinical treatment plans, clinician decision-making, and patient outcomes. In research studying medication adherence, approximately 80% of patients demonstrated medication compliance when digital therapeutics were utilized versus 50% of patients taking pharmacotherapy [13,14].

Digital therapeutics integrates comprehensive artificial intelligence, data analytics, and predictive models, enabling clinicians and clinical care teams to detect patient changes, monitor progressions, forecast earlier, implement advanced interventions and care plan revisions, and encourage lifestyle changes more readily. Various means of data collection (asynchronous, real-time, and continuous data monitoring) within DTx enable clinicians to monitor disease metrics and provide efficient, individualized care solutions to aid in averting poor health outcomes [11,15].

DTx empowers healthcare teams and clinicians with advanced opportunities to collect and assess data before patient medical appointments. Enabling subsequent patient visits to be more focused and time-efficient and creating time for clinicians to enhance patient relations and engagement.[9]Cumulatively speaking, digital therapeutics allows clinicians and healthcare teams to close several healthcare gaps while expanding their scope of services and care to patients.

Patients: Many digital therapeutics effectively promote behavior and lifestyle changes to help users manage, stabilize, or treat their medical conditions and prevent poor health outcomes. Unlike pharmacotherapies, digital therapeutics do not produce drug toxicity, medication side effects, drug-to-drug interactions, or major adverse events. Digital therapeutics' side effects are considered minor and are primarily associated with side effects related to digital device usage to access DTx software applications [8,16].

DTx real-time data collection generates time-sensitive digital insights, which guide, promote, and prompt patient-specific behavior changes. Digital therapeutics embody interactive and proactive software that, in turn, generates information specific to the patient, empowering patients and encouraging users to take a more active role and responsibility in their care, health goals, and outcomes [11,15].

Patients and caregivers can also access DTx software platforms and quality care solutions from the convenience of their homes or private workplaces. Digital therapeutics' ease of accessibility increases access to care, especially for patients who have to contend with transportation or geographical barriers [15].

Barriers

When comparing DTX versus pharmacotherapies from a patient perspective, limitations primarily revolve around preutilization requirements (i.e., training, digital literacy, and cognitive abilities), patient accessibility, and patient information security. The drawbacks of DTXs from a financial and clinical perspective are more focused on training, patient engagement, and data security [6,8].

Economic: Compared with pharmacotherapy, digital therapeutics have added costs to support education and training for clinicians, healthcare team members, patients, and caregivers. There are also financial burdens to support the technological architecture, data, and cybersecurity measures, including proper digital equipment and software, ongoing IT maintenance and preventive support, and integration of electronic health records [8,9,15].

Clinicians and Clinical Settings: Training, integration into clinical and practitioner workflows, and educating patients are common barriers affecting DTx clinician prescribing and incorporating DTx into clinical practice care plans [6,8,15].

Properly incorporating DTx into clinical practice workflows and getting patient buy-in require clinicians and supporting healthcare team members to obtain additional training. Training can be multifaceted, time- and labor-extensive, and entails learning about reimbursement, the intricacies of a wearable device, a digital health application, research studies, patient education measures, data retrieval, cybersecurity, and more.

Because digital therapeutics demands advanced data storage and utilization of personal health data, it involves added cybersecurity and information technology measures to be supported, employed, and accounted for by clinicians and clinical practices, which is an additional barrier for clinicians and clinical trials versus traditional pharmaceuticals [8,9].

Patients: Although digital therapeutics offers patients many healthcare benefits, some patients will encounter digital barriers related to DTx. Digital technology obstructions include access to supporting digital devices (i.e., phone, computer, or tablet), broadband

Internet availability, digital hardware costs, low technology literacy, and fears of compromising personal health data.

Low cognitive abilities, literacy levels, lack of patient education, and medical conditions that hinder one's cognitive ability are additional DTx barriers clinicians, patients, and caregivers must contemplate when considering a DTx for treatment, prevention, or management of a medical condition [8,15].

Challenges to adoption

Most DTx adoption challenges are rooted around organizational changes and clinical adoption, correlating to supporting regulatory and administrative policies [15]. The following reading highlights adoption challenges straddled by the industry at publication.

Payment/Reimbursement: Digital therapeutics have multiple payment pathways, including patients (direct-to-consumer), pharmacy benefits, insurance payers, and employers. The various methods of DTx reimbursement complicate the adoption of digital therapeutics because policies, regulations, and organizational processes must be defined, formulated, and standardized to support each mode of reimbursement [6,15,17]. Refer to the Digital Therapeutics II chapter in this book for further details of the impact regulatory issues and agencies have on DTx industry.

Workflow Integration: DTx into clinical practice and practitioner workflows hinder health systems, healthcare teams, and individual practitioners from capitalizing and utilizing DTx to their fullest [6,15]. In fact, integrating digital health tools into electronic health records was the second highest contributing factor influencing physicians' adoption of digital health tools, including digital therapeutics [18]. A reluctance to adopt and integrate DTx in care plans because of associated patient education needs and the impact this has on clinical practice workflows also exists among clinicians.

Providers: According to the 2022 American Medical Association Physician Adoption of Digital Health Tools study, only one in nearly 10 physicians reported utilizing digital therapeutics in clinical practice, demonstrating a low adoption rate of digital therapeutics at the time of the survey [18]. Physicians reported malpractice insurance coverage of digital health tools (including DTx) and integration into electronic health records as the most significant factors affecting their adoption of DTx [18].

Patients: Patients' fears about the safety of their medical information, digital literacy, and cognitive abilities impact patient engagement and adoption. Most DTx entail complex tasks versus traditional pharmacological and biologic agents (i.e., taking a pill). Therefore, patients accessing DTx resources must maintain baseline technological and cognitive abilities to utilize effectively and adopt DTx [8,15].

Trends and innovations

Current and future trends

In the realm of digital health, the convergence of technology and medicine has given rise to the transformative field known as digital therapeutics (DTx). Leveraging the power of digital platforms, data-driven insights, digital biomarkers, and evidence-based interventions, DTx are redefining the way medical conditions are managed and treated [6,19]. This section delves into the current trends, growth trajectory, and potential future prospects of DTx.

Current trends

Diverse Applications: DTx have evolved far beyond their initial conception as mere smartphone applications. They now encompass a wide spectrum of conditions, ranging from mental health disorders such as anxiety and depression to chronic diseases such as diabetes and cardiovascular conditions. These solutions provide evidence-based, personalized interventions and support, enhancing patient engagement and adherence [6].

Clinical Validation: The credibility of DTx has surged as a result of rigorous clinical validation. Companies are investing in robust research to prove the effectiveness of their solutions, aligning with traditional pharmaceutical standards. Regulatory bodies, such as the FDA and Notified Bodies in the European Union, have also started granting approvals to certain DTx as medical treatments [6].

Remote Patient Monitoring: The COVID-19 pandemic accelerated the adoption of remote patient monitoring, driving the demand for DTx solutions. Patients and healthcare providers now recognize the value of continuous remote monitoring, allowing for early intervention and real-time adjustments to treatment plans [6].

Growth and proliferation

Investment Influx: The DTx market has witnessed a substantial influx of investments from venture capital firms, pharmaceutical companies, and technology giants. This influx of funds is propelling research, development, and commercialization efforts, thereby fueling the growth of the field [6].

Global Accessibility: DTx hold the promise of making healthcare more accessible and affordable worldwide. With the ubiquity of smartphones and the Internet, patients in remote and underserved areas can benefit from therapeutic interventions that were previously out of reach.

Collaborative Ecosystem: A synergy between technology companies, healthcare providers, regulators, and patients is essential for the growth of DTx. According to the 2022 survey conducted by the AMA, only 11% of physicians are already incorporating digital therapeutics into clinical application; however, 40% intend to incorporate digital therapeutics into their practices within 1 year [18]. Collaborative efforts are paving the way for streamlined regulations, interoperability standards, and seamless integration into existing healthcare systems [6].

Future prospects

Personalized Interventions: As our understanding of genetics and individual variability deepens, DTx will likely become more personalized. Treatment plans will be tailored to a patient's genetic makeup, lifestyle, and preferences, optimizing outcomes [20].

Integration with AI and IoT: The integration of artificial intelligence (AI) and the Internet of Things (IoT) will enhance the capabilities of DTx [21]. AI-driven algorithms will analyze vast amounts of patient data to provide real-time insights and predictive analytics for better decision-making [22].

Behavioral Health Focus: The field of mental health will significantly benefit from DTx. As societies prioritize mental well-being, digital solutions will play a pivotal role in providing accessible and effective interventions for a range of mental health conditions [6].

The growth and proliferation of DTx mark a paradigm shift in healthcare. Current trends such as diverse applications and clinical validation, coupled with their widespread adoption and promising future prospects, paint a picture of a dynamic and transformative field that has the potential to revolutionize healthcare delivery, making it more patient-centered, accessible, and effective. As the DTx landscape continues to evolve, collaboration among stakeholders will be pivotal in realizing the full potential of these groundbreaking interventions.

Expand your knowledge

JOGO is a PDTx product composed of wearable wireless sensors and a mobile app utilizing artificial intelligence (AI) and virtual reality (VR) to "… help healthy brain cell networks rewire themselves to work with muscles that have become inactive due to stroke and other neuromuscular conditions." [23] One of the many patient testimonials found on JOGO's website relates how JOGO enabled the rehabilitation of the use of a poststroke patient's fingers after 3 months in a rehab clinic failed to produce results.

As traditional medical approaches intertwine with cutting-edge digital solutions, the need for the clinician to access accurate and reliable information becomes paramount. This section provides a curated collection of resources that will not only aid in unraveling the complexities of DTx but also empower the student/clinician to make informed clinical decisions and pass along innovative and evidence-based DTx options to patients.

From reputable websites and research repositories to academic journals, this compilation paves the way for an enriched understanding of the intersection between technology and healing. Embark on a journey of discovery using these tools and activities to chart your course through the dynamic world of DTx.

Medical education and instructor resources

General websites

- The Digital Therapeutic Alliance, https://dtxalliance.org/
- The Center For Technology and Behavioral Health (C4tbh), https://www.c4tbh.org/programreviews/?f=true&category=mix&commercially_available=mix
- Digital Health Center of Excellence, https://www.fda.gov/medical-devices/digital-health-center-excellence

Journals

- *The Lancet Digital Health*, https://www.thelancet.com/journals/landig/home,
- *Nature Partner Journals Digital Medicine* (NPJ Digital Medicine) https://www.nature.com/npjdigitalmed/

Research: ***Clinical Trials*** To access an up-to-date online database of DTx clinical research studies, consider surveying ClinicalTrials.gov. This open-access repository stores DTx trials in a record format, allowing one to view clinical trial investigators, sponsors, medical condition(s), study inventions, and study format, also, if the study needs healthcare practitioners or patients to join, and researcher results if the study was completed [24]

- ClinicalTrials.gov, https://clinicaltrials.gov/search?term=%22digital%20therapeutics%22

Regulatory information

The SaMD section of the FDA Digital Health Center of Excellence offers viewers a broad range of information to understand, define, and gain detailed insights about regulatory aspects impacting SaMDs, which influence the development of PDTx and DTx.

- FDA-Digital Health Center of Excellence: Software as a medical device, https://www.fda.gov/medical-devices/digital-health-center-excellence/software-medical-device-samd

DTx products and companies

Explore the links below to quickly search, seek out, and get a glimpse of digital therapeutic products and companies.

- DTx Alliance: DTx product library https://dtxalliance.org/understanding-dtx/product-library/
- Digital Health: Sampling of DTx companies https://digital.health/digital-therapeutics
- Dealroom: DTx companies by therapeutic area https://app.dealroom.co/lists/20489/

Learner sample activities

Activity 1: Is this a DTx?

Focus: Identification of a digital therapeutic product.

Objectives:

- Recognize the steps and actions involved in developing a DTx
- Determine if a health product most likely qualifies as a digital therapeutic
- Evaluate digital health products to make informed decisions

Instructions: Provide learners with a list of digital health tools and digital therapeutics. Utilizing the DTA flowsheet available at https://dtxalliance.org/wp-content/uploads/2022/09/DTA_FS_Is-This-Product-a-DTx.pdf, instruct learners to work through the flowsheet, to determine if a product meets the established criteria by the DTA to be determined a DTx.

Activity 2: Journal club

Focus: Clinical Research.

Objective:

- Review and discuss completed research studies on digital therapeutic products to determine personal conclusions, limitations, feasibility of application of product to practice, study design, and bias.

Instructions: Complete an online search for a free journal club template, like the one found at https://www.ashp.org/-/media/assets/new-practitioner/docs/Sample-Journal-Club-Presentation-Template.pdf Search ClinicalTrials.gov for a trial evaluating a DTx product or choose a DTx product and find the trial data using an alternative source. Fill out the journal club template and present the information to a group.

Activity 3: Thinking about digital therapeutics and care plans

Focus: Integration of Digital Therapeutics.

Objectives:

- Identify DTx products and services to better care for patients
- Converse with colleagues and patients about DTx products for treatment, prevention, or management of specific medical disorders
- Consider and evaluate DTx products for future care plans

Instructions: Provide learners a list of medical conditions that have an approved digital therapeutic. Ask learners to select one medical condition for this activity. Instruct learners to research current DTx products that support their selected therapeutic focus area, create a list of supporting DTx, select one DTx to highlight (preferably not from Table 13.2), and submit an electronic document that comments on the following:

- Learner name and selected medical condition
- A list of available DTx that support the learner's selected medical condition of focus
- Name resources utilized to identify the above list of DTx
- Highlight the below information
- DTx Name, Website, supporting company, and date/year DTx went on market
- Rationale of what attracted or influenced your decision to highlight this DTx
- Brief product overview
- Clinical research studies conducted and outcomes
- Target population (age groups, comorbidities, etc.)

References

[1] Ronquillo Y, Meyers A, Korvek SJ. Digital health [Updated 2023 May 1]. In: StatPearls [internet]. Treasure Island (FL): StatPearls Publishing; January 2023. Available from: https://www.ncbi.nlm.nih.gov/books/NBK470260/.

[2] Digital Medicine Society. DiMEsociety.org. [Accessed 30 November 2023]. http://www.dimesociety.org/about-us/defining-digital-medicine/.

[3] Digital Therapeutics Alliance. www.dtxalliance.org/DTA_DTx-Definition-and-Core-Principles.pdf. [Accessed 30 November 2023]. https://dtxalliance.org/wp-content/uploads/2021/01/DTA_DTx-Definition-and-Core-Principles.pdf.

[4] Digital Therapeutics Alliance. DTxAlliance.org/DTA_FS_DTx-Product-Categories_010521.pdf. [Accessed 30 November 2023]. https://dtxalliance.org/wp-content/uploads/2021/01/DTA_FS_DTx-Product-Categories_010521.pdf.

[5] Frank SR. Digital health care–the convergence of health care and the Internet. Journal of Ambulatory Care Management April 2000;23(2):8–17. https://doi.org/10.1097/00004479-200004000-00003.

[6] IQVIA Institute for Human Data Science. Digital health trends 2021: innovation, evidence, regulation, and adoption. July 2021.

[7] Digital Therapeutics Alliance. www.dtxalliance.org/US-Regulatory-and-Reimbursement-Pathways.pdf. [Accessed 30 November 2023]. https://dtxalliance.org/wp-content/uploads/2022/01/US-Regulatory-and-Reimbursement-Pathways.pdf.

[8] Wang C, Lee C, Shin H. Digital therapeutics from bench to bedside. NPJ Digital Medicine 2023;6(1):38. https://doi.org/10.1038/s41746-023-00777-z.

[9] Patel NA, Butte AJ. Characteristics and challenges of the clinical pipeline of digital therapeutics. NPJ Digital Medicine 2020;3(1):159. https://doi.org/10.1038/s41746-020-00370-8.

[10] Van Norman GA. Drugs, devices, and the FDA: part 2: an overview of approval processes: FDA approval of medical devices. JACC Basic to Translational Science 2016;1(4):277–87. https://doi.org/10.1016/j.jacbts.2016.03.009.

[11] Adatia C, et al. The health benefits and business potential of digital therapeutics. McKinsey & Company; January 2023. https://www.mckinsey.com/industries/life-sciences/our-insights/the-health-benefits-and-business-potential-of-digital-therapeutics. [Accessed 26 September 2023].

[12] Widmer RJ, Allison TG, Lerman LO, Lerman A. Digital health intervention as an adjunct to cardiac rehabilitation reduces cardiovascular risk factors and rehospitalizations. Journal of Cardiovascular Translational Research 2015;8(5):283–92. https://doi.org/10.1007/s12265-015-9629-1.

[13] Kamat T. Digital therapeutics can improve medication adherence in diabetes. Journal of Family Medicine and Primary Care 2020;9(11):5806–7. https://doi.org/10.4103/jfmpc.jfmpc_1252_20.

[14] Ahmed I, Ahmad NS, Ali S, et al. Medication adherence apps: review and content analysis. JMIR Mhealth Uhealth 2018;6(3):e62. https://doi.org/10.2196/mhealth.6432.

[15] Aylward B. Digital therapeutics adoption: advancing from concept into practice. https://healthcare.rti.org/insights/prescription-digital-therapeutics-challenges. [Accessed 26 September 2023].

[16] Chung JY. Digital therapeutics and clinical pharmacology. Translational Clinical Pharmacology 2019;27(1):6–11. https://doi.org/10.12793/tcp.2019.27.1.6.

[17] Aylward B. Addressing 3 challenges to prescription digital therapeutics. RTI Health Advance; March 02, 2023. https://healthcare.rti.org/insights/digital-therapeutics-dtx-adoption. [Accessed 26 September 2023].

[18] AMA (American medical association) Digital Health Research. Physicians' motivations and Key requirements for adopting digital health adoption and attitudinal shift from 2016 to 2022. September 2022.

[19] Babrak LM, Menetski J, Rebhan M, Nisato G, Zinggeler M, Brasier N, Baerenfaller K, Brenzikofer T, Baltzer L, Vogler C, Gschwind L, Schneider C, Streiff F, Groenen PMA, Miho E. Traditional and digital biomarkers: two worlds apart? Digital Biomarkers September 5, 2019;3(2):92–102. https://doi.org/10.1159/000502000.

[20] Corridon PR, Wang X, Shakeel A, Chan V. Digital technologies: advancing individualized treatments through gene and cell therapies, pharmacogenetics, and disease detection and diagnostics. Biomedicines 2022;10(10):2445. https://doi.org/10.3390/biomedicines10102445.

[21] National Institute of Standards and Technology. Information Technology Laboratory: Computer Security Resource Center. [Accessed 30 November 2023]. csrc.nist.gov/glossary/term/internet_of_things.

[22] Stanojevic C, Bennett CC, Sabanovic S, et al. Conceptualizing socially-assistive robots as a digital therapeutic tool in healthcare. Front Digit Health 2023;5:1208350. https://doi.org/10.3389/fdgth.2023.1208350.

[23] JOGO Health. About Us: Science. JOGOhealth.com/science. [Accessed 30 November 2023]. https://www.jogohealth.com/science.

[24] National Library of Medicine. ClinicalTrials.Gov. [Accessed 30 November 2023]. https://clinicaltrials.gov.

CHAPTER 14

Digital therapeutics: A new era of technology for treatment

Whitney Kay Stewart
Independant author

Introduction

Digital therapeutics (DTx), an emergent industry over the past decade, offer low risk, easy to deliver, and effective evidence-based treatments for a variety of conditions and diseases. The DTx story is quite captivating, as it navigates a stringent regulatory framework against the unique global backdrop of the COVID-19 pandemic and subsequent economic downturn. This chapter explores the history and evolution of the industry, discusses the regulatory framework for these products, and details the process of generating clinical evidence. We will touch on the challenges unique to DTx products, examine the international landscape, and review key commercialization strategies. After reading this chapter, you should understand:

- What are DTx?
- How has the DTx industry evolved?
- What regulations apply to DTx?
- What type of clinical evidence do DTx use?
- Commercialization strategies for DTx companies
- Ongoing challenges in the DTx industry as of 2023

Definitions and keywords

Digital therapeutics (DTx): health software intended to treat or alleviate a disease, disorder, condition, or injury by generating and delivering a medical intervention that has a demonstrable positive therapeutic impact on a patient's health [1].

Prescription digital therapeutics (PDTs): a subcategory of DTx intended to be prescribed by a clinician. This category may require more robust clinical evidence and must follow a strict pathway to approval.

Digital Health. https://doi.org/10.1016/B978-0-443-23901-4.00014-3

Software as a medical device (SaMD): software intended to be used for one or more medical purposes that perform these purposes without being part of a hardware medical device. SaMD is a regulatory categorization and DTx is a subcategorization.

Background

History and evolution of the industry

The world has experienced a transformative digital revolution that continues to propel society into uncharted territory. The integration of computers, mobile applications, artificial intelligence, and other cutting-edge technologies has ushered in a period of boundless potential, particularly in the domain of healthcare and medical interventions. Among the many applications of technology in healthcare, digital therapeutics (DTx) stand out as a significant evolution in the realm of medicine. In this chapter, we embark on a comprehensive exploration of the field of digital therapeutics.

In order to understand DTx, you must understand the larger landscape of the digital products available to modern consumers. DTx are a part of the larger system of Digital Health, which is a term that "applies to all technologies that engage patients around their health and wellness" [2]. The expansive realm of Digital Health encompasses various elements such as mobile health (mHealth), telehealth (also known as telemedicine), devices, sensors, wearables, health information technology (HIT), personalized medicine, and DTx. According to a report published in 2021, there are more than 350,000 mobile apps available on app stores that can be divided into subcategories of medical, health, and fitness [3].

A subset of digital health is digital medicine, which "consists of software or hardware products, typically supported by evidence, to measure or intervene in the service of human health." [4] Examples of digital medicine include digital biomarkers and remote patient monitoring systems. DTx are a specific category within digital medicine.

The term "Digital therapeutic" has been in use since 2012 and appeared in print for the first time in a 2015 article by Sepah et al. defined as "evidence-based behavioral treatments delivered online that can increase accessibility and effectiveness of healthcare." The first formal and specific definition of DTx appeared in 2017, set forth by the Digital Therapeutics Alliance (DTA), a global nonprofit trade association of industry leaders and stakeholders engaged in the evidence-driven advancement of digital therapeutics. The Digital Therapeutics Alliance defined DTx as "evidence-based therapeutic interventions that are driven by high-quality software programs to treat, manage, or prevent a disease or disorder" [5]. Defining these products was pivotal for the industry in an attempt to increase awareness and understanding of this new type of product.

In 2023, the DTA, in an attempt to "ensure industry and global alignment" adopted the International Standardization Organization (ISO)'s new definition for digital therapeutics—"*health software intended to treat or alleviate a disease, disorder, condition, or injury by generating and delivering a medical intervention that has a demonstrable positive therapeutic impact on a patient's health*" [1]. Despite this attempt to formalize a definition for DTx, there is still no international definition, and the term continues to be interpreted and defined differently in different countries.

DTx largely appear in the form of software (e.g., mobile applications) and can also be a combination of software and hardware. For DTx, the software is the generator of the therapy.

Examples of DTx solutions

- Mobile applications employing CBT therapies to treat mental conditions such as major depressive disorder, insomnia, general anxiety disorder, and substance abuse disorders
- Virtual reality programs used to treat ADHD in children or chronic lower back pain—these require VR headsets (hardware), but the product is the VR software
- A combination of a music training program and gate measurement tools used to improve walking in stroke victims—this also requires hardware to measure footsteps, but the treatment comes from the software

Unique characteristics of DTx

There are many considerations for the development and implementation of DTx within the larger regulatory and general healthcare landscape. Note that the following are general characteristics of digital therapeutics and the specifics differ between actual products.

- DTx undergo an *agile development process*—companies can easily update and change the product to get better outcomes or to improve the patient experience. Similarly, these products can be iterated upon rather rapidly, leading to constant improvement. Although this does lead to regulatory challenges, overall it is a strength of the product types.
- DTx have *novel mechanisms of action*. Perhaps one of the more exciting prospects of the industry, DTx may target pathways that are otherwise untargetable by pharmaceuticals or traditional medical devices. Although some mechanisms of action are well known, such as Cognitive Behavioral Therapy (CBT) and auditory-motor entrainment, others will require additional studies to fully understand.

- DTx have the ability to generate *real-time outcomes*. Both patients and clinicians may have access to real-time data to measure the effectiveness of the therapy, allowing for more immediate treatment changes or adjustments. DTx companies can gather Real-World Data (RWD) and conduct Real-World Evidence (RWE) studies with their products inherently.
- DTx have *lower risk profiles*. Generally, there are few immediate safety risks that come with the use of DTx products other than those associated with the use of technology. Although risks with treatment depend on the patient population, DTx tend to minimize risks relative to traditional interventions
- DTx have a *varied place in therapy*—they can be used in place of traditional treatments, or as a supplement either concurrently with, before, or after other treatments. There are many opportunities to fit DTx into treatment plans to get better overall outcomes.

First approval and on

The first DTx approved in the United States was the Pear Therapeutics reSET program for the treatment of substance use disorders, which was cleared in 2017 [6]. Since then, the industry has grown and changed rapidly.

The COVID-19 pandemic catalyzed the implementation of digital health as a strategy to address limited healthcare access. For example, mental health care needs in the world dramatically increased (e.g., approximately 25% increase in the prevalence of anxiety and depression), and there was no longer sufficient coverage to meet demand [7]. During this time, DTx offered the potential for easily accessible, low-risk mental health services. The temporary regulations put in place during the pandemic allowed for accelerated marketing of products that would otherwise have taken years to be made widely available. The next section will address the regulatory landscape for DTx.

As a category of treatment, DTx continues to grow and products are being rapidly commercialized. As of 2022, there were over 40 DTx approved by the FDA [8] and more continue to move through the regulatory approval process.

International landscape

Although the first digital therapeutic was approved in the United States, diagnostic therapeutics are now part of an international industry. In fact, as of 2023, many other countries have established processes for getting DTx approved and in the hands of patients. Germany was the first country to establish DTx-specific regulations using their

DiGA regulatory infrastructure [9]. Other countries have followed suit, attempting to clarify regulations and pave the path for appropriate oversight and expanded access. There has been active participation in the industry within the United Kingdom, Japan, Australia, China, France, and South Korea.

Regulatory landscape

DTx are most commonly considered and regulated as medical devices. In the United States, there are well-defined pathways for seeking and granting approval of medical devices.

Digital therapeutics are regulated by the Center for Devices and Radiological Health (CDHR) within the FDA. Unlike most health apps, which are unregulated, DTx delivers medical care without clinician involvement and thus requires stricter regulatory requirements. Not all DTx seek regulatory approval or clearance, but only those approved by the FDA can be prescribed and reimbursed in the same way as traditional medical devices and therapies. DTx companies initially faced many challenges in getting approval through the traditional medical device pathways, but after many successes, they can now confidently navigate the framework already established.

Medical devices, and therefore DTx, are classified by their risk category and fall into the following three categories: exempt devices, class II, and class III [10].

Exempt devices

Exempt devices include both Class I and Class II devices that do not require a premarket approval (PMA) to the FDA but must register with the FDA and pay an annual registration fee. General control requirements must be met.

Class II

Class II devices can follow one of two categories:

1. **510(k) clearance**—requires substantial equivalence to a predicate device. Special controls are required and may require a clinical trial. Once the process is complete, the device will be considered FDA-cleared.
2. **De novo**—requires reasonable assurance of safety and efficacy. Typically, a prospective clinical trial is required. Once completed, the device will be considered FDA-granted. The first FDA-cleared DTx, Pear Therapeutics this route.

Class III

Class III are the highest-risk devices and require a premarket approval, the most stringent submission subtype, to demonstrate safety and efficacy. In general, prospective clinical trials will be required for this category. This process is similar to traditional higher-risk medical devices, where an IND is required in order to conduct a clinical trial.

Software as a medical device (SaMD) [11]

Software as a Medical Device (SaMD) is defined as software intended to be used for one or more medical purposes that perform these purposes **without** being part of a hardware medical device. For regulatory purposes, DTx are typically considered a subcategory of SaMD; however, from a practical perspective, SaMD is a unique category. Examples of SaMD include [12].

- Software that allows a healthcare professional to view and interpret radiographic images remotely on a smartphone.
- Software that collects and analyzes data, then uses an algorithm to develop a treatment plan for a specific condition or illness.

Another subcategory of SaMD that is DTx-adjacent is "Around-the-Pill" solutions in the form of companion software applications. These are apps intended to be used alongside a pharmaceutical or traditional treatment to provide supportive services such as medication compliance support, symptom tracking, and other disease-specific features. In general, these solutions are utilized by Pharma companies.

A helpful distinction between the larger category of SaMD and DTx is that DTx require engagement from users, so the intervention is not solely the software itself, but the entire package of the experience. You cannot, therefore, control the outcome with software programming alone.

There are specific software companies within the DTx industry that help these Pharma companies develop companion solutions. SaMD Regulatory requirements for these devices must be met in order for them to be approved for use on the market so some Pharma companies elect to use these companies instead of building software from the ground up internally. Some examples of these companies active in 2023 include Voluntis and Bright Insight.

For example, to support patients with hemophilia taking Hemgenix, CSL Behring released a companion app called BSUPPORT. The application supports the patient on their hemophilia journey and provides features such as eligibility assessment, guided gene therapy support, reminders, and a patient journal to track important information a patient may want to share with their clinician [13].

Enforcement discretion

The first approval of a DTx came in 2017 [6], but the growth of the industry and adoption of this new category of treatment options were slow through 2019. Starting in 2020, the COVID-19 pandemic expedited adoption as the need for more easily accessible treatment options increased.

In April 2020, during the government-established COVID-19 Public Health Emergency, in order to "expand the availability of digital health therapeutic devices for psychiatric disorders to facilitate consumer and patient use while reducing user and healthcare provider contact and potential exposure to COVID-19 during this pandemic" [14], the FDA released an enforcement discretion policy. Enforcement discretion applies to low-risk products that meet the definition of a medical device. Instead of requiring regulatory submission and approval or clearance, the company is allowed to go to market but must have the evidence generated to support that they are complying with the applicable regulations. Several DTx companies used this policy to release their products to the public before FDA approval or clearance. However, the policy ended with the end of the public health emergency, and all companies are now required to follow the traditional regulatory pathways.

For more information on EUAs, visit the FDA's website https://www.fda.gov/emergency-preparedness-and-response/mcm-legal-regulatory-and-policy-framework/emergency-use-authorization.

Iterative development

One challenge many DTx companies face is how to maintain regulatory approval as their products are constantly evolving and improving. The FDA has taken a proactive approach to addressing this issue, including its Precertification (Pre-cert) Pilot Program, outlined as follows. As of 2023, this is an ongoing discussion with guidance and regulations continuing to evolve.

DTx that use machine learning/artificial intelligence (ML/AI)

2023 has been a year of incredible growth in the use of AI in all facets of life. It has been applied to the practice of medicine and has been incorporated into digital health products, including digital therapeutics. However, the premise of AI, that a product could be "continually learning", is hard to fit within the existing regulatory frameworks.

For DTx products utilizing AI or ML algorithms, the FDA requires that the sponsor provide detailed data and information about the source of the data, the methods by which the algorithm was trained, and how the resulting algorithms were validated [15]. There is also an increasing concern about health equity and a need to demonstrate that the algorithms are trained on data from a diverse patient population.

In January 2021, the FDA released an *Artificial Intelligence/Machine Learning-based Software as a Medical Device (SaMD) Action Plan* that included multiple actions intended to advance the agency's oversight of these products captured in Table 14.1 [16].

We can expect further changes and clarifications to the regulatory framework as the FDA continues to issue guidance documents on various topics including draft guidance on "Computer Software Assurance for Production and Quality System Software" and final guidance "Clinical Decision Support Software" in September 2022.

Table 14.1: FDA's AI/ML actions.

Action #	Action title	Action plan
1	**Tailored regulatory framework for AI/ML-based SaMD**	The FDA committed to providing guidance to support a new framework, specifically related to the "predetermined change control plan." The plan would include types of anticipated modifications and the associated methodology for implementing those changes.
2	**Good machine learning practice (GMLP)**	The FDA said they will "encourage harmonization" and the creation of a set of AI/ML best practices. The FDA is actively engaged in multiple efforts to move this forward.
3	**Patient-centered approach incorporating transparency to users**	The FDA wants to promote transparency of these devices to users and patients. Transparency may include information on the source of the data used in the algorithm training and clarity around the benefits, risks, and limitations of the devices.
4	**Regulatory science methods related to algorithm bias and robustness**	The FDA acknowledged that there are concerns about the bias and generalizability of use with these devices and the data forming the basis of their functions. The FDA will support regulatory science research efforts to ensure factors such as race, ethnicity, and socioeconomic status are incorporated into the development and maintenance of these devices.
5	**Real-world performance (RWP)**	Recognizing the increasing significance of real-world data in medical device development and regulation, the FDA acknowledged that this is particularly relevant due to the continuous learning and utilization of real-world data-driven algorithms in AI/ML-based devices. The FDA has expressed its dedication to initiating voluntary pilot programs aimed at monitoring real-world performance with the goal of establishing consistent principles for assessing the real-world performance of AI/ML-enabled devices.

DTx intended to be used in combination with prescription drugs

DTx can be used in many ways, including in combination with prescription drugs. There are special regulations for software intended to be associated with prescription drugs, known as prescription drug use-related software (PDURS). Unlike medical devices and standalone DTx, which are regulated by CDHR, these combination products, and specifically the colabeling, are regulated by the Center for Drug Evaluation and Research (CDER). In 2018, the FDA posted a proposed framework for the regulation of PDURS [17]. The goal was to "promote the development of digital technologies that can … help guide the safe and effective use of medicines, to help patients improve their health" and "to modernize our approach to overseeing software products that are designed to be used in conjunction with prescription drugs" [18]. In September 2023, the FDA released draft guidance "Regulatory Considerations for Prescription Drug Use-Related Software" [18a]. The draft guidance proposes relaxed regulatory requirements for placing PDURS on drug labels and discusses labeling requirements. It must be noted that these regulations are independent from the framework for medical device software and that DTx may still need to go through the traditional medical device pathways even if they are intended to be used in combination.

Special FDA programs impacting DTx

The FDA has been an excellent partner to the DTx industry and is actively engaged in clarifying requirements across digital health. The FDA does not want to be seen as a roadblock in the digital health revolution, but also must ensure it protects the public by adequately reviewing and regulating products within digital medicine. They created two submission programs that help accelerate the approval process—the Breakthrough Devices Program and the Safer Technologies Program.

Breakthrough devices program [19]

FDA approval can take many years, so to speed up the process, the FDA established the Breakthrough Devices Program in 2017. This program assists companies by providing timely premarket feedback on and offering design assistance with clinical trials to increase trial flexibility.

The FDA released updated guidance on September 15, 2023, which expanded inclusion criteria for the Breakthrough Devices Program to include devices that improve health disparities and accessibility in addition to devices that improve clinical outcomes. In order to qualify for the program, companies need to demonstrate that their device improves access to receive breakthrough device designation [20].

Safer technologies program (SteP) [21]

In 2021, the FDA created the STeP program for devices “reasonably expected to significantly improve the safety of currently available treatments or diagnostics that target an underlying disease or condition associated with morbidities and mortalities less serious than those eligible for the Breakthrough Devices Program” [21].

Both programs are intended to reduce the regulatory burden and time to approval and get products into the hands of patients quicker, activities that are in alignment with the FDA’s mission to protect and serve the public health.

Precertification (Pre-cert) pilot program

In 2017, the FDA created the pilot Pre-cert program to establish a new regulatory framework aligned with the iterative nature of medical software, including DTx. Many software products evolve quickly and become a product beyond what was originally approved by the FDA; however, the foundational idea of the program was that products should not be required to be reapproved after each significant change as that slows progress. Under the program, the FDA piloted regulating the companies rather than individual products. The program concluded in September 2022, and their final report stated, first, that there were numerous limitations with the program, and that the FDA encountered “challenges with implementing the proposed approach under our current statutory authorities.” It claimed a need for new federal legislation to allow for more flexible regulations [22]. It was a proactive approach to adapt regulatory processes as technology advances, but was ultimately unsuccessful.

International considerations

Companies considering expanding their DTx product beyond its current market, particularly a global market, need to develop action plans for meeting localization requirements and international regulations. DTx products present unique challenges for globalization compared with pharmaceuticals or traditional medical devices.

Localization requirements

User engagement is critical to efficacy of DTx products, and similar levels of engagement across user locations is crucial for effective global deployment. Therefore, localization requires DTx to be adapted to the specifics of the location of the user. Adaptions can include providing the product in multiple languages, adjusting the product to align with cultural norms, and other regionally specific features. Without proper localization strategy, DTx companies could face significant barriers to adoption and scalability.

Product-level adaptations aim to foster end-user engagement in various local settings. However, DTx products also need to obtain regulatory approval in each country.

International regulations

The process for regulatory approval is complex. One significant barrier for obtaining regulatory approval is each country's requirement for the location of the clinical trials whose evidence supports the product. Some countries will accept an evidence dossier without location requirements while others require a specific percentage of clinical evidence from their country. The following case series with Germany and South Korea demonstrates the heterogeneity of international regulations.

Each country has its own regulatory body and regulations, and DTx products have had a challenging time navigating all the different frameworks. Some countries have made significant progress in providing a clear path for digital therapeutics.

Germany

Germany's DiGA (digital health applications) initiative is part of the 2019 Digital Healthcare Act (DVG). The DVG set the legal framework for reimbursement for providers who prescribe DiGAs to the German citizens covered by the government-mandated health insurance. Digital health applications are low-risk medical devices that have been approved by Germany's Federal Institute for Drugs and Medical Devices (BfArM) [9]. Some examples of DiGAs are an application by the company Hello Better for Diabetes and Depression, an application by Oviva for patients with obesity, and an application by the company GAIA called Elevida for patients with multiple sclerosis (MS) [23].

The first "DiGAs" were authorized for use in October 2020, and as of September 2023, the DiGA library, a list of approved applications, had 55 applications listed [23]. Outside of regulations, companies producing DiGAs for the German market face similar barriers as DTx companies in the United States, such as adoption by clinicians and a sustainable revenue stream. Although DTx companies do not have to negotiate with each insurance provider, they still have to negotiate a reimbursement price with the insurers' representative body. For most companies, that price is below what is necessary to sustain the business. To complicate things further, price negotiations start after the DTx has been listed for 12 months, during which time the company can choose the price to charge. Once the negotiations are completed, the company has to pay back the difference between their original price and the new set price [24].

South Korea [25]

As of 2023, South Korea was the only country outside of the United States that has specifically used the term DTx within their regulations. South Korea defines DTx as "software as a medical device that provides evidence-based therapeutic intervention to patients to prevent, manage, or treat a medical disorder or disease." In South Korea, the regulatory pathways are clearly defined; devices are classified by risk into Class I and Class II. For Class I devices, no approval is required. For Class II devices, the regulations specifically require evidence-based data, including at least one of the following: a clinical article published in a peer-reviewed journal, clinical trial, or clinical guideline recognized by the Korean Academy of Medical Sciences to support the claim [26].

In February 2023, the Korean Ministry of Food and Drug Safety (MFDS) approved its first digital therapeutic for the treatment of insomnia. This approval marks the beginning of a new era in South Korea regarding DTx. The MFDS took a proactive approach to digital therapeutics by providing clinical trial guidelines and deploying dedicated staff to facilitate the approval of this DTx. The collaborative approach of the MFDS will likely encourage other DTx companies to pursue product development or implementation in South Korea.

The DTA's website provides up-to-date information on multiple countries' regulations, including Australia, China, France, and the United Kingdom at https://dtxalliance.org/understanding-dtx/dtx-by-country/.

Clinical evidence generation

An important component of DTx is the *"demonstrable positive therapeutic impact"* [1]. For a product to be considered a DTx, there must be sufficient clinical evidence to support the product claims.

The extent and type of clinical evidence required for approval of DTx across various countries have been challenging for government agencies to clearly define. Pharmaceutical products must undergo Phase 1, Phase 2, and Phase 3 clinical trials before being considered for approval. While this process is extensive, it also provides clear expectations for pharmaceutical companies to meet. As of the time of this writing, no standardized clinical evidence expectations have been developed for DTx. The heterogeneity of DTx products makes it challenging to define and/or standardize substantive clinical evidence. DTx companies' clinical evidence approach depends on many factors including the specifics of the device, the claims being made, and the commercialization strategy. Initially, the primary endpoints may just focus on demonstration of efficacy over other options, such as standard of care. That may be sufficient to get approval or go to market. As a product matures, companies may investigate more details about the novel mechanism of action or compare two different programs ("doses"). The clinical evidence required also depends on the stakeholder requiring to see it—whether it be regulators, payers, or clinicians. Some regulators may require you to compare the active product to a sham or inactive product, as is typical with pharmaceuticals. Payers may want to see both clinical efficacy and evidence that the product improves outcomes in real-world settings. Designing an effective evidence-generation plan requires consideration of all of these elements and stakeholders.

Regulatory-wise, without clear guidelines, companies rely on frequent interactions with the FDA to understand the evidence needed for obtaining authorization. In general, the company will have needed to complete a pivotal study with positive evidence. Pivotal studies are most commonly randomized-controlled trials since RTCs are considered the gold standard of evidence generation in medicine. As of 2023, nearly 80% of the pivotal trials for DTx were RCTs. One barrier for DTx companies to conduct RCTs is creating an appropriate control group. DTx are software-based, so creating a "placebo" and maintaining a double-blind strategy can be difficult [27]. For DTx product studies, the placebo is a "sham application" that replicates the DTx experience without the therapeutic effect. However, many companies opt to forgo using a sham application in their study design because sham applications are time-consuming, complex, and expensive to create. Lack of clear guidelines outlining the criteria for reasonable control arms in DTx product studies remains a challenge for the DTx industry [28].

To complicate matters more, payers require different evidence from regulators. Whereas regulators require DTx companies to demonstrate positive therapeutic impact, payers require DTx companies to demonstrate efficacy and economic viability. Health Economics Outcomes Research (HEOR) and Real-World Evidence (RWE) are two strategies for providing evidence of efficacy and economic viability. Health Economics Outcomes Research (HEOR) attempts to measure the link between treatment and actual outcomes. Real-World Evidence (RWE) takes data available outside of trials, such as insurance claims, to look at product impact in real-world settings. Both types of research are particularly powerful in demonstrating impact as companies strive for reimbursement. Typically, those types of studies come after efficacy-focused trials. In 2022, the DTA published the guide, "Setting the Stage for a Fit-For-Purpose DTx Evidentiary Standard" [29], which aimed to align the clinical-evidence requirements across the healthcare stakeholders involved in decision-making. More work needs to be done to streamline the process for companies wanting to demonstrate the therapeutic effect, efficacy, and economic viability of their DTx products.

There are postapproval/postmarketing expectations for DTx. One benefit of DTx is the real-time access to data, which can feed Real-World Data (RWD) and RWE studies. This is also when a company may conduct HEOR studies in an attempt to expand its reimbursement potential. In this stage, the company will continue to analyze its product and iterate for better outcomes.

Now that we have reviewed the complex system of providing clinical evidence, let us explore a generic example of the clinical trial journey a DTx company may go through. Early in development, companies are evaluating their product's risks and benefits, including behavior change with experimental trials. These trials aim to understand and improve the product's mechanism of action (MoA). Once a company is satisfied with the DTx's risk–benefit profile, the next step is for the company to explore their product's usability through user testing and collecting usability data. After these early stages, a company may enter the pivotal data collection stage. This will be the core evidence collected for regulatory submissions and initial data for early conversations with payers.

Commercialization strategies

There are multiple strategies for commercializing a DTx, and companies have been known to change their strategy based on roadblocks, learnings, or a changing market. Implementing a successful go-to-market strategy remains a key challenge for the industry. Here, we will discuss some of the major categories of strategies seen across the DTx industry.

Direct-to-consumer

As distinguished previously, there is a difference between PDTs and non-PDTs. Any company that decides to market and take their product direct-to-consumer will not require a prescription for its use. Instead, it will charge consumers for the use, typically in the form of a subscription. Companies may elect to use this model based on reach and because of challenges related to reimbursement. For example, Akili Therapeutics announced in September 2023 that it was moving from a PDT model to a direct-to-consumer model with its product for ADHD EndeavorRx after struggling to find financial success with a prescription model. They reported challenges with convincing payers to cover the product, a challenge that has been seen across the industry. This will still require them to submit data to the FDA but should open the door to higher accessibility [30].

Employer partnerships

This is a business-to-business-to-consumer route to market that holds particular promise in the US market, especially if the DTx is aimed at prevention and would apply to a large percentage of a product's user base. This strategy requires individual negotiations with each self-insured employer. This strategy may also create a need for account managers and other team members to manage individual relationships.

Payer reimbursement

Payer reimbursement enables billing for DTx to go through insurance companies or payers("payers"). This strategy allows healthcare providers to prescribe a digital intervention to their patients without needing the patients to pay for it out of pocket. This strategy also allows DTx companies to be reimbursed for the use of their product. In the United States, with privatized healthcare, coverage for drugs and other services depends on the specific insurance company and the contracts that the company has in place with pharmaceutical and medical device companies. DTx companies are therefore required to negotiate with each private insurance company for coverage and to set unique pricing, which can be a slow and arduous process. In countries with socialized medicine, this process can be less intense. For example, in Germany, DTx companies negotiate with one entity, the government, to establish reimbursement status and set reimbursement prices. Although it hasn't necessarily resulted in pricing that fits the individual circumstances of each DTx product, it has simplified the process.

Partnering with pharma

As the DTx industry continues to grow and the commercial viability of products is realized, Pharma companies have shown interest in incorporating DTx solutions into their overall product dossier. The Pharma industry has started to branch into digital medicine in a number of ways, including investing in DTx products for disease areas they have products in and by developing unique digital companion apps for their approved pharmaceutical products. These digital solutions help the Pharma companies differentiate themselves as digital products continue to evolve.

There have been some successful DTx/Pharma partnerships. With a partnership, DTx companies get access to the vast resources of a Pharma company, which results in easier routes to market, more success with reimbursement, and other benefits. For example:

- In 2018, Novartis became the first pharmaceutical company to partner with a DTx company when they announced a go-to-market deal with Pear Therapeutics [31].
- In 2021, Eisai and Voluntis announced a partnership to develop novel DTx for oncology patients [32].
- In 2022, Bayer invested $9.5 million in Woebot Health, a company delivering AI-powered DTx solutions in the mental health space [33].

Some partnerships have failed, as is the case with the Novartis and Pear Therapeutics deal. The original plan had Novartis leading the sales and marketing and had Pear continuing to focus on updating and iterating on the products reSET and reSET-O [31]. In October 2019, the end of the partnership was announced as Novartis changed strategies and Pear resumed complete ownership of the commercialization of their products [34].

Alternate strategies

There is always room for unique strategies, including combination strategies. The best path to commercialization depends on the specifics of the product and successful DTx companies typically utilize multiple commercialization strategies. For example, Floreo, whose VR system facilitates learning for people with autism spectrum disorder (ASD), ADHD, anxiety, and other conditions, has focused its commercialization strategy on an enterprise license system. The product is used by state-licensed professionals so it does not require FDA approval, and the company has successfully launched without it. As of early 2023, the products are used by more than 100 healthcare enterprises [35].

Other challenges for DTx companies

Cybersecurity

Cybersecurity is a large challenge for DTx due to the ubiquitous use of mobile technology and frequent transmission of sensitive data over the Internet. Transparency and risks surrounding cybersecurity have become increasingly important to users and patients. As tools within the medical ecosystem, DTx may create or capture protected health information (PHI) and thus have a responsibility to ensure data are being captured, stored, and transmitted securely.

Cybersecurity risk and mitigation are a major consideration during the regulatory review of DTx products. In the United States, all device manufacturers must consider cybersecurity risks for their devices. The FDA released guidance titled "Cybersecurity in Medical Devices: Quality System Considerations and Content of Premarket Submissions" on September 27, 2023 [22], which provides detailed recommendations for medical devices. The guidance covers components such as a Secure Product Development Framework (SPDF) and expands on their expectations around security risk management. An SPDF is defined as a "set of processes that reduce the number and severity of vulnerabilities in products throughout the device lifecycle" and may be one way of satisfying the regulations [22]. It also recommends "threat modeling" as a process for identifying risks and vulnerabilities and defining countermeasures to "prevent, mitigate, monitor, or respond to the effects of threats to the medical device system throughout its lifecycle." It calls for transparency and providing device users with information related to cybersecurity controls, risks to the system, and other pertinent information. During the submission process, robust documentation on cybersecurity needs to be included and should scale with the risk of the device.

Reimbursement

A lack of defined benefit categories and a general lack of consistency across different payers has limited the ability of DTx companies to reach a sustainable level of revenue on their products. Traditional methods of reimbursement focus on reimbursing pharmaceuticals or medical devices, which does not align with the unique qualities of DTx.

Coding is an embedded process in the US reimbursement process. Initially, DTx did not have a specific code. The recent establishment of a Level II Healthcare Common Procedure Coding System (HCPCS) code has been helpful in clarifying the role of DTx in this infrastructure. Code A9291 covers an FDA-cleared, prescription digital behavioral therapy and provides the option for payers to reimburse PDTs as either a pharmacy or a durable medical equipment Medicare benefit. Payers reported that the establishment of the code will increase the likelihood of covering PDTs, with most classifying them as a medical benefit [36].

In 2022, the *Access to Prescription Digital Therapeutics Act of 2022* was introduced to the Senate. It would create a new benefit category for digital therapeutics and ensure coverage and reimbursement by Medicare and Medicaid. This would increase reimbursements and allow DTx companies to earn a return on their investments in these products. As of Dec 2023, the law has still not been passed [37].

Adoption

A significant barrier to widespread success for DTx has been the overall adoption seen by the industry since its creation. It has been challenging to distinguish DTx from the larger landscape of digital health products. It has also been hard to formalize reimbursement pathways and incentives for the companies, clinicians, and payers. This has led to slow adoption by all stakeholders. Healthcare systems are complex, and adoption requires both an understanding of the products and their place in care and the establishment of the necessary frameworks within clinical practices.

Sustainability/profitability

DTx companies, like all other businesses, need to become profitable and financially sustainable to survive. As of 2023, there has yet to be a true success story in the DTx industry, but the industry is young. Still, there is much to be learned from the trials of DTx companies.

Case study—Pear Therapeutics [38]

We have mentioned Pear Therapeutics multiple times throughout this chapter. As one of the earliest DTx companies and owner of the first FDA-cleared DTx product, they are a useful case study for the journey of a DTx company. As one of the first major DTx companies and a company that helped pave the way for the industry, it is worthwhile to examine the timeline and the successes and failures of Pear specifically.

Pear was founded in 2013. They had a vast product development pipeline, but saw the approval of three DTx products.

1. reSET (2017)—designed for treating substance use disorder
2. reSET-O (2018)—aimed at helping patients with opioid use disorder as an adjunct to outpatient treatment
3. Somryst (2020)—designed for the treatment of insomnia using a CBT-based digital platform

They experienced many challenges during their active period.

- Adoption challenges—the healthcare industry is often slow to adapt, and there was much resistance to the novel concept of PDTs
- Reimbursement—the company had a hard time obtaining adequate coverage from insurance companies
- Costs—developing PDTs is an expensive endeavor, and the company had to put a lot of capital into marketing as the industry was still very early—this proved to be detrimental to their overall revenue
- COVID-19 pandemic—the era slowed the progress of the DTx industry as healthcare priorities were focused elsewhere

On April 7, 2023, Pear therapeutics filed for bankruptcy, and their story now serves as a cautionary tale for the rest of the industry.

Benefits of DTx

We've discussed the history of DTx, the regulatory landscape, the clinical evidence process, and the ongoing industry challenges. We will conclude with a review of the benefits of DTx, outlined in Table 14.2. These benefits are based on evidence and presented as an expert opinion. They highlight why digital therapeutics could be such a powerful area of medicine and why it is worth continuing to push and overcome the barriers.

Table 14.2: Benefits of DTx.

Benefit category	Benefit details
Accessibility	DTx are very easily accessible, and the majority are intended to be used at home. The benefit of effective therapies that are not anchored to an individual clinician or a medical appointment cannot be emphasized enough.
Cost-effective	DTx can reduce overall healthcare costs by reducing the need for in-person visits. Studies must be conducted to collect confirmatory data, and for many products, this is a confirmed benefit.
Real-time data	DTx can collect and report on real-time data as they continuously monitor patient progress. Instead of relying on infrequent time-points of lab draws or in-person appointments for data to make treatment decisions, both clinicians and patients are empowered to make more frequent adjustments that can lead to better treatment outcomes.
Engagement	DTx engage patients in their treatment and in their overall healthcare by requiring active ongoing participation. Personalization offered by many DTx products increases overall engagement that may lead to better outcomes.

Conclusion

Digital therapeutics are an innovative tool coming out of the digital health revolution. They hold near unlimited potential to support, treat, and help patients manage a wide variety of diseases. Since 2015, the industry has grown tremendously, and while some challenges have been resolved, many challenges still exist that will need to be overcome to increase widespread adoption. As the value and understanding of digital therapeutics become mainstream and embedded into healthcare, the path ahead will become less challenging.

References

[1] Digital Therapeutics Alliance. "DTA's Adoption & Interpretation of ISO's DTx Definition". https://dtxalliance.org/wp-content/uploads/2023/06/DTA_FS_New-DTx-Definition.pdf.

[2] Rastegayeva I. The rise of digital therapeutics. Dassault Systèmes Dassault Systèmes North America; 2019. Available from: https://blog.3ds.com/industries/life-sciences-healthcare/the-rise-of-digital-therapeutics/.

[3] mHealth Apps Market Size, Share & Trends Analysis Report By Type (Fitness, Medical), By Region (North America, Europe, Asia Pacific, Latin America, Middle East & Africa), and Segment Forecasts, 2023 - 2030. Grand View Research. https://www.grandviewresearch.com/industry-analysis/mhealth-app-market.

[4] Dang A, Arora D, Rane P. Role of digital therapeutics and the changing future of healthcare. Journal of Family Medicine and Primary Care May 31, 2020;9(5):2207–13. https://doi.org/10.4103/jfmpc.jfmpc_105_20. PMID: 32754475; PMCID: PMC7380804.

[5] Digital Therapeutics Alliance. Digital therapeutics definition and core principles. 2019. https://dtxalliance.org/.

[6] Comstock J. Pear Therapeutics gets de novo FDA clearance for reSET. A Digital Therapeutic for Substance Abuse September 14, 2017.

[7] COVID-19 pandemic triggers 25% increase in prevalence of anxiety and depression worldwide. World Health Organizaiton; March 02, 2022. https://www.who.int/news/item/02-03-2022-covid-19-pandemic-triggers-25-increase-in-prevalence-of-anxiety-and-depression-worldwide.

[8] Aylward B. Digital therapeutics adoption: advancing from concept into practice. RTI Health Advance; October 25, 2022. https://healthcare.rti.org/insights/digital-therapeutics-dtx-adoption#:~:text=Although%20there%20are%20currently%20more,integration%20into%20standard%20clinical%20workflows.

[9] Wels-Maug C. Digital health apps in Germany - an update on the DiGA journey. Healthcare IT News; November 29, 2021. https://www.healthcareitnews.com/news/emea/digital-health-apps-germany-update-diga-journey.

[10] Digital Therapeutics Alliance. "DTx regulatory and reimbursement pathways" - United States. https://dtxalliance.org/wp-content/uploads/2022/01/US-Regulatory-and-Reimbursement-Pathways.pdf.

[11] Software as a Medical Device (SAMD)." FDA, https://www.fda.gov/medical-devices/digital-health-center-excellence/software-medical-device-samd. Current as of 12/04/2018.

[12] Goerlich D. 7 examples of software as a medical device (SaMD). The Refinery; August 09, 2022. https://the-refinery.io/blog/7-examples-of-software-as-a-medical-device-samd.

[13] CSL behring: supporting hemophilia B patients on a journey toward a life-changing gene therapy treatment." BrightInsight, www.brightinsight.com/resources/csl-behring-supporting-hemophilia-b-patients-on-a-journey-toward-a-life-changing-gene-therapy-treatment. (Accessed 26 September 2023).

[14] Enforcement policy for digital health devices treating psychiatric disorders during Coronavirus disease." FDA, www.fda.gov/regulatory-information/search-fda-guidance-documents/enforcement-policy-digital-health-devices-treating-psychiatric-disorders-during-coronavirus-disease. Released April 2020.

[15] Scott J, Levy S. The next era of digital therapeutics. Hogan Lovells; May 16, 2023. https://www.engage.hoganlovells.com/knowledgeservices/viewContent.action?key=Ec8teaJ9Vao1rZsRe%2FRDnV7eOOGbnAEFKCLORG72fHz0%2BNbpi2jDfaB8lgiEyY1JAvAvaah9lF3dzoxprWhI6w%3D%3D&nav=FRbANEucS95NMLRN47z%2BeeOgEFCt8EGQ0qFfoEM4UR4%3D&emailtofriendview=true&freeviewlink=true.

[16] Artificial intelligence/machine learning (AI/ML)-based software as a medical device (SaMD) action plan. FDA; January 2021. https://www.fda.gov/media/145022/download.

[17] Prescription drug-use-related software; establishment of a public docket; request for comments. Federal Register 2018. https://www.federalregister.gov/documents/2018/11/20/2018-25206/prescription-drug-use-related-software-establishment-of-a-public-docket-request-for-comments.

[18] FDA in Brief: FDA takes steps to advance a new framework to promote development of digital tools that can inform the safe and effective use of prescription drugs. FDA; November 19, 2018. https://www.fda.gov/news-events/fda-brief/fda-brief-fda-takes-steps-advance-new-framework-promote-development-digital-tools-can-inform-safe.

[18a] Regulatory considerations for prescription drug UseRelated software guidance for industry - draft guidance. FDA; September 2023. https://www.fda.gov/media/172165/download.

[19] Breakthrough Devices Program." FDA, www.fda.gov/medical-devices/how-study-and-market-your-device/breakthrough-devices-program#s8. Current as of 9/14/2023.

[20] Breakthrough devices program: guidance for industry and Food and Drug Administration staff. FDA; September 2023. https://www.fda.gov/media/162413/download.

[21] Safer Technologies Program for Medical Devices." FDA, www.fda.gov/medical-devices/how-study-and-market-your-device/safer-technologies-program-step-medical-devices. Current as of 03/15/2021.

[22] The software precertification (Pre-Cert) pilot program: tailored total product lifecycle approaches and key findings. FDA; September 2022. https://www.fda.gov/media/161815/download?attachment.

[23] DiGA Directory. DiGA - Digital health applications directory. diga.bfarm.de/de/verzeichnis?type=%5B%5D. (Accessed 27 September 2023).

[24] Nicol-Schwarz K. DiGA promised German healthtechs access to 73M patients, but insurer roadblocks and slow adoption are limiting its potential. Sifted; July 06, 2023. https://sifted.eu/articles/diga-promised-

german-healthtechs-access-to-73m-patients-but-insurer-roadblocks-and-slow-adoption-are-limiting-its-potential.

[25] Cho CH. The beginning of the era of digital therapeutics in Korea: challenges and opportunities. Journal of Korean Medical Science May 29, 2023;38(21):e166. https://doi.org/10.3346/jkms.2023.38.e166. PMID: 37270919; PMCID: PMC10226848.

[26] Digital Therapeutics Alliance. "DTx regulatory and reimbursement pathways" - South Korea. https://dtxalliance.org/wp-content/uploads/2022/01/South-Korea-Regulatory-and-Reimbursement-Pathways.pdf.

[27] Huh KY, Oh J, Lee S, Yu KS. Clinical evaluation of digital therapeutics: present and future. Healthcare Informatics Research July 2022;28(3):188–97. https://doi.org/10.4258/hir.2022.28.3.188.

[28] Wang C, Lee C, Shin H. Digital therapeutics from bench to bedside. npj Digital Medicine March 10, 2023;6(1):38. https://doi.org/10.1038/s41746-023-00777-z.

[29] Digital Therapeutics Alliance. "Setting the stage for a fit-for-purpose DTx evidentiary standard". https://dtxalliance.org/wp-content/uploads/2022/12/DTA-Clinical-Evidence-Paper_12.22.pdf.

[30] Anderson M. Digital therapeutics company Akili ditches prescription business model. Healthcare Brew; September 15, 2023. https://www.healthcare-brew.com/stories/2023/09/15/digital-therapeutics-company-akili-ditches-prescription-business-model.

[31] Snyder Bulik B. In a digital first for pharma, Novartis signs on to market Pear's drug-abuse therapies. Fierce Pharma; April 24, 2018. https://www.fiercepharma.com/marketing/novartis-and-pear-therapeutics-partner-again-time-for-commercialization-deal-substance.

[32] Voluntis and Eisai to collaborate on digital therapeutics for oncology patients. Business Wire 2021. https://www.businesswire.com/news/home/20210426005910/en/Voluntis-and-Eisai-to-Collaborate-on-Digital-Therapeutics-for-Oncology-Patients.

[33] Buntz B. Decoding Bayer's digital health leap and its implications on drug discovery and personalized medicine. Drug Discovery and Development; June 01, 2023. https://www.drugdiscoverytrends.com/bayers-digital-health-strategy/.

[34] Muoio D. Novartis is cutting off its digital therapeutics commercialization partnership with Pear Therapeutics. MobiHealthNews; October 16, 2019. https://www.mobihealthnews.com/news/north-america/novartis-cutting-its-digital-therapeutics-commercialization-partnership-pear.

[35] Digital therapeutics explained. HTD Health March 27, 2023. https://htdhealth.com/insights/digital-therapeutics-explained/.

[36] The time is right for commercializing prescription digital therapeutics. AmerisourceBergen; November 10, 2022. https://www.amerisourcebergen.com/insights/manufacturers/time-is-right-for-commercializing-prescription-digital-therapeutics?&utm_source=fierce&utm_medium=paid-media&utm_campaign=bps_fy23_014_dtx&utm_content=fierce-native-article.

[37] Hanaman D. A crossroads for the digital therapeutics industry. Now is the time to Act. June 12, 2023. Pharmexec.com. https://www.pharmexec.com/view/crossroads-digital-therapeutics-industry-time-act.

[38] Wrzosinksi P. Pear therapeutics: the rise and fall of a digital therapeutics. Pioneer. Disrupting Healthcare; April 12, 2023. https://disrupting.healthcare/2023/04/12/pear-therapeutics-the-rise-and-fall-of-a-digital-therapeutics-pioneer/.

CHAPTER 15

The future of preventive primary care

Dipu Patel[1] and Amit Kumar Dey[2]

[1]Department of PA Studies, University of Pittsburgh, Pittsburgh, PA, United States; [2]Department of Diabetology, Apollo Sugar Clinics, Kolkata, India

> *Sensors will not replace senses, electronics will not replace embraces, screens will not replace smiles. But, we will need to learn how to use sensors, electronics, and screens to inform our sensibility, warm our embraces, and share our smiles.*
>
> **Dipu Patel.**

Introduction

According to the Centers for Disease Control and Prevention (CDC) [1], 7 out of 10 deaths in the United States are caused by chronic disease. Furthermore, according to the World Health Statistics: monitoring health for the SDGs, Sustainable Development Goals report [2], written by the World Health Organization (WHO), "The impact of NCDs (noncommunicable diseases) grew from causing 61% of global deaths (equivalent to 31 million, UI: 24−40 million) in 2000 to causing 74% (or 41 million, UI: 29−57 million) in 2019, and from causing 47% (or 1.3 billion, UI: 0.8−1.7 billion) of global disability-adjusted life-years (DALYs) in 2000 to causing 63% (or 1.6 billion, UI: 1.0−2.2 billion) of DALYs in 2019."

To put a finer point on the issue, "Four major NCDs collectively killed about 33.3 million (UI: 24.5−43.3 million) people in 2019, a 28% increase compared to 2000. These major NCDs are cardiovascular disease (17.9 million, UI: 13.4−22.9 million), cancer (9.3 million, UI: 6.9−12.2 million), chronic respiratory disease (4.1 million, UI: 2.9−5.6 million) and diabetes (2.0 million, UI: 1.4−2.7 million)." [2].

As the global population continues to struggle with chronic diseases and the long-term burdens of care, clinicians equally struggle to mitigate the burdens of disease and provide care that truly impacts outcomes. No matter the country or healthcare system, the current model of primary care is not sustainable for the patient or the provider. Patients have limited access to timely, cost-effective care, and providers are being pushed to see more patients in smaller increments of time. The future of preventive and primary care needs to

Digital Health. https://doi.org/10.1016/B978-0-443-23901-4.00015-5

be reenvisioned. This chapter focuses on the future of preventive and primary care and how digital health can perhaps make an impact on care delivery, reshape how care is delivered, and how outcomes may be measured.

Although the future of primary care is virtual, there will be times when patients will need to be seen in a physical space, and healthcare will always need the human touch. Imagine stepping into a primary care clinic of the future. As you approach the entrance of the office, a warm voice welcomes you by your preferred name and reassures you about your visit. This voice is your personal AI-powered receptionist, a friendly digital assistant named "Willow" who knows you, your preferences, and your habits. Willow will help you and your healthcare provider make the best decisions for your care. As you continue to the reception area, virtual reality (VR) technology surrounds you in a landscape that is tailored to your mood or preference; whether it's a serene forest, a peaceful beach, or even the cozy comfort of your own living room. You notice that there is no waiting room; there isn't one! This is because AI algorithms have been working behind the scenes, predicting and optimizing appointment schedules so that you don't have to wait for your appointment. Furthermore, no paperwork or forms to fill out. The clinic, powered by AI, already has reviewed our medical history, appointment details, and any specific concerns you might have, ensuring that your visit is tailored to your unique healthcare needs. Your healthcare provider already has the information she needs to help take care of you and your needs. The focus is wholly on you, not the computer screen, or the paperwork. You spend an hour with your healthcare provider having every concern addressed, care coordinated, and digital health prescriptions managed.

This is the future of primary care: patient-centered, technology-driven, and provider-focused. The future of preventive care is a seamless integration of precision medicine, personalized medicine, and coordination of care with interprofessional teams and caregivers with technology enabling empathy and human touch.

Let's walk through this clinic of the future.

AI in the future clinic

AI-powered reception area

The AI-powered receptionist is the communications hub of the ecosystem [3]. The AI-powered receptions also serve as the first point of contact in the collaborative care ecosystem [4,5]. Harnessed with facial recognition, it will have the ability to adapt the environment to your symptoms and concerns. For example, if parents are bringing in their child for a visit, the AI receptionist would engage the child with coloring games, storytelling, and age-appropriate games based on their developmental milestones. For elderly patients, the AI receptionist would have any assistive devices, such as wheelchairs and walkers, ready before the appointment. Furthermore, the waiting rooms of the future will be equipped with VR headsets [6,7]. Although patients will not wait long, the VR headsets will help enhance the patient experience. AI receptionists and VR waiting rooms are a promising area of research and growth in primary care [8]. This patient-facing technology has the potential to transform the patient experience in primary care.

Healthcare in the metaverse

As technology continues to evolve, so will healthcare providers. The seamless integration of technology and collaborative team-based practice will come to fruition in the primary care setting. In a single visit, patients and caregivers will be able to be taken care of by primary care providers, physical therapists, nutritionists, pharmacists, and case workers. The patient will have personalized care wrapped around all the services and tools needed to be healthy.

"A 'metaverse' is a three-dimensional shared virtual space in which users may carry out all actions via the use of augmented reality (AR), mixed reality (MR) and virtual reality (VR) technology." [9] The metaverse holds immense potential for revolutionizing healthcare systems by enabling shared and immersive virtual worlds, allowing for interoperability across various platforms [9]. It facilitates the creation and transfer of content between virtual healthcare settings while preserving user identities. These technologies serve as the foundational elements of the metaverse. While the metaverse offers promising healthcare applications, there are significant challenges to address, such as identity security and hardware limitations. Additionally, as it aims to seamlessly integrate with physical reality and relies on advanced technologies such as AR, VR, MR, AI, high-speed networks, edge computing, and blockchain caution and deliberate thought in its use are essential.

While there are technical hurdles to address, such as security, patient privacy, network speed, and data sharing, the metaverse's potential to enhance healthcare lies in its ability to create immersive, interconnected virtual environments where healthcare professionals can collaborate and patients can receive safe, high-quality care, no matter where they are.

Patient education and research with generative AI

In the future, patient education about their healthcare will be tailored not only to their specific disease but also to their genetics, environment, and culture. Healthcare providers will be able to utilize AI algorithms and provide patients with recommendations on lifestyle, medication, and treatment options in the language that the patient understands while keeping in mind the cultural context, grade level, and regional dialects. The future of primary care patient education will allow patients to access care 24/7 through the use of chatbots and offer guidance in real time using risk stratification [10]. This guidance will be evidence-based right down to the patient's genetics.

Generative AI and Natural Language Processing (NLP) have elevated the demand for contextual care and brought what was once thought to be sci-fi to reality. Although we are still early in the era of generative AI and the models are still far from perfect, they do hold a lot of promise. Current models still hallucinate information and require human supervision. For example, the following prompt response was generated using OpenAI's ChatGPT [10]. The content is generally accurate; however, three out of the four sources cited are hallucinations. This phenomenon has been acknowledged by OpenAI in its technical report, "Despite its capabilities, GPT-4 has similar limitations to earlier GPT models: it is not fully reliable (e.g., can suffer from "hallucinations"), has a limited context window, and does not learn from experience. Care should be taken when using the outputs of GPT-4, particularly in contexts where reliability is important." [11].

ChatGPT prompt: Write me a paragraph on how GPT will accelerate scientific research and cite sources

The following paragraph is written wholly by Chat-GPT-3.

"Generative Pre-trained Transformer (GPT) has the potential to accelerate scientific research in a multitude of ways. One of the primary ways that GPT can accelerate research is through its ability to analyze and synthesize large volumes of data from a variety of sources. GPT models have been trained on vast amounts of text data, including scientific articles, research papers, and patents, which enables them to identify patterns and insights that would be difficult to identify through traditional methods. GPT can also assist in the discovery of new scientific concepts and hypotheses by generating novel combinations of ideas based on existing research. Additionally, GPT can facilitate collaboration and knowledge sharing among researchers by providing a platform for natural language communication and document sharing. By automating time-consuming tasks such as literature reviews and data analysis, GPT can allow researchers to focus on more complex and creative aspects of scientific discovery. Several studies have demonstrated the potential of GPT in scientific research, including in the fields of drug discovery, biomedical research, and natural language processing. However, there are also challenges associated with the use of GPT in research, such as the need for high-quality data, model interpretability, and ethical considerations. Nonetheless, GPT has the potential to transform the scientific research landscape and enable new discoveries that would have been otherwise impossible."

"Generated Sources:

- Belthangady C, Roy D. Transforming drug discovery with machine learning and AI models. Drug Discovery Today 2020;25(5):804–11.

- Karimi S, Karami J, Yazdi MA. Deep learning approaches in biomedical research: a review. Artificial Intelligence in Medicine 2020;104(101):822.
- Dai X, Yang Z, Yang Y, Carbonell JG, Le QV, Salakhutdinov R. Transformer-XL: attentive language models beyond a fixed-length context. arXiv preprint arXiv. https://doi.org/1901.02860.
- Hagendorff T, Yoo Y. Ethical implications of language models trained on biomedical data. BMJ Health & Care Informatics 2021;28(1):e100333."

While hallucinations can be reduced by more specific prompting and techniques such as Retrieval Augmented Generation, it is not perfect [12,13]. The current readily available models such as ChatGPT, Bard, and Bing are not trained on medical information, there are a number under development that will no doubt improve trust, safety, and reliability of patient education.

Generative AI holds the promise of transforming patient education into a highly personalized, accessible, and continuously updated experience. By harnessing the power of AI-driven content generation and language translation, primary care providers can empower patients with the knowledge and information they need to make informed decisions about their health, leading to improved healthcare outcomes and enhanced patient satisfaction.

The future state of primary care

Technology will drive changes in practice style and modalities. Table 1 highlights the transformative journey that primary care is poised to undergo in the near future with the integration of digital health technologies. It illustrates the differences between the current primary care model and the promising future model, emphasizing how digital health is set to revolutionize patient care across diverse populations. Three examples are discussed briefly further to highlight this transformation. The following section dives deeper into chronic disease care, specifically diabetes care through the AI lens after briefly touching on other areas of family practice care.

Elderly care

For an elderly patient struggling with hypertension, the current primary care model often involves sporadic in-person visits and a reactive approach to disease management. However, in the future, digital health technologies will enable continuous remote monitoring of blood pressure, personalized medication management, and proactive interventions. AI-driven diagnostics will detect anomalies in real time, and telehealth consultations will ensure more regular check-ins with healthcare providers. This approach not only enhances the patient's well-being but also optimizes healthcare costs by preventing costly hospitalizations and the downstream complications of this chronic disease.

Pediatric care

Similarly, for pediatric patients with asthma, the current model relies heavily on episodic office visits and limited engagement. In contrast, the future model will leverage digital health to provide continuous monitoring through smart inhalers and wearable devices. Pediatric patients (and their parents) will benefit from interactive, age-appropriate educational virtual tools that help them understand and manage their condition. Furthermore, virtual reality consultations will be used to address anxiety related to asthma, making the entire experience more child-friendly and less anxiety-provoking for the parents and caregivers.

LGTBQ+ care

For an LGBTQ patient dealing with depression, the current primary care model may lack sensitivity and specialized support. However, the future model will place a strong emphasis on patient empowerment and inclusivity. LGBTQ+ individuals will have access to tailored mental health apps, online support groups, and AI chatbots that provide understanding and guidance. Teletherapy sessions with LGBTQ-affirmative therapists will be readily available, ensuring that mental healthcare is not only accessible but also sensitive to the unique needs of this population.

In summary, Table 15.1 underscores how the future of primary care is poised to embrace digital health to improve patient care, access, engagement, and outcomes across diverse demographics. Examples in hypertension, asthma, and depression highlight the shift from reactive and sporadic care to proactive, continuous, and patient-centered approaches that leverage technology to enhance both health and patient experience.

Chronic disease

Artificial intelligence in diabetes and metabolic syndrome care

The influx of artificial intelligence (AI) into healthcare propels a transformative era where innovative solutions, technological integration, and data analytics converge to revolutionize patient care and medical research. Among myriad medical conditions, diabetes stands out as a critical focal point for such innovations, given its widespread prevalence and intricate management needs. This section looks into AI's capabilities, prospects, challenges, and ethical quandaries, specifically in the field of diabetes care.

AI navigating through diabetic retinopathy challenges

Diabetic retinopathy, a compellingly complex domain within diabetes management, emerges as a notable beneficiary of AI's prowess. The intervention of AI in screening and

Table 15.1: The current state and the future potential of primary care.

Aspect	Current primary care model	Future primary care model with digital health
Access to care	Sometimes limited by geographical proximity, physical location, and office hours	Enhanced access through telehealth, AI-powered virtual clinics, and 24/7 availability
Patient engagement	Relatively passive patient engagement with limited access to health data	Active patient engagement with access to personalized health data, wearables, and health apps
Interactions	Mainly in-person office visits, emails, and phone calls	Diverse interactions, including telehealth, chatbots, virtual reality consultations, and AI-driven messaging
Diagnostic tools	Reliance on traditional diagnostic tools with delays in results in the context of symptomology	Integration of AI-driven diagnostics, remote monitoring devices, and real-time health data analysis
Collaborative care	Limited, delayed, and difficult collaboration between primary care physicians and specialists	Seamless interprofessional collaboration through virtual team meetings, leveraging the metaverse, and data sharing
Chronic disease management	Reactive and single-visit management with occasional check-ups and follow-ups	Proactive management with continuous monitoring, personalized care plans, and early intervention
Patient empowerment	Limited patient empowerment and involvement in care decisions	Empowered patients with access to health information, self-management tools, and shared decision-making
Preventive care	Limited focus on preventive care due to time and cost constraints	Emphasis on preventive care with tailored health recommendations, reminders, and proactive outreach
Cost efficiency	High costs associated with in-person visits and inefficiencies	Improved cost efficiency through reduced hospitalization, streamlined care pathways, and optimized resource allocation
Patient experience	Varies widely but often includes long wait times and administrative hassles	Improved patient experience with shorter waiting times, personalized care, and virtual engagement
Data security and privacy	Concerns about data security and privacy in electronic health records	Enhanced data security and privacy measures, including blockchain technology and encrypted health records

early diagnosis of diabetic retinopathy, particularly in communities where medical resources are constrained, is pivotal. Ingenious applications, such as the deployment of deep learning (ANN) in image analysis and the utilization of smartphone-embedded fundus cameras, articulate a future where technology and accessibility coalesce to democratize diabetes and metabolic care. The scalability and efficiency of AI-fueled screening protocols suggest an avenue where early detection and nuanced management of diabetic retinopathy become easily attainable.

Predictive models: Gazing into the future of diabetes and metabolic care

Unleashing machine learning models into predictive analysis within the landscape of diabetes and metabolic syndrome signifies a leap toward preventive healthcare and personalized medicine. The capacity of AI to foresee outcomes, ranging from the onset of diabetes to intricate correlations such as the link between type II diabetes and other comorbidities, unlocks new dimensions in risk management and therapeutic interventions. The proliferation of predictive models not only augments clinical decision-making but also creates a framework where patient outcomes are perpetually optimized through dynamic, data-driven strategies.

Technological symbiosis in comprehensive diabetes management

AI's amalgamation with diverse technological advancements shapes a future where diabetes management transcends traditional boundaries, venturing into integrated and patient-centric care. The harmonization of digital health technologies and AI leverages the gargantuan volumes of diabetes data, crafting a milieu where intelligent decision-making and digital health symbiotically elevate patient outcomes and resource utilization. AI-powered solutions, ranging from intelligent chatbots (virtual health assistants) to adaptive screening systems, illuminate a trajectory where patients and healthcare providers are continually supported by a digital infrastructure that is both intelligent and intuitive. This will lead to better dietary and lifestyle recommendations, resulting in behavior modification, thus enabling the possibility of better patient outcomes in chronic metabolic care.

Elevating detection and mitigating complications with AI

The inception of AI in diagnostic protocols and the management of diabetic complications casts a spotlight on the preventive and mitigative potentials embedded within intelligent algorithms. The multidisciplinary impact of AI, as witnessed in its applications in renal damage and kidney disease management associated with diabetes, highlights the cross-domain efficacy of AI. This epitomizes a scenario where AI doesn't merely serve as a diagnostic tool but evolves holistically, mitigating complications and enhancing life quality across the diabetic population.

AI interfacing with insulin pumps and continuous glucose monitoring systems

AI's interface with insulin pumps and continuous glucose monitoring systems (CGMS) emerges as a beacon of transformative diabetic management. Model predictive control (MPC) algorithms with proportional-integral-derivative (PID) controllers guided by the fuzzy logic control approach intertwined with insulin delivery and glucose monitoring are already available in the latest advanced insulin pumps crafting a milieu that takes us a step toward "closing the loop." The integration of AI with insulin pumps has unlocked the door to automated insulin delivery (AID) systems, also known as artificial pancreas systems, which meticulously monitor glucose levels, ensuring that insulin delivery is perpetually attuned to the patient's physiological needs. Moreover, the convergence of AI and CGMS inaugurates a paradigm where real-time glucose data become a catalyst for dynamic insulin management strategies, mitigating risks and enhancing life quality for diabetic individuals. This has resulted in better clinical outcomes with excellent time in range (TIR) in patients on AID.

AI in diabetic foot care

AI is revolutionizing diabetic foot care with the advent of smartphone-based camera systems. Such systems empower patients to take an active role in their daily wound care. The potential benefits include faster wound healing and a reduction in associated travel and health costs. Additionally, researchers are harnessing the power of low-cost thermal imaging systems to swiftly evaluate the risk diabetic patients have of developing foot ulcers.

A notable innovation in this domain is the development of "Smart Insoles." These specially designed insoles are embedded with multiple pressure sensors to monitor the varied pressures exerted across the foot's plantar region. With the structured data these insoles capture, AI algorithms can predict the onset of diabetic foot syndrome and identify risks associated with diabetic foot ulcer (DFU).

Multimodal generative AI (ChatGPT) in diabetes and metabolic care

ChatGPT has emerged as a valuable tool in the realm of diabetes care. Currently, it offers immediate responses to diabetes-centric queries, ensuring timely reminders for medication and insulin, and tailoring dietary advice for individual patients. Beyond just answering questions, the AI lends emotional and psychological support to patients, recommends suitable physical activities, and clarifies intricate details about treatments and medications. Furthermore, it acts as a bridge, guiding patients to essential resources and support groups while continuously evolving based on ongoing patient interactions. Looking ahead, the future of ChatGPT in diabetes care seems even more promising. It aims to seamlessly integrate with advanced devices for real-time glucose monitoring and use AI capabilities to predict blood sugar levels and associated risks. The horizon includes personalized coaching for diet and exercise, automated follow-ups for treatment adherence, and an expanded accessibility range to cater to diverse patient groups. Additionally, the platform is gearing toward a more integrated healthcare experience by synchronizing with telehealth services, facilitating robust community interactions, and empowering patients with vital self-management tools. All of these advancements will be undertaken with a keen eye on adhering to and influencing future healthcare regulations and standards.

Cost-effectiveness: A balancing act in resource utilization

The confluence of cost-effectiveness and resource optimization within the AI-diabetes nexus imparts an essential perspective, especially considering global healthcare disparities. AI's potential to rationalize resource allocation underscores the viability of intelligent healthcare solutions even within resource-constrained environments. Thus, AI enables a beacon of equitable, accessible, and sustainable management of chronic metabolic and diabetes healthcare, potentially dissolving geographical and socioeconomic barriers that have historically impeded universal healthcare access for chronic diseases.

Ethical and practical conundrums in AI deployment

As we navigate through the variegated landscape of AI in diabetes care, ethical considerations and pragmatic challenges emerge as inevitable counterparts to technological advancements. The imperative for validating AI models, ensuring explainability, and fortifying ethical deployment threads through the discourse, offering a subtle reminder that technological advancements must be perpetually anchored in ethical and practical realities. The evolution of AI in healthcare mandates a delicate balance where innovations are ceaselessly aligned with ethical, clinical, and social expectations, ensuring that technological progress does not inadvertently spawn new dilemmas or exacerbate existing disparities.

Gazing forward: Nurturing the future of AI in diabetes care

The prospective pathways unfolding within the AI—diabetes paradigm evoke a future where intelligent algorithms, ethical considerations, and innovative solutions intertwine to shape a new epoch in diabetic care and research. From advancing machine learning models for predictive analytics to exploring nascent technologies that might redefine diabetes care by 2030, the forward momentum within this domain encapsulates a spirit of perpetual evolution, guided by research, innovation, and an unwavering commitment to enhancing patient outcomes and experiences.

Summary

AI, with its profound implications, intricate challenges, and unparalleled prospects, commands a pivotal role in the ongoing and future narratives of diabetes and metabolic care. Through the lenses of screening, predictive modeling, comprehensive management, ethical deployment, and future research, AI materializes as a multifaceted entity, capable of orchestrating transformative changes across the diabetes care continuum. However, the journey ahead mandates a collective vigilance, ensuring that as we navigate through the enthralling possibilities of AI, we remain steadfastly anchored in ethical, clinical, and social realities, ensuring that the future we sculpt is not only technologically advanced but also ethically sound, clinically validated, and universally accessible. Thus, as we tread forward, let us weave a tapestry where technology, ethics, and humanity converge to redefine the future of diabetes care in a manner that is as compassionate and equitable as it is innovative and transformative.

Conclusion

The primary care clinic of the future will be a vastly different place than the clinics of today. It will be a place where patients are treated as individuals, where prevention is a top priority, and where Fig. 15.1 is used to enhance the patient experience. As we begin to untether ourselves from the four walls of a clinic to seek and provide care, our norms will shift. We will shift practice from seeing patients once or twice a year for chronic conditions they live with on a daily basis to continuous remote patient monitoring with

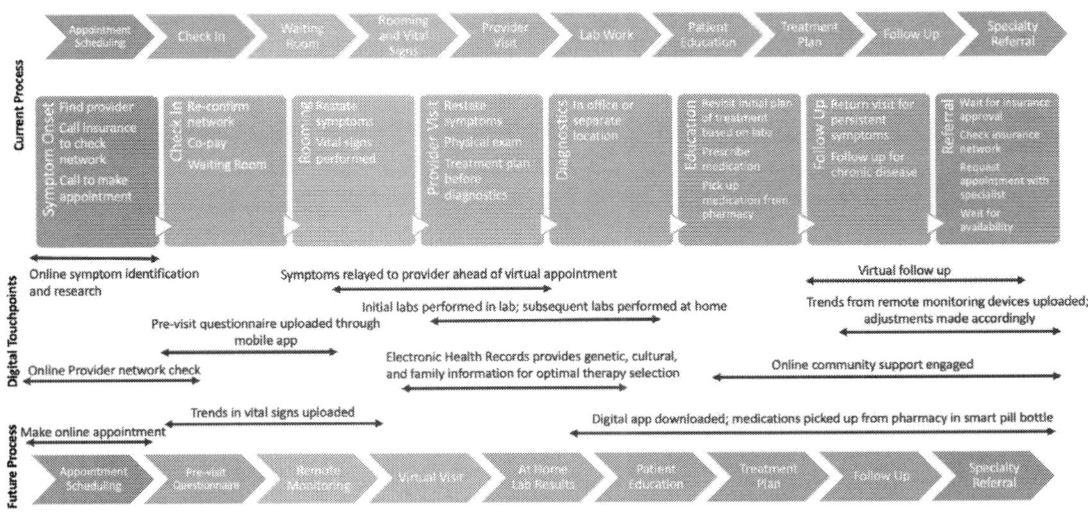

Figure 15.1
Overview of current and future patient journey with digital touchpoints.

real-time interventions to promote a healthy lifestyle and avoid downstream complications. All of this care will be coordinated by interprofessional collaborative teams in synergy with specialists, PTs, OTs, nutritionists, and pharmacists. This will bring to reality true patient-centered care, decrease healthcare costs, and improve provider and patient satisfaction.

Not too far in the future, care in the metaverse will be the norm, Apps for all disease states will be on formulary and first-line options, and AI assistants will go the extra mile to help you make the most informed decision for your health. This is the future of primary care, and I am excited for it.

Assessment options

1. **Virtual Clinic Design Challenge**: Write or draw the future virtual clinic. Be creative and imagine what the future of primary care clinics will need. Think about the layout and features of this futuristic primary care clinic powered by digital health technologies. You can incorporate AI-powered receptionists, VR waiting rooms, and other innovative elements discussed in the chapter.
   Objectives:
   1. Apply understanding of chapter content Assess and evaluate the ability to comprehend the key concepts of how digital health technologies can transform the primary care clinic experience.
   2. Encourage readers to think creatively and innovatively about the future of healthcare design.
2. **Patient-Centered Digital Health Story**: Write a story of a patient visit from both the patient and provider perspectives. You may include technologies discussed in the chapter or other technologies and digital health tools. Include specific examples.
   Objectives:
   1. Assess and evaluate the ability to empathize with patient and provider experiences and how digital health can impact both and provider and the patient's lives.
   2. Encourage effective communication skills through storytelling and convey complex healthcare concepts in a clear manner.
3. **Digital Health Impact Analysis**: Conduct an impact analysis of digital health on primary care. Choose one specific aspect discussed in the chapter (e.g., patient engagement, preventive care, collaborative care) and write a short essay or report on how the integration of digital health technologies is likely to impact that aspect. Consider the benefits, challenges, opportunities, implications, and potential outcomes.
   Objectives:
   1. Assess and evaluate the ability to analyze the impact of digital health on primary care and

2. Apply knowledge to discuss the benefits, challenges, opportunities, and implications of digital health implementation and how to make informed predictions on how digital health will shape the future of primary care.

References

[1] iHealthcareAnalyst I. Global Preventive Healthcare Market $345 Billion by 2029. iHealthcareAnalyst, Inc. - Healthcare Market Research. (Accessed 15 November 2023). https://www.ihealthcareanalyst.com/government-initiatives-public-awareness-propel-preventive-health-care-technologies-services-market/.

[2] World Health Organization. World health statistics 2023. World Health Organization; 2023. (Accessed 15 November 2023). https://www.who.int/publications/i/item/9789240074323.

[3] Schneider J. AI-powered virtual people can now take over office receptionist duties. (Accessed 15 November 2023). https://petapixel.com/2021/03/11/ai-powered-virtual-people-can-now-take-over-office-receptionist-duties/.

[4] AimeReception: AI virtual receptionist, virtual human based on Multimodal AI. (Accessed 15 November 2023). https://www.aimesoft.com/aimereception.html.

[5] Digital Doctors and Robot Receptionists | Extended Abstracts of the 2019 CHI Conference on Human Factors in Computing Systems. ACM Conferences. 2019. https://dl.acm.org/doi/abs/10.1145/3290607.3312916.

[6] Al-Nerabieah Z, Alhalabi M-N, Owayda AM, Alsabek L, Bshara N, Kouchaji C. Effectiveness of using virtual reality eyeglasses in the waiting room on preoperative anxiety: a randomized controlled trial. Perioperative Care and Operating Room Management 2020;21:100129. https://doi.org/10.1016/j.pcorm.2020.100129.

[7] de Tommaso M, Ricci K, Laneve L, Savino N, Antonaci V, Livrea P. Virtual visual effect of hospital waiting room on pain modulation in healthy subjects and patients with chronic migraine. Pain Research and Treatment 2013;2013:1–8. https://doi.org/10.1155/2013/515730.

[8] Baki Kocaballı A, Ijaz K, Laranjo L, et al. Envisioning an artificial intelligence documentation assistant for future primary care consultations: a co-design study with general practitioners. Journal of the American Medical Informatics Association 2020;27(11):1695–704. https://doi.org/10.1093/jamia/ocaa131.

[9] Bansal G, Rajgopal K, Chamola V, Xiong Z, Niyato D. Healthcare in metaverse: a survey on current metaverse applications in healthcare. IEEE Access 2022;10:119914–46. https://doi.org/10.1109/access.2022.3219845.

[10] Patel, D. ChatGPT and the future of health care. Clinical Advisor. (Accessed 15 November 2023). https://www.clinicaladvisor.com/home/topics/practice-management-information-center/chatgpt-future-health-care-medicine/.

[11] OpenAI. GPT-4 Technical Report 2023. https://cdn.openai.com/papers/gpt-4.pdf.

[12] Zhang P. Maged. Generative AI in medicine and healthcare: promises, opportunities and challenges. Future Internet 2023;15(9):286. https://doi.org/10.3390/fi15090286.

[13] Mitigating LLM Hallucinations: a multifaceted approach. AI, software, tech, and people, not in that order… by X. (Accessed 15 November 2023). https://amatriain.net/blog/hallucinations#advancedprompting.

Further reading

[1] Ahmed A, Aziz S, Abd-Alrazaq A, Farooq F, Househ M, Sheikh J. The effectiveness of wearable devices using artificial intelligence for blood glucose level forecasting or prediction: systematic review. Journal of Medical Internet Research 2023;25:e40259.

[2] Ahmed A, Aziz S, Abd-Alrazaq A, Farooq F, Sheikh J. Overview of artificial intelligence-driven wearable devices for diabetes: scoping review. Journal of Medical Internet Research 2022;24(8):e36010.
[3] Ahuja A, Kewlani D. Commentary: artificial intelligence - a game changer. Indian Journal of Ophthalmology 2020;68(2):405–6.
[4] Nomura A, Noguchi M, Kometani M, Furukawa K, Yoneda T. Artificial intelligence in current diabetes management and prediction. Current Diabetes Reports 2021;21(12):61.
[5] Derozier V, Arnavielhe S, Renard E, Dray G, Martin S. How knowledge emerges from artificial intelligence algorithm and data visualization for diabetes management. Journal of Diabetes Science and Technology 2019;13(4):698–707.
[6] Sng GGR, Tung JYM, Lim DYZ, Bee YM. Potential and pitfalls of ChatGPT and natural-language artificial intelligence models for diabetes education. Diabetes Care 2023;46(5):e103–5.
[7] Spänig S, Emberger-Klein A, Sowa JP, Canbay A, Klaus M, Heider D. The virtual doctor: an interactive clinical-decision-support system based on deep learning for non-invasive prediction of diabetes. Artificial Intelligence in Medicine 2019;100:101706. https://doi.org/10.1016/j.artmed.2019.101706.
[8] Gold JI, Annick ET, Lane AS, Ho K, Marty RT, Espinoza J. "Doc McStuffins: doctor for a day" virtual reality (DocVR) for pediatric preoperative anxiety and satisfaction: pediatric medical technology feasibility study. Journal of Medical Internet Research 2021;23(4):e25504. https://doi.org/10.2196/25504.
[9] Veling W, Lestestuiver B, Jongma M, Hoenders R, van Driel C. Virtual reality relaxation for patients with a psychiatric disorder: crossover randomized controlled trial. Journal of Medical Internet Research 2021;23(1):e17233. https://doi.org/10.2196/17233.
[10] Haleem A, Javaid M, Khan IH. Holography applications toward medical field: an overview. Indian Journal of Radiology and Imaging 2020;30(3):354. https://doi.org/10.4103/ijri.ijri_39_20.
[11] Javaid M, Haleem A. Industry 4.0 applications in medical field: a brief review. Current Medicine Research and Practice 2019;9(3):102–9. https://doi.org/10.1016/j.cmrp.2019.04.001.
[12] Imagining the Future of Primary Care: A Global Look at Innovative Health Care Delivery | NEJM Catalyst. NEJM Catalyst Innovations in Care Delivery. (Accessed 15 November 2023). https://catalyst.nejm.org/doi/full/10.1056/CAT.20.0481.
[13] Eysenbach G. The role of ChatGPT, generative language models, and artificial intelligence in medical education: a conversation with ChatGPT and a call for papers. JMIR Medical Education 2023;9:e46885. https://doi.org/10.2196/46885.
[14] Jeha GM, Qiblawi SH, Jairath N, et al. ChatGPT and generative artificial intelligence in Mohs surgery: a new frontier of innovation. Journal of Investigative Dermatology 2023;143(11):2105–7. https://doi.org/10.1016/j.jid.2023.05.018.
[15] Chow CK, Redfern J, Hillis GS, et al. Effect of lifestyle-focused text messaging on risk factor modification in patients with coronary heart disease. JAMA 2015;314(12):1255. https://doi.org/10.1001/jama.2015.10945.

CHAPTER 16

Integrating digital medicine in rural communities

Susan McDiarmid[1] and Sonia V. Otte[2]
[1]Westfield State University PA Program, Westfield, MA, United States; [2]California State University - San Bernardino, San Bernardino, CA, United States

Introduction

Continued healthcare access issues in the United States (US) have made it challenging and seemingly impossible for communities to achieve *health equity*—the "attainment of the highest level of health for all people." [1] Inequitable differences in health and quality-of-life outcomes (i.e., *health disparities*) can be attributed to environmental factors known as the *social determinants of health*. Examples of social determinants of health include safe housing, education, socioeconomic status, access to nutritious foods, racism, air and water pollution, and literacy level [2]. The individual and combined effect of these environmental conditions can have a profound impact on the health and well-being of communities, particularly those located in rural areas.

According to the Centers for Disease Control (CDC), more than 46 million Americans living in rural areas experience poorer health outcomes than their urban counterparts [3]. Residents of rural US communities face a greater risk of death "from heart disease, cancer, unintentional injury, chronic lower respiratory disease, and stroke." [3] In addition, disparities in mental healthcare access in rural communities contribute to higher rates of death "due to drugs, alcohol, and suicide" [4] (dubbed as *deaths of despair*). This increasing gap between rural and urban communities is largely linked to a fragmented healthcare delivery system, lack of healthcare providers, limited preventive care, and transportation concerns [5,6].

A significant contributor to the fractured healthcare delivery is the closure of remote hospitals. Since 2010, a total of 152 hospital closures and conversions have occurred within rural US communities, primarily in Texas and across the Southeast [7]. The affected communities are typically racially and ethnically diverse, as well as have an increased number of uninsured, publicly insured, and socioeconomically disadvantaged

Digital Health. https://doi.org/10.1016/B978-0-443-23901-4.00016-7

residents [6]. These closures force rural residents to travel even farther for care. The increased distance may lead to critical delays in emergent care access and poorer health outcomes, including "increased length of stay (LOS) and in-hospital mortality." [7] In addition to emergent care, rural emergency departments (EDs) are often utilized for acute and nonurgent conditions due to limited access to primary care services. Following hospital/ED closures and their associated job reduction, the number of clinicians and health professionals may also decrease in the surrounding area leading to a smaller healthcare workforce. Therefore, the cumulative impact of remote hospital closures is significant to the health of rural communities.

In order to mitigate these existing disparities in rural areas, both government agencies and the private sector have sought out and implemented traditional and innovative approaches. Traditional approaches include scholarships, loan forgiveness, and loan repayment programs for physicians and advanced practice providers who commit to working in rural communities postgraduation. Although effective for recruitment, these efforts have not always led to long-term retention. Rural communities are then faced with an inconsistency in care each time a provider leaves following a fulfilled obligation (e.g., 2–5 years).

One more innovative approach is the integration of community health workers (CHWs). CHWs are often highly involved members of the community they serve, so they are uniquely positioned to connect patients with providers, support services, and resources [5]. The level of training varies on location but may be as little as a few hours or days [5]. Although there is no standardized training, CHWs provide a cost-effective method to address access to care issues and improve health outcomes. Through facilitated engagement, CHWs have the potential to decrease ED visits and promote preventive and chronic care [5].

Finally, a newer area of development in rural communities is digital medicine. Rural communities within the United States and around the world have started integrating the use of telemedicine, mobile applications, self-monitoring devices, and more. Studies evaluating the effectiveness of these digital medicine interventions (DMIs) continue to grow [8]. The success of each intervention can vary depending on the patient population, field of medicine, geographic location, and if supplemented with a healthcare professional (e.g., CHW).

Barriers and challenges to DMI adoption in rural communities

Although digital medicine interventions are increasingly found to be beneficial, its adoption in rural communities has been slow due to several identified factors [8]. These barriers are largely related to patient factors and issues related to cost and infrastructure.

Patient preferences and needs

Through interviews and focus groups, studies noted that patients have concerns about digital medicine due to a general resistance to change [8—10]. In a qualitative study of 30 participants, Slevin et al. [9] found that a lack of perceived usefulness dissuaded patients from accepting DMIs. The study noted that patients with chronic disease (i.e., chronic obstructive pulmonary disease) felt too overwhelmed and time-constrained from their current care routine to add more complexity with a DMI [10]. Patients in this study [10] also noted a concern over replacing face-to-face clinical visits with digital interactions. Babbage et al. [8] evaluated rural communities and noted a similar preference among its 114 study participants for face-to-face conversation with their healthcare providers. However, this preference was primarily noted by the study's older participants [8].

Beyond patient preference, the development of DMIs must focus on the needs of individual patients or patient groups. When DMIs do not incorporate a target group's needs, their adoption rate may be limited and lead to an exacerbation of health disparities [11]. For example, studies found that DMIs known to improve the health outcomes of patients with long-term conditions led to minimal or no improvement in health outcomes for patients with lower socioeconomic status [12]. Therefore, use of a one-size-fits-all model should be avoided to help support a wide range of patient needs. An individual's or group's socioeconomic status, ethnicity, language, geographic location, and culture should all be integrated into the development of a DMI.

Usability and adherence

Even when DMIs are created with a specific population in mind, usability and adherence are often overlooked [9]. Examining how a patient would interact with the technology may better predict their rate of adherence. Low patient adherence will likely lead to a limited health benefit [9]. Therefore, DMI development should also consider patient usability, including technological skills, comfort (e.g., wearable technology), and physical ability (e.g., poor vision; musculoskeletal and neurological conditions). In rural communities, limited access to technology often prohibits the development of the technological skills (i.e., *digital literacy*) required to use DMIs effectively. This inequitable access further contributes to the digital divide and health disparities [12]. In the study by Slevin et al. [10], some participants stated that the adoption of DMIs could be more seamless with the individual support of a trained professional (such as a CHW) or a group learning environment.

Cost and infrastructure

Utilizing DMIs may reduce healthcare costs for rural residents by decreasing travel expenses and related fees. However, these benefits are often negated by the prohibitive cost of digital medicine technology, internet access, and an access point (i.e., smart phone, tablet, computer) [8]. Residents of significantly isolated communities are at times required to purchase an expensive satellite internet service. Elevated costs can also be attributed to a fee-for-service approach to DMI implementation. Although the research and development of digital medicine technology are costly, a fee-for-service approach should be avoided to promote equitable access [12].

A primary challenge for many rural communities is poor internet connectivity or a general lack of internet access. According to the Federal Communications Commission, approximately 17% of rural households in the United States lack the internet access required to support video-based telehealth services [13]. Therefore, support from federal and state governments is needed to continue to develop the telecommunications infrastructure and offer free internet access to rural and underserved communities. In the interim, many rural communities have created designated locations (e.g., community health centers, public libraries) to offer access to digital medicine technology and other health resources.

Preventative care and disease management in rural communities

Digital medicine interventions (DMIs) have emerged as promising tools to bridge the gap between the needs of rural communities and the availability of primary care, women's health, behavioral health, and substance use disorder services. DMIs allow individuals in rural communities to connect with healthcare professionals and access healthcare without the need to travel long distances.

Behavioral health and substance use disorder conditions

Behavioral health and substance use disorders are significant public health concerns that affect individuals across diverse geographic and demographic backgrounds. Substance use disorders, including alcohol and opioid use disorders, are prominent issues in rural communities. According to the CDC, the drug overdose rate was 26.2 per 100,000 standard population in rural counties with the rate of female overdose deaths being higher in rural counties than urban counties [14]. The rate of overdose deaths involving psychostimulants was 31% higher, and semisynthetic opioids was 13% higher in rural counties than urban counties.

According to the American Psychological Association (APA), rural areas often have fewer behavioral health professionals per capita, leading to reduced access to vital services, timely interventions, and evidence-based treatments (e.g., medication-assisted treatment for substance use disorders) [15]. Limited access to comprehensive healthcare services, including addiction treatment programs, can contribute to the persistence of substance misuse. Furthermore, the interconnectedness of behavioral health and substance use disorders can lead to a cycle of co-occurring conditions that are particularly challenging to address in remote areas with limited healthcare professionals [16].

Utilizing telemedicine is one effective approach to improving access to mental health services in rural communities. Overall, DMIs offer anonymity and convenience, which can help reduce the stigma often associated with treatment for behavioral health and substance use disorders. Online support groups and self-help applications provide individuals with a space to share their experiences, seek advice, and develop coping strategies in a nonjudgmental environment. Some of the applications utilized for behavioral health concerns include opportunities for patients to document their mental health status and be directly connected to emergency services if warranted. Applications also exist for patients with substance use disorders to help manage and monitor their medication-assisted treatment and symptoms, as well as connect them with available community resources. However, it's essential to address challenges such as the security and privacy of personal health information in digital platforms.

Primary care and women's health

Primary care and access to women's health services in rural communities are critical components of ensuring comprehensive and equitable healthcare delivery. However, numerous challenges persist in providing adequate care to women residing in these underserved areas. According to the United States Department of Health and Human Services, as of June 2023, 65.6% of primary care health professional shortage areas in the US were located in rural areas [17]. Limited geographical access, healthcare workforce shortages, and socioeconomic disparities contribute to the complexity of addressing women's health needs in rural regions.

The shortage of healthcare providers, particularly obstetricians and gynecologists, in rural areas compounds the challenges of delivering appropriate women's healthcare. Research by the American College of Obstetricians and Gynecologists (ACOG) reveals that approximately 49% of US counties lack even a single obstetrician, and 68% lack a gynecologist [18]. This scarcity is even more pronounced in rural locales, where obstetric services are often unavailable, forcing women to travel considerable distances for prenatal care, deliveries, and postpartum follow-up.

Socioeconomic factors also play a pivotal role in limiting women's health access in rural areas. Financial constraints, lower health literacy rates, and cultural norms can impede women's utilization of healthcare services. The ACOG highlights that rural women are more likely to face economic challenges, including lower median incomes and higher rates of individuals who are uninsured or underinsured, which ultimately hinder their ability to seek timely and appropriate care [19]. Additionally, cultural stigmas and prevailing norms around women's health topics can discourage open discussions and preventative screenings, further contributing to health disparities among rural women.

An innovative approach to prenatal care utilizing a DMI and CHWs was explored by Cramer et at [20]. In a sample size of 98 pregnant women living in rural communities, participants were enrolled in either an intervention or a control group. The intervention group received prenatal care and patient education through a smartphone containing a specific prenatal platform texting functionality, hyperlinks with patient education, and weekly contact from a CHW. Participants in the intervention group were able to easily navigate pregnancy and community resources while also having direct contact with a healthcare team member (CHW). The control group received prenatal care and printed educational materials without interaction with a CHW. After analysis of the 77 women who completed the study, Cramer et al. [18] concluded that this DMI in conjunction with CHW involvement showed promise for improving health outcomes and medical care adherence. Financially, a positive return on investment (i.e., DMI and CHW compensation) was demonstrated under the two scenarios [20], which could help organizations in rural communities replicate and fund this intervention.

Toolkit and recommendations for success of DMI in rural communities

Healthcare organizations and community leaders should consider collaborations to incorporate DMIs into the healthcare delivery options for rural communities. Catering healthcare access to a rural community's patient population is important, including expanding office hours for farm workers [21], improving internet connectivity, and options for telemedicine appointments. Following is a list of recommendations to consider when incorporating DMIs into rural communities (adopted and modified from Buyting et al.) [22]:

1. **Infrastructure**: know the geographical context of each rural community and adjust the implementation plan of the DMI accordingly. This includes internet and technology access as well as transportation to the locations of routine and emergent healthcare (including CHWs).
2. **Community stakeholder involvement**: be sure to include all of those invested in the success of the DMI. To start, the voice and needs of rural health patients should be heard and incorporated into the implementation plan. Then, the integration of healthcare organization administrators and healthcare professionals (physicians, physician associates, nurse practitioners, CHWs, registered nurses, medical assistants, psychologists, mental health counselors, social workers, etc.) should follow. Finally, consider including community elected officials, technology companies, nonprofit organizations, town municipality departments, and utility companies. It is important not to duplicate initiatives already available. Communication and collaboration are keys to success!

3. **Anticipate and address implications of DMI integration**: incorporating DMIs into an organization's workflow can be challenging. Plan ahead for expected patient compliance barriers and clarification of team members' roles and responsibilities.
4. **Easy to navigate resources and training**: DMI programs need to be intuitive and easy to manage so all healthcare workers and patients, regardless of education or technological skill level, can utilize the platforms. Orientation to any new technology is going to be required for all healthcare employees and patients utilizing the DMI platforms and services. Electronic health system, interpersonal communication, collaboration, data privacy, and telemedicine skills training may help drive success of DMI initiatives. Initial and ongoing plans for technological support and efficiently troubleshooting any issues are essential.
5. **Importance of patient education**: digital and paper patient educational material should be provided for all visits, including telemedicine visits, as rural health community patients often have internet connectivity issues at their primary residencies. Development of these materials should consider health literacy levels, the use of multiple languages, and accessibility to deliver the most effective patient education.

Conclusion

The way in which medicine is being accessed and delivered in rural health settings has been fundamentally changed by recent events including healthcare worker shortages, epidemics, and pandemics. It is well known that health disparities in rural communities disproportionately impact communities with high racial and ethnic diversity [6]. Advancements in DMIs including healthcare innovations and technology can have a substantial impact on rural patient population access to healthcare and health outcomes. What remains uncertain, at this time, is the impact of artificial intelligence.

Ensuring access to healthcare in rural communities is a multifaceted challenge that necessitates systemic changes, policy support, and innovative digital health solutions. Removing barriers to healthcare access begins with collaboration of all community and healthcare stakeholders in rural communities. Addressing geographical barriers, healthcare workforce shortages, and socioeconomic disparities are paramount in closing the gap in healthcare access and improving patient outcomes in rural communities. Shared initiatives between healthcare organizations, educational institutions, and government agencies are also essential to incentivize healthcare providers to practice in rural areas through loan forgiveness programs and improved infrastructure [23].

Digital medicine interventions, including telemedicine and online support systems, hold the potential to mitigate these challenges by improving access to services, reducing stigma, and offering flexible modes of care delivery. Collaborative efforts between healthcare organizations, policymakers, and technology developers are crucial to ensure that digital medicine solutions are effectively integrated into rural communities. Moreover, tailored DMIs can empower rural communities with the knowledge and resources needed to prioritize their health and engage in preventative care practices, which helps promote health equity.

Questions and opportunities for additional research

1. With the continued growth of digital medicine, should access to broadband be considered a public health issue?
2. Are there resources that rural health communities could collaborate on to improve access to care?
3. How can artificial intelligence be utilized to positively impact rural healthcare communities and health outcomes?

References

[1] U.S. Department of Health and Human Services, Office of Disease Prevention and Health Promotion. Health equity in healthy people 2030. (Accessed 6 July 2023). https://health.gov/healthypeople/priority-areas/health-equity-healthy-people-2030.

[2] U.S. Department of Health and Human Services, Office of Disease Prevention and Health Promotion. Social determinants of health. (Accessed 6 July 2023). https://health.gov/healthypeople/priority-areas/social-determinants-health.

[3] Centers for Disease Control and Prevention. About rural health. Updated May 9, 2023. (Accessed 11 July 2023). https://www.cdc.gov/ruralhealth/about.html.

[4] Myers CR. Using telehealth to remediate rural mental health and healthcare disparities. Issues in Mental Health Nursing 2019;40(3):233–9. https://doi.org/10.1080/01612840.2018.1499157.

[5] Berini CR, Bonilha HS, Simpson AN. Impact of community health workers on access to care for rural populations in the United States: a systematic review. Journal of Community Health 2022;47(3):539–53. https://doi.org/10.1007/s10900-021-01052-6.

[6] Khushalani JS, Holmes M, Song S, et al. Impact of rural hospital closures on hospitalizations and associated outcomes for ambulatory and emergency care sensitive conditions. The Journal of Rural Health 2023;39(1):79–87. https://doi.org/10.1111/jrh.12671.

[7] The Cecil G. Sheps Center for Health Services Research at the University of North Carolina at Chapel Hill. Rural hospital closures. (Accessed 6 July 2023). https://www.shepscenter.unc.edu/programs-projects/rural-health/rural-hospital-closures.

[8] Babbage DR, van Kessel K, Terraschke A, et al. Attitudes of rural communities towards the use of technology for health purposes in New Zealand: a focus group study. BMJ Open 2020;10(6):e037892. https://doi.org/10.1136/bmjopen-2020-037892.

[9] Fraser MJ, Gorely T, O'Malley C, et al. Does connected health technology improve health-related outcomes in rural cardiac populations? systematic review narrative synthesis. International Journal of Environmental Research and Public Health 2022;19(4):2302. https://doi.org/10.3390/ijerph1904230.

[10] Slevin P, Kessie T, Cullen J, et al. A qualitative study of chronic obstructive pulmonary disease patient perceptions of the barriers and facilitators to adopting digital health technology. Digit Health 2019;5:1–10. https://doi.org/10.1177/2055207619871729.

[11] Al-Dhahir I, Reijnders T, Faber JS, et al. The barriers and facilitators of eHealth-based lifestyle intervention programs for people with a low socioeconomic status: scoping review. Journal of Medical Internet Research 2022;24(8):e34229. https://doi.org/10.2196/34229.

[12] Graham-Brown MPM, Smith AC, Greenwood SA. Digital health interventions in chronic kidney disease: levelling the playing field? Clinical Kidney Journal 2023;16(5):763−7. https://doi.org/10.1093/ckj/sfac259.
[13] Federal Communications Commission. Fourteenth broadband deployment report. Published January 19, 2021. (Accessed 7 August 2023). https://docs.fcc.gov/public/attachments/FCC-21-18A1.pdf.
[14] Spencer MR, Garnett MR, Miniño AM. Urban-rural differences in drug overdose death rates, 2020. National Center for Health Statistics 2022;440. https://doi.org/10.15620/cdc:118601.
[15] Edwards AM, Hung R, Levin JB, et al. Health disparities among rural individuals with mental health conditions: a systematic literature review. Journal of Rural Mental Health 2023;47(3):163−78. https://doi.org/10.1037/rmh0000228.
[16] Parker RD, Meyer JA, Abram MA. National data and the applicability to understanding rural and remote substance use. Journal of Prevention 2023;44:491−500. https://doi.org/10.1007/s10935-023-00734-2.
[17] Bureau of Health Workforce, Health Resources and Services Administration. Designated health professional shortage areas statistics. U.S. Department of Health & Human Services. (Accessed 20 July 2023). https://data.hrsa.gov/topics/health-workforce/shortage-areas.
[18] Rayburn WF, Klagholz JC, Murray-Krezan C, et al. Distribution of American Congress of Obstetricians and Gynecologists fellows and junior fellows in practice in the United States. Obstetrics & Gynecology 2012;119(5):1017−22. https://doi.org/10.1097/AOG.0b013e31824cfe50.
[19] American College of obstetricians and gynecologists committee opinion No. 586. Health disparities in rural women. Obstetrics & Gynecology 2014;123:384−8.
[20] Cramer ME, Mollard EK, Ford AL, Kupzyk KA, Wilson FA. The feasibility and promise of mobile technology with community health worker reinforcement to reduce rural preterm birth. Public Health Nursing 2018;35(6):508−16. https://doi.org/10.1111/phn.12543.
[21] Bloss JE, LePrevost CE, Zahra AG, et al. Advancing the health of migrant and seasonal farmworkers in the United States: identifying gaps in the existing literature, 2021. Health Promotion Practice 2022;23(3):432−44. https://doi.org/10.1177/15248399211033308.
[22] Buyting R, Melville S, Chatur H, et al. Virtual care with digital technologies for rural Canadians living with cardiovascular disease. CJC Open 2022;4:133−47.
[23] National Health Service Corps. Who we are. Health Resources & Services Administration. (Accessed 15 June 2023). https://nhsc.hrsa.gov/.

CHAPTER 17

CMS telehealth coding and guidelines

Aditi U. Joshi
Nagamed Digital Consulting, Paris, France

Objectives

1. Understand the background of CMS and its history of telehealth
2. Learn about the changes and how they affected the populations, billing, and telehealth reimbursement
3. Identify key codes and where to find them for current and future utility

Introduction

Background of CMS and its structure: Medicare and Medicaid

Healthcare billing and reimbursement have been a barrier to the growth and use of telemedicine due to the complexity of the current system as well as the lack of recognition of telehealth as a viable modality to deliver care (ref). The general theory is that the pandemic was the driving force for reimbursement changes; however, there had been expansions and recognition of the needed coding and regulations even before the pandemic. This was most recognized by the Centers for Medicare and Medicaid Services (CMS).

CMS is a federal agency within the United States Department of Health and Human Services (HHS). CMS is responsible for administering the Medicare and Medicaid programs, which provide health insurance to millions of Americans. CMS is responsible for enrolling beneficiaries, paying providers, setting payment rates, monitoring the quality of care, enforcing program rules and relevant to telehealth, promoting innovation. It covers millions of Americans with health insurance and increases access to care for certain populations.

As a standard for much of how the US healthcare market thinks about innovations, billing, and changing regulations, the goal of this chapter is to provide an overview of this agency and how it affected telehealth growth. This chapter will go through a brief background of

Digital Health. https://doi.org/10.1016/B978-0-443-23901-4.00017-9

CMS, telehealth codes, and how they have been developed. After reading the chapter, the objective is to understand how telehealth billing works for a federal agency.

Background of Medicare

Medicare is a federal program funded by Social Security payroll deductions. It is implemented by the US government and was created to cover people who are over 65, living with disabilities, debilitating chronic diseases, and/or a variety of other conditions. The Medicare program has doubled the number of patients over 65+ who have health insurance under their coverage. It has decreased the financial burden and increased health access for the senior population.

Medicare is divided into four parts: Parts A and B, a.k.a. "Original Medicare," which allows more flexibility in terms of choosing services and doctors. Part A covers hospital care, Part B covers outpatient services (and whatever's not covered by Part A). Parts C and D are optional and require extra funding. Part C, a.k.a Medicare Advantage, is technically privately paid, and Part D covers prescriptions and includes MediGap, a bridge insurance program that works with private insurance to handle items that don't fall under general coverage [1].

Medicare has an outsized influence on the healthcare reimbursement policy. While Medicare covers a smaller percentage of the population than health insurance and Medicaid, it is the largest payer for inpatient encounters and hospitalizations, primarily due to the elderly and sick populations it covers using the most expensive healthcare services. As a result, Medicare is a standard bearer for most other paper programs in the United States. It has an influence over innovations including telehealth. For example, when Medicare expanded telehealth policies, other payers tended to follow suit.

Background of Medicaid

Medicaid is a joint federal and state program for vulnerable populations and those with limited resources including those with disabilities, the terminally ill, children (CHIP), and pregnant women. The program itself improves access—those with Medicaid eligibility in childhood have fewer emergency visits and hospitalization later in life, better educational attainment, and reduced teen mortality.

Due to Medicaid falling under the CMS umbrella, there are federal rules that Medicaid programs must follow. Each state technically runs its own programs under its own name. States are required to cover certain services through their Medicaid programs—these include doctor visits, hospital visits, mental health, prenatal and maternity care, preventive care, and more. Aside from those guidelines, eligibility and benefits for other services vary by state as long as they don't conflict with superseding federal laws. Naturally, this makes Medicaid coverage and reimbursement more complicated [1].

Overview of the history of telehealth reimbursement within CMS

CMS and telehealth services

Prepandemic: CMS was one of the first government organizations to use telehealth for patients outside of aerospace and the military. It has been reimbursing telehealth services since 2002. The expansion was slow and deliberate, which in turn the efforts have helped to establish telehealth's foundation, particularly with respect to regulatory laws and the expansion of access. They approached telehealth reimbursement and policy in a conservative way. Early on, payments were restricted to rural and Health Professional Shortage Areas (HPSAs), where people, hospitals, and clinics were scarce. Reimbursement was further restricted to only certain types of clinicians: physicians, nurse practitioners, physician assistants, midwives, psychologists, social workers, and registered dieticians. Asynchronous telehealth was not covered, so images or chats were not included in the coverage [2].

There were restrictions placed on where a given patient happened to be physically while participating in a telehealth visit, called an "originating site." Initially, the originating site for patients had to be within some type of healthcare facility, whether a physician's office, a rural health clinic, hospital, skilled nursing facility, or other health center, and could not be from their homes.

Many of these regulations were implemented to help expand telehealth access, but their complicated nature ultimately hindered it, especially as the technology advanced. The restrictions created confusion among providers, particularly with billing. Most providers would rather bill patients directly than deal with CPT codes, originating sites, documentation, and restrictions. The headaches and chaos created by all of the restrictions led many to leave a substantial amount of Medicare money on the table. Between 2008 and 2016, telehealth visits grew from 0.81 to 5.23 per 1000 patients, which only represents 0.5% of all visits reimbursed [3]. The most common beneficiaries were under 65, disabled, dual Medicare/Medicaid eligible, and living in rural areas.

There were governmental entities and individuals who recognized telehealth's potential and attempted to expand it. The CONNECT (Creating Opportunities Now for Necessary & Effective Care Technologies) Act was introduced in 2016. The legislation sought to significantly expand Medicare telehealth coverage by removing the geographic restrictions and expanding originating sites to include patients' homes. The goal was to be able to practically change the offerings of telehealth companies, expand access, and attempt to be able to serve more patients. Despite bipartisan and broad external support, it was never passed, even after several attempts at reintroduction [4].

Despite this setback, the CONNECT Act produced a framework for how telehealth could be expanded and informed subsequent legislation. CMS has expanded telehealth in intervals ever since. In 2017, many Medicare patients chose to include telehealth visits as part of their care. In 2018, certain patients with chronic conditions could opt for telehealth instead of an in-person follow-up, though they were still required to be seen in person every 3 months. Although changes were slow in coming, most efforts aimed at expanding telehealth failed to take hold until the pandemic hit.

Medicaid and parity laws

Medicaid has had a different trajectory in relation to telehealth. Due to Medicaid programs being state-specific, each state could determine what type of telehealth services were reimbursed and for what amounts. As early as 2015, 46 of the 50 states had various telehealth services covered by Medicaid—36 allowed primary care, 17 allowed text-based communication, and 16 even allowed for physical and occupational therapy to be delivered over telehealth [5].

This created a wide array of parity laws, which predate COVID, and are a common topic of discussion in the telehealth industry. *Parity* essentially refers to what is or isn't considered *equal or comparable* care; in terms of telehealth, the primary distinction is between remote and in-person visits. If a law determines telehealth to be equal or comparable with in-person care, they've effectively stated that telehealth *is* a viable and equal type of healthcare service modality, and payment parity should ostensibly follow close behind [6].

Telehealth parity is further divided into *payment parity* and *service parity,* and the latter does not guarantee the same rate of payment. Each state has different parity laws—any given state may offer payment parity, service parity, or both, and how much each state pays influences how laws are written, as well as how payment works through Medicaid and private insurance [6].

By 2020, many Medicaid programs were expanding telehealth coverage to certain patients in rural and underserved areas. The aim was to improve access, reduce costs, and most importantly, to distribute care more equitably to vulnerable populations, many of whom struggle to find clinicians who accept Medicaid. Because Medicaid telehealth expansion varied by state, it ultimately became an easy way to test and compare results between states. For example, one study found that states that had Medicaid expansion had 54% more telemental health claims than those that did not [7]. In those where private insurers paid for telehealth, adoption rates were much higher than in states that didn't [8].

Medicaid beneficiaries had more flexibility in terms of using telehealth as compared with Medicare. State restrictions continued to impact what programs they could use, which influenced overall outcomes. This paved the way for many of the changes that came about during and after the pandemic.

COVID and the rapid expansion of CMS telehealth codes

CARES act and PHE

The quickest and largest change in telehealth billing and reimbursement was a result of the pandemic. This occurred principally through the passing of the $2.2 trillion CARES (Coronavirus Aid, Relief, and Economic Security) Act in March 2020. While most of the package was related to preventing the economic fallout of COVID-19, the act also included provisions aimed at improving COVID-related healthcare, including vaccine development, testing, treatment, resource allocation, and ultimately an expansion of telehealth services in Medicare.

COVID brought about the largest-ever sea change in telehealth policy, specifically in regard to reimbursement. Clinicians were able to bill Medicare for treatment and waive cost-sharing for telehealth visits, which meant that patients no longer had to pay copays or deductibles. Even though telehealth wasn't always paid at the same rates, it was paid, which led to enormous changes and growth. New patients were now able to receive telehealth care without having a previously established relationship. The "originating site" restrictions were also removed, and clinicians, from their own homes, were free to see patients. Coverage expanded from rural areas to everywhere.

The act's waivers also expanded, and clinicians were permitted to deliver telehealth and now included social workers, psychologists, physical and occupational therapists, etc. For emergency department patients, medical screening exams could even be conducted through telehealth. Reimbursement for remote patient monitoring, mental health, and chronic care expanded, as did telephone visits, which increased access for seniors without internet connections.

The CARES Act dramatically increased the use of telehealth. In April 2020, nearly half (43.5% or 1.28 million per week) of Medicare primary care visits were conducted through telemedicine, compared with only 0.1% 2 months prior. By the summer and fall of 2020, more than 25% of Medicare beneficiaries had had a telehealth visit. There were 840,000 total telehealth visits in 2019, compared with 52.7 million in 2020—a staggering 63-fold increase [9]. Notably, telehealth use was the highest among Medicare beneficiaries with long-term disabilities, Black and Hispanic populations, and those with multiple comorbid conditions, all of which are populations that telehealth benefited the most [10].

Medicaid expanded just as rapidly as Medicare during the pandemic; however, the state-specific nature of Medicaid made some of the resulting changes predictably more complicated. The federal emergency waivers declared that there was parity between telehealth and in-person care nationwide. Each state could decide which type of parity they were delivering, whether service or payment. Physicians still had to hold a license in the states in which their patients were located, and at the beginning of the pandemic, some of these license restrictions were relaxed so clinicians could continue seeing patients across state lines, despite varying rules from state to state [6,7,11].

As predicted, this rapid change led to varying degrees of adoption and rollout success. Primary care practices identified reimbursement confusion as a top barrier to telehealth use [12] and many clinics struggled with telehealth implementation [13]. To alleviate some of this confusion, the CMS created a Telehealth Toolkit, which provided information on regulations, barriers, reimbursement, and what state was generally doing, but its utility was limited, and few gained value from it [5].

As the pandemic waned, the number of telehealth visits among Medicare beneficiaries correspondingly fell. As a result, some of the telehealth initial expansions have expired, or are set to expire, while others have been continuously extended. In turn, Medicaid has expanded in some ways and backed off in others. COVID-era waivers will change significantly in the coming years, but the forward movement of telehealth within Medicare during the pandemic and beyond cannot be ignored [14,15].

Telehealth coding and billing

Overview of current procedural terminology (CPT) codes for telehealth services

It is worth diving into how codes and services are generally determined within the healthcare system. In general, CPT codes are a standardized system developed and maintained by the American Medical Association (AMA) to represent medical, surgical, and diagnostic services provided by healthcare professionals. These codes enable accurate documentation of services rendered, facilitate reimbursement processes, and assist in tracking healthcare trends. With the rise of telehealth, the AMA has adapted its CPT code system to encompass a comprehensive range of remote medical services, ensuring that healthcare providers are appropriately compensated for their virtual care efforts [16].

The application for new codes is a stepwise process that allows petitioning for new codes, an evaluation by a committee, and a process to determine which codes are necessary and then send them through various committees for evaluation [17]. Essentially CPT codes can be requested, changed, and improved upon as new information, and innovations occur, which affected telehealth coding.

The coding system has defined telehealth categories into selected services with codes specifically being used for each of them (Table 17.1). The codes are constantly changing, and it is required to be up to date on the current guidelines for reimbursement. For example, in E and M codes, the AMA points out that the appropriate place of service must be defined and some payers require determining the second place of service (Fig. 17.1). As it is payer-dependent, it requires knowing and contracting with each different payer.

Telehealth Visits

Synchronous audio/visual visit between a patient and clinician for evaluation and management (E&M)

Code	Description
CPT Code 99202-99205	Office or other outpatient visit for the evaluation and management of a new patient
CPT Code 99211-99215	Office or other outpatient visit for the evaluation and management of an established patient

*A list of all available codes for telehealth services can be found here:

https://www.cms.gov/Medicare/Medicare-General-Information/Telehealth/Telehealth-Codes

Please note—Check with your payer to determine the appropriate Place of Service (POS) code for your telehealth visits. The AMA is aware that some commercial payers are requiring the use of POS 02—Telehealth (The location where health services and health related services are provided or received, through a telecommunication system.) This is important to ensure your telehealth E/M visits are accurately associated with the care of patients for suspected or diagnosed COVID-19.

Figure 17.1
Codes from the AMA on telehealth visits [18] codes from AMA. *The American Medical Association.*

This, in turn, causes much confusion limiting the extent of telehealth growth and creating an entire industry around fixing this problem.

Of note, CPT codes can be reevaluated and changed based on both updated market and clinical forces and require an application to the AMA [20]. This is especially true as CMS, payers, and telehealth companies may have input or feedback. Advocacy and lobbying for these changes are an essential part of improvement and worked to expand the extent of telehealth codes.

CPT codes for telehealth were created as a necessity and reaction to the growing list of services, the need to increase access, and response to the growing number of telehealth companies petitioning for improved reimbursement.

The current codes were created as early as the 2010s, and a task force at the AMA was convened in 2015 to continue to improve the codes as telehealth expanded. In line with the CMS expansions prepandemic, the CPT codes also had to change as more use cases were examined and created [21]. For example, CMS began to cover peritoneal dialysis check-in visits in a stepwise plan to expand access, requiring an investigation into whether current codes work. As any entity can petition the AMA to evaluate a digital medicine use case, these new expansions were taken into account as more telehealth codes were created [22]. Most of these codes are precursors to current codes, and those discussions were instrumental in expanding the codes during the pandemic. Added to the CONNECT Care Act and advocacy from specialty organizations, the growth of these codes has helped define billing and reimbursement. They serve as a fundamental tool for accurately documenting and billing these remote medical services. By encompassing various

Table 17.1: Categories of services for telehealth CPT codes [19].

• Telehealth visits (virtual check-ins)	• These codes cover brief, patient-initiated communications with healthcare providers through platforms like phone calls or secure messaging. They are useful for assessing patient status, providing advice, and determining the need for further medical attention.
• E-visits	• E-visit codes are employed for non—face-to-face interactions between patients and providers via online portals or secure email. These interactions involve the exchange of medical information and can aid in diagnosis and treatment planning.
Telehealth consultations	• these codes apply to comprehensive telehealth consultations where healthcare professionals provide expert opinions, analysis, and recommendations to patients or referring providers. These consultations often involve reviewing medical records and diagnostic information.
Remote physiologic monitoring	• CPT codes for remote patient monitoring are used when healthcare providers collect and interpret patient data, such as vital signs, using monitoring devices. This ongoing monitoring allows for timely interventions and adjustments to treatment plans.
Behavioral health services	• these codes encompass remote mental health and behavioral therapy sessions, catering to the growing need for virtual mental healthcare options.
Chronic care management	• for patients with chronic conditions, CPT codes for telehealth enable healthcare providers to remotely manage and coordinate their care, ensuring regular check-ins and adjustments to treatment plans.
• online digital evaluation and management (E/M) services	• these codes address the evaluation and management of patient conditions conducted through online platforms, including history-taking, assessment, and treatment recommendations.

categories of telehealth interactions, these codes enable healthcare providers to capture the nuances of virtual care and ensure that patients receive the necessary medical attention regardless of geographical limitations.

Overall, researching and monitoring CPT codes aid in evaluating which digital health codes and practices will be utilized currently and in the future. This process informs CMS billing and reimbursement.

Billing and reimbursement through Medicare and Medicaid

For clinicians to become eligible for reimbursement from Medicare, they need to apply for an NPI (National Provider Identifier) through their regional Medicare office. To do so, one must generally be a physician, nurse, pharmacist, physical therapist, psychologist, dentist, or chiropractor, or work for a lab, health maintenance organization, hospital, ambulance company, pharmacy, or a few other entities [23]. To become a Medicaid provider, you have to apply within every state you want to cover, which becomes especially complicated for those who are practicing telehealth across state lines.

Once approved, Medicare billing is straightforward (though not always at the level some providers would prefer!). Medicare sets prices through a set fee schedule for clinicians, as well as a list of costs for other common services, whether ambulance services, labs, medical equipment, supplies, orthotics, and beyond. After a service or procedure has been rendered to the patient, five-digit Current Procedural Terminology (CPT) codes are used to identify services and procedures for billing and reporting purposes. Medicaid billing is state-specific but has similar processes and requirements to Medicare.

To bill using a particular code, the medical record documentation must reflect the corresponding level of care. For example, if one is delivering critical care services to an ER patient and wants to add a CPT code on the corresponding bill, the documentation has to include certain things to support that claim, such as a certain amount of time spent in providing undivided care to that patient. If documentation doesn't support the criteria of critical care, that patient cannot and will not be billed for those services provided.

Healthcare providers that bill Medicare need to keep up with annual changes in fee schedules. It's complicated, a lot of work, and as a result, an entire ecosystem has developed around the world of billing, coding, reimbursement, and documentation. Documentation and billing services are a huge industry, and providers are constantly trained and retrained on how precisely to document. The administrative overhead of billing is one of the many reasons American healthcare costs are so high.

Review of recent CMS policy changes impacting telehealth services and evaluation of temporary versus permanent telehealth policy changes since PHE

Through the PHE and updates from the AMA, CMS codes for telehealth services have had constant updates. Through the pandemic, the Emergency waivers had been extended multiple times as the government recognized the value of telehealth. Both through CMS extensions and the Consolidated Appropriations Act (CAA) of 2023, certain telehealth provisions are covered or extended (Table 17.2) [25,26].

CMS decided to continue paying certain telehealth codes through 2023 after the PHE, with the proposed plan to look into future policy to make certain codes permanent. CMS also suspended plans to require physicians who provide care from home to report their home address on Medicare enrollment. In response to AMA advocacy, CMS agreed to

Table 17.2: Coding changes post PHE and CAA [24].

Covered through 2023
Category 3 telehealth services. Nonfacility payment rates for telehealth services will remain the same through 2023, i.e., telehealth payments will remain the same as in-person through 2023. Direct supervision may continue to be provided virtually through 2023.
Extensions through 2024
The acute hospital care at home model is extended through 2024. Medicare coverage and payment of audio only services will continue through December 31, 2024. Geographic and originating site restrictions on Medicare telehealth services are waived through December 31, 2024. Codes for reimbursement for audio-only telebehavioral health services which will only be covered through December 31, 2024. An in-person visit will not be required for a patient to be eligible for behavioral health services via telehealth through December 31, 2024.
Extensions through 2025
The in-person requirement on Medicare telemental health services is delayed until on or after January 1, 2025.
Permanent changes
The ability of opioid treatment programs (OTPs) to provide patient counseling and therapy by phone is permanent. RPM can permanently be used for both chronic and acute conditions. Rural ERs can be originating sites.

continue to allow teaching physicians to provide virtual supervision of residents through 2023 and will address future policy in future rulemaking. They also will not enforce frequency limits of telehealth visits.

Some of these changes are being extended as CMS will address them in future policymaking, likely the 2024 Medicare physician payment regulation. As noted, AMA lobbying aided in changing CMS policy and is a reminder to lobby CMS for changes one wants to make permanent [24].

Other changes relevant to CMS coding include RPM services that will continue to be allowed for established patients and must be for 16 days. As of this publication, RPM codes are being reevaluated by AMA's DMPAG and will likely be edited for those codes with CMS input.

Other government agencies are also adding to make certain policy changes expand after the PHE, many of which will inform Medicare policy. The DEA extended PHE policies on prescribing controlled substances. Physician licensure remains deferred to state law and has more hold over Medicaid policy because of this [18].

As of this publication, this remains current policy; however, this is an ongoing and rapidly changing process. The goal was to understand some of the motivations and current CMS policies that are leading to policy changes. However, most of the permanent changes remain to be seen as very few have been adopted as permanent.

Other CMS-based reimbursement policies

While the aforementioned covers the telehealth video or audio-based codes, there have been other CMS-based regulations worth noting, namely asynchronous telehealth and RPM/RTM coding. Both of these are newer areas of consideration and remain to be seen what changes are going to be made.

Asynchronous telehealth

Asynchronous store and forward tech means the transmission of a patient's medical information from an originating site to the physician or clinician without the patient being present, nor being a real-time interaction. Some examples include chat-based applications and text messaging. Of note, this does not include telephone calls, facsimile messages, and emails. There has been growth of this form of telehealth as more consumer-driven telehealth companies are taking advantage of being able to message and offer care to patients with fewer staffing hours, leading to potentially more efficiency.

Federal law and CMS only have paid for certain store and forward programs in Hawaii and Alaska. In these programs, Medicare has been known to cover them in the absence of other forms of communications technology.

For other states, there has been a movement to include this form of telehealth; however, it is not covered by CMS, but by commercial payers. This is also changing as some states have adopted the asynchronous codes permanently. For example, NY and AZ have adopted asynchronous telehealth into their Medicaid payment coverage. Because these are not federally mandated, each state has the ability to determine for themselves whether they will cover them and will remain a changing landscape [27].

RPM/RTM codes

Remote patient monitoring (RPM) and remote therapeutic monitoring (RTM) have been a growing and natural progression to basic telehealth visits (note that Medicare uses Remote *physiologic* monitoring in its coding parlance despite the more common definition). RPM is the use of digital health solutions to capture patient information and data outside of traditional clinical environments, i.e., home. The data can then be used to inform care, intervene when patients are worsening, monitor treatments, and gives both patient and clinician further health information [28]. HHS categorizes RPM under telehealth as an adjunct part of care, recognizing that using wearables and information from devices expands the utility of telehealth [29]. The most common current use cases are for chronic diseases such as hypertension, diabetes mellitus, heart disease, COPD, and asthma. Studies show some results that state that RPM programs can reduce hospitalizations, shorten hospital stays, and decrease ED visits [28,30–32].

The RPM codes were created by a task force convened by the AMA's Digital Medicine Payment Advisory Group in 2019 for digitally stored RPM codes [33]. These codes include those for the cost of devices, training on the devices when required, and the evaluation and treatment codes, the latter of which is based on a certain number of days per month that the patient has been monitored. RTM CPT codes were launched in 2022 and are also used for device supply, device setup, and patient education in their use, plus patient adherence and response to therapy. RTM is geared toward evaluating particular treatments and regimens. Current RTM codes focus on respiratory, musculoskeletal systems, CBT, therapy adherence and response, and monitoring therapeutic response to gathered data [34]. While the use of digital therapeutics is low, the number of physicians wanting to incorporate them is high with the hope that these codes will be utilizable [35,36].

To bill Medicare for RPM, the patient must be established, the clinician must be eligible to bill for E/M services, the data must be electronically collected and automatically uploaded, and the location must be secure for analysis and interpretation by the clinician. The device must be defined as a medical device by the FDA. RPM data must be collected for at least 16 days out of 30 days and the services must monitor an acute care or chronic condition [29]. Medicaid is state-dependent, and each state has specific conditions for billing RPM coding, similar to other telehealth coding [6].

Because of the changing nature of RPM and the expansion of the types of clinicians that are using these codes, the AMA has been editing the current codes to reflect the updated clinical needs. This is yet another example of the constantly evolving nature of digital health, telehealth, and CPT billing.

Future of CMS codes in telehealth

Given the enormity of the aging population in the United States, the use of telehealth and RPM codes will likely increase. While the future of telehealth billing with CMS is complicated to predict, the government has shown time and again that they are willing to continuously extend many of its recent changes to keep telehealth in effect. In December of 2022, the government passed the Omnibus Bill, which extends telehealth flexibilities until the end of 2024. In January 2023, President Biden announced that the public health emergency waivers would end on May 11 of the same year. While these appear to be at odds with one another, the Omnibus Bill has introduced some of the waivers into a federal spending bill, effectively decoupling them from the emergency waivers. In other words, even when the emergency waivers expire, many of their telehealth reimbursements and flexibilities will remain. Because each state can determine what they want Medicaid to cover, it is understandably more complicated to predict. However, many states have already made some Medicaid telehealth flexibilities permanent or are planning to [37]. As CMS goes into 2024 policy changes, there is a chance some of these flexibilities will become permanent.

CMS's Medicare and Medicaid are major healthcare payers in the United States, and as a result, both are strong influencers of reimbursement, in general. While permanent changes to telehealth are largely incumbent on Congress, continuing and billing for telehealth services whenever they're available help as when services fall out of use, they're more likely to be cut. CMS aggregates telehealth-related utilization and results, including cost-effectiveness and impact, and uses them to convince legislators and lawmakers to extend telehealth beyond the pandemic [38].

Overall, the codes for telehealth, RPM, and RTM are continuing to be expanded by CMS despite the changes in the COVID flexibilities. While programs and systems billing for services can find information online, they need to stay up to date on those codes to stay compliant.

References

[1] History. Available from: https://www.cms.gov/about-cms/who-we-are/history.

[2] Harkey K, Kaiser N, Zhao J, Gutnik B, Kelz R, Matthews BD, et al. Utilization of telemedicine to provide post-discharge care: a comparison of pre-pandemic vs. pandemic care. The American Journal of Surgery August 2023;226(2):163–9.

[3] Chapter 8: Telehealth services and the Medicare program (June 2016 report) Available from: https://www.medpac.gov/document/http-www-medpac-gov-docs-default-source-reports-chapter-8-telehealth-services-and-the-medicare-program-june-2016-report-pdf/.

[4] ATA. American Telemedicine Association. Schatz, wicker introduce resolution to mark telehealth awareness week. 2021. Available from: https://www.americantelemed.org/ata-news/schatz-wicker-introduce-resolution-to-mark-telehealth-awareness-week/.

[5] Trump Administration Releases COVID-19 Telehealth Toolkit to Accelerate State Use of Telehealth in Medicaid and CHIP. Available from: https://www.cms.gov/newsroom/press-releases/trump-administration-releases-covid-19-telehealth-toolkit-accelerate-state-use-telehealth-medicaid.

[6] CCHP. Home. 2021. Available from: https://www.cchpca.org/.

[7] Harju A, Neufeld J. The impact of the Medicaid expansion on telemental health utilization in four Midwestern states. Telemedicine Journal and e-Health November 2021;27(11):1260–7.

[8] Adler-Milstein J, Kvedar J, Bates DW. Telehealth among US hospitals: several factors, including state reimbursement and licensure policies, influence adoption. Health Affairs February 2014;33(2):207–15.

[9] 2021-12-30 15:27. Available from: https://www.hhs.gov/about/news/2021/12/03/new-hhs-study-shows-63-fold-increase-in-medicare-telehealth-utilization-during-pandemic.html.

[10] Koma W, Cubanski J, Neuman T, KFF. Medicare and telehealth: coverage and use during the COVID-19 pandemic and options for the future. 2021. Available from: https://www.kff.org/medicare/issue-brief/medicare-and-telehealth-coverage-and-use-during-the-covid-19-pandemic-and-options-for-the-future/.

[11] Austin AE, Tang L, Kim JY, Allen L, Barnes AJ, Chang CCH, et al. Trends in use of Medication to treat opioid use disorder during the COVID-19 pandemic in 10 state Medicaid programs. JAMA Health Forum June 2, 2023;4(6):e231422.

[12] Chang JE, Lai AY, Gupta A, Nguyen AM, Berry CA, Shelley DR. Rapid transition to telehealth and the digital divide: implications for primary care access and equity in a post-COVID era. The Milbank Quarterly June 2021;99(2):340−68.

[13] Payán DD, Frehn JL, Garcia L, Tierney AA, Rodriguez HP. Telemedicine implementation and use in community health centers during COVID-19: clinic personnel and patient perspectives. SSM - Qualitative Research in Health December 2022;2:100054.

[14] Shachar C, Engel J, Elwyn G. Implications for telehealth in a postpandemic future: regulatory and privacy issues. JAMA June 16, 2020;323(23):2375−6.

[15] Wang J, Patel V, Salek S, Abbaszadegan H, Rehman S, Garcia-Filion P. Impact of expanding telephonic codes in a state Medicaid program during COVID-19. Telemedicine Journal and e-Health March 2023;29(3):408−13.

[16] American Medical Association. Telehealth Coding. Available from: https://www.ama-assn.org/topics/telehealth-coding.

[17] Dotson P. CPT® codes: what are they, why are they necessary, and how are they developed? Advances in Wound Care December 2013;2(10):583−7.

[18] American Medical Association. American Medical Association. AMA telehealth policy, coding & payment. 2023. Available from: https://www.ama-assn.org/practice-management/digital/ama-telehealth-policy-coding-payment.

[19] List of telehealth services. Available from: https://www.cms.gov/medicare/coverage/telehealth/list-services.

[20] American Medical Association. American Medical Association. CPT® code change applications. 2022. Available from: https://www.ama-assn.org/practice-management/cpt/cpt-code-change-applications.

[21] Wicklund E, MobiHealthNews. AMA workgroup targets telemedicine and CPT codes. 2015. Available from: https://www.mobihealthnews.com/news/ama-workgroup-targets-telemedicine-and-cpt-codes.

[22] Wicklund E, MobiHealthNews. CMS boosts telehealth in 2015 physician pay schedule. 2014. Available from: https://www.mobihealthnews.com/news/cms-boosts-telehealth-2015-physician-pay-schedule.

[23] Become a Medicare provider or supplier. Available from: https://www.cms.gov/medicare/enrollment-renewal/providers-suppliers.

[24] Calendar year (CY) 2023 Medicare Physician Fee Schedule final rule. Available from: https://www.cms.gov/newsroom/fact-sheets/calendar-year-cy-2023-medicare-physician-fee-schedule-final-rule.

[25] Khera N, Knoedler M, Meier SK, TerKonda S, Williams RD, Wittich CM, et al. Payment and coverage parity for virtual care and in-person care: how do we get there? Telemedicine Reports May 18, 2023;4(1):100−8.

[26] Hamadi HY, Zhao M, Haley DR, Dunn A, Paryani S, Spaulding A. Medicare and telehealth: the impact of COVID-19 pandemic. Journal of Evaluation in Clinical Practice February 2022;28(1):43−8.

[27] CCHP. Store-and-forward. Available from: https://www.cchpca.org/topic/store-and-forward/.

[28] Steinberg R, Anderson B, Hu Z, Johnson TM, O'Keefe JB, Plantinga LC, et al. Associations between remote patient monitoring programme responsiveness and clinical outcomes for patients with COVID-19. BMJ Open Quality September 2021;10(3). Available from: https://doi.org/10.1136/bmjoq-2021-001496.

[29] telehealth.hhs.gov. Telehealth and remote patient monitoring. Available from: https://telehealth.hhs.gov/providers/preparing-patients-for-telehealth/telehealth-and-remote-patient-monitoring.

[30] Whitehead D, Conley J. The next frontier of remote patient monitoring: hospital at home. Journal of Medical Internet Research March 16, 2023;25:e42335.

[31] Coutu FA, Iorio OC, Ross BA. Remote patient monitoring strategies and wearable technology in chronic obstructive pulmonary disease. Frontiers of Medicine August 17, 2023;10:1236598.

[32] Park S, Kum HC, Zheng Q, Lawley MA. Real-world adherence and effectiveness of remote patient monitoring among Medicaid patients with diabetes: retrospective cohort study. Journal of Medical Internet Research August 22, 2023;25:e45033.

[33] Kvedar JC, Mittermaier M, Pritzker J. The industry impact of the American medical association's digital medicine payment advisory Group (DMPAG). npj Digital Medicine December 24, 2022;5(1):193.

[34] American Medical Association. CPT code set moving at the speed of digital health innovation. 2022. Available from: https://www.ama-assn.org/practice-management/cpt/cpt-code-set-moving-speed-digital-health-innovation.

[35] Velez FF, Colman S, Kauffman L, Ruetsch C, Anastassopoulos K. Real-world reduction in healthcare resource utilization following treatment of opioid use disorder with reSET-O, a novel prescription digital therapeutic. Expert Review of Pharmacoeconomics & Outcomes Research February 2021;21(1):69–76.

[36] Torous J, Hsin H. Empowering the digital therapeutic relationship: virtual clinics for digital health interventions. npj Digital Medicine May 16, 2018;1:16.

[37] KFF. How the pandemic continues to shape Medicaid priorities: results from an annual Medicaid budget survey for state fiscal years 2022 and 2023 - telehealth. 2022. Available from: https://www.kff.org/report-section/medicaid-budget-survey-for-state-fiscal-years-2022-and-2023-telehealth/.

[38] United States. Government Accountability Office. Medicaid: CMS should assess effect of increased telehealth use on beneficiaries' quality of care: report to congressional committees. United States Government Accountability Office; 2022. p. 59.

CHAPTER 18

ICD-10 and SNOMED CT: The role of healthcare classification systems in digital health

Sara Gallo
Clinical Insighters Consulting, Health Equity & Transformation Consultant, Denver, CO, United States

Introduction

In the intricate realm of healthcare, efficient communication, and data management are paramount. The two cornerstones of this digital bridge are the International Classification of Diseases, 10th Revision (ICD-10), and the Systematized Nomenclature of Medicine—Clinical Terms (SNOMED CT). These coding systems have played a pivotal role in ensuring standardized classification and interpretation of medical conditions, procedures, and clinical data [1—3]. This chapter explores the origins and development of ICD-10 and SNOMED CT, their profound significance in healthcare, and how the ever-expanding horizons of digital health are poised to transform their roles [4]. Layered with the common uses of ICD-10 and SNOMED CT coding for claims purposes, this chapter will also explore use cases and how billing and coding can help to identify trends in digital health and guide future diagnostic definitions, population health management, and fee schedule improvements as digital health utilization grows.

The historical context of ICD-10 and SNOMED CT

ICD-10: A global standard

The lineage of healthcare coding can be traced back to the late 19th century when it became evident that a standardized system for classifying diseases and medical procedures was desperately needed [4,5]. This realization culminated in the inception of the International Classification of Diseases (ICD) by the World Health Organization (WHO) in 1948. The initial version, ICD-6, was followed by several revisions, each striving to enhance the accuracy and comprehensiveness of healthcare coding. The ICD-10 serves as

Digital Health. https://doi.org/10.1016/B978-0-443-23901-4.00018-0

a universal framework for precisely classifying diseases, medical conditions, and healthcare procedures [6,7]. It was adopted by the World Health Organization (WHO) and has become the gold standard for healthcare coding worldwide.

ICD-10 was first adopted by WHO member states in 1994. It represented a leap in healthcare coding. ICD-10 is a comprehensive system that encompasses a vast array of diseases, conditions, and healthcare procedures. Its alphanumeric codes provide a standardized language that transcends borders, facilitating international communication among healthcare professionals, researchers, insurers, and policymakers. The adoption of ICD-10 has streamlined everything from clinical diagnoses to epidemiological tracking, reshaping healthcare documentation and administration worldwide.

The alphanumeric designations provide a common language for healthcare professionals, researchers, insurers, public health officials, and policymakers. These codes are essential for various purposes:

Diagnosis and Treatment: Clinicians use ICD-10 codes to document patient diagnoses and procedures accurately. This standardized language ensures clarity and consistency in medical records.

Billing and Reimbursement [8]: Health insurance claims are processed using ICD-10 codes to determine the validity of medical services provided. Accurate coding is vital for healthcare providers to receive proper reimbursement for their services.

Epidemiology and Public Health [8]: Public health officials rely on ICD-10 codes to track and analyze disease trends, enabling early detection of outbreaks and the development of targeted interventions.

Medical Research: ICD-10 codes facilitate medical research by enabling researchers to analyze large datasets of patient records, aiding in the discovery of trends, treatment efficacy, and potential areas for innovation.

SNOMED CT: Precision in clinical terminology

While ICD-10 excels in classifying diseases and procedures, a complementary system was needed to capture the nuanced world of clinical practice. This need gave rise to the Systematized Nomenclature of Medicine—Clinical Terms (SNOMED CT), which emerged in the late 20th century [9].

SNOMED CT is not merely a coding system: it is a comprehensive clinical terminology that encapsulates the rich tapestry of clinical concepts. Designed to be utilized in electronic health records (EHRs) and clinical documentation systems, SNOMED CT comprises a vast vocabulary of clinical terms, from signs and symptoms to anatomical structures and clinical findings [10,11]. It allows healthcare professionals to document patient information with precision and specificity, paving the way for enhanced patient care, research, and data exchange.

SNOMED CT complements ICD-10 by providing clinical granularity. Its importance in healthcare can be seen in various aspects [12,13].

Clinical Documentation [13]: SNOMED CT allows for precise documentation of patient conditions, symptoms, and clinical findings, fostering more accurate and detailed electronic health records.

Interoperability: As healthcare becomes increasingly digital, SNOMED CT facilitates interoperability between different EHR systems, ensuring a seamless exchange of clinical information.

Research and Decision Support [14]: Researchers and healthcare providers use SNOMED CT to enhance decision support systems, making clinical practice more evidence-based and efficient. Table 18.1.

Digital health's impact on ICD-10 and SNOMED CT

As digital health technologies continue to advance, their integration with ICD-10 and SNOMED CT becomes pivotal [15]. Digital health encompasses telemedicine, wearable devices, health apps, and more, all of which generate a wealth of clinical data and help to inform clinical medical decision-making. ICD-10 and SNOMED CT are poised to adapt and expand in response to these changes:

Data Integration, interoperability, and exchange [15]: ICD-10 and SNOMED CT will incorporate codes and terminologies related to digital health interventions, ensuring that these technologies are seamlessly integrated into electronic health records and clinical practice.

Quality Assurance: The use of these coding systems will play a crucial role in ensuring the quality and safety of digital health interventions through standardized documentation and data analysis.

Research Advancements: The wealth of data generated by digital health technologies will provide researchers with unprecedented opportunities to study the impact of these interventions on patient outcomes and healthcare delivery.

Healthcare Delivery [15]: The integration of ICD-10 and SNOMED CT with digital health technologies will facilitate more precise and efficient healthcare delivery, enabling providers to make data-driven decisions and enhancing patient care.

Table 18.1: ICD-10 and SNOMED CT comparison.

Traits	ICD-10	SNOMED CT
Purpose	Primarily used for coding diseases, conditions, and procedures for billing, epidemiology, and medical records.	Designed for clinical documentation, capturing detailed clinical concepts and findings for electronic health records (EHRs) and clinical practice.
Scope	Focuses on diseases, conditions, and healthcare procedures.	Encompasses a wide range of clinical concepts, including diseases, symptoms, anatomical structures, clinical findings, procedures, and more.
Organization	Organized in chapters and sections based on disease categories.	Organized hierarchically in a more complex and interconnected manner, allowing for detailed clinical descriptions.
Coding	Utilizes alphanumeric codes (e.g., ICD-10-CM for clinical modification).	Uses a combination of numeric and alphanumeric identifiers for concepts (e.g., SNOMED CT concept IDs).
International adoption	Globally recognized and used for billing and epidemiological purposes in many countries.	Widely adopted but often used more in EHRs and clinical documentation, with significant adoption in some countries.
Level of detail	Provides less detailed clinical information but focuses on coding diseases and procedures precisely.	Provides a high level of clinical detail, enabling precise description of clinical findings and concepts.
Clinical use	Used for coding diagnoses and procedures for billing, insurance claims, and statistical reporting.	Used for detailed clinical documentation, supporting clinical decision-making, data exchange, and interoperability among EHRs.
Flexibility	Less flexible in capturing nuanced clinical concepts beyond specific diagnoses and procedures.	Highly flexible in describing clinical nuances, making it suitable for a wide range of healthcare scenarios.
Integration	Often integrated with healthcare billing systems and claims processing.	Integrated into EHRs, clinical decision support systems, and clinical data exchange standards.
Coding updates	Regularly updated by WHO and national authorities to reflect advances in medicine and new diseases.	Continuously updated to accommodate evolving clinical knowledge and terminology.
Use cases	Used in medical coding for billing and reimbursement, epidemiology, and research.	Primarily used for clinical documentation, interoperability, and supporting clinical care decisions.

ICD-10 codes play a pivotal role in documenting diagnoses and procedures related to digital health interventions, enabling data collection and analysis for patient care and research, and are often used to risk adjust for the complexity of a patient and the journey throughout a number of chronic conditions using standardized coding. The adoption of digital health and the appropriate use of digital health care can be relayed through appropriate ICD-10 and CPT coding. The use of these technologies is being analyzed often only through claims data that would be reporting only ICD-10 and CPT coding versus encounter data. As the coding sets expand to include not only more digital health intervention-related actions/statuses but also lifestyle circumstances (social determinants of health; SDOH) that potentially impact the importance of incorporating digital health into the care of the patient, there will be a significant opportunity to better define the value of digital health interventions when implementing coding intentionally.

To further discuss ICD-10 and SNOMED CT, let us consider the following scenario for coding a visit for Este, a 45 year-old-female with Type II Diabetes Mellitus being seen by Dr. Louis [16].

ICD-10 Coding: [16].

In this scenario, ICD-10 codes are used to document what the patient encounter was for. In the case of Este, the provider saw Este for her chronic medical condition, specifically her diagnosis of Diabetes Mellitus Type 2. Here's how it works:

ICD-10 Diagnosis Code for Diabetes Mellitus Type 2: E11.9.

ICD-10 code E11.9 represents "Type 2 diabetes mellitus without complications." This code is used to classify Este's primary medical condition, which is Type 2 diabetes. Because Este has a controlled disease state and has not had any complications such as chronic renal disease or microalbuminuria, the ICD-10 code can also provide that information.

SNOMED CT Coding: [17].

SNOMED CT is used for *more detailed clinical documentation, allowing healthcare providers to capture specific clinical concepts and findings related to the patient's condition and care*. Here's how SNOMED CT might be used in this scenario:

SNOMED CT Clinical Finding for Diabetes Diagnosis:

SNOMED CT provides clinical terms to describe the characteristics and details of a patient's condition. In this case, an SNOMED CT code, 44054006 (Diabetes Mellitus Type 2), might be used to provide additional information about Este's diabetes diagnosis, such as the, severity, or any associated complications. Example: "Diabetes Mellitus Type 2 without complication."

SNOMED CT Observation for Blood Glucose Level: [17,18] SNOMED CT can be *used to record specific clinical observations*. If Este had her blood glucose level checked during her visit, an SNOMED CT code could be used to document this observation.

Example: "Blood Glucose Level—[Result] mg/dL"

SNOMED CT Procedure for Diabetes Education: [17,18]

If Dr. Louis provided Este with diabetes education during the visit, an SNOMED CT procedure code might be used to document this educational intervention.

Example: "Diabetes Education and Counseling Provided."

These codes help ensure that Este's medical condition and the care she received are accurately documented in her electronic health record (EHR). They also enable precise communication between healthcare providers, insurers, and researchers, contributing to improved patient care and better health outcomes.

See Table 18.2 below to compare and contrast the use of ICD-10 and SNOMED CT in Este's scenario. Note that ICD-10 is primarily used for coding Este's diagnosis and any associated procedures and is essential for billing and reimbursement purposes, as well as for epidemiological studies and research that rely on standardized disease classification. On the other hand, SNOMED CT is used for comprehensive clinical documentation, capturing specific clinical concepts related to Este's condition. It provides flexibility in describing clinical nuances and supports clinical decision-making, research, and quality improvement initiatives. However, it is not used for billing purposes.

Table 18.2: Purpose of ICD-10 and SNOMED CT in clinical visit.

Traits	ICD-10	SNOMED CT
Purpose	Coding for billing and reimbursement	Detailed clinical documentation
ICD-10 (primary diagnosis)	E11.9 (type 2 diabetes mellitus)	N/A
SNOMED CT concept (primary diagnosis)	N/A	44054006 (diabetes mellitus type 2)
Additional ICD-10 codes (if applicable)	E11.65 (type 2 diabetes with hyperglycemia)	N/A
Additional SNOMED CT concepts	N/A	420099009 (hyperglycemia)
Clinical findings (if recorded)	N/A	Elevated blood sugar levels
Procedures (if applicable)	Hemoglobin A1c test (ICD-10 procedure code)	N/A
Billing and reimbursement	ICD-10 codes used for insurance claims	SNOMED CT not used for billing
Clinical documentation	Limited to diagnosis and billing codes	Comprehensive clinical details recorded
Clinical decision support	Basic information for billing and coding	Detailed clinical information for decision support
Data integration	Integrated into billing and financial systems	Integrated into EHRs and clinical decision support
Flexibility	Limited flexibility in describing clinical nuances	Highly flexible for precise clinical descriptions
Research and quality improvement	Data used for epidemiological studies and research	Data supports clinical research and quality improvement initiatives

**Disclaimer for coding discussed in this book: Always consult the latest coding guidelines and regulations to ensure compliance with the specific requirements of the payer you are dealing with.

Telemedicine

Telemedicine, which encompasses virtual visits, remote consultations, and telehealth services, has experienced significant growth, especially in the era of digital health. It offers patients remote access to healthcare professionals, eliminating geographical barriers and increasing healthcare accessibility. ICD-10 and SNOMED CT are crucial in telemedicine for several reasons:

Billing and Reimbursement: Telemedicine services must adhere to a structured coding system such as ICD-10 to facilitate accurate billing and reimbursement. These codes are used to classify the patient's condition and the services provided during the virtual visit. Health insurers rely on ICD-10 codes to determine the appropriate level of reimbursement for the telehealth encounter. This ensures that healthcare providers are fairly compensated for their services, promoting the sustainability of telemedicine practices.

Diagnosis and Treatment Documentation: In telemedicine, detailed documentation is crucial for patient care continuity and legal purposes. While ICD-10 codes provide a high-level diagnosis, SNOMED CT allows clinicians to capture nuanced clinical details and care plan interventions. For example, SNOMED CT can describe specific symptoms, physical exam findings, or treatment recommendations discussed during a telehealth visit. This comprehensive documentation supports clinical decision-making and patient management.

Tracking and Monitoring Chronic Conditions: For patients with chronic conditions, telemedicine offers a convenient way to manage their health remotely. ICD-10 codes help in tracking and identifying these conditions for billing, while SNOMED CT codes record specific clinical data such as lab results, medication adjustments, and lifestyle advice. Over time, this data assists healthcare providers in assessing the effectiveness of treatments and making informed adjustments to the care plan.

Prescription Management: Telemedicine often involves prescription management, where clinicians prescribe medications during virtual visits. ICD-10 codes identify the primary reason for the prescription, such as a mental health disorder or a chronic condition. In contrast, SNOMED CT may be used to document the specific details of the prescribed medication, including dosage, frequency, and instructions. Accurate recording of this information is vital for patient safety and medication management.

Cross-Provider Communication: Telemedicine encounters often require seamless communication among healthcare providers. SNOMED CT aids in creating detailed clinical summaries, capturing the essence of the telehealth consultation. These summaries, securely shared among providers, enable efficient cross-provider communication. This ensures that primary care physicians, specialists, and other healthcare professionals are informed about the patient's telemedicine interactions, promoting coordinated and patient-centered care.

Examples of common ICD-10 codes used in telemedicine

1. J06.9—Acute upper respiratory infection, unspecified [19]: Acute visits especially during the winter months when patients may not be able to make it into the office depending on weather, schedule availability to incorporate travel, need to reduce risk of infection in the waiting room, or lack of childcare present a perfect alternate opportunity to diagnose and treat virtually. This ICD-10 code is a common code used for upper respiratory infections including viral infections and would be appropriate given that POC testing is limited in a virtual care environment.
2. F32.9—Major depressive disorder, single episode, unspecified [20]: For mental health telehealth visits, this code may be applicable when diagnosing a patient with depression.
3. I10—Essential (primary) hypertension [21]: If a patient with high blood pressure is managed through telehealth, the ICD-10 code for essential hypertension (I10) is used in the documentation.
4. M54.5—Low back pain [22]: This code can be used for telehealth visits where a patient's complaint or condition is related to low back pain.

*Please note that the choice of ICD-10 code should be based on the specific diagnosis or condition being treated during the telehealth encounter.

Complementing the ICD-10 codes, Current Procedural Terminology (CPT) codes describe the services provided during telehealth encounters, ranging from routine follow-ups to telephone evaluations. Place of Service (POS) codes, notably POS 02, denote that healthcare services were delivered via telehealth [23]. Additionally, modifiers such as Modifier 95 indicate synchronous telemedicine services, while Modifier GQ signifies asynchronous communication, and Modifier GT indicates interactive audio and video systems. These codes and modifiers, when applied correctly, contribute to the seamless functioning of telehealth, supporting precise documentation, transparent billing, and efficient reimbursement processes.

Remote patient monitoring

Remote patient monitoring (RPM) has become a critical component of telehealth, enabling healthcare providers to continuously track patients' health data and manage chronic conditions from a distance [24]. ICD-10 and SNOMED CT play vital roles in this process.

ICD-10 codes are used to identify and document chronic conditions that are being monitored remotely. For example, patients with chronic diseases such as diabetes (E11.9—Type 2 diabetes mellitus without complications) or hypertension (I10—Essential (primary) hypertension) have these codes associated with their diagnoses [25]. These codes are important for tracking the specific chronic conditions being managed through RPM.

SNOMED CT comes into play when capturing detailed clinical data during remote monitoring. Healthcare providers can use SNOMED CT concepts to record specific clinical findings, such as blood glucose levels, blood pressure readings, or cardiac rhythm abnormalities. This level of granularity allows for a comprehensive and precise record of the patient's health status over time.

Both ICD-10 and SNOMED CT codes facilitate the establishment of monitoring parameters and alert thresholds for patients under remote observation. For instance, a patient with heart disease (ICD-10 code I25.10—Atherosclerotic heart disease of native coronary artery without angina pectoris) may have set ranges for cholesterol levels and blood pressure. If these values exceed or fall below certain limits, the RPM system can trigger alerts for timely intervention.

Furthermore, remote patient monitoring systems often incorporate clinical decision support (CDS) tools. These tools analyze the data collected through SNOMED CT-coded observations and ICD-10-coded diagnoses. If significant changes or concerning trends emerge, CDS alerts healthcare providers, enabling them to make informed decisions about adjusting treatment plans or contacting the patient.

Accurate ICD-10 coding ensures that healthcare providers can bill for remote monitoring services effectively. ICD-10 codes represent the chronic conditions or reasons for monitoring, supporting proper reimbursement for RPM services, which are becoming increasingly essential for managing population health and reducing healthcare costs.

RPM ICD-10 and SNOMED CT coding examples

Here are examples of how ICD-10, CPT codes, and SNOMED CT codes are used for remote patient monitoring (RPM).

1. Hypertension Monitoring:

ICD-10 Code for Hypertension: I10 (Essential (primary) hypertension) [26].

Scenario: A patient with hypertension is enrolled in an RPM program for ongoing monitoring. Each data point collected from the RPM device is tagged with ICD-10 code I10 to indicate the patient's primary diagnosis of hypertension.

SNOMED CT Code: 38341003 (Hypertension) [27].

Scenario Explanation: For a patient enrolled in an RPM program for hypertension monitoring, each data point collected from the RPM device can be tagged with SNOMED CT code 38341003 to specify the clinical concept of hypertension.

2. Diabetes Remote Monitoring:

ICD-10 Code for Type 2 Diabetes: E11.9 (Type 2 diabetes mellitus without complications) [28].

Scenario: A patient with type 2 diabetes participates in RPM to track blood glucose levels. The RPM data is associated with ICD-10 code E11.9 to denote the patient's diabetes diagnosis.

SNOMED CT Code: 44054006 (Diabetes mellitus type 2) [29].

Scenario Explanation: In the context of diabetes remote monitoring, the RPM data related to blood glucose levels can be associated with SNOMED CT code 44054006, which represents the specific diagnosis of diabetes mellitus type 2.

3. Heart Failure Management:

ICD-10 Code for Heart Failure: I50.9 (Heart failure, unspecified) [20].

Scenario: A patient with heart failure is on RPM to monitor vital signs, weight, and symptoms. The RPM data is linked to ICD-10 code I50.9, which indicates the presence of heart failure.

SNOMED CT Code: 84114007 (Congestive heart failure) [30].

Scenario Explanation: For a patient on RPM to manage heart failure, the RPM data encompassing vital signs, weight, and symptoms can be linked to SNOMED CT code 84114007, signifying the clinical concept of congestive heart failure.

In the context of remote patient monitoring (RPM), healthcare providers benefit from a streamlined process that involves automating data collection, remote data monitoring, alerting and intervention, and comprehensive documentation and billing [31]. RPM devices continuously gather patient data, which can be automatically assigned ICD-10 codes based on the patient's diagnoses. This data is then remotely monitored in real-time or at scheduled intervals, enabling healthcare providers to gain insights into the patient's health trends. RPM systems can trigger alerts when data points deviate from established thresholds or indicate worsening health, prompting timely interventions. The combination of RPM data and associated ICD-10 codes serves as a valuable tool for comprehensive documentation and accurate billing, ensuring appropriate reimbursement for RPM services [32].

Additionally, CPT coding examples highlight the specific codes used for various RPM-related services. For instance, CPT code 99,453 represents the initial setup of an RPM device and patient education, while code 99,454 corresponds to the monthly monitoring service with data transmission and alerts [33]. Code 99,457 covers the monthly data review and interactive communication with the patient or caregiver. Furthermore, CPT code 99,458 is employed when additional time beyond the initial 20 min is spent on RPM review during the month. These CPT codes play a crucial role in properly documenting and billing for the different facets of remote patient monitoring, ensuring that healthcare providers are appropriately compensated for their services [34,35].

These examples illustrate how ICD-10 codes are used to link RPM data to the patient's specific diagnoses, while CPT codes are employed to bill for various aspects of remote patient monitoring, including setup, ongoing monitoring, and data review. Accurate coding is essential for documenting the patient's condition and services provided, as well as for reimbursement purposes.

When submitting claims for telehealth services, ensure that the relevant social determinants of health (SDOH) codes are included in the documentation [36]. This helps in justifying the need for telehealth visits, especially when social factors significantly impact the patient's ability to access in-person care. By incorporating SDOH codes into your telehealth documentation, you can provide a more comprehensive view of the patient's health and better justify the necessity of telehealth visits in addressing the unique challenges posed by social determinants of health. This approach can support more effective and patient-centered care [37].

Hospital services through telehealth/remote patient monitoring

In a hospital setting, including Tele-ICU (Tele-Intensive Care Unit) services, the application of ICD-10 coding and CPT billing to telehealth is vital for accurate documentation and billing practices [38,39]. While there is some overlap, telehealth coding in the hospital requires special attention [40].

ICD-10 Coding for Telehealth in the Hospital [41]

ICD-10 codes are employed to document diagnoses and conditions for patients receiving telehealth services within the hospital. This includes Tele-ICU services. Key points for ICD-10 coding in this context include.

1. Diagnosis Coding for Telehealth Patients: ICD-10 codes are used to record the patient's primary diagnosis and relevant comorbidities. For instance, if a patient in the ICU is receiving Tele-ICU monitoring for sepsis, the primary diagnosis might be ICD-10 code A41.9 (Sepsis, unspecified organism), and any related comorbidities should be documented using the appropriate ICD-10 codes [42].
2. Additional ICD-10 Coding for Telehealth-Related Conditions: Beyond the primary diagnosis, healthcare providers should use ICD-10 codes to document conditions directly linked to the telehealth service. For example, if Tele-ICU involves remote monitoring of

a ventilated patient, relevant ICD-10 codes for respiratory conditions and ventilator management should be applied.
3. Telehealth Encounter Documentation: Proper documentation of the telehealth encounter and the patient's condition is crucial for accurate ICD-10 coding. It's essential to clearly indicate in the medical record that the encounter took place via telehealth, the start and end of the visit, the total time spent on the encounter, if there were other assistants present or caregivers present as well as that you obtained consent. It is also important to state limitations due to virtual settings versus in-person settings.

It's crucial to adhere to the specific coding and billing guidelines of your hospital, as well as those of the payer, to ensure accurate and compliant billing for Tele-ICU and other telehealth services provided within the hospital setting. Additionally, stay informed about any changes in coding and billing regulations, as they may evolve over time.

ICD-10 coding for E-consults

ICD-10 coding for e-consults involves documenting diagnoses and conditions related to the consultation process [41,43–45]. The primary purpose is to specify the patient's primary diagnosis or the reason for the consult, with additional codes used for relevant comorbidities. Accuracy and specificity in code selection are essential to support medical decision-making. Clear and comprehensive documentation of e-consult details, including clinical questions and recommendations, should align with diagnoses/clinical conditions managed with appropriately chosen ICD-10 codes that correlate.

Here's how ICD-10 coding applies to e-consults

1. Primary Diagnosis: The primary purpose of ICD-10 coding in e-consults is to document the patient's primary diagnosis or the reason for the consult. This code should reflect the condition or issue for which the consulting healthcare provider is seeking guidance.
2. Additional Diagnoses: If there are comorbidities or other relevant conditions that impact the patient's care and are discussed during the e-consult, they should be documented using additional ICD-10 codes. These codes provide a comprehensive picture of the patient's health status.
3. Code Selection Accuracy: Ensuring the accuracy and specificity of the ICD-10 codes is crucial. The codes should precisely represent the patient's condition to support appropriate medical decision-making and care recommendations.
4. Documentation of E-Consult Details: It is essential to have clear and comprehensive documentation of the e-consult, including the clinical questions asked, the consulting provider's recommendations, and the rationale for those recommendations. The ICD-10 codes should align with this documentation.

It's essential for healthcare providers to follow the specific coding and billing guidelines of their healthcare system, payer, and jurisdiction when conducting e-consults. Accurate coding and documentation support appropriate reimbursement and ensure compliance with regulatory requirements.

Challenges of ICD-10 and SNOMED CT codes in digital health

The accurate identification of Hierarchical Condition Category (HCC) codes during telehealth visits is essential for determining the Risk Adjustment Factor (RAF) score in healthcare. To achieve precise RAF scoring, healthcare providers should begin by identifying and thoroughly documenting relevant chronic conditions under HCC categories during telehealth encounters. Assigning the appropriate ICD-10 codes that accurately represent the patient's diagnoses is crucial. Additionally, documenting clinical data related to these chronic conditions, such as laboratory results and treatment plans, is essential, as it influences the RAF score. Providers must ensure comprehensive documentation of telehealth encounters, including medical history, physical examination findings, assessments, and plans, while clearly indicating changes in health status and management. Staying informed about evolving coding guidelines, verifying telehealth eligibility for RAF scoring, coordinating with coding and billing teams, and continuously monitoring and updating RAF scores are integral components of this process. Ultimately, accurate HCC code identification in telehealth plays a vital role in risk adjustment and reimbursement within the healthcare landscape.

SNOMED CT, a robust clinical terminology system, brings precision and granularity to clinical data in digital health, yet it poses notable challenges. Its intricate complexity demands extensive learning and training for healthcare professionals. Integrating SNOMED CT into existing health IT systems can be resource-intensive, raising concerns about compatibility and upgrades. Ensuring uniform code usage across diverse healthcare settings is challenging and vital for interoperability. Regular updates require active system management, but maintaining accurate cross-referencing with other coding systems, such as ICD-10, can be complex. Cost, data privacy, and security considerations weigh on healthcare organizations, while the system's extensive terminology can overwhelm users. Additionally, international variations and migrating from legacy systems introduce further complexities. Despite these hurdles, SNOMED CT enhances standardized clinical terminology, data interoperability, and clinical decision support, incentivizing healthcare organizations to invest in its integration for improved patient care and data-driven decision-making.

The reimbursement process in healthcare is a multifaceted system that heavily depends on precise coding, mainly ICD-10 and CPT codes, which play a crucial role in determining whether a healthcare appointment is eligible for reimbursement. ICD-10 codes are employed to document a patient's diagnosis or condition, with accuracy being paramount. The specificity of these codes is vital, as vagueness may result in lower reimbursement rates or claim denials. Additionally, demonstrating the medical necessity of the appointment through the ICD-10 code is essential. On the other hand, CPT codes describe the specific healthcare services provided during the appointment, whether it's an evaluation, procedure, or diagnostic test. The choice of the appropriate CPT code is determined by the complexity and duration of the service, documented through elements such as history, examination, and medical decision-making. Modifiers can provide extra information about the service, further justifying reimbursement. Reimbursement is influenced by factors such as payer guidelines, coding accuracy, medical necessity, comprehensive documentation, adherence to guidelines, and timely claim submission. Should a claim be denied, healthcare providers can appeal by providing additional documentation to support their reimbursement request. In essence, precise coding and documentation practices are integral to ensuring that healthcare providers are fairly reimbursed for their services within the intricate reimbursement landscape.

The future of codes in digital health

Digital transformation in healthcare is ushering in new trends and concepts such as digital determinants of health [46]. However, there are significant challenges related to reimbursement through ICD-10 and CPT coding, which can disproportionately affect patients. Access disparities are a critical concern, with some patients lacking the necessary technology or digital literacy for digital health services. Insurance coverage for digital health varies widely, leaving underinsured or uninsured patients potentially with limited access. Provider reimbursement rates for digital health services can vary widely and commonly have been associated with lower payment, particularly impacting business models for providers in underserved areas. With uncertainty surrounding reimbursement and coverage, providers and their administration commonly have to adjust their digital health offerings based on sound business capacity. Because of the additional structural inequities and disparities that exist in society, if insurance coverage/reimbursement and/or digital access are not equitable, digital health disparities may worsen, particularly among vulnerable populations who could benefit from virtual access. The digital divide, which separates those with and without access to technology, can widen due to reimbursement policies favoring digital health. Cultural and linguistic barriers can hinder the effective use of these services, while data privacy concerns may be heightened for marginalized communities. Addressing these disparities in reimbursement for digital health services is essential to promoting health equity. Policymakers, payers, and healthcare providers must work together to develop reimbursement models that prioritize equitable access to these services, especially for underserved and vulnerable populations. This may include revising reimbursement rates, expanding coverage, and addressing digital literacy and technology access challenges.

In an increasingly digital healthcare landscape, ICD-10 codes, particularly those related to social determinants of health (SDOH), play a crucial role in justifying the need for telehealth visits and improving patient care outcomes. These SDOH Z codes within ICD-10 help capture factors beyond medical conditions that influence a patient's health [47]. Healthcare providers can use them to assess and document relevant social factors during telehealth visits, such as housing instability, food insecurity, and poverty. By explaining how these social factors impact the patient's health and care plan, providers can emphasize the necessity of telehealth services. Collaborating with interdisciplinary teams and planning telehealth interventions that consider SDOH challenges further enhances patient care. Continuous evaluation of progress and, when necessary, referrals to community resources can address persistent barriers. Adequately combining SDOH z-codes in telehealth and ICD-10 coding could further define the patient journey and justify the need for more digital health services, especially when social factors significantly affect a patient's ability to access in-person care. By incorporating SDOH codes into telehealth documentation, you can provide a more comprehensive view of the patient's health and better justify the necessity of telehealth visits in addressing the unique challenges posed by social determinants of health. This approach can support more effective and patient-centered care. Please reference the further reading section for more information regarding SDOH Z-Codes and how to implement them when providing patient care, especially telehealth.

The planned expansion of ICD-10 coding for digital health services is a response to the growing integration of digital health technologies into healthcare delivery. Key aspects of this expansion include the development of new CPT codes to cover a broader range of digital health services, particularly in areas such as telehealth, remote patient monitoring, and virtual care visits. The coding and billing for these services will become more specific and granular as the use of digital health technologies continues to grow. This expansion also encompasses areas such as digital therapeutics, integration with electronic health records (EHRs), improved data collection and reporting, and alignment with value-based care models. Policy and regulatory changes, as well as a focus on patient-centered care and interoperability, will shape the evolution of digital health coding and billing practices. Ultimately, these changes aim to ensure that healthcare providers can accurately document and be reimbursed for the full spectrum of services provided through digital health technologies, thereby enhancing patient care and access. Healthcare professionals and organizations should stay informed about these developments to navigate the evolving landscape of digital health reimbursement effectively.

Conclusion

In conclusion, ICD-10 and the eventual shift to ICD-11 and SNOMED CT have evolved over decades to become foundational pillars of healthcare coding and clinical documentation [48]. Their adaptability and expanding roles in the digital health era reflect their enduring importance in ensuring the accuracy, efficiency, and quality of healthcare delivery. As digital health technologies continue to revolutionize the healthcare landscape, these coding systems will remain indispensable in navigating the ever-evolving world of healthcare data. As the clinician, it is important to optimize the value of claims-based data by effectively using ICD-10 and CPT coding to correlate the use of telehealth as a modality with condition management. Using the coding systems with intention can highlight the array of conditions and circumstances in which telehealth is applied as a modality and it will be important for further understanding of telehealth utilization to represent the applications of telehealth directly with the condition management scenarios it is being applied. The more that can be presented in coding system level data, the more reliable and predictive the data can be to develop additional codes along with reimbursement fee schedule rates for future digital health services.

AI disclosure

During the preparation of this work the author(s) used ChatGPT in order to For readability and formating. After using this tool/service, the author(s) reviewed and edited the content as needed and take(s) full responsibility for the content of the publication.

References

[1] Fung. Achieving logical equivalence between SNOMED CT and ICD-10-PCS surgical procedures. AMIA annual symposium proceedings AMIA symposium. 2018. 2017. https://pubmed.ncbi.nlm.nih.gov/29854138/. [Accessed 28 September 2023].

[2] Ternois I, Billard-Pomarès T, Carbonelle E, Franchinard L, Duclos C. Using SNOMED-CT to help the transition from microbiological data to ICD-10 sepsis codes. HAL (Le Centre pour la Communication Scientifique Directe). 2019;264:1604–5. https://doi.org/10.3233/shti190556.

[3] Lena Suryani D, Ernawati F, Barsasella D. Diversity of medical terminology based on SNOMED-CT to support the accuracy of COVID-19 diagnostic code on ICD-10. In: The 8th international conference on public health Solo, Indonesia; 2021.

[4] Vikström A, Nyström M, Åhlfeldt H, Lars-Erik S, Nilsson G. Views of diagnosis distribution in primary care in 2.5 million encounters in Stockholm: a comparison between ICD-10 and SNOMED CT. Journal of Innovation in Health Informatics 2010;18(1):17–29. https://doi.org/10.14236/jhi.v18i1.750.

[5] History of the Development of the ICD. https://cdn.who.int/media/docs/default-source/classification/icd/historyoficd.pdf.

[6] Hirsch JA, Nicola GN, McGinty G, et al. ICD-10: history and context. American Journal of Neuroradiology 2016;37(4):596–9. https://doi.org/10.3174/ajnr.a4696.

[7] ICD—ICD-10-CM—International Classification of Diseases. ICD-10-CM/PCS Transition; 2023. Published, https://www.cdc.gov/nchs/icd/icd10cm_pcs_background.htm. [Accessed 28 September 2023].

[8] Holman T, Wallask S, Lee K. ICD-10 (international classification of diseases, tenth revision). Health IT; 2018. Published, https://www.techtarget.com/searchhealthit/definition/ICD-10#:~:text=ICD%2D10%20purpose%20and%20uses,assist%20in%20medical%20reimbursement%20decisions. [Accessed 28 September 2023].

[9] Overview of SNOMED CT. Nih.gov. 2013. Published, https://www.nlm.nih.gov/healthit/snomedct/snomed_overview.html#:~:text=SNOMED%20CT%20originated%20from%20the,to%20describe%20morphology%20and%20anatomy.&text=Under%20Dr.,the%20growing%20needs%20of%20medicine. [Accessed 28 September 2023].

[10] Kalet IJ. Biomedical information access. Elsevier eBooks; January 1, 2009. p. 223–50. https://doi.org/10.1016/b978-0-12-369438-6.00008-8. Published online.

[11] Chang E, Mostafa J. The use of SNOMED CT, 2013-2020: a literature review. Journal of the American Medical Informatics Association 2021;28(9):2017–26. https://doi.org/10.1093/jamia/ocab084.

[12] 5-Step briefing | SNOMED International. SNOMED international. 2016. Published, https://www.snomed.org/five-step-briefing#:~:text=SNOMED%20CT%20supports%20the%20development,enables%20automatic%20interpretation%20of%20these. [Accessed 28 September 2023].

[13] National Library of Medicine. Overview of SNOMED CT. National Library of Medicine; 2016. Published, https://www.nlm.nih.gov/healthit/snomedct/snomed_overview.html. [Accessed 28 September 2023].

[14] Introduction of systematized nomenclature of medicine–clinical terms coding into an electronic health record and evaluation of its impact: qualitative and quantitative study. JMIR Preprints 2015. Published, https://preprints.jmir.org/preprint/29532. [Accessed 28 September 2023].

[15] Nath S. The role of standards for digital health and health information management. https://jbcr.net.in/JBCR-VOL-6-issue-1-2019-20/pdf/1.pdf.

[16] 2024 ICD-10-CM Diagnosis Code J06.9: Acute upper respiratory infection, unspecified. 2024. Icd10data.com. Published, https://www.icd10data.com/ICD10CM/Codes/J00-J99/J00-J06/J06-/J06.9. [Accessed 3 May 2024].

[17] 38341003—hypertensive disorder—SNOMED CT. 2022. Findacode.com. Published, https://www.findacode.com/snomed/38341003–hypertensive-disorder.html. [Accessed 3 May 2024].

[18] 2024 ICD-10-CM Diagnosis Code A41.9: sepsis, unspecified organism. 2024. https://Icd10data.com. Published, https://www.icd10data.com/ICD10CM/Codes/A00-B99/A30-A49/A41-/A41.9. [Accessed 3 May 2024].

[19] 2023 ICD-10-CM Diagnosis Code E11.9: type 2 diabetes mellitus without complications. 2023. Icd10data.com. Published, https://www.icd10data.com/ICD10CM/Codes/E00-E89/E08-E13/E11-/E11.9#:~:text=Type%202%20diabetes%20mellitus%20without%20complications,-2016%202017%202018&text=As%20Admission%20Dx-,E11.,effective%20on%20October%201%2C%202022. [Accessed 28 September 2023].

[20] 73211009—diabetes mellitus—SNOMED CT. 2022. Findacode.com. Published, https://www.findacode.com/snomed/73211009–diabetes-mellitus.html. [Accessed 28 September 2023].

[21] 44054006 SNOMED code | Diabetes mellitus type 2 (disorder) | Systematized nomenclature of medicine code directory | Medical coding library www.hipaaspace.com. http://www.HIPAASpace.com © 2023. www.hipaaspace.com. Published 2023. Accessed September 28, 2023.| https://www.hipaaspace.com/medical_billing/coding/snomed/44054006.

[22] 2023 ICD-10-CM diagnosis code F32.9: Major depressive disorder, single episode, unspecified. 2023. Icd10data.com. Published, https://www.icd10data.com/ICD10CM/Codes/F01-F99/F30-F39/F32-/F32.9. [Accessed 28 September 2023].

[23] 2023 ICD-10-CM diagnosis code I10: essential (primary) hypertension. 2023. Icd10data.com. Published, https://www.icd10data.com/ICD10CM/Codes/I00-I99/I10-I16/I10-/I10. [Accessed 28 September 2023].

[24] Published 2023 ICD-10-CM diagnosis code M54.5: low back pain. 2023. Icd10data.com. https://www.icd10data.com/ICD10CM/Codes/M00-M99/M50-M54/M54-/M54.5. [Accessed 28 September 2023].

[25] Coding scenario: telehealth. 2021. Aafp.org. Published, https://www.aafp.org/family-physician/patient-care/current-hot-topics/recent-outbreaks/covid-19/covid-19-telehealth/coding-scenarios-during-covid-19/telehealth.html. [Accessed 28 September 2023].

[26] ThoroughCare. 2023 remote patient monitoring (RPM) CPT codes, billing, and reimbursements. 2023. Thoroughcare.net. Published, https://www.thoroughcare.net/blog/2023-remote-patient-monitoring-cpt-codes-99453-99454-99457-99458. [Accessed 28 September 2023].

[27] Definitive Healthcare. Top 20 remote patient monitoring related diagnoses. Definitive Healthcare 2020. Published, https://www.definitivehc.com/resources/healthcare-insights/top-remote-patient-monitoring-diagnoses. [Accessed 28 September 2023].

[28] Beckman KD. How to document and code for hypertensive diseases in ICD-10. Family Practice Management 2014;21(2):5–9. https://www.aafp.org/pubs/fpm/issues/2014/0300/p5.html. [Accessed 28 September 2023].

[29] 2023 ICD-10-CM Diagnosis Code E11.9: type 2 diabetes mellitus without complications. 2023. Icd10data.com. Published, https://www.icd10data.com/ICD10CM/Codes/E00-E89/E08-E13/E11-/E11.9. [Accessed 28 September 2023].

[30] 2023 ICD-10-CM diagnosis code I50.9: heart failure, unspecified. 2023. Icd10data.com. Published, https://www.icd10data.com/ICD10CM/Codes/I00-I99/I30-I5A/I50-/I50.9. [Accessed 28 September 2023].

[31] 56675007—Acute heart failure—SNOMED CT. Findacode.com. 2022. Published, https://www.findacode.com/snomed/56675007–acute-heart-failure.html. [Accessed 28 September 2023].

[32] Billing for telehealth encounters: introductory guide for medicare fee for service. 2022. https://www.cchpca.org/2022/03/2022BillingGuidefinal.pdf.

[33] Billing and coding medicare fee-for-service claims. 2023. telehealth.hhs.gov. Published, https://telehealth.hhs.gov/providers/billing-and-reimbursement/billing-and-coding-medicare-fee-for-service-claims. [Accessed 28 September 2023].

[34] 99091, 99453, 99454, 99457 and 99458: a guide to RPM codes in 2022 from CareSimple. CareSimple. March 2, 2022. Published, https://caresimple.com/new-rpm-codes-99091-99453-99454-99457-99458/. [Accessed 28 September 2023].

[35] Gross GN. Coding telemedicine visits for proper reimbursement. Current Allergy and Asthma Reports 2020;20(11). https://doi.org/10.1007/s11882-020-00970-0.

[36] ThoroughCare. 2023 Remote Patient Monitoring (RPM) CPT codes, billing, and reimbursements. Thoroughcare.net. Published 2023. Accessed September 28, 2023. https://www.thoroughcare.net/blog/2023-remote-patient-monitoring-cpt-codes-99453-99454-99457-99458#:~:text=RPM)%20%7C%20CPT%20codes-,2023%20Remote%20Patient%20Monitoring%20CPT,99453%2C%2099454%2C%2099457%2C%2099458&text=Understanding%20the%20CPT%20billing%20codes,the%20patient%20and%20by%20Medicare.

[37] Coding for social determinants of health (SDOH). Accessed September 28, 2023. https://downloads.aap.org/AAP/PDF/SDOH.pdf.

[38] Social determinants of health and medical coding: what to know. American Medical Association; May 13, 2022. Published, https://www.ama-assn.org/practice-management/cpt/social-determinants-health-and-medical-coding-what-know. [Accessed 28 September 2023].

[39] Critical care documentation and billing update: COVID-19 pandemic. Accessed September 28, 2023. https://www.sccm.org/getattachment/5e30fe35-2dde-43db-8935-4ce41b8c7e5b/Critical-Care-Documentation-and-Billing-Update-CO.

[40] Managing patients remotely: billing for digital and telehealth services. 2023. Acog.org. Published, https://www.acog.org/practice-management/coding/coding-library/managing-patients-remotely-billing-for-digital-and-telehealth-services. [Accessed 28 September 2023].

[41] Esposito TJ, Reed R, Adams RC, Fakhry SM, Carey D, Crandall M. Acute care surgery billing, coding and documentation series part 3: coding of additional select procedures; modifiers; telemedicine coding; robotic surgery. Trauma surgery & acute care open 2020;5(1):e000587. https://doi.org/10.1136/tsaco-2020-000587.

[42] Billing for telehealth in emergency departments. 2023. telehealth.hhs.gov. Published, https://telehealth.hhs.gov/providers/best-practice-guides/telehealth-for-emergency-departments/billing. [Accessed 28 September 2023].
[43] Telemedicine CPT codes. February 8, 2022. Curogram.com. Published, https://blog.curogram.com/telemedicine-cpt-codes. [Accessed 28 September 2023].
[44] E-consults. 2021. telehealth.hhs.gov. Published, https://telehealth.hhs.gov/providers/best-practice-guides/telehealth-for-emergency-departments/e-consults. [Accessed 28 September 2023].
[45] AMA telehealth policy, coding and payment. American Medical Association; July 19, 2023. Published, https://www.ama-assn.org/practice-management/digital/ama-telehealth-policy-coding-payment. [Accessed 28 September 2023].
[46] Atreja A, Francis S, Kurra S, Kabra R. Digital medicine and evolution of remote patient monitoring in cardiac electrophysiology: a state-of-the-art perspective. Current Treatment Options in Cardiovascular Medicine 2019;21(12). https://doi.org/10.1007/s11936-019-0787-3.
[47] Truong HP, Luke AA, Hammond G, Wadhera RK, Reidhead M, Joynt KE. Utilization of social determinants of health ICD-10 Z-codes among hospitalized patients in the United States, 2016–2017. Medical Care 2020;58(12):1037–43. https://doi.org/10.1097/mlr.0000000000001418.
[48] Fung KW, Xu J, Bodenreider O. The new International Classification of Diseases 11th edition: a comparative analysis with ICD-10 and ICD-10-CM. Journal of the American Medical Informatics Association 2020;27(5):738–46. https://doi.org/10.1093/jamia/ocaa030.

Further reading

Digital health policy and reimbursement

TELEHEALTH FOR PROVIDERS: WHAT YOU NEED TO KNOW (cms.gov).
Resources—ATA (americantelemed.org).
Home | Center for Connected Health Policy (cchpca.org).
National Consortium of Telehealth Resource Centers | Home.
Executives for Health Innovation | A Catalyst for Healthcare Transformation (ehidc.org).

Social Determinants of Health

Social Determinants of Health Information Exchange Toolkit (healthit.gov).
Social Determinants of Health Use Case Implementation Guide (mihin.org).
Gravity Project (thegravityproject.net).

Digital Health research and standardization

Digital Medicine Society (DiMe)—Advancing digital medicine to optimize human health. (dimesociety.org).
Home—Digital Therapeutics Alliance (dtxalliance.org).

CHAPTER 19

Digital health law

Jeremy Sherer and Amy Joseph
Orrick, Herrington & Sutcliffe LLP, Boston, MA, United States

Introduction and terminology

"Digital health" is an umbrella term that generally references the delivery of healthcare services from a distance involving the use of telecommunications technology. Terms such as "telehealth" and "telemedicine" are not universally defined and have different meanings depending on the state or sector of the healthcare industry in which a practitioner operates. Here, we use "telehealth" to reference a range of healthcare services that can be delivered through telecommunication technology, while "telemedicine" is specific to medical services furnished through digital health modalities. Remote patient monitoring (RPM) is another digital health modality that fits under the "digital health" umbrella but is nevertheless distinct from telehealth and telemedicine in common parlance (though certain states define RPM as a type of telehealth technology). RPM is the most common type of monitoring technology where a user wears or carries a data-collecting tool that transmits large volumes of clinical data to be analyzed by a clinical team operating at a distance, usually asynchronously (i.e., not in real time). And, of course, digital health involves more than the delivery of care by clinicians, as artificial intelligence (AI) tools continue to expand the types of information and decision support delivered to practitioners and patients alike.

Overview of legal framework

At its core, oversight of digital health falls under the same rubric that applies to other aspects of healthcare. Without providing an overview or getting into the complexity of the US legal system and the interplay between federal and state legal frameworks, when looking to understand what is permitted, what is restricted, what parameters are in place, and in some cases, what is simply not addressed, with respect to digital health offerings, there are four key areas of legal authority and guidance: (1) State law and regulations, as

Digital Health. https://doi.org/10.1016/B978-0-443-23901-4.00019-2

well as state agency oversight; (2) federal law, regulations, and federal agency oversight; (3) applicable contractual terms and conditions; and (4) case law in federal and state jurisdictions.[1]

State oversight

Just as a licensed healthcare professional must be licensed in each state where they furnish professional services, the practitioner must comply with the laws of such states. That seemingly straightforward task becomes nuanced and complex when delivering care virtually, as providers can (and often do) treat patients in multiple jurisdictions in the span of a single day. The legal authorities that govern the provision of care on a state-by-state basis include statutes, regulations, and subregulatory guidance. Statutes are legal codes that are passed by state lawmakers (i.e., the legislature) while regulations are promulgated by state agencies with subject matter expertise. Subregulatory guidance, meanwhile, includes advisory opinions, frequently asked questions (or FAQ) documents posted on board websites, and even professional board newsletters. Subregulatory guidance can be particularly instructive in understanding how a professional board or other regulator *interprets* the laws and regulations on the books.

Federal oversight

Much of the regulation of virtual care or other digital health tools occurs at the state level, as addressed earlier. However, certain federal laws, regulations, and subregulatory guidance may apply, depending on the context. The key federal agencies providing oversight are described herein, though this summary is far from the universe of areas of federal oversight that could apply to any particular healthcare business model. Each of the following is within the U.S. Department of Health and Human Services (HHS), except for the Federal Trade Commission.

Centers for Medicare & Medicaid Services (CMS). CMS is a federal agency that, among other things, administers the Medicare program and works in conjunction with state governments in the administration of state Medicaid programs. CMS is the largest payer for healthcare in the United States, and there has been a continuing expansion of reimbursement available for digital health in this context. Although the applicable Medicare and Medicaid statutes, regulations, and other regulatory guidance do not apply to every instance of the use of a digital health solution, they are often looked to as examples by state regulators and other third-party payers as a benchmark for best practices and therefore play a prominent role in the industry.

[1] This chapter does not address international laws, which would apply if seeking to deploy or implement a digital health solution in any international jurisdiction.

For example, the Medicare program has long recognized the value of telehealth in limited situations, but since the COVID-19 pandemic, there has been significant expansion in the contexts under which Medicare will reimburse for telehealth through services.[2] Many of those expanded coverage policies have been extended through the end of the calendar year 2024; however, it remains to be seen whether Medicare will permanently cover telehealth services outside of largely rural areas, where telehealth services are generally available. Separately, the CMS Innovation Center is constantly testing new payment and service delivery models, and many such models incorporate and provide additional flexibility to utilize digital health.[3]

Food and Drug Administration (FDA). The FDA regulates a broad variety of products, including food, drugs, biologics, and notably, medical devices, under the Federal Food, Drug, and Cosmetic Act of 1938 (the FD&C Act) and regulations promulgated thereunder. A common question that arises in developing certain digital health software solutions providing clinical decision support is whether the software constitutes a device regulated by the FDA or falls within an applicable exception. If the clinical decision support tool meets four criteria, it is excluded from the definition of a device and not subject to FDA approval, with key requirements including that the tool is intended for use by a healthcare professional (not use by the patient), where the tool is intended to enable the healthcare professional to independently review any recommendations presented, but is not intended for the professional to primarily rely on the recommendations with respect to clinical decision making for individual patients.[4] In other words, from a regulatory oversight perspective, a line is drawn between tools that might help *supplement*, but not *substitute* or *supplant*, a healthcare professional's independent professional judgment.

Office of Inspector General (OIG). OIG is an oversight unit within HHS that seeks to prevent fraud, waste, and abuse.[5] Some key activities include audits and investigations of individuals and entities that participate in and receive reimbursement from governmental healthcare programs, including the Medicare and Medicaid programs. OIG also engages in educational activities and issues guidance, such as through the issuance of voluntary compliance guidance, toolkits, and advisory opinions.[6] As digital health has grown within the industry, so has OIG's attention in this area of healthcare delivery and reimbursement. OIG has expressly acknowledged the value that digital health solutions can provide in efforts to promote access to care, improve the quality of care, and reduce costs, on

---

[2] See 42 U.S.C. §1395(m) (m); 42 C.F.R. § 410.78; List of Telehealth Services | CMS.

[3] CMS Innovation Center Homepage | CMS Innovation Center.

[4] 21 U.S.C. § 360j(o); see also Clinical Decision Support Software Guidance for Industry and Food and Drug Administration Staff (Sept. 28, 2022).

[5] The U.S. Department of Justice is also extremely active in investigation and enforcement activity in the healthcare industry, including a robust criminal healthcare fraud unit.

[6] See https://oig.hhs.gov/compliance/.

multiple occasions, including as part of its significant rulemaking in 2020 to provide more flexibility to promote value-based arrangements.[7] However, as with any other modality by which healthcare is delivered, there is the potential for fraud, waste, and abuse in digital health, and OIG has been increasing its scrutiny—in particular, with respect to telehealth—in recent years.[8]

Office for Civil Rights (OCR). Among other things, OCR enforces the federal Health Insurance Portability and Accountability Act and regulations promulgated thereunder (HIPAA).[9] These provisions apply to most, but not all, healthcare providers and their contractors that create, receive, maintain, or transmit "protected health information" on their behalf, and include robust requirements with respect to the privacy and security of such information, as well as breach notification obligations to affected individuals, the government, and in some cases, the media. While healthcare providers are also subject to state data privacy and security laws in appliable jurisdictions and may also be subject to other federal data privacy laws (including, without limitation, 42 U.S.C. Section 290dd and 42 C.F.R. Part 2, applicable to certain substance use disorder patient records), HIPAA has been influential in setting consumer and industry expectations as to best practices for protection of health information, given its broad applicability, detailed requirements, and amount of guidance and enforcement actions to draw from. Digital health solutions involve the utilization of significant utilization of patient data, whether it is the exchange and storage of such information through a telehealth platform or utilizing data to help build and train generative AI tools, to which HIPAA and other applicable privacy and security laws apply.

Federal Trade Commission (FTC). FTC's focus is consumer protection, and it engages in oversight and enforcement to prevent anticompetitive, deceptive, and unfair business practices. Among other things, the FTC has promulgated a Health Breach Notification Rule and engaged in a series of enforcement actions, with a particular recent focus on health apps and connected devices that collect or use consumers' health information.[10] FTC also provides oversight of advertising and marketing, such as with respect to claims

[7] 85 Fed. Reg. 77684 (Dec. 2, 2020) (finalizing proposals that "aim to support innovative methods and novel arrangements, including the use of digital health technology such as remote patient monitoring and telehealth").

[8] See, e.g., https://oig.hhs/gov/reports-and-publications/featured-topics/telehealth/(providing an overview of telehealth, telefraud schemes, OIG enforcement actions, and other OIG oversight activity); see also OIG's Toolkit: Analyzing Telehealth Claims to Assess Program Integrity Risks, OEI-02-20-00723 (Apr. 20, 2023).

[9] 42 U.S.C. § 1320d et seq.; 45 C.F.R. Part 160−164.

[10] 16 C.F.R. Part 318.

regarding health-related products, and online advertising and marketing, which would apply to any digital health solution being offered to consumers.[11]

Contractual terms and conditions

As addressed earlier, the Medicare and Medicaid programs are large payers that have established requirements to be eligible for reimbursement for services, including services provided through digital health solutions, such as virtual video or audio-only visits and remote patient monitoring. In addition to statutory and regulatory rules and regulations, terms and conditions of these payers may be set forth in provider agreements. Similarly, healthcare providers contracting with other third-party payers, which could include Medicare Advantage organizations, Medicaid Managed Care organizations, and commercial insurance companies or health maintenance organizations, will also be subject to contractual terms and conditions that will apply for a service to be eligible for reimbursement. Rules can vary from payer to payer and often will require review of the contractual terms as well as other policies and procedures, to determine the specific requirements established by the particular payer.

Case law

When disputes in any area of law escalate, they are ultimately decided by courts of law (subject to resolution through mediation, arbitration, or other agreed upon process to reach a settlement of the dispute). Litigation is uncommon in the context of the state-level scope of practice issues; however, there have been situations where important legal precedent involving digital health has been established through such proceedings. As one example in the digital health context, as telehealth utilization grew in the United States, tensions emerged between those representing "brick and mortar" provider facilities and the telehealth practices providing virtual care. That came to a head in Texas, where the Texas Medical Board's (TMB's) regulations prohibited establishing a physician—patient relationship through telehealth.[12] In practice, that meant that telehealth could only be utilized in scenarios where a physician had previously treated the patient in person. Teladoc and two physicians working with its affiliated medical practice sued the TMB in the US District Court for the Western District of Texas, seeking an injunction and monetary damages alleging that the TMB telemedicine rules were anticompetitive and restricted trade.[13] Their position was that the TMB rules stifled competition in violation of

[11] See, e.g., 16 C.F.R. Part 255; FTC's Health Products Compliance Guidance (updated guidance issued in 2022); FTC's Guides Concerning Use of Endorsements and Testimonials in Advertising, 88 Fed. Reg. 48092 (July 26, 2023).

[12] 28 TAC § 190.8(1) (L) (since rescinded).

[13] Teladoc, Inc. v. Texas Medical Board, 112 F. Supp. 3d 529, 533 (W.D. Tex. 2015).

federal antitrust laws and prevented Teladoc's affiliated medical practices from establishing a foothold in the Texas market. After the District Court rejected Teladoc's assertion that its decision-making was protected by principles involving sovereign immunity of state governments, Texas adopted new regulations allowing practitioner–patient relationships to be established through telehealth, and Teladoc dropped its lawsuit.[14] Though unusual, this episode highlights the role that courts can play in establishing crucial standards and guideposts as the role of digital health technology in care delivery continues to evolve.

Front of mind legal issues in digital health

A myriad of laws apply to digital health, making the legal landscape broad and complex. Additional complexity can arise given the pace at which digital health innovation is growing and the sometimes slower ability of legislatures and agencies to keep up. There are times when bright line answers might not exist and innovators are left to use their best reasoned judgment as to how to structure their business to comply—such as where the applicable law contemplates healthcare delivery in "brick and mortar" locations only. In addition, given the broad scope of items and services that can fall under the umbrella of digital health, the legal issues that arise vary between business models. The following provides a summary of "frequent flier" legal considerations that tend to arise, and which legal practitioners keep front of mind, but should not be taken as the universe of legal issues at play. To name just a few examples, this chapter does not address topics such as compliance with antikickback laws, physician self-referral laws, or other laws intended to prevent fraud, waste, and abuse, which generally apply in the healthcare context.

Licensure considerations

A central function of state professional boards is consumer protection. Specifically, state boards must know who is treating residents of their state and be able to verify that those professionals are appropriately qualified to do so. Boards utilize state licensure processes to achieve that goal, with the overarching principle being that a practitioner must be licensed in the jurisdiction where the patient is located at the time of treatment.[15] Some states have registration processes for out-of-state providers, rather than requiring full licensure for virtual care.[16] At the bottom, this means that a practitioner treating patients nationwide must hold a license or similar registration across dozens of jurisdictions. There are state compact efforts underway that seek to create reciprocal licensure among

[14] 22 TAC § 174.2.

[15] *See*, e.g., Cal. Bus. & Prof. Code § 2290.5(b).

[16] *See*, e.g., Ariz. Rev. Stat. § 36–3606.

participating states, such as the Interstate Medical Licensure Compact, which is currently active in 34 states, and the Nurse Licensure Compact, which is established in 39 jurisdictions. A PA Licensure Compact has been established; however, it has only been enacted by the states of Delaware and Utah.[17]

Most states have exceptions to their licensure requirements; however, states vary widely as to what categories of exceptions they recognize. Common exceptions include emergency situations, caring for an established patient, providing an interprofessional consult to another practitioner, and providing care as staff to a traveling sports team. Any practitioner providing care across state lines should familiarize themselves with the licensure requirements of the states in which their patients are located, as well as any applicable exceptions.

Consent

As telehealth utilization has grown, states have expanded their efforts to ensure that patients understand the risks and benefits associated with telehealth, which objective is generally accomplished through telehealth consent. States vary in what they require in terms of patient consent, but common features include confirming that patients who receive care through telehealth can still receive care in person, recognizing that telehealth may not be appropriate for all types of clinical treatment, and that connectivity issues can arise in virtual care. Practitioners should familiarize themselves with the consent standards of the state in which their patient is located when delivering virtual care. One particular issue to assess is whether the state simply requires consent to be obtained, but does not specify whether it needs to be in writing, or instead requires that the consent be in writing.

Prescribing and supervision

Delivering clinical services across state lines is already complex from a legal perspective; however, care that involves prescribing medication introduces yet another layer of complexity in the form of state pharmacy laws. Like any other care delivered through telehealth, providers must be licensed in the state where the patient is located when prescribing medication. For nonphysician practitioners with prescriptive authority, it is essential to ensure that both the prescribing nonphysician practitioner *and* the supervising physician are licensed in the state in which the patient is located. Federal and state-controlled substances prescribing registrations are equally important. Federal law requires practitioners prescribing controlled medication to register with the DEA in any state where the practitioner will prescribe controlled substances to a patient, and approximately half of the states have separate, state-level controlled substances prescribing registrations, which also need to be completed.[18]

---

17 www.pacompact.org.

18 21 C.F.R. 1306.03; *see*, e.g., Massachusetts Controlled Substances Registration.

One further wrinkle is that federal law, rather than state law, governs prescribing involving controlled substances. Historically, the Controlled Substances Act as amended by the Ryan Haight Act has prohibited prescribing schedule II-V controlled substances without first examining the patient in person, unless one of a series of fairly narrow exceptions is satisfied.[19] Those standards are being revisited by the DEA as this chapter was written in the fall of 2023. Specifically, issues the DEA is assessing include whether to implement a special telemedicine registration that would allow practitioners to prescribe controlled substances through telehealth, whether rules surrounding buprenorphine treatment should be different than other controlled substances, and whether a "telemedicine referral" from a patient's primary care provider should be sufficient to allow a specialist to prescribe controlled substances from a distance. This is an important area for telebehavioral health, obesity medicine, and gender-affirming care practitioners, among others, who regularly utilize controlled medication in their practices, to monitor moving forward.

Modalities and practitioner—patient relationship establishment

As discussed herein, what constitutes "telehealth" varies, both in terms of how the terms are utilized colloquially and as a matter of state law. Legally, the main issue for practitioners to consider is what types of communication are permitted when furnishing clinical services in a particular state. Since the Teladoc-TMB dispute discussed earlier, synchronous audio—video technology utilized in "video visits" has become widely accepted, and is permitted by all 50 states as well as their Medicaid programs. Instead, other, less interactive forms of telecommunication technology are now the subject of questions around how practitioners can legally practice their professions in the eyes of state professional boards. One of the modalities under examination is asynchronous online questionnaires, which gather information about a patient's symptoms for a clinician to review, make a diagnosis, and if clinically appropriate, prescribe medication. Some online questionnaires are "smart" or "adaptive" questionnaires, meaning that the tools are interactive, and the questions presented to the patient are determined using algorithm-driven workflows designed by clinicians to gather the information that a practitioner requires to treat the patient consistent with the applicable standard of care. Some state laws and regulatory guidance criticize or expressly prohibit treating patients through the use of a questionnaire alone. For example, the Oregon Medical Board's Telemedicine Policy states, in relevant part, "[t]reatment based solelyon an online questionnaire without individualized review and assessment does not constitute an acceptable standard of care".[20]

[19] 21 U.S.C. § 829(e).

[20] Oregon Medical Board Statement of Philosophy, Telemedicine (as amended Oct. 2, 2020) (emphasis added).

Other states' approaches to telehealth are deliberately broad, seeking to accommodate, and in some cases encourage, increased utilization of telehealth by implementing modality-agnostic telehealth definitions. Massachusetts, for example, introduced a new definition of telehealth in early 2021: "Synchronous or asynchronous audio, video, electronic media or other telecommunications technology, including, but not limited to: (1) interactive audio-video technology; (2) remote patient monitoring devices; (3) audio-only telephone; and (4) online adaptive interviews, for the purpose of evaluating, diagnosing, consulting, prescribing, treating, or monitoring of a patient's physical health, oral health, mental health or substance use disorder condition".[21] Ultimately, it is important to verify that any modality used to treat a patient is permitted under applicable state law to avoid potential scrutiny from state regulators.

Corporate practice of medicine prohibition

Many states expressly prohibit the so-called "corporate practice of medicine," which prohibits entities owned and controlled by unlicensed individuals from engaging in the practice of medicine.[22] In many states, this means that as a general rule, companies cannot employ or contract with physicians to provide professional services (with some exceptions, including where the company is owned by licensed physicians and specifically formed under state law to provide professional services). The public policy rationale behind such prohibition is to prevent such entities from exerting too much control over physicians, to avoid interfering with a physician's professional judgment, and prioritizing profit over patient care. In some states, this prohibition also extends to other healthcare professionals, such as dentists and psychologists.

Though this concept has broader applicability than in the digital health context, it is mentioned here as it has a significant impact on how digital health companies are structured. Often, a so-called "lay entity" that is not owned by physicians develops a digital health solution, but would not be permitted to utilize that solution to deliver care to patients. Such companies may enter into contractual arrangements with a closely aligned professional entity that is owned and controlled by an appropriate healthcare professional, where the company then licenses its technology and otherwise provides turn-key administrative services to facilitate the provision of care by the professional entity using the digital health company's technology. This model is very common across all states but can invite scrutiny if not structured and implemented in compliance with laws.

[21] MGL ch. 112 § 5O(a) (emphasis added).

[22] See, e.g., Cal. Bus. & Prof. Code §§ 2052, 2400.

Privacy laws

Beyond HIPAA (which is summarized in section Federal oversight of this chapter), each state has its own privacy and security laws. In some instances, these laws may be more stringent than HIPAA, including more restrictive provisions regarding when individually identifiable information can be disclosed without patient consent. One example is in the context of telebehavioral health since information about a person's mental health or the fact that a person has or has had a substance use disorder (or even simply the fact that a patient has sought behavioral health treatment) is often considered sensitive information that warrants additional protection.[23]

Artificial intelligence

While AI is nothing new to healthcare, there has been an exponential increase in interest in the use of such tools in a wide variety of ways, ranging from virtual assistants and other administrative practice management tools to complex clinical decision support tools. Many existing laws regulate key risks that have been raised with respect to AI. For example, with respect to data protection, the various federal and state privacy laws referenced earlier would apply. With respect to concerns of bias, unlawful discrimination laws potentially apply. As another example, depending on the specific clinical decision support tool, it might be considered a "device" that is subject to the Food & Drug Administration (FDA) oversight. Multiple federal agencies have signaled intent to utilize the existing legal framework to regulate the development and deployment of AI.[24] However, as of the date this chapter is being written, there is no overarching federal legal framework specific to AI in healthcare. This is not necessarily surprising, as sometimes it can take time for lawmaking efforts to catch up to innovation. It is anticipated that the legal landscape with respect to AI in healthcare will look very different in the years to come.

[23] See, e.g., Cal. Welf. & Inst. Code § 5328.

[24] See, e.g., US Consumer Financial Protection Bureau et al., "Joint Statement on Enforcement Efforts Against Discrimination and Bias in Automated Systems (issued Apr. 25, 2023).

CHAPTER 20

Use and reuse of data: Access, ownership, value, and trust

Danny Van Roijen
EU, Brussels, Belgium

Introduction

As our society becomes more digital, an exponential amount of data is being created. This is not different within the healthcare market. According to a 2020 RBC Capital Markets article [1], the healthcare industry generated about 30% of the world's total data volume. The global healthcare data storage market [2] grew to $5.7 billion in 2023. The healthcare data storage market includes revenues earned by entities onsite data storage, public cloud data storage, and hybrid cloud data storage solution. The market value includes the value of related goods sold by the service provider or included within the service offering. The data storage is used by the healthcare sector for patient records, electronic medical records (EMR) and backups, radiological images, insurance claims, and office documents. The data storage solutions are also used by healthcare companies to store data about manufacturing products and their processes. It is expected to grow from $4.88 billion in 2022 to $10.52 billion in 2027 at a compound annual growth rate of 16.6%.

Widespread use of electronic health record systems has supported the shift from paper to electronic records. This evolutionary process is still in progress as primary, secondary, and tertiary care, as well as pharmacies, home care, and other settings are undergoing this digital transformation. Next to that, existing care processes and methodologies are benefiting from new technological innovations, such as medical devices offering enhanced accuracy, functionality, and capability. For instance, within the field of pathology, a microscope slide can be scanned into a high-resolution file. Such whole slide image can easily take up a few gigabytes of storage. By use of digital pathology platforms, researchers can collaborate remotely, make image annotations, and train algorithms to support better detection and diagnosis.

Digital Health. https://doi.org/10.1016/B978-0-443-23901-4.00020-9

Wearables and sensors can capture data at more frequent intervals or even perform continuous measurements in a more frictionless or remote way. The miniaturization and integration of technology in new and user-friendly form factors not only help to expand the types of data generated but also facilitate data capture beyond the walls of the traditional care setting. Whether or not these data are being generated within a medical context or with medical-grade equipment may even be less relevant for certain use cases. An example could be a health assessment through face analysis using a conventional smartphone camera.

On top of this, the digitalization of administrative and operational processes within the healthcare sector provides an additional layer of information. The availability of this information, in combination with health data from patients or patient populations, can create meaningful insights to support clinical decisions, to efficiently allocate resources, or to evaluate health policies and outcomes.

Emerging fields of research feed the need for more data, such as omics research or the development of digital biomarkers. A lot of new data points are being uncovered and studied. While the promise of data-driven healthcare is not solely based on volume, it is not expected any time soon that there will come an end to the data explosion within healthcare.

With larger volumes of data comes more responsibility. Obviously, there are practical challenges in terms of data management and security, but more important than the generation or storage of data, are aspects of interoperability and accessibility, which will enable the use, reuse, and exchange of data. Only if we are able to link, trace, compare, and recombine data, will we be able to unlock its real potential and value.

Complexities and boundaries of data

Before discussing the value of data, let us first address some general concepts about it.

The Data—Information—Knowledge—Wisdom pyramid

The Data—Information—Knowledge—Wisdom pyramid (see Fig. 20.1), often used within the context of information management, represents in a very visual way the relationship between data, information, knowledge, and wisdom. Information can be gathered by collecting, combining, and collating data. Taking into account the context and meaning of this information, one can gain a better understanding and reach a level of Knowledge. The most important step forward in this process is to move from the Knowledge stage to the Wisdom stage, where previous insight can be meaningfully applied to expected future challenges.

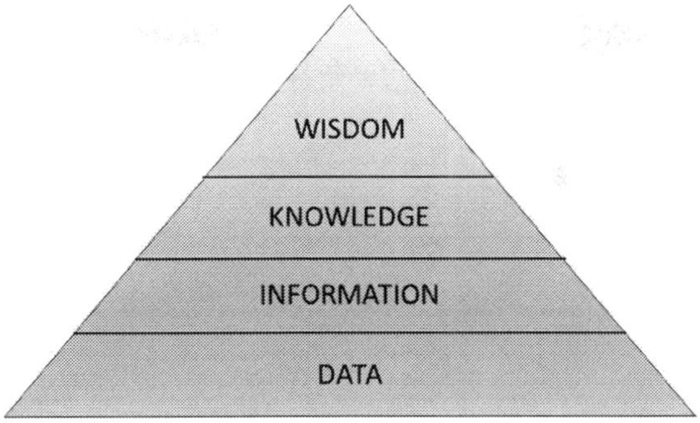

Figure 20.1
Data—Information—Knowledge—Wisdom pyramid.

When applying the DIKW model to the healthcare setting, however, it becomes quickly apparent that this simplified representation does not capture the multidimensional complexities we see around data in the context of health. We can distinguish between different types of data, based on the source of input and the way the data relates to a person's health situation. There is also a complexity and sensitivity to the extent data can be revealing and, unknowingly or unintentionally, lead to the (re)identification of a person. The reuse of data in a different context may trigger new information, changing perspectives that can be translated into new knowledge.

Health data, health-related data, and other data

In its most narrow definition and application, we can consider health data as data stemming from direct observations or measurements of a person's health condition, typically captured within a medical context, such as medical imaging or vital signs.

A more broadly defined group of health-related data will further complete the understanding of those factors that directly or indirectly impact the health condition of a patient. These include information that is being gathered through anamnesis or health symptoms and lifestyle parameters, from which valuable insight can be inferred for patient diagnosis and treatment. Such information, however, is not always readily available or routinely considered within the context of current care.

Further, there is an unexplored ocean of other data that may or may not be relevant to the patient's health condition or outcome. The World Health Organization (WHO) in this respect lists various determinants of health [3], which include the social and economic environment, the physical environment, and the person's individual characteristics and behaviors. According to the WHO, social determinants of health account for between 30% and 55% of health outcomes, and population health outcomes may be more affected by sectors outside the health sector than by the health sector itself [4].

Considering the low data maturity level of current health systems, such as the inability to issue, access, or share electronic patient summaries or lab results, most of the ongoing efforts are focusing on making health data more easily available. While this may seem to be the "low-hanging fruit" in turning *data* into *information* according to the DIKW model, ultimately with a positive impact on the patient, this is not an easily accomplished feat. Although typically clinical data enjoy a higher level of standardization and reliability, semantic and technical interoperability issues hamper the smooth exchange of health data.

From a technical perspective, it may not always be technically possible or practical to share data. There are scenarios where a report in a PDF format may be sufficient, whereas in other scenarios, for instance, when developing algorithms, direct access to the raw data may be more useful. Regarding semantic interoperability, there is a lack of consistency, for instance, in the use of coding and terminology systems, which may lead to incomplete or incorrect understanding of the clinical information being shared [5].

The inclusion of health-related data faces even higher hurdles as, especially in the case of data generated outside a clinical context, standardization is lacking and the reliability and accuracy of measurements are being questioned. At the same time, the use of real-world data is seen as crucial in gaining better insights in the efficacy of medicines and treatments.

Personal versus nonpersonal data

Another important dimension especially relevant for the health sector is the distinction between personal and nonpersonal data. While this may seem trivial, in practice, the interpretation is very important as it raises legal obligations and can require specific measures.

In Europe, the legal basis for processing personal data is being defined by the General Data Protection Regulation (GDPR) [6], which defines inter alia "personal data" (see Box 20.1) and "data concerning health" (see Box 20.2).

It is important to note that more stringent data protection measures apply to the processing of special categories of personal data, including the processing of genetic data, biometric data for the purpose of uniquely identifying a natural person, data concerning health, or data concerning a person's sex life or sexual orientation.

The possibility of reidentification and the understanding of what is considered data concerning health is under constant strain due to the ever-shifting landscape of new technologies. Some of these technologies include the increasing availability of new data sources, the development and accessibility of computational power, data analytics and artificial intelligence tools, and scientific progress. These changing boundaries of what

Box 20.1 EU General Data Protection Regulation, Article 4. Definitions, personal data

Art.4(1) "personal data" means any information relating to an identified or identifiable natural person ("data subject"); an identifiable natural person is one who can be identified, directly or indirectly, in particular by reference to an identifier such as a name, an identification number, location data, an online identifier, or to one or more factors specific to the physical, physiological, genetic, mental, economic, cultural, or social identity of that person.

Box 20.2 EU General Data Protection Regulation, Article 4. Definitions, data concerning health

Art.4(15) "data concerning health" means personal data related to the physical or mental health of a natural person, including the provision of health care services, which reveal information about his or her health status.

constitutes personal data and data concerning health have made it even more difficult to agree on a correct, or even uniform, interpretation of the legal requirements established under the GDPR, which consequently has impacted data holders' ability or willingness to share data. High penalties enacted by legislation for breaches of data protection have further exacerbated the situation, leading to a more risk-averse approach by data holders who then, in turn, lock up the information at their disposal.

Primary and secondary use of data

When looking at the purposes for which data can be used, typically a distinction is being made between the primary and secondary use of data. Within the healthcare context, the primary use of data should be understood as data that is being used for the provision of care to the patient. In the case of secondary use of data, the data are being used for purposes other than the original purpose for which the data were collected. The secondary use of data will help to support research, innovation, development, and policymaking. This may also include personal electronic health data that have been initially collected in the context of primary use. For instance, a medical imaging report can support the diagnosis or treatment of a patient (primary use), whereas the same imaging report might be used for research (secondary use) helping to better identify and classify lesions.

The distinction is important for two reasons. First of all, from a legal perspective, different obligations [7] may apply, for instance, regarding the necessity and validity of consent or information to be communicated on the further processing of data. Next to that, there is a more person-centric aspect, where in the case of primary use of the data, the person/patient is the direct beneficiary. In the case of secondary use of data, there may or may not be a direct or indirect impact for the person. Therefore, one may be more cautious or even unwilling to share data, balancing his/her personal interest against other or more public interests, also taking into account possible risks, such as data loss or unauthorized access.

Ownership of and access to health data

Traditional care pathways already involve multitudinal actors. The rise of noncommunicable diseases, for example, and the existence of multiple comorbidities are leading to more specialized needs that necessitate input from multidisciplinary teams. Integrated or coordinated care approaches require better data exchange between different care environments, often between primary and secondary care.

Data ownership

Within the context of the existing relationship between a patient and care providers, in principle, the patient is the owner of the data. With medical devices and digital health technologies increasingly being used as an important channel for monitoring and treating patients, there is a noticeable shift in the data relationship between patient and clinician. This raises the question what is the relationship between the healthcare providers, the technology providers, and the patients? Who controls what and how does this impact the use of data?

Another question regarding data ownership relates to the scope of data being considered. Should this only relate to the data that is being generated for the original purpose? What about other layers of data that can be of particular relevance, such as logging data, use and maintenance information, incident reporting, or metadata? Data generated by a medical device or digital health technology that is being used to support the diagnosis or treatment of the patient (primary use) may at the same time be valuable to improve the performance of the technology (secondary use).

Similar questions arise when it comes, for instance, to informal notes, summary reports, or inferred data. If a psychologist takes some informal notes to support or prepare a report, does that information belong to him or the patient? If a medical device measures different endpoints, would any aggregation, manipulation, or scoring of these values be considered data of the patient as well? How to deal with inferred data where the output may be the result of the combination of the patient data with other data sources?

The development and use of artificial intelligence applications further raise questions along the entirety of the data pipeline, including how data curation, annotation, or labeling may impact discussions around ownership and intellectual property.

Another element to consider is how to treat data that can also be revealing about others, such as in the case of genetic data. Direct-to-consumer genetic tests have given people more accessible options in learning about their genetic predispositions or specific phenotypes. Given the nature of this information, the sharing of this data with other parties may to a certain extent disclose information on the person's relatives and their health condition, without their prior information or consent. This can have unintended and far-reaching consequences, be it related to genetic diseases, questions of kinship, law enforcement, or more malicious use of the information.

From the aforementioned, it is clear that there can be no uniform response to these questions, as there are a multitude of channels and processes through which data are being generated and processed. All things considered, it begs the question if ownership is the most relevant question in order to unlock the value of data use and reuse within health. Some of the most stringent regimes regarding data and data protection do not define or assign data ownership. Instead, through a number of different initiatives and frameworks, there is a specific focus on control, accessibility, and data portability.

Data access and patient empowerment

Access to data improves the patient journey and experience, as it supports a more seamless transition from one care provider to the other, eliminating unfavorable health issues due to incorrect or incomplete data. Access to health data is also considered an essential element empowering patients, as they are enabled to more actively and proactively manage their health conditions and outcomes by acting on the (now expanded) information made available to them. Data can be more supportive in moving to a more personalized and preventive approach, with digital health technologies providing the ability for self-care and home care. In this regard, wider availability of data in the context of lifestyle and well-being will have a positive contribution.

One important initiative on access to data in the interest of the patient is the Digital Decade program [8] within Europe. As part of the digitalization of public services [9], the European Commission has set the target of 100% of EU citizens to have access to their medical records online. A first baseline assessment explores several dimensions of this target, such as the accessibility of electronic patient summaries, ePrescriptions, and electronic results and reports. For the moment, on average within EU Member States, this level of accessibility stands at 72%, measured against 12 subindicators that aim to reflect the implementation level of citizens' access to electronic health records, the categories of accessible health data, and the mechanisms and channels to securely connect and grant access [10].

The value of data

While data may seem to be everywhere in the health sector, much of that data has been locked up in siloes with no easy way to share it or reuse it. A lot can be learned, however, from linking or combining different datasets or building longitudinal datasets. At the same time, the pooling of data may help, for instance, to mitigate data bias or improve the representation of minority groups and vulnerable people.

Faced with technical, organizational, or even legal barriers, it is challenging to build the necessary environment or incentives to stimulate data reuse and sharing. In many cases, additional steps will be needed by the holder to prepare or manipulate the data in such a way that it can directly contribute to the envisioned purpose of the data user. Such steps may include actions to determine and warrant the accuracy, specificity, quality, and interoperability of the data. In the context of the to-be-established European Health Data Space [11], the current proposals foresee the development of a data quality and utility label.

Referring to the DIKW model, information and knowledge can only be extracted if we add meaning and context to the data. Therefore, in itself data points, or to a certain extent, datasets, will only hold little or no value. Consequently, the valorization of data can only be appropriately considered when looking at the overall contribution of the dataset to the purpose and realized outcomes. This raises the question of whether you can or should put a price on data. Within our data economy, several business models exist that monetize the use and sharing of data. In the context of health, this is, however, a much more sensitive issue, as many consider their health data as deeply personal, representing their identity and vulnerability.

Monetization versus data as a public common good

In response to the commercial interests of the pharmaceutical, medtech, or technology industry, some believe patients should be able to monetize their health data to regain some level of control and possibly get a cut on the industry's revenues. In such case, one question that presents itself is: "what amount of money would be considered meaningful to the patient while also being realistic in terms of the actual contribution the data presents to the overall outcome," in particular, when the latter is unknown at the time of data acquisition.

Monetization may not always be in the best interest of the patient. From an ethical perspective, it may create a divide between those that can afford to share or not share, and those that cannot afford such a decision. Some may decide to share their data against their own interests, for instance, out of financial need or attracted by short-term gains. Furthermore, under- or overrepresentation of particular population groups may negatively impact people on a larger scale.

At the same time, a monetization approach may perpetuate or aggravate existing imbalances or concentration of information, with less favorable access to health data for, for instance, smaller companies, nongovernmental organizations, and academia.

Considering the impact on society and the general population, various stakeholders are of the opinion that sharing of health data should be considered as a public common good. One example is the belief that data that have been produced by the public sector, or by extension partially or fully funded with public means, should be made freely available. Within Europe, the Open Data Directive [12] is a regulatory framework that defines the conditions for use of public sector information, including the prohibition to grant exclusive rights to a third party. Data should be made available free of charge, except for where applicable some marginal costs to prepare, anonymize, or protect certain data. The Open Data Directive will also cover some specific high-value datasets in the area of health, such as figures on mortality, fertility, and hospital admissions.

Another initiative to support the voluntary sharing of data is the Data Governance Act [13] in Europe. While there have been data trusts and other types of data cooperatives before, in order to build trust, the Data Governance Act will give legal backing to data intermediary services and data altruism organizations (see Box 20.3), clearly defining how they should handle data in a transparent way.

Box 20.3 EU Data Governance Act, Article 2. Definitions, data altruism

"... the voluntary sharing of data on the basis of the consent of data subjects to process personal data pertaining to them, or permission of data holders to allow the use of their non-personal data without seeking or receiving a reward that goes beyond compensation related to the costs that they incur where they make their data available for objectives of general interest as provided for in national law, where applicable, such as healthcare, combating climate change, improving mobility, facilitating the development, production and dissemination of official statistics, improving the provision of public services, public policy making or scientific research purposes in the general interest."

Even more ambitious, Europe is currently working on the legal and operational establishment [14] of a European Health Data Space with the aim of unlocking massive amounts of data in a secure way, in line with European values, in order to facilitate secondary use of data to support better health outcomes.

At the same time, within the public and private sector, we see new initiatives emerging, developing personal information management systems, digital wallets or data vaults, whether or not decentralized, which give citizens more control [15] to manage and share their personal data with authorities, caregivers, family, or third parties.

Aspects of trust

Due to the personal and often sensitive nature of health data, trust is crucial in promoting the use and reuse of health data. Trust is difficult to gain, but is also easily lost. Clearly, technical and organizational measures are necessary to ensure an adequate level of data protection and security.

Data minimization and purpose limitation are some key principles to which we must adhere. There is more ambiguity on the legal basis of processing health data. Whereas informed consent is a well-established concept, consent may not always be necessary or favorable from a data protection perspective, in particular when it comes to the secondary use of data.

Notwithstanding the fact that in some cases, there is no need to inform a person on the further processing of his or her personal data, such as in the case of anonymization, it is always better to clearly and transparently communicate how personal data are being used and shared.

A broad survey [16], in support of the European Health Data Space initiative, found that citizens support the secondary use of health data when it matches their ethical values. Citizens considered health data as a part of themselves, whether anonymized or not. If their data were being used for purposes not supported by them, they felt being made complicit and exploited.

Healthcare has also proven vulnerable to cyberattacks [17] due to several factors, such as the underresourcing and -financing of cyber resilience measures, the societal and critical impact of the sector (especially in times of a pandemic crisis), and the sensitive nature of data making it both attractive for extortion and identity fraud. "Security by design" is therefore paramount in order to convince people that they can reliably and securely access and share their most personal data through digital and remote health technologies.

Although data protection and security measures are essential, the COVID-19 crisis has demonstrated that more is needed to get people on board. Even in the case of COVID-19 apps that used anonymized data, that were strongly vetted from a security perspective, and that were the subject of broad media campaigns and public debate, there was still reluctance among different populations to install and use the application [18]. This goes to show that other aspects of trust matter as well.

Many studies have indicated, for instance, that people demonstrate varying levels of trust toward different stakeholders, with general practitioners and other clinicians overall being considered the most trustworthy, while people may be putting less confidence in industry or even government organizations.

Trust is not a one-off action. Trust needs to be built on the basis of mutual respect through open and transparent communication with the opportunity to meaningfully provide and consider feedback, envisioning a long-term partnership between different actors. Only within such an environment will the use, reuse, and sharing of health data flourish and take us from the Data stage, through the Information and Knowledge stage, to the Wisdom stage.

Conclusion

In sum, we postulate that the health sector is a dynamic landscape of changing factors and data points, each featuring a different actor with a likely different motivation and/or goal. Each one of them holds a piece of the puzzle to uncover new insights that will lead to better health outcomes. The question of ownership is therefore less relevant than the willingness to share and make data accessible. While the idea of health data as a public common good is gaining traction, it will be important to further consider and strengthen strategies targeting the underlying aspects of trust, and in particular how they can help to ensure inclusivity, both in terms of the health data that is being shared and in terms of the population groups that stand to benefit from newly gained insights thereof.

References

[1] RBC Capital Markets. The heallthcare data explosion; 2020. Available at: https://www.rbccm.com/en/gib/healthcare/episode/the_healthcare_data_explosion (Accessed 25 September 2023).
[2] The Business Research Company. Healthcare Data Storage Global Market Report 2023; 2023. Available at: http://The Business Research Company, https://www.reportlinker.com/p06284262/Healthcare-Data-Storage-Global-Market-Report.html (Accessed 25 September 2023).
[3] World Health Organization. Determinants of health; 2017. Available at: https://www.who.int/news-room/questions-and-answers/item/determinants-of-health (Accessed 25 September 2023).
[4] World Health Organization. Social determinants of health; no date. Available at: https://www.who.int/health-topics/social-determinants-of-health#tab=tab_1 (Accessed 25 September 2023).
[5] European Commission Study on eHealth, interoperability of health data and artificial intelligence for health and care in the European Union : final study report. Lot 1, Interoperability of Health Records in

the EU; 2021. Available at: https://ec.europa.eu/newsroom/dae/redirection/document/79897 (Accessed 25 September 2023).

[6] Regulation (EU) 2016/679 of the European Parliament and of the Council of 27 April 2016 on the protection of natural persons with regard to the processing of personal data and on the free movement of such data, and repealing Directive 95/46/EC (General Data Protection Regulation); 2016. Available at: https://eur-lex.europa.eu/legal-content/EN/ALL/?uri=CELEX:32016R0679 (Accessed 25 September 2023).

[7] European Commission Assessment of the EU Member States' rules on health data in the light of GDPR; 2021. Available at: https://health.ec.europa.eu/system/files/2021-02/ms_rules_health-data_en_0.pdf (Accessed 25 September 2023).

[8] European Commission. Europe's Digital Decade: digital targets for 2030; 2023. Available at: https://commission.europa.eu/strategy-and-policy/priorities-2019-2024/europe-fit-digital-age/europes-digital-decade-digital-targets-2030_en (Accessed 25 September 2023).

[9] Commission Implementing Decision 2019/1765 of 22 October 2019 providing the rules for the establishment, the management and the functioning of the network of national authorities responsible for eHealth, and repealing Implementing Decision 2011/890/EU; 2019. Available at: https://eur-lex.europa.eu/legal-content/EN/ALL/?uri=CELEX:32019D1765 (Accessed 25 September 2023).

[10] European Commission. Digital decade e-Health indicators development : final report, Publications Office of the European Union; 2023. https://data.europa.eu/doi/10.2759/530348. Available at: https://data.europa.eu/doi/10.2759/530348 (Accessed 25 September 2023).

[11] European Commission. European Health Data Space; 2023. Available at: https://health.ec.europa.eu/ehealth-digital-health-and-care/european-health-data-space_en (Accessed 25 September 2023).

[12] Directive (EU) 2019/1024 of the European Parliament and of the Council of 20 June 2019 on open data and the re-use of public sector information (Open Data Directive) (2023). Available at: https://eur-lex.europa.eu/legal-content/EN/TXT/?uri=CELEX:32019L1024 (Accessed 25 September 2023).

[13] Regulation (EU) 2022/868 of the European Parliament and of the Council of 30 May 2022 on European data governance and amending Regulation (EU) 2018/1724 (Data Governance Act); 2022. Available at: https://eur-lex.europa.eu/legal-content/EN/TXT/?uri=CELEX:32022R0868 (Accessed 25 September 2023).

[14] HealthData@EU Pilot – Piloting an infrastructure for the secondary use of health data (2023). Available at: https://ehds2pilot.eu/ (Accessed 25 September 2023).

[15] SOLID project (no date). Available at: https://solidproject.org/ (Accessed 25 September 2023).

[16] Towards a European Health Data Space (TEHDAS) (2023) TEHDAS consultation: Citizens support the secondary use of health data when it matches their ethical values. Available at: https://tehdas.eu/results/tehdas-consultation-citizens-support-the-secondary-use-of-health-data-when-it-matches-their-ethical-values/ (Accessed 25 September, 2023).

[17] EU Agency for Cybersecurity (ENISA), 2023. Health Threat Landscape. Available at: https://www.enisa.europa.eu/publications/health-threat-landscape (Accessed 25 September 2023).

[18] European Commission, Directorate-General for Communications Networks, Content and Technology. Study on lessons learned, best practices and epidemiological impact of the common European approach on digital contact tracing to combat and exit the COVID-19 pandemic; 2022. Available at: https://data.europa.eu/doi/10.2759/146050 (Accessed 6 December 2023).

CHAPTER 21

Ethical issues for AI in medicine

Derek Leben
Tepper School of Business, Carnegie Mellon University, Pittsburgh, PA, United States

Introduction

AI has many exciting prospects for medical use, but along with these prospects come significant ethical risks and challenges. In the opening of their recent book, *The AI Revolution in Medicine: GPT-4 and Beyond* [1], Peter Lee, Carey Goldberg, and Isaac Kohane begin with a hypothetical example:

"Suddenly, the patient was crashing. His heart rate rocketed to over 160 beats per minute, but his blood pressure fell dangerously to 80 over 50 … [the medical staff] plunged syringe after syringe into his IV to inject pressors-pressure-boosting drugs – to add to the saline that would support his blood pressure, but to no avail."

Exasperated and desperate, a medical resident pulls out her phone and describes the situation to GPT-4, which responds:

"The experimental antibiotic [the patient] is on is associated with a drop in white blood cells in 5% of patients in a paper recently published from the Phase II study. His counts have dropped over the last three blood draws in the past 2 days. The article reports that G-CSF infusion was highly effective in reversing the drop in white blood cells. That is a tactic that could be considered."

Quickly, the medical resident "phoned the pharmacy to send a dose of the G-CSF infusion and then double-checked the research," which she asked GPT-4 to summarize for her. Convinced that G-CSF is the best option, she gives him the drug, as suggested by GPT-4.

In their imaginary scenario, the advice of GPT-4 winds up saving the life of the patient. But what if, rather than saving the patient's life, the infusion of G-CSF had worsened the patient's condition? What if GPT-4 had not provided this paper citation but just made the pure recommendation of G-CSF without any other explanation? Or, even worse, what if the paper recently published is entirely fictional, the result of a tendency that AI models have for boldly fabricating realistic-sounding medical information? How many errors like

Digital Health. https://doi.org/10.1016/B978-0-443-23901-4.00021-0

this would we say were unacceptable? And when they do occur, would we hold the resident, the hospital, or OpenAI liable for these errors?

This is an example applying large language models to medical uses, which we can categorize as "generative AI." Yet this is a relatively new development, and the vast majority of medical AI applications are still what we can categorize as "predictive AI" (e.g., 75% of the AI systems approved by the FDA in the past 2 years are image recognition models for radiology). Both are AI, in the sense that they are systems that make human-like decisions based on machine learning procedures over large datasets. However, while predictive AI produces a specific value to some input, such as a risk score or label, generative AI will produce novel strings of text, image, or sounds, based on an instruction or prompt. For our discussion, we will consider ethical issues that arise with the application of both types.

In response to the increasing demand for ethical AI, companies and governments have devoted considerable resources toward developing AI ethics policies. Two recent meta-analyses, one from ETH Zurich's Health Ethics and Policy Lab [2] and another from Harvard's Berkman-Klein Center [3], have surveyed dozens of AI ethics declarations from companies, governments, and nonprofit organizations. According to the Zurich team's paper, the most frequent values across 84 of these documents are:

- Transparency and Explainability (73/84)
- Fairness (68/84)
- Nonmaleficence (60/84)
- Responsibility (60/84)
- Privacy (47/84)
- Beneficence (41/84)
- Autonomy (34/84)

On their own, these values are just a label for what people find important in each step of implementing an automated system. Without defining exactly what is meant by "fairness" or "privacy" and developing a theoretical framework for how these all fit together, there are no real constraints placed on the use of AI. However, these can serve an important practical purpose as methods of segmenting the ethical terrain, and this chapter will be organized roughly in this way, considering ethical challenges around Autonomy, Explainability, Fairness, Harm, and Responsibility.

We will mostly ignore data privacy and security issues, not because they are irrelevant, but because they fall under the domain of "data ethics," rather than specifically "AI ethics." It is still important to remember that all machine learning methods involve training data, and those who design or deploy AI models often ignore the source of this training data. As many companies such as Stability and Midjourney have discovered in their use of artworks to train image generators, the artists whose data are used for building a model have not explicitly consented to that particular usage of their data and often believe that this constitutes a violation of consent. The same problem can and will apply to the use of medical data to train AI models. Even when patients have given a generic or blanket form of consent for their medical data to be used for something like "research purposes," the use in building an AI model may go beyond this original understanding and represent a new usage that requires additional layers of consent. The ethical issue here is not only security (it may be possible to "recover" a person's medical information from an AI model) but also data ownership. Even if a patient's data cannot be recovered from a model, if we think of medical data as property that has been "leased" to organizations and individuals for certain uses, then anything going beyond those original uses is a violation of that contract with patients. This problem becomes even more important when tech companies are making profits from selling these AI models to medical practitioners; the patients who have (unknowingly) provided the training data for these models have a case for demanding some fair share of these profits.

The rest of this chapter will focus on the challenges of meeting minimal standards in the domains of explainability, fairness, safety, and liability. These challenges apply to all parties involved in the design and deployment of medical AI systems: the tech companies designing a system, the hospital or practice purchasing a system, and the practitioners deploying a system. All parties have an ethical obligation of due care to ensure that an AI system meets these standards. For this reason, I will deliberately be using the more neutral word "system" rather than words such as "device" or "tool," each of which implies some greater responsibility on the part of manufacturers or practitioners, respectively (the recent debate about the FDA classification of AI as a "tool" or "device" is motivated by these interests; tech companies want them to be called "tools," while hospitals want them to be called "devices")

Transparency

In the mid-1990s, a group of researchers at the University of Pittsburgh conducted a large trial (78 hospitals) for a neural network trained to predict the mortality risk for patients with community-acquired pneumonia. The AI system was tested on over 4000 patients with pneumonia, and from a perspective of pure accuracy, the results seemed encouraging, with accuracy rates around 98.5% [4,5]. However, when inspecting these models, the researchers found a shocking assumption: pneumonia patients with a history of asthma were assigned *lower*-risk scores than pneumonia patients without a history of asthma! The problem, described by a group of Microsoft researchers, was in the training data:

The relationship between asthma and lower mortality rates reflected a true pattern in the training data: patients with a history of asthma who presented with pneumonia usually were admitted not only to the hospital but directly to the ICU (Intensive Care Unit). The good news is that the aggressive care received by asthmatic pneumonia patients was so effective that it lowered their risk of dying from pneumonia compared with the general population. The bad news is that because the prognosis for these patients is better than average, models trained on the data incorrectly learn that asthma lowers risk, when in fact asthmatics have much higher risk (if not hospitalized) [6].

Thus, the AI system came to "believe" that patients with asthma were at lower risk of mortality, which is exactly wrong. As another AI researcher, Marco Ribeiro, remarked in an interview: "If they'd relied on this system to triage, those people would have just be sent home to die."

This feature of the AI system was only recognized because the team from the University of Pittsburgh compared it with more traditional rule-based triage models. However, the danger of transparency in AI systems is that it is often difficult or impossible to identify this sort of rule in a complex AI model, such as "Has Asthma (x) -> Lower Risk (x)." Indeed, there is no such rule in a neural network. Instead, there are large sets of numerical weights or connections between features, where the weights may reflect a relationship between one feature (asthma) and the target variable (risk), but that relationship is not something that is easy to identify from the network itself unless one is doing hard work to try and discover it. This lack of transparency is what led the Pittsburgh team to recommend against the neural network, despite its higher accuracy levels.

To some extent, the issue of transparency for AI systems is analogous to the old problem of transparency in the doctor–patient relationship. When a human doctor makes a diagnosis or prescription, we expect that they will also provide some information about their reasoning to the patient, attempt to foster an understanding of this reasoning in the patient, and allow the patient an opportunity to ask questions and be provided satisfying answers. For our purposes, let's call the first part of this process "interpretability," the second part "explainability," and the third part "verification." The entire process as a whole will be called "transparency." But the problem for AI models such as Watson and GPT-4 is that they often lack transparency in the sense that it is difficult or impossible to trace the reasoning that led to its conclusions or foster any sort of understanding and verification of this process. Instead, these models are called *black boxes*, meaning that we can only say something like: "they produce highly accurate responses, but we don't understand why."

The lack of transparency is often justified by designers as a necessary loss for the purpose of producing more accurate AI systems. In a now-infamous graph produced by a 2019 DARPA report [7], machine learning methodologies are represented on a graph that plots what we are calling "interpretability" and "accuracy," demonstrating a linear trade-off between the two. Instead of trying to achieve all three components of transparency, many researchers have abandoned interpretability and instead focused on developing methods for providing explainability and verification through other means. These methods are called "xAI (explainable AI) tools" (for reviews, see [8,9]). Some of these xAI tools, such as LIME and SHAP, involve creating a secondary or surrogate model for estimating the influence of inputs on the outputs [10,11]. Others, such as Counterfactual Methods, will create alternative models to estimate the changes in inputs that would lead to a different output [12]. What all of these xAI methods have in common is that they are not "opening the black box" to show you how it works, but instead, trying to foster some sort of understanding of the decision in terms of the features used and their relationships to the output.

Many computer scientists have challenged this supposed trade-off between transparency and accuracy, arguing that we can in principle design very powerful AI systems that are also highly transparent in every sense [13]. Without wading into this technical debate, let's assume that we currently have available a set of AI systems, some of them more powerful and less transparent, and some of them less powerful but more transparent. Obviously, medical professionals have a duty to deploy the most accurate systems possible, but at what point should we rule out some of these powerful systems as failing to provide the right sort of transparency?

This question cannot be answered without addressing the reasons why patients can and should care about transparency in the first place. As [14] describes, we might care about transparency because of its instrumental value (i.e., what sorts of goods it creates), or because of its inherent value (i.e., the intrinsic good of access and understanding). Generally, if you think that transparency is valuable because it is useful in getting other sorts of goods, then you might be more willing to abandon interpretability and settle for an xAI method that provides that sort of good. For instance, certain xAI methods such as LIME and SHAP can provide some information about the most important and relevant features in a decision, while Counterfactual Methods can provide justification for why some features were used and not others. If we think that explainability is valuable for the comfort it provides to patients, then we should be concerned primarily with what sorts of explanations patients find most satisfying. Both [15] and Byrne [16] have argued that counterfactual methods provide the most psychologically satisfying answers. However, if we think that explainability is valuable because it provides some window into the actual mechanisms of a system (interpretability) that those impacted by the system have a right to know, then this may rule out the usage of certain types of complex AI models from any medical applications.

Fairness

In 2019, a study published in Science alleged that there was racial bias in a system developed by Optum for assigning risk scores to patients. Despite the fact that race was not actually used as a feature in the Optum system, Black patients were systematically assigned lower-risk scores than equally sick White patients. A few months later, this was reported in the Washington Post with the headline: *Racial Bias in a Medical Algorithm Favors White Patients Over Sicker Black Patients.* It turns out that this disparity was caused by measurement choices: the Optum system used healthcare costs as a way of measuring medical needs. Generally, this assumption makes sense: people who spend more on healthcare tend to have greater medical needs. However, because White patients have greater wealth and access to care than Black patients, they will spend disproportionately more on healthcare.

The first thing to note in discussions of AI fairness is that even a system that is "blind" to protected features such as gender and race can still produce systematically unequal outcomes for groups, especially when the training data for a system contain inequalities between these groups. A focus on merely "pure procedural justice" might sometimes accept these inequalities as "unfortunate, but not unfair," as the Libertarian philosopher Robert Nozick once remarked. From this perspective, it's true that there are inequalities in the training data that are the result of historical injustices, but those historical injustices are not the fault of current practitioners, and they have no positive obligations to correct those injustices. This is also the approach that the current Supreme Court has been taking to discrimination cases in the past 10 years. However, US discrimination law has historically acknowledged both an obligation to avoid "disparate treatment" in a pure procedural sense and also an obligation to avoid "disparate impact." The latter is a positive obligation to provide equal outcomes to equally qualified members of different groups and necessarily involves taking measures to correct for historical injustices in the data that one uses. From this perspective, merely claiming that an AI system is "blind" to protected features, i.e., that inequalities produced by the system are unintended, is not enough.

Even if we are convinced that parties have obligations to avoid both disparate treatment and disparate impact, there are many different ways to measure fair impacts [17]. The headlines about the Optum case were careful to note that the unequal outcomes produced by the system were for *error rates* between groups, rather than rates of correct predictions. There are several different statistical metrics for equality between groups, and one of the key findings from the field of Algorithmic Fairness has been that it is typically impossible to satisfy all of these metrics simultaneously. For example, in the well-known debate about the COMPAS algorithm used to assign risk scores to prisoners eligible for parole, journalists at ProPublica alleged that the system is biased because it has higher error rates for Black prisoners compared with White prisoners. However, the company that designs the system, Northpointe (now Equivant), defended their system by noting that there are equal rates of correct predictions for qualified White and Black prisoners in testing data. It is entirely possible that Optum could have made the same sort of claim if their system correctly assigned high-risk scores to White and Black patients who did need care at equal rates. This shows that it's not enough to demand that the outcomes of a model are "equal" between groups since it is generally impossible, but rather, that they must specify "equal with respect to what?" Each party that designs and deploys AI systems must consider which outcomes are those for which it is important to seek equality [18,19].

Researchers have developed several mitigation methods for the purpose of enforcing some metric of equality between groups in an AI system. For example, one can make use of Microsoft's "Fairlearn" package to constrain the model used by an AI system such that we move closer to equality in some statistical metric. However, just like achieving greater transparency often comes with an accuracy loss, achieving greater equality often comes with an accuracy loss as well. Given that accuracy losses translate into serious harm, we should be extremely concerned about this and ask ourselves what sacrifices in accuracy we are willing to accept. Furthermore, as noted by researchers like [20], those who design AI systems in medicine will often solve the problem of fairness by producing worse outcomes for an advantaged group rather than better outcomes for a disadvantaged group, a solution called "leveling down." Although these outcomes are more fair, they do not actually make anyone better off, and thus, we should be careful to avoid superficial solutions to fairness problems.

Fairness is an issue not only for the process and outputs of an AI model but also for access. Even if an AI model treats all individuals and groups equally, it is still unjust if the model is only available to members of advantaged groups. In February 2023, the CEO of OpenAI, Sam Altman, posted a set of possible uses for GPT-4 on social media, which included: "AI medical advisors for people who can't afford care." In response, the AI ethicist Timnit Gebru responded by characterizing this as an "AI utopia where the poor get chatbots as doctors because they can't access the care the rich get." While automation may seem like a promising way to provide low-cost healthcare, if people prefer human treatment to AI treatment, then it may also provide a lower-quality alternative that acts as an excuse to avoid providing all citizens with equal levels of care.

Safety and liability

No AI system is perfect, and there will always be some rate of error. In medical applications, these errors translate into mistaken diagnoses and prescriptions, which can result in serious harm. As with any medical product, such as pharmaceuticals and medical devices, AI systems must clear a minimal threshold for product safety. However, unlike these other medical products, there are few standards for how to evaluate minimal safety thresholds for AI systems. For instance, what constitutes an acceptable error rate in an AI diagnostic system? In 2023, a medical research group from the Department of Radiology at Bispebjerg-Frederiksberg University Hospital in Copenhagen reported an incident where the hospital began using an AI system for diagnosing knee osteoarthritis, with less than impressive results:

"In our case, a low-risk AI algorithm misclassified the first patient in the knee osteoarthritis diagnostic conclusion for no obvious reasons, and it surprised the implementation group how skeptical they became after the misinterpretation by the AI algorithm" [21].

Following this inconspicuous start, the team surveyed employees in the Department of Radiology about what they believed to be an acceptable error rate for both AI and humans. The average threshold for an acceptable error rate in humans was 11.3%, while the average expectation for AI was 6.8%. The researchers note that the AI system they used for diagnosing knee osteoarthritis had a 13% error rate in external studies [22].

One interesting thing to note about AI errors is that they can often be "crazy," meaning that they are not the sorts of errors that a human would make. For example, when Watson was being tested by oncologists at Sloan Kettering Memorial, they reported that the system recommended that a patient with severe bleeding be given a drug that would worsen the bleeding. This may be compared with when an earlier version of Watson played the "Jeopardy! Challenge" against the two human champions and defeated both of them, but lost the final question when it answered "Toronto" for a question under the category of "U.S. Cities." We might forgive understandable errors, but these sorts of crazy errors might be something unacceptable, even if the frequency of errors overall is lower than humans.

Even with a benchmark for frequency and type of errors, we might worry about the validity of measurement for these errors in an AI system. In a 2020 paper from Nature Medicine, Eric Topol notes that most of the evidences presented for the efficacy of medical AI systems are retrospective rather than prospective studies:

There are currently hundreds of published retrospective reports that fall under the rubric of "clinical trials" of AI, but they are not really trials at all. While essential for laying the groundwork, these are in silico assessments of datasets to determine how well a deep neural network performs a clinical task, compared with a small number of physicians. Such AI reports do not simulate clinical practice but instead work from a cleaned, relatively pristine, annotated dataset. The real world of medicine, in contrast, is messy, with plenty of missing data, lots of it unstructured, and its focus is caring for patients rather than developing an analytical substrate. The stark contrast between a clinical environment and an in silico one cannot be overemphasized, and hence, clinical trials of AI are needed.

Beyond just developing benchmarks for safety, there must be consensus on the methods for validating these benchmarks. This is analogous to some of the challenges in validating safety for other AI systems, such as autonomous vehicles, where companies such as Waymo have argued for the use of "simulated" miles driven as a substitute for real miles driven on the road. IBM argued for something similar in evaluating the diagnoses of Watson, insisting that "synthetic" data could be used in the validation process along with real patient data.

Assuming that consensus is reached about safety benchmarks and a validation process, the question of liability for errors still remains. When the system inevitably results in harm, who is to blame, both ethically and legally? Several legal scholars have begun to weigh in on this question, mostly focusing on the issue of liability in predictive AI systems [23]. Sullivan [24] describes the ways in which current tort liability laws and case histories can be applied to predictive AI systems. Like medical devices, AI systems in medicine involve both product liability and medical liability. Beyond just the minimal due care that we expect companies to devote to testing the safety of their products, the doctrine of strict liability holds that companies such as IBM could still be liable for the errors of a well-validated AI system. Of course, IBM will note that their system is sold to medical practitioners who also bear some responsibility for usage, which is the doctrine of "learned intermediaries." This is the point at which standards of medical malpractice may also become more relevant than standards for product safety. If a practitioner is not properly using an AI system as directed, perhaps relying too much on its results and not properly checking them, then that practitioner may be liable under medical malpractice standards. Similarly, if a hospital is not properly training its medical staff in the appropriate usage of an AI system, they may be held liable under "vicarious negligence (respondeat superior)" standards.

One of the most important dangers of AI systems is that their human-like performance or interface can lull practitioners into greater levels of trust than a standard diagnostic tool. This goes beyond just standard "automation bias," and into a sort of anthropomorphic bias, where practitioners may be less likely to challenge the recommendations of a system that appears human-like. This is especially dangerous for generative AI systems such as GPT-4, which can express their opinions with the appearance of confidence and sophistication. In the imaginary scenario of Lee et al. [1], where a medical resident seeks advice from GPT-4, the system recommends an infusion of G-CSF, and this turns out to be good advice, saving the patient's life. However, if it turns out that this was the wrong recommendation, would we hold the resident or OpenAI responsible? This is still unclear within the law. Furthermore, they describe how the medical resident "double-checks" the research, but also uses GPT-4 to summarize the articles. We've seen many cases where GPT-4 will "double-down" on fabrication by continuing to fabricate information and relying on AI to check the results of AI is verging on reckless practices.

Another liability risk for medical AI is in direct-to-consumer approaches, which bypass the expertise of a medical professional. Sam Altman's statements encouraging people without access to healthcare to use GPT-4 to diagnose their medical symptoms opens the door to this risk. Many people already turn to search engines such as Google and social media platforms such as Facebook for answers to their medical questions, but the companies that make these products (Alphabet and Meta) can always claim that they are merely allowing people to discover content generated by others and cannot be held responsible for the effects of that content (this was upheld in the recent 2023 Supreme Court decision about Section 230). However, GPT-4 is not allowing people to find content generated by others, but generating its own content, and can plausibly be held responsible for the effects of that content. OpenAI might insist that users bear some responsibility for appropriate usage, but expectations about responsible use are very different when users are laypersons compared with medical professionals. Clearly, there are some domains where OpenAI has drawn the line and placed constraints around usage, such as information about how to make bombs. If companies allow people to make use of AI systems for self-diagnosis and treatment, they must make the case that laypeople have the capacity for responsible use at a large scale or place constraints around the use of AI systems for that purpose.

Conclusion

The ethical issues for medical AI are not new. Instead, they are applying the traditional ethical issues in medicine to a new domain. Medical practitioners constantly make judgments about how to respect the autonomy and privacy of patients, how to be transparent in their decision-making, how to treat patients fairly, and how to avoid unreasonable risks and take responsibility for errors. However, automation tends to magnify and accelerate preexisting issues. Medical AI may intensify the lack of understanding that patients have about how they are treated, the inequalities in healthcare created by historical injustices, and the difficulties of attributing responsibility to distributed actions. On the other hand, these ethical challenges also may force us to be precise in areas where standards were previously vague. If any party is implementing AI for medical purposes, they must present to patients and the public a clear policy about how they will be addressing these challenges.

References

[1] Kohane I, Lee P, Goldberg C. The AI revolution in medicine: GPT-4 and beyond. Pearson Press; 2023.

[2] Jobin A, Ienca M, Vayena E. The global landscape of AI ethics guidelines. Nature Machine Intelligence 2019;1:389−99.

[3] Fjeld J, Achten N, Hilligoss H, Nagy A, Srikumar M. Principled artificial intelligence. Berkman Klein Center Publications; 2020.

[4] Cooper G, Aliferis RA, Aronis J, Buchanan B, Caruana R, Fine M, Glymour C, Gordon G, Hanusa B, Janosky J, Meek C, Mitchell T, Richardson T, Spirtes P. An evaluation of machine-learning methods for predicting pneumonia mortality. Artificial Intelligence in Medicine 1997;9(2):107−38.
[5] Cooper G, Abraham CA, Aronis J, Buchanan B, Caruana R, Fine M, Janosky J, Livingston G, Mitchell T, Montik S, Spirtes P. Predicting dire outcomes of patients with community acquired pneumonia. Journal of Biomedical Informatics 2005;38(5):347−66.
[6] Caruana R, Lou Y, Gehrke J, Koch P, Sturm M, Elhadad N. Intelligible models for HealthCare: predicting pneumonia risk and hospital 30-day readmission. In: KDD, vol 15. ACM Publications; 2015.
[7] Gunning D, Aha D. DARPA's explainable artificial intelligence (XAI) program. AI Magazine 2019;40(2):44−58.
[8] Arrieta A, Díaz-Rodríguez N, Del Ser J, Bennetot A, Tabik S, Barbado A, Garcia S, Gil-Lopez S, Molina D, Benjamins R, Chatila R, Herrera F. Explainable Artificial Intelligence (XAI): concepts, taxonomies, opportunities and challenges toward responsible AI. Information Fusion 2020;58:82−115.
[9] Guidotti R, Monreale R, Ruggieri S, Turini F, Giannotti F, Pedreschi D. A survey of methods for explaining black box models. Association for Computing Machinery 2019;21(5).
[10] Lundberg S, Lee S. A unified approach to interpreting model predictions. Advances in Neural Information Processing Systems 2017;(30):4765−72.
[11] Ribeiro M, Singh S, Guestrin C. Why should I trust you? Explaining the predictions of any classifier. Proceedings of the 22nd ACM SIGKDD International Conference on Knowledge Discoveryand Data Mining 2016;1:1135−44.
[12] Wachter S, Mittlestadt B, Russell C. Counterfactual explanations without opening the black box: automated decisions and the GDPR. Harvard Journal of Law and Technology 2018;31:1−47.
[13] Rudin C. Stop explaining black box machine learning models for high stakes decisions and use interpretable models instead. Nature Machine Intelligence 2019;(1):206−15.
[14] Colaner N. Is explainable AI intrinsically valuable? AI & Society 2022;(37):231−8.
[15] Miller T. Explanation in artificial intelligence: insights from the social sciences. Artificial Intelligence 2019;267:1−38.
[16] Byrne R. Counterfactuals in explainable artificial intelligence (XAI): evidence from human reasoning. Proceedings of the 28th international joint conference on artificial intelligence 2019:6276−82.
[17] Barocas S, Hardt M, Narayanan A. Fairness in machine learning. 2023. https://fairmlbook.org/.
[18] Binns R. Fairness in ML: lessons from political philosophy. Journal of Machine Learning Research 2019;(81):1−11.
[19] Morse L, Teodorescu M, Awwad Y, Kane G. Do the ends justify the means? Variation in the distributive and procedural fairness of machine learning algorithms. Journal of Business Ethics 2021;181.
[20] Mittelstadt B, Wachter S, Russell C. The unfairness of fair machine learning: levelling down and strict egalitarianism by default. Michigan Technology Law Review; 2023.
[21] Lenskjold A, Nybing JU, Trampedach C, Galsgaard A, Brejnebøl MW, Raaschou H, Rose MH, Boesen M. Should artificial intelligence have lower acceptable error rates than humans? BJR Open 2023;5(1).
[22] Brejnebøl MW, Hansen P, Nybing JU, Bachmann R, Ratjen U, Hansen IV, et al. External validation of an artificial intelligence tool for radiographic knee osteoarthritis severity classification. European Journal of Radiology 2022;(150).
[23] Vladeck D. Machines without Principles: liability rules and AI. Washington Law Review 2019;(89):117−50.
[24] Sullivan H, Schweikart S. Are current tort liability doctrines adequate for addressing injury caused by AI? AMA Journal of Ethics 2019;(21):160−6.

CHAPTER 22

Health policy

Christine Rodgers, Nathan Miracle, Kathryn Reed, and Amy Brown
Department of Physician Assistant Studies, University of Pittsburgh, Pittsburgh, PA, United States

Introduction

This chapter explores the recent history and multifaceted dimensions of digital health policy, shedding light on its impact on diverse concerned parties. The narrative begins by elucidating the global context, emphasizing the World Health Organization's call for standardized eHealth strategies, and subsequently delves into the United States' struggle to form a cohesive digital health policy framework.

This chapter will also review the 2030 Agenda for Sustainable Development established by the World Summit on Information Society, organized by UNESCO, advocating for the strategic use of digital technology to achieve universal health coverage and improved well-being. A critical analysis of the World Health Organization's global strategy on digital health 2020–25 follows, emphasizing the importance of treating digital technologies as public goods to ensure equity, privacy, and ethical use.

The discussion then turns to ethical considerations in health policy, underlining the need for robust governance structures and enhanced digital health capacity. This chapter will scrutinize the evolution of digital health policies within the Centers for Medicare & Medicaid Services (CMS), tracing significant milestones from the American Recovery and Reinvestment Act (ARRA) to the recent shifts catalyzed by the COVID-19 pandemic.

The impact of digital health policies on Federally Qualified Health Centers (FQHC) and Rural Health Clinics (RHC) is meticulously examined, highlighting their role in bridging healthcare gaps and the challenges posed by policy reversals post-COVID-19.

Private payer perspectives on digital health are explored, focusing on the transformation of reimbursement policies and the integration of digital tools in chronic disease management. This chapter concludes with a forward-looking perspective, identifying barriers to digital health implementation and advocating for increased regulation to harness the full potential of this transformative force in healthcare.

Digital Health. https://doi.org/10.1016/B978-0-443-23901-4.00022-2

Recent history of digital health policy

Digital health is a broad term that encompasses using computing platforms, connectivity, software, and sensors for healthcare and related uses. The scope of digital health includes several categories such as mobile health (mHealth), health information technology (HIT), wearable devices, telehealth and telemedicine, and personalized medicine. These technologies span a wide range of uses and can include technologies intended for use as a medical product, in a medical product, as companion diagnostics, or as an adjunct to other medical products (devices, drugs, and biologics). They may also be used to develop or study medical products. From mobile medical applications and software that support the clinical decisions providers make every day to artificial intelligence and machine learning, digital technology has been driving a revolution in healthcare. Digital health tools have the vast potential to improve our ability to accurately diagnose and treat disease and to enhance the delivery of healthcare for the individual [1].

Digital health policy recent history overview

Despite the adoption of resolution WHA66.24 by the World Health Organization (WHO) Health Assembly in 2013 aiming to standardize the global eHealth strategy and recommending Member States to develop policies and legislative mechanisms linked to a national eHealth strategy, this goal remains unfulfilled in the United States of America (USA) [2]. In the USA, policymakers and concerned users have struggled to reach a consensus on enacting health policy in the digital realm, resulting in minimal and inconsistent recommendations for invested parties.

The 2030 Agenda for Sustainable Development, established during the World Summit on Information Society in 2015, acknowledges that the dissemination of information and communication technologies can expedite human progress by fostering interconnectedness. Following this meeting, the global health community increasingly agrees that the strategic and innovative utilization of digital technology, coupled with advanced information and communication technologies, will play a vital role in ensuring that a larger population benefits from universal health coverage, improved protection against health emergencies, and enhanced overall well-being [2].

The global strategy on digital health 2020–25 encompasses four guiding principles designed to establish global standards within national health sectors and strategies, promoting the appropriate and sustainable adoption of digital health technologies. While all principles are important, this chapter focuses on promoting the appropriate use of digital health technologies. The global strategy advocates for digital technologies to be treated as public goods, adaptable to different countries and contexts to promote equity and address crucial challenges within healthcare systems. By promoting digital technology as public goods, it also safeguards individuals, populations, healthcare professionals, and systems against misinformation, information misuse, malicious cyber activities, fraud, exploitation, inappropriate use of health data, racism, and human rights violations. As digital health gains prominence, digital determinants of health become increasingly vital. Therefore, global strategies should prioritize establishing digital foundations within national strategies, collaborating with various sectors and system users at all levels. The appropriate use of digital health should encompass health promotion, disease prevention, patient safety, ethics, interoperability, intellectual property, data security, privacy, cost-effectiveness, patient engagement, and affordability [2].

Ethical considerations in health policy

Strengthening the governance of digital health at global, regional, and national levels is an essential construct that needs to occur. This is one of four strategic objectives intended to provide guidance and coordination on global digital health transformation per the World Health Organization (WHO). This objective could be achieved through the establishment of sustainable and robust governance structures and the enhancement of digital health capacity. The governance framework should aim to empower countries in promoting, innovating, and scaling up digital health technologies. Furthermore, this objective emphasizes the importance of standards encompassing safety, security, privacy, interoperability, and ethical data usage within and beyond the healthcare sector. The proposed policy options and actions encompass leveraging existing structures, creating sustainable governance frameworks, coordinating investments, promoting digital health competencies, and facilitating informed decision-making. Anticipated outcomes include establishing governance frameworks, global interoperability standards, guidance for digital healthcare facilities and interventions, and recommendations for the pseudonymization and anonymization of health data.

CMS policy in the digital age—National picture

The Centers for Medicare & Medicaid Services (CMS) were established by President Lyndon B. Johnson on July 30, 1965. Under the collective efforts of Medicare, Medicaid, the Children's Health Insurance Program (CHIP), and Health Insurance Marketplace, health coverage is provided to more than 100 million people in the USA [3]. There are specific groups of individuals covered by these services, including Medicare's coverage of individuals who are aged 65 or older, those with End-Stage Renal Disease (ESRD), and certain younger individuals with disabilities. Medicaid and CHIP provide coverage based on income and family size for individuals and families that qualify. Medicaid and CHIP qualifications and benefits differ state-to-state but must adhere to certain federal guidelines. The Health Insurance Marketplace allows individuals, families, and small businesses to compare coverage and the cost of health insurance plans.

Although the CMS have undergone several federal alterations since their inception, the formal convergence of digital health and the CMS did not occur officially until 2009. On February 17, 2009, President Barack Obama signed the American Recovery and Reinvestment Act (ARRA) into law. The ARRA effectively formalized the nation's acknowledgment that health information technology (HIT) is a component of national health policy while establishing federal government oversight. Importantly, the ARRA's provisions on HIT included incentive payments for "eligible professionals (EPs), eligible hospitals, and critical access hospitals (CAHs) participating in Medicare and Medicaid programs that adopt and successfully demonstrate meaningful use of certified electronic health record (EHR) technology" [4]. These ARRA HIT provisions and their subsequent amendments are considered part of the "Health Information Technology for Economic and Clinical Health Act" or the "HITECH Act" [4].

In subsequent years, the HITECH Act spurred the development of additional CMS programs. In 2011, the CMS established additional incentive programs to encourage the use of certified electronic health record technology (CEHRT). Initially called the Medicare and Medicaid Electronic Health Record Incentive Programs, the name was changed in April 2018 to the Medicare and Medicaid Promoting Interoperability Programs to emphasize a commitment to interoperability and the exchange of healthcare data. This program ended in 2022 [5]. The CMS also introduced an eHealth Initiative in 2013 to improve coordination and communication efficacy for providers related to the regulatory burden of information technology, especially the adoption and use of ICD-10 codes [6]. In 2020, CMS created a new Part D e-prescribing electronic prior authorization standard allowing providers to see that a prior authorization is required as they are prescribing the medication, thereby decreasing provider burden and delays in patient prescribing [7].

However, the most recent and significant alteration to the CMS and digital health policies occurred in response to the COVID-19 pandemic. Throughout the COVID-19 pandemic, the Trump Administration expanded telehealth benefits for Medicare recipients, allowing providers to complete and be paid for "virtual check-ins" to decrease the likelihood of COVID-19 exposure. On March 6, 2020, the Trump Administration additionally expanded Medicare's telehealth coverage, temporarily, by paying providers to evaluate and treat Medicare patients across the country via telehealth while giving providers the ability to reduce or waive any cost-sharing for those telehealth visits. Prior to this, Medicare would only pay clinicians for specified telehealth visits under certain conditions (i.e., rural patients traveling to a local medical facility to receive telehealth services from a remote provider). This expansion allowed a range of healthcare providers (clinical psychologists, licensed clinical social workers, nurse practitioners, etc.) to provide care for Medicare patients via telehealth with visits that could be completed from the patient's home or a clinic or hospital [8]. Of note, Medicaid has more flexible telehealth reimbursement options, even pre-COVID-19, which were able to be altered at the state level.

After COVID-19's designation as a public health emergency ended, the CMS telehealth policy shifted again with some Medicare changes being incorporated as permanent and some changes remaining temporary with new specified end dates. Permanent Medicare changes include the provision of telehealth services for behavioral/mental healthcare in the home and the optional provision of those services through audio-only communication platforms. On December 31, 2024, several temporary Medicare changes will end including Medicare patients receiving non-behavioral/mental healthcare in the home and telehealth services being provided by all eligible Medicare providers to patients across the USA.

Digital health policy impacts—FQHC, RHC

Federally Qualified Health Centers (FQHC) were initially established by President Lyndon B. Johnson in 1965 as part of his purported "War on Poverty." These medical centers were created to combat a growing need, found across the nation, of an increasing portion of the populace that was unable to afford the medical care that they required. FQHCs were envisioned to bridge the gap of access to medical care regardless of the patient's ability to pay for services. This, coupled with an open-door policy, resulted in a newfound avenue for patients to receive medical care, especially in rural and underserved areas. The high percentage of individuals who lacked medical insurance or who wholly relied on Medicaid services for care in certain geographic areas created a healthcare void that was filled by the health centers. As defined by Healthcare.gov [9], FQHCs are "Federally funded nonprofit health centers or clinics that serve medically underserved areas and populations. Federally qualified health centers provide primary care services regardless of your ability to pay. Services are provided on a sliding scale fee based on your ability to pay."

These health centers are in a unique position to provide care to some of the most vulnerable patients with the least access to care in the country. Considering this, FQHCs have specific guidelines from both the CMS and the individual state Medicaid systems that govern their delivery and the reimbursement of digital health services. As previously mentioned, FQHCs most commonly function in locations where access to healthcare services is absent or severely limited, so policies enabling the use of telehealth visits and other digital health such as remote patient monitoring can further increase the positive impact of increase access to care in the locations. This impact was made even more evident during the global COVID-19 pandemic in 2020 and the Public Health Emergency (PHE) declaration that accompanied it. Early in the pandemic's timeline, reimbursable services at FQHCs were expanded to allow continued access to much-needed chronic disease management for patients and to maintain a revenue stream for healthcare centers.

However, since the resolution of the PHE surrounding the COVID-19 pandemic, there has been a slow rollback of the policies that enabled FQHCs to provide care via various digital health pathways.

Currently, there are several different providers that are approved by the Federal government to provide care in FQHCs and Rural Health Clinics (RHCs), which reflects the significant role that advanced practitioners play in providing care in these underserved areas. Physicians, Physician Assistants, Nurse Practitioners, and Certified Midwives can all provide care via digital means through these specialized healthcare facilities. Mental health visits can also be facilitated via digital modalities with the practitioners listed above in addition to Clinical Psychologists and Clinical Social Workers [10]. The modalities approved for rendering care via digital visits include both live video and audio, as well as audio-only visits. These visits may be reimbursed at a slightly different pay rate than traditional in-person visits, however, the substantial benefits to patients, especially in sites where access to medical care is already severely limited, may outweigh any financial pitfall for these institutions. Remote patient monitoring services are not separately billable by FQHCs and RHCs since these institutions and providers are already reimbursed for these services via a separate built-in pay scale.

As previously mentioned, the COVID-19 pandemic and the subsequent PHE rapidly accelerated the use of digital communication to facilitate patient care. Specifically, within FQHCs and RHCs these policy changes allowed for new patient visits with previously unestablished patients to take place via digital means. Before this COVID-19-related policy change, only patients seen in the healthcare facility during the past year were eligible for visits to be completed through digital means. However, with the end of the PHE declaration on May 11, 2023, the expansion of digital health services has been reverted to a pre-COVID-19 policy state.

FQHCs and RHCs play an increasingly vital role in the current medical landscape. As healthcare resources continue to conglomerate around metropolitan areas, increasing access to care for patients who choose to live in a more rural setting is vitally important to ensure that the medical needs of the entire populace are met. Increased allowance for and reimbursement of medical visits provided through digital means could greatly impact the health of patients who seek care at FQHCs and RHCs.

Digital health policy impacts: Private payers

When discussing the impact digital health has had on private payers, one recurring theme heavily discussed is reimbursement for services. More specifically, digital health has greatly impacted the expansion and subsequent reimbursement of telehealth services. Historically, private payers have traditionally provided minimal, if any, reimbursement for telemedicine services. As we have recently seen, the COVID-19 pandemic drastically changed the reimbursement policies of private payers. This relatively quick shift to the utilization of telemedicine services demonstrated that we had competent providers and sufficient technology, but that a shift in policy was needed to ensure the appropriate resources were provided. Existing policy requires private payers to provide some portion of reimbursement for telehealth services and often have parity requirements associated with them. One example is "service parity" which requires that the same standard of care be met as when delivering services in-person. However, this type of parity does not guarantee the same rate of payment [11]. The other type of parity, which is less common among states, is "payment parity." This is a requirement for the same payment rate or amount to be reimbursed via telehealth as it would be if it had been delivered in-person [11]. There are also often requirements for utilization reviews and for cost sharing to be the same as they would have been if the service had not been provided via telehealth.

An additional way that private payers have utilized digital health is to achieve their primary goal of keeping member costs down without impacting the quality of care. As discussed in "US Healthcare spending by payer and health condition," we see that the chronic disease of diabetes mellitus is one of the biggest cost burdens for private payers [12]. As a result of this, many health plans have developed diabetes management initiatives, but have integrated the use of digital health to improve member outcomes. Examples of these new innovations include dedicated health coaches, improvement in care coordination, member data collection, and utilization to personalize initiatives and innovative technologies such as real-time glucose monitoring and intervention. These innovations have helped health plans deliver consistent and improved outcomes by reducing members diabetes-associated costs and improving health markers (i.e., reducing BMI and A1C levels) [12].

Digital health literacy considerations

Digital health literacy is another important component to take into account when discussing the implementation of digital health policies. When viewed from the perspective of patients functioning in a digital healthcare realm, health literacy needs to address other important aspects of healthcare delivery. For technology to make a meaningful impact, it must surpass basic literacy and numeracy enhancement. It should encompass functional and critical skills like navigating healthcare systems, facilitating communication with healthcare providers, and fostering shared decision-making [13].

There are currently various technologies that can improve digital health literacy including artificial intelligence, remote monitoring devices, wearable devices, and improved communications with voice-optimizing devices; however, all of these devices require their own individual levels of technological savvy for patients to be able to fully utilize and actualize the benefits of this technology in their healthcare decision making [13].

Although the above discussions denote the challenges associated with expanding digital health use and an ever-increasing reliance on the use of these technologies, several of these factors may actually support the improvement of digital health literacy across populations. As patients access and participate in the use of wearable health technology and health-related apps, familiarity with these types of medical technology and the potential for positive health-related outcomes should be viewed as part of the solution [14].

Finally, given the potential cost to patients to acquire the technological devices to actively participate in video conferencing and telecommunication, even the most robust of policy enhancements, at the federal, state, or private payer level, to improve the access to these services will all be for naught if the economic disparities between patients are not taken into account and remedied [15].

Steps for the future of digital health

While we continue to see the cost of treating chronic conditions steadily increases and healthcare provider shortages persist, it is apparent that the healthcare system requires substantial transformation. The implementation of digital health could aid in this long overdue healthcare system update. As we have discussed, digital health has gradually become recognized as a method of improving patient outcomes and providing best practice healthcare. Unfortunately, digital health implementation and utilization is slowed by strict and often archaic policy, shareholders' resistance to change within healthcare, and disregard for cultural and workplace changes in an increasingly technological world. These barriers result in an increase in unregulated health technology, which can be alluring to patients seeking a solution to their health concerns. With these concerns already present, and threatening to worsen, it is apparent that we can improve our healthcare system by investing in digital health and increasing regulation of digital health policies.

Self-directed further investigation

Now that you have learned about various aspects of digital health policies, please review the individual state-level policies governing digital health for the states that you work and/or practice in.

Consider reviewing these resources as part of this exercise:

https://www.frontiersin.org/articles/10.3389/fdgth.2023.1069410/full

https://www.ncbi.nlm.nih.gov/pmc/articles/PMC6859518/

https://bmcmedicine.biomedcentral.com/articles/10.1186/s12916-019-1377-7

https://www.who.int/docs/default-source/documents/gs4dhdaa2a9f352b0445bafbc79ca799dce4d.pdf

https://journals.ukzn.ac.za/index.php/JISfTeH/article/view/170/791

https://link.springer.com/article/10.1007/s11948-020-00175-8

https://www.cchpca.org/all-telehealth-policies/

https://link.springer.com/article/10.1007/s10865-018-9966-z

https://21259815.fs1.hubspotusercontent-na1.net/hubfs/21259815/Health%20Systems%20Assets/The%20Promise%20of%20Digital%20Health%20Then%20Now%20and%20the%20Future.pdf

https://www.fda.gov/medical-devices/digital-health-center-excellence/what-digital-health

https://www.healthit.gov/topic/health-equity

https://www.ncbi.nlm.nih.gov/pmc/articles/PMC5682364/

https://www.ncbi.nlm.nih.gov/pmc/articles/PMC3920473/

https://www.samhsa.gov/blog/digital-access-super-determinant-health#:~:text=Internet%20access%20is%20increasingly%20recognized,%2C%20employment%2C%20and%20healthcare%20access

https://sdgs.un.org/goals

References

[1] FDA. What is Digital Health? FDA. September 22, 2020. https://www.fda.gov/medical-devices/digital-health-center-excellence/what-digital-health.

[2] Global strategy on digital health 2020-2025. Geneva: World Health Organization; 2021. License: CC BY-NC-SA 3.0 IGO.

[3] History. Centers for Medicare & Medicaid Services. https://www.cms.gov/about-cms/who-we-are/history. (Accessed on 11 September 2023).

[4] 25324 Federal Register. vol. 75, no. 88 https://www.govinfo.gov/content/pkg/FR-2010-05-07/pdf/2010-8159.pdf. (Accessed 11 September 2023).

[5] Promoting Interoperability Programs | CMS. www.cms.gov. https://www.cms.gov/medicare/regulations-guidance/promoting-interoperability-programs?redirect=/ehrincentiveprograms/. (Accessed 11 September 2023).

[6] https://global-factiva-com.pitt.idm.oclc.org/ga/default.aspx?page_driver=.

[7] CMS names an e-prescribing standard to reduce provider burden and expedite patient access to needed medications | CMS. https://www.cms.gov/newsroom/news-alert/cms-names-e-prescribing-standard-reduce-provider-burden-and-expedite-patient-access-needed. (Accessed 11 September 2023).
[8] President Trump Expands Telehealth Benefits for Medicare Beneficiaries During COVID-19 Outbreak | CMS. March 17, 2020. https://www.cms.gov/newsroom/press-releases/president-trump-expands-telehealth-benefits-medicare-beneficiaries-during-covid-19-outbreak.
[9] Federally Qualified Health Center (FQHC) - HealthCare.gov Glossary. https://www.healthcare.gov/glossary/federally-qualified-health-center-fqhc/.
[10] All telehealth policies. CCHP. https://www.cchpca.org/all-telehealth-policies/.
[11] Parity Requirements for Private Payer Telehealth Services. CCHP. https://www.cchpca.org/topic/parity/.
[12] Dieleman JL, Cao J, Chapin A, et al. US health care spending by payer and health condition, 1996-2016. JAMA 2020;323(9):863−84. https://doi.org/10.1001/jama.2020.0734.
[13] Dunn P, Hazzard E. Technology approaches to digital health literacy. International Journal of Cardiology 2019;293:294−6. https://doi.org/10.1016/j.ijcard.2019.06.039.
[14] Meskó B, Drobni Z, Bényei É, Gergely B, Győrffy Z. Digital Health is a cultural transformation of traditional healthcare. mHealth 2017;3:38. https://doi.org/10.21037/mhealth.2017.08.07.
[15] Turcios Y. Digital access: a super determinant of health. SAMHSA March 22, 2023. https://www.samhsa.gov/blog/digital-access-super-determinant-health#:~:text=Internet%20access%20is%20increasingly%20recognized,%2C%20employment%2C%20and%20healthcare%20access.

CHAPTER 23

Regulatory considerations

Caitlin Kelley and Mona Kelley
Kelley Medical Consultants LLC/RAIsonance Group, Springfield, TN, United States

Key Terms

Regulatory Agency	Any government body that regulates the approval and marketing of medical devices and pharmaceuticals
Food and Drug Administration	The government body within the United States that regulates food, cosmetics, pharmaceuticals, biological products, and medical devices
Medical Device	Any instrument, machine, contrivance, implant, or in vitro reagent that's intended to treat, cure, prevent, mitigate, or diagnose a disease
Mobile Medical Applications	Software programs that run on smartphones that are an accessory to a medical device or transform a mobile platform into a regulated medical device.
Artificial Intelligence	The theory and development of computer systems able to perform tasks that normally require human intelligence
Machine Learning	The use and development of computer systems that can learn and adapt using algorithms and statistical models rather than explicit instructions.

Common Regulatory Standards

Common standards for digital health technology medical device manufacturers	
21 C.F.R.	Legal requirements in the U.S. for medical devices and therapeutics, enforced by the FDA
ISO 13485	Standard for the design, development, and production of all medical devices
ISO 14971	Delineates the requirements to manage risk in all medical devices
ISO 62366	Describes requirements for including usability/human factors engineering as a part of the design and validation of medical devices
IEC 62304	Standard for the design, development, and evaluation of software medical devices

Introduction

While digital health technologies are continuously becoming more mainstream in our everyday lives, uptake in the healthcare sector is not as expedient. For digital health to truly expand in the healthcare setting, the regulatory landscape must first adapt and become more hospitable to these technologies. Globally, the Food and Drug Administration is considered one of the more friendly regulatory agencies regarding any new technology, including digital health. Despite multiple commitments from the agency to ensure that new technologies are considered within the correct context and implemented

Digital Health. https://doi.org/10.1016/B978-0-443-23901-4.00023-4

quickly when proven safe and effective, large agencies have difficulty moving at the increasingly frantic pace of technological innovation. Digital health technologies can be designed, coded, and released in a fraction of the time that is required for a more traditional medical device that includes hardware. While this is a clear advantage for innovation, the quick production time has created difficulties for manufacturers within the regulatory landscape. The software development process (the only manufacturing required for a software-only device) is also much more agile than that of writing extensive guidance documents, which is the primary method for regulatory agencies to communicate their standing on various topics to stakeholders. These documents are drafted over time, released in draft format for comments from stakeholders, and then finalized, all of which can take years.

Digital Health Center of Excellence

The FDA has made several strides in this area, however, to facilitate more digital health technologies to enter the market. The Digital Health Center of Excellence (DHCoE) was founded in September 2020 with the goal of empowering digital stakeholders to advance healthcare through research, partnerships, regulatory innovation, and developing appropriate policy [1]. While the center does work to serve other departments within the FDA that may need to review submissions regarding digital health, manufacturers, patients, and healthcare providers are also included in the department's stakeholders as expediting the advancement of safe and effective digital health technologies that improve patient care benefits all parties. Before the launch of the DHCoE, 13 guidance documents had been released (from 2005 to 2019) that included some level of digital health information or guidance. However, the general consensus among stakeholders was that these guidance documents were cumbersome and not well-informed to the issues faced in the development of these technologies. Since the launch, the DHCoE has assisted in updating existing guidance documents to reflect a more modern approach as well as informing the 10 new guidance documents that have been released in just 3 years. Currently, the main interests of the DHCoE are cybersecurity, Artificial Intelligence/Machine Learning (AI/ML), Augmented Reality/Virtual Reality (AR/VR), and wireless medical devices. Research is ongoing in these areas as are the publications of guidance documents.

Mobile Medical Applications

One huge stride to assist digital health technologies in getting to market more quickly was the release of the *Policy for Device Software Functions and Mobile Medical Applications* guidance document in 2022 [2]. The document provided a notable increase in clarity around what would be regulated in terms of both software and mobile applications. In that document, the FDA made it clear that no regulation would be applied to smartphones, tablets, or other general-purpose hardware on which these types of software would be run. While the hardware may be needed to perform adequate software or usability testing, this statement allows the manufacturer to focus on the development of a safe and effective software function without concern for the regulation of the necessary hardware. More importantly, the FDA made it very clear that they did not intend to regulate every mobile medical application (MMA) on the market. The intent was to only regulate MMAs, which "could pose a risk to a patient's safety if the software applications were to not function as intended."

Two subsets of software are specifically discussed in the document as functions that the FDA does not intend to regulate. The first is any software that helps a patient to self-manage a disease process in some way (i.e., an app that allows a patient to journal and track symptoms). This has allowed the market to be saturated with a variety of smartphone apps that promote wellness whether generally or specific to a disease condition. These apps are expressly allowed to coach patients with specific medical conditions as well as communicate information about the patient to their healthcare provider. This provision has also allowed certain applications for tracking, such as heart rate variability, to become very popular as this type of software does provide some objective data, but does not provide diagnosis or treatment information. The second set of software that is not expressly regulated is that which automates tasks for a healthcare provider. One example of this type of software is an app or other software that performs a basic calculation, such as body mass index, NIH stroke scale, or other similar scales. The provider is able to make these calculations without the tool but can provide more efficient care by having this type of tool. Of note, these are also thought to not pose a risk to the patient if functioning incorrectly because the calculation is performed by or under the direct supervision of the provider, meaning that the healthcare provider would question an incorrect calculation rather than act on it. Finally, the guidance gave specific information that the FDA had no intentions to regulate electronic health record software, any applications strictly focused on fitness, health, or wellness, medical dictionaries, or any type of software that allows the healthcare provider to search for evidence-based treatment or pharmacologic intervention information. The guidance was a massive step toward ensuring that healthcare providers have the technology to deliver more efficient and effective care without sacrificing patient safety.

Regulatory concerns: Artificial Intelligence/Machine Learning devices

One of the most popular topics in the news today surrounding digital health is that of Artificial Intelligence/Machine Learning (AI/ML). AI/ML-enabled devices are also one of the most common digital health technologies that must obtain regulatory approval to enter the market. While certain use cases for this type of technology, such as ChatGPT, are making AI seem commonplace to the general population, most healthcare providers have some type of pause with the thought of incorporating the technology into mainstream practice. However, the reality is that AI technology is already assisting healthcare providers in making complex medical decisions, reviewing medical images, and ensuring documentation is complete. To date, the FDA has approved approximately 692 devices that include some level of AI/ML technology. Of those, 531 are related to radiology, which has long been the leader in medical specialties using AI. Of the remaining 161 devices, 71 are related to cardiology, and the rest are split between many different specialties. Of the 155 new AI/ML devices on the market in the last year, it bears noting that only three of those were from the De Novo pathway [3].

When seeking approval from the FDA, there are three main pathways to get a medical device to market [4]. First, premarket authorization is used only for devices that are considered of the highest risk (i.e., implanted devices or those that could cause death in the case of malfunction). Three devices on the market include some type of AI/ML function that was approved using this pathway although none of the three were approved during the last year. The second and certainly the most common pathway is the 510K. When submitting this application, the manufacturer has to provide enough safety and efficacy data to prove the device in question is equivalent to devices that are already on the market. This pathway, by far, requires less time and resources. Often, manufacturers are not required to complete a new clinical validation trial and can receive their clearance to get the device to market much more quickly than the other pathways. The final pathway for approval is the De Novo pathway. This is a newer pathway, but includes all medical devices that would be considered low or moderate risk with no device currently on the market that is comparable. Because of the novelty of the devices being considered in this pathway, a plethora of safety and effectiveness data are required to be granted the designation. Because of this, the development stage is rather costly and resource-intensive.

Based on this information, what does it mean that less than 2% of the AI/ML devices on the market came through the De Novo pathway? The remaining 98% are devices that are new to the market but have the same intended use as devices that are already on the market, meaning the technology is not novel nor are the diseases being diagnosed or treated. For instance, there are many devices on the market that utilize AI/ML-enabled image detection to assist radiologists in making certain diagnoses. A company that already has this type of software may want to update their device with an improved algorithm, or another company may develop software that does the exact same thing but uses a different AI/ML algorithm. In either of these situations, the company would submit a 510K application to prove that the new algorithm is equally safe and effective (or better) than the one that is already on the market. This means that more than 98% of the AI/ML devices that have come to market in the last year were not providing a new use or indication to the market. In contrast, only three AI/ML-enabled devices within the last year provided a new type of value and innovation to healthcare.

After the realization that only a few devices are making it to market for new indications, it bears discussion of the barriers that AI/ML-enabled devices experience in making it to market. Before 2021, there was no AI/ML-specific formal guidance for manufacturers to consider when creating these algorithms. Guidance related to cybersecurity and software functions is certainly applicable and helpful for those components of the device, but with no guidance for the algorithm itself, stakeholders were left guessing as to what the agency would consider safe, effective, and worthy of approval. In 2021, the FDA, in conjunction with Health Canada, released *Good Machine Learning Practice for Medical Device Development: Guiding Principles*, in an attempt to provide some level of support for the development of AI/ML-enabled devices [5]. While many of the guidelines, such as the separation of training datasets and testing datasets, were components of basic data science, others made positive strides toward the collaboration of these manufacturers with the correct stakeholders. One of the most important principles in that document for this discussion is the use of multidisciplinary expertise from the conception of the product all the way through release and ongoing maintenance. The guidance provided a clear need for healthcare providers to work with AI/ML software manufacturers to ensure that the end product is useable and meaningful for patient care. Of course, the engagement of stakeholders is key to any project, and in the world of medical devices, the provider and patient's abilities to interact with the device are of the utmost importance.

However, this particular principle also helped to solve another key issue in the world of AI/ML. Data scientists are the primary discipline responsible for developing, training, and testing the models that comprise an AI/ML algorithm. This new and evolving field, however, often relies on strategies, such as data mining, that require review of large amounts of data for patterns, rather than a more linear working approach [6]. As such, the focus for data scientists is the research of patterns, rather than linear development as would be defined by the scientific method or even software development standards. Healthcare providers are in the perfect position to provide context to datasets that allow the data scientist to better understand what patterns are meaningful within the data. Furthermore, the knowledge of the healthcare providers helps to predict what patterns in data have the potential to exist. For instance, data scientists may be encouraged to look for similar patterns in similar disease processes to assist with diagnosis or, conversely, may need to look for specific differences between two disease processes when reviewing images. Regulatory agencies are rooted in more traditional scientific methods as are healthcare providers. By including healthcare providers from the very conception of the development of digital health technologies, the technology is developed in a more effective manner: a manner in which the patient is better served by the outcome and the regulatory agency is more able to understand the technology and therefore, approve it for use.

Another huge issue facing the world of AI/ML is the ability to obtain the amount and quality of data required to train models adequately. Models that are trained on too little data do not generalize well to the population rendering the expected outcome invalid [7]. However, the cost and resources required to obtain data, especially new data for indications not previously explored, can be exorbitant. This overextension of resources in combination with particularly long regulatory timeframes has led to some companies going out of business before receiving an approval. This issue is a predominant reason that the leading companies with approved AI/ML-enabled medical devices are major players in the field, including GE, Siemens, and Phillips [8]. These companies have the capital to acquire the necessary data and wait for the regulatory approval. The FDA did address some of the data issues, stating that datasets should be representative of the patient population, separating the training and testing datasets, and designing the models in a way that is tailored to the available data [5]. While these issues assist in the development of quality AI/ML algorithms, they do not address the need for an extensive quantity and quality of data. These decisions must be made by the data science professionals who are developing, training, testing, and validating the models.

The final issue that pertains to AI/ML digital health technologies centers on the issue of allowing the machine to learn, evolve, and improve. Machine Learning algorithms are designed to learn and improve over time. This type of learning can be supervised, unsupervised, semisupervised, and reinforcement [9]. However, the FDA and other regulatory agencies understandably have concerns about an algorithm providing predictions regarding diagnoses and treatment of diseases from an algorithm that is constantly changing. This possibility opens a significant risk for performance degradation, meaning an algorithm with a sensitivity of 90% could degrade to a sensitivity of 70% without the user of the device having any knowledge of the change. However, in an ideal scenario, the learning potential of the device may also cause that same sensitivity of 90% to rise to 95%. Due to an abundance of caution, the FDA has only approved AI/ML algorithms that are completely locked, meaning they cannot learn or improve. The 2021 guidelines specified that a human should always be in the loop when allowing a machine to learn [5], implying that learning could take place, be tested, and then the improved algorithm released. In 2023, a draft guidance was released beginning to specify requirements for submitting such a plan that will allow AI/ML manufacturers to improve their algorithms regularly and in a sensible manner [10]. This major change and improvement to the regulations will allow healthcare providers and patients to benefit from the full abilities of AI/ML-enabled digital health technologies.

Regulatory concerns: Cybersecurity

Cybersecurity is the major inherent risk associated with digital health technologies. Stakeholders often first consider the possibility of patient data privacy breaches, which of course is absolutely a concern. Beyond that, medical devices and hospital systems can be rendered inoperable in the case of a cybersecurity incident [11]. These types of incidents are more threatening than data privacy issues in that they can delay the diagnosis and treatments of patients, thereby posing a more immediate or life-threatening risk. Management of more traditional medical device risks is well-defined both in 21CFR [12] and ISO 14971 [13]. However, managing cybersecurity risks is not as established. The FDA released the first guidance document regarding cybersecurity in 2014. An updated document entitled *Cybersecurity in Medical Devices: Quality System Considerations and Content of Premarket Submissions* was finally released in 2023 [14]. This obvious delay confirms the concerns posed in the introduction of the chapter regarding the difficulty faced by regulatory agencies when trying to keep pace with the constantly changing environment of digital health. Nine years in digital health is a proverbial lifetime with many iterations of new and evolving issues within cybersecurity as well as software function in a broader sense.

This latest guidance document did, however, provide valuable insight into the way that digital health medical device manufacturers should be handling cybersecurity. Cybersecurity is to be considered a part of patient safety and is regulated within the company's quality system. As such, the user, which could be the patient or the healthcare provider, is to be fully informed of a device's cybersecurity controls through device labeling, such as instructions for use of the device. This transparency allows the user and more likely the healthcare system to ensure cybersecurity safeguards are in place at all levels. The guidance document also provided a framework for both the documentation to be submitted to the FDA and expectations for the entire life cycle of the product. This means that companies are held liable for not only testing before market entry, but maintenance of those cybersecurity safeguards when the device is in the hands of the user. These ongoing requirements allow the healthcare provider to utilize and prescribe the use of digital health medical devices without concern for unnecessary risk to the patient or the healthcare system.

Regulatory concerns: Usability

Human factors and usability engineering are concerns for all medical devices. IEC 62366 is the standard that outlines the process for medical device manufacturers to evaluate the usability of a device [15]. The primary regulatory concern for digital health technologies is the usability of the user interface. Usability considerations are specific to the intended user population, which could be healthcare providers or patients. Many software-based medical devices are intended to be used by the healthcare provider. In these situations, the users are smaller in number and usually have a greater familiarity with technology. Medical device manufacturers can train these individuals in person or remotely to ensure they are able to operate the software correctly. However, digital health technology medical devices that are to be used as over-the-counter devices pose a different problem entirely as well as a greater risk. Most of these software applications are accessed through smartphone or other handheld device that is the user's personal property. While regulatory agencies are clear that they are not regulating smartphones or tablets, the user must be able to utilize the associated screens.

The FDA guidance document *Applying Human Factors and Usability Engineering to Medical Devices*, while not entirely focused on digital health technology, does address this need [15]. Manufacturers must perform usability testing to ensure that critical tasks, those that must be performed correctly for the device to function safely and effectively, are able to be performed successfully. This testing and any resulting design changes to the technology are considered part of risk management for the device. With almost 50% of healthcare spending in the United States attributed to patients age 65 and older [16], the likelihood that patients utilizing a medical device are not comfortable with digital health technology is quite high. For this reason, this population should always be included in usability testing. The task of manufacturers is to ensure that the user interface for the technology is very clear with no assumption that the user will intuitively be able to manage the screens.

Conclusion/key takeaways

- The pace of the development of digital health technologies is far more agile than the development of regulations, standards, and guidance documents that can inform the safe and effective development of potential medical devices.
- The FDA has begun to pick up momentum in supporting digital health technology manufacturers with more accurate guidance to ensure successful submissions that allow new devices to enter the market.
- Healthcare providers are important stakeholders in the development of digital health technologies and should be at the forefront of development to help ensure that technologies can be used safely and effectively, are clinically meaningful, and can be incorporated successfully into clinical workflows.

References

[1] U.S. Food and Drug Administration. Digital Health Center of Excellence; 2023. https://www.fda.gov/medical-devices/digital-health-center-excellence. [Accessed 2 January 2024].

[2] U.S. Food and Drug Administration. Policy for Device Software Functions and Mobile Medical Applications. 2022. https://www.fda.gov/regulatory-information/search-fda-guidance-documents/policy-device-software-functions-and-mobile-medical-applications. [Accessed 2 January 2024].

[3] U.S. Food and Drug Administration. Medical Device Databases. 2023. https://www.fda.gov/medical-devices/device-advice-comprehensive-regulatory-assistance/medical-device-databases3. [Accessed 2 January 2024]. pathways for FDA.

[4] U.S. Food and Drug Administration & HealthCanada. Good Machine Learning Practice for Medical Device Development: Guiding Principles. 2021. https://www.fda.gov/media/153486/download. [Accessed 2 January 2024].

[5] O'Sullivan C. Data science is not science: How to incorporate the scientific process in your data science analysis. Towards Data Science 2023. https://towardsdatascience.com/data-science-is-not-science-bb95d783697a. [Accessed 6 January 2024].

[6] Dagaev N, Roads BD, Luo X, Barry DN, Patil KR, Love BC. A too-good-to-be-true prior to reduce shortcut reliance. Pattern Recognition Letters 2023;166:164–71. https://doi.org/10.1016/j.patrec.2022.12.010.

[7] Koncz A. The current state of almost 700 FDA-approved, AI based medical devices. The Medical Futurist 2023. https://medicalfuturist.com/the-current-state-of-fda-approved-ai-based-medical-devices/. [Accessed 4 January 2024].

[8] Nichols JA, Herbert Chan HW, Baker MAB. Machine Learning: applications of artificial intelligence to imaging and diagnosis. Biophysical Reviews 2019;11(1):111–8. https://doi.org/10.1007/s12551-018-0449-9.

[9] U.S. Food and Drug Administration. Marketing Submission Recommendations for a Predetermined Change Control Plan for Artificial Intelligence/Machine Learning (AI/ML)-Enabled Device Software Functions. 2023. https://www.fda.gov/regulatory-information/search-fda-guidance-documents/marketing-submission-recommendations-predetermined-change-control-plan-artificial. [Accessed 6 January 2024];

[10] International Medical Device Regulators Forum. Medical Device Cybersecurity Guide 2023. https://www.imdrf.org/working-groups/medical-device-cybersecurity-guide. [Accessed 3 January 2024].

[11] 21 C.F.R. Part 820 Quality System Regulation. 2023.

[12] Medical devices: Application of risk management to medical devices. ISO Standard No. 14971:2019. https://www.iso.org/standard/72704.html [Accessed 8 January 2024]

[13] U.S. Food and Drug Administration. Cybersecurity in Medical Devices: Quality System Considerations and Content of Premarket Submissions. 2023. https://www.fda.gov/regulatory-information/search-fda-guidance-documents/cybersecurity-medical-devices-quality-system-considerations-and-content-premarket-submissions. [Accessed 3 January 2024].

[14] Medical devices. Part 1: Application of usability engineering to medical devices. IEC Standard NO. 62366-1:2015. https://www.iso.org/standard/63179.html [Accessed 8 January 2024].

[15] U.S. Food and Drug Administration, Applying Human Factors and Usability Engineering to Medical Devices. 2016. https://www.fda.gov/regulatory-information/search-fda-guidance-documents/applying-human-factors-and-usability-engineering-medical-devices. [Accessed 4 January 2024].

[16] Kalseth J, Halvorsen T. Health and care service utilization and cost over the life-span: a descriptive analysis of population data. BMC Health Services Research 2020;20(435). https://doi.org/10.1186/s12913-020-05295-2.

CHAPTER 24

Data validation and verification and IRB process

David Beck[1], Christina Davis[2], and Jeffrey C. Cooper[3]

[1]School of Health and Rehabilitation Sciences (SHRS), Department of PA Studies, University of Pittsburgh, Pittsburgh, PA, United States; [2]Department of PA Studies, University of Pittsburgh, Pittsburgh, PA, United States; [3]University of Pittsburgh, Pittsburgh, PA, United States

Data validation, data verification, and clinical validation considerations

Data validation

Over the years, digital health has gained momentum. It has expanded to newer technologies in medicine to manage diseases and health risks, provide clinical decision support, and promote wellness. It is reported that over 200 health apps are added daily and that billions of dollars in funding are invested yearly in the digital health sector [1]. But how can we ensure that this digital health explosion is safe and does not cause harm? Are digital health products validated and verified? Although some products have been rigorously studied, not all have been widely evaluated [1]. A unified approach needs to be taken to create a framework for the validation, verification, and clinical validation of digital health products.

At a basic level, data validation is the process of verifying that data will represent what it claims to represent. As with other products, this validation needs to be objective and transparent, with the goal of bringing enhanced clarity to a product. For digital health products, this means that the information aligns with its intended use and that the technology aligns with the user's needs. This process will likely evolve over time and may be influenced by regulatory bodies since establishing a standardized approach to data validation is challenging. Digital health products have often been implemented, with the thought that validation would occur later. Validation has become a priority, and developments are underway to better validate digital health products. One approach, the Digital Health Scorecard, has been created to objectively define requirements and standards for digital health products [1].

Digital Health. https://doi.org/10.1016/B978-0-443-23901-4.00024-6

With the large volume and quick growth of new digital health products, the process of evaluation of all these products remains a challenge and will continue to unfold. Voluntary accreditation agencies certifying apps, provider-based efforts to validate apps, independent third parties, as well as algorithmic validation will evolve as well as real-world testing [2]. How digital health projects move from validation to use needs to be consistently and carefully reviewed.

Data verification

Evaluation of new digital health products should involve two steps: validation and verification. At a basic level, verification is the process of checking if a product was built according to specification [3]. This process will check the data to make sure it is not only accurate but also a reflection of its intended purpose. This process will add to the overall trustworthiness of a product, in the eyes of a consumer. For some digital health products, computational simulation has been performed for product evaluation, which involves simulated outcomes based on synthesized cases [3]. However, at present, much of the digital health industry lacks verification measures. The creation and implementation of standardized and consistent methodologies for the verification of digital health products remain an industry-wide challenge; however, it is necessary to distinguish between products and promote a higher standard of quality.

Clinical validation considerations

All digital health products should demonstrate clinical validation, which is the clinical safety, effectiveness, and efficacy of a product [4]. This process is normally done by clinical trials. Although in other healthcare products, there is a clear path on how to evaluate these areas, the path is more complex in digital health products. Some groups have offered guidelines in the clinical validation of electronic patient-recorded outcome measures (ePROMs), including The International Society for Pharmacoeconomics and Outcomes Research (ISPOR) [4]. Additionally, a product can receive an ORCHA seal of approval, to show that a company has achieved validation. But what level of safety, effectiveness, and efficacy is necessary to consider a digital health product meaningful?

Clinical validation usually occurs after a digital health product has been validated and verified and is conducted to promote a certain product for a certain subset of the population. This validation should evaluate the correlation between a product and clinical condition. This process should answer the following questions—Who? What? When? Where? Why? This process should also ensure that there are no biases involved. Due to the large number and many different types of questions asked for clinical validation, developing a standardized framework is difficult.

Risk assessment process

The risk assessment process dates back to many years ago. One can find papers and scientific journals with ideas on how to assess and manage risk. Assessing and managing risk support decision-making. New analysis methods and techniques along with risk analysis approaches are used in many sectors. Not only various techniques but also various tools are often used in this process. Regarding digital health products, there again needs to be a systematic evaluation of these products, which also can be challenging. This should involve an evaluation of hazards, and one may add ethical considerations with their use. To assess risk, not only do risks need to be identified but also an analysis of these risks.

Additionally, when focusing on digital health products, these products themselves can play a critical role in early risk assessment, in clinical settings. During the COVID-19 pandemic, chatbots digitally helped patients in performing risk assessment, by receiving a score indicating the level of COVID-19 risk [5]. Risk assessment for cardiovascular disease can also be done with digital health products. Machine learning and natural language processing algorithms have been found to have comparable levels of accuracy in assessing acuity risk in ERs to skilled providers [2]. Although digital health tools can support risk stratification, there is concern about the risk of loss of privacy for those individuals sharing their sensitive data through digital health products and lack of human engagement.

But what risk assessment processes are in place for digital health products? The Digital Health Checklist for Researchers (DHC-R), described later in this chapter, is an example of one tool that was developed as a decision support tool. The risk of the use of a digital health product is compounded by the anticipated value, which often leads to fast-paced experimentation [1]. The onus to identify risk has often shifted to the clinician and patient. Although the data should undergo validation and verification, the necessity for a risk assessment tool is crucial in high-risk clinical scenarios with complex products [1]. Although many advancements have been made regarding risk assessment and digital health products, further development is underway and encouraged.

Digital health scorecard

While the number and complexity of digital health products continue to grow, the ability to measure quality remains a challenge. As mentioned earlier, one reason for this challenge is the lack of a standardized approach to validation [1]. The Digital Health Scorecard has been created to objectively define requirements and standards for digital health products. It can help to discriminate between products. This is felt to be a hybrid approach, which defines requirements and standards, then discloses them and evaluates and reports them to the industry and public [1]. It can also be used to refine existing products or help in the creation of new ones. As digital health products continue to evolve, so shall this approach.

The digital health scorecard consists of four components, called domains: technical, clinical, usability, and cost [1]. Technical validation will focus on the functionality and accuracy of the product and solution [1]. Clinical usability or validation will demonstrate efficacy [1]. The purpose of usability is to assess if the technology will align with user needs and preferences. And cost, although many products are low cost or free, will be assessed about value [1]. By gathering together the individual domain assessments from the digital health scorecard, a Global Digital Health Score can be created [1]. This score can help with the initial selection of digital health products.

Digital health checklist for researchers (DHC-R)

As health research continues to grow, and digital health products offer an opportunity for continued sensible, systemic, and measured expansion. For example, a wearable fitness tracker can collect real-time data to assess the effectiveness of an intervention. However, using technologies for research purposes requires an awareness of known risks. Researchers themselves should be part of the risk assessment process; however, there is little guidance on this. Because of this gap, the Digital Health Checklist for Researchers (DHC-R) was created as one tool used to help with research planning and potential problems associated with digital health research [6]. It was created as a decision-support tool by behavioral scientists and was created to promote informed decision-making, especially regarding social and ethical responsibilities for those conducting the research [6].

The DHC-R supports the following four domains: access and usability, privacy, data management, and risks and benefits [7]. It is available through the Research Center for Optimal Digital Ethics (ReCODE) Health research webpage, which supports those individuals conducting digital health research [7]. Access and usability focus on whether or not the participant can access and use the product [7]. It takes into consideration the cost, such as the need to purchase Internet. Privacy focuses on the types of personal information that is gathered from participants [7]. Risks and benefits focus on the probability of potential harm versus the benefits gained from the study [7]. With the evolution of new digital health products, additional "checklists" will evolve, especially as new gaps surface.

Generated research abstracts with ChatGPT

Having both practical application and intellectual property features, digital health products require scholarly evidence along with usage-based measures for validation and verification.

The simplest demand versus availability market arguments explain the advent of complex tools and methods to help verify and validate new digital health utilities and resources. To satisfy demand, new meta-applications entered the scene to navigate an otherwise overwhelming wealth of data sources.

At this moment, is anyone not thinking of ChatGPT? In the old days of card catalogs and friendly reference librarians, a given research inquiry might prompt scholars and students to perceive a daunting prospect. Researchers may share a greater aversion to replying, "I don't know" than to fabricate an answer. To avoid that indignity, now robots can help. If AI is old news regarding fast thinking, ChatGPT in its infancy represents an arguably rampant but widespread solution—boasting more than 100 million users 2 months after launch (in comparison to TikTok requiring nine months and Instagram 2-1/2 years) ([8], citing Sensor Tower) Hu (2013). "ChatGPT sets record for fastest growing user base—analyst note," Reuters, February 1, 2023—for this necessary validation process

Another economic argument holds that great innovations arrive with costs. Before balancing those risks with rewards, and rendering ChatGPT perhaps "too good to be true," our discussion traces historical framings.

How did we get here?

Big Data

An irony of the advent of the "information explosion," a term first used in 1941 [9] Oxford English Dictionary; cited in Press [9], Forbes, "A Very Short History Of Big Data," https://www.forbes.com/sites/gilpress/2013/05/09/a-very-short-history-of-big-data/?sh=7d07787965a1, 2013, and Big Data, first coined in October 1997 [10]; "Application-controlled demand paging for out-of-core visualization," Proceedings of the IEEE 8th conference on Visualization, 1997, is that ideals of conduct had not changed from centuries before nor decades since. What else has not changed is that there are always cheaters, borrowers, and line cutters. This chapter explores how patrolling measures have adapted and grown to keep pace with digital abuse and neglect made easier and tempting with technological advancements.

In attempting to make life better for humankind, health, resources, animal kingdoms, and economy, research has not only historical legitimacy but also an element of intellectual property. "Hey, that's mine!" remains a frequent and rightful protest. What to do, when opportunities to claim partial or full ownership of something not original are plentiful and accessible? This study does not investigate how the legal field offers ethical protections or else tidy escapes from accountability. Instead, we look at organizational bodies, foundations, and principles that promote fairness in research behaviors and sharing knowledge in digital health systems.

Start with the premise that digital policing would be unnecessary if organic, interpersonal measures worked. If not everyone can behave, then either everyone or no one must referee. That range is wide; somewhere in between lies a manageable, reliable, and consistent network of watchers. One example is Facebook's implementation of self-contained enforcement by reporting and restricting accesses, when trolls emerged from various digital swamps.

The phrase "information explosion" may be misleading if taken literally as one event. Rather, information continues to reexplode, with new inventions and unprecedented features. Paraphrasing Brian Basgen, CIO at Emerson College, Taylor Swaak contends "that when people hear the word 'AI' right now, they think of ChatGPT, a tool that, while imperfect, boasts capabilities most people have never seen before, like the power to pass an M.B.A. exam" [11] Swaak, Taylor (2023). "First Came ChatGPT. Then Came the Over-the-Top Sales Pitches," the Chronicle, 8/7/23. https://www.chronicle.com/article/first-came-chatgpt-then-came-the-over-the-top-sales-pitches. ChatGPT may currently be the most visible example of a system utility designed with best intentions, and effectiveness, but hence inviting abuse like anything else. Accordingly, reactions to ChatGPT range from "Wow, this is great!" to "What hath Hades spawned now?"

The title of the cited recent article in the Chronicle of Higher Education summarizes current digital phenomena: "First Came ChatGPT. Then Came the Over-the-Top Sales Pitches." Crediting G2 with this measurement, Swaak notes, "... Out of 145,000 software products, the top three fastest-growing ones are AI tools," with higher education as a target market. According to Basgen and Swaak, amidst the onslaught of email promotions, "for the most part, there's more noise than there is signal," followed by a lot of clicking "delete" or wondering, "Who's the expert?" Ibid [11]. Other value judgments of good or bad aside, ChatGPT is popularly perceived as another wave of annoyance.

If higher education is indeed a primary target market, good thing that academics always conduct themselves honorably in their insulated ivory tower, right? Nay! - Now trolls, ingrates, and sycophants have joined specious AI "experts" to infest research communities—along with the usual careless participants who have always needed coaching away from "traditional" plagiarism. If this depiction of the digital human seems cynical, confining remedies to carelessness and neglect still signals a problem with integrity, attributions, and credit. The ordinarily dutiful researcher discovers a vital snippet of information; but then in this age of remote learning and conduct, her phone rings, or her dog barks, or her soufflé explodes in the oven. That she forgets or perhaps loses that key reference seems more probable than thinking, "Hmm, heck with it, I need this insight whether or not I thank So-and-So. Just don't get caught." Even with this benefit of the doubt, someone gets caught every day, either because of negligence or a deliberate informational heist. Both could be actionable.

IRB process

To determine whether AI integrity requires more formal monitoring, and given that no such global body exists, perhaps we draw parallels with other organizations that have proven effective and gained trust in setting standards, along with repercussions for not following those standards. One possible source of precedent is institutional review boards (IRBs). The National Institutes of Health (NIH) defines the Institutional Review Board as "research ethics committees provid[ing] a core protection for human research participants through advance and periodic independent review of the ethical acceptability of proposals for human research." [12]. National Library of Medicine, https://www.ncbi.nlm.nih.gov/pmc/articles/PMC4631034/#: ~ :text=Institutional%20review%20boards%20(IRBs)%20or,of%20proposals%20for%20human%20research, 2015 [12]. Does this make the IRB a collective, a network, an expectation for any research university, or simply a righteous concept that research shenanigans *upon human subjects* shall be dealt with? The very mention of the abbreviation "IRB" causes some to shudder as they might at "internal audit." Some meanwhile contend, providence and research bless the IRB. A reasonable interpretation is that any research institute creates an IRB or equivalent out of obligation for research credibility—with some autonomy. For example, Pitt's website does not specifically identify an "institutional review board"; rather, the concept of IRB and its enforcements are entrusted to the Human Research Protection Office, complete with its own, protected acronym (HRPO).

Ethical and regulatory review

A brief history may help clarify existing standardization and rationale. Margaret R. Moon, MD, MPH, notes, "Immanuel Kant's second maxim defines the tension that drives and bedevils IRBs. Human-subjects research uses humans as subjects, as a means to an end. The imperative that it is never merely as a means, but always also an end in itself, makes IRBs necessary. The history of human-subjects research is replete with horrid examples of what happens when investigators fail to respect humans as ends in themselves." Moon, Margaret (2009). "The History and Role of Institutional Review Boards: A Useful Tension," AMA Journal of Ethics, https://journalofethics.ama-assn.org/article/history-and-role-institutional-review-boards-useful-tension/2009-04, 2009 [13]. UT Houston shares related wisdom that IRB sources arose also from the Nuremberg trials. "… Abuses of World War II Nazi doctors came to public attention. This led to the creation of the Nuremberg Code in 1945, the first legal attempt to deal with ethical issues of modern research. As biomedical research efforts expanded the international need for a more specific code of ethics was formulated in the 1964 Declaration of Helsinki." [14]; https://www.uth.edu/cphs/for-researchers/history-of-irb.htm, 2008 to present [14] to present.

Word spread, even without Twitter (Aka, X) or other modern familiar means to share knowledge (or unsubstantiated claims) instantaneously. Action in the United States commenced at NIH HQ in Bethesda in 1953 Expansion of rules on "extramural" research "led to the establishment of institutional review boards (IRBs) at hundreds of institutions receiving federal funding for research." Ibid [14] to present. However, numerous sources cite the Tuskegee Syphilis Study, proceeding through 1972 (how was this humanly possible?), as the final statement subsequently calling for the establishment of the IRB system with the passage of the National Research Act of 1974 (finally, a law—and one directed by Senator Ted Kennedy and signed into law by President Richard Nixon in an interesting alliance). The National Commission for the Protection of Human Subjects of Biomedical and Behavioral Research publication in 1979 of the Belmont Report represents a culmination of "three general ethical principles that continue to be applied to the research of human subjects:

Beneficence: To maximize benefits for science, humanity, and research participants and to avoid or minimize risk or harm.

Respect: To protect the autonomy and privacy rights of participants.

Justice: To ensure the fair distribution among persons and groups of the costs and benefits of research" [15]. National Commission for the Protection of Human Subjects of Biomedical and Behavioral Research, https://www.hhs.gov/ohrp/regulations-and-policy/belmont-report/read-the-belmont-report/index.html, April 18, 1979 [15].

These seem noble and memorable guidelines, if broad and idealistic. How should they be enforced?

Continuing a rational evolution with momentum, more than 80 countries hosted IRBs or "equivalent bodies" through 2015 McCarthy and Grady (2008). "The origins and policies that govern institutional review boards," cited in: Emanuel E, Grady C, Crouch R, Lie R, Miller F, Wendler D, eds. The Oxford Textbook of Clinical Research Ethics. New York, NY: Oxford University Press; 2008:541−550, https://www.ncbi.nlm.nih.gov/pmc/articles/PMC4631034/, 2008 [16]. Although IRBs deal specifically with human subjects, digital and communications scientists and policymakers might aspire to create a similar guide, with teeth. Consider as a comparison that legal argument often enlists similar case facts and circumstances as *precedent* to justify the proposed policy. Also consider in contrast that protection of animal subjects remains often organic and activist, hence also unenforceable except by social media slamming and activist shaming. Do we want those actions to be the only recourse?

Another debate is whether medical *research* on human diseases and conditions, indeed, is protected and enforced by IRBs—or to what extent. If the IRB has been conceived to restrict direct contacts and interventions (in vivo) on human subjects, the scope may or may not necessarily cover research and practice that cures or manages those conditions (in vitro). If medical research depends instead on legal systems to determine that line and scope, we are left with debate, not resolution.

Determination of appropriate risk management strategies

Aside from intellectual property ownership and compensations, utilities such as ChatGPT, flaws, and misuse notwithstanding could be considered primarily a great benefit for the expediency and breadth of digital research. Machine learning has been designed and enhanced by humans to gather and sort at nearly inconceivable speeds. Is that process not more effective than weary researchers continuing to dig, probe, and publish—all reliant on grant status? Besides, freeware is cheaper and faster than soft money. Misattribution of sources may be a worthy sacrifice for faster access to knowledge, cures, and treatment. Much like a person must rely on a car to go 60 mph, we depend on machines that human beings invented to muster the speed and discernment we otherwise cannot. As articulated earlier, ChatGPT is a timely example and impossible to ignore.

Urgency to draw and enforce lines of conduct and attribution has lagged because nobody dies or suffers physically as a direct result of digi-theft or -laziness in itself, only in context. But it's still wrong, and contrary to the spirit and traditions of betterment. While 80 countries adopting IRB standards is commendable, standard conduct for AI and digital health must cover the whole world of 195 countries (some of which may not have medical and research systems strengthened by IRB). One way to proceed with "enforcing" data integrity and protecting against digital banditry might be to build and test a system here, wherever "here" may be. Then spread the word, and watch it carry. This is very much in the research tradition of presenting, sharing, and proceeding upon any valuable discovery. Maybe such systems already exist, yet have not been widely tapped. Would it be ironic or predictable that ChatGPT itself might be the entity that discovers universal systems to keep its own digital conduct in check? Binary system, heal thyself!

However this may occur, the most important priority is achieving or at least approaching shared goals to harness and direct AI searches that inform digital health theory and application with proper attribution and efficiency. The incentives for such global collaboration are well articulated in Dr. Dipu Patel's "10 Themes" in this volume's Introduction: expanding populations, healthcare worker shortages, data that inform medical research, new innovations, interdisciplinary teamwork, AI-powered diagnostics, "smart living", training, adding mental health to medical treatments, and impacting climate change. These are ideals worth defending and promoting.

One goal of this chapter has been to address questions whether ChatGPT is a scholarly friend or foe. The correct answer seems, "Yes," or "Both"—ally with dutiful and ethical enforcements; scourge without.

Hence, a call to action: Let's build a Digital Health IRB!

References

[1] Mathews SC, McShea MJ, Hanley CL, Ravitz A, Labrique AB, Cohen AB. Digital health: a path to validation. Npj Digital Medicine 2019;2(1). https://doi.org/10.1038/s41746-019-0111-3.

[2] Abernethy A, Adams L, Barrett M, Bechtel C, Brennan P, Butte A, Faulkner J, Fontaine E, Friedhoff S, Halamka J, Howell M, Johnson K, Long P, McGraw D, Miller R, Lee P, Perlin J, Rucker D, Sandy L, Savage L, Stump L, Tang P, Topol E, Tuckson R, Valdes K. The promise of digital health: then, now, and the future. NAM Perspectives 2022;6(22). https://doi.org/10.31478/202206e.

[3] Guo C, Ashrafian H, Ghafur S, Fontana G, Gardner C, Prime M. Challenges for the evaluation of digital health solutions—a call for innovative evidence generation approaches. Npj Digital Medicine 2020;3(1). https://doi.org/10.1038/s41746-020-00314-2.

[4] Shah SS, Gvozdanovic A. Digital health; what do we mean by clinical validation? Expert Review of Medical Devices 2021;18(1):5−8. https://doi.org/10.1080/17434440.2021.2012447.

[5] Fagherazzi G, Goetzinger C, Rashid MA, Aguayo GA, Huiart L. Digital health strategies to fight COVID-19 worldwide: challenges, recommendations, and a call for papers. Journal of Medical Internet Research 2020;22(6). https://doi.org/10.2196/19284.

[6] Ellis RB, Wright J, Miller LS, Jake-Schoffman D, Hekler EB, Goldstein CM, Arigo D, Nebeker C. Lessons learned: beta-testing the digital health checklist for researchers prompts a call to action by behavioral scientists. Journal of Medical Internet Research 2021;23(12). https://doi.org/10.2196/25414.

[7] Nebeker C, Ellis RJB, Behavioral Informatics and Technology SIG. Making responsible choices in digital health research. Society of Behavioral Medicine 2023;2023.

[8] Hu K. "ChatGPT sets record for fastest growing user base − analyst note," Reuters, February 1, 2023. In: comparison, TikTok required nine months and Instagram 2-1/2 years (citing Sensor Tower); 2023.

[9] Oxford English Dictionary; cited in Forbes. Press, Gil (Sr. Contributor). A Very Short History of Big Data 2013. https://www.forbes.com/sites/gilpress/2013/05/09/a-very-short-history-of-big-data/?sh=7d0778 7965a1.

[10] Cox M, Ellsworth D. Application-controlled demand paging for out-of-core visualization. In: Proceedings of the IEEE 8th conference on visualization, 1997; 1997.

[11] Swaak T. First came ChatGPT. Then came the over-the-top sales pitches. The Chronicle 2023. https://www.chronicle.com/article/first-came-chatgpt-then-came-the-over-the-top-sales-pitches.

[12] Christine G. National library of medicine. 2015. https://www.ncbi.nlm.nih.gov/pmc/articles/PMC4631034/#:~:text=Institutional%20review%20boards%20(IRBs)%20or,of%20proposals%20for%20human%20research.

[13] Moon M. The history and role of institutional review boards: a useful tension. AMA Journal of Ethics 2009. https://journalofethics.ama-assn.org/article/history-and-role-institutional-review-boards-useful-tension/2009-04.

[14] UTHealth Houston. (2008 to present). https://www.uth.edu/cphs/for-researchers/history-of-irb.htm .

[15] Ryan KJ, et al. National commission for the protection of human subjects of biomedical and behavioral research. 1979. https://www.hhs.gov/ohrp/regulations-and-policy/belmont-report/read-the-belmont-report/index.html.

[16] McCarthy C, Grady C. The origins and policies that govern institutional review boards. In: Emanuel E, Grady C, Crouch R, Lie R, Miller F, Wendler D, editors. The Oxford textbook of clinical research ethics. New York, NY: Oxford University Press; 2008. p. 541−50. https://www.ncbi.nlm.nih.gov/pmc/articles/PMC4631034/.

CHAPTER 25

Healthcare, trials, and digital impact

Samarth Kashyap[1] and Shambhavi Singh[2]

[1]DS Digital Consulting, Digital Evolution and Implementation, Delhi, India; [2]DS Digital Consulting, Digital Health and Research, Mumbai, Maharashtra, India

If any area of the healthcare industry was more directly impacted by the global pandemic and digital technology, it was clinical trials and studies. Both are integral components of drug development and approval.

Prepandemic, the industry began taking baby steps toward digital and patient-centric design with the concept of Hybrid Trials. With the advent of COVID-19 interfering with access to patients on-site, the entire industry and infrastructure were forced to pivot and expeditiously leverage the power of digital technology.

Trial design

As healthcare professionals, it's crucial to understand the significance of research trials in improving healthcare outcomes. They are systematic investigations that help us gather evidence, make informed decisions, and advance medical knowledge.

Study versus trial

Scientific study is a broad term encompassing any systematic examination or investigation aimed at generating new knowledge. A trial is a specific type of study that involves testing a particular intervention or treatment. Clinical trials, in particular, focus on evaluating the safety and efficacy of medical interventions in human subjects. They follow a structured protocol and often proceed through distinct phases before potential approval and widespread use of the intervention. So, while all clinical trials are studies, not all studies are trials.

Types of trials

Broadly, from an epidemiological perspective, study designs can be of two types: Observational (for hypothesis generation) and Experimental (for hypothesis testing).

Digital Health. https://doi.org/10.1016/B978-0-443-23901-4.00025-8

Observational studies can be descriptive and analytical. Examples include cross-sectional, case–control, cohort study, etc. **Experimental studies** involve an intervention that specifically examines the connection between exposure (risk) and outcome (disease/outcome), allowing researchers to make more definitive conclusions about causation/causal pathways. Examples include clinical trials, field trials, and community trials [1]. Each one has many other subtypes. The choice of trial design depends on multiple factors, like study objectives, characteristics of the disease of interest, timeframe, ethical considerations, resources at disposal, etc.

Gathering evidence in medical science is a rigorous process that goes through multiple stages. Each stage has an objective and serves a different purpose in the ladder of evidence generation. Progression to the next level requires a thorough evaluation of the evidence's quality and reliability at the current stage and adherence to established research methodologies and ethical standards. Various tiers of evidence generation can be delineated in a hierarchy, beginning with Expert opinion at one end and progressing upwards through case reports, case–control studies, cohort studies, Randomized Controlled Trials (RCT), critically appraised topics, systematic reviews, culminating with meta-analysis at the top.

Clinical trial

Clinical trials or Interventional trials are done to test new drugs, treatment regimens, drug dosages, procedures, biological products, medical devices, behaviors, preventive care, etc [2]. The purpose is the assessment of efficacy, safety, or risk–benefit ratio while the overall goal may be to establish superiority, noninferiority, or equivalence [3]. These trials prospectively assign human participants or their groups to health-related interventions and evaluate their effects on health outcomes.

Broadly, clinical trials can be categorized as uncontrolled (without a control arm) and controlled (with a control arm/s). The former could be used for Phase I trials focusing on the understanding of pharmacokinetics of new drugs while latter are more commonly used in advanced phases. Controlled trials are used to distinguish between a participant outcome due to intervention from the outcome caused due to other factors. Control plays an important role and must be defined carefully. These can be a placebo (when no effective treatment exists), active treatment (when comparing a new drug to the standard available), dose comparison (when comparing different doses of the same drug), or "no-treatment" (when testing against no treatment) [3].

Phases in clinical trial

The journey of drug discovery comprises several crucial stages, each one rigorously designed and serving a specific purpose. The first stage starts with testing new molecular compounds, followed by animal testing. Stage three comprises of clinical trials (described below) followed by United States Food and Drug Administration (FDA) review to ensure safety for marketing of the drug. The final stage involves postmarketing monitoring conducted over several years to adjust the dose and frequency of the drug [4].

Clinical trials have the following phases:

1. **Phase I (Safety)**. Involves 20–100 healthy volunteers and test new drugs, and their dosage and identify any side effects.
2. **Phase II (Effectiveness)**. Involves 100–300 patients (with disease of interest) and studies efficacy and side effects of the drug.
3. **Phase III (Generalizability)**. Involves 300–3000 patients and studies efficacy and side effects with larger populations to achieve generalizability of the drug.
4. **Phase IV (Surveillance)**. Involves several thousand people with disease of interest and conducted once FDA approvals are received and done for testing over longer time-frames in population at large [5].

Public health trials

These are done only after the intervention of interest has passed the laboratory's test safety and dosage measures are under acceptable ranges for larger populations. The purpose is to test the efficacy and effectiveness in community settings or real-world scenarios. Whatever the intervention, for a public health trial to be conducted, it requires prior evidence of noninferiority to the standard available to be able to recommend it in community settings for testing.

Sponsor, clinical research organizations, and participant

Conducting clinical trials involves multiple stakeholders. The three key ones are Sponsors, Clinical Research Organizations (CROs), and Participants.

Sponsors

Sponsors are typically organizations or entities that initiate, manage, and finance clinical trials. They can transfer any or all of their trial-related duties to a CRO, but the final responsibility for the quality and integrity of the trial always resides with the sponsor. According to guidelines for Good Clinical Practices (GCP) 2023, the sponsor is generally responsible for selection of investigators, monitoring progress of trial as per protocol, monitoring safety, maintaining records and reports, etc. [6].

Clinical research organizations (CROs)

CROs are independent entities contracted by sponsors to assist in various aspects of conducting clinical trials. They provide expertise in study design, site selection, data management, and regulatory compliance, as outlined in GCP guidelines. These days, many CROs provide complete clinical trial management support including creating protocols for conducting site feasibility, project management, and medical monitoring services.

Participants

They encompass a diverse group of individuals who voluntarily enroll in clinical research studies. The involvement of participants varies based on the type and phase of the trial and their recruitment, privacy, and safety are guided by the International Council For Harmonization Of Technical Requirements For Pharmaceuticals For Human Use (ICH) GCP guidelines.

Types of participants

- **Healthy Volunteers**: Studies, often in Phase 1 trials, involve healthy individuals. These focus on safety, dosing, and side effects.
- **Patients**: Trials in later phases, such as Phase 2 and Phase 3, include patients with the target medical condition to assess treatment safety and efficacy.
- **Vulnerable Populations**: Some trials encompass vulnerable populations like children, the elderly, pregnant women, or those with cognitive impairments to cater to the specific needs of these groups. Special protections are in place to ensure their rights and welfare.
- **Specific Demographics**: Researchers may seek participants from specific demographic groups, such as gender, race, or ethnicity, to assess treatment responses across diverse populations to ensure that the benefits of the medicine are distributed more equitably and to enhance the generalizability of the results [4].

Ensuring that participants understand the purpose of the study, procedures, risks, and benefits is imperative before they enroll in the trial. Informed Consent (written, verbal through audio or video) is a mandatory step and is done early on while inviting participants. If the study involves children or those below 18 years of age, seeking consent from their parents or legal guardians followed by assent from the participant is essential.

Bias

A tendency that can lead to unprejudiced consideration is a bias. In research, it can be a systematic error that can be introduced at any stage of the study (study design, data collection, or analysis) [1]. They can be of several types. An example is selection bias (participants are not representative of the target population). Biases cannot be eliminated but measures can be taken to minimize them. For example, randomization and blinding techniques in study design can help reduce selection bias. Ensuring a well-defined study protocol and employing standardized data collection methods reduces the risk of information bias. Additionally, careful statistical analysis and control for potential confounding variables can help address confounding bias. Transparency in reporting research methods and findings also aids in bias reduction.

Institutional review board (IRB) and protocol

All trials should be reviewed by an ethics committee/review board to ensure that the appropriate ethical standards are being upheld. This ethical oversight is particularly vital in today's clinical research landscape, where digital technology plays a big role. It helps ensure that issues such as safeguarding data privacy, obtaining informed consent online, and making sure algorithms are fair are given the attention they deserve.

As per FDA guidelines, an Institutional Review Board (IRB) is a formally designated group responsible for assessing and overseeing biomedical research involving human participants. An IRB holds the power to grant approval, request necessary adjustments (for approval assurance), or reject research proposals. This evaluation plays a crucial role in safeguarding the rights and well-being of individuals participating in research. IRBs must adapt their review processes to assess the unique ethical considerations associated with data collection, storage, and sharing in the digital realm. Moreover, they must scrutinize data security measures, compliance with FDA regulations, and equitable access to digital interventions. Ethical considerations in biomedical and clinical research are not mere formalities, they are the moral compass that guides the entire research process and are based on the principles of beneficence, justice, and autonomy.

A protocol is a detailed action plan for conducting clinical research. It is a blueprint that the research team must follow to ensure research integrity, minimize the potential for bias, and enhance the validity and reliability of the study [7]. According to ICH Good Clinical Practice guidelines (2023), the key elements that a protocol must include are rationale and significance, study objectives and its design, selection and exclusion of participants, data collection and record keeping, adverse events and discontinuation, quality control and assurance, ethical considerations, timelines, and publication plan [6].

On-site, hybrid, and decentralized clinical trials (DCTs)

Clinical trials have evolved into three distinct approaches: On-Site, Hybrid, and Decentralized Clinical Trials (DCTs), each offering unique advantages and challenges. On-site trials, the traditional model, maintain strict control over data quality but can be geographically limiting and demanding for patients. Hybrid trials blend on-site and remote elements, offering increased flexibility and broader patient recruitment while still requiring some physical visits. Decentralized trials minimize or sometimes eliminate the need for physical sites, leveraging technology for remote recruitment, consent, monitoring, and data collection, enabling wider patient recruitment and real-world data collection. The choice among these approaches hinges on factors such as the nature of the trial, patient demographics, regulatory requirements, budget, and available technology. With advancements in digital health technology, decentralized trials are gaining momentum. While traditional on-site trials continue to play a vital role when precise control is essential, hybrid trials provide a middle ground for many research scenarios.

Data privacy

Data privacy for participants is an integral and essential aspect of clinical research. Regulatory frameworks like HIPAA (Health Insurance Portability and Accountability Act) in the United States and GDPR (General Data Protection Regulation) in Europe are in place to safeguard the privacy of clinical trial or study participants. HIPAA, specifically, imposes stringent requirements on healthcare organizations and their associates, mandating compliance with its key components, including the Privacy Rule (standards for the protection of individuals' medical records and personal health information), Security Rule (mandates safeguards for the electronic storage and transmission of health data), and Breach Notification Rule (outlines requirements for reporting data breaches) through routine technical and nontechnical assessments. These regulatory measures underscore the critical importance of protecting participant data throughout the course of clinical research.

Digitization of trials

The practice of medicine has evolved over the past few years with the onset and application of Electronic Health Records, medical devices, and various Wearable IoT devices (e.g., Garmin Watch Apple watch, etc.), which allow tracking health vitals and other records easily and swiftly. The impact of digital advancements on the Clinical and Public health trials has been tremendous from induction, recruitment, and enrollment to intervention via robust and fast data collection. As the technological boundaries are pushed, newer methods and processes are being defined to make the platforms seamless.

Electronic records

Electronic health record (EHR) versus electronic medical record (EMR)

EMR is a digital version of paper charts that are typically maintained by a single care provider/Clinician's office. They can contain lab results, allergies, demographic information, medications/vaccines, visits, etc.

EHR is a patient's medical history inclusive of a broader view of a patient's care. EHRs can be shared between multiple healthcare providers, laboratories, or specialists. Hence, it contains information from all the clinicians involved in the patient's care.

The main difference between EHR and EMR is that EHRs are maintained by multiple care providers while EMRs aren't. Hence, making EHR interoperable between multiple caregivers; giving them complete access to patient's medical history [8].

Electronic trial records

Electronic source data (eSource)

During a trial or public health research, any Electronics Source Data (eSource) is defined as any combination of text, graphics, data, audio, pictorial, or other information represented in digital form that is created, modified, maintained, archived, retrieved, or distributed by a computer system per The United States Food and Drug Administration (FDA). They include information in original records and certified copies of original records of clinical findings, observations, or other activities captured prior to or during a clinical investigation used for reconstructing and evaluating the investigation. There are multiple ranges of ways eSource can be captured—Electronic Diaries, Digital Devices, Sensors/Wearables etc. As the data are electronic in nature, it allows researchers to have high consistency and legitimacy to the collected data thereby reducing the risk of submission errors.

Clinical outcome assessment (COA) and electronic patient reported outcomes (ePRO)

The FDA defines a clinical outcome assessment (COA) as a measure that describes or reflects how a patient feels, functions, or survives. There are various types of COAs depending upon the person reporting the patients' symptoms (Observers, Clinicians, or Patients/Participants).

Trial participants can use digital devices like tablets or Smartphones to answer designed surveys and provide reports through an app or other electronic platform then the reported outcomes are called ePRO. Since the data directly come from the participant/patient, this allows better reliability than otherwise provided by paper forms.

Electronic data capture (EDC)

EDCs are a type of Web platforms/Mobile apps/tools typically implemented by trial Sponsors/CROs/Sites for participants to collect trial data. They collect key data needed for analysis and reporting. EDCs are usually very efficient in maintaining much cleaner data than paper forms, they have various validation checks programmed in place to ensure data meets its minimum desired requirements. This also allows for greater organization and higher compliance of the data.

EDC is typically owned by the sponsors and is a subset of eSource as it does not collect Protected Health Information (Patient) of the patient. ePRO is considered another type of eSource; while eSource is collected by the researchers ePRO is generated by participants directly [9].

Wearables and IoT for data collection

In recent years, we have seen an extensive increase in the use of wearables. Wearables act as sensors and EDC platforms act as Software applications on digital devices that can collect data remotely. They come in a wide variety, some are worn either as wristbands/headbands which collect actigraphy, blood pressure, heart rate, and electromyography while others are applied as skin patches or as a form of clothing to monitor ECG or skin temperature. As wearables can be worn throughout the day, it is a big step forward to traditional means of data collection, especially in vital signs and telemetry. These also provide objective measures over subjectively reported outcomes such as pain/fatigue [10]. Sleep studies have benefitted tremendously from wrist-worn actigraphy devices [11].

Wearables have proved to be a boon for the safety monitoring of patients to detect early alarms, dose, and frequency adjustments or drugs under discovery. Though there is promising potential for wearable devices, the major impact has yet to be realized. The reasons behind the lack of transformation include scientific, regulatory, ethical, legal, data management, and security challenges [12].

Cybersecurity

When discussing digital clinical trials, one of the biggest items of concern is the safety and security of the patient data. Since a lot of sensitive PHI and other patient data are collected and stored, cybersecurity is one of the biggest aspects that one must consider when setting up a trial in addition to regulatory standards such as the Health Insurance Portability and Accountability Act (HIPAA), General Data Protection Regulation (GDPR), etc. Encrypted storage, data backups, controlled access, and regular reviews are some common steps employed by trial teams to ensure data integrity, privacy, and regulatory standards. The National Institute of Standards and Technology (NIST) Cybersecurity Framework is one of the most popular approaches to establishing these measures in a flexible and cost-effective manner [13].

The NIST Cybersecurity Framework helps in identifying, preventing, and mitigating cybersecurity incidents and attacks [13]. Due to its flexible and cost-effective approach, it is one of the most commonly used frameworks. The NIST framework consists of five primary steps [13]:

- Identify the resources and elements that need to be protected from potential cybersecurity attacks
- Protect these at-risk resources by applying appropriate safeguards

- Detect any cybersecurity incidents or attacks via regular reviews
- Respond swiftly and accurately to contain the impact of the incident
- Recover from the incident and restore capabilities and services

Moreover, in response to the dynamic cybersecurity landscape, trial teams are exploring innovative solutions. Technologies such as blockchain, with its decentralized and tamper-resistant nature, provide an additional layer of security and transparency in managing clinical trial data. Artificial intelligence (AI) and machine learning (ML) are leveraged for predictive threat analysis and real-time monitoring, allowing for the proactive identification of potential security breaches.

As the digital transformation of clinical trials continues, the commitment to cybersecurity remains paramount. Integrating traditional best practices with cutting-edge technologies ensures that clinical trials not only meet but exceed the highest standards of data protection, privacy, and regulatory compliance. This proactive and adaptive approach is essential to safeguarding the integrity of clinical trial data in an ever-evolving cybersecurity landscape.

Data lake

While managing Trial data, Real-World Data (RWD) are used to generate Real-World Evidence (RWE) as evidence of a medical product's safety and efficacy. With digitization, the world has transformed how Clinical Trials are conducted. Ever-growing expanse of the EHR and other patient monitoring, data are available in multiple formats or sizes. Data lakes aim to adopt a structural architecture to house these Big Data and allow collection of data from multiple heterogeneous sources thereby employing a pivotal role.

In an ecosystem of Data Lake for Sponsors, this approach allows for the democratization of access to data, ensures transparency, and allows the entire organization to use one authoritative data source without being bogged down by the format it was initially collected. For such data lakes, Metadata (data about data) managers can routinely review external standards and update the internal metadata as necessary. The scalability of data is tremendous; Machine Learning capabilities are further enhanced to forecast outcomes or predict a range of prescribed actions. A comprehensive analysis can be performed by researchers upon combining similar datasets of multiple studies [14].

Digital players

With the ever-evolving digital world, there have been significant players over the recent years, here are some of the bests in the industry.

Medable

Medable's mission is to get effective therapies to patients faster by providing an end-to-end, global cloud platform with a flexible suite of tools that allows sponsors, patients, providers, and contract research organizations to work together as a team in clinical trials. Medable's solutions enable more efficient clinical research, more effective healthcare delivery, and more accurate precision and predictive medicine. Medable's clinical assessment phase promotes the provision of healthcare services directly to patients by facilitating clinical applications and securely storing individuals' personal health information for use by healthcare providers and researchers. Additionally, developers can employ the platform to enhance or develop applications for use on mobile devices, tablets, and desktop computers [15].

Medidata

Medidata offers essential functionalities of an Electronic Health Record (EHR) system, allowing the storage of patients' medical records. It encompasses four distinct account types: patient, physician, pathologist, and pharmacist. Furthermore, this system extends its capabilities by providing additional features, including pharmacy searches within a specified area, locating doctors in a given region, and identifying local pathologists. Users can also book doctor appointments, request home visits from physicians, and verify medical practitioners. Medidata serves various purposes, primarily focusing on the secure storage of crucial medical data. Safeguarding such data is of paramount importance, as it not only ensures security but also facilitates accessibility from any location and at any time for future use [16].

Thread

It is a leading decentralized clinical trials technology and consulting service provider, helping biopharma and CROs decentralize clinical research and enable eCOA for sites, participants, caregivers, and home health professionals [17]. Through its unified platform, THREAD is making studies 30% more efficient and five times more inclusive and diverse. Sponsors and CROs can remotely capture data from participants and sites during, in-between, and in-clinic visits. Through its comprehensive platform and scientific expertise, THREAD supports studies to be patient-centered, accessible, and efficient.

Science 37

Science 37 proprietary unified platform Metasite is transforming clinical research by enabling patients to participate in trials from the comfort of their homes [18]. It delivers trial orchestration and data capture in a single, end-to-end platform that guides the workflow for patients and study staff and electronically captures study data. The platform enables eConsent, ePRO, telemedicine, scheduling, and wearable/device integration to deliver clinical trials directly to patients, wherever they are. The result is consistent user journeys, greater compliance, and high-quality data. The platform has in-house medical and operational experts who drive uniform study orchestration, enabling greater compliance and high-quality data. From enrollment through to study completion, the patient follows intuitive, app-based processes using their everyday mobile devices or provisioned devices [18].

Data are king! benefits of digital health tools in clinical trials or studies

Digital health tools use has seen exponential growth in the last few years, especially around the COVID-19 pandemic with companies using Digital health technologies to switch to decentralized clinical trials. The availability of various devices, implantable, ingestible, wearable, and sensors and information technology and computing platforms help in getting data directly from patients. Portable tools such as implanted or worn collect real-time data from remote locations that are away from clinical study sites.

Evolution of digital health tools in clinical trials

Pre-20th century, operational challenges such as identifying, recruiting, acquiring data, and follow-ups drive up the trial cost and timelines along with increasing burden on enrolled participants (distance from the clinical site and other constraints). All this resulted in low participation. However, now with Digital tools, the whole process has become less cumbersome and patient data can be collected from any location as they continue with their day today lives. This new era of DHT-generated data can allow for digital phenotyping, i.e., the quantification of individual patients using multimodal data from personal digital devices [19].

The adoption of telemedicine as a tool has benefitted the clinical trial industry and played a big role in streamlining the trial process and easing the participant onboarding from across geographies by including features like remote consenting, video/remote assessment, etc. The telemedicine platforms also support remote patient monitoring and management. Remote patient monitoring (RPM) is a type of telehealth in which healthcare providers monitor patients outside the traditional care setting using digital medical devices, such as weight scales, blood pressure monitors, pulse oximeters, and blood glucose meters. The data collected from these devices are then electronically transferred to the clinical trial team.

Currently, Digital tools are being used through various stages of drug development like computer-aided drug design, computational modeling for predictive toxicology, and big data analytics for clinical trial management.

Masanneck et al. analyzed the evolution of the use of DHTs in trials registered on ClinicalTrials.gov for four chronic neurological disorders: epilepsy, multiple sclerosis, Alzheimer's disease, and Parkinson's disease [20]. They found that the relative frequency of clinical trials using DHTs increased from 0.7% in 2010 to 11.4% in 2020 [20].

Digital trials are changing how clinical trials are carried out by successfully managing them with the least resources to achieve timely and cost-effective completion of clinical studies. Regulatory organizations such as the FDA, Health Canada, and others are pressing sponsors to digitize their clinical trials by providing several guidelines for specific digital tools and data security.

Technical consideration for using digital tools in clinical trials

Measurements, verification, and validation are used to assess the technical features of digital tools [21]. For Data captured through DHT, it is necessary to clearly understand and standardize the software and hardware specifications.

The U.S. Food and Drug Administration (FDA) 2021 draft guidance on "Digital Health Technologies for Remote Data Acquisition in Clinical Investigations" makes recommendations on endpoint collection using digital tools, validation, and verification of the tools in trials [22].

Benefit of digital health tools in clinical trials

Clinical trials are usually lengthy, costly, and have lots of complexities. The use of digital tools leads to cost reductions, less complex processes, and reduced overall burden.

For patients, they can bring down the pressure of trial participation including reduced time and travel costs and hassle-free onboarding. They also automate the data collection along with maintaining its quality.

According to the FDA other potential advantages of these DHTs include the ability to [23]:

- make continuous or frequent measurements of clinical features.
- record or measure novel clinical features that could not be captured during traditional study visits.
- decentralize clinical trial activities by obtaining clinical data from study participants remotely.

Challenges to data security

Data Privacy—with the increasing use of digital tools in the trials data privacy poses one of the biggest challenges. Identifiable patient data such as GPS/location data, may expose trial participants to legal action and financial damage as a result of social stigma.

Authentication and data reliability—virtual trials collecting data remotely face authentication challenges, e.g., wearables can be worn by a person other than the participant compromising the validity of the data collected. The data quality poses another challenge that impacts data reliability in real-world settings e.g., artifacts can be derived from the environment (e.g., increased temperature sensing when the device is worn under a blanket), the device itself, or from the patient (e.g., improperly worn devices) [24].

The near future—AI/ML in clinical trials

Developments in technology are fostering the creation of new forms of AI/ML and the field of medicine and healthcare research is no longer an exception, with AI tools rapidly being explored from laboratory to clinical trials. Clinical trials allow drug testing and medical interventions on humans and are thus considered a gold standard for the development of safe and effective medications. Despite this fact, they are not without challenges as they involve high investments, lengthy timelines, complex protocols, data quality, data sharing, monitoring issues, and many more [25].

Use cases of AI/ML in the clinical trials

Patient recruitment and eligibility screening

The integration of AI technologies in patient recruitment and eligibility screening brings a transformative impact. Employing sophisticated algorithms, AI scrutinizes electronic health records (EHRs), medical histories, and genetic profiles to pinpoint individuals who align with the specific criteria of clinical trials. Additionally, Natural Language Processing (NLP) delves into unstructured clinical notes, extracting pertinent information to further refine participant eligibility. This automated approach not only significantly trims down the time and costs traditionally associated with manual screening but also contributes to the cultivation of a more diverse and well-suited participant pool, fostering efficiency and inclusivity in the clinical trial process.

Predictive analytics for trial outcomes

In the domain of predictive analytics for trial outcomes, the application of machine learning (ML) proves instrumental. ML models meticulously dissect historical clinical trial data, incorporating diverse elements such as biomarkers, patient demographics, and trial characteristics. Through this comprehensive analysis, predictive models emerge, offering a valuable tool to estimate the probability of success or failure for a new trial. This predictive capability plays a pivotal role in informed decision-making processes related to investment strategies and resource allocation, empowering stakeholders with insights that enhance the overall efficacy and strategic planning of clinical trials.

Optimizing trial design

When it comes to optimizing trial design, Machine Learning (ML) algorithms wield their analytical prowess to scrutinize extensive datasets. This meticulous analysis allows these algorithms to discern the most suitable trial parameters, encompassing factors like dosages, patient demographics, and trial duration. The outcome of this optimization is profound, steering clinical trials toward more efficient trajectories Optimized trial designs not only facilitate faster results but also yield substantial cost savings. By honing in on the most effective parameters, ML-driven optimization in trial design stands as a catalyst for enhanced study efficiency, streamlining processes, and contributing to the overall success of clinical trials.

Data quality and integrity assurance

In the critical aspect of data quality and integrity assurance, Artificial Intelligence (AI) algorithms play a pivotal role. These sophisticated algorithms are adept at discerning inconsistencies, errors, and potential instances of fraud within clinical trial datasets. The implementation of AI in this capacity serves as a robust safeguard, ensuring the reliability and integrity of the data at every stage of a clinical trial. This reliability is paramount for regulatory compliance, adhering to stringent standards set by authorities such as the FDA, and is equally vital for informed decision-making by stakeholders involved in the trial. By fortifying data quality and integrity, AI contributes significantly to the credibility and success of clinical trials.

Drug safety monitoring

For drug safety monitoring, Artificial Intelligence (AI) systems play a crucial role by continuously scrutinizing patient data. Through meticulous analysis, these AI systems are adept at detecting adverse events, safety concerns, and unexpected side effects that may arise during the course of a clinical trial. The real-time monitoring capabilities of AI empower swift identification of safety issues, enabling timely intervention and effective risk mitigation strategies. By providing an early warning system for potential safety concerns, AI contributes significantly to ensuring the well-being of trial participants and bolsters the overall safety and integrity of the clinical trial process.

Drug discovery and target identification

In the dynamic landscape of drug discovery and target identification, Artificial Intelligence (AI) emerges as a transformative force. Leveraging its analytical capabilities, AI delves into genetic, genomic, and proteomic data to discern potential drug candidates and therapeutic targets. This comprehensive analysis accelerates the traditionally time-intensive drug discovery process by efficiently identifying promising compounds and elucidating mechanisms of action. By navigating vast datasets with speed and precision, AI becomes an invaluable tool in the quest for innovative pharmaceuticals, contributing to the expedited identification of viable candidates and streamlining the early stages of drug development. The integration of AI in drug discovery endeavors marks a paradigm shift, promising greater efficiency and success in the quest for novel therapeutic interventions.

Challenges and limitations of AI/ML implementation

Data privacy and security concerns

Data Sensitivity: Clinical trial data, including patient health records and genomic information, are highly sensitive and subject to strict privacy regulations such as HIPAA (Health Insurance Portability and Accountability Act) in the United States. AI/ML systems require access to this sensitive data, raising concerns about unauthorized access, data breaches, and patient privacy violations.

Interoperability and data integration

Heterogeneous Data Sources: Clinical trial data are often sourced from various platforms, including electronic health records (EHRs), wearables, and lab equipment, which may use different data formats and standards. Integrating and harmonizing these diverse data sources for AI/ML analysis can be challenging and time-consuming.

Regulatory and compliance challenges

Regulatory Approval: Getting regulatory approval for AI/ML algorithms in clinical trials can be a complex process. Regulators like the FDA (U.S. Food and Drug Administration) require thorough validation and documentation of AI/ML models, which can slow down trial timelines.

Ethical and Legal Considerations: Ethical issues, such as informed consent for AI-driven interventions or the need for human oversight, can pose challenges. Legal liabilities in case of algorithmic errors or adverse events are also areas of concern.

Bias and fairness issues

Data Bias: AI/ML models can inherit biases present in the training data. If historical clinical data contains biases related to gender, race, or socioeconomic factors, these biases can perpetuate and lead to unfair treatment recommendations in clinical trials.

Fairness Concerns: Ensuring that AI/ML algorithms provide fair and equitable treatment recommendations is an ongoing challenge. Researchers need to carefully assess and mitigate bias to prevent unjust disparities in clinical trial outcomes.

Addressing these disadvantages requires a comprehensive approach that includes robust data governance, strong security measures, regulatory compliance, transparency in AI/ML models, and ongoing efforts to mitigate bias and ensure fairness in clinical trial processes [1].

References

[1] Chidambaram AG, Josephson M. Clinical research study designs: the essentials. Pediatric Investigation 2019;3(4):245–52. https://doi.org/10.1002/ped4.1216.

[2] Clinical Trials. Newsroom. Questions and answers. World Health Organization; 2020. www.who.int. https://www.who.int/news-room/questions-and-answers/item/clinical-trials.

[3] Nair B. Clinical trial designs. Indian Dermatology Online Journal 2019;10(2):193. https://doi.org/10.4103/idoj.idoj_475_18.

[4] FDA. The drug development process. U.S. Food and Drug Administration; January 4, 2018. https://www.fda.gov/patients/learn-about-drug-and-device-approvals/drug-development-process.

[5] Bowen M, et al. A beginner's guide to the clinical research organization. 2015.

[6] International council for harmonisation of technical requirements for pharmaceuticals for human use ICH harmonised guideline good clinical practice (GCP) E6(R3). 2023. https://database.ich.org/sites/default/files/ICH_E6%28R3%29_DraftGuideline_2023_0519.pdf.

[7] Al-Jundi A, Sakka S. Protocol writing in clinical research. Journal of Clinical and Diagnostic Research January 1, 2016;10(11):ZE10. https://doi.org/10.7860/jcdr/2016/21426.8865.

[8] Garrett P, Seidman J. EMR vs EHR – What is the difference? Healthit.gov. January 4, 2011. https://www.healthit.gov/buzz-blog/electronic-health-and-medical-records/emr-vs-ehr-difference.

[9] Hosely M. Understanding eSource, ePRO, and EDC. Advarra; August 25, 2021. https://www.advarra.com/blog/understanding-esource-epro-and-edc/.

[10] U.S. Department of Health and Human Services. Guidance for industry patient-reported outcome measures: use in medical product development to support labeling claims. Food and Drug Administration (FDA) 2009;(Dec 2009):7–8. Available at: https://www.fda.gov/media/77832/download.

[11] Izmailova ES, Wagner JA, Perakslis ED. Wearable devices in clinical trials: hype and hypothesis. Clinical Pharmacology and Therapeutics 2018;104(1):42–52. https://doi.org/10.1002/cpt.966.

[12] Guidance for industry electronic source data in clinical investigations. 2013. https://www.fda.gov/media/85183/download.

[13] Standards | NIST. NIST. June 30, 2016. https://www.nist.gov/standards.

[14] Cappiello C, Gribaudo M, Plebani P, Salnitri M, Tanca L. Enabling real-world medicine with Data Lake Federation: a research perspective. Lecture Notes in Computer Science January 1, 2022:39–56. https://doi.org/10.1007/978-3-031-23905-2_4.

[15] Faridi F, Sarwar H, Ahtisham kumar S, Jamal K. Cloud computing approaches in health care. Materials Today: Proceedings 2022;51:1217–23. https://doi.org/10.1016/j.matpr.2021.07.210.

[16] Choudhary R, Marodkar M, Chaoji K, et al. Implementation on Online Health System (MediData), EHR System with Additional Features. International Journal of Trend in Research and Development 2024;5(2):2394–9333. https://www.ijtrd.com/papers/IJTRD16301.pdf.

[17] THREAD. Decentralized clinical trial and eCOA platform. 2024. https://www.threadresearch.com/.

[18] Science 37 Wins 2023 MedTech Breakthrough Award for "Best Overall Clinical Trial Platform." Science37.com 2023. https://www.science37.com/science-37-wins-2023-medtech-breakthrough-award-best-overall-clinical-trial-platform.

[19] Torous J, Kiang MV, Lorme J, Jukka-Pekka O. New tools for new research in psychiatry: a scalable and customizable platform to empower data driven smartphone research. JMIR Mental Health 2016;3(2):e16. https://doi.org/10.2196/mental.5165.

[20] Masanneck L, Gieseler P, Gordon WJ, Meuth SG, Stern AD. Evidence from ClinicalTrials.gov on the growth of digital health technologies in neurology trials. Npj Digital Medicine 2023;6(1). https://doi.org/10.1038/s41746-023-00767-1.

[21] Coravos A, Khozin S, Mandl KD. Developing and adopting safe and effective digital biomarkers to improve patient outcomes. Npj Digital Medicine 2019;2(1). https://doi.org/10.1038/s41746-019-0090-4.

[22] Digital Health Technologies for Remote Data Acquisition in Clinical Investigations Guidance for Industry, Investigators, and Other Stakeholders DRAFT GUIDANCE. https://www.fda.gov/media/155022/download.

[23] Center. Digital health technologies. U.S. Food and Drug Administration; 2023. https://www.fda.gov/science-research/science-and-research-special-topics/digital-health-technologies-dhts-drug-development.

[24] Böttcher S, Vieluf S, Bruno E, et al. Data quality evaluation in wearable monitoring. Scientific Reports 2022;12(1). https://doi.org/10.1038/s41598-022-25949-x.

[25] Singh S, Loke YK. Drug safety assessment in clinical trials: methodological challenges and opportunities. Trials 2012;13(1). https://doi.org/10.1186/1745-6215-13-138.

CHAPTER 26

The future of digital health

Arta Bakshandeh[1,2,3]

[1]Alignment Health, Orange, CA, United States; [2]USC Keck School of Medicine, Los Angeles, CA, United States; [3]Global Physicians Corps, CA, United States

As we stand at the cusp of a new era, the landscape of medicine is undergoing a paradigm shift unparalleled in history, steering rapidly toward an epoch defined by the seamless integration of technology and healthcare. By 2100, digital medicine is poised to redefine our very understanding of health and wellness, revolutionizing diagnostics, treatment, and even the fabric of life itself. This assumes that artificial general intelligence, otherwise known as human intelligence, mimicked by a machine, is still a fantasy. In this chapter, we delve into the fascinating realm of futuristic digital medicine, envisioning a world where the boundaries between the physical and the virtual blur, where artificial intelligence synergizes with human ingenuity to birth unprecedented medical marvels, and where the digitalized nexus of healthcare promulgates a golden era of personalized, preventive, and precise medical interventions. As we journey into the heart of what the 22nd century has to offer, we shall unlock the visions and aspirations grounding the future of digital medicine, unfolding a tapestry of innovations that promises to elevate human health to uncharted echelons.

Envisioning the rapid evolution of medicine calls for a deep introspection of our journey thus far and the exponential growth trajectory we find ourselves on. If we look back nearly a century, the discovery of penicillin marked a pivotal milestone, heralding an era of antibiotics and drastically changing the landscape of medicine. Fast forward to today, we stand amid an era of relentless innovation fueled by the advent of artificial intelligence which has accelerated the rate at which medical knowledge doubles, now estimated to be every few years. This brisk pace of development makes predicting the medical landscape 75 years from writing this a complex yet exhilarating endeavor.

As we look toward the year 2100, it becomes increasingly apparent that we are venturing into uncharted territory, venturing further than we could have ever imagined a century ago. The integration of artificial intelligence in healthcare is not just a technological advancement; it is a revolution that promises to redefine the paradigms of medical science. It conjures a future where predictive analytics could preempt illnesses before they manifest, where treatment plans are tailored down to individual genetic makeups, and

Digital Health. https://doi.org/10.1016/B978-0-443-23901-4.00026-X

where digital avatars might guide individuals on personalized wellness journeys. Yet, amidst this whirlwind of advancements, lie intricate webs of ethical dilemmas, privacy concerns, and the ever-looming question of accessibility. As we navigate the exciting path of foresight, this chapter seeks not just to paint a picture of the marvels that await but to engage deeply with the nuanced tapestry of challenges and opportunities that pave the road to 2100, a journey toward a future echoing with the harmonious blend of technology and the human spirit, reaching for the pinnacle of health and wellbeing.

Artificial Intelligence (AI) and Machine Learning (ML)

As we look into the future of digital health, deep learning algorithms stand as one of the pivotal forces spearheading the revolution in the healthcare sector. These sophisticated algorithms have the innate ability to sift through massive datasets, identifying intricate patterns and anomalies that can often elude the human eye. For instance, predictive analytics harness large datasets to identify potential health risks before they become severe, guiding preventative healthcare into unprecedented territories of precision. In today's world, it is largely around chronic conditions like chronic kidney disease and the progression to dialysis or hospital admission risk. Other examples illustrate AI's promising capabilities in analyzing electronic health records (EHRs) to forecast the likelihood of chronic diseases such as diabetes or heart disease, thereby facilitating early interventions and perhaps, in the long run, alleviating healthcare systems from the burden of late-stage chronic disease management [1]. The future should be exciting, with the increased use of wearable technology streaming data and convolutional neural networks being able to capture vital signs with just seconds of video to analyze.

Beyond diagnostics, the realm of healthcare administration is witnessing a transformation with the integration of Natural Language Processing (NLP). NLP has come to play a pivotal role in automating a myriad of administrative tasks such as transcribing doctor—patient conversations, significantly improving efficiency, and reducing the administrative burden that often hampers healthcare delivery [2]. This, coupled with deep learning's foray into medical imaging, where it is employed to identify conditions from diabetic retinopathy to various forms of cancer with remarkable precision, signals a transformative era in healthcare. You can imagine a future where imaging is done in real-time from your own device, read by a computer vision model as normal and done or abnormal and sent to a radiologist for human confirmation. Large language models integrated into the patient population's longitudinal health record are found in unified data platforms without silos where patients can ask questions about their health and results with the precision of a medical doctor without ever interacting with another human.

Deep learning promises to foster methodologies and tools that are hyper-personalized to individual patient profiles, integrating and analyzing multidimensional data including genomics, proteomics, consumer information, EHRs, and more. These advancements promise a shift from a reactive healthcare system to a proactive one, grounded in preventative strategies and early interventions. Moreover, deep learning algorithms promise to open new avenues in real-time monitoring and just-in-time interventions using wearable and implantable devices, effectively extending healthcare beyond the confines of hospitals and clinics as eluded too before. Yet, the rapid pace of this transformation necessitates a vigilant eye on ethical considerations including data privacy and algorithmic fairness to ensure an inclusive, equitable, and human-centric healthcare future. A promising frontier in this regard is the exploration of federated learning, which ensures data privacy while facilitating algorithm training across decentralized devices, hinting at a future healthcare landscape that is both technologically advanced and grounded in ethical practices.

As we look into the future of digital health, deep learning algorithms stand as one of the pivotal forces spearheading the revolution in the healthcare sector. These sophisticated algorithms have the innate ability to sift through massive datasets, identifying intricate patterns and anomalies that can often elude the human eye. For instance, predictive analytics harness large datasets to identify potential health risks before they become severe, guiding preventative healthcare into unprecedented territories of precision. In today's world, models largely center around chronic conditions like chronic kidney disease and the progression to dialysis or hospital admission risk. Other examples illustrate AI's promising capabilities in analyzing electronic health records (EHRs) to forecast the likelihood of chronic diseases such as diabetes or heart disease well before disease onset, thereby facilitating early interventions and perhaps, in the long run, alleviating healthcare systems from the burden of late-stage chronic disease management [1]. With the integration of EHRs and the increased use of wearable technology, streaming data, and convolutional neural networks will be vital in capturing patient telemetry with just seconds of video to analyze.

Deep learning algorithms are the linchpin of this transformation, possessing the innate ability to unravel intricate patterns and anomalies within enormous datasets. These algorithms herald an age of predictive analytics that leverages the wellspring of personal health data—encompassing genetics, lifestyle, and environmental factors—to craft personalized health interventions. Individualized treatment plans can already be tailored to the unique genetic makeup of each person, setting the stage for more precise and effective therapies [3]. In introduction of genomics and proteomics as signals for deep learning exemplifies a monumental shift from a one-size-fits-all paradigm to a nuanced, tailored care model that is responsive to individual health narratives, thereby steering preventative healthcare into an era characterized by unprecedented precision [4].

Beyond diagnostics, the healthcare administration landscape is witnessing a seismic shift with the integration of Natural Language Processing (NLP). This technology has rapidly become indispensable, easing the administrative burden and enhancing efficiency by automating tasks such as the transcription of doctor–patient conversations [2]. Meanwhile, deep learning forays further into the medical imaging domain, where it has been employed to identify a spectrum of conditions with remarkable precision, from diabetic retinopathy to various forms of cancer.

Imagine a near future where healthcare transcends the conventional boundaries of hospitals and clinics. Picture a scenario where personalized medicine and tailored therapies are not just concepts, but everyday realities bolstered by wearable technology that continuously streams vital health data, enabling real-time monitoring and just-in-time interventions through convolutional neural networks. These networks have the potential to analyze complex datasets in mere seconds, paving the way for instantaneous feedback and immediate consultations with healthcare professionals. It is a future where individualized health data serves as the cornerstone, guiding medical imaging analyses carried out right from your personal device, offering a seamless and almost instantaneous interpretation of results.

As we look forward, deep learning promises a paradigm where tools and methodologies are hyper-personalized to individual patient profiles, weaving in a rich tapestry of multidimensional data including genomics, proteomics, and comprehensive consumer information. This landscape propels us from a reactive to a proactive healthcare model, grounded in preventative strategies and early interventions, leveraging the detailed insights from individual health data to craft treatment plans that are as unique as each individual's DNA.

Yet, with the immense potential comes the pressing need for vigilance, ensuring ethical considerations are at the forefront, encompassing data privacy and algorithmic fairness. This rapid evolution in healthcare beckons a future grounded in responsible innovation, fostering a healthcare landscape characterized by inclusivity, equity, and a patient-centric approach. Federated learning emerges as a promising frontier, offering a framework that ensures data privacy while fostering algorithm training across decentralized devices, promising a healthcare landscape that marries technological advancements with ethical foundations, guiding us toward a future where healthcare is not just a service, but a personalized experience, evolving continuously with each stride in technological advancement.

The symbiotic relationship between healthcare professionals and advancing technologies such as large language models and robotic process automation (RPA) is critical to the advancement of AI in healthcare and scaling practitioners by decreasing administrative tasks and allowing providers to practice medicine again. Automation technologies stand primed to shoulder routine tasks, substantially reducing administrative burdens that have long plagued healthcare settings [5]. This not only promises a leaner and more efficient operational landscape but heralds a substantive shift in the roles and responsibilities of healthcare professionals. As automation impeccably takes over repetitive chores, it paves the way for healthcare workers to engage more profoundly in strategic and decision-making roles. This evolution necessitates a fresh skill set where professionals are adept at supervising AI systems and interpreting their outputs with discernment. Moreover, with large language models (LLMs) at the helm, there is the promising potential for enhanced communication and understanding, as these models can facilitate nuanced understanding and processing of natural language in clinical settings, fostering a more holistic and informed approach to patient care. The average clinician today spends an average of 10 hours a week charting and looking for data in various data sets. LLMs herald a promising shift toward a healthcare ecosystem where professionals can leverage the prowess of AI to enhance their strategic input, fostering a landscape of collaborative intelligence where man and machine work in unison to reach the zenith of efficiency and efficacy in healthcare delivery.

As we transition from a focus on the in-house adjustments brought about by automation technologies, our attention shifts to the broader global landscape redefined by the emergence of remote work in healthcare. While automation fortifies the internal mechanics of healthcare systems, the remote work frontier expands its boundaries, breaking geographical barriers to ensure continuity and accessibility in healthcare delivery. This encompasses a growing telemedicine sector, which has seen an exponential rise, fueled in part by the necessity born during the COVID-19 pandemic, a period that significantly accelerated the adoption of virtual healthcare teams and remote consultations, cementing its role as an indispensable facet of modern healthcare [6]. Alongside telemedicine, remote monitoring and healthcare delivery have emerged as potent tools in the healthcare armamentarium, facilitating real-time health data monitoring and fostering timely interventions, thus promising to curtail unnecessary hospital visits and re-admissions, enhancing the efficiency and effectiveness of healthcare delivery [7]. The future most certainly consists of virtual care where clinical-type avatars communicate via chatbot with patients.

Privacy, security, and regulatory issues

In the coming 75 years, the digital health landscape is set to undergo transformative changes, heralding advancements and posing significant challenges in the realms of privacy, security, and regulatory frameworks. Privacy concerns will largely revolve around data ownership, with individuals striving for greater control and say in the management and utilization of their health data. The concept of informed consent will undergo evolutions, gravitating toward a more granular approach, enabling patients to dictate the specific uses of their health data. Meanwhile, genomic privacy will surge to the fore, necessitating robust protective measures against genetic discrimination and ensuring the safeguarding of sensitive genomic data.

On the security front, the uptick in cyber threats will command a comprehensive strategy focusing on breach prevention and incident response plans tailored to shield health data ecosystems effectively. The securing of communications will be paramount, with end-to-end encryption becoming a standard in data transmission, coupled with secure messaging platforms for healthcare professionals and patients. As authentication and authorization mechanisms become more sophisticated, there will be a concerted move toward biometric authentication, supported by role-based access control to delineate and restrict access based on individuals' roles within healthcare settings.

Regulatory frameworks will evolve to govern emerging technologies effectively and foster interoperability through the standardization of health information systems, thereby promoting data portability. The integration of AI and machine learning in healthcare will raise pressing issues concerning bias, discrimination, and the efficacy of these technologies, calling for stringent regulatory oversight. Telemedicine will forge ahead, bringing to the forefront questions surrounding licensing, accreditation, and quality assurance. As the digital health space expands globally, there will be an urgent need to address cross-border data flows and work toward establishing global standards, all while maintaining an ethical lens focusing on bridging the digital divide and pondering the ramifications of health surveillance technologies.

Ethics and social impact

As digital health evolves in the next 75 years, ethical considerations and the social impact of emerging technologies will become focal points of discussion. Bridging the digital divide will be an essential ethical task, seeking to ensure that all individuals, regardless of their socioeconomic status, have equal access to digital health advancements. This endeavor will encompass efforts to make technologies accessible, understandable, and useable across different demographics. Surveillance technologies, which might be leveraged to monitor health metrics continuously, will bring forth ethical dilemmas, balancing the fine line between maintaining public health and respecting individual privacy rights.

Moreover, the deployment of artificial intelligence in healthcare will necessitate a deep ethical introspection into the questions of bias and discrimination that could potentially be amplified by these technologies. Careful development and deployment of AI systems will be vital to ensure that they do not reinforce existing societal inequalities and disparities in healthcare access and outcomes. Attention will also be needed toward ensuring the safety and effectiveness of these technologies, warranting regulations that mandate rigorous testing and validation before widespread adoption.

A significant area of focus will also be the international harmonization of digital health standards to ensure uniform quality and safety of healthcare services globally. This will entail working on frameworks that allow for cross-border data flows while ensuring the highest level of security and privacy of individual health data. Global collaborations will be encouraged to foster environments where knowledge and expertise are shared, promoting a cohesive approach to digital health that respects the sociocultural nuances of different regions. Together, these efforts in addressing the ethical and social implications of digital health will pave the way for a future where technology serves to enhance health outcomes while respecting and upholding the fundamental rights and dignity of all individuals.

Education and training

In the foreseeable future, medical and nursing school curricula are poised to undergo substantial transformations, with an infusion of AI, VR, and AR technologies in the education ecosystem. AI has the capability to craft individualized learning pathways for students, meticulously designed to cater to their strengths and address their areas of improvement. This technology would not only aid in diagnosing and planning treatments but would also encourage students to develop a robust understanding grounded in data analysis and critical thinking. This would foster a generation of medical professionals adept at leveraging AI to support their decision-making processes.

VR and AR technologies are gradually becoming a staple in medical education, providing immersive and interactive learning experiences that transcend the confines of traditional textbook learning. For instance, students can now engage with detailed 3D models of human anatomy, navigating through the complex structures in a virtual space. This hands-on approach promotes a deeper understanding of the intricate systems within the human body, allowing students to explore and learn in an environment that closely mirrors real-life scenarios.

Within clinical settings, AR and VR are envisioned to redefine practical learning. These technologies create realistic simulations, offering a safe haven for students to practice and hone their skills before stepping into real-world medical environments. Moreover, AR can facilitate enriched learning experiences during live surgeries, with students having access to a rich repository of educational content overlaid on the live procedure, making for an immersive learning experience. Such interactive and immersive training modules are expected to nurture more confident and competent professionals, ready to take on the complexities of real-life medical situations with a well-rounded educational background.

As we forge ahead, it becomes evident that fostering agility and adaptability in healthcare professionals will be integral to their education. The future calls for a culture of continuous learning, where curricula are dynamic and evolve in tandem with the rapid advancements in the healthcare sector. This approach will ensure that medical and nursing students are not only grounded in foundational knowledge but are also in step with the latest developments, ready to work in harmony with AI systems, and adept at utilizing AR and VR technologies for informed, data-driven decision-making and complex procedures. This harmonious blend of technology and education envisages a future where healthcare professionals are equipped with both knowledge and the skill to leverage cutting-edge technologies for improved patient outcomes.

Conclusion

As we stand on the threshold of a digital health revolution, this chapter has elucidated the profound transformations we can anticipate in the healthcare landscape, fueled by the integration of AI technologies such as deep learning algorithms, NLP, and VR/AR in diagnostics, administration, and medical education.

In diagnostics, AI holds the promise of early detection and preventative care, leveraging the analysis of massive datasets to identify potential health risks before they escalate. Deep learning will unlock highly personalized approaches to medicine, tapping into multidimensional data to foster preventative strategies grounded in real-time monitoring and early interventions. The integration of AI in healthcare administration promises to streamline processes and reduce burdens, facilitating a seamless healthcare experience that could reshape our expectations of medical consultations and interactions with healthcare professionals. Moreover, the educational realms of medical and nursing schools stand to witness a revolutionary transformation, with technology infusing curricula with interactive, individualized, and immersive learning experiences, nurturing a new generation of medical professionals adept at navigating the digital health landscape.

Yet, this frontier is not without its challenges. While the coming era holds much promise, it demands a concerted and ethical approach to ensure inclusivity, equity, and privacy in the face of rapid advancements. The integration of AI and machine learning in healthcare brings to the fore critical ethical considerations regarding bias, discrimination, and the overarching efficacy of these technologies. It becomes imperative to develop stringent regulatory frameworks that encourage innovation while safeguarding individual rights and promoting ethical usage.

Moreover, as AI fosters autonomous patient-management platforms and advances in wearable technologies make real-time health monitoring a reality, we venture into uncharted territories where ethical considerations around data privacy and surveillance technologies come to the fore. The pivotal role of federated learning, promising a future that respects data privacy while fostering advancements, emphasizes the necessity for a well-balanced approach that honors ethical principles.

Looking forward, the global community must rally toward establishing international standards that address cross-border data flows and work toward mitigating the digital divide, fostering a landscape where digital health technologies are accessible, comprehensible, and useable across diverse demographic groups.

As we envision the future of digital health, an integrated approach that embraces the dynamic synergies of technology and human expertise emerges as the beacon of hope. AI stands not as a replacement but as a sophisticated tool in the hands of skilled professionals, guiding them toward more precise, preventative, and personalized healthcare interventions. The next 75 years beckon a healthcare landscape characterized by unprecedented innovations, driving toward a horizon where the boundaries between physical and virtual blur, making access to care and issues of the past, and ushering in an era of medical marvels that could redefine life and longevity as we know it.

References

[1] Shameer K, et al. Translational bioinformatics in the era of real-time biomedical, health care and wellness data streams. Briefings in Bioinformatics 2017;18(1):105–24.

[2] Pons E, et al. Natural language processing in radiology: a systematic review. Radiology 2016;279(2):329–43.

[3] Manolio TA. Bringing genome-wide association findings into clinical use. Nature Reviews Genetics 2013;14(8):549–58.

[4] Van Rheenen W, et al. Genetic correlations of polygenic disease traits: from theory to practice. Nature Reviews Genetics 2019;20(10):567–81.

[5] Singhal S, et al. The next wave of healthcare innovation: the evolution of ecosystems. McKinsey & Company; 2020.

[6] Hollander JE, Carr BG. Virtually perfect? Telemedicine for COVID-19. New England Journal of Medicine 2020;382(18):1679–81.

[7] Dorsey ER, Topol EJ. State of telehealth. New England Journal of Medicine 2016;375(2):154–61.

CHAPTER 27

Battling misinformation

Michael Robert Smith[1] **and Chelsea Backer**[2]

[1]Chobanian and Avedisian School of Medicine, Boston University, Boston, MA, United States;
[2]Access Sports Medicine and Orthopaedics, Concussion Management, Exeter, NH, United States

Objectives

Recognition of the harmful effects of misinformation on societal cohesion and behaviors can help public health officials devise effective strategies to protect public health.

The increasing quantity and improved quality of misinformation among the vast amount of digital content during an infodemic requires novel and effective approaches to identify, refute, and mitigate its negative effects.

Public health officials should balance public health measures against civil liberties so as to concurrently protect the population and preserve individual freedoms.

Definitions

Backfire Effect—a phenomenon where people continue to believe misinformation despite being presented with evidence to the contrary.

C2PA—The Coalition for Content Provenance and Authenticity.

CDC—Centers for Disease Control and Prevention.

Change Blindness—a phenomenon of visual perception that occurs when a stimulus undergoes a change without being noticed by its observer.

Distributed Amplification—strategy whereby a disinformation campaign operator directs participants to rapidly and widely disseminate campaign materials via their own personal social media accounts.

Illusory Truth Effect—the tendency to believe false information to be correct after repeated exposure.

Digital Health. https://doi.org/10.1016/B978-0-443-23901-4.00027-1

Implied Truth Effect—a phenomenon whereby headlines that fail to get tagged as false by fact checkers are assumed validated and thus are seen as accurate even if they are indeed false.

Manipulated media—any image or video with content or context edited along the "cheap fake" to "deepfake" spectrum with the potential to mislead and cause harm.

NIAID—National Institute of Allergy and Infectious Diseases.

Picture Superiority Effect - phenomenon whereby people are more likely to remember images than written or spoken words.

Synthetic media—aka "deepfakes" are digital falsifications of images, video, and audio created using an editing process that is automated through AI techniques.

Battling misinformation

> *"The trouble with most folks isn't their ignorance. It's knowin' so many things that ain't so."*
>
> ***Josh Billings.***

Prior to the development of written language, historical accounts and information were passed down through word of mouth. Not only was this form of communication inefficient and fraught with potential for factual errors, but it also limited the acquisition and sharing of knowledge by the general public. The development of written language allowed for more widespread dissemination of knowledge, but consequently increased the potential for misleading or factually incorrect information to be shared as well. With the invention of the printing press by Gutenberg in the 1400s, a multitude of tomes could be produced on any subject and provide a source of reference for further research. This of course meant that false and distorted news and information could be disseminated that much more quickly and accepted as truth by a greater number of people.

In the 1890s, publishers Joseph Pulitzer and William Hearst competed for readers by reporting rumors as truth and sensationalizing stories in a practice coined "yellow journalism." Similar to social media today, those sensationalized headlines grabbed more attention and sold more newspapers, which increased advertising revenue or advanced an agenda. In response, thoughtful readers sought out reliable news sources, and more authoritative publications like The New York Times came into the public fold.

In the 21st century, the spread of misleading or false information not only still remains a problem, but with widespread internet access, social and mass media sites have the ability to propagate exponentially greater amounts of information immediately to a worldwide audience. So great is the volume of information that currently traverses the internet, that it is impossible for medical and scientific authorities to verify all of this data for accuracy, much less to be able to correct inaccuracies or refute misinformation.

Compounding the problem of increased misinformation being propagated is that historically in the United States, mistrust of the government has been an underlying trait of the general public. Thus, it should not be surprising that during the uncertainty of a worldwide pandemic, a segment of the population would seek out and believe alternative sources of information. Unfortunately, with the current ability of misinformation to be rapidly and widely transmitted through the internet, public distrust of government and public health officials has increased to the point where a large number of people reject advice or directives meant to protect their health and that of those around them. The increasing danger is that preventative medicine measures will be ignored, and public health crises may be exacerbated in the short term and drawn out in the long.

Infodemic

The "infodemic" that resulted from the global COVID-19 pandemic overwhelmed the ability of public health officials and political leaders to provide accurate scientific data and authoritative public health directives. The term infodemic was coined by Washington Post columnist David Rothkopf in 2003 [2] and describes the overflow of information that occurs during an acute public health event. The vast amount of media content in an infodemic causes confusion among the populace, encourages mistrust of health authorities and undermines the effectiveness of the public health response. Indeed, sowing confusion and distrust is the primary goal of some of the spreaders of medical misinformation.

Early on in the COVID-19 pandemic, the frequent announcements, directives, and necessary corrections in recommendations by public health officials contributed to a decrease in the general public's acceptance of sound infection control and medical advice. Directives to help "flatten the curve" and decrease the rate of transmission of the virus were harmed by the tsunami of information, often contradictory, which was available through the traditional mainstream and social media.

For example, advice from former National Institute of Allergy and Infectious Diseases (NIAID) Director Dr. Anthony Fauci in the initial stage of the COVID-19 pandemic that people need not wear masks was meant to minimize the chance that there would not be enough personal protective equipment (PPE) to supply frontline US healthcare workers. But by the time production of PPE was ramped up and newer evidence indicated that the general public could benefit from mask wearing, there had been so much contradictory information that a segment of the population did not trust the veracity of his claims that COVID was indeed a serious health emergency and mask wearing became a political, rather than public health, issue.

Misinformation

Social media and digital news have not only changed how quickly information is spread but have given rise to a large number of unreliable or counterfeit sources which can spread "misinformation" or "disinformation" instantaneously to a worldwide audience. Even if there is no malintent on the part of a person distributing information through social media, the vast amount of information churned out in an infodemic increases the risk that the information will not be accurate or impartial. The contemporary term "fake news" has been coined to describe misleading information from a presumably reliable source presented as factual, verifiable information.

Misinformation is false information that is spread, regardless of whether there is intent to mislead, whereas disinformation defines intentional falsehoods engineered to make a person question the truth and click and share, with the goal to generate profit [3]. Misinformation can change perceptions and cause people to believe ideas that are contrary to established facts. Disinformation has been used in many ways to report false information with goals ranging from damaging reputations of political rivals, generating income through clicks, or derogatively referring to information someone simply finds unfavorable. Misinformation can be innocently distributed such that the source genuinely thinks it is factually accurate. Whereas disinformation would be where the source intentionally spreads harmful or false information with the purpose of causing harm or damage [4].

Organized social media manipulation campaigns have been found to operate throughout the world. A report by the University of Oxford found that governments, public relations firms and political parties are producing misinformation on an industrial scale. Reportedly, 93% of the 81 countries surveyed use disinformation as part of political communication. Alarmingly, 76 countries actively used disinformation and media manipulation as part of their political campaigns [5].

At the same time that the number of online information sources has exploded in number and influence, the distribution and influence of traditionally respected print media has diminished. A study found that in 2009, the Baltimore Sun produced a total of 23,668 news stories. "That is 32% *fewer* than it did for all of 1999, when it produced 34,852. And it is 73% fewer than in 1991, when the Baltimore Sun newsrooms produced 86,667 stories." [6] It should be noted that in 1991 the Sun actually still had a morning and evening newspaper which, even at that time, was uncommon as most US cities only had morning edition newspapers.

Rational people would be justified in asking: "why would someone spread false medical or scientific information? Especially during the course of a public health emergency?" Among the more insidious goals of misinformation is not simply to get people to distrust a certain official, or reject a recommended safety initiative, but rather to make citizens not trust anything at all. The increasing use of Artificial Intelligence, AI, only heightens this danger. Advances in large-scale language models will soon make it possible for AI bots to eliminate some of their obvious signs, like grammar errors and poor punctuation. AI can make it possible to produce an unlimited number of distinct messages in a disinformation campaign [7].

It is critical to keep in mind, however, that online or social media should not be labeled misinformation simply because one disagrees with it or finds it objectionable. In a democratic society, healthy civil discourse requires government and societal leaders to avoid early assumptions and to avoid labeling opposing viewpoints as automatically false. Medical providers in particular must always strive to find the truth and test our assumptions so as to optimize care for our patients.

For example, early on in the COVID-19 pandemic, the scientific community, and subsequently the news media, derogatively referred to people who believed that the virus was created in the Wuhan Institute of Virology as being conspiracy theorists. Yet in February 2023, FBI Director Christopher Wray revealed that "the FBI has for quite some time now assessed that the origins of the pandemic are most likely a potential lab incident in Wuhan." [8] It only perpetuates the fracturing of our civil society when one group is depicted as extremists by the mainstream media, but then reputable government officials later affirm their views.

Spreading misinformation

An obvious question is: "How does misinformation spread so quickly?" The spreader of misinformation uses a tactic called "Distributed Amplification" whereby a campaign operator implicitly or explicitly directs viewers and participants to rapidly and widely disseminate campaign materials via their own personal social media accounts. This information may include propaganda and misinformation as well as activist messaging or verified information [9]. For example, a deepfake image or other false story could be posted in a fringe Facebook account or other media. It could then be disseminated by followers and picked up by a prominent media source and amplified. This wide dissemination of material is meant to overwhelm the "information ecosystem with a specific narrative or message" [10] so as to mitigate clarification or invalidating efforts.

Images are a particularly useful tool for spreaders of misinformation. Numerous studies have shown a "Picture Superiority Effect" whereby images are more likely to be remembered than words. Manipulated photos and videos can overwhelm the information ecosystem. These manipulated media range from AI-generated deepfakes to simply using older images with new captions under a different context. Research shows that images tend to be both more memorable and more widely shared than text-only posts, heightening their potential to cause real-world harm [11].

Since people view and receive targeted news due to their previous internet searches and sites visited, they frequently encounter the same information from numerous sources. This gives rise to the "Illusory Truth Effect." This is a psychological mechanism whereby when one is repeatedly exposed to information of a certain narrative, then that person is more likely to accept it as true. People simply confuse the familiarity they have with information as affirmation that it is the truth [12]. Distributed Amplification relies on participants frequenting certain sources to receive the misinformation, accept it as true, and then to individually circulate it through their own online and offline communities as widely as possible.

In order to first reach a person or group to utilize Distributed Amplification, the source of that misinformation must know who or where to send it to. It is important to keep in mind that we do not all see the same version of the internet. People live in information bubbles seeing only what they read/look out for. This makes people vulnerable to targeted information or content that is promoted via algorithms. These algorithms are designed to catch a person's attention and hook him/her in with an emotional response. This puts factual information at a disadvantage, particularly if the source of any correction is a person that the consumer of misinformation does not like or think trustworthy.

In her 2018 book, The Age of Surveillance Capitalism, Harvard Business School Professor Shoshana Zuboff described how big tech companies "systematically and relentlessly extract information and data from the activities of 'users' of the various 'services' [13]. Prof Zuboff coined the term "surveillance capitalism" and describes what the tech companies are doing as "an antidemocratic and anti-egalitarian juggernaut." What happens is that when an individual uses Google as a search engine, a 'behavioral surplus' is produced which, on account of machine intelligence, can be harvested to predict which products are likely to attract that person as a consumer. In addition to keywords, each Google search query produces a wake of collateral data such as the number and pattern of search terms, how a query is phrased, spelling, punctuation, dwell times, click patterns, and location. Such information is commodified and traded to companies aiming to better target customers [14].

The goal of all this information harvesting is in the end, accumulation of capital. During the initial months of the COVID-19 pandemic, the leading surveillance capitalist CEOs experienced extraordinary increases in their wealth. The US-based Institute for Policy Studies reported that between January 1, 2020, and April 10, 2020, the total reported wealth of Jeff Bezos had increased by an estimated $25 billion. At Facebook, Mark Zuckerberg's personal wealth increased about $22 billion during that time [15]. It must be recognized that at the same time that leading government political and health officials were instructing people to stay home and socially distance, Jeff Bezos' corporation, Amazon, was a direct beneficiary of the expanded use of home delivery services for its goods. That Bezos was also the owner of the Washington Post media corporation was seen as proof by many that COVID was indeed a "plandemic."

In addition to harvesting users' personal data for profit, the social media companies have changed the landscape for receiving misinformation and creating like-minded groups of media consumers. When a user visits certain posts propagating misinformation, a recommendation algorithm can nudge that user to similar content thereby creating an echo chamber for misinformation and fake news [16]. In addition to social media, many mainstream news outlets, like MSNBC or Fox News, will cater to a specific political ideology, which can further disseminate misinformation or biased content. Consumers of that media are more likely to be persuaded by information coming from messengers they trust, or messages that already align with their beliefs. This is especially true when the information comes from political leaders they support. Leaders whom they do not support on the other hand, may dissuade them from believing the information [17].

Public trust

In order to understand why acceptance of medical misinformation has become so widespread in the United States, it is necessary to look at the key role that trust plays in public perception. It is a widely held axiom that distrust of politicians is the historical norm in the United States. Certainly, the belief among a segment of the American public that the government is composed of opportunists who use their power and positions of influence in order to enrich themselves or to misinform or manipulate the American public is not new. In the 1800s, Mark Twain was quoted to have quipped: "We have the best Congress that money can buy."

During the COVID-19 infodemic, when the sheer amount of information available could overwhelm a citizen's ability to evaluate conflicting claims, trust and trustworthiness took on even greater importance. Trust involves an individual making him or herself "vulnerable to another individual, group, or institution that has the capacity to do her harm or to betray her. Trust is seldom unconditional; it is given to specific individuals or institutions over specific domains." [18] Since government has the ultimate power to cause harm to the individual citizen, it follows that this trust is not given unconditionally.

The crucial attributes historically identified as necessary for public officials to possess in order to ensure social trust are the capacities to:

- make credible commitments
- design and implement policies nonarbitrarily
- demonstrate competence

The more trustworthy citizens perceive government to be, the more likely they are to consent to its demands and regulations. Simply, when government is perceived as trustworthy, citizens are more likely to comply in behavior, thus reinforcing the Social Contract whereby individuals give up some personal freedoms in order to live in a stable civil society [19]. Unfortunately, it appears that Americans currently hold such negative views toward their elected officials that this loss of trust in government is likely to continue into the foreseeable future. "People … lost confidence because time after time political authorities, Democrats and Republicans alike, demonstrated through their decisions and actions that they were not competent, not efficient, not honest, not fair, and certainly not to be trusted to make the right policy decisions." [20].

Elected officials, bureaucrats, and other government and public health officials must not only be "trustworthy, but they must also possess "competence in the domain over which trust is being given, (and that they) will not betray the trust as a consequence of either bad faith or ineptitude." [21] Thus when President Biden said: "You're not going to get COVID if you have these vaccinations," his exaggeration was seen by many, not so much as common political grandstanding, but as a case of disinformation. Others felt that his words reflected his lack of competence over the handling of the COVID-19 pandemic.

To be sure, he was technically correct when he extoled his administration's success since at that point there had been only 5492 vaccinated people who tested positive for coronavirus and were hospitalized or died. That was out of more than 159 million vaccinated Americans in total. Indeed, the director of the Centers for Disease Control and Prevention, Dr. Rochelle Walensky, noted that "99.5% of all deaths from COVID-19 (were) in the unvaccinated." [22].

Medical professionals can help restore trust in the public health arena by always acting professionally, utilizing evidence-based medicine to guide their medical decision making, and by always respecting patient autonomy. We can engender trust in our recommendations, and improve adherence, if our patients see as us honest brokers and not as trying to set an agenda. We must be mindful of how a large number of people have come to distrust the advice of the medical community.

During the initial stages of the COVID-19 vaccine rollout, it was noted that "Black people (were) underrepresented in vaccinations, and with Black, Native American, Asian, and Hispanic COVID-19 patients still dying at disproportionately alarming rates." [23] There were numerous reasons for this including the fact that many African Americans were initially hesitant to receive the vaccine. Some in the media ascribed this hesitancy to conspiracy theories and misinformation. But this was simplistic. It must be acknowledged that in the historical context of anti-Black racism within the US public health system a lack of trust has developed. "The truth is, Black people have *every* right to legitimately fear and be skeptical of the U.S. healthcare system as it has continually failed to provide Black patients with the assurance that their health and safety is a concern, much less a priority." [24].

Strategies

What strategies can we use to battle misinformation and ensure that the public understands and believes current medical science and standards of medical care? Of course, we must start by viewing all official statements with skepticism until confirmed by other sources. Since people live in information bubbles seeing only what they read/look out for, we must seek out numerous sources for information. Even, or especially, from sources whose viewpoint we may disagree with. We should obtain information from reliable sources such as government health agencies, medical associations and peer reviewed journals. Keep in mind though, that if content users are already prone to viewing misinformation, algorithms are designed to provide users with further false content, and they are less likely to engage in fact checking. Indeed, users inclined to fact check stories or assertions are those people least likely to be duped by misinformation.

In their 2021 feature article, Drew Shenkman and Kelli Slade examined the mass media's reliance on official police pronouncements when reporting local news events. They found numerous instances where police departments had either omitted critical details, or blatantly lied, when disclosing information in officer involved shootings. Shenkman and Slade noted that all of the journalists whom they spoke with said they "Never rely solely on police records or statements when reporting on incidents involving law enforcement." [25] Journalists recounted circumstances in which the official version of events was inaccurate, including where the police were not forthright or complete in the retelling of events, they had engaged in wrongdoing, litigation was pending, investigations were open and ongoing, or there was inherent police bias [26].

Besides one's own personal efforts at limiting the spread, and belief, of misinformation, there are Preemptive Strategies which can be used on a wide scale. Preemptive Strategies are aimed at limiting the effect and spread of misinformation before it is encountered. When information is shared, many users might not even realize the information is inaccurate. Recall the "Illusory Truth Effect," whereby when one is exposed to additional information of a certain narrative, then the more likely that person is to perceive that it is true. Among the preemptive strategies are techniques such as fact checking, prebunking, and debunking.

Mike Caulfield, a digital information literacy expert at Washington State University created the SIFT method to critically analyze content on news and social media. Using the SIFT tool, Caulfield recommends that people:

- Stop when they feel a strong emotion or desire to share information
- Investigate the source through any fact-checking platform
- Find better coverage by looking for the information from multiple independent reputable outlets (especially from different political ideologies).
- If needed, trace information back to the original source [27].

Fact-checking

Fact-checking and debunking techniques focus on corrective strategies. Fact-checking has become professionalized and has its own code of principles published by the International Fact-Checking Network (IFCN). Large organizations such as wikipedia.com, snopes.com, factCheck.org, and PolitiFact are useful resources to check accuracy of information and identify the initial source. Independent reviewers and journalists can also fact-check information on an individual basis. Through years of education, many health professionals have completed the training needed to ensure an adequate level of background knowledge to adequately fact check information [28]. Most of the time mistakes are honest mistakes, but misinformation spreads fast and needs to be debunked quickly.

We in the medical field can encourage fact-checking organizations and healthcare professionals to actively debunk false medical claims and then share accurate information. Many news sites have created fact checking divisions already. For example, on Saturday 10/7/23, Reuters showed video of an Israeli airstrike on the Gaza strip from May 2023, which had been mislabeled on social media as showing a retaliatory strike in response to the attack on Oct. 7 by the Palestinian terrorist group Hamas. Reuters then labeled it as "miscaptioned." [29].

Debunking, however, is made more difficult when images are subtly manipulated. The growing sophistication of photo-editing tools means that nearly anyone can make a convincing forgery. Studies have shown that people have an extremely limited ability to detect and locate manipulations of real-world scenes. The term "change blindness" is used to describe the phenomenon where a person is unable to perceive a difference in appearance when a visual image undergoes an alteration. The results of their 2017 experiment offer an important first step in understanding people's inability to identify photo forgeries and highlight the need to bring current guidelines and policies governing the acceptable standards for the use of photos into the digital age [30].

A preemptive strategy called prebunking inoculates people before they are even exposed to misinformation by teaching them how to spot and become resilient to misinformation.

Prebunking has been shown to be effective at reaching large groups of people across political divides [31]. Prebunking generally focuses on how manipulation and misinformation work rather than directly fact-checking or debunking information. In general, it follows a more educational than accusatory format. Prebunking is based on inoculation theory, first described in the 1960s by social psychologist William McGuire to be used as a psychological "vaccine for brainwashing." This inoculation theory has been shown to be effective across boundaries and during public health crises. Inoculation occurs in two parts. The first is by alerting viewers that the information they are about to witness is false or misleading. The second step is to provide users with tools when they encounter misleading information in the future such as counterarguments [32].

Fact-checking organizations and healthcare professionals can be encouraged to actively debunk false medical claims and share accurate information, both in person and virtually. Accurate information can be obtained from reliable sources such as government health agencies, medical associations and peer reviewed journals. Fact-checking can be an intervention that lasts days to weeks [33].

When fact-checkers find an example of misinformation or disinformation, the label identifying it as such should be neutral, or at least not confrontational. It should not insult a reader's intelligence or worldview. There is no better way to entrench someone in their belief than to belittle them. More effective is to utilize softer language when presenting information that debunks a post. If possible, fact-checkers should provide an explanation for why the manipulated media is false. If the manipulated media is a picture or includes an image, using an image will be helpful as is shown by the "picture superiority effect."

It is important to keep in mind that with the sheer magnitude of content on social and mass media, it is not possible to fact-check every news story or item on social media. Thus, fact-checking can itself have the unintended consequence of implying accuracy if an article or news item does not have a label that the information has been verified or has been found to be of questionable veracity. Recent research suggests that labeling only a subset of fact-checkable content on social media may do more harm than good by increasing users' beliefs in the accuracy of unlabeled claims. It is the phenomenon of "the implied truth effect" whereby false headlines that fail to get tagged are considered validated and thus are seen as more accurate even if they are indeed false [34]. The implied truth effect is perhaps the most profound challenge of labeling as it is impossible for fact-checkers to check all media posted to platforms. Because of this limitation in fact-checking at scale, fact-checked media on platforms will always be a subset, and labeling that subset will always have the potential to boost the perceived credibility of all other unchecked media, regardless of its accuracy [35].

Users should take time to critically evaluate the information encountered before sharing. They should determine whether the information is accurate and trustworthy, and if not, the user should not share. In fact, asking users to hesitate and evaluate information and headlines before sharing can reduce the amount of misinformation shared online, regardless of whether the information aligns with political beliefs. When speaking with friends and family about misinformation and fake news, listen, show empathy and guide people to sources that can provide more accurate information. Encourage users to verify information before sharing it and to be cautious of sensationalist headlines and anecdotal claims.

Healthcare professionals, professional organizations, and tech companies should collaborate to develop campaigns and tools to combat misinformation. There are top-down and bottom-up approaches to combating misinformation within a community and both should be utilized so as to avoid the feeling that an individual's beliefs, culture, or preferences are being marginalized.

People should consider where information comes from, such as the media, government officials, religious leaders, school and social media such as Facebook, Instagram, TikTok, and X (Twitter). Those who spread misinformation are more likely to have mistrust of science and academic expertise and top-down approaches like government health campaigns are less likely to be successful for those individuals. Public health organizations should help identify trusted messengers within a community or social network and work with them to promote accurate information and debunk misinformation. We should encourage doctors and medical experts to engage in online discussions to provide accurate information and counter misinformation. People are more likely to be persuaded by messages that might not align with their political beliefs and values when that information comes from messengers they trust and routinely engage with and repealed by those that they don't. Misinformation can be corrected by trusted political leaders. Lastly, we should encourage transparency in healthcare communication, where healthcare providers openly discuss risks, uncertainties, and benefits with patients.

As a society, we should invest in and expand education programs to help with digital literacy, health literacy, and interest in science, technology, engineering, and math (STEM). Exposure to critical thinking and scientific investigation can help provide a toolkit to understand and evaluate information. We should provide education to our patients and the general public in order to help them discern credible sources from unreliable ones. Early and continuing education will help build resilience to misinformation and disinformation, especially as information becomes more easily spread through communities and boundaries.

Social media platforms should enforce strict policies against the spread of misinformation and provide easy to use tools to identify and report false claims. For example, on large platforms such as Facebook and Instagram, misinformation can be identified and flagged by both individual users and third-party fact checking organizations. If false information is identified, it is labeled as false information, and users are notified as such if they choose to share the post or have shared it in the past. Content that is flagged as false or altered will appear lower on feeds, which reduces the number of viewers. Platforms should modify algorithms to prioritize trustworthy sources and reduce the visibility of misinformation. Platforms should be held accountable for the spread of misinformation.

These strategies, when implemented collectively, can help address the challenge of medical misinformation in the digital age.

Conclusion

Throughout human history, technological advances in distributing information have seen corresponding increases in the ability of various actors to use media sources to distribute misinformation. As each technology extended the distribution of knowledge, it increased the risk that factually inaccurate information would be accepted as truth and perpetuated.

Our current time, however, is particularly fraught with danger. Large tech companies use bots and algorithms to redirect internet users to similar content reinforcing the tendency for people to have their own version of the internet and live in information bubbles. The practice of "surveillance capitalism" engaged in by the big tech companies reinforces this trend by ensuring people encounter only that content which is similar to what they search for.

The COVID-19 pandemic magnified the problem of misinformation in the medical field because so much information was being issued by reputable, and reputable-appearing, sources that the average person had difficulty separating fact from fiction. Necessary corrections on infection control measures or treatment, based on updated, evidence-based medicine, were at once attacked by nefarious sources as government lies, or simply further caused confusion and doubt in the general public.

Yet medical and public health professionals, government officials, and societal leaders can fight back against misinformation and its effects. It will take a whole of society effort, but it can be done. We must start by constantly striving for truth and not accepting at face value every pronouncement or assertion by any government official, even if we agree with their ideology. We must ourselves fact-check information we encounter and not share it with colleagues until its veracity has been confirmed.

Governments must pressure big tech and social media companies to fact-check, and not give a platform to promoters of disinformation who strive to create doubt or to promote ideas that harm the public health. Utilizing the tools we have to battle disinformation; we can limit the spread of misinformation and disinformation and mitigate its deleterious effects.

Medical professionals, public health professionals, government officials, and societal leaders all have a responsibility in helping to limit the dissemination of misinformation which enters the public discourse through social and mass media. In addition, we all share an obligation to our patients and to society as a whole to ensure that our patient counseling and treatment is accurate and based on evidence-based medicine. We must constantly strive to ensure that false or biased medical information is not accepted as fact.

The medical community must respect patient autonomy in ultimately deciding their health choices, even if we disagree with them. We must present factual, evidence-based medicine, in a respectful and supportive manner, and then allow our patients to make their own choices.

Medical professionals should always be mindful that in our zeal to protect the public health, we cannot allow civil liberties and human rights to be abused by those who would do so for their own selfish purposes. We cannot support invasive policies similar to the one enacted in Poland in 2021 whereby smartphones were used to enforce a quarantine with individuals mandated to remain home and compelled them send a photograph of themselves within "20 minutes of receiving a prompt from government officials". If the individual missed the deadline, a police visit was triggered [13]. We must always balance public health and reduction of disease spread against expanding the surveillance capabilities of government authorities who may be loath to give up such power once the medical crisis has passed.

References

[1] Jacobs M. Fake News in the 1890s: Yellow Journalism. 2018. Retrieved from the Digital Public Library of America, https://production.dp.la/primary-source-sets/fake-news-in-the-1890s-yellow-journalism.

[2] Ansolabehere S. The paradox of minimal effects: University of Michigan Press, https://www.press.umich.edu/pdf/0472099213-ch2.pdf.

[3] Caulfield M. The SIFT method: Pressbooks.

[4] Cohen GL. Party over policy: the dominating impact of group influence on political beliefs. Journal of Personality and Social Psychology 2003;85(5):808–22. https://doi.org/10.1037/0022-3514.85.5.808.

[5] Dengler V. COO., Digital news innovation fund impact report, Google News Initiative. DNI_Fund_Impact_Report_v3.pdf.

[6] Dictionary.com.

[7] Dowling CM, Henderson M, Miller MG. Knowledge persists, opinions drift: learning and opinion change in a three-wave panel experiment. American Politics Research 2020;48(2):263–74. https://doi.org/10.1177/1532673X19832543.

[8] European Commission. The digital services act package. (Accessed 12 October 2023). Shaping Europe's digital future (europa.edu).

[9] Garrett PM. 'Surveillance capitalism, COVID-19 and social work': a note on uncertain future(s). British Journal of Social Work April 2022;52(3):1747–64. https://doi.org/10.1093/bjsw/bcab099.

[10] Gordon M, Strobel W. FBI director says Covid pandemic likely caused by Chinese lab leak. The Wall Street Journal February 28, 2023.

[11] Guess AM, et al. Misinformation review. Harvard Kennedy School of Government; January 14, 2020. https://misinforeview.hks.harvard.edu/article/fake-news-limited-effects-on-political-participation/.

[12] Hassan A, Barber SJ. The effects of repetition frequency on the illusory truth effect. Cognitive Research: Principles and Implications May 13, 2021;6(1):38. https://doi.org/10.1186/s41235-021-00301-5. PMID: 33983553; PMCID: PMC8116821.

[13] Hamilton IA. Poland made an app for quarantined Coronavirus patients which forces them send a selfie or face police. (businessinsider.com).

[14] International Fact Checking Network. IFCN code of principles (poynter.org).

[15] Lee HJ. How to distinguish between reliable and unreliable sources online. Inkspire.org.

[16] Levi M, Stoker L. Political trust and trustworthiness. Annual Review of Political Science 2000;2000.

[17] McGuire WJ. Resistance to Persuasion conferred by active and passive prior refutation of the same and alternative counterarguments. Journal of Abnormal and Social Psychology September 1961;63(2):326–32. https://doi.org/10.1037/h0048344.

[18] Merkley E, Loewen P. Science and health misinformation in the digital age, public policy forum. July 2021.

[19] Mr. Bot goes to Washington, the economist. September 2, 2023. https://www.economist.com/united-states/2023/08/31/ai-will-change-american-elections-but-not-in-the-obvious-way.

[20] Nightingale SJ, Wade KA, Watson DG. Can people identify original and manipulated photos of real-world scenes? Cognitive Research 2017;2:30. https://doi.org/10.1186/s41235-017-0067-2.

[21] Pariser E. The filter bubble: what the internet is hiding from you, London. Viking; 2011.

[22] Pennycook G, Rand DG. Lazy, not biased: susceptibility to partisan fake news is better explained by lack of reasoning than by motivated reasoning. Cognition 2019;188:39–50. https://doi.org/10.1016/j.cognition.2018.06.011.

[23] Pennycook G, et al. The implied truth effect: attaching warnings to a subset of fake news headlines increases perceived accuracy of headlines without warnings. Management Science 2020;66(11):4944–57. https://doi.org/10.1287/mnsc.2019.3478.

[24] Reuters fact check, fact check: Israel's may Gaza strike video falsely shared as October. Reuters.

[25] Rock D. A bias against bias. Psychology Today October 26, 2016.

[26] Roozenbeek J, et al. Prebunking interventions based on the psychological theory of 'inoculation' can reduce susceptibility to misinformation across cultures. Harvard Kennedy School Misinformation Review February 3, 2020. https://doi.org/10.37016//mr-2020-008.

[27] Rothkopf D. When the buzz bites back, Washington post. May 11, 2003.

[28] Saltz E, et al. It matters how platforms label manipulated media. Here are 12 principles designers should follow, first draft news, it matters how platforms label manipulated media. Here are 12 principles designers should follow. firstdraftnews.org.

[29] Shenkman D, Slade K. Police reports shouldn't set the news agenda: a guide to avoiding systemic racism in reporting. Fall: Communications Lawyer, American Bar Association; 2020. https://www.americanbar.org/groups/communications_law/publications/communications_lawyer/fall2020/police-reports-shouldnt-set-news-agenda-guide-avoiding-systemic-racism-reporting/#23.

[30] Social media manipulation by political actors an industrial scale problem, University of Oxford, News and Events. January 13, 2021.

[31] van der Linden S, et al. Inoculating the public against misinformation about climate change. Global Challenges February 2017;1(2):1600008. https://doi.org/10.1002/gch2.201600008.

[32] Watson-Daniels J. Black health in America: exploring racial disparities in COVID-19 vaccination data, data for black lives, February 25, 2021. Black health in America: exploring racial disparities in COVID-19 vaccination data - D4BL.

[33] Wood T, Porter E. The elusive backfire effect: mass attitudes' steadfast factual adherence. Political Behavior 2019;41(1):135–63. https://www.jstor.org/stable/48688420.

[34] Woodward C, Yen H., AP FACT CHECK: Biden goes too far in assurances on vaccines, Associated Press Online, July 22, 2021.

[35] World Health Organization, Infodemic management 101, online course. OpenWHO.

Further reading

[1] Pasquetto I, et al. MisinfoRx, a toolkit for health care providers. Harvard Global Health Institute. https://misinforx.com/download/.

CHAPTER 28

Educating the next generation in digital medicine

Vanessa Bester[1] and Eric Van Hecke[2]
[1]Augsburg University, Department of PA Studies, Minneapolis, MN, United States; [2]Concordia University, Department of PA Studies, St. Paul, MN, United States

Introduction

In the ever-evolving landscape of healthcare, digital medicine has emerged as a transformative force, reshaping the way healthcare is delivered, managed, and experienced. The integration of digital technologies into healthcare systems has the potential to enhance patient outcomes, improve access to care, streamline administrative processes, and reduce costs. As we stand at the precipice of a digital healthcare revolution, it is imperative that healthcare providers are equipped with the knowledge and skills necessary to navigate this new paradigm.

While the promise of digital medicine is vast, its realization hinges on the preparedness of healthcare providers. Without proper education and training, the full potential of digital medicine may remain untapped, and patients could be deprived of the benefits it offers [1]. In this chapter, we will review some of the key components of digital healthcare, explore the current trends in digital medicine education, and address future directions in standardized curricula, core competencies, and strategies for its effective integration into healthcare education.

Understanding the key components of digital medicine

Healthcare is in the midst of a profound revolution, driven by the integration of digital technologies that promise to transform the way healthcare is delivered, accessed, and experienced. Digital medicine encompasses a broad spectrum of technologies and practices that leverage digital tools and data to enhance healthcare delivery and patient outcomes. It extends beyond the confines of traditional medical practice and embraces innovations that are revolutionizing healthcare, from electronic health records (EHRs), Telemedicine and Virtual Care, Health Monitoring Devices and Wearables, Artificial Intelligence (AI) and

Digital Health. https://doi.org/10.1016/B978-0-443-23901-4.00028-3

Table 28.1: Key components of digital medicine.

Component	Description
Electronic health records (EHRs)	EHRs have become the backbone of modern healthcare, allowing healthcare providers to access patient data seamlessly and facilitate coordinated care
Telemedicine and virtual care	Telemedicine connects patients and healthcare providers remotely, offering convenience and expanding access to healthcare services, particularly in underserved areas
Health monitoring devices and wearables	Wearable devices, such as smartwatches and fitness trackers, collect real-time health data, enabling continuous monitoring and early intervention
Artificial intelligence (AI) and machine learning in healthcare	AI algorithms assist in diagnosis, treatment planning, and predictive analytics, enhancing the precision and efficiency of healthcare
Digital therapeutics and Mobile health Apps	These digital interventions offer therapeutic benefits and support patients in managing chronic conditions, mental health, and lifestyle choices
Internet of Things (IoT)	IoT devices and sensors in healthcare enable the seamless collection of patient data from various sources, enhancing monitoring and treatment planning.

Machine Learning, to Digital Therapeutics and Mobile Health Apps (Table 28.1). Each of these elements plays a unique and indispensable role in shaping the future of healthcare, offering an array of benefits that will improve patient outcomes, enhance healthcare access, and revolutionize the wellness journey. However, as digital healthcare technologies continue to evolve, they also face ongoing challenges and obstacles in realizing their full potential.

Healthcare is undergoing significant change, driven by an array of digital technologies that collectively promise a more patient-centric, efficient, and interconnected future of medicine. The transformation also presents a compelling need for healthcare education to evolve in parallel, and it is crucial to address the associated challenges with educating the next generation. In the following section, we will delve into the current challenges faced in educating healthcare providers on digital medicine, recognizing that overcoming these obstacles is essential for the successful implementation of these innovative tools in healthcare education and practice.

Current challenges in educating healthcare providers in digital medicine

The transformative potential of digital medicine in healthcare necessitates addressing shared challenges in educating both healthcare providers and students effectively. By recognizing these challenges, educational programs can develop comprehensive strategies encompassing tailored training, resource allocation, interdisciplinary collaboration, ethical awareness, and the preservation of patient-centric care. This holistic approach is essential to prepare the healthcare workforce and future professionals for success in the ever-changing digital healthcare setting.

Resistance to change and varied levels of digital literacy

One of the fundamental challenges in digital medicine education is the resistance to change among entrenched healthcare providers. These seasoned professionals may hesitate to embrace digital technologies, while incoming students possess diverse levels of digital literacy. Some adapt easily to digital tools, while others require more support. To address these intertwined challenges, tailored training programs must accommodate varying digital literacy levels. Active engagement and hands-on experiences should be integral to the learning process, encouraging both providers and students to embrace the digital revolution in healthcare [2].

Resource constraints and technological advancements

Resource limitations, a common predicament for educational institutions and healthcare organizations, can hinder effective digital medicine education. Tight budgets, limited access to digital infrastructure, and rapid technological advancements pose formidable challenges. Overcoming these barriers demands a strategic approach to resource allocation, prioritizing investments that facilitate comprehensive digital medicine education. Institutions must remain agile to adapt to ever-evolving technology, ensuring their educational programs stay current and relevant [3].

Interdisciplinary collaboration and ethical/regulatory complexities

Digital medicine often necessitates collaboration among healthcare professionals from diverse backgrounds. This interdisciplinary teamwork is pivotal to unlocking the full potential of digital tools and technologies. However, it presents a shared challenge in teaching providers and students to function seamlessly within multifaceted teams. Moreover, the introduction of digital tools introduces intricate ethical and regulatory considerations, including patient data privacy and compliance with healthcare laws. Education programs must incorporate interdisciplinary exercises simulating real-world scenarios, fostering effective teamwork. Emphasis on ethical and regulatory awareness ensures that providers and students navigate digital health with integrity and compliance at the forefront [4–7].

Balancing traditional and digital skills and patient-centered care

Achieving a harmonious balance between traditional clinical skills and digital competencies stands as a pivotal aspect of digital medicine education. It is imperative that healthcare providers and students learn to seamlessly integrate digital tools into their practice while upholding the timeless principles of patient-centered care. This delicate equilibrium calls for a carefully designed curriculum that fosters a holistic approach to healthcare. Within such a curriculum, technology is viewed not as a replacement for the human touch but as a facilitator that enhances the patient experience. This approach ensures that patients remain at the core of the healthcare journey, where the synergy of human compassion and digital efficiency creates the optimal healthcare outcome [8,9].

Data security and privacy and assessment and evaluation

Data security and patient privacy take center stage as paramount concerns. Both healthcare providers and students must possess a profound understanding of these issues to ensure the responsible practice of digital medicine. Additionally, assessing and evaluating competence in digital medicine present its own set of challenges. Traditional assessment tools may need a substantial transformation to accurately gauge the proficiency of individuals in digital competencies. Therefore, it is incumbent upon educational institutions to adapt their assessment methods, ensuring that they are reflective of digital health's complexities and the multifaceted skills and knowledge required for success.

Navigating the challenges in digital medicine education for healthcare providers and students is essential for preparing them to deliver high-quality care in the digital age. Whether addressing resistance to change, limited resources, interdisciplinary collaboration, or the delicate balance between traditional and digital skills, a holistic approach encompassing tailored training, resource allocation, interdisciplinary collaboration, ethical awareness, and a patient-centric focus is paramount. By proactively addressing these challenges, healthcare institutions and educators can empower providers and students to leverage digital tools effectively, enhancing patient care and driving positive outcomes [10,11].

Integrating digital medicine into healthcare education

The imperative of educating the upcoming cohort in the domain of digital medicine concurrently necessitates the alignment of current healthcare professionals with this evolving paradigm. The field of digital medicine is in a state of constant evolution, characterized by rapid advancements and innovative breakthroughs. From artificial intelligence-driven diagnostic tools to wearable health devices and telemedicine platforms, new technologies continually emerge to enhance patient care and healthcare delivery. Digital medicine is rapidly becoming a critical component of modern healthcare delivery, offering numerous benefits for both patients and healthcare providers.

Integrating digital and telemedicine into a healthcare curriculum is an imperative step in preparing the next generation of healthcare professionals. As the field of digital medicine continues to experience rapid advancements and innovation, educators must take proactive measures to ensure that healthcare students are well equipped with the knowledge and skills needed to harness the potential of telemedicine effectively. Before embarking on the journey of curriculum development and integration, educators must first gain a comprehensive understanding of telemedicine's multifaceted role in modern healthcare. This understanding extends to recognizing the myriad advantages it offers, including enhanced patient access to care, increased engagement, and more efficient healthcare delivery. Equally important is familiarity with the various modalities within telemedicine, ranging from synchronous, real-time interactions to asynchronous, store-and-forward methods, as this knowledge forms the cornerstone for creating a well-rounded and effective telemedicine curriculum [12–14].

In this section, we delve into the intricacies of incorporating telemedicine into healthcare education, exploring key considerations and strategies that guide the development of a comprehensive curriculum. From defining clear learning objectives that form the foundation of any curriculum to practical approaches such as integrating telemedicine into existing courses or creating dedicated modules, we provide insights into crafting an educational framework that empowers students to excel in telemedicine practice. We also emphasize the critical role of hands-on training, ethical and legal awareness, and tailored assessment methods to ensure that students emerge from their education prepared to navigate the ethical, legal, and practical aspects of telehealth as part of those curricular objectives. Furthermore, we shed light on the significance of interdisciplinary learning, fostering collaboration among healthcare professionals from various disciplines, and how industry partnerships can augment the curriculum by providing real-world perspectives and insights from the rapidly changing digital medicine environment. Finally, we underline the importance of ongoing evaluation and adaptation to ensure that the telemedicine curriculum remains relevant, aligned with emerging technologies, and responsive to the dynamic needs of both patients and healthcare providers. In essence, this section serves as a comprehensive guide for educators and institutions striving to integrate telemedicine seamlessly into their healthcare curriculum.

One approach to incorporating telemedicine into a healthcare curriculum is to integrate it into existing courses. For example, educators can incorporate telemedicine simulations into clinical skills training to help students become familiar with virtual patient encounters. They can also include modules on telemedicine ethics and regulations within courses that cover medical ethics and healthcare law. Additionally, educators can develop case studies or scenarios that require students to assess and manage patients using telemedicine. Another approach is to create dedicated telemedicine courses or elective modules. These courses can cover various aspects of telemedicine in-depth, providing students with a comprehensive understanding of the field. Key topics to include are telemedicine technologies and platforms, legal and ethical considerations, telemedicine in different specialties (e.g., telepsychiatry, telecardiology), hands-on experience with telemedicine equipment and software, and interprofessional collaboration in telehealth teams.

Once a curricular approach has been determined, a foundation of clearly defined learning objectives should be established. Educators should identify specific educational outcomes related to telemedicine. These objectives may include understanding the principles and history of telemedicine, proficiency in using telemedicine technologies, adherence to ethical and legal guidelines in telemedicine practice, effective communication and patient engagement in virtual encounters, assessment and management of patients through telehealth (often based upon organ system or common complaints), and evaluation of data, outcomes and quality improvement in the practice of digital medicine. A critical component of integrating telemedicine into a healthcare curriculum is the allocation of curriculum space dedicated to the ethical and legal aspects of telemedicine. Within this framework, it is essential to emphasize pertinent topics, including but not limited to, patient consent, privacy regulations, data security, licensure prerequisites, documentation, and reimbursement policies. This focus ensures that students develop a comprehensive understanding of the ethical and legal dimensions specific to telemedicine practice within their respective regions. By delving into these aspects, students are better equipped to navigate complex telemedicine scenarios while adhering to regulatory requirements and maintaining ethical integrity. The objectives should be clear and measurable, yet flexible and versatile enough to evolve with technology. The objectives should also align with the program's mission and vision along with input from stakeholders and experts in digital medicine practice [15–20].

It is also imperative to create tailored assessment methods that align with the unique learning objectives required in the realm of telemedicine. These assessments should aim to evaluate students' capacity to perform virtual patient consultations effectively, communicate proficiently through telehealth platforms, and navigate intricate ethical and legal dilemmas inherent to telemedicine practice. To achieve a comprehensive evaluation, educators should consider a diverse range of assessment tools. These may include telemedicine-focused case presentations, wherein students analyze and present telehealth cases, making diagnostic and treatment recommendations. Specialized examinations can assess their knowledge of telemedicine regulations, ethics, and best practices. Furthermore, the utilization of objective structured clinical examinations (OSCEs) can create real-life telehealth scenarios for students to navigate, covering various aspects of virtual patient care. By integrating these assessments into the curriculum, educators can gauge students' readiness and competence in delivering telehealth services while ensuring their ethical and legal acumen in the practice of telemedicine [21–24].

Hands-on training and experiential learning stand as indispensable pillars in the endeavor to equip healthcare students with the practical skills and confidence needed to effectively leverage telemedicine technologies. These immersive approaches bridge the gap between theoretical knowledge and real-world application, fostering a deep understanding of telehealth's intricacies. Simulations and role-playing exercises, for instance, create a structured and risk-free environment wherein students can engage in virtual patient encounters. These exercises not only enable students to become proficient in using telemedicine platforms but also encourage them to fine-tune their communication skills. Effective patient engagement in virtual settings requires distinct communication strategies, including active listening and nonverbal cues, which students can hone through repeated practice. Moreover, hands-on experiences extend beyond simulated scenarios into the realm of telemedicine practicums and clinical rotations. These opportunities provide students with genuine exposure to telehealth in action, mirroring real-world telehealth teams and the complexities of remote patient care. By partnering with healthcare institutions that offer telemedicine services, students have the privilege of working alongside seasoned telemedicine practitioners. In such environments, they can apply their acquired knowledge in practical settings, manage patient consultations, and confront the unique challenges posed by remote healthcare delivery [25–27].

Interdisciplinary learning lies at the core of a well-rounded telemedicine curriculum. Telemedicine often involves collaboration among healthcare professionals from various disciplines, including physicians, nurses, pharmacists, and allied health providers. Therefore, incorporating telemedicine into the curriculum naturally lends itself to interprofessional education (IPE). Students from diverse healthcare fields can come together to work on telemedicine projects, participate in telehealth case studies, and engage in collaborative problem-solving. This mirrors real-world telehealth teams, where healthcare professionals with different expertise collaborate to provide comprehensive care. Taking IPE further, developing industry partnerships also plays a pivotal role in enhancing the telemedicine curriculum. Collaborating with healthcare organizations, telemedicine technology companies, and telehealth service providers can provide invaluable insights and resources. Industry experts can offer students real-world perspectives on telemedicine implementation, share best practices, and expose them to the latest telehealth technologies. Given telemedicine technologies evolve rapidly, industry collaboration offers an opportunity for educators and students to stay informed about the latest telemedicine platforms, devices, and best practices. This also sets a standard that encourages students to stay updated even after graduation through continuous learning [28–30].

Systematic evaluation of the telemedicine curriculum is an indispensable component of its long-term success and relevance. This evaluation process involves a meticulous and ongoing assessment of the curriculum's various elements, such as content, teaching methodologies, and assessment methods. Through regular feedback mechanisms involving students, faculty, and healthcare practitioners, educational institutions can identify areas for improvement, adaptation, and change. This rigorous evaluation ensures that the curriculum aligns with emerging technologies, healthcare practices, and the dynamic needs of patients and providers alike. By systematically reviewing and enhancing the curriculum, institutions can continuously optimize the quality of telemedicine education, equipping students with the knowledge and skills required to excel in this transformative field of healthcare [31−33].

As the field of digital medicine continues to advance at an unprecedented pace, the development of a comprehensive curriculum becomes increasingly crucial. Such a curriculum equips the next generation of healthcare professionals with the skills and knowledge needed to navigate the intricate intersection of healthcare and technology.

Challenges and ethical considerations faced in digital medicine education

While digital medicine holds immense promise for improving patient care and healthcare delivery, it also presents several challenges and ethical considerations that educators and curriculum designers must carefully address. Before closing this section, we feel it imperative to address critical cautions and considerations that underscore the creation of a digital medicine curriculum. We present these vital facets, aiming to provide educators and stakeholders with valuable insights into crafting a curriculum that not only imparts technical proficiency but also nurtures an unwavering commitment to patient welfare, ethical practice, and health equity [34−37]

1. **Bias and Fairness in AI**: AI algorithms can inherit biases present in training data, potentially leading to disparities in healthcare outcomes. Curriculum designers must educate students about the risk of bias in AI and emphasize the importance of continuous monitoring and evaluation of AI systems for fairness and equity.
2. **Data Privacy and Security**: Digital medicine relies heavily on patient data, which raises concerns about privacy and security. Curriculum should instill a deep understanding of data protection laws and ethical considerations to ensure that students respect patients' privacy and maintain data security.
3. **Health Disparities**: Addressing health equity is crucial. Curriculum designers should emphasize the role of digital medicine in reducing disparities while acknowledging that technology can exacerbate them if not applied thoughtfully. Teach students to identify and rectify potential biases in data and algorithms.
4. **Ethical Dilemmas**: Digital medicine may present students with ethical dilemmas, such as balancing data-driven decisions with patient autonomy. Prepare students to navigate these complex issues, emphasizing shared decision-making and ethical AI development.
5. **Human-Centered Care**: Technology should complement, not replace, human-centered care. Stress the importance of maintaining the patient-provider relationship and using digital tools to enhance, not hinder the healthcare experience.
6. **Interdisciplinary Collaboration**: Encourage interdisciplinary education to foster collaboration among healthcare professionals, data scientists, and engineers. Address the challenges of effective communication and teamwork in the digital healthcare context.

7. **Resource Accessibility**: Ensure that students understand the potential disparities in access to digital healthcare tools and technologies. Teach them to consider solutions that can mitigate these disparities, such as telehealth options for underserved communities.
8. **Cultural Competence**: Digital medicine should be culturally sensitive and respectful of diverse patient populations. Include cultural competence training to help students navigate cultural differences and provide equitable care.
9. **Regulatory Compliance**: The regulation of digital medicine and AI is evolving. Teach students about current regulations and encourage them to stay informed about changes. Emphasize the importance of ethical and legal compliance.
10. **Continuous Learning**: Digital medicine is a rapidly advancing field. Encourage a culture of lifelong learning, where healthcare providers continuously update their knowledge and skills to adapt to new technologies and best practices.

In summary, a comprehensive telemedicine curriculum should encompass various critical elements. These include fostering a profound understanding of telemedicine's role within modern healthcare through delineating clear and well-defined modalities of learning, concise learning objectives and assessments that guide learning, facilitating immersive and hands-on training experiences and clinical exposure in telehealth settings, promoting interprofessional education to mirror real-world telehealth teams, and addressing the ethical and legal dimensions of telemedicine practice. These actions are focused on staying abreast of rapid technological advancements in digital medicine while maintaining a rigorous process of continuous evaluation and improvement to ensure the curriculum remains both current and effective in preparing future healthcare professionals for the telemedicine era.

Competencies in digital medicine education

In the previous section, we explored how to plan to incorporate digital medicine into a health profession education program. As we transition into discussing the core competencies necessary for healthcare providers in the realm of digital medicine, it's essential to recognize that overcoming these challenges is fundamental to achieving proficiency in this care modality. Building on the foundation of addressing educational hurdles and resistance to change, we present a simple framework for digital health competencies that will empower healthcare providers to excel in the digital age of medicine (Table 28.2).

These competencies encompass the knowledge, skills, and attitudes necessary for healthcare students to excel in telemedicine practice and provide high-quality, patient-centered care in virtual healthcare settings while adhering to ethical, legal, and quality standards. Educators may take a reverse-design approach, beginning first with the

Table 28.2: Competencies in digital medicine education.

Competency domain	Example competency
Telemedicine technology proficiency	Proficient use of telemedicine technologies (videoconferencing, EHRs, remote monitoring, apps)
Patient assessment through telehealth	Comprehensive virtual patient assessments
Communication skills in telehealth	Effective communication in virtual encounters
Ethical and legal considerations	Understanding telemedicine ethics and legal requirements
Interprofessional collaboration	Collaborative teamwork in telehealth practice
Telemedicine documentation	Accurate and comprehensive documentation in EHRs
Telehealth clinical skills	Adaptation of clinical skills to virtual patient care
Telemedicine ethics and advocacy	Advocating for responsible telemedicine practice
Telehealth quality improvement	Implementing quality improvement initiatives in telehealth
Telehealth assessment and evaluation	Evaluating telehealth outcomes and patient feedback
Continuous learning and adaptability	Commitment to ongoing professional development in telemedicine
Cultural competency in telehealth	Cultural sensitivity and adaptability in virtual patient encounters

competencies and mapping backward through to the curricular delivery, content, and assessments. Limitations often encountered are related to the perception of the need for funding, time for curricular development, and expertise, however, approaching digital medicine in a stepwise fashion, leveraging resources through sharing experiences and expertise provides ample opportunity to begin introducing digital medicine to the next generation of learners [32,38–42].

Best practices

Centering upon a standard history and physical assessment curriculum, programs can form a comprehensive plan to achieve a seamless integration effectively. Here we outline steps involved toward comprehensive curricular integration of telehealth and digital medicine that can be employed within an individual program [43–46].

Step 1: Needs Assessment and Goal Setting

- **Conduct a Needs Assessment:** Begin by evaluating the current curriculum, student expectations, and present-day telehealth practices. Identify gaps in knowledge and skills related to telehealth and virtual patient encounters.
- **Set Clear Learning Objectives:** Define specific learning objectives for integrating telehealth into the physical examination course. Ensure alignment with program goals and accreditation requirements.

Step 2: Curriculum Design

- **Identify Integration Points:** Determine where telehealth topics can be seamlessly integrated into the existing physical examination course. Consider both didactic and practical components of the course.
- **Develop Telehealth Modules:** Create dedicated telehealth modules or lessons that cover essential topics, such as telehealth technology, ethical and legal considerations, communication skills in virtual encounters, and conducting virtual patient assessments.
- **Incorporate Case-Based Learning:** Design case studies and scenarios that require students to apply telehealth principles in patient assessment, diagnosis, and communication.

Step 3: Faculty Training and Development

- **Provide Faculty Training:** Offer training and professional development opportunities to instructors to ensure they are proficient in telehealth technologies and best practices. Faculty should understand telehealth's ethical and legal aspects.
- **Facilitate Interdisciplinary Collaboration:** Encourage collaboration between faculty from different healthcare disciplines to bring diverse perspectives into the telehealth curriculum.

Step 4: Resources and Infrastructure

- **Secure Telehealth Tools:** Ensure access to telehealth technology platforms, video conferencing software, and electronic health records (EHRs) for both faculty and students. Collaborate with IT departments to facilitate this access.
- **Create a Telehealth Simulation Lab:** Establish a dedicated telehealth simulation lab where students can practice virtual patient encounters using standardized patients and telehealth equipment.

Step 5: Integration into the Course

- **Integrate Telehealth Didactics:** Embed telehealth didactics into relevant sections of the physical examination course. These can include lectures, seminars, or online modules.
- **Hands-on Telehealth Practice:** Allocate time for hands-on telehealth practice in the telehealth simulation lab. Students should conduct virtual patient assessments, practice communication skills, and use telehealth equipment. Table 28.3 demonstrates a case example of a student Telehealth encounter with a simulated patient.
- **Assessment Methods:** Develop assessment methods that evaluate students' proficiency in telehealth competencies. This may include virtual patient encounter evaluations, written exams, or case presentations. Table 28.4 demonstrates an example of an evaluation tool to assess students during Telehealth encounters with simulated patients.

Table 28.3: Case example — student/simulated patient teleheath encounter.

Simulated Patient Information: **Name: Mr. John Smith** **Age: 55** **Sex: Male** **Chief Complaint: Persistent Cough** **Student: Sarah Miller** **Supervising Provider: Emily Rodriguez**
Scenario:
Sarah Miller, a healthcare provider student, is participating in a telemedicine training session under the guidance the supervising medical provider, Emily Rodriguez. They are conducting a virtual patient encounter with Mr. John Smith, a 55-year-old male who presents with a persistent cough. This encounter is designed to help Sarah develop her telemedicine skills and patient communication.
Setting:
The encounter takes place in a secure telemedicine platform where Sarah and Dr. Rodriguez can see and interact with Mr. Smith through video conferencing.
Telehealth simulated patient encounter Progression:
Introduction and establishing Rapport:
• Sarah initiates the session by introducing herself and her supervising provider, Emily Rodriguez. • She explains the purpose of the encounter as a learning experience for her and seeks Mr. Smith's consent to discuss his medical concerns. She confirms Mr. Smith's identity by asking for his date of birth. • She acknowledges the encounter as a telehealth encounter and explains to Mr. Smith general instructions and expectations. • Mr. Smith agrees and shares that he's been experiencing a persistent cough for the past 2 months.
Medical history and Symptoms:
• Sarah asks Mr. Smith about his medical history, including any preexisting conditions, allergies, and medications. • She inquires about the nature of the cough, including when it started, whether it's associated with any other symptoms (fever, shortness of breath, sputum production), and if he has any triggers. • Mr. Smith mentions that he has no known medical conditions, is not on any medications, and the cough is dry and occurs throughout the day.
Physical examination:
• Since Sarah cannot physically examine the patient, she asks Mr. Smith to describe any visible symptoms or changes, such as changes in his skin color, swelling, or weight loss. • Mr. Smith reports no visible changes but mentions that he's lost a few pounds unintentionally.
Assessment and Differential diagnosis:
• Sarah formulates a preliminary assessment and differential diagnosis: • Assessment: Persistent cough • Differential diagnosis: Allergies, asthma, chronic obstructive pulmonary disease (COPD), gastroesophageal reflux disease (GERD), lung infection, lung cancer. • She discusses these possibilities with Mr. Smith, explaining that further evaluation is necessary to diagnose the specific etiology.

Table 28.3: Case example – student/simulated patient teleheath encounter.—cont'd

Further evaluation and next steps:
• Sarah discusses the need for additional tests, such as a chest X-ray, pulmonary function tests, and bloodwork. • She schedules a follow-up appointment for Mr. Smith to discuss the results and potential treatment options.
Patient education and Counseling:
• Sarah provides Mr. Smith with information about lifestyle modifications, such as avoiding smoking (if applicable), staying hydrated, and using a humidifier. • She emphasizes the importance of adhering to the follow-up appointments and any prescribed treatments.
Closing the encounter:
• Sarah summarizes the key points of the encounter and asks if Mr. Smith has any questions or concerns. • She reassures him that they will work together to uncover the cause of his cough and develop an appropriate treatment plan.

Table 28.4: Case example – telehealth simulated patient encounter evaluation form.

Student Information **Student Name:**____________________ **Date of Evaluation:**__________________ **Evaluator Name:**___________________ **Patient Scenario** **Patient's Simulated Case Number:**________ **Patient's Simulated Name:**____________ **Chief Complaint:**____________________
Student performance assessment
Communication and Rapport Building:
• Introduced themselves, including their professional title, and addressed the patient by name. • Confirmed the patient's identity by asking for their date of birth (or another confirmatory identification method). • Acknowledged the encounter as a telehealth visit and clearly provided directions and expectations. • Demonstrated active listening and components of empathy-forward patient communication. • Used clear and appropriate language, avoided medical jargon. • Overall, established patient rapport and made the patient feel comfortable.
History taking:
• Gathered an appropriately comprehensive medical history based on the chief complaint. • Asked relevant and open-ended questions. • Followed up on the patient's responses with probing questions, reflecting questions, or summary statements. • Demonstrated sensitivity when asking about sensitive topics.
Clinical knowledge:
• Demonstrated an understanding of the relevant medical concepts. • Formulated an appropriate differential diagnosis.

Continued

Table 28.4: Case example – telehealth simulated patient encounter evaluation form.—cont'd

• Discussed potential diagnostic tests or assessments. • Explained medical concepts in an understandable manner.
Physical examination:
• Clearly explained the purpose of the examination and outlined instructions for the patient. • Demonstrated or simulated the proper technique (e.g., inspection, palpation) • Asked for the patient's verbal consent before proceeding.
Assessment and care Planning:
• Formulated a clear assessment based on the gathered information. • Discussed treatment options and recommendations. • Provided an understandable rationale for the recommended plan. • Addressed the patient's concerns and preferences in the care plan.
Patient education:
• Provided relevant health education tailored to the patient. • Checked the patient's understanding in a respectful manner and encouraged questions. • Gave clear instructions regarding medications or lifestyle modifications. • Emphasized the importance of follow-up and treatment compliance.
Professionalism:
• Maintained a respectful and nonjudgmental attitude and communication style. • Respected and maintained patient confidentiality and privacy. • Managed time effectively during the encounter. • Demonstrated professionalism in appearance and demeanor.
Technical proficiency:
• Displayed knowledge of the necessary hardware and software components related to conducting the telehealth encounter. • Utilized technology appropriately during telehealth encounter. Student was not "multitasking" or searching unrelated or nonrelevant information.
Overall assessment:
• Outstanding • Good • Satisfactory • Needs improvement
Comments and feedback (Strengths and areas for improvement):
Additional Comments (if any):

Step 6: Evaluation and Continuous Improvement

- **Gather Student Feedback:** Collect feedback from students regarding the integration of telehealth into the course. Use their input to make necessary adjustments.
- **Evaluate Learning Outcomes:** Assess whether students meet the defined learning objectives related to telehealth. Analyze data on their performance and adapt the curriculum accordingly.

Step 7: Ongoing Faculty Development

- **Stay Current:** Encourage faculty to stay updated on telehealth advancements by participating in continuing education and engaging in telehealth-related research or projects.
- **Peer Collaboration:** Foster a culture of peer collaboration among faculty members by sharing best practices and experiences related to telehealth education.

Step 8: Ethical and Legal Considerations

- **Emphasize Ethical and Legal Training:** Ensure that students understand the ethical and legal aspects of telehealth practice, including patient consent, privacy, and compliance with telehealth regulations.

Step 9: Quality Assurance

- **Quality Improvement Initiatives:** Establish quality improvement programs to monitor and enhance the telehealth curriculum continually.
- **Accreditation Compliance:** Ensure that the telehealth curriculum aligns with relevant accreditation standards and guidelines.

Step 10: Integration Across the Curriculum

- **Expand Telehealth Integration:** Consider expanding telehealth integration beyond the physical examination course to other healthcare courses, ensuring a comprehensive approach to telehealth education.

Conclusion

In this chapter, we've explored the importance of digital medicine in modern healthcare and the need for healthcare providers to be educated in this field. Digital medicine is not a static field; it evolves continuously. Healthcare professionals must commit to lifelong learning to remain effective in their roles. To meet the demands of modern healthcare, healthcare institutions must prioritize digital medicine education to ensure that healthcare providers are well-equipped to deliver the best possible care in this digital age.

References

[1] Shaffer DW, Kigin CM, Kaput JJ, Scott Gazelle G. What is digital medicine? Studies in Health Technology and Informatics 2002;80:195–204. https://doi.org/10.3233/978-1-60750-924-0-195.

[2] Schreiweis B, Pobiruchin M, Strotbaum V, Suleder J, Wiesner M, Bergh B. Barriers and facilitators to the implementation of eHealth services: systematic literature analysis. Journal of Medical Internet Research 2019;21(11). https://doi.org/10.2196/14197.

[3] Cullen MW, Geske JB, Anavekar NS, McAdams JA, Beliveau ME, Ommen SR, Nishimura RA. Reinvigorating continuing medical education: meeting the challenges of the digital age. Mayo Clinic Proceedings 2019;94(12):2501−9. https://doi.org/10.1016/j.mayocp.2019.07.004.

[4] Keasberry J, Scott IA, Sullivan C, Staib A, Ashby R. Going digital: a narrative overview of the clinical and organisational impacts of eHealth technologies in hospital practice. Australian Health Review 2017;41(6):646−64. https://doi.org/10.1071/AH16233.

[5] Sinsky CA, Jerzak JT, Hopkins KD. Telemedicine and team-based care: the perils and the promise. Mayo Clinic Proceedings 2021;96(2):429−37. https://doi.org/10.1016/j.mayocp.2020.11.020.

[6] Clark PA, Capuzzi K, Harrison J. Telemedicine: medical, legal and ethical perspectives. Medical Science Monitor 2010;16(12):RA261−72.

[7] Solimini R, Busardò FP, Gibelli F, Sirignano A, Ricci G. Ethical and legal challenges of telemedicine in the era of the COVID-19 pandemic. Medicina 2021;57(12). https://doi.org/10.3390/medicina57121314.

[8] Record JD, Ziegelstein RC, Christmas C, Rand CS, Hanyok LA. Delivering personalized care at a distance: how telemedicine can foster getting to know the patient as a person. Journal of Personalized Medicine 2021;11(2):1−11. https://doi.org/10.3390/jpm11020137.

[9] Piette JD, Newman S, Krein SL, Marinec N, Chen J, Williams DA, Edmond SN, Driscoll M, Lachappelle KM, Kerns RD, Maly M, Kim HM, Farris KB, Higgins DM, Buta E, Heapy AA. Patient-centered pain care using artificial intelligence and mobile health tools: a randomized comparative effectiveness trial. JAMA Internal Medicine 2022;182(9):975−83. https://doi.org/10.1001/jamainternmed.2022.3178.

[10] Shah S, Diwan S, Kohan L, Rosenblum D, Gharibo C, Soin A, Sulindro A, Nguyen Q, Provenzano D. The technological impact of COVID-19 on the future of education and health care delivery. Pain Physician 2020;23(4):S367−80.

[11] Katznelson G, Gerke S. The need for health AI ethics in medical school education. Advances in Health Sciences Education 2021;26(4):1447−58. https://doi.org/10.1007/s10459-021-10040-3.

[12] Mantas J. Biomedical and health informatics education − the IMIA years. Yearbook of Medical Informatics 2016:S92−102. https://doi.org/10.15265/IY-2016-032.

[13] Mantas J, Ammenwerth E, Demiris G, Hasman A, Haux R, Hersh W, Hovenga E, Lun KC, Marin H, Martin-Sanchez F, Wright G. Recommendations of the International Medical Informatics Association (IMIA) on education in biomedical and health informatics. Methods of Information in Medicine 2010;49(2):105−20. https://doi.org/10.3414/ME5119.

[14] Bichel-Findlay J, Koch S, Mantas J, Abdul SS, Al-Shorbaji N, Ammenwerth E, Baum A, Borycki EM, Demiris G, Hasman A, Hersh W, Hovenga E, Huebner UH, Huesing ES, Kushniruk A, Hwa Lee K, Lehmann CU, Lillehaug S-I, Marin HF, Marschollek M, Martin-Sanchez F, Merolli M, Nishimwe A, Saranto K, Sent D, Shachak A, Udayasankaran JG, Were MC, Wright G. Recommendations of the International Medical Informatics Association (IMIA) on Education in Biomedical and Health Informatics: second revision. International Journal of Medical Informatics 2023;170. https://doi.org/10.1016/j.ijmedinf.2022.104908.

[15] Aungst TD, Patel R. Integrating digital health into the curriculum—considerations on the current landscape and future developments. Journal of Medical Education and Curricular Development 2020;7. https://doi.org/10.1177/2382120519901275.

[16] Bulik RJ, Shokar GS. Integrating telemedicine instruction into the curriculum: expanding student perspectives of the scope of clinical practice. Journal of Telemedicine and Telecare 2010;16(7):355−8. https://doi.org/10.1258/jtt.2010.090910.

[17] Bonney A, Knight-Billington P, Mullan J, Moscova M, Barnett S, Iverson D, Saffioti D, Eastland E, Guppy M, Weston K, Wilson I, Nicky Hudson J, Pond D, Gill G, Hespe C. The telehealth skills, training, and implementation project: an evaluation protocol. JMIR Research Protocols 2015;4(1). https://doi.org/10.2196/resprot.3613.

[18] Love R, Carrington JM. Introducing telehealth skills into the Doctor of nursing practice curriculum. Journal of the American Association of Nurse Practitioners 2021;33(11):1030–4. https://doi.org/10.1097/JXX.0000000000000505.

[19] Emerson MR, Buchanan L, Golden A. Telehealth simulation with graduate nurse practitioner students. Nurse Educator 2021;46(2):126–9. https://doi.org/10.1097/NNE.0000000000000843.

[20] Costich M, Robbins-Milne L, Bracho-Sanchez E, Lane M, Friedman S. Design and implementation of an interactive, competency-based pilot pediatric telemedicine curriculum. Medical Education Online 2021;26(1). https://doi.org/10.1080/10872981.2021.1911019.

[21] Phillips TA, Munn AC, George TP. Assessing the impact of telehealth objective structured clinical examinations in graduate nursing education. Nurse Educator 2020;45(3):169–72. https://doi.org/10.1097/NNE.0000000000000729.

[22] Quinlin L, Clark Graham M, Nikolai C, Teall AM. Development and implementation of an e-visit objective structured clinical examination to evaluate student ability to provide care by telehealth. Journal of the American Association of Nurse Practitioners 2021;33(5):359–65. https://doi.org/10.1097/JXX.0000000000000409.

[23] Farrell SE, Junkin AR, Hayden EM. Assessing clinical skills via telehealth objective standardized clinical examination: feasibility, acceptability, comparability, and educational value. Telemedicine and e-Health 2022;28(2):248–57. https://doi.org/10.1089/tmj.2021.0094.

[24] Kumra T, McGuire M, Stein A, Pahwa AK. Telemedicine clinical skills needs assessment in early medical students. Family Medicine 2022;54(4):294–7. https://doi.org/10.22454/FamMed.2022.904873.

[25] Murphy EM, Stein A, Pahwa A, McGuire M, Kumra T. Improvement of medical student performance in telemedicine standardized patient encounters following an educational intervention. Family Medicine 2023;55(6):400–4. https://doi.org/10.22454/fammed.2023.523442.

[26] Mulcare M, Naik N, Greenwald P, Schullstrom K, Gogia K, Clark S, Kang Y, Sharma R. Advanced communication and examination skills in telemedicine: a structured simulation-based course for medical students. MedEdPORTAL: The Journal of Teaching and Learning Resources 2020;16. https://doi.org/10.15766/mep_2374-8265.11047. undefined.

[27] Pfeil SA, Shellhaas CS. Using simulation to train clinical providers in the effective use of telehealth. Nutrition in Clinical Practice 2023;38(3):520–30. https://doi.org/10.1002/ncp.10977.

[28] Fox BI, Umphress DA, Hollingsworth JC. Development and delivery of an interdisciplinary course in mobile health (mHealth). Currents in Pharmacy Teaching and Learning 2017;9(4):585–94. https://doi.org/10.1016/j.cptl.2017.03.005.

[29] Skiba DJ, Barton AJ, Knapfel S, Moore G, Trinkley K. Infusing informatics into interprofessional education: the iTEAM (interprofessional technology enhanced advanced practice model) project. Studies in Health Technology and Informatics 2014;201:55–62. https://doi.org/10.3233/978-1-61499-415-2-55.

[30] Estes K, Gilliam E, Knapfel S, Lee C, Skiba D. Discovering eHealth technology: an innovative interprofessional graduate student learning experience. Studies in Health Technology and Informatics 2016;225:242–6. https://doi.org/10.3233/978-1-61499-658-3-242.

[31] Harendza S, Gärtner J, Zelesniack E, Prediger S. Evaluation of a telemedicine-based training for final-year medical students including simulated patient consultations, documentation, and case presentation. GMS Journal for Medical Education 2020;37(7):1–8. https://doi.org/10.3205/zma001387.

[32] Brebner EM, Brebner JA, Ruddick-Bracken H, Wootton R, Ferguson J. The importance of setting and evaluating standards of telemedicine training. Journal of Telemedicine and Telecare 2003;9(1_Suppl. l):7–9. https://doi.org/10.1258/135763303322196150.

[33] Jones HM, Ammerman BA, Joiner KL, Lee DR, Bigelow A, Kuzma EK. Evaluating an intervention of telehealth education and simulation for advanced practice registered nurse students: a single group comparison study. Nursing Open 2023;10(6):4137–43. https://doi.org/10.1002/nop2.1620.

[34] Sabin JE, Skimming K. A framework of ethics for telepsychiatry practice. International Review of Psychiatry 2015;27(6):490–5. https://doi.org/10.3109/09540261.2015.1094034.

[35] Bramstedt KA, Prang M, Dave S, Shin PNH, Savy A, Fatica RA. Telemedicine as an ethics teaching tool for medical students within the nephrology curriculum. Progress in Transplantation 2014;24(3):294–7. https://doi.org/10.7182/pit2014289.

[36] Chunara R, Zhao Y, Chen J, Lawrence K, Testa PA, Nov O, Mann DM. Telemedicine and healthcare disparities: a cohort study in a large healthcare system in New York City during COVID-19. Journal of the American Medical Informatics Association 2021;28(1):33–41. https://doi.org/10.1093/jamia/ocaa217.

[37] Lyles CR, Sharma AE, Fields JD, Getachew Y, Sarkar U, Zephyrin L. Centering health equity in telemedicine. The Annals of Family Medicine 2022;20(4):362–7. https://doi.org/10.1370/afm.2823.

[38] Hart A, Romney D, Sarin R, Mechanic O, Hertelendy AJ, Larson D, Rhone K, Sidel K, Voskanyan A, Ciottone GR. Developing telemedicine curriculum competencies for graduate medical education: outcomes of a modified Delphi process. Academic Medicine 2022;97(4):577–85. https://doi.org/10.1097/acm.0000000000004463.

[39] Noronha C, Lo MC, Nikiforova T, Jones D, Nandiwada DR, Leung TI, Smith JE, Lee WW. Telehealth competencies in medical education: new Frontiers in faculty development and learner assessments. Journal of General Internal Medicine 2022;37(12):3168–73. https://doi.org/10.1007/s11606-022-07564-8.

[40] Hersh WR, Gorman PN, Biagioli FE, Mohan V, Gold JA, Mejicano GC. Beyond information retrieval and electronic health record use: competencies in clinical informatics for medical education. Advances in Medical Education and Practice 2014;5:205–12. https://doi.org/10.2147/AMEP.S63903.

[41] Powers BB, Van Zuilen RM, Schwartz AW, Dang S, McLaren JE, Hoang-Gia D, Moo LR. Competencies for video telemedicine with older adult patients. Journal of the American Geriatrics Society 2023;71(4):1283–90. https://doi.org/10.1111/jgs.18246.

[42] Rutledge CM, O'Rourke J, Mason AM, Chike-Harris K, Behnke L, Melhado L, Downes L, Gustin T. Telehealth competencies for nursing education and practice. Nurse Educator 2021;46(5):300–5. https://doi.org/10.1097/nne.0000000000000988.

[43] GMS. Journal for Medical Education | Digital Teaching and Digital Medicine: A National Initiative is Needed. 2018.

[44] Perry CK, Damschroder LJ, Hemler JR, Woodson TT, Ono SS, Cohen DJ. Specifying and comparing implementation strategies across seven large implementation interventions: a practical application of theory. Implementation Science 2019;14(1). https://doi.org/10.1186/s13012-019-0876-4.

[45] Grimshaw JM, Eccles MP, Lavis JN, Hill SJ, Squires JE. Knowledge translation of research findings. Implementation Science 2012;7(1).

[46] Foy R, Eccles MP, Jamtvedt G, Young J, Grimshaw JM, Baker R. What do we know about how to do audit and feedback? Pitfalls in applying evidence from a systematic review. BMC Health Services Research 2005;5. https://doi.org/10.1186/1472-6963-5-50.

CHAPTER 29

Incorporating AI and ML into the classroom

Carlos Gutierrez[1,2,3], Stephanie Jalaba[4], Ryan Kingsley[5], and Sarah Bolander[6]

[1]Department of Physician Assistant Studies, University of Pittsburgh, Pittsburgh, PA, United States; [2]A.T. Still University, Kirksville, MO, United States; [3]InclusiCare Medical, Phoenix, AZ, United States; [4]Department of PA Medicine, Michigan State University, East Lansing, MI, United States; [5]Mayo Clinic College of Medicine and Science, Hospital Internal Medicine, Rochester, MN, United States; [6]Department of Physician Assistant Studies, Northern Arizona University, Phoenix, AZ, United States

Introduction

The prevalence of information, communication, and technology has transformed the nature of learning and teaching. Traditional teaching practices, which were previously limited to printed text and direct face-to-face interaction, are now being disrupted by technological tools and advances. The advancement of technology provides a more flexible learning environment, accommodating diverse learning styles and needs. For instance, the use of videos in education offers an authentic experience, simulating real-world scenarios without the need for physical presence. Such tools enhance the learning experience, promote understanding of various community development issues, and stimulate analytical thinking and problem-solving. Nonetheless, more advanced and more capable tools are now available.

The integration of AI/ML into digital health education is ushering in a transformative era of technology-enhanced learning experiences. AI/ML tools are redefining the boundaries of digital health education, offering innovative methodologies such as immersive simulations, which complement traditional teaching techniques and address the unique challenges presented by the rapidly evolving healthcare landscape. This section delves into specific examples of these tools, highlighting their potential benefits and applications in the classroom as well as some challenges to consider.

Digital Health. https://doi.org/10.1016/B978-0-443-23901-4.00029-5

Ways to incorporate AI/ML into the classroom

AI/ML in interactive teaching methods

In the realm of digital health education, interactivity emerges as a cornerstone for effective and enriching learning experiences. The integration of engaging elements in the educational process facilitates active learning with course content and establishes real-time interactions between students and instructors. By incorporating these tools and methods, educators can create an immersive and participatory environment that enhances the learning journey.

One of the key components of interactive digital health education is the utilization of multimedia instruments. AI can create adaptive multimedia presentations that adjust to individual learning styles and paces of individual students. For example, AI algorithms can analyze student engagement using various types of content and provide personalized recommendations, ensuring complex concepts are undersood through the most effective medium for each student.

Quizzes and assessments integrated into digital health education platforms serve as valuable interactive tools. Imagine AI-powered assessents in which a tool can dynamically adjust the difficulty of questions using biometrics to read a student's confidence level and based on performance. This can provide a customized testing experine that accurately measures student understanding and progression. Additionally, ML algorithims may analyze student responses to idenify other potential knowledge gaps and suggest targeted review materials or provide immediate tutoring. Intelligent tutoring systems, a component of AI/ML often integrated into quiz and assessment platforms, will be discussed further in this chapter.

Online discussions are another vital aspect of interactivity in digital health education. Interactive platforms and discussion boards provide a virtual space for students to exchange ideas, share perspectives, and engage in meaningful conversations. These discussions enable learners to explore different viewpoints, refine their arguments, and deepen their understanding through constructive dialog with peers and instructors. As healthcare education shifted to a digital approach during the onset of the COVID-19 pandemic, many students began to engage in asynchronous online discussion, leading to an improved understanding of medicine [1,8]. AI tools can moderate online discussions suggesting relevant resources, questions, and topics based on the context of the situation. Additionally, AI can analyze the sentiment of student posts to gauge engagement and emotional response, providing important insights about student satisfaction and knowledge gaps.

Simulations offer an immersive and hands-on approach to learning in the field of digital health education. By simulating real-world scenarios and patient interactions, learners can apply their knowledge and skills in a safe and controlled environment. Simulations foster critical thinking, decision-making, and problem-solving abilities, allowing students to gain practical experience and confidence before entering clinical settings. One example of simulation in the digital setting is the use of an interactive simulator tool to engage students in medical communication scenarios. Further discussion on simulations will be provided in this chapter.

While embracing collaboration in digital health education, instructors should empower students to take an active role in their own learning process. Self-directedness has been shown to be an important factor in effective learning, particularly in a blended learning environment. AI can analyze a student's learning habits, peformance data, and preferences to create customized study plans. This allows each student to receive the most relevant and effective resources and activities, promoting self-directed learning. The participatory nature of interactive methods fosters deeper engagement, critical thinking, and a profound understanding of the course material. It encourages students to apply knowledge in practical scenarios, enhances collaboration and communication skills, and prepares them for challenges in the digital health landscape.

As digital health continues to evolve, the integration of interactive elements in education becomes increasingly essential. Medical educators should emphasize the value of collaboration and provide practical guidance on incorporating interactive multimedia presentations, online discussions, simulations, and quizzes into the curriculum. By leveraging these interactive methods, educators can nurture a new generation of healthcare professionals who are well-equipped to navigate the complexities of the digital age.

High-fidelity and virtual reality simulation

High-fidelity simulation allows for impactful educational opportunities in healthcare training. Highly sophisticated manikins can replicate human physiology and offer feedback on complex and immersive scenarios, creating a unique teaching environment. This modality enables the integration of medical knowledge with the complexities of clinical practice in a safe and replicable environment. High-fidelity simulators can be used across the educational spectrum, from initial didactic instruction in the classroom to clinical education, and beyond into postgraduate training.

Computerized case scenarios can be used in a similar fashion to traditional high-fidelity simulation, depending on the unique objectives of the activtity. These are typically structured, text-based simulations that present clinical cases with a series of questions and decision points. Platforms for these case scenarios may offer lower cost options and increased accessibility at institutions where high-fidelity simulators cannot be purchased or the simulator(s) are used by multiple students and programs making the availability limited. Examples of clinical situations particularly amenable to computerized case scenarios include handling medical errors, emergent conditions, surgical procedures, technical skills, and specific populations such as infants. Utilizing computerized case scenarios allows for a safe environment to build critical thinking skills, offer immediate feedback, and opportunities toremediate learners. These simulations should be developed and assessed by content experts. If utilizing an educational platform with pre-made case scenarios, some items to consider include assuring the cases have learning objectives appropriate for the level of learner, and ensuring the cases are kept up to date with changing clinical practices.

High-fidelity simulation is evolving rapidly, and costs to maintain the updated technology may be a challenge to sustain. Low-fidelity simulators, though they have less functionality, are still great tools for simulation, paticularly procedural skill practice. Traditional in-person simulation, with either high-fidelity manikins or standardized patient actors, hold tremendous benefits for learners; however, increasing costs, faculty demands, and declining availability limit use, especially in areas with fewer resources. Despite advancements, these teaching and assessment methods should be combined with human oversight to adjust for errors, enhance communication, and facilitate prebriefs and debriefs, which are critical components of quality simulation learning [4].

Virtual reality (VR) can offer a more cost-effective approach to enhancing clinical knowledge, skills, and attitudes [2]. Some common applications of virtual reality simulation include virtual patients, clinical skill simulators, conversational models, and environmental immersion, each of which has its particular strengths and applicability.

Virtual patients, a specific form of virtual medical training characterized by simulation of clinical scenarios that prompt clinical decision-making, have been found to be particularly well-suited to training and assessing clinical reasoning [18,21]. With increasing demands placed on healthcare providers and the associated increases in healthcare worker burnout, clinical education requirements are outpacing capabilities of faculty [14,24]. Employing effective clinical learning experiences such as virtual patients and virtual reality can reduce the reliance of healthcare education programs on clinical educators, preceptors, and sites, thereby, advancing clinical education stewardship.

Clinical skill simulators focus on the development and assessment of clinical and technical skills, such as endoscopy, central line placement, and surgical skills in medical training. Virtual reality offers several advantages to educational programs, including cost-effectiveness, replicability, and safety. A recent systematic review by Mao et al. [9] on virtual reality in surgical training found that high-quality studies supported the use of virtual reality, showing improvements in procedural times, accuracy, cost-effectiveness, and task completion.

Conversational models, defined here as virtual reality applications that employ Large Language Models (LLMs) to conduct realistic conversational interactions with participants, represent a powerful emerging application at the intersection of virtual reality and artificial intelligence. Educational programs employ this technology to train in empathic communication techniques, conflict negotiation, history-taking, and interprofessional communication. Learning outcomes for students using this approach are equivalent to traditional methods, with increased student satisfaction and engagement [10].

Environmental immersion, another type of virtual reality tool, draws from robust data on clinical applications of virtual reality and the theoretical framework of immersion and presence as core components of effective learning in virtual reality [11,12]. A common example of this approach is the use of 360-degree videos, which allow learners to see and hear an environment of interest. This method has been used to orient students to labor and delivery, surgical preparation, and street medicine. While this technique does not allow for interactivity, it serves as valuable support for students unfamiliar with specific contexts prior to clinical learning experiences.

Intelligent tutoring systems

Learning in medical education consists of various layers and applications of knowledge. Learners begin with obtaining basic knowledge and as they progress through different layers of learning, they eventually reach a point where they can apply the knowledge to patient care scenarios. Not all learners enter into medical education with the same level of knowledge or learning abilities, and similarly, not all learners progress through the different layers of learning along the same timeline. Educators adapt to these differences using the pedagogical approach known as scaffolding, which is a student-centered method that requires awareness of students' existing knowledge and skills with subsequent implementation of learning activities structured to enable optimal learning [13]. This is intended to advance students from their zone of proximal development over time, which represents the range of tasks a learner can perform with the help and guidance of a more knowledgeable individual but cannot yet perform independently. A key challenge with this approach is accurately determining a student's zone of proximal development.

Intelligent tutoring systems can effectively mitigate differences in knowledge and skill level by meeting students at their current level and assisting them in their learning progression, eliminating the need for educators to develop multiple layers of curriculum. These systems can be applied in various learning capacities. Some online learning platforms use intelligent learning systems to help students master content by using an algorithm based on a student's correctness and level of confidence (selected by the student when they answer a question) to continually tailor the quiz questions in real time to meet their needs in learning.

Other intelligent learning systems can assist healthcare education students in developing critical thinking skills within clinical scenarios by using real, deidentified patient cases in a zero-risk environment. These platforms are designed to provide multidimensional evaluations and address learner deficiencies. Students are challenged with multifaceted decision-making and assessment at each level of a patient's case, from information collection to analysis and observations. In one particular program, cases are tailored according to difficulty levels and structured within a four-level framework to progress through [14].

Intelligent learning systems may also have the ability to improve a student's "feeling-of-knowing" judgment, which is the learner's certainty of their actual performance. When the "feeling-of-knowing" is mismatched with correctness, this is known as bias. Research has shown that bias can result in more clinical errors. Bias often takes the form of either underconfidence or overconfidence. Underconfidence might lead to treatment delays, while overconfidence might result in ineffective decision-making. A study by Feyzi-Benagh et al. [15] found that metacognitive scaffolding and immediate feedback through intelligent tutor systems led to cognitive improvements from the pretest to the posttest. Conversely, in the study group without immediate feedback tutoring, no significant change in scores was observed from pretest to posttest [15].

Chatbots and virtual assistants

In the rapidly evolving landscape of digital health education, chatbots, and virtual assistants have emerged as powerful tools to enhance learning experiences and provide personalized support. These technologies leverage artificial intelligence to interact with users, offering real-time responses and tailored information based on individual needs.

Educators should first be aware of the virtual assistants available to patients to properly prepare students for the new digital health landscape. A virtual assistant named "Vitoria" was designed to promote education and adherence to antidiabetic medications in older people [16]. The study by Isa Brito Félix et al. [16] presents an innovative approach to improving medication adherence among older adults with diabetes. They achieved this by using this virtual assistant, developed on the a platform for Android devices. This anthropomorphic virtual assistant is rooted in the behavior change wheel framework, targeting psychological capability and reflective motivation to influence behavior. The assistant employs a well-defined set of behavior change techniques, such as problem-solving, to interact with users both verbally and nonverbally. This research underscores the growing potential of chatbots and virtual assistants in digital health education, offering a theory-based, interactive, and personalized approach to addressing the critical issue of medication adherence [16].

The metaverse, a concept that has gained significant attention recently, is another domain in which chatbots and virtual assistants can play a pivotal role, particularly for medical education [17]. As a fully immersive parallel digital reality, the metaverse offers opportunities for health education and training. For instance, platforms such as Second Life, a virtual world video game first launched in 2003, have been used for diverse health initiatives [17]. Platforms like Second Life have demonstrated the potential for health education initiatives. With the integration of augmented reality, virtual reality, and artificial intelligence, the metaverse can transform educational experiences. Chatbots and virtual assistants in the metaverse can facilitate interactive learning, provide instant feedback, and simulate complex clinical scenarios. These technologies enable healthcare education students to engage in realistic, hands-on training environments, enhancing their learning and preparedness for real-world healthcare challenges. While chatbots play an incredible role in virtual and simulation settings, educators can incorporate chatbots to assist with coursework, provide instant feedback on assignments, and facilitate virtual discussions.

Chatbots and virtual assistants are not just technological novelties; they are increasingly being used as transformative agents in healthcare, and in healthcare education. As these tools continue to evolve, they will undoubtedly play a more central role in shaping personalized, interactive, and effective learning experiences for students at any level.

Benefits of incorporating AI/ML in the classroom

Personalized learning

AI and ML provide many advantages to the personalization of learning, defined as learning activities designed and implemented in ways that consider individual learner needs and help them construct their own knowledge [18,19]. By its nature, personalized learning requires a large amount of student data, and this is precisely a fundamental strength of AI and ML technologies.

Large language models (LLMs) are a form of AI, which use deep machine learning systems to collect and analyze large language datasets and create human-like responses [20]. Implementation of LLM-powered chatbots in educational programs, for example, can provide real-time, useful responses to common questions on the learner-facing side while simultaneously offering the ability to collect large and detailed datasets that may be leveraged to tailor instruction and curricular design to meet the needs of specific types of learners and even to individuals. The University of Murcia in Spain, Staffordshire University in the United Kingdom, and Georgia Institute of Technology in the United States have all introduced chatbots designed to provide 24/7 management of student questions with impressive accuracy [20].

ChatGPT, one of the most popular types of LLM, has seen rapid adoption and increasing popularity in education, especially in educational fields that require interpretation and production of peer-reviewed literature. A 2023 systematic review by Malik Sallam [21] found one of the chief benefits of ChatGPT was its ability to help nonnative English speakers interpret and produce scholarly work.

Improved student engagement

Although AI/ML is increasingly being used in academia, most educators may not be fully aware of the benefits of incorporating these opportunities for students. Given the many benefits, faculty should thoughtfully augment current learning strategies with AI, which may improve student engagement. Machine learning has the ability to identify distinct needs of a learner, which can direct more meaningful engagement. ML enhances personalized learning, which in turn supports competency-based medical education. Real-time assessment, immediate feedback, and intelligent tutoring cater to student learning and are often delivered as edutainment, which has emerged as an effective and engaging method of instruction in certain circumstances [22]. During the COVID-19 pandemic, many students learned to thrive in educational environments that fostered various ways of learning, including these engaging methods.

Students are in a unique setting that may allow them to become both educated consumers and users of AI/ML resources, enhancing both their educational experience and their future clinical practice. Enhancing the current curriculum to integrate components of artificial intelligence will likely engage students in the modernization of health science systems and patient care, and pique interest in a generation of learners who have come to embrace the many benefits of advanced technology. This adaptation and implementation may be onerous on faculty, but AI actually has the ability to offset workload if used efficiently.

Increased efficiency and accuracy

AI-powered educational tools are transforming the realm of assessments. They offer the ability to enhance the precision of evaluations, provide tailored feedback for students, and allow educators to adapt their teaching methodologies to cater to the individual needs of each student [23]. Such advancements promise to redefine the delivery and assessment of education, leading to improved outcomes for learners. Large language AI models, in particular, have shown potential in various areas of classroom assessment, from determining the purpose of tests to interpreting the results.

In the context of AI/ML applications, the importance of efficiency and accuracy cannot be overstated. Similar trends are seen in other industries. In the field of technological predictions, experts prioritize making forecasts that are not only timely but also highly accurate. A study by Wang et al. [14] in 2023 highlighted that in technological predictions, the focus isn't solely on predicting what will happen, but also on getting that information as quickly and precisely as possible. This is because timely and accurate information can make the difference between success and failure.

Similarly, in healthcare applications of AI/ML, there is an emphasis on providing quick and accurate results, diagnoses, or treatment suggestions, as they can directly impact patient outcomes. This principle can also be applied to educational contexts, underscoring the importance of prompt and accurate feedback and assessments in the learning process.

In essence, the integration of AI/ML in educational settings heralds a new era. By harnessing these technologies, we have the opportunity to achieve unparalleled efficiency, accuracy, and personalization. AI and ML can help ensure students experience timely, relevant, individualized feedback, with increased engagement, thereby enhancing the overall learning experience.

Navigating the ethical and practical labyrinth: Challenges and considerations for implementing AI/ML in the classroom

The technological leap of integrating AI and MIL into educational experiences does not come without challenges. Educators, policymakers, and technologists must grapple with a range of ethical and practical questions to ensure responsible and effective use of these technologies.

One of the most pressing ethical concerns is the collection and use of student data. AI and ML systems often require large datasets for effective operation, raising questions about data ownership and usage [23,24]. Before deploying any AI or ML tools in the classroom, educators must obtain the appropriate informed consent from students and/or guardians, clearly outlining what data will be collected and how it will be used [25].

While AI and ML technologies are often touted for their accuracy, many of these systems have not undergone rigorous testing in real-world educational settings. Concerns arise regarding the reliability of information generated by these technologies, particularly when used for high-stakes decisions such as student assessments.

Another significant concern is the potential for misuse of AI and ML technologies. For example, students might use AI-generated content to complete assignments, undermining the educational process and violating academic integrity. Tools designed to detect such unethical usage are still in their infancy and are not entirely reliable, posing challenges for educators in maintaining the authenticity of student work and preserving the learning process.

AI and ML technologies are not neutral; they can reflect and perpetuate societal biases and inequalities. Educators must be aware of these broader implications and strive to use these technologies in a manner that is inclusive and equitable.

As AI and ML technologies continue to evolve, ongoing research and dialogue are essential for addressing these challenges. Feedback mechanisms should be put in place to assess the effectiveness of these technologies in the educational setting and to make necessary adjustments [25].

Assessment

Reflective journal

As you reach the end of this chapter, it's time to pause and reflect on the transformative role of Artificial Intelligence (AI) and Machine Learning (ML) in digital health education. The chapter has covered a wide range of topics, from interactive teaching methods and high-fidelity simulations to intelligent tutoring systems and ethical considerations. Now, let's take a moment to assess your understanding and thoughts on these subjects. How do you see AI/ML contributing to personalized learning in digital health education? What are some ethical challenges you foresee in the integration of AI/ML into digital health education? How do you envision the future of digital health education with the integration of AI/ML?

AI disclosure

During the preparation of this work, the author(s) used Chat GPT. We asked chat to review the chapter after peer review to edit any issues with flow or grammar. After using this tool/service, the author(s) reviewed and edited the content as needed and take(s) full responsibility for the content of the publication.

References

[1] Akgun S, Greenhow C. Artificial intelligence in education: addressing ethical challenges in K-12 settings. AI and Ethics 2022;2(3):431–40. https://doi.org/10.1007/s43681-021-00096-7.

[2] Barteit S, Lanfermann L, Bärnighausen T, Neuhann F, Beiersmann C. Augmented, mixed, and virtual reality-based head-mounted devices for medical education: systematic review. JMIR Serious Games 2021;9(3):e29080. https://doi.org/10.2196/29080.

[3] Caponnetto P, Triscari S, Maglia M, Quattropani MC. The simulation game—virtual reality therapy for the treatment of social anxiety disorder: a systematic review. International Journal of Environmental Research and Public Health 2021;18(24):13209. https://doi.org/10.3390/ijerph182413209.

[4] Carl E, Stein AT, Levihn-Coon A, Pogue JR, Rothbaum B, Emmelkamp P, Asmundson GJG, Carlbring P, Powers MB. Virtual reality exposure therapy for anxiety and related disorders: a meta-analysis of randomized controlled trials. Journal of Anxiety Disorders 2019;61:27–36. https://doi.org/10.1016/j.janxdis.2018.08.003.

[5] Christoforaki M, Beyan O. AI ethics—a bird's eye view. Applied Sciences 2022;12(9):4130. https://doi.org/10.3390/app12094130.

[6] Cook DA, Triola MM. Virtual patients: a critical literature review and proposed next steps. Medical Education 2009;43(4):303–11. https://doi.org/10.1111/j.1365-2923.2008.03286.x.

[7] Cook DA, Erwin PJ, Triola MM. Computerized virtual patients in health professions education: a systematic review and meta-analysis. Academic Medicine: Journal of the Association of American Medical Colleges 2010;85(10):1589–602. https://doi.org/10.1097/acm.0b013e3181edfe13.
[8] Daulatabad V, Kamble P, John N, John J. An overview and analogy of pedagogical approaches in online–offline teaching tactics in COVD-19 pandemic. Journal of Education and Health Promotion 2022;11(1):341. https://doi.org/10.4103/jehp.jehp_11_22.
[9] Feyzi-Behnagh R, Azevedo R, Legowski E, Reitmeyer K, Tseytlin E, Crowley RS. Metacognitive scaffolds improve self-judgments of accuracy in a medical intelligent tutoring system. Instructional Science 2014;42(2):159–81. https://doi.org/10.1007/s11251-013-9275-4.
[10] Félix IB, Guerreiro MP, Cavaco A, Cláudio AP, Mendes A, Balsa J, Carmo MB, Pimenta N, Henriques A. Development of a complex intervention to improve adherence to antidiabetic medication in older people using an anthropomorphic virtual assistant software. Frontiers in Pharmacology 2019;10. https://doi.org/10.3389/fphar.2019.00680.
[11] Kayingo G, Gordes KL, Fleming S, Cawley JF. Thinking outside the box: advancing clinical education in an era of preceptor shortage. Journal of Physician Assistant Education 2023;34(2):135–41. https://doi.org/10.1097/JPA.0000000000000500.
[12] Komasawa N, Yokohira M. Simulation-based education in the artificial intelligence era. Cureus 2023. https://doi.org/10.7759/cureus.40940.
[13] Lee D, Huh Y, Lin CY, Reigeluth CM, Lee E. Differences in personalized learning practice and technology use in high- and low-performing learner-centered schools in the United States. Educational Technology Research & Development 2021;69(2):1221–45. https://doi.org/10.1007/s11423-021-09937-y.
[14] Mao RQ, Lan L, Kay J, Lohre R, Ayeni OR, Goel DP, Sa D. Immersive virtual reality for surgical training: a systematic review. Journal of Surgical Research 2021;268:40–58. https://doi.org/10.1016/j.jss.2021.06.045.
[15] Masava B, Nyoni CN, Botma Y. Scaffolding in health sciences education programmes: an integrative review. Medical Science Educator 2023;33(1):255–73. https://doi.org/10.1007/s40670-022-01691-x.
[16] Mittelstadt B. Near-term ethical challenges of digital twins. Journal of Medical Ethics 2021;47(6):405–6. https://doi.org/10.1136/medethics-2021-107449.
[17] Murthy VH. Confronting health worker burnout and well-being. New England Journal of Medicine 2022;387(7):577–9. https://doi.org/10.1056/NEJMp2207252.
[18] Qiu CS, Majeed A, Khan S, Watson M. Transforming health through the metaverse. Journal of the Royal Society of Medicine 2022;115(12):484–6. https://doi.org/10.1177/01410768221144763.
[19] Rodrigues MAM, Zornoff D, Kobayasi R. Remote Pathology teaching under the COVID-19 pandemic: medical students' perceptions. Annals of Diagnostic Pathology 2022;56:151875. https://doi.org/10.1016/j.anndiagpath.2021.151875.
[20] Ryan GV, Callaghan S, Rafferty A, Higgins MF, Mangina E, McAuliffe F. Learning outcomes of immersive technologies in health care student education: systematic review of the literature. Journal of Medical Internet Research 2022;24(2):e30082. https://doi.org/10.2196/30082.
[21] Sallam M. ChatGPT utility in healthcare education, research, and practice: systematic review on the promising perspectives and valid concerns. Healthcare 2023;11(6):887. https://doi.org/10.3390/healthcare11060887.
[22] Shemshack A, Spector JM. A systematic literature review of personalized learning terms. Smart Learning Environments 2020;7(1). https://doi.org/10.1186/s40561-020-00140-9.
[23] Wolfensberger A, Anagnostopoulos A, Clack L, Meier MT, Kuster SP, Sax H. Effectiveness of an edutainment video teaching standard precautions - a randomized controlled evaluation study. Antimicrobial Resistance and Infection Control 2019;8(1). https://doi.org/10.1186/s13756-019-0531-5.
[24] Wang H, Zhuge Q, Sha EH-M, Xu R, Song Y. Optimizing efficiency of machine learning based hard disk failure prediction by two-layer classification-based feature selection. Applied Sciences 2023;13(13):7544. https://doi.org/10.3390/app13137544.
[25] van Dis EAM, Bollen J, Zuidema W, van Rooij R, Bockting CL. ChatGPT: five priorities for research. Nature 2023;614(7947):224–6. https://doi.org/10.1038/d41586-023-00288-7.

CHAPTER 30

Incorporating digital health into the curriculum

Carlos Gutierrez[1,2], Sarah Bolander[3], Ryan Kingsley[4], and Stephanie Jalaba[5]
[1]Department of Physician Assistant Studies, University of Pittsburgh, Pittsburgh, PA, United States; [2]InclusiCare Medical, Phoenix, AZ, United States; [3]Department of Physician Assistant Studies, Northern Arizona University, Phoenix, AZ, United States; [4]Mayo Clinic College of Medicine and Science, Hospital Internal Medicine, Rochester, MN, United States; [5]Department of PA Medicine, Michigan State University, East Lansing, MI, United States

Use of artificial intelligence (AI) and machine learning (ML) in the healthcare setting has expanded significantly in the last decade, and even more rapidly in the past few years. The global spread of Coronavirus Disease 2019 (COVID-19) undeniably contributed to the significant and rapid progress in digital health made since 2020. Because of restrictions on in-person interactions, the healthcare industry shifted to using telemedicine and various digital health technologies for remote monitoring. The pandemic highlighted the importance of data and analytics in healthcare and increased the investment in digital health [1]. Since 2020, most healthcare organizations are now involved in developing or adopting healthcare-related AI/ML products that are changing the system as we know it.

The World Health Organization (WHO) has structured the classification of various digital health interventions (DHIs) into four different categories based on the ways in which these technologies are being used to support healthcare needs. The four categories that make up this framework include *Interventions for Clients, Interventions for HealthCare Providers, Interventions for Health System or Resource Managers, and Interventions for Data Service*s [2]. This tool recognizes the diversity of communities working in digital health and the many different facets of healthcare affected. Each of the four categories contains specific interventions and discrete examples of real-life applicability, many using AI and/or ML. For example, *Provide prompts and alerts based according to protoco* is one identified decison support intervention for healthcare providers, with an illustrative example being the Mobile App for Management of HIV in Pregnancy. Clinical and administrative flags are generated on both patient-specific and clinic population-specific bases for missed appointments, concerning laboratory analysis values, and missing information [2].

Digital Health. https://doi.org/10.1016/B978-0-443-23901-4.00030-1

Machine learning was recognized over 70 years ago to describe the ability of a machine to perform a task and to improve its performance over time with acquired experience. Simply put, it requires the input of statistical tools that learn about relationships between data based on inputs and outputs with repeated usage. Over time it has evolved into technology that can perform high-functioning tasks, sometimes even those that are difficult or impossible for humans. AI in healthcare has taken two forms. Assistive AI requires the clinician to make a final decision, while autonomous AI makes a clinical decision without the involvement of a clinician. There are potential benefits and drawbacks of both systems.

In 2018, the FDA approved the first autonomous ML system, accompanying a fundus camera for the detection of diabetic retinopathy [3]. This tool was created to increase access to screening and improve outcomes in diabetic patients by allowing healthcare professionals who did not specialize in eye care to employ the screening and detect diabetic retinopathy with increased efficacy. A clinical trial established the safety and efficacy of the tool and the exact parameters of when the algorithm could be appropriately used [3]. One study proved the diabetic retinopathy screening algorithm could detect referable diabetic retinopathy with high sensitivity and specificity [4].

Artificial Intelligence is currently being tested to improve almost every aspect of healthcare from research to diagnosis, treatment, and patient care. In its simplest functionality, AI can automate a mundane task such as data entry or appointment scheduling, and free up human personnel to focus on more complex and rewarding tasks. With more complex functionality, AI can process information to make diagnoses that a human cannot yet predict. For example, AI electrocardiogram screening has proven the ability through varied studies to detect left ventricular systolic dysfunction, hypertrophic cardiomyopathy, and silent atrial fibrillation by using information beyond what is visible to the eye of an experienced clinician [5,6]. Despite robust testing and proven accuracy of many AI tools, their practical applicability into medicine is not as simple. Factors such as differences between testing populations and applied populations, variability in applied settings, and lack of understanding, trust, or accessibility by clinicians must all be considered before many of these tools can have meaningful impacts on healthcare [5].

The application of AI/ML into healthcare has many favorable implications, such as the ability to improve patient care and outcomes with early detection and improved prediction of disease; and some being less favorable, such as potential harm with a missed diagnosis or a misdiagnosis. For these reasons, the regulation and oversight of AI/ML products being used in digital healthcare is a current topic of interest and debate.

As the field of healthcare continues to evolve, it has become increasingly important to educate the next generation of healthcare professionals in digital health. With the advent of digital health technologies, such as mobile health (mHealth) apps, wearable devices, and telehealth platforms, a growing need exists for both future and current healthcare professionals to be trained on the use of these tools to be able to provide high-value care. Therefore, medical schools and healthcare education programs must incorporate digital health training into their curricula. This chapter will explore the best practices for integrating digital health education into medical schools and healthcare programs, discuss the challenges faced, and offer solutions for effective implementation.

First steps in incorporating digital health education into the curriculum

Developing a digital health education curriculum requires an understanding of the subject matter, pedagogical strategies, and the unique needs of learners. Educators must ensure that the curriculum is designed to equip students with the necessary skills and knowledge to navigate the digital health landscape effectively.

As educators begin crafting a digital health education curriculum, they must center their attention on comprehending the learning context, or where and how the learning takes place. First, educators must outline clear and measurable learning objectives. These objectives serve as the roadmap for the curriculum, detailing what students need to know or be able to accomplish upon completing the course. Learning objectives should be tailored to fit the digital age. For example, some learning objectives may include understanding how to use electronic health records or telemedicine platforms, while others may highlight the use of digital diagnostic tools and how these should or should not be incorporated into patient care.

Next, educators should appreciate the digital health learners' needs. As students have roots in various backgrounds, they each have varying levels of familiarity with digital health technologies and the curriculum should be flexible enough to accommodate this diversity. When engaging in curriculum design, educators should consider practice-specific differences. For example, a student in a rural healthcare setting and a student in an academic hospital with state-of the-art technology have different experiences and require training on health delivery at different levels. Most patients in a rural setting will rely on technologies such as remote monitoring from a digital device or telemedicine delivery, whereas this may be different for the urban student. Tailoring the curriculum to meet these varied needs ensures that all students can benefit and effectively serve their patients. Those developing curricula must also consider the broader social, cultural, and economic factors that may influence the learning process, including varying attitudes toward technology [7].

Next, educators should become aware of the resources available for teaching and learning. This includes not just the technological tools like online platforms and digital textbooks but also human resources such as instructional technology specialists and educators experienced in digital learning. These resources will play a significant role and how effectively the curriculum can be delivered.

Lastly, the term *learning context* also extends to the environment and conditions in which the learning will occur. This could mean the physical setting like a classroom or remote online platform as well as the broader sociocultural factors that might influence learning.

As educators come to understand these various aspects of the learning context, they can design a digital health education curriculum that is both comprehensive and adaptable to the unique needs and conditions of their student population.

Examples of integration of digital health into the curriculum

Digital problem-based learning in digital health education

In our rapidly evolving medical landscape, digital health education must be integrated into training the next generation of healthcare practitioners. One instructional approach that has shown promise in this regard is Problem-Based Learning (PBL), particularly its digital variant—Digital Problem-Based Learning (DPBL).

DPBL is an instructional method combining the principles of PBL with digital technologies. This instructional approach aims to improve health professionals' knowledge, skills, attitudes, and satisfaction by presenting them with real-world problems in a digital format. Approaches have varied, as the pandemic struck the globe, forcing the use of a blended approach of face-to-face delivery and digital experiences. A systematic review and meta-analysis conducted by Tudor Car, et al. [8] provides compelling evidence for the effectiveness of DPBL in health professions education. The study included randomized controlled trials comparing DPBL with traditional learning methods. The findings suggest that DPBL is as effective as traditional PBL and improves post intervention knowledge outcomes. Furthermore, when compared to traditional learning methods, DPBL showed significant improvement in both knowledge and skill development.

Digital problem-based learning, particularly in hybrid learning programs, has various advantages that are important in digital health education. First, DPBL enhances knowledge retention through engaging students in active problem-solving. DPBL helps address skill development by allowing students to develop their practical skills, including critical thinking and decision-making. Lastly, DPBL lends to student satisfaction and efficiency of resources.

Implementing DPBL in the digital health education curriculum provides robust, efficient, and effective approache to help prepare students for the challenges of their professional careers in healthcare. As digital health continues to expand the role of DPBL in shaping competent, satisfied, and resource-efficient professionals should not be overlooked.

Use of real-world case studies

Another method of integrating digital health in the curriculum involves educators using real-world case studies through a digital platform. Using these tools help to tie theory into practice. For example, students may understand that an extremely elevated hemoglobin A1c is associated with diabetes symptoms, but their understanding is heightened when they are presented with a case of an individual presenting with polyuria, polydipsia, and weight loss and are required to utilize critical thinking. Case-based learning is prominent in various professions, including digital health education, and is implemented to provide students with a better understanding of the healthcare subject matter and its clinical applications through emphasizing critical thinking skills [9].

When educators use authentic case studies in digital health education, they have been shown to improve student engagement and deepen their understanding of complex health concepts. During the COVID-19 pandemic, healthcare professions institutions and other universities had implement novel solutions to facilitate the learning process. These changes included transitioning from in-person classes to online learning and incorporating virtual simulations (discussed in this book) and telehealth experiences for clinical training. In these situations, case studies were often implemented [9]. Students were able to connect the clinical application to the knowledge they were learning in class.

Along with the benefit from better engagement, healthcare students also foster critical thinking and problem-solving skills when exposed to case studies. For example, integration of sustainability concerns into curricula through a process-oriented approach found students could solve problems more effectively when they were presented with concrete project scenarios [10].

On the other hand, educators should note that successful integration of real-world case studies into a curriculum requires careful planning and execution. Educators must ensure that case studies are relevant, engaging, and aligned with the learning objectives of the course. They must also provide adequate support and resources for students to effectively engage with case studies and apply their learnings to real-world scenarios.

There are many promising approaches for digital health in the classroom. These approaches promote active engagement, foster critical thinking, and prepare students for challenges in the digital health landscape. However, to maximize their benefits, educators should carefully consider the design of the case studies and provide adequate context, support, and resources for students.

Challenges and potential solutions for implementing digital health education into the curriculum

Implementing digital health education into the classroom does not come without challenges. Educators should consider factors such as resource availability, diversity of learners, and the rapid pace of technological advancements. Additionally, many educators themselves may need significant education on these tools before incorporating them into their curricula.

The costs associated with advanced technologies often make them inaccessible to some. Some institutions may not have the financial means or support to implement advanced technological tools into a curriculum. This disparity in resources leads to incongruent learning experiences with only a fraction of healthcare students currently having access to novel digital health tools. Grants and supplemental funding are methods to help prevent this barrier to implementing digital health in a classroom. Educators should consider seeking external funding and grants if institutions cannot support the implementation of digital health and learning into the classroom. Additionally, many free or discounted training programs and resource centers exist online or as part of society memberships that relate to digital health.

If not previously attempted, educators should consider bringing the importance of the evolving digital health landscape to institutional leadership's attention to promote its inclusion in budgetary spending and allocation of resources. This is important as the diversity of learners in any medical education program continues to increase [11]. Each group of students brings its own set of experiences, expectations, and skill levels, especially when it comes to technology.

Adaptive teaching methods are essential in ensuring each student can engage with the material in a meaningful way, rather than implementing a universal approach that may not meet the needs of each student. For example, some students may be digital natives, while others may be digital immigrants who are new to using technology tools for learning.

For those students who are less familiar with technology, introductory workshops at the beginning of a program are an excellent resource. Workshops can cover the basics of digital literacy, such as navigating online platforms, and even simple tasks like sending emails or using cloud storage services. This can help to ensure that all students, regardless of their prior experience with technology, start on an even footing.

Similarly, the pace of technological advances may pose a challenge for educators. New tools and platforms continue to emerge, creating a need for continuous training and adaptation. In order to assist with ongoing educational needs for faculty because of the dynamic nature of technology, institutional leadership should consider investing in regular training sessions for educators to ensure they are equipped with the latest knowledge and skills. Some great ideas for institutions include *Tech Days* or *Digital Health Weeks*. These events could include hosting technology companies to highlight their latest products and provide training sessions. Effectively, both educators and students can be exposed to latest technological discoveries in digital health. Additionally, leaders should consider online platforms that offer courses on the latest technology trends. Educators should also be willing to engage, understandchallenges, and construct appropriate feedback for students so that they can appropriately engage with the advancing digital health age.

Despite costs of technological equipment and trainings already being a significant burden, more barriers do exist. The time-intensive nature of these trainings makes them less feasible or desirable for many educators. Educators may already be facing burnout and feel overburdened in their current roles. However, educators cannot be expected to teach a subject they have not had the resources, time, or ability to learn. Additionally, institutions may not provide financial support when the tangible benefits are not readily visible. One solution to this problem involves outsourcing educational endeavors for implementing digital health in the classroom when it is not feasible for the instructor to teach. Using free resources, as well as cost-effective resources, may be reasonable solutions. Educators can also partake in group learning, or an institution may commit to a multi-year package to bargain a better rate. Some healthcare professions programs may even allow instructors to learn about digital health technologies alongside students to offset future costs.

The numerous benefits of digital health education are apparent; however, we must address the challenges head on to ensure an up-to-date, effective, and inclusive learning environment for students. As technology evolves, educators and institutions must also evolve. Teaching methods and curricula need to be adapted in order to harness the full potential of digital tools. This requires a commitment to continued learning, an investment in resources, and a focus on student-centric learning.

Assessment

Reflective Journal

Having explored the intricacies of digital health education, its integration in the classroom, and the challenges faced by users, take a moment to reflect on your personal experiences or observations. How do you see the role of digital health evolving in familiar educational settings? Are specific AI/ML tools or strategies discussed in this chapter that resonate with your experiences or aspirations? How might you apply the best practices and overcome the challenges discussed in your own educational or professional context? Jot down your thoughts, insights, and any questions that arise.

References

[1] Chen T, Peng L, Yin X, Rong J, Yang J, Cong G. Analysis of user satisfaction with online education platforms in China during the COVID-19 pandemic. Healthcare (Basel) 2020;8(3):200. https://doi.org/10.3390/healthcare8030200.

[2] World Health Organization. Classification of digital health interventions. 2018. https://apps.who.int/iris/bitstream/handle/10665/260480/WHO-RHR-18.06-eng.pdf. [Accessed 12 September 2023].

[3] Channa R, Wolf R, Abramoff MD. Autonomous artificial intelligence in diabetic retinopathy: from algorithm to clinical application. Journal of Diabetes Science and Technology 2021;15(3):695–8. https://doi.org/10.1177/1932296820909900.

[4] Gulshan V, Peng L, Coram M, et al. Development and validation of a deep learning algorithm for detection of diabetic retinopathy in retinal fundus photographs. JAMA 2016;316(22):2402–10. https://doi.org/10.1001/jama.2016.17216.

[5] Attia ZI, Harmon DM, Behr ER, Friedman PA. Application of artificial intelligence to the electrocardiogram. European Heart Journal 2021;42(46):4717–30. https://doi.org/10.1093/eurheartj/ehab649.

[6] Noseworthy PA, Attia ZI, Behnken EM, et al. Artificial intelligence-guided screening for atrial fibrillation using electrocardiogram during sinus rhythm: a prospective non-randomised interventional trial. Lancet 2022;400(10359):1206–12. https://doi.org/10.1016/S0140-6736(22)01637-3.

[7] Al-Shorbaji N, Atun R, Car J, Majeed A, Wheeler E. Elearning for undergraduate health professional education: a systematic review informing a radical transformation of health workforce development. https://apps.who.int/iris/bitstream/handle/10665/330089/9789241508261-eng.pdf?sequence=1&isAllowed=y. [Accessed 12 September 2023].

[8] Tudor CL, Kyaw BM, Dunleavy G, et al. Digital problem-based learning in health professions: systematic review and meta-analysis by the digital health education collaboration. Journal of Medical Internet Research 2019;21(2):e12945. https://doi.org/10.2196/12945.

[9] Gardanova Z, Belaia O, Zuevskaya S, Turkadze K, Strielkowski W. Lessons for medical and health education learned from the COVID-19 pandemic. Healthcare (Basel) 2023;11(13):1921. https://doi.org/10.3390/healthcare11131921.

[10] Fleaca B, Fleaca E, Maiduc S. Framing teaching for sustainability in the case of business engineering education: process-centric models and good practices. Sustainability 2023;15(3):2035. https://doi.org/10.3390/su15032035. [Accessed 19 September 2023].

[11] Association of American Medical Colleges. 2022 Fall applicant, matriculant, and enrollment data tables. AAMC; 2022. https://www.aamc.org/media/64176/download?attachment. [Accessed 19 September 2023].

CHAPTER 31

Student perspectives of digital health: Learning through quality improvement

Megan Gallagher and Allison Bakowicz
University of Pittsburgh, Department of PA Studies, Pittsburgh, PA, United States

Doctorate of physician assistant studies: Digital health initiatives

Physician assistants or physician associates (PAs) are medical professionals that are highly trained in critical thinking. We are repeatedly taught to examine evidence, apply best-practice standards, and explore treatment options to achieve positive outcomes for our patients. Current PA graduates fulfill the standard expectations to be capable medical providers; however, there is a lack of instruction regarding advancement in PA lifelong professional timeline. Specifically, students are not routinely instructed on the skills required to step into a leadership role or taught to apply quality improvement science within their clinical practice. In 2022, the University of Pittsburgh developed a Doctorate of Physician Assistant Studies (DPAS) program to change this narrative. We decided to pursue this degree to grow as leaders who initiate and advocate for important change regarding both our patients and our healthcare system. In doing so, we will have gained the tools necessary to advance our careers in various industries, including the administrative or academic realms of medicine. These are changes that we believe to benefit both patients and providers in our places of employment. This chapter discusses our journey in the DPAS program and the project we deployed using quality improvement science. All reference to the project are a reference to the work of Bakowicz and Gallagher [1].

The mainstay of the DPAS degree program is quality improvement science. Although we work in different states, at two separate health systems, we have observed similar flaws in the patient discharge process within our workplaces. The current practice negatively impacts flow and patient experience and causes daily frustration to staff. Megan Gallagher has been working in trauma surgery for 2 years and Allison Bakowicz has been working in emergency medicine for 16 years. It was our desire to improve upon this antiquated standard practice that brought us together for our capstone project at the University of Pittsburgh.

Digital Health. https://doi.org/10.1016/B978-0-443-23901-4.00031-3

The discharge process has many working parts. We narrowed our study to focus on the patient education portion of hospital discharge instructions. Currently, an after-visit summary can be digitally accessed; however, the actual patient education/instructions are not digitally available. Our goal was to improve the patient's perception of both accessibility and comprehension by providing the educational information in a digital format. Often, we have seen the current printed discharge papers haphazardly discarded or reportedly lost by patients. Our hypothesis was that by giving the patient digital access to this written education, they would have it more readily accessible on their smartphone device for convenient reference. This would make it easier for the patient to apply the information and improve the home care of their condition. Digital delivery also allowed the included educational images to be viewed in color, rather than in black and white, thus improving their utility and advancing the patient's health literacy.

The use of digital document technology has steadily advanced in nonmedical areas of business such as the entertainment, real estate, shopping, and travel industries. De' et al. [2] reported in mid-2020 that companies have improved software and increased their technological infrastructure due to the rapid growth of digital requirements secondary to COVID-19 and the change in the population's daily norm. This forward progress was greatly advanced out of necessity during the COVID-19 pandemic, requiring the general population to comply with new digital initiatives during lockdown and strict social distancing measures. Although the field of medicine has pushed forward on digital health initiatives such as telemedicine visits, patient access to healthcare documentation has lagged behind at our hospitals. We focused our quality improvement efforts on creating digital patient education discharge instructions after an inpatient stay or emergency department visit. This digital health initiative was adopted with the hypothesis that a digital copy can improve patient accessibility and understanding of the information within the document, therefore increasing patient-perceived health literacy [1].

Quality improvement capstone project

Due to the complexity of providing an effective, concise, and comprehensive discharge process, there were many potential areas to target when developing our quality improvement project. We designed and studied a root cause analysis through a fishbone diagram, seen in Fig. 31.1, to uncover and visualize the issues within the discharge process. We identified six main problematic factors with current printed discharge instructions. This visual exercise helped us as principal investigators to focus our study within the larger, multifaceted discharge process problem. We narrowed our project to specifically target accessibility and readability, which in turn has an effect on health literacy. Future quality improvement work may include other main ideas within the

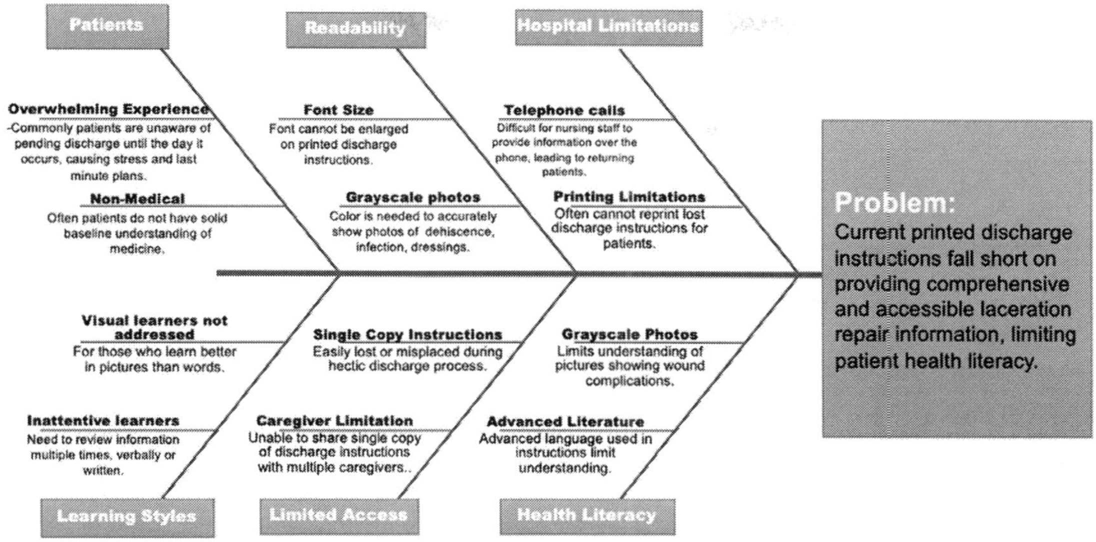

Figure 31.1

Root cause analysis - issues with the discharge process [1]. This is a fishbone diagram outlining the multiple problems with current printed discharge instructions. Our study focused on the accessibility and understandability of the document and how it would relate to improved health literacy. *From Bakowicz, A. A. & Gallagher, M. M. (2023). Digital discharge instructions: Surveying patient perceived health literacy of laceration care discharge instructions with digital document delivery.*

problem of practice; however, our limited implementation period during the DPAS program required concentration on a few key points within the overarching issue.

Bakowicz and Gallagher [1] reported that when a patient's medical visit has ended, they are provided ample education on the proper care and precautions regarding their condition. Poor discharge instructions prevent patients from adequately caring for themselves after discharge from the hospital [3]. When these instructions are insufficient, health outcomes and patient experience decline [4]. Additionally, studies have shown that many patients may not read or understand their discharge instructions [5]. Unfortunately, when patients do not understand their discharge instructions, they become unable to self-manage their recovery process and outcomes can be negatively affected [3]. This is especially important regarding wound care. Patients with healing lacerations and surgical incisions are sent home and expected to adequately care for wounds without previous medical training. Studies have long shown that many patients exhibit a knowledge deficit when it comes to their discharge instructions, specifically concerning home care and return-to-hospital parameters [6].

Currently, patients are provided with a standard set of printed discharge instructions in black-and-white ink when they are discharged from an emergency department or inpatient hospital stay. These papers contain written instructions for care of their condition and often include images to further describe the information. Unfortunately, we have both experienced patients disposing of the large packets of discharge paperwork on the way out of the hospital, reportedly finding them cumbersome and not useful. Patients will often contact the hospital with questions about home care of their condition; during these calls, patients are referred back to their discharge instructions by staff. Commonly, patients report they have discarded, misplaced, or do not understand the information within the instructions.

Printed discharge instructions are given to patients in one standard-size font and include only grayscale images in the patient education. Choi [7] has found that pictures are an essential part of complete discharge instructions. Not only do images provide support for visual learners, but they also allow for increased health literacy beyond the recommended eighth-grade reading level of the instruction text [8]. However, current black-and-white printing parameters decrease the utility of these important instructional images.

Since we both routinely care for patients requiring sutured wound care in our areas of medicine, laceration care patient education was the focus of our quality improvement capstone project. These current discharge instructions contain two images, in black-and-white, which visually compare an infected wound to a normal appearing wound. These important images are meant to demonstrate and educate patients on visual signs of an infected wound, such as erythema. It is much easier to identify an infected wound by the erythema seen in a colored image, while the grayscale image looks completely normal. While researchers Mueller et al. [9] have shown that electronic discharge instructions may increase the readability of these documents, it is unknown how these efforts would specifically benefit wound care patients.

Based on our real-life experiences and review of the literature, it is clear that the current discharge paperwork lacks accessibility and limits understanding, hindering patients' ability to maximize the utility of the information. Multiple studies have identified the impact that poor discharge instructions may have on patient outcomes and the vital role discharge instructions play in healthcare and health outcomes [3–7]. Digital copy discharge instructions have been shown to improve outcomes in pain medication advice [10]. However, there is a lack of research on the impact of digital discharge instructions regarding patient understanding of home wound care and preferred media for discharge instructions.

The change project idea was centered around the hypothesis that providing patients with a digital copy of discharge instructions would be beneficial in reaching our process improvement goal. The intention was not to evaluate the instructions themselves, but rather to survey the patient's perception of improved accessibility and understanding of the digital document, and query their preference for a digital version of this document in the future. The hospital systems involved in this quality improvement project use the same automated patient education document for laceration care through Cerner, an electronic medical record service. A portable delivery file (pdf) of this education was created to distribute as a digital copy. There were no changes made to the document: all language, text, and photos are identical to the original. The only differences between the printed and digital versions are that the digital version was readily accessible through smartphone and the images were inherently visible in color rather than black and white. This allowed the measurement of patient responses to be accurate, as they were only able to comment on the effects of digitizing the paper copy.

Email, QR codes, and SMS (short message service) texts were considered for implementation of our study; however, studies have shown that patients prefer SMS text messages over emails when it involves private health information [11,12]. Over a period of approximately seven weeks, 20 sutured wound care patients were enrolled in the quality improvement study. During the study, the patients still received the standard set of printed discharge instructions, but they were concurrently enrolled in an online messaging platform that sent a text message with a link to the pdf file of the digital patient education.

An independently validated, unique survey instrument was created to evaluate if enrolled patients perceived the digital copy to be easier to find and/or increased their understanding of laceration care at home. In addition to collecting demographic data on the patient's age range, gender identity, and education level, the survey also recorded patient preference for discharge document type in the future [1].

Of the 20 participants, 14 completed the survey. Our participants varied in age, education level, and gender identity. All 14 participants stated that the digital copy was more accessible than the printed copy. Nearly all participants responded that the digital copy increased their understanding of the information. In the future, all but one patient answered that they would prefer to receive a digital copy, either on its own or in conjunction with a printed copy; see Fig. 31.2 [1].

Although our sample population size was too small to allow for generalization to the greater patient population, the results did show that patients of varying ages, education levels, and gender identities responded positively to this digital shift in their healthcare information. The Center for Disease Control (CDC) defines personal health literacy as "the degree to which individuals have the ability to find, understand, and use information and services to inform health-related decisions and actions for themselves and others" [13]. Based on the CDC definition of health literacy, the participants did exhibit an improvement in perceived health literacy. While small, our research is an encouraging first step in continuing to investigate digital discharge instructions on a larger scale [1].

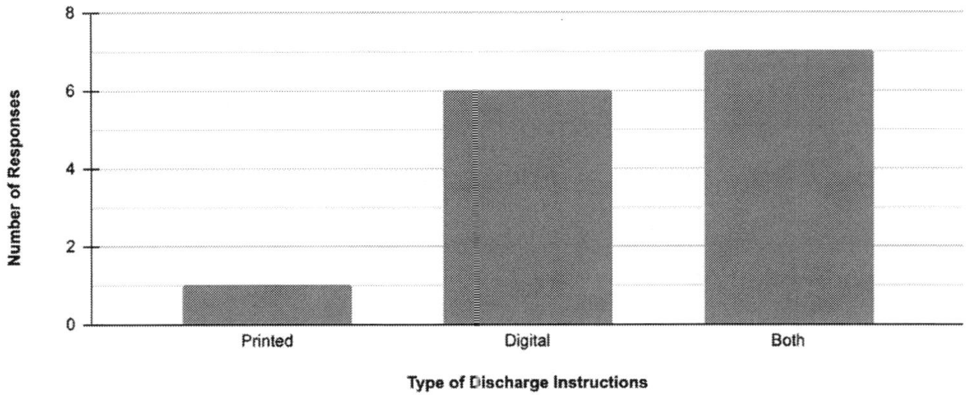

Figure 31.2
Patient preference for discharge document type [1]. The majority of patients in our study preferred to receive either a digital copy either alone or in conjunction with current printed discharge papers [1]. *From Bakowicz, A. A. & Gallagher, M. M. (2023). Digital discharge instructions: Surveying patient perceived health literacy of laceration care discharge instructions with digital document delivery.*

Patient equity in digital health literacy

Our project focused on advancing technology in medicine. As this occurs, the general patient population must also advance in their use of technology as well. The World Health Organization states that health is multifactorial and affected by determinants of health, which are: the social and economic environment, the physical environment, and a person's individual characteristics and behaviors [14]. Richardson et al. [15], defined digital determinants of health (DDoH) as access to technological devices, comprehension on the use of these tools, internet access in the home and community, as well as greater digital literacy. This group of researchers also reported that DDoH interacts with social determinants of health (SDoH), which further impact health outcomes in the population [15].

SDoH are defined by the Centers for Disease Control and Prevention as "conditions in the environments in which people are born, live, learn, work, play, worship, and age that affect a wide range of health, functioning, and quality-of-life outcomes and risks" [16]. The SDoH falls into five key categories: healthcare access and quality, education access and quality, social and community context, economic stability and the neighborhood, and the built environment [15]. Social and digital determinants of health intersect and are a large contributing cause of health inequalities among the population. Despite these inequalities, the COVID-19 pandemic has encouraged, and often required, widespread use of technology. The surge in technology use has highlighted vast inequalities in the patient population.

When implementing our project, we learned that accessibility to a digital platform is not universal within the patient population. Patients without a smartphone device were unable to be enrolled in our quality improvement study, as a smartphone was required to open the digital discharge instruction document. This proved to be a limiting factor in our study; several patients were excluded from the study on this criterion alone. DDoH and SDoH impact and highlight digital health inequalities throughout the population. As described, access to the internet and digital tools is not equal among the population; equitable access and working toward improving digital literacy is important in improving health outcomes.

Future initiatives in digital health documents

Although there are unavoidable digital health inequalities, as mentioned above, it is important to prioritize equality as digital health continues to progress forward. As the digital world continues to evolve, it is imperative that the use of technological platforms in the medical field grows with it. When designing our quality improvement project, we wanted to create a framework that could be easily replicated and applied to other types of patient education upon discharge, beyond laceration care. Although small, our patient population indicated perceived benefits to the use of digital discharge instructions, indicating that they were more accessible and they perceived an increased understanding of the educational material [1]. Our project was an initial step in improving and digitizing the discharge process, which we hope is built upon in the future.

There are advancements within the realm of digital discharge instructions that have the potential to further improve patient discharge experience. For example, digital instructions allow the possibility of increasing the number of full-colored educational photos included within the document; Choi [7] has found that pictures are an essential part of complete discharge instructions. Importantly, additional images allow for the inclusion of photos with an array of skin tones; as dark and ethnic skin tones are commonly excluded from patient education images. The inclusion of photos of a variety of skin tones is crucial to make discharge instructions more relatable and relevant to everyone in the patient population [1].

As digital media and access to this media advances, educational videos on platforms such as YouTube are exponentially increasing. This is a potential area of digital medical growth and could target visual learners in the population. If digital instructions become more widely used and available, there is potential to create instructional videos to show patients how to care for their medical condition at home [1]. Patients may benefit from viewing a wound dressing video, rather than reading a description on how to perform the dressing change. Technology is versatile and has the ability to reach a wide range of patients as long as the digital and social determinants of health are considered and addressed to maximize the benefit for all. The future of digital healthcare is vast and growing, with the potential to improve both patient experience and health literacy.

This chapter reflects our work in the Doctorate of Physician Assistant Studies program. All references to the program is a reference to our work and owned by Bakowicz and Gallagher [1].

References

[1] Bakowicz AA, Gallagher MM. Digital discharge instructions: Surveying patient perceived health literacy of laceration care discharge instructions with digital document delivery. University of Pittsburgh, Department of Physician Assistant Studies; 2023.

[2] De' R, Pandey N, Pal A. Impact of digital surge during covid-19 pandemic: a viewpoint on research and Practice. International Journal of Information Management 2020;55. https://doi.org/10.1016/j.ijinfomgt.2020.102171.

[3] Kang E, Gillespie BM, Tobiano G, Chaboyer W. General surgical patients' experience of hospital discharge education: a qualitative study. Journal of Clinical Nursing 2020;29(1−2):e1−10. https://doi.org/10.1111/jocn.15057.

[4] Kang E, Gillespie BM, Tobiano G, Chaboyer W. Discharge education delivered to general surgical patients in their management of recovery post discharge: a systematic mixed studies review. International Journal of Nursing Studies 2018;87(1−13). https://doi.org/10.1016/j.ijnurstu.2018.07.004.

[5] Topham EW, Bristol A, Luther B, Elmore CE, Johnson E, Wallace AS. Caregiver inclusion in IDEAL discharge teaching: implications for transitions from hospital to home. Professional Case Management 2022;27(4):181−93. https://doi.org/10.1097/ncm.0000000000000563.

[6] Yadav AK, Budathoki SS, Paudel M, Chaudhary R, Shrivastav VK, Malla GB. Patients understanding of their diagnosis and treatment plans during discharge in emergency ward in a tertiary care centre: a qualitative study. JNMA J Nepal Med Assoc 2019;57(219):357−60. https://doi.org/10.31729/jnma.4639.

[7] Engel KG, Buckley BA, Forth VE, McCarthy DM, Ellison EP, Schmidt MJ, Adams JG. Patient understanding of emergency department discharge instructions: where are knowledge deficits greatest? Academic Emergency Medicine 2012;19(9):E1035−44. https://doi.org/10.1111/j.1553-2712.2012.01425.x.

[8] Choi J. Literature review: using pictographs in discharge instructions for older adults with low-literacy skills. Journal of Clinical Nursing 2011;20(21−22):2984−96. https://doi.org/10.1111/j.1365-2702.2011.03814.x.

[9] Skaggs D. My website reads at an eighth grade level: why plain language benefits your users (and you). Journal of Library & Information Services in Distance Learning 2017;11(1−2):96−105. https://doi.org/10.1080/1533290X.2016.1226581.

[10] Mueller SK, Giannelli K, Boxer R, Schnipper JL. Readability of patient discharge instructions with and without the use of electronically available disease-specific templates. Journal of the American Medical Informatics Association 2015;22(4):857−63. https://doi.org/10.1093/jamia/ocv005.

[11] Doyle SK, Rippey JC, Jacques A, Rea AM, Kaiser EN, Miller SM, Anstey MHR. Effect of personalised, mobile-accessible discharge instructions for patients leaving the emergency department: a randomised, controlled trial. Emergency Medicine Australasia 2020;32(6):967−73. https://doi.org/10.1111/1742-6723.13516.

[12] Abraham E, Chow EPF, Fairley CK, Lee D, Kong FYS, Mao L, Goller JL, Medland N, Bavinton BR, Sudarto B, Joksic S, Wong J, Phillips TR, Ong JJ. eSexualHealth: preferences to use technology to promote sexual health among men who have sex with men and trans and gender diverse people. Frontiers in Public Health 2022;10. 1064408. https://doi.org/10.3389/fpubh.2022.1064408.

[13] Chow, Fairley CK, Lee DM, Ong JJ, Rahman R, Afrizal A, Phillips TR. Is SMS text or email more effective for recruitment into sexual health research? Sexually Transmitted Infections 2022;98(5). https://doi.org/10.1136/sextrans-2022-055436.

[14] Centers for Disease Control and Prevention. What is health literacy? Centers for Disease Control and Prevention; February 2, 2022. Retrieved, https://www.cdc.gov/healthliteracy/learn/index.html#: ~ :text=Personal%20health%20literacy%20is%20the,actions%20for%20 themselves%20 and%20 others.
[15] World Health Organization. Determinants of health. World Health Organization; 2017. https://www.who.int/news-room/questions-and-answers/item/determinants-of-health.
[16] Richardson S, Lawrence K, Schoenthaler AM, Mann D. A framework for digital health equity. Npj Digital Medicine 2022;5(1). https://doi.org/10.1038/s41746-022-00663-0.

CHAPTER 32

From classroom to clinic: A student's perspective

Dua Abbas
School of Medicine, Yale Univeristy, New Haven, CT, United States

Introduction

I wait 6 min before my patient joins UpDox, the video software PracticeFusion utilizes for patients. My patient is panting through the screen trying to catch her breath. "Thank you for taking me in, I just got off work and my second shift starts in 30 min." My patient from Chicago, IL, tells me that if it were not for this video visit, she wouldn't be able to see a provider for months. She is a single mother of two, juggling two jobs and trying to make ends meet.

A few states over in Pittsburgh, PA, an Uzbeki family brings their 4-month-old newborn for a wellness check. They have recently immigrated to the state and have no family or friends. My preceptor and I speed-dial our Uzbeki translator, who is able to smoothly translate our visit, and the parents leave with a smile on their face.

More than 2000 miles away in Milpitas, CA, I join the Zoom appointment for my 60-year-old patient who was recently diagnosed with hypertension and hyperlipidemia. We go over his lab results and discuss his medications. Before having the ability to meet with me through Zoom, the patient would have to take two buses to reach our office when the patient's children were unable to take him to his appointments. The option of having his appointments in the comfort of his home brings ease to him and his children. I am overjoyed to see his improvement 1 month later at our follow-up appointment.

For my elective rotation, I opted for a virtual behavioral medicine rotation. Seeing more than 25 patients a day through Zoom, I am amazed at the care we can provide in the comfort of our homes. My preceptor is able to spend more time talking to patients, follow up with patients whenever necessary, is able to prescribe necessary medications and perform evaluations/assessments as needed.

Digital Health. https://doi.org/10.1016/B978-0-443-23901-4.00032-5

All over the country, digital medicine is being utilized in a variety of specialties. However, we must ask ourselves if the transition from schooling to joining the workforce prepares us to join the digital health world. Do we have the tools to effectively see patients? Is there online etiquette we should know beforehand? Are there any techniques to prepare for virtual visits? In education and healthcare, these important questions are left unaddressed *and should be tackled.*

Background

The healthcare landscape is being revolutionized through technological advancements. A vital component of this revolution is telemedicine, which plays a huge role in the future of healthcare. Learning telemedicine is in line with the worldwide movement toward patient-centered treatment and improved access to healthcare. Telemedicine streamlines healthcare delivery: it reduces wait times, minimizes administrative overhead, and optimizes resource allocation. Technological advancements in telemedicine are driving innovations in diagnostics, remote monitoring, and treatment modalities. Staying informed about these developments allows healthcare professionals to offer cutting-edge care to their patients. Healthcare providers who are proficient in telemedicine contribute to a technologically competent workforce that allows for continuous education and professional development. Analysts project the telemedicine market to be US $520 billion by 2023, with over 100 million e-visits every year [1]. We should take advantage of the familiarity medical students have with technology and implement it into the standardized health curriculum.

Methods

A database search was completed (Fig. 32.1) in August 2023 using the terms "*telehealth* OR *telemedicine* OR *eHealth* OR "*online health*" OR "*on-line health*" OR *ehealth* OR *e-health* AND *education* OR *curriculum,* which resulted in 1220 articles. The databases searched included PubMed, Scopus, and Cochrane. Articles were then narrowed down by year, language, article type, and disciplines; titles and abstracts were screened. The remaining studies were reviewed, and records older than 2013 were excluded. This resulted in 15 articles that were then thoroughly analyzed. These articles were then narrowed down to include three articles that discussed:

- patient education as a definition
- the use of telehealth for education (rather than education about telehealth itself)
- technical aspects
- the level of knowledge and skills of practitioners in telehealth

Preferred Reporting Items for Systematic Reviews and Meta-Analyses flow diagram

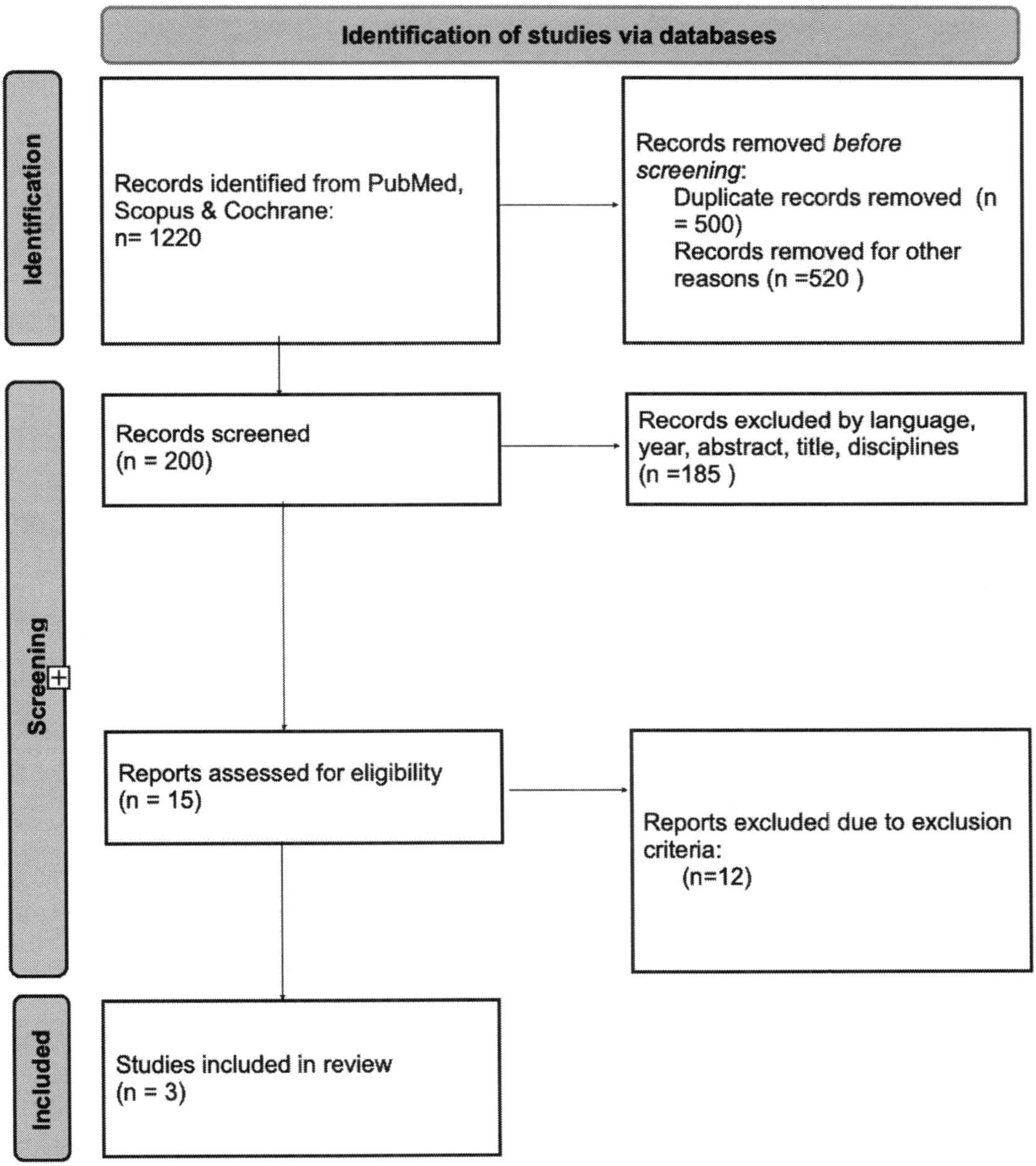

Figure 32.1
Identification of studies. *Flow chart created on PRISMA.*

Results

Study 1

In February 2018, third-year medical students received telehealth training by the Uniformed Services University of Health Sciences to improve telehealth knowledge.

Study design

A 9-h training program was developed for a cohort of 149 third-year medical students who had recently completed their core clinical clerkships. The course structure encompassed several key components. First, a mandatory pretest with 21 multiple-choice questions was administered a week before the course started. The training then comprised 4 h of interactive lectures delivered asynchronously. These lectures covered a wide range of telehealth-related topics, including its historical evolution, practical applications, ethical considerations, safety protocols, military utilization, and proper etiquette. Additionally, 3 h of in-person interactive instruction were required. This segment discussed ethical dilemmas, patient selection criteria, the current landscape of telehealth usage, risk management strategies, and appropriate telehealth etiquette. The curriculum also included two standardized, faculty-supervised mock patient encounters conducted through videoconference, each lasting 30 min. Finally, to put what they learned in practice, students gained hands-on operational experience, practicing the diagnosis of common medical conditions through telehealth. A mandatory posttest, consisting of 21 multiple-choice questions, and a course evaluation were also required to be completed at the end [2].

Study results

Among the medical students who took part in the study, a significant majority of 119 individuals (80%) expressed their intentions to incorporate telehealth into their future practice. The study's findings indicated a positive increase in telehealth knowledge as shown by: (1) An average improvement of 10.1% was observed in pre- and posttest scores among the participants. (2) Competency was demonstrated through the completion of a competency-based checklist. and (3) Postcourse feedback from students and preceptors.

Study 2

Nurse researchers initiated a quality improvement project with the goal of enhancing telehealth in the graduate nursing curriculum. They created a two-part evidence-based curriculum designed for graduate Family Nurse Practitioner (FNP) students.

Study design

A total of 57 s- and third-year family nurse practitioner students participated in this project. It was delivered in two distinct parts: part one consisted of an online lecture, while part two involved a telehealth simulation. In the first part of the telehealth curriculum, students were instructed on various clinical skills, including history-taking and assessment, the identification of diagnoses and potential differential diagnoses, and the accurate documentation of telehealth visits. For the second part of the curriculum, each simulation group comprised six students, one mediator, and one instructor. Each scenario presented a patient vignette that included details such as age, gender, medication history, chief complaint, past medical/surgical history, and allergies. These simulations were conducted over a 2-h period, with a total of six patient scenarios for the students to work through [3]. After this, the instructor and mediator facilitated a debriefing session with the students that encompassed discussions on including key health history details, visual examinations, differential diagnoses, diagnostic procedures, treatment options, red flags, and proper documentation practices.

Study results

Following their participation in the online lecture and virtual simulation, participants were asked to complete an anonymous survey. Upon an analysis of the qualitative survey data, it became evident that the students found the telehealth simulation to be highly engaging. The mean score for the question "please tell me how useful you found this simulation to be to your future practice as an FNP" was 4.9. And for the question "please tell me in your opinion if we should continue this simulation for future cohorts," the mean score was 4.8[3]. These scores, rated on a scale of 1−5, indicate a strong endorsement of the program for their future roles as Family Nurse Practitioners. Table 32.1.

Table 32.1: Study results.

Author	Publication year	# Of participants	Study group	Results
Jonas, Christopher et al.	2018	149 students	Third-year medical students	+
Olivia A. Cassiday et al.	2020	57 students	2nd- and 3rd-year family NP students	+
David Bunnell et al.	2021	26 educators of 17 universities	PA students	+

Study 3

The purpose of this study was to gauge interest and create a telehealth framework that could be used in other PA programs.

Study design

A curriculum was designed utilizing learning outcomes and instructional objectives for PA graduates. The curriculum was designed to meet the accreditation standards and was evaluated by local and national PA educators. The curriculum was distributed to 17 different programs and 26 educators [4].

Study results

Survey responses showed that 75% of participants strongly approve of the curriculum. Of this group, 100% stated it should be integrated into PA education [4].

*note for table "+" indicates positive results and are in support of adding this to existing medical curricula.

Discussion

It is clear through these studies that implementing a telehealth curriculum during schooling for all health professionals will not only make the transition to the workforce easier but also be a valuable tool to future employers.

My first two rotations in internal medicine were a great sneak peek into what telemedicine could entail. While the practice was mainly in person, we saw a few telemed patients daily. The practice owner would send Zoom links to her patients the day of and have them join at an allotted time. Minor nuances such as setting up Zoom waiting rooms and only admitting patients during their appointment were common mishaps. Although I was familiar with Zoom, I had to learn certain nuances over time. For example, there was an instance where a patient accidentally joined the meeting too early, which resulted in them joining a meeting with a different patient. This could have been a dangerous situation if we had not noticed and could have gone against HIPAA guidelines. Additionally, the setting of where the meeting was taking place was important, as video calls were only allowed in rooms where no other patient information could be heard or seen.

For my third rotation, I was lucky enough to rotate at a Behavioral Health telemedicine site. I chose this rotation as my elective because I was intrigued by the digital care we provided in internal medicine. It was during this rotation where I truly saw the capability of telemedicine. I saw a multitude of diagnoses and treatments for schizophrenia, ADHD, major depressive disorder, generalized anxiety, and more. My preceptor took additional time out of his schedule to explain different scenarios and how we deal with patients over the digital platform. For example, when a schizophrenic patient decided to turn off his room lights and stop answering our questions, I was stuck on what I should do. Thankfully, my preceptor dealt with the situation, and we debriefed afterward.

Four months later, at a primary care site that utilized Practice Fusion, I was introduced to Updox—the telehealth software partnered with the EMR system. Initially, I was only utilizing the basic video chat feature to speak to our patients. Thankfully, the medical student who was on her third week of the rotation enlightened me with her knowledge on other features of the platform. For example, I learned how to simultaneously create digital documents during the visit, take screenshots, and have the information compiled into a summary that can be uploaded to the patient's chart. I saved so much time and learned about features I would have otherwise been oblivious to.

Had I had a simulation of similar scenarios before the clinical year, I may have been better prepared for these telemedicine encounters. This is why I believe it is so important to have some sort of training, whether in the didactic year or simultaneously during the clinical year.

So what should this training address? Table 32.2 showcases just a few questions that must be further discussed in a learning environment. Content can be delivered in person or virtually over a span of multiple modules. Students should also be able to observe digital cases and learn from them before applying them in rotations or their workplace. By incorporating this training into the standardized medical, PA, nursing, or any health professional school curriculum, students will approach challenges in telemedicine with confidence.

As students, it is vital for us to be comfortable with telemedicine considering the new digital age we are living in. Internet of Things (IoT), artificial intelligence (AI), and

Table 32.2: Potential teaching points for telehealth curriculum.

Telehealth etiquettes—background/visuals, audio, lighting, equipment, cultural awareness, etc.
Introduction—appropriate applications of telehealth/most common applications of both outpatient and inpatient telehealth.
Common systems—how to navigate the most common EMR/video and digital health systems used in healthcare. How to utilize the specific features.
Structure—what happens before, during and after telehealth visits? What kinds of staff are needed on both sides of the camera?
Privacy concerns—what issues are unique to telehealth and to HIPPA compliance?
Reimbursement—what is required to secure reimbursements for telehealth visits?
Troubleshooting—common network, telecommunications, connection, audio, picture, and call or quality issues.
Examine regulatory standards and ethical principles of virtual healthcare.

blockchain are just a few advancements that have been made in digital technology. Health professional students must stay up to date to better serve their patients. These advancements are increasing accessibility for all patients, regardless of financial status. Barriers such as transportation, mobility challenges, and taking days off from work, which results in less income, are all addressed with digital health.

Not only is accessibility increased, but also outcomes are improved for both patients and providers. Telemedicine has been shown to possibly reduce burnout rates in providers. It offers the opportunity for providers to work remotely and have flexible schedules, ultimately improving work–life balance. Mitigating commute times alone is enough to substantially reduce burnout rates in providers. For instance, my preceptor in the Bay Area would often schedule her telemed appointments from home first thing in the morning so she could avoid morning traffic. Instead of 1.5 h of commute at 7:00 a.m., she could have a 30-minute commute leaving at 9:00 a.m. Saving time, gas, and money not only helps her personal life, but the prevention of burnout makes her a better provider as well. Additionally, telemedicine allows for streamlined administrative processes, creating efficiency for charting and allowing providers to focus more on patient care.

Conclusion

Considering the increasing demand and importance of telehealth in delivering patient care, it's very likely that the majority of healthcare providers will incorporate some form of digital medicine into their practice throughout their careers. With the increasing focus on value-based care, healthcare providers are looking for ways to provide high-quality care while accommodating their patients' needs. These needs can range from timely and convenient access to healthcare to coordinated care for chronic conditions.

If we know providers will be utilizing some form of digital health, why have we not established a curriculum during their training? Imagine how much more prepared students would be in their rotations if they had some previous training. Not only would it benefit the students, but also students could spread the knowledge to preceptors and fellow colleagues. The impact of not teaching students can lead to consequences that could be otherwise avoidable. As a patient myself, I expect all my medical visits to be professional, whether in person or virtually. For some, online etiquette may not come instinctively. Without an established curriculum, it is difficult to take advantage of all the benefits digital medicine has to offer. I firmly believe in the positive rewards telemedicine provides both patients and providers and urge all providers to incorporate some aspect of digital medicine into their practice. As a student, I have seen the tangible benefits of telemedicine. The immigrant Uzbeki family, the grandfather without transportation, and the single mother taking her appointment during her lunch break are all real-life examples of the positive outcomes digital health brings and will continue to bring.

References

[1] Global Telemedicine Strategic Analysis Report 2023: Market Set to Grow by a Staggering $450+ Billion by 2030 - Impacts of COVID-19 Provides Grounds for a Flourishing Future. Published September 8, 2023. https://www.businesswire.com/news/home/20230908618768/en/Global-Telemedicine-Strategic-Analysis-Report-2023-Market-Set-to-Grow-by-a-Staggering-450-Billion-by-2030—Impacts-of-COVID-19-Provides-Grounds-for-a-Flourishing-Future—ResearchAndMarkets.com.

[2] Jonas CE, Durning SJ, Zebrowski C, Cimino F. An interdisciplinary, multi-institution telehealth course for third-year medical students. Academic Medicine 2019;94(6):833−7. https://doi.org/10.1097/acm.0000000000002701.

[3] Cassiday OA, Nickasch BL, Mott JD. Exploring telehealth in the graduate curriculum. Nursing Forum 2021;56(1):228−32. https://doi.org/10.1111/nuf.12524.

[4] Bunnell D, Gordes KL. Building a PA telehealth curriculum. Journal of the American Academy of Physician Assistants 2021;34(12):1. https://doi.org/10.1097/01.jaa.0000800612.20279.91.

CHAPTER 33

Interpreting the future: Navigating the tele revolution in healthcare language access

Muhiyadin Aden
Augsburg University, Department of PA Studies, Minneapolis, MN, United States

Introduction

"I will not let you operate on my boy! I need to be with him!" Hani, a Somali refugee, insisted when the doctor told her that her son needed surgery to remove a portion of his intestine injured during a bike accident. Obviously, she could not go into the OR with her son. She looked at me and said, "He will go with him, then." As the interpreter and cultural liaison, I accepted her offer to end the stalemate. The surgeon agreed after I explained the inherent distrust toward Western medical providers in the Somali refugee community due to a fear of organ harvesting—a reality many migrants have faced in developing countries.

When I think about Hani's story, I can't help but remember the shock of coming to America and going to my first clinical encounter as a teenage Somali refugee. Arriving in the USA, my entire family was mandated to have a medical exam. However, in Somalia, there are no medical facilities, only traditional medicine, so from the moment we arrived at the hospital, every experience was foreign, confusing, and disorienting—from the automatic sliding doors and unintelligible language to the inappropriate hand gestures. We were not even sick; I cannot imagine how much harder this would be for people whose child or loved one was suffering a life-threatening injury or illness.

For me and my family, the chaos of the hospital system coalesced into clarity the moment Mahad—our medical interpreter—stepped into the exam room. His presence is all I remember from that medical encounter. Sharing our language, culture, and skin color, we suddenly felt at ease as he interpreted for the medical staff, who seemed to fade into the background. While this is not what we strive for now in medical interpreting, the reality is that they are the source of safety and comfort, especially in that first experience in the American medical system. Though the memory of that medical encounter remains blurry, the impact of the medical interpreter's assistance remains crystal clear. Mahad was a

Digital Health. https://doi.org/10.1016/B978-0-443-23901-4.00033-7

community liaison, telling us what to do, normalizing the experience, and guiding us toward understanding and care. Ultimately, he became a mentor to me in the USA and the healthcare system. The role of a medical interpreter cannot be understated. They not only facilitate communication but also provide a sense of belonging and dignity.

Hani's story, my story, is not unique. I can think of thousands of patients just like Hani in the 10 years I have spent in interpreter services. It is these limited English proficiency (LEP) patients that led me to become a leader in interpretive services as a manager and supervisor. When patients began asking me for medical advice that I was not qualified to provide, I remembered where my journey began—as a CNA, before being recruited to interpret for patients—and decided to take the next step in my career journey to become a physician assistant (PA) and provide medical care to refugee, LEP, and marginalized communities. Having completed my didactic PA training, I recognize the need to help providers and healthcare administrators establish more efficient and sustainable systems for language access. The goal for language access is for patients to have meaningful access that is quick, suitable for each patient, useful, and preferred.

Despite rapid advances in utilizing technology-based solutions post-COVID-19 pandemic, there is still a need to develop a more adaptable hybrid model that utilizes interpreting resources to the benefit of all stakeholders—patients, providers, hospitals, and interpreters. The question is, how do we develop standards? Do we need standards? Has the switch to technology fixed all our problems? What are the limitations of technology-based interpreting? Is it appropriate for all patients? Is it cost-effective; is it worth the investment/up-front costs? How do we best utilize it? Are there inefficiencies that still need to be addressed?

Background

In America, there are over 25 million LEP individuals who require adequate language accommodations for effective healthcare [1–4]. Multiple laws (Title VI in 1964, plus American Disability, Joint Commission, and Executive Order 13,166 of August 11, 2000) require public healthcare facilities to provide meaningful access to language services [1–3]. Medical education often fails to provide adequate awareness and training on how to work with interpreters and the laws that govern these services. This puts both the healthcare systems and providers at risk of lawsuits and losing their medical licensing. The failure to provide language access is not only illegal but also results in negative health outcomes for LEP patients and builds distrust in communities.

Researchers have shown that LEP patients face significant challenges in accessing healthcare due to language barriers [1,4,5]. Ji et al. examined the existing literature and concluded that results in misunderstandings of both diagnosis and therapeutic plans in clinical encounters leading to [6]

- Medication omission
- Missed appointments
- Dissatisfaction of care
- Wasteful resource utilization, including:
- increased emergency room visits
- excessive testing
- misdiagnoses
- unnecessary invasive procedures
- inappropriate medication and intervention
- increased hospitalization

Medical literature also highlights the significant impact of trained professional interpreters in reducing medical errors, making access to medical interpreters with continued medical education essential. In a study conducted by Flores et al., the results demonstrated that encounters with professional interpreters had significantly fewer errors of potential consequence (12%) compared with ad hoc (22%) and no interpreters (20%). Moreover, among professional interpreters, those with more than 100 hours of training made significantly fewer errors, with their proportion of errors of potential consequence being much lower (2% vs. 12%) [7]. These findings underscore the importance of ensuring that medical interpreters receive comprehensive training and ongoing education to improve patient safety and enhance the quality of care for LEP patients in healthcare settings.

Hani's story goes even further than the literature to illustrate that the consequences of miscommunication could lead to increased rates of mortality. If I had not been there as a trusted cultural liaison and interpreter, her son would have died because a piece of his intestine was dead, and he was nearly septic. These barriers not only hinder the provision of quality care but also contribute to health disparities among vulnerable populations.

As a refugee who has personally experienced the challenges of language barriers in healthcare, my journey has led me to a career dedicated to bridging these gaps. Starting as a medical interpreter and progressing to the role of Supervisor and Manager in one of the largest hospital-based interpreter departments at Hennepin Healthcare System (HHS), I have witnessed firsthand the transformative power of language access. Now, as a PA student, I am passionate about exploring how healthcare providers and organizations can leverage different technologies to further enhance cultural understanding and overcome language barriers.

While working for the Interpreter Services Department (ISD) at HHS, I surveyed to gather data from our system and three others in the Twin Cities metro area. These data will be utilized to demonstrate the change and evolution in technology use and in-person interpreting before and after the COVID-19 pandemic. These metro hospitals provide a good model for how to deliver quick and robust language access for LEP individuals utilizing technology. However, the current challenge is that there are no expectations or rules that automatically prioritize the type of interpreter service modality that a patient should receive. I will utilize the survey data and case studies from my experiences as an interpreter to illustrate both the challenges and the opportunities for developing flexible, patient-centered, community-based standards.

Interpreter Services Department at Hennepin Healthcare System

Hennepin Healthcare System (HHS) is the largest Safety Net organization in Minnesota. [With] only 73.5% of ambulatory encounters in these clinics were performed with English as the primary language, HHS has one of the largest LEP patient populations in Minnesota [6]. Additionally, 20%–30% of this level 1 trauma hospital's patients require a language interpreter. Hennepin Healthcare System patients utilize over 7.4 million interpretation minutes each year with over 100 staff interpreters and vendor partners providing over 90 languages with an annual budget of about $10M. The top language serviced at HHS is Spanish, followed by Somali, comprising 89% of total languages serviced; however, the remaining 11% is composed of multiple rare and unique languages, which are difficult to provide timely interpreter services (Fig. 33.1) [8].

To meet the tremendous demand for language services and comply with language access requirements, ISD provides qualified professional interpreters in three modalities: over-the-

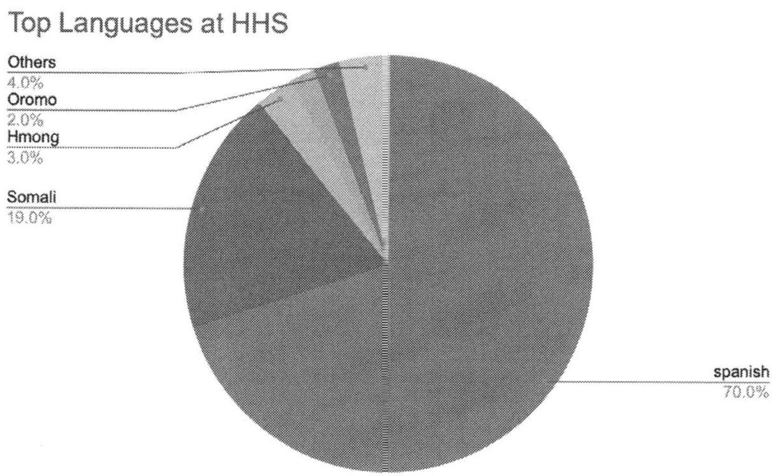

Figure 33.1
Percentage of languages serviced at HHS. Other languages include French, Mandarin, Mina, Ewe, Swahili, Kisii, and American Sign language (ASL) [8].

phone (OPI), video remote (VRI), and in-person interpreting. These modalities are integrated seamlessly, allowing medical providers and patients to quickly access their preferred mode of interpretation according to their needs. The integration of these modalities has enabled the organization to effectively meet the high demand for language access in a sustainable, cost-effective, and equitable manner. Hennepin Healthcare System is now considered to have one of the premier interpreter services departments in the USA. Hennepin Healthcare System's success has served as a model for other large hospitals. It is the result of a decade of innovation in various approaches.

Transitioning from in-person to tele-interpreting: Challenges and opportunities

In 2012, when I joined the ISD, we had over 130 full-time equivalents (FTE), and the only modality of interpreting was in-person. The department had been over budget by $1.5M every year for over a decade, which prompted the higher leadership to pressure the middle management to make necessary budget cuts. Yet, medical providers and patients frequently complained about long wait times for interpreters. Interpreters and their union complained that they were overworked and tired walking from clinic to clinic or waiting for patients and providers who were not ready to start the visit. We quickly realized that this model of in-person interpreting was not sustainable and that we had to search for a language access model that supports our staff in delivering care in a timely, effective, efficient, and equitable manner while not compromising our patient safety.

We set up an interpreter-stakeholder committee consisting of interpreters, IT, providers, and department leaders to utilize the Lean problem-solving strategies to not only identify modifiable gaps but also propose practical solutions. We also visited many organizations to search and learn the best particles in providing language access. Finally, after a long tedious process, we settled for the following strategy to create a hybrid model that provides VRI, OPI, and in-person utilizing our 130 FTE but also partners up with other similar hospitals in order to share interpreter resources.

The HHS leadership team decided to implement, and I gradually executed over the next decade the following changes.

- Create a Language Center (LC) located within HHS and staffed with some of our interpreters who could take video and phone calls from the 100s of iPad-on-carts (also known as VRI units) that were deployed to patient care areas throughout the hospital.
- Join a network of LCs across 50 hospitals—Health Care Interpreter Network (HCIN)—to share interpreters when idling too long due to low demand.
- Prioritize some of our in-person interpreters for acute areas.
- Implement an on-demand dispatching system for in-person interpreters instead of prescheduling to eliminate inefficiencies due to patient no shows.

The immediate benefits of implementing this strategy, such as quick and diverse language modalities, were evident. This was a win all around: interpreters were more productive; demand for services was met; patients and providers were more satisfied with having access to better qualified and higher quality, medically trained interpreters; and HHS saved money.

Achieving full implementation, however, took several years due to challenges that arose when attempting to integrate in-person interpreters into the language center to handle video and phone calls. Some healthcare providers, in solidarity with the interpreter union, expressed concerns that technology would replace their jobs and professions. This group wrote petition letters to the hospital CEO, protesting against the implementation of these remote technologies.

The fear of this new technology isn't particularly new or specific to HHS. Marshall et al. evaluated the process of implementing VRI in a hospital that already used in-person and OPI. The study examined the impact on the utilization of language services, efficiency, and costs, as well as implementation challenges. "After overcoming initial challenges, VRI implementation, as part of the provision of comprehensive language services, can potentially yield several benefits, including immediate extensive use, decreased OPI, reduced wait times for language services, rapid uptake in clinics previously lacking in-person interpreter access, and increased average minutes per encounter by in-person interpreters" [1]. Despite its clear benefits in both increasing access and decreasing costs, the greatest barrier to its full implementation was the discomfort with change.

In March 2020, everything changed overnight. We were in the middle of union contract negotiations where the sticking point was putting limits on tele-interpreting (VRI and OPI) because they were afraid it would replace their jobs. All of this resistance was erased overnight. I was literally in a meeting with the union when the hospital chief nursing officer (CNO) called to inform us that, due to COVID-19, we would be shutting down all ambulatory areas and that all ancillary staff must go home due to limited PPE availability.

Many hospitals were laying off their interpreting staff. Concerned with the uncertainty of contracting the deadly virus and hoping to avoid layoffs, we sent about 30% of our staff interpreters home with video phones. The others worked from our language center, which already met the infection prevention requirements of social distancing. In response, the union representatives changed their opposition to VRI. Ironically, the reality was that tele-interpreting saved their jobs.

As the leader of interpretive services, the thought of the impact layoffs would have on our valuable staff, their families, and our vulnerable LEP patients, who were disproportionately affected by the virus, was sickening. I quickly urged our organization's upper management for support in expanding the language center's capacity to handle technology-based interpreting by adding an additional 100 OPI/VRI stations. I will forever be grateful for their unequivocal support and their resounding "yes" to my proposal.

Due to the low demand for patient care, we shared 100% of our interpreters with HCIN, taking calls for other hospitals. This turned out to be a pivotal moment, as providers, interpreters, and patients came to accept technology-based interpreting and telehealth in general as safe and effective alternatives. As a result, interpreter productivity drastically improved, and wait times for interpreters virtually disappeared (Fig. 33.2 and Table 33.1). Financially, the department went from being chronically over budget by $1.5M each year to making over a $900K surplus. While the changes were already in process toward a more efficient and economical system utilizing technology-based solutions for 80% of encounters, the pandemic served as a catalyst to achieving our goals.

Our staff productivity, defined as the number of minutes interpreted per hour for LEP patients and providers, increased by 30% compared with 2018 (Fig. 33.1). In 2021, internal data analysis revealed that an HHS remote interpreter (VRI and OPI modalities) was more than twice as productive as an in-person interpreter; the average duration of an in-person encounter, excluding walking time, was approximately 32 minutes, while a VRI encounter lasted around 14 minutes (Table 33.1). The improvements in productivity illustrate the increased efficiencies of the implementation of technology-based interpreting modalities.

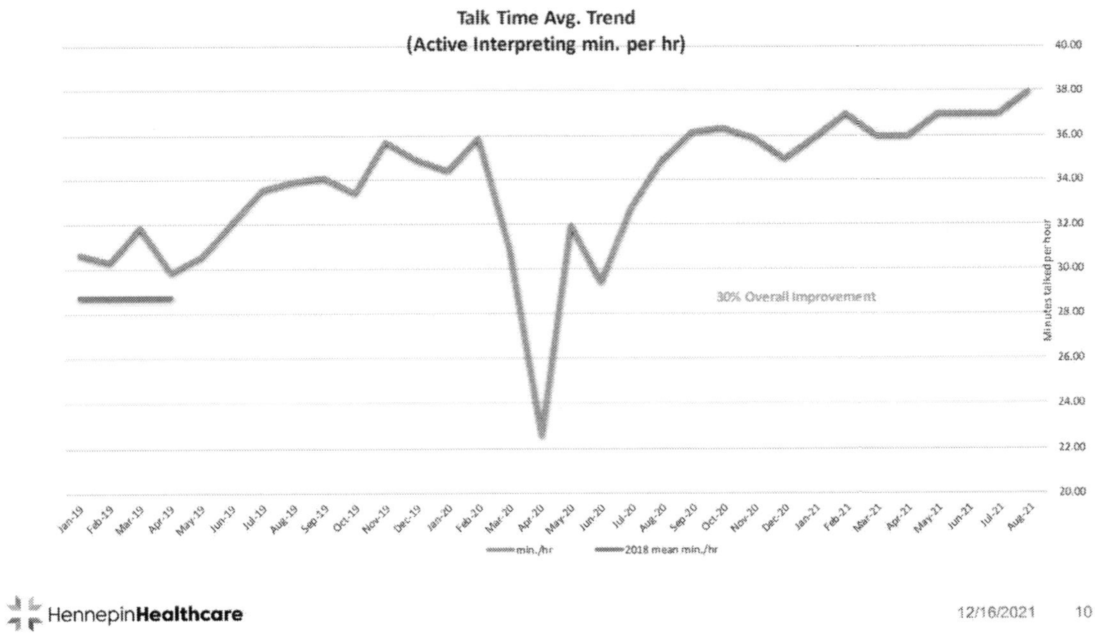

Figure 33.2
Productivity of interpreters from 2018 to 2021 [8]. Graphic data showing interpreter productivity in minutes of talk time interpreting.

Table 33.1: Comparison of interpreting modality efficiencies [8].

	VRI	OPI	In-person
Average encounter time (minutes)	14	12	32

Researchers elsewhere have found that efficiencies in remote interpreting versus in-person extend beyond the length of the encounter. Burkle et al. found that the mean wait time for "an in-person interpreter request until their arrival was 19 min.... but the range extended out to 100 min," demonstrating a high variability [3]. When factoring in the walk time and the average talk time of in-person interpreters, their productivity is 3.6 times lower compared to technology-based interpreters. Inefficiencies like these, Ji et al. stated, are why "healthcare workers are often 'getting by,' which is thought to be due to the current models of interpreter delivery, namely the time and effort required to request an interpreter, as well as inflexible scheduling." They concluded, "Mobile applications [VRI] may be used to facilitate access to medical interpreters with high clinician and patient satisfaction" [5].

By the end of 2021, our goals were met with approximately 80% of the total interpreter demand met through remote modalities, while the remaining 20% involved in-person interpretation. On the surface, this looked like a win; however, several concerns and questions were raised.

The Pendulum Swing: Going too far with remote modality

The HHS leadership team met regularly through 2021 to monitor our progress through data and feedback from our stakeholders. Though our goals for relative proportions of interpreting modalities were met, two primary areas of concern came to the surface. Complaints from unions, patients, and providers highlighted the reality that, in some ways, the remote modalities had swung too far. Two specific areas of concern were raised: vulnerable patients and inadvertent inefficiencies.

It is essential to determine which vulnerable patients will benefit more from in-person interpretation versus technology-based. For example, medical teams may unintentionally default to technology-based modalities for all their LEP patients, potentially overlooking the needs of those who require in-person interpreters. Some LEP patients are more vulnerable due to factors such as age or disabilities and may not be best served by remote technology. Some medical conditions or cases would best be served using the physical presence of an in-person interpreter to ensure effective communication and understanding between healthcare professionals and patients.

The consequences of too much access can cause inadvertent inefficiencies. We have witnessed unintentional "double-dipping" when two interpreters—in-person and technology-based—were requested for a single patient. While this may appear to provide greater access to language services from the medical team's perspective, it creates inefficiencies from the interpreter's standpoint.

In reflecting on these concerns, it becomes apparent that healthcare workers are uncertain about how to balance and prioritize specific interpreter modalities (in-person or remote). This points to the lack of clear guidelines regarding when and where each modality should be accessed, further complicating the interpretation process and hampering efficiency. This is not a new problem. Schiaffino et al. noted "a lack of uniformity in the need and offering of language services, which varied by hospital location and ownership". Additionally, Schiaffino et al. stated, "the offering of language services remains inconsistent: Fewer than two out of three US hospitals provided language services to patients living in their service areas" [9,10].

Realizing that there are no guidelines nor research on this topic, let alone benchmarking to help guide the budget for ISD, I decided to conduct a survey with the goal of comparing HHS to other local hospitals and developing unofficial community standards to help guide decisions and priorities in our hospital and region.

Methods

Four hospital systems in the Twin Cities metro area were surveyed through email between 2018 and 2021. Three out of the four hospital systems provide most of the LEP patient care, averaging over 360K contacts yearly. Permission and support letters to publish their data have been obtained in 2023 (Augsburg University IRB **#2023-06-04**). These data were analyzed in combination with the case report and Hennepin County Medical Center Interpreter Services Data using a modified Standards-Based Management and Recognition (SBM-R) quality improvement approach.

The survey included the following questions.

1. How many total LEP patient contacts/encounters do you handle on an annual basis?
2. What is the relative proportion/breakdown of in-person versus technology-based modalities (%)?
3. Do you have criteria for prioritizing in-person for certain medical encounters?
4. What modalities do you prioritize in your pediatric area?

Results

The results of the hospital survey are shown in Fig. 33.3, which highlights the different approaches of four major hospitals in the Twin Cities and how they leverage technology and innovation to meet and prioritize communication access for our diverse patient

2021 Remote vs In-person Benchmhark Categories	A	B	C	D
Total Patient Contacts	363058	334000	46000	385000
% remote	79%	67%	80%	90%
% in-person	21%	33%	20%	10%
How is your out-patient Pediatric Clinic covered? In-Person or Remote?	Mixed (67% remote and 33% in-person)	Mixed, 13 and under all in-person. Remote dependent upon visit-type for over 13 years, percent unknown	100% remote, unless staff specifically request in-person interpreson due to reasons such as cognitive delays or had-of-hearing	Not a tracked metric
Criteria for In-person for your system?	ED Stabilization room All OR locations Procedures (i.e., IR & Cath Lab, Radiology with Contrast, CT, and MRI) Care Conferences (End of Life) Complex Clinic ICU units Patients who are hard of hearing Pediatric & Pedo Dentistry	New patients Patients 13 and younger Deaf patients MRI Consults Care Conferences Procedures Consents determvisit typesit-type and department, defaulted in Epic	MRI (Magnetic Resonance Imaging) Interventional radiology neuropsychic evaluations Video Speech swallow study Nuclear medicine HVI Stress Test Stab room (ED trauma room per staff request only Pulmonary function test Cardiac Rehab Palliative (per Palliative team request only)	Safe and Healthy Kids, Audiology, Rehab Evaluation Visits, Care Conference, Labor and Delivery, MRI, Neuropsych Evals, Autism Clinic, Inpatient Chemical Dependency, Cath Lab, Gamma Knife, All procedures with conscious sedation (Peds Sedation, Endoscopy, Colonoscopy, etc.)

Figure 33.3

Interpreter utilization in 2021 [8]. Benchmarking data on interpreter utilization in four major hospitals in the metro Twin Cities area, in aggregate and deidentified.

population. I was consistently impressed with my colleagues and their creativity and dedication to utilizing technology-based solutions for the betterment of their patients. On average, the hospitals met 79% of language access demand with remote technology and 21% with in-person [8]. It is well known that this is a big shift from the majority in-person utilization pre-COVID. The managers that were surveyed indicated that they will continue the current status due to efficiencies and cost-effectiveness realized through the use of this technology. One hospital shared that they saved about $3M and was planning to build a brand new language center for their staff.

The survey findings make clear that face-to-face interpreters may be more suitable for complex medical encounters involving noise and multiple care team members. Examples of such encounters include Trauma Emergency Rooms (Stab room), light sedation procedure rooms (such as interventional radiology, GI, and eye surgery ORs), CT and MRI scans, emotionally complex cases such as end-of-life care conferences, ICUs, and challenging diagnoses such as new cancer diagnoses. While valuable information was obtained, it is not the whole story.

We can show how many LEP patients received language services and the proportion of interpreting modalities used; however, we cannot tell you which specific patients were served and which were not. For instance, there is currently no data indicating the percentage of LEP patients who rely on family members, bilingual providers, medical interpreters, or no interpreter at all. The problem is that there is no requirement and no system for providers to track how each LEP patient's language needs were met. The lack of interpreter documentation not only poses potential risks to patient outcomes but also exposes the medical team to legal jeopardy.

Despite laws that encourage tracking data on language access, there is no requirement forcing providers to document in the electronic systems. This points back to the need for flexible community standards for the use of interpreter services because we have to have data to develop and monitor benchmarks, hold hospitals accountable, and continuously improve and innovate. Further research is necessary to establish standardized protocols for accessing interpreters in a medical setting.

Analysis: The case for an adaptable hybrid model

As a former manager of the ISD at HHS who was also on the front-line interpreting, I have personally experienced and gathered feedback from various stakeholders including medical providers, patients, and hospital administrations regarding interpreter modalities. There is a range of perspectives, including those from the interpreter union and language access activists who often advocate for in-person interpretation over technology-based options. However, literature shows that there is no significant difference in patient satisfaction between in-person, VRI, and OPI [Joseph et al.] [11] I want to address the persisting misconceptions about technology-based interpreting that I want to address utilizing case studies from my experiences as an interpreter.

One misconception is that meaningful connections with patients are only possible through in-person interpreters. While being a prevailing assumption, this is far from true. The success of virtual interpreting lies in the medical provider's willingness to adapt and their comfort working with both virtual and in-person interpreters. While at HHS, I facilitated a conversation between caring parents in Los Angeles and the medical team using VRI. The parents sought to discuss an experimental medical trial for their child's incurable condition, still awaiting FDA approval.

During the emotionally charged and intricate 2-hour encounter, I worked diligently to explain the concept of experimental treatment to these recent immigrants who were unfamiliar with the term "experimental drug." The lead medical provider employed the "teach back" method to ensure the parents comprehended the treatment plan, including its benefits and potential side effects. The parents articulated the plan, including their comprehension of the benefits and potential side effects of the experimental therapy, demonstrating their willingness to proceed. The family expressed gratitude toward the medical team for their kindness and compassion. In a profound moment, they expressed to me, the interpreter, "We are so glad you are part of our community."

Despite the physical distance between Minnesota and California, their acknowledgment affirmed that interpreters can establish meaningful connections between providers and patients through stable video communication, transcending physical distances. This experience underscored the significance of healthcare providers embracing and adapting to virtual interpreting technologies and countering the assumption that in-person interpretation is the sole means of establishing genuine connections with patients.

On the other extreme, many believe that telehealth interpreting can be used for anything. One of our fantastic Spanish interpreters shared with me during my time as manager at HHS a story that disproves this assumption. The interpreter came to my office to debrief, telling me:

"I found myself involved in a telehealth encounter that unfolded in an unsuccessful manner. The video call commenced midway through the encounter, with a PA attending to a 15-year-old girl and her mother at a community clinic. To my surprise, the PA began the conversation abruptly by stating, 'Yes, the pregnancy test was positive, you are pregnant.' The ensuing chaos in the room revealed that the mother was unaware of the PA's decision to order a pregnancy test. The atmosphere became fraught with screams, tears from both mother and daughter, and a general sense of distress. I was taken aback by the PA's choice to utilize a video interpreter for this highly sensitive encounter, especially when there were available in-person interpreters who could have provided support."

This case demonstrates an example of a time when technology was chosen inappropriately. Due to the sensitivity of this topic, in-person should have been the modality of choice for both the provider and the interpreter. Other factors that should be considered when choosing a modality include cultural considerations, which play a significant role in medical settings. For example, within the Hispanic population, including LEP individuals, religious beliefs hold great importance. Consequently, a teenage pregnancy can have devastating consequences within their communities and for the patient, specifically.

Another misconception is that the medical team will lose the power of cultural brokering due to a decrease in interactions between the medical provider and the interpreter in a remote setting. This assumes that the only way to have cultural competency is to have the interpreter present in the room. While interacting with interpreters promotes "cultural humility," virtual interpreting does not undermine this aspect. Professional medical interpreters are skilled in transitioning from being a "mouthpiece" for patients and medical teams to becoming cultural brokers if it enhances communication [1,12]. However, there are other models that achieve the same goals

Effective teaching of cultural humility requires intentional facilitation and the active participation of supervising attending physicians, residents, and interpreters in a culturally conducive environment. A group of emergency medicine providers (Paetow et al.) [13] sought to determine the impact of a brief cultural immersion experience on emergency medicine residents' knowledge, attitudes, and behaviors when caring for Somali patients in HHS' emergency department. A culinary cultural immersion brought small groups of residents together with Somali interpreters to share a meal at a Somali restaurant. The results of this study demonstrated increased knowledge of Somali culture, healthcare paradigms, and diet. Behavioral changes included adjusting clinical visits to patient expectations and using interpreters as cultural brokers. Positive attitudinal changes were also reported, including an increased acceptance of cultural differences and a sense of connectedness to the Somali population.

What these cases highlight is the pitfalls of all or nothing approaches. It is essential to strike a balance between remote and in-person interpretation to cater to the specific needs of patients and medical encounters. That is why I recommend a hybrid model that is flexible and integrated in its approach. Standards and guidelines must take into account the vulnerability of the patient, the community and cultural needs, the acuity of the medical condition, and the sensitivity of the issue. Certainly, providing language access is a complex process, but the key to success is an administrative culture, which encourages innovation through continuous experimentation, failure, and learning.

Recommendations for flexible, patient-centered, community-based standards

The goal for patients is to have very quick access to interpreters that are also suitable (patient-centered) for each patient that is useful that they prefer and provides meaningful access. This could be technology-based or in-person. In-person might be best for patients, but it is also resource-intensive and fraught with delays. This is not an easy decision.

It's going to take a lot of work to develop standards, guidelines, and protocols, but once implemented, it should be seamless. Create criteria based on location or type of medical encounter.

1. Researchers must study problems around language access to help develop recommendations and protocols. We need to know more about the connection between language access and health outcomes. We have seen providers making language access decisions based on their preconceptions and the lack of information. Data will help develop better protocols, which will better guide the medical providers.
2. Prioritized in-person should include complex medical encounters where cognition is an issue, sensitive topics, emergency stabilization. Special consideration should be given to patient preference and provider preference.
3. Ideally, when choosing an interpreting modality, the process must be collective, utilizing input from all stakeholders—patients, providers, and interpreters.
4. Hospitals must create criteria for when to use in-person and when to use technology based on location or type of medical encounter.

5. Hospitals must require modality preferences to be listed in the electronic charts so that it can be used at the time of scheduling appointments, resulting in less confusion about which modality to use at the time of the appointment.
6. Providers must learn to use the technology to avoid patient care delays. We have experienced providers tending to non-LEP patients before LEP because they are waiting for interpreters. That is an inequity that is avoidable with technology.
7. Hospitals must hire and train interpreters from the community and utilize them in the most effective and efficient manner: a hybrid model.
8. Providers must be trained in how to work with an interpreter, the legal requirements for meaningful language access, how to utilize the technology so they are more proficient and the issue of language access on the whole. The how, why, and the value of using interpreters.
9. Providers should participate in regular, ongoing cultural training with interpreters such as lunch and learns. Topics could include religion, food, traditional medicine such as herbs that act as blood thinners, parenting practices, language nuances such as words that have interchangeable meanings, and other medically relevant practices such as genital manipulation.
10. Interpreters need regular training, education resources, and support to ensure that they stay on top of best practices and medical knowledge. Ideally, they would learn anatomy and physiology. Interpreters tend to burn out after about 5 years in the field, so training related to mental health and self-care as well as regular debriefing and counseling will support their success.
11. All stakeholders must advocate for increased investment in language access resources and technologies in healthcare organizations to meet the diverse needs of LEP patients. Medical facilities must have technology-based access to interpreters throughout the hospital. Simply, there needs to be iPAD screens everywhere—welcome area, waiting areas, patient rooms—readily available to LEP patients. In addition, new facilities should be designed with technology-based access from the beginning to avoid the cost of retrofitting.
12. Language access leaders in each community should have at least quarterly, if not monthly, meetings to build their own, community-based standards for language access.
13. To help bring costs down, which reduces barriers to access and provides money to implement new strategies, hospitals must work with insurance and government agencies to get reimbursed for language access costs. This would require hospitals to accurately document language access encounters.

Conclusions

The role of medical interpreters is crucial in providing meaningful access to healthcare for LEP patients. They serve as cultural liaisons, bridging the gap between patients and medical providers, and offering a sense of safety and comfort to vulnerable populations.

Language barriers in healthcare can lead to incomplete understanding, miscommunication, and potential negative healthcare outcomes. By ensuring effective communication through interpreters, we can improve patient satisfaction and reduce healthcare disparities.

The use of technology-based interpreting modalities (VRI and OPI) has revolutionized language access, making it more efficient and cost-effective. Adding technology-based solutions to interpretation services has had a positive impact on each stakeholder. However, we know that not all LEP patients' language needs are being met despite the legal requirements, with potential risk to patient outcomes and legal liabilities for healthcare organizations. There are clear limitations to the use of technology-based interpreters. The next phase in the evolution of improving language access in medical settings is to create a standardized protocol for accessing interpreters in medical settings. However, to do this effectively, more data are required.

It is crucial for hospitals to implement a mandatory requirement within LEP electronic medical records that medical providers indicate how they access interpreters for each LEP patient. Mandatory interpreter documentation would provide desperately needed data that can be utilized to meet multiple goals. Knowing whether or not medical interpreters were utilized provides insight into legal compliance. The ability to link interpreting modality to patient vulnerability and medical acuity would allow decision-makers to determine the effectiveness of interpreter modalities in specific medical encounters and establish community standards and guidelines for prioritizing in-person or remote interpreting.

Striving toward a balanced, hybrid system of language access modalities requires cultural humility. Immersive experiences and cultural training can strengthen the role of medical interpreters as cultural brokers and educators. Promoting cultural competency training and facilitating interactions between interpreters and medical providers outside the hospital environment develops the empathy and understanding required for effective cross-cultural communication among healthcare providers, interpreters, and patients.

Encouraging collaboration and knowledge-sharing among hospitals and healthcare organizations will improve interpreter resource sharing and reduce inefficiencies in interpreter utilization. Gathering data from other hospital systems in the area was effectively a method of checking the health of our ISD against our neighbors. At HHS, interhospital cooperation and coordination allowed us to build more effective and efficient systems together.

HHS and similar hospital systems have made incredible advances in technology-based solutions for language access, but more work needs to be done. Thinking back to my first experience in the American hospital system, I can imagine a welcome kiosk with multiple languages inviting patients to receive interpreter assistance upon first entering the hospital or medical facility. Beyond that, hospital systems will ideally develop flexible, patient-centered, community-based standards that balance the use of technology and in-person interpreters to provide timely, effective, efficient, and equitable language access without compromising safety. By implementing these recommendations and embracing technology while maintaining the human touch, healthcare organizations can further enhance language access for LEP patients, improve healthcare outcomes, and reduce disparities among vulnerable populations.

References

[1] Marshall LC, Zaki A, Duarte M, Nicolas A, Roan J, Colby AF, Noyes AL, Flores G. Promoting effective communication with limited English proficient families: implementation of video remote interpreting as part of a comprehensive language services program in a children's hospital. The Joint Commission Journal on Quality and Patient Safety 2019;45(7):509−16. https://doi.org/10.1016/j.jcjq.2019.04.001.

[2] Youdelman MK. The medical tongue: U.S. Laws and Policies on Language Access. Health Affairs 2008;27(2):424. https://doi.org/10.1377/hlthaff.27.2.424.

[3] Burkle CM, Anderson KA, Xiong Y, Guerra AE, Tschida-Reuter DA. Assessment of the efficiency of language interpreter services in a busy surgical and procedural practice. BMC Health Services Research 2017;17:456. https://doi.org/10.1186/s12913-017-2425-7.

[4] Tran AV, Roberts KP. Language accommodations for limited English proficient patients in rural health care. Journal of Immigrant and Minority Health 2023;25:674−9. https://doi.org/10.1007/s10903-022-01416-7.

[5] Ji X, Chow E, Abdelhamid K, Naumova D, Mate KKV, Bergeron A, Lebouché B. Utility of mobile technology in medical interpretation: a literature review of current practices. Patient Education and Counseling 2021;104(9):2137−45. https://doi.org/10.1016/j.pec.2021.02.019.

[6] Jelinek R, Pandita D, Linzer M, Bikah Bi Nguema Engoang J, Rodin H. An evidence-based roadmap for the provision of more equitable telemedicine. Applied Clinical Informatics Journal 2022;13(03):612−20. https://doi.org/10.1055/s-0042-1749597.

[7] Flores G, Abreu M, Barone CP, Bachur R, Lin H. Errors of medical interpretation and their potential clinical consequences: a comparison of professional versus ad hoc versus no interpreters. Annals of Emergency Medicine 2012;60(5):545−53. https://doi.org/10.1016/j.annemergmed.2012.01.025.

[8] Aden M. Minnesota metro hospital surveys and HCMC interpreter productivity. De-identified institutional data set 2021.

[9] Executive Order 13166 of August 11. Improving access to services for persons with limited English proficiency. Title 3, The President. Federal Register 2000;65(159). . [Accessed 16 August 2000].

[10] Schiaffino MK, Al-Amin M, Schumacher JR. Predictors of language service availability in U.S. hospitals. International Journal of Health Policy and Management 2014;3(5):259−68. https://doi.org/10.15171/ijhpm.2014.95.

[11] Joseph C, Garruba M, Melder A. Patient satisfaction of telephone or video interpreter services compared with in-person services: a systematic review. Australian Health Review 2017;42(2):168−77. https://doi.org/10.1071/AH16195.

[12] Schiaffino MK, Nara A, Mao L. Language services in hospitals vary by ownership and location. Health Affairs 2016;35(8). https://doi.org/10.1377/hlthaff.2015.0955.

[13] Paetow G, Scott N, Panning A, Hopkins J, Aden M, Hart D. Culinary cultural immersion: a qualitative analysis of resident knowledge, attitudes, and behavioral changes following a brief Somali cultural immersion experience. Academic Medicine 2023. https://doi.org/10.1002/aet2.10844.

CHAPTER 34

Organizational perspective

Amy Haller[1] and Ben Reynolds[2]
[1]University of Pittsburgh, Department of PA Studies, Pittsburgh, PA, United States; [2]UPMC, Pittsburgh, PA, United States

Healthcare workforce implications

In recent years, integrating Digital Medicine and Artificial Intelligence (AI) into the healthcare ecosystem has brought a transformative shift, redefining how healthcare is delivered, managed, and experienced. The integration of AI in healthcare has emerged as one of the most powerful transformative advances. This chapter examines AI integration from the perspective of healthcare institutions, focusing on strategic considerations for leaders charged with implementation and then the downstream process to adopt. This integration offers remarkable benefits to the healthcare industry, from improved healthcare outcomes and increased efficiency to substantial cost savings and heightened patient satisfaction but requires a well-organized change management skillset to cause the least disruption in the delivery of quality of patient care.

Organizational benefits of digital health and AI leveraging digital health and AI for organizational advantages in healthcare: A strategic approach

In today's healthcare landscape, the fusion of digital health and artificial intelligence (AI) won't be just a choice but a necessity for healthcare institutions aspiring to remain competitive while delivering high-value care. The organizational benefits of embracing digital health and AI are well described and encompass nearly every aspect of healthcare operations, from streamlined administrative processes to more efficient supply chain management to clinical improvement of patient outcomes. As a healthcare business leader, grasping the strategic aspects of adopting these technologies will be a requirement to be successful. We will discuss how to make well-informed business-based decisions regarding software and algorithm selection and how to evaluate AI products in alignment with specific healthcare system needs. Finally, we will outline an action plan and explore the critical factors underpinning the success of implementing digital health and AI solutions within a healthcare organization.

Digital Health. https://doi.org/10.1016/B978-0-443-23901-4.00034-9

The healthcare leader's case for AI integration

Before implementing a potentially resource-consumptive integration of AI into your healthcare organization, it's important to present a persuasive case to stakeholders, including executives, board members, and clinicians, just like any other novel and disruptive change. A leader's argument should be fixed around the core advantages digital health and AI can deliver across the spectrum of process improvement and the administrative efficiencies it facilitates.

Because AI-powered tools can automate administrative tasks, streamline workflows, and alleviate the administrative workload on healthcare professionals, there is an enormous opportunity to embed greater efficiency into this space. The most persuasive case will demonstrate cost savings while allowing the healthcare workforce to concentrate more on patient care and less on burdensome administrative tasks. This application could have the added benefit of improving wellness and decreasing burnout.

While administrative efficiencies may have the greatest impact immediately, the downstream effect of giving healthcare providers more time to care for patients will provide more of an opportunity to improve outcomes and quality. Making the clinical case of using AI to enhance diagnostic accuracy, customize treatment plans, and predict disease outbreaks will make a compelling argument and can translate into improved patient outcomes and satisfaction. The deeper integration of AI analytical tools can sift through vast troves of patient data to identify trends, optimize resource allocation, and enhance decision-making across all healthcare operations and business levels. All these benefits must be underpinned by a comprehensive cost–benefit analysis demonstrating how the initial AI technology investment will yield long-term savings. This can be demonstrated through AI helping to reduce errors, fewer readmissions, and optimize resource utilization.

Once the decision has been made to begin the journey of AI utilization, it is vital to chart a comprehensive action plan. Planning and implementation are essential, as is evaluating the various AI products' value.

Implementation begins with a needs assessment. What are the specific challenges your organization faces that AI can help you overcome? Where can AI have the most significant impact? Is the need in business or operations? Or is it in the clinical space, like decision support? Prioritizing these areas based on their potential to enhance patient care and streamline operations will help leaders build an implementation blueprint to guide further actions.

A needs assessment will also help organizations understand what AI platform best fits the problem that will need to be solved. It cannot be overstated how robust the emerging AI product space is, and so vigorously assessing the various AI platforms and solutions currently available in the market is key to understanding what they can do and what they can't. Consider factors such as scalability, compatibility with existing systems (such as the EHR and revenue cycle technologies), ease of integration, and the product's reputation. Engage IT experts and data scientists in this process to ensure technical viability.

When evaluating AI products, assess how well the AI product aligns with the identified need. Does it address the specific challenges you've identified during the needs assessment? Evaluate the quality and availability of data required for the AI product to function effectively. Do the data align with your system policies, healthcare regulations, and ethical standards? Establish clear performance benchmarks to measure the AI product's effectiveness in addressing your needs. These metrics should be directly tied to your organizational goals, such as improved patient outcomes, cost reduction, or provider efficiency.

One of the most important steps in implementation is to establish robust data governance protocols to manage patient data ethically and securely. With the proper representation of an AI governance team, healthcare systems can establish robust data governance protocols that enhance the accuracy and reliability of AI decision-making models. Choosing an AI product that can adhere to critical healthcare regulations such as HIPAA (Health Insurance Portability and Accountability Act) to maintain patient trust and legal compliance is important. Invest in training programs to equip all staff with the necessary skills to utilize AI-powered tools effectively. This includes both clinical and nonclinical staff who will interact with the technology.

AI implementation is disruptive from making the decision to proceed, to the end-user experience. Leaders must recognize that integrating AI will necessitate a cultural shift within the organization. Using change management strategies that can gain buy-in up and down the user spectrum, focusing a significant representation from the clinically facing healthcare workforce to minimize resistance to change. Consider implementing small-scale pilot programs to validate the selected AI solution in real-world scenarios while gathering real-time feedback from end users. This will enhance implementation and the buy-in process and empower leaders to make any necessary changes for larger-scale rollouts past the pilot phase. Leaders should also account for the organization's scalability and expansion of AI applications.

Integrating digital health and AI into healthcare organizations can offer important benefits, provided the meticulous decision-making process and the chosen AI products are well-suited to the specific need. As a healthcare leader, one must advocate for this transformative change and ensure the selected software and algorithms align closely with your organization's mission and objectives. Following a structured evaluation and implementation approach, as outlined here, can position your healthcare institution to thrive in an increasingly data-driven and technologically advanced healthcare landscape.

Implementing digital health

Implementing digital health technologies has revolutionized the healthcare industry, promising enhanced patient care, streamlined processes, and improved outcomes. However, this transition has its challenges and benefits from an organizational standpoint. This section explores the various facets of implementing digital health, including talent acquisition, resource allocation, financial considerations, training and education, and its implications on the healthcare workforce.

Talent acquisition

One of the primary challenges in implementing digital health is the acquisition of skilled personnel capable of developing, managing, and utilizing these technologies effectively. For instance, the Mayo Clinic, a renowned healthcare institution, established the Center for Digital Health, recognizing the need for specialized expertise in digital health. They invested in training programs and collaborated with academic institutions to cultivate a pool of experts in this field. This proactive approach enabled them to implement various digital health solutions successfully.

Time and resource allocation

Digital health implementation requires a significant commitment of time and resources. The transition from traditional systems to digital platforms necessitates careful planning and allocation of resources. The Boston Children's Hospital exemplifies this, investing heavily in a comprehensive electronic health record (EHR) system. This involved a substantial financial commitment and a multiyear timeline for implementation. However, the benefits of increased efficiency and improved patient care justified the investment.

Financial considerations

Implementing digital health technologies often requires a substantial financial investment. However, the return on investment (ROI) can be significant. For example, the Cleveland Clinic implemented a telemedicine program, enabling virtual visits for certain specialties. This expanded their reach to patients in remote areas and reduced operational costs associated with physical infrastructure. The ROI was evident in increased patient satisfaction scores and reduced overhead expenses [1].

Training and education

The successful integration of digital health technologies hinges on comprehensive training and education programs for healthcare professionals. Vanderbilt University Medical Center recognized this and established the HealthIT Accelerate program. This initiative provides extensive training to clinicians and staff on the effective use of digital health tools. The program has been instrumental in ensuring a smooth transition to a digitally enabled healthcare environment.

Workforce implications

Implementing digital health technologies can have profound implications for the healthcare workforce. While it may lead to increased efficiency and expanded capabilities, it can also necessitate a shift in roles and responsibilities. For instance, adopting robotic process automation (RPA) at Intermountain Healthcare led to the redeployment of administrative staff to more patient-facing positions. This not only optimized their workforce but also improved patient engagement.

Conclusion

Implementing digital health technologies presents both challenges and benefits from an organizational perspective. Strategic talent acquisition, prudent resource allocation, careful financial planning, robust training programs, and thoughtful consideration of workforce implications are crucial components of a successful implementation. Organizations that navigate these challenges effectively stand to reap the rewards of improved patient care, enhanced efficiency, and a sustainable healthcare ecosystem.

Outcomes that matter

Benefits of digital medicine/AI in the healthcare ecosystem

Improved healthcare outcomes

One of the most significant advantages of incorporating Digital Medicine and AI into healthcare practices is the substantial enhancement of healthcare outcomes. By harnessing AI algorithms to process vast amounts of patient data, healthcare providers can uncover valuable insights that aid in early disease detection, accurate diagnosis, and personalized treatment plans. These insights, often inaccessible to the human eye due to the complexity and volume of data, empower healthcare professionals with a deeper understanding of patient conditions, allowing for more informed and targeted interventions.

Moreover, AI-driven predictive models assist in identifying potential health risks and forecasting disease progression. This proactive approach enables clinicians to intervene earlier in a patient's journey, resulting in better disease management and prevention. The seamless integration of patient data, medical history, and real-time monitoring through Digital Medicine further facilitates continuous tracking and adjustment of treatment plans, ultimately leading to improved patient outcomes. Studies such as the systematic review and metaanalysis conducted by Meng et al. have demonstrated the positive impact of patient-reported outcome tracking and health information provision through remote patient monitoring software on patient outcomes, particularly in oncology care [1]. This research highlights how integrating digital tools can improve healthcare outcomes by enhancing patient engagement, enabling personalized interventions, and facilitating timely interventions based on real-time data.

The effectiveness of remote patient monitoring extends beyond oncology care. Bai et al. conducted a randomized clinical trial showing the beneficial effects of home blood pressure telemonitoring and additional support on blood pressure control [2]. This study exemplifies how remote monitoring and supportive measures can improve healthcare outcomes, particularly in managing chronic conditions.

Additionally, using machine learning approaches to administrative claims data, as demonstrated by MacKay et al., illustrates how data-driven insights can predict clinical outcomes in diverse medical and surgical patient populations [3]. This approach aids healthcare professionals in making informed decisions, optimizing treatment plans, and tailoring interventions to individual patients, thus contributing to improved healthcare outcomes.

In neurorehabilitation, Moon et al. conducted a scoping review highlighting the potential of artificial neural networks in enhancing patient outcomes [4]. These networks offer the ability to analyze complex data and provide personalized rehabilitation strategies, ultimately improving neurorehabilitation outcomes.

Furthermore, using telemedicine networks has shown promise in improving clinical outcomes. Sinha and Bettermann investigated the clinical outcomes of acute ischemic stroke patients within a telemedicine network, demonstrating the feasibility and effectiveness of telemedicine in delivering timely and efficient care, which can positively impact patient recovery and outcomes [5].

Nomura et al. conducted a multicenter open-label randomized controlled trial comparing telemedicine to face-to-face clinic visits for smoking cessation [6]. The study demonstrated the noninferiority of telemedicine in achieving smoking cessation, highlighting how digital interventions can yield comparable outcomes to traditional in-person approaches.

Moreover, wearable technology has been explored to predict health outcomes. Burnham et al. conducted a literature review on wearable technology, emphasizing its potential to provide real-time health data that can be leveraged to predict health events and optimize interventions, leading to improved healthcare outcomes [7].

These studies underscore the transformative impact of Digital Medicine and AI on healthcare outcomes. Through early detection, personalized interventions, and data-driven decision-making, these technologies contribute to a paradigm shift in healthcare, fostering improved patient outcomes across various medical contexts.

Increased efficiency

Integrating Digital Medicine and AI into healthcare practices has revolutionized efficiency across the entire spectrum of care. Administrative tasks that were once time-consuming and prone to errors are now streamlined through AI-powered automation. For instance, AI applications have made scheduling appointments and managing EHRs more efficient and accurate. This streamlined approach saves time and reduces the likelihood of errors, ultimately contributing to improved patient care.

The application of machine learning has also extended to predicting patient no-shows in various clinical settings. Chen et al. conducted a study in an academic pediatric ophthalmology clinic using machine learning techniques to predict patient no-shows, as documented in their work "Application of Machine Learning to Predict Patient No-Shows in an Academic Pediatric Ophthalmology Clinic" [8]. By leveraging historical data and patterns, their model aimed to enhance appointment scheduling and resource allocation, enhancing operational efficiency.

In addition, telehealth services have demonstrated notable impacts on efficiency. The study conducted by Stefos et al., "The Effect of Telehealth Services on Provider Productivity," explored how telehealth implementation influenced provider productivity [9]. By allowing remote consultations and reducing the need for in-person visits, telehealth can optimize time utilization for healthcare providers and patients. The transformative potential of telehealth is further emphasized in the article "Telehealth: Enhancing Care through Technology" [10]. By leveraging technological advancements, telehealth enhances access to care, enabling healthcare professionals to provide medical services, consultations, and follow-ups remotely. This approach improves patient convenience and contributes to optimizing healthcare delivery processes. The efficient utilization of telemedicine technology for presurgical assessment is highlighted by Mullen-Fortino et al. in their study "Presurgical Assessment Using Telemedicine Technology: Impact on Efficiency, Effectiveness, and Patient Experience of Care". By conducting assessments remotely, healthcare providers save time and resources, making the process more efficient for patients and medical professionals [11].

AI-driven algorithms have also shown their prowess in optimizing resource allocation within healthcare facilities, thus minimizing wait times, and improving patient experiences. A study by Kinberg et al., "Modernizing the Otolaryngology Referral Workflow: The Impact of Electronic Consultation," exemplifies this with their investigation into the impact of electronic consultation on the referral process [12].

Integrating electronic consultations improved the referral workflow's efficiency, reducing waiting times for patients seeking specialized care.

Furthermore, the integration of AI and machine learning in surgical settings has brought about significant improvements in efficiency and patient outcomes. In their work, Rozario and Rozario discussed the potential of machine learning in optimizing operating room efficiency: "Can machine learning optimize the efficiency of the operating room in the era of COVID-19?" [13]. By considering factors such as case complexity and surgeon availability, AI algorithms can aid in scheduling surgeries more efficiently, contributing to better resource utilization and patient care.

Moreover, AI technologies have also impacted the realm of nursing, as highlighted by Clancy in "Artificial Intelligence and Nursing: The Future Is Now" [14]. These technologies help nurses manage administrative tasks more efficiently, allowing them to allocate more time to direct patient care and enhancing overall workflow efficiency.

The integration of machine learning has also demonstrated its effectiveness in streamlining specialty care access. In their study, Winchester et al. investigated electronic consults to improve specialty care access for veterans [15]. Electronic consultations reduce delays and streamline the process of obtaining specialized care by facilitating communication between primary care providers and specialists. Furthermore, studies have examined the impact of AI on specific medical procedures. Kyono et al.'s work "Improving Workflow Efficiency for Mammography Using Machine Learning," delved into how machine learning enhances mammography workflow efficiency [16]. AI algorithms assist radiologists in interpreting mammograms, leading to more accurate diagnoses and efficient patient management.

In conclusion, integrating AI, machine learning, and telehealth technologies into healthcare systems has significantly improved efficiency. These technologies have streamlined administrative tasks, optimized resource allocation, and improved various aspects of patient care, ultimately contributing to enhanced workflow efficiency and overall patient experiences.

Cost savings

Digital Medicine and AI technologies offer substantial cost-saving opportunities across the healthcare landscape. By automating administrative tasks and streamlining processes, healthcare organizations can significantly reduce operational costs associated with manual labor and paperwork. The recent shift to virtual clinics during the COVID-19 era has highlighted the potential benefits of such approaches, as demonstrated by Croghan et al. in their study on virtual urology clinics [17]. This shift has saved time and costs and brought about environmental benefits through reduced carbon emissions.

The development of innovative algorithms further contributes to cost savings. Scheinker et al. designed and evaluated an automated preference card optimization algorithm that has implications for cost-effective resource utilization within medical settings [18]. Similarly, the study by de Carvalho et al. showcased how machine learning can identify individuals with higher morbidity and avoidable health costs after acute coronary syndromes, leading to targeted interventions and cost-effective healthcare delivery [19]. In line with these findings, AI technologies facilitate evidence-based decision-making, guiding clinicians toward the most effective and cost-efficient treatments. Golding and Nicola discussed the business case for AI tools, emphasizing their potential to improve quality while reducing costs in medical settings [20]. Furthermore, the elusive quest for cost savings in digital health, as highlighted by Rahimi, underlines the ongoing efforts to harness the benefits of technology for financial efficiencies [21].

The integration of AI-driven approaches also extends to specialized areas of care. Fritzen et al. conducted a pan-European economic analysis, identifying potential cost savings by integrating glucose monitoring-based telemedical approaches into diabetes management [22]. Similarly, Soto-Varela et al. conducted a study on optimizing costs in reducing falls among older individuals through vestibular rehabilitation, showcasing the potential of technology-driven interventions for cost-effective geriatric care [23].

As healthcare systems strive for value, big data analytics capabilities are crucial. The review by Brossard et al. explores the path from big data analytics capabilities to value in hospitals, emphasizing the importance of data-driven strategies in achieving cost-effective and quality-focused healthcare [24].

In summary, integrating AI and digital technologies in healthcare offers diverse avenues for cost savings. These technologies automate tasks, enable early disease detection, support evidence-based decisions, and optimize resource allocation, ultimately leading to more efficient and cost-effective healthcare delivery. Through these advancements, healthcare systems can better allocate resources, reduce unnecessary expenses, and ultimately, enhance patient care and financial sustainability.

Patient satisfaction

Digital Medicine and AI technologies can potentially elevate patient satisfaction by enhancing the healthcare experience. Integrating telemedicine and remote monitoring empowers patients to access medical advice and consultations without the constraints of geographical barriers [25]. This convenience is particularly valuable for individuals with limited mobility, chronic conditions, or remote areas.

AI-driven chatbots and virtual health assistants provide patients with round-the-clock support, answering queries and offering guidance on managing their health. These tools improve communication between patients and healthcare providers, increasing patient engagement and empowerment. Additionally, the personalized treatment plans generated by AI algorithms demonstrate a commitment to individual patient needs, further enhancing patient satisfaction [26].

Moreover, patient preferences for different modes of healthcare delivery play a crucial role in overall satisfaction. Schneider et al. explored patient preferences for handheld autoinjectors versus wearable large-volume injectors, shedding light on the importance of aligning technology choices with patient preferences [27]. Similarly, Tharion et al. conducted a randomized clinical trial to evaluate patient satisfaction through an immersive experience using a mobile phone-based head-mounted display during arthroscopic knee surgery, showcasing the impact of technology on patient experience [28]. Furthermore, analyzing patient feedback comments using natural language processing and machine learning techniques contributes to understanding patient preferences and improving their experiences [29]. This approach not only enhances patient satisfaction but also informs healthcare providers about areas for improvement.

While AI technologies can enhance patient satisfaction, avoiding pitfalls such as paternalism and considering patient autonomy is crucial [30]. The evaluation of an AI cloud-based platform's impact on patient satisfaction with therapy, as demonstrated in the CINDERELLA trial, exemplifies the efforts to assess technology-driven interventions in real-world healthcare scenarios [31].

In summary, the integration of Digital Medicine and AI technologies in healthcare has the potential to improve patient satisfaction significantly. From remote consultations and monitoring to AI-driven communication tools and personalized treatment plans, these technologies offer enhanced convenience, engagement, and patient-centered care.

Conclusion

The benefits of integrating Digital Medicine and AI into the healthcare ecosystem are profound and multifaceted. From improved healthcare outcomes to increased efficiency, substantial cost savings, and heightened patient satisfaction, these technologies are revolutionizing how healthcare is delivered and experienced. As the healthcare industry continues to embrace the potential of Digital Medicine and AI, patients, providers, and healthcare systems stand to reap the rewards of a more advanced and patient-centered approach to care.

References

[1] Meng WW, Bai YY, Yan L, Zheng W, Zeng Q, Zheng YS, Zha L, Pi HY, Sai XY. Effects of patient-reported outcome tracking and health information provision via remote patient monitoring software on patient outcomes in oncology care: a systematic review and meta-analysis. Biomedical and Environmental Sciences: Biomedical and Environmental Sciences 2023;36(6):517–26.

[2] Bai YY, Yan L, Meng WW, et al. Effect of home blood pressure telemonitoring plus additional support on blood pressure control: a randomized clinical trial. Biomedical and Environmental Sciences: Biomedical and Environmental Sciences 2023;36(6):517–26.

[3] MacKay EJ, Stubna MD, Chivers C, Draugelis ME, Hanson WJ, Desai ND, Groeneveld PW. Application of machine learning approaches to administrative claims data to predict clinical outcomes in medical and surgical patient populations. PLoS One 2021;16(6):e0252585.

[4] Moon S, Ahmadnezhad P, Song HJ, Thompson J, Kipp K, Akinwuntan AE, Devos H. Artificial neural networks in neurorehabilitation: a scoping review. NeuroRehabilitation 2020;46(3):259–69.

[5] Sinha K, Bettermann K. Clinical outcomes of moderate to severe acute ischemic stroke in a telemedicine network. Journal of Clinical Neuroscience 2019;69:160–5.

[6] Nomura A, Tanigawa T, Muto T, Oga T, Fukushima Y, Kiyosue A, Miyazaki M, Hida E, Satake K. Clinical efficacy of telemedicine compared to face-to-face clinic visits for smoking cessation: multicenter open-label randomized controlled noninferiority trial. Journal of Medical Internet Research 2019;21(4):e13520.

[7] Burnham JP, Lu C, Yaeger LH, Bailey TC, Kollef MH. Using wearable technology to predict health outcomes: a literature review. Journal of the American Medical Informatics Association 2018;25(9):1221–7.

[8] Chen J, Goldstein IH, Lin WC, Chiang MF, Hribar MR. Application of machine learning to predict patient no-shows in an academic pediatric ophthalmology clinic. AMIA Annual Symposium Proceedings. 2021;2020:293–302. https://doi.org/10.1093/20000/amykba.

[9] Stefos T, Carey K, Shen ML, Poe S, Oh DH, Moran E. The effect of telehealth services on provider productivity. Medical Care 2021;59(5):456–60. https://doi.org/10.1097/MLR.0000000000001529.

[10] Manocchia A. Telehealth: enhancing care through technology. Rhode Island Medical Journal 2020;103(1):18–20.

[11] Mullen-Fortino M, Rising KL, Duckworth J, Gwynn V, Sites FD, Hollander JE. Presurgical assessment using telemedicine technology: impact on efficiency, effectiveness, and patient experience of care. Telemedicine Journal and e-Health 2019;25(2):137–42. https://doi.org/10.1089/tmj.2017.0133.

[12] Kinberg EC, Kirke DN, Trosman SJ. Modernizing the otolaryngology referral workflow: the impact of electronic consultation. The Laryngoscope 2021;131(6):E1792–6. https://doi.org/10.1002/lary.29333.

[13] Rozario N, Rozario D. Can machine learning optimize the efficiency of the operating room in the era of COVID-19? Canadian Journal of Surgery 2020;63(6):E527–9. https://doi.org/10.1503/cjs.016520.

[14] Clancy TR. Artificial intelligence and nursing: the future is now. The Journal of Nursing Administration 2020;50(3):125–7. https://doi.org/10.1097/NNA.0000000000000855.

[15] Winchester DE, Wokhlu A, Vilaro J, Bavry AA, Park K, Choi C, Panna M, Kaufmann M, McKillop M, Schmalfuss C. Electronic consults for improving specialty care access for veterans. American Journal of Managed Care 2019;25(5):250–3.

[16] Kyono T, Gilbert FJ, van der Schaar M. Improving workflow efficiency for mammography using machine learning. Journal of the American College of Radiology 2020;17(1 Pt A):56–63. https://doi.org/10.1016/j.jacr.2019.05.012.

[17] Croghan SM, Rohan P, Considine S, Salloum A, Smyth L, Ahmad I, Lynch TH, Manecksha RP. Time, cost and carbon-efficiency: a silver lining of COVID era virtual urology clinics? Annals of the Royal College of Surgeons of England 2021;103(8):599–603. https://doi.org/10.1308/rcsann.2021.0097. PMID: 34464571.

[18] Scheinker D, Hollingsworth M, Brody A, Phelps C, Bryant W, Pei F, Petersen K, Reddy A, Wall J. The design and evaluation of a novel algorithm for automated preference card optimization. Journal of the American Medical Informatics Association 2021;28(6):1088–97. https://doi.org/10.1093/jamia/ocaa275. PMID: 33497439.

[19] de Carvalho LSF, Gioppato S, Fernandez MD, Trindade BC, Silva JCQE, Miranda RGS, de Souza JRM, Nadruz W, Avila SEF, Sposito AC. Machine learning improves the identification of individuals with higher morbidity and avoidable health costs after acute coronary syndromes. Value in Health 2020;23(12):1570–9. https://doi.org/10.1016/j.jval.2020.08.2091. PMID: 33248512.

[20] Golding LP, Nicola GN. A business case for artificial intelligence tools: the currency of improved quality and reduced cost. Journal of the American College of Radiology 2019;16(9 Pt B):1357–61. https://doi.org/10.1016/j.jacr.2019.05.004. PMID: 31492415.

[21] Rahimi K. Digital health and the elusive quest for cost savings. Lancet Digit Health 2019;1(3):e108–9. https://doi.org/10.1016/S2589-7500(1930056-1. PMID: 33323258.

[22] Fritzen K, Basinska K, Rubio-Almanza M, Nicolucci A, Kennon B, Vergès B, Zakrzewska K, Schnell O. Pan-European economic analysis to identify cost savings for the health care systems as a result of integrating glucose monitoring based telemedical approaches into diabetes management. Journal of Diabetes Science and Technology 2019;13(6):1112–22. https://doi.org/10.1177/1932296819835172. PMID: 30917691.

[23] Soto-Varela A, Gayoso-Diz P, Faraldo-García A, Rossi-Izquierdo M, Vaamonde-Sánchez-Andrade I, Del-Río-Valeiras M, Lirola-Delgado A, Santos-Pérez S. Optimising costs in reducing rate of falls in older people with the improvement of balance by means of vestibular rehabilitation (ReFOVeRe study): a randomized controlled trial comparing computerised dynamic posturography vs mobile vibrotactile posturography system. BMC Geriatrics 2019;19(1):1. https://doi.org/10.1186/s12877-018-1019-5.

[24] Brossard PY, Minvielle E, Sicotte C. The path from big data analytics capabilities to value in hospitals: a scoping review. BMC Health Services Research 2022;22(1):134. https://doi.org/10.1186/s12913-021-07332-0.

[25] Rhoden PA, Bonilha H, Harvey J. Patient satisfaction of telemedicine remote patient monitoring: a systematic review. Telemedicine Journal and e-Health 2022;28(9):1332–41. https://doi.org/10.1089/tmj.2021.0434.

[26] Jayakumar P, Moore MG, Furlough KA, Uhler LM, Andrawis JP, Koenig KM, Aksan N, Rathouz PJ, Bozic KJ. Comparison of an artificial intelligence-enabled patient decision aid vs educational material on decision quality, shared decision-making, patient experience, and functional outcomes in adults with knee osteoarthritis: a randomized clinical trial. JAMA Network Open 2021;4(2):e2037107. https://doi.org/10.1001/jamanetworkopen.2020.37107.

[27] Schneider A, Kolrep H, Horn HP, Jordi C, Gierig S, Lange J. Understanding patient preferences for handheld autoinjectors versus wearable large-volume injectors. Expert Opinion on Drug Delivery 2023;20(2):273–83. https://doi.org/10.1080/17425247.2022.2162037.

[28] Tharion JG, Kale S. Patient satisfaction through an immersive experience using a mobile phone-based head-mounted display during arthroscopic knee surgery under spinal anesthesia: a randomized clinical trial. Anesthesia & Analgesia 2021;133(4):940–8

[29] Khanbhai M, Anyadi P, Symons J, Flott K, Darzi A, Mayer E. Applying natural language processing and machine learning techniques to patient experience feedback: a systematic review. BMJ Health Care Inform 2021;28(1):e100262. https://doi.org/10.1136/bmjhci-2020-100262.

[30] Ferrario A, Gloeckler S, Biller-Andorno N. AI knows best? Avoiding the traps of paternalism and other pitfalls of AI-based patient preference prediction. Journal of Medical Ethics 2023;49(3):185–6. https://doi.org/10.1136/jme-2023-108945.

[31] Kaidar-Person O, Antunes M, Cardoso JS, Ciani O, Cruz H, Di Micco R, Gentilini OD, Gonçalves T, Gouveia P, Heil J, Kabata P, Lopes D, Martinho M, Martins H, Mavioso C, Mika M, Montenegro H, Oliveira HP, Pfob A, Rotmensz N, Schinköthe T, Silva G, Tarricone R, Cardoso MJ, CINDERELLA Consortium. . Evaluating the ability of an artificial-intelligence cloud-based platform designed to provide information prior to locoregional therapy for breast cancer in improving patient's satisfaction with therapy: the CINDERELLA trial. PLoS One 2023;18(8):e0289365. https://doi.org/10.1371/journal.pone.0289365.

CHAPTER 35

Patient perspectives on digital health

Debra Maria Ruh
Ruh Global IMPACT, Rockville, VA, United States

Introduction—The patient perspective

Why patient perspectives matter

Patient perspectives are indeed crucial in the shift toward digital health, especially for vulnerable patients such as persons with disabilities and elders. Overall patient perspectives are essential to ensure that digital health and telehealth solutions are not only technologically advanced, but also human-centric, inclusive, and responsive to the diverse needs of all patients. By valuing all patient input and involving them in the design and implementation of these technologies, we can create a more accessible, inclusive, effective, and equitable healthcare system.

Let's explore how persons with disabilities encounter various barriers in the realm of digital health, highlighting the essential reasons for including disability perspectives in this field:

1. Inaccessible Digital Tools: Many digital health platforms, websites, and mobile applications are not designed with accessibility features. This can include issues such as nonoptimized screen readers, lack of keyboard navigation options, or insufficient contrast for those with visual impairments.
2. Limited Compatibility: Some individuals with disabilities may rely on specific assistive technologies or devices that may not be compatible with certain digital health systems. This compatibility gap can hinder their ability to access vital health information and services.
3. Complex User Interfaces: Complex and convoluted user interfaces can pose challenges for individuals with cognitive or learning disabilities. Simplifying interfaces and providing clear instructions can make digital health resources more accessible.
4. Communication Barriers: People with speech or hearing impairments may face difficulties in using digital health platforms that rely heavily on verbal communication, audio instructions, or lack sign language support.

Digital Health. https://doi.org/10.1016/B978-0-443-23901-4.00035-0

5. Data Privacy and Security: Ensuring data privacy and security in digital health is essential, but overly complex security measures can be challenging for individuals with certain disabilities, such as those with limited dexterity or who use assistive technology to input information.
6. Limited Content Representation: Digital health content may not always address the specific needs or concerns of individuals with certain disabilities. This can result in a lack of relevant information or guidance for managing their health effectively.
7. Awareness and Training: Healthcare providers and digital health developers may lack awareness and training in accessibility and disability-related issues, leading to unintentional barriers.
8. Cost and Affordability: Some assistive technologies or devices that could enhance access to digital health services may be costly, creating financial barriers for individuals with disabilities.
9. Stigmatization: There can be social stigma associated with disabilities, which may discourage individuals from seeking out digital health services or disclosing their needs and preferences to healthcare providers.
10. Regulatory Compliance: Ensuring that digital health platforms comply with disability-related regulations and standards can be a significant challenge for developers and organizations.

Including disability perspectives in digital health is essential to address these barriers comprehensively. It not only promotes equitable access to healthcare but also drives innovation in creating more inclusive and user-friendly digital health solutions that benefit everyone, regardless of their abilities or disabilities.

Here are several reasons why their input and feedback are essential:

Essential reasons for including disability perspectives in digital health

- **Accessibility**: Makes platforms compatible with assistive technologies.
- **Usability**: Reveals overlooked barriers and interface improvements.
- **Tailored Solutions**: Addresses the unique needs of diverse disabilities.
- **Empowerment**: Increases patient autonomy in managing conditions.
- **Care Gaps**: Highlights shortcomings in healthcare services.
- **Ethical Concerns**: Ensures rights and privacy are respected.
- **Quality Improvement**: Refines offerings based on feedback.
- **Policy Impact**: Informs inclusive healthcare regulations.

Overall, involving patients with disabilities in the shift toward digital health is essential to creating a more patient-centered and inclusive healthcare ecosystem. Their perspectives help shape solutions that better meet their needs and contribute to a more equitable healthcare system for everyone.

Digital health versus traditional in-person care

The transformative potential of digital health

Digital health is revolutionizing the healthcare landscape by providing numerous advantages over traditional in-person care. From enhanced accessibility to personalized treatments, this innovative approach offers a myriad of benefits for a diverse patient population.

Key benefits of digital health

- **Accessibility and Convenience**: Digital health eliminates geographical barriers, making healthcare accessible to everyone, especially those in remote or underserved areas.
- **Cost-Effectiveness**: By accommodating patients' schedules and offering remote consultations, digital health reduces costs.
- **Personalization**: Tailored treatment plans and continuous monitoring empower patients to take an active role in managing their health.
- **Communication and Collaboration**: Secure, real-time communication between patients and providers improves treatment adherence and outcomes.
- **Inclusivity**: Features such as multilingual support and accessibility settings cater to diverse needs, including those of patients with disabilities.
- **Health Education and Stigma Reduction**: Digital platforms offer educational resources for preventive care and can also help reduce the stigma associated with certain medical conditions.

Bridging the gap: Digital versus traditional care

While traditional in-person care remains indispensable for certain medical needs, digital health complements and amplifies these services. The convenience of digital tools enables flexible scheduling, reduced travel, and immediate care, creating a more efficient and effective healthcare ecosystem.

In-person medical care remains indispensable in several critical situations where digital healthcare cannot adequately replace the need for hands-on expertise and specialized equipment. Emergencies such as heart attacks and severe injuries demand immediate attention from healthcare professionals in a hospital setting. Physical examinations and diagnostics often rely on visual and tactile assessments, making in-person visits essential for accurate diagnoses and treatments. Surgeries, procedures, and complex interventions require controlled environments and the skilled hands of surgeons and medical staff, ensuring patient safety and optimal outcomes.

Furthermore, various medical procedures, including vaccinations, injections, and IV treatments, necessitate the expertise of healthcare professionals to administer them safely. Conditions such as pregnancy, obstetrics, and childbirth demand continuous monitoring and in-person care to ensure the well-being of both mother and child. In mental health emergencies, such as severe crises or suicidal ideation, immediate intervention by mental health professionals is vital, which cannot be achieved through digital means alone.

While digital healthcare offers convenience and accessibility for many healthcare needs, it complements rather than substitutes traditional in-person care. Both approaches are integral to a comprehensive healthcare system, ensuring patients receive the right level of care, whether it involves physical examinations, surgical interventions, or specialized treatments, to optimize health outcomes and well-being.

Conclusion

Digital health is not just an alternative but an enhancement to traditional healthcare systems. By broadening access, fostering patient empowerment, and ensuring equity, digital health is setting the stage for improved health outcomes across diverse patient populations.

Does the shifting aging of society's demographics impact digital health?

The shifting aging of society's demographics has a significant impact on digital health. As populations around the world continue to age, there is a growing demand for healthcare services and solutions that cater to the unique needs of older individuals. Digital health technologies play a crucial role in addressing these needs by providing remote monitoring, telehealth services, and tools for managing chronic conditions.

Furthermore, the adoption of digital health among older adults is increasing as they become more tech-savvy and comfortable with digital devices. This trend is reshaping the healthcare landscape, driving the development of user-friendly apps, wearable devices, and telemedicine platforms tailored to older users.

However, it's important to consider accessibility and inclusivity in digital health solutions to ensure that older individuals can fully benefit from these technologies. Addressing the challenges of usability, affordability, and privacy concerns for this demographic is crucial for the successful integration of digital health into an aging society. In summary, the aging demographics are not only impacting digital health but also shaping its evolution to better serve the needs of older populations.

Benefits of embracing an aging population

- **Community and Economy**: Experience, mentorship, and workforce contributions.
- **Social Impact**: Volunteering, cultural preservation, and social cohesion.
- **Innovation**: Market opportunities and enhanced creativity in the workforce.

Digital health advantages for aging society

- **Improved Access**: Telehealth and mobile apps.
- **Health Management**: Remote monitoring and chronic disease care.
- **Convenience**: Medication reminders and teleconsultations.
- **Social and Mental Well-being**: Virtual social activities and cognitive apps.
- **Specialized Features**: Accessibility for disabilities and caregiver support tools.

Embracing aging as a society has the potential to trigger a series of substantial societal transformations. First and foremost, healthcare would take center stage, with a heightened focus on preventive healthcare and the management of age-related health issues. Healthcare systems may reallocate resources toward geriatric care, and research into age-related diseases and conditions would garner increased attention, leading to advancements in elder care and overall health outcomes.

In parallel, there would be a growing demand for age-friendly housing and infrastructure, tailored to the needs of older adults. This would encompass everything from more accessible transportation options to housing designs that accommodate aging in place, as well as the development of public spaces that promote active aging and community engagement.

As society embraces aging, the need for robust social support systems for older adults will become evident. This would include the expansion of caregiving services, enhanced mental health support, and the creation of community programs aimed at combating social isolation and loneliness among seniors.

Moreover, encouraging intergenerational relationships would become a societal priority. Such a shift would foster mutual understanding and cooperation between different age groups, promoting a more cohesive and interconnected society.

Governments, too, would need to adapt public policies in response to changing demographics and the needs of an aging population. This might involve reforms in areas such as pensions, healthcare, and social services to ensure the well-being and security of older individuals.

Lastly, embracing aging could ignite innovation in products and services tailored to older adults, spanning technology, entertainment, and leisure activities. By acknowledging and valuing individuals at all stages of life, society would take a holistic approach toward fostering inclusivity, creating an age-friendly environment, and nurturing intergenerational bonds—a recipe for a more connected and harmonious society.

In summary, an inclusive approach to aging populations enriches society economically and culturally. Accessible digital health tools further empower them for healthier, more independent lives.

Current aging statistics (2022)

- Globally, the number of people aged 60 and older is expected to more than double by 2050, reaching 2.1 billion (Source: United Nations).
- In many developed countries, the proportion of the population aged 65 and older is already around 20% or higher (Source: World Bank).

Projected aging statistics (by 2050)

- The global median age is projected to increase from 31 years in 2020 to 36 years in 2050 (Source: United Nations).
- In some countries, the proportion of the population aged 65 and older is projected to exceed 30% by 2050 (Source: World Bank).

Benefits and obstacles of aging populations

Understanding the importance of catering to aging populations in digital health is vital because it allows healthcare providers and technology developers to create solutions that meet the unique needs of older individuals. As the elderly population grows, addressing their healthcare requirements becomes crucial for maintaining their well-being. It can benefit aging populations by promoting access to healthcare services, monitoring chronic conditions remotely, and facilitating early interventions. Additionally, working closely with aging individuals and integrating their perspectives into digital health solutions fosters user-centered design, ensuring that technology is user-friendly and tailored to their specific needs.

Digital health can be particularly advantageous for aging populations as it overcomes geographical and mobility barriers. It allows older individuals to access healthcare services from the comfort of their homes, reducing the need for strenuous travel. It also promotes regular check-ups and consultations, improving the management of chronic conditions and reducing the risk of complications.

However, several obstacles need to be addressed to fully harness the benefits of digital health for aging populations. These obstacles include issues related to digital literacy, access to technology, affordability, and concerns about data privacy and security. Bridging the digital divide among older adults and ensuring that telehealth services are affordable and user-friendly are essential steps toward maximizing the potential benefits of digital health for this demographic.

Let's explore the benefits and obstacles:

Benefits:

1. **Experience and Wisdom**: Older adults offer valuable knowledge in decision-making.
2. **Active and Productive Aging**: Many contribute to the workforce and economy.
3. **Intergenerational Support**: They often mentor and care for younger generations.
4. **Market Opportunities**: Creates business potential in sectors such as healthcare and leisure.

Obstacles:

1. **Healthcare Costs**: Aging populations can drive up national healthcare costs.
2. **Pension and Social Security**: Strains pension and social systems, needing reforms.
3. **Labor Market Challenges**: Older workers may face discrimination and employability issues.
4. **Dependency Ratios**: Fewer working-age people to support the growing older population.

It's important to note that perspectives on aging can vary widely based on cultural, economic, and social factors. Addressing the challenges and maximizing the benefits of an aging society requires a collaborative effort that involves all generations working together toward an inclusive and sustainable future.

Can the inclusion of diverse patients' perspectives help society shift to digital health?

Patient perspectives are indeed crucial in the shift toward digital health and telehealth, especially for vulnerable patients such as persons with disabilities. Aging and disabilities can present several challenges for digital health, making it crucial to address these issues to ensure inclusivity and equitable access to technology-driven healthcare. At the same time, the unique perspectives of aging populations and persons with disabilities can help create better global solutions that cater to a wider range of individuals, helping ensure that all patients have full access to digital health.

Obtaining diverse patient perspectives, including those of aging adults and people with disabilities, is crucial to ensure that digital health solutions are truly inclusive and effective for all individuals. Firstly, diverse perspectives contribute to the development of technology that caters to a wide range of user needs and preferences. By understanding the unique challenges and requirements of aging populations and individuals with disabilities, digital health developers can create more accessible, user-friendly, and accommodating platforms and applications.

Secondly, involving diverse patient perspectives helps in identifying potential biases and barriers within digital health systems. It enables the healthcare industry to proactively address issues related to accessibility, usability, and equity, ensuring that no one is left behind in the shift toward digital healthcare. By engaging with these populations, digital health can better meet the overarching goal of improving healthcare outcomes and enhancing the overall well-being of all patients, regardless of age or ability.

Challenges

- **Digital Literacy**: Limited tech experience hampers use among older and disabled people.
- **Physical Limitations**: Impairments affect traditional device use.
- **Cognitive Impairments**: Complex interfaces can be hard for those with memory or attention issues.
- **Visual/Hearing Loss**: Age-related sensory loss affects engagement.
- **Connectivity**: Poor internet in rural areas limits digital health adoption.

Creating better global solutions

- **Inclusive Design**: Involve diverse users in design for broader accessibility.
- **Accessibility Standards**: Use guidelines to make tools usable for all.
- **Assistive Tech**: Support devices such as screen readers for enhanced usability.
- **Personalization**: Offer tailored experiences to suit individual needs.
- **Education**: Boost digital literacy among older adults and disabled persons.
- **Telehealth**: Facilitates easier access for aging populations.
- **Policy Support**: Government incentives and regulations promote inclusivity.

By considering the challenges faced by aging individuals and persons with disabilities and actively involving them in the development process, digital health can become a more inclusive and supportive tool for healthcare globally. Embracing accessibility in digital health ensures that no one is left behind in benefiting from advancements in healthcare technology.

How can learning from the patient's perspective be of paramount importance in the digital health journey?

Gaining insights from the patient's perspective plays a pivotal role in the digital health journey for numerous compelling reasons. Patients, as the ultimate end-users, provide invaluable input that contributes to the development of user-friendly and highly effective solutions. Their perspectives serve as a compass, pointing out unmet needs and steering the creation of personalized, engaging, and impactful technologies. Furthermore, involving patients in the process empowers them to take an active role in managing their health, simultaneously mitigating biases and circumventing stigmatization in the design and implementation phases.

Patient feedback ensures continuous improvement and addresses ethical considerations such as data privacy. Ultimately, patient-centric outcomes lead to better healthcare experiences and an inclusive healthcare system.

Learning from the patient's perspective is of paramount importance in the digital health journey for several reasons:

- **User-Centric Design**: Makes tech user-friendly and relevant.
- **Unmet Needs**: Helps identify and fill healthcare gaps.
- **Engagement and Adoption**: Increases patient use and satisfaction.
- **Empowerment**: Encourages active health management.
- **Customization**: Allows for tailored healthcare solutions.
- **Bias and Stigma**: Ensures inclusivity and fairness.
- **Accessibility**: Fosters equitable healthcare access.
- **Improvement**: Enables ongoing tech refinement.
- **Ethics**: Upholds data privacy and builds trust.

In summary, incorporating patient perspectives in the digital health journey is crucial for user-centered design, addressing unmet needs, enhancing engagement, empowering patients, and tailoring solutions. Patient input ensures accessible, unbiased, and ethical digital health technologies that lead to better healthcare outcomes and a more patient-centric healthcare system.

Need for digital solutions

Accessible digital solutions hold a central position in tackling worldwide health issues, offering numerous advantages that encompass:

- **Global Reach**: Extends healthcare to remote and underserved areas.
- **Inclusivity**: Accessible designs benefit people with disabilities.
- **Enhanced Delivery**: Streamlines healthcare processes for better focus.
- **Remote Monitoring**: Enables telemedicine and remote patient care.
- **Patient Empowerment**: Increases access to data and self-management tools.
- **Preventive Care**: Uses analytics for early detection and prevention.
- **Data Insights**: Supports research and evidence-based practices.
- **Crisis Management**: Aids in emergency coordination and real-time info.
- **Continuous Improvement**: Drives healthcare innovation.

In conclusion, accessible digital solutions promote equity, inclusivity, and patient empowerment while enhancing healthcare delivery, remote care, preventive efforts, crisis management, and research. They ensure that advancements benefit everyone, leaving no one behind in the pursuit of better global health.

The power of accessible information

The power of accessible information in digital health cannot be overstated. Accessible information is a cornerstone of inclusive healthcare, and it plays a crucial role in transforming the patient experience and achieving equitable outcomes for all individuals, regardless of their abilities or backgrounds.

Transitioning from the need for digital solutions to the transformative power of accessible information in digital health, it becomes evident that the integration of technology and information accessibility is nothing short of revolutionary. By harnessing the capabilities of digital solutions, we have the opportunity to empower patients, bridge disparities, and enhance the overall healthcare experience for everyone.

This includes:

- **Patient Empowerment**: Clear information enables informed health decisions.
- **Informed Consent**: Accessibility aids shared decision-making in digital care.
- **Reduced Disparities**: Diverse formats and languages level the healthcare field.
- **Enhanced Communication**: Accessible info improves patient-provider dialog.
- **Digital Literacy**: Understandable digital health info boosts tech proficiency.
- **Improved Adherence**: Clear info enhances treatment compliance and outcomes.
- **Caregiver Support**: Accessible info benefits both patients and caregivers.
- **User-Centered Design**: Accessibility fosters inclusive digital platforms.
- **Legal and Ethics**: Accessible info meets legal and ethical standards.

In conclusion, accessible information in digital health is a powerful enabler of patient empowerment, shared decision-making, reduced disparities, enhanced communication, improved adherence, and better health outcomes. Embracing accessibility as a core principle drives innovation and inclusivity in the healthcare landscape, aligning with a societal commitment for many people around the world to advocate for accessibility and inclusion in all aspects of life, including digital health. Every person has the right to be meaningfully included.

Empowerment through knowledge: Accessing reliable health information

Empowerment through knowledge is a fundamental aspect of providing reliable health information to patients around the world. Access to accurate and trustworthy health information is a powerful tool that enables individuals to take charge of their health, make informed decisions, and actively participate in their healthcare journey. Here's why accessing reliable health information is so crucial:

- **Information Access**: Get reliable health resources.
- **Remote Consults**: Consult doctors from home.

- **Health Monitoring**: Track vitals and activities.
- **Personalized Plans**: Receive tailored care.
- **Self-Management**: Set and track health goals.
- **Data Empowerment**: Make decisions based on your data.
- **Preventive Care**: Utilize tools for prevention.
- **Communication**: Directly talk to healthcare providers.
- **Informed Consent**: Make educated medical choices.
- **Community Engagement**: Join research and support networks.

In summary, empowering patients around the world through reliable health information is an essential aspect of ensuring patient-centered, inclusive, and effective healthcare. Access to accurate knowledge enables patients to make informed decisions, advocate for their health, and actively participate in their care journey. By promoting global health literacy and fostering trust in the healthcare system, we can work toward a healthier and more empowered global community.

Digital health and our health

Digital health enhances healthcare by providing easy access to information, facilitating remote care, and improving communication between patients and providers. It offers personalized, efficient, and inclusive solutions for preventive care and early detection, leading to better health outcomes. These solutions include:

- **Information**: Access reliable health info.
- **Remote Consults**: Skip travel for healthcare.
- **Monitoring**: Track health metrics in real-time.
- **Personal Plans**: Get tailored care.
- **Self-Management**: Set and monitor goals.
- **Data Use**: Make informed decisions.
- **Prevention**: Utilize preventive tools.
- **Communication**: Speak directly to providers.
- **Consent**: Choose treatments knowingly.
- **Community**: Join research and support groups.

In conclusion, digital health presents you with the tools and resources to take control of your health journey actively. By accessing information, participating in digital health consultations, monitoring your health, and engaging in self-management, you can make informed decisions and play a proactive role in maintaining and improving your health. Embracing digital health aligns with the United Nations (UN) Sustainable Development Goals (SDGs) for inclusivity and empowerment, where individuals can harness technology to achieve better health outcomes and lead more fulfilling lives.

Digital tools for health monitoring

Digital health tools offer a robust way to self-monitor and track your health in real-time, from capturing vital signs to personalized health insights. Benefits include:

1. **Real-Time Data**: Monitor vital signs, activity, and more.
2. **Personalized Insights**: Receive tailored health advice.
3. **Chronic Disease Management**: Easily track and manage chronic conditions.
4. **Goal Tracking**: Set and monitor health objectives.
5. **Early Detection**: Identify health issues early.
6. **Healthy Habits**: Receive reminders and rewards to encourage positive behavior.
7. **Preventive Care**: Engage in preventive health practices.
8. **Remote Monitoring**: Enable healthcare providers to monitor you remotely.
9. **Record Management**: Maintain and access your electronic health records (EHRs).
10. **Increased Literacy**: Better understand your health data.

In summary, digital health tools offer a comprehensive solution for proactive health management, aligning with societal goals of accessibility and empowerment.

Simplifying medication and appointments

Digital health streamlines medication and appointment management with:

1. **Medication Reminders**: Get timely reminders for medication.
2. **Medication Tracking**: Monitor adherence to prescribed treatments.
3. **Interaction Alerts**: Receive alerts for potential medication interactions.
4. **Electronic Refills**: Refill prescriptions online.
5. **Appointment Scheduling**: Easily book or modify appointments.
6. **Telehealth**: Access healthcare from a distance.
7. **Access to Records**: View your health records online.
8. **Data Integration**: Connect health data from various devices.
9. **Provider Communication**: Message healthcare providers securely.
10. **Family Involvement**: Involve caregivers in healthcare management.

Overall, digital health offers a convenient and efficient way to manage healthcare tasks, enhancing medication safety and healthcare accessibility.

Centralizing personal health records

Digital health centralizes personal health records (PHRs), allowing:

1. **Comprehensive Information**: Consolidate all health data in one place.
2. **Care Coordination**: Facilitate seamless communication among healthcare providers.
3. **Patient-Centered Care**: Engage in your healthcare journey.
4. **Safety and Error Reduction**: Minimize the risk of medical errors.

5. **Efficient Telehealth**: Streamline telehealth consultations.
6. **Medication Management**: Track medication usage and interactions.
7. **Data Privacy**: Benefit from secure health information storage.
8. **Self-Advocacy**: Empower yourself to make informed decisions.
9. **Continuity of Care**: Access consistent healthcare across settings.
10. **Health Insights**: Analyze PHR data for preventive care.

In conclusion, digital health provides a secure, centralized hub for managing health information, promoting patient engagement, and safer healthcare outcomes.

Streamlining communication and collaboration in healthcare

Digital health and telemedicine improve communication and collaboration among patients and healthcare providers by providing:

1. **Remote Consults**: Access healthcare from anywhere, making it convenient and inclusive.
2. **Accessibility**: Overcome geographical limitations to healthcare access.
3. **Secure Messaging**: Enable direct, secure communication between patients and providers.
4. **Data Sharing**: Share health data for more accurate diagnoses and treatments.
5. **Patient Education**: Access educational resources for better health understanding.
6. **Joint Decision-Making**: Engage patients and providers in collaborative care.
7. **Care Coordination**: Centralize health data for better team collaboration.
8. **Fast Test Results**: Access medical reports quickly through digital platforms.
9. **Medication Alerts**: Receive reminders and alerts for medication management.
10. **Multidisciplinary Virtual Consults**: Consult multiple specialists virtually.

In summary, digital health fosters better patient-provider communication and collaboration, enabling a patient-centered and coordinated healthcare experience. These technologies align with society's goals of inclusivity and empowerment.

Navigating challenges and opportunities

Digital health and telemedicine offer valuable support to patients in navigating challenges and opportunities related to their health and interactions with medical professionals.

Here's how these technologies can help:

- **Reliable Information**: Stay informed on health matters.
- **Remote Consults**: Seek medical advice without visits.
- **Chronic Management**: Track and manage chronic conditions.

- **Tailored Plans**: Get personalized healthcare.
- **Self-Management**: Use apps for meds and symptoms.
- **Care Coordination**: Streamline communication among providers.
- **Mental Health**: Access counseling and therapy remotely.
- **Empowerment**: Make informed healthcare decisions.
- **Second Opinion**: Consult global specialists.
- **Data Insights**: Gain trends for early issue detection.
- **Virtual Support**: Join groups for shared experiences.
- **Accessibility**: Reach healthcare anywhere; ensure full access to all resources.

In conclusion, digital health offers a wide range of tools and services to support patients in navigating their health challenges and opportunities. From accessing reliable information and remote consultations to personalized care plans and mental health support, these technologies empower patients to take control of their health and foster collaborative relationships with medical professionals. Embracing digital health aligns with the world's vision of an inclusive and patient-centered healthcare ecosystem, where patients are equipped with the accessible resources they need to thrive and lead healthier lives.

Privacy and security concerns

Balancing trust and convenience digital health ensures privacy and trust through

In the realm of digital health, the careful consideration of privacy and security concerns stands as a paramount imperative. Achieving a delicate equilibrium between trust and convenience, digital health endeavors to uphold the fundamental values of privacy and reliability. This foundation of trust is essential in fostering patient confidence and engagement, as individuals must feel assured that their sensitive health data is safeguarded while benefiting from the convenience and innovation that digital technologies offer. This delicate balance is what enables digital health to revolutionize the healthcare landscape while maintaining the sanctity of personal information, ensuring a future where privacy and trust are inseparable from healthcare innovation.

For example:

- **Data Encryption**: Protects sensitive info.
- **Patient Consent**: Gives control over data sharing.
- **HIPAA Compliance**: Meets regulatory standards.
- **User Authentication**: Verifies patient identity securely.
- **Transparency**: Clarifies data handling practices.
- **Security Audits**: Addresses vulnerabilities.
- **Privacy Education**: Teaches best practices.
- **Privacy by Design**: Builds in privacy features.
- **Encrypted Channels**: Secures patient-provider talks.

- **Data Anonymization**: Preserves privacy in research.
- **Third-Party Assessments**: Validates security.
- **Accessible Support**: Easy reporting of privacy concerns.

In conclusion, digital health prioritizes patient privacy and security by implementing robust data protection measures, transparent practices, and compliance with regulations. This fosters trust in the system while ensuring that patients can conveniently access healthcare services and manage their health information confidently. Striking this balance between trust and convenience aligns with the world's vision of an inclusive and secure accessible healthcare environment, where patients can embrace digital health with confidence in their privacy and safety.

Overcoming technological barriers and digital literacy challenges

Digital health can play a significant role in overcoming technological barriers and digital literacy challenges for patients. Here's how digital health helps:

- **User-Friendly Design**: Easy navigation for all tech levels.
- **Health Literacy Programs**: Educational resources for effective tool use.
- **Assistive Tech**: Inclusive features for disabilities.
- **Multilingual Support**: Language options for diverse users.
- **Tech Support**: Help for technical issues.
- **Mobile Apps**: Intuitive, easy-to-use apps.
- **Telehealth Training**: Guides for using telehealth services.
- **Remote Monitoring Guidance**: Assistance in tracking health data.
- **In-Person Support**: Direct help for those struggling with digital literacy.
- **Engaging UX**: Interactive, exploratory interfaces.
- **Custom Support**: Tailored help for vulnerable groups.
- **Public Campaigns**: Awareness efforts to boost digital literacy.

By addressing technological barriers and offering support for digital literacy, digital health empowers patients to embrace technology confidently and use it as a valuable tool to manage their health effectively. Embracing digital health aligns with the world's vision of inclusivity and accessibility, where all patients can harness the benefits of technology to improve their health and well-being.

Advocating for access and equity in digital health

The pursuit of equity and inclusion in digital health is a critical mission for both moral and practical reasons:

- **Universal Access**: Ensuring digital health is accessible to all, irrespective of age, ability, or location, is foundational to its success.

- **Empowerment and Trust**: Focusing on equity fosters patient empowerment, improves health outcomes, and builds trust.
- **Information Equality**: The technology should facilitate informed choices and shared decision-making for all users.
- **Eliminating Barriers**: Advocacy and equity-focused design can make healthcare accessible to underserved and isolated communities.
- **Data Integrity and Security**: Addressing bias and prioritizing data privacy are essential for trustworthy and effective solutions.
- **Socio-Economic Impact**: Equitable digital health technologies have the potential to reduce healthcare disparities, improve overall societal health, and offer economic benefits.
- **Legal and Ethical Responsibility**: Fair and transparent digital health solutions are not just ethical imperatives but also legal necessities.

In summary, advocating for access, equity, and the removal of bias in digital health technologies is crucial for creating a healthcare landscape that is inclusive, effective, and sustainable. This aligns with the vision of a healthcare system where all individuals can lead healthier, more fulfilling lives through the ethical and equitable use of technology.

Ethical Responsibilities of healthcare providers and technology developers

Digital health can play a crucial role in supporting the ethical responsibilities of healthcare providers and technology developers. Here's how digital health can assist in upholding ethical standards:

- **Data Privacy**: Robust measures protect sensitive patient information.
- **Informed Consent**: Tools ensure patients understand and control data usage.
- **Transparency**: Platforms clarify how patient data is used and held accountable.
- **Bias Prevention**: Monitoring and audits aim for equitable treatment.
- **Patient-Centered**: Design empowers patient participation in care.
- **Education**: Platforms offer resources for informed health decisions.
- **Quality Monitoring**: Tools help evaluate and improve healthcare quality.
- **Ethics Training**: Modules raise ethical awareness among providers.
- **Risk Management**: Solutions identify and mitigate data and ethical risks.
- **Regulatory Compliance**: Supports adherence to privacy and ethical laws.

By integrating ethical considerations into the design, development, and implementation of digital health technologies, healthcare providers and technology developers can build trust, enhance patient engagement, and uphold ethical responsibilities in the delivery of healthcare services. Digital health has the potential to amplify ethical practices and ensure that technology is a force for good in healthcare, benefiting both patients and the healthcare ecosystem as a whole.

The importance of user experience and patient-centered design

User experience (UX), accessibility, and patient-centered design are crucial considerations in digital health for several reasons:

- **Engagement**: Positive UX boosts patient use of digital health tools.
- **Improved Outcomes**: Easy-to-use design leads to better health management.
- **Inclusivity**: Accessible tech serves diverse user needs, reducing disparities.
- **Empowerment**: User-friendly tools let patients actively manage their health.
- **Trust**: Well-designed platforms gain patient trust and confidence.
- **Compliance**: Intuitive design improves treatment adherence.
- **Safety**: Design minimizes user errors for safer healthcare.
- **Customization**: Tailored experiences enhance patient engagement.
- **Efficiency**: Streamlined UX aids healthcare provider workflows.
- **Continuous Improvement**: User feedback drives ongoing enhancements.

By prioritizing user experience, accessibility, and patient-centered design, digital health solutions can be more effective, inclusive, and impactful. These considerations ensure that technology serves as a supportive tool in patient care, fostering better communication, and engagement, and ultimately leading to improved health outcomes.

Societies expectations have changed

Society's expectations of our healthcare providers dramatically changed after COVID-19. What insights can we glean from the experience of being marginalized during the pandemic, and how might this inform your journey in the realm of digital health?

The COVID-19 pandemic brought about significant changes and challenges in the healthcare industry, leading to altered expectations from healthcare providers. From the perspective of being excluded or facing barriers during the pandemic, several insights can be gained, reflecting on the importance of digital health in the journey ahead:

- **Digital Health's Role**: Pandemic showcased the value of remote healthcare.
- **Equitable Access**: Digital health must be inclusive to bridge healthcare disparities.
- **Remote Monitoring**: Pandemic accelerated use for early detection and fewer hospital visits.
- **Data Privacy**: Increased digital health use underscores the need for robust data protection.
- **Interoperability**: Seamless data exchange became crucial during the pandemic.
- **Workforce Resilience**: Tech can ease provider burnout and improve collaboration.
- **Digital Literacy**: The pandemic highlighted the need for user training.
- **Adaptability**: Digital health offers agility to adapt to healthcare changes.

- **Human-Centric**: Technology should not replace empathy and patient relationships.

In conclusion, the pandemic underscored the significance of digital health in modern healthcare, particularly in ensuring accessibility, inclusivity, and resilience. As we move forward, the lessons learned from being excluded during the pandemic can shape a more patient-centered and equitable digital health journey that addresses the needs of all individuals and supports healthcare providers in delivering high-quality care.

Call to action: Amplifying patient voices in digital health

The time has come for a resounding call to action: the amplification of patient voices within the realm of digital health. Undoubtedly, the moment has arrived when we must unite in our collective effort to prioritize the inclusion of patients as the central focal point of healthcare.

Their invaluable perspectives, diverse needs, and unique experiences must serve as the guiding force behind the conception, design, and adoption of digital health technologies.

Here are some key actions that can help amplify patient voices in digital health:

- **Patient-Centered Design**: Involve patients in usability testing to meet their needs.
- **Advisory Boards**: Use panels for ongoing, diverse patient feedback.
- **Education**: Boost digital health literacy for patient empowerment.
- **Patient-Reported Outcomes**: Use PROs to measure digital health impact.
- **Health Advocacy**: Involve patient groups in policy and initiative shaping.
- **Diverse Research**: Include all patient groups to avoid bias.
- **Data Transparency**: Clearly explain patient data rights and usage.
- **Cocreated Resources**: Develop patient-led educational materials.
- **Accessible Design**: Advocate for usability by those with disabilities.
- **Feedback Loop**: Use patient feedback for continuous improvement.
- **Ethics**: Prioritize privacy, consent, and patient well-being.

By taking these actions, we can create a patient-centric digital health ecosystem that addresses the diverse needs and perspectives of patients. Amplifying patient voices in digital health leads to more relevant, inclusive, and effective solutions that ultimately contribute to improved healthcare outcomes and patient experiences (Fig. 35.1).

Digital health focuses on enhancing and improving accessibility and user experience for patients through technology. This includes user-friendly designs that simplify navigation of the technology, educational programs for patient training, assistive technology for those with disabilities, and language support for diverse linguistic needs. Furthermore, it involves reliable tech support, intuitive mobile apps, telehealth guides, remote monitoring

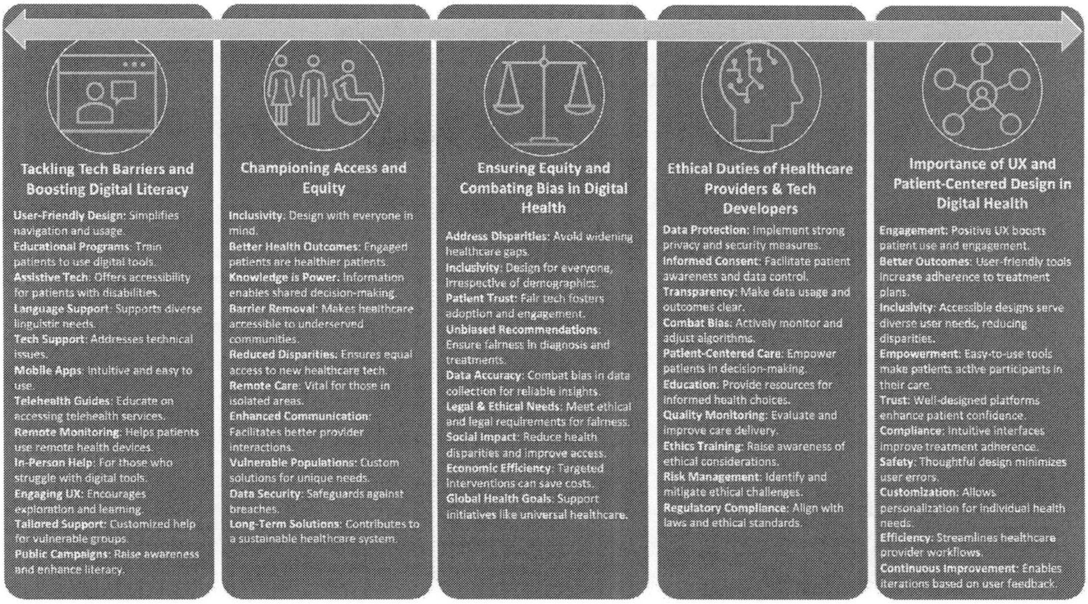

Figure 35.1
Aspects of amplifying patient voices in digital health. *Debra Ruh.*

devices, and in-person assistance for those who need help with digital literacy. Engaging user experiences (UX) and tailored support, particularly for vulnerable groups, should be emphasized with the overarching goal of overcoming technological barriers and empowering patients to confidently manage their health.

Advocating for access to equity is crucial. This encompasses inclusivity in design, patient engagement, shared-decision making by leveraging real-time information, and removing barriers to accessing care. Digital health seeks to reduce disparities, provide remote care for isolated areas, and improve provider-patient communication. This is further done by improving the infrastructure and prioritizing data security and patient privacy.

Lessons from COVID-19 on digital health

COVID-19 reshaped expectations for healthcare, emphasizing:

- **Telemedicine**: Bridged gaps during lockdowns, making healthcare more accessible.
- **Equitable Access**: Revealed disparities, calling for inclusive digital health designs.
- **Remote Monitoring**: Proved valuable for early detection and reducing hospital visits.
- **Data Privacy**: Raised concerns that must be addressed to build trust.
- **Interoperability**: Highlighted the need for seamless data exchange.

- **Workforce Resilience**: Digital tools can reduce provider burnout.
- **Digital Literacy**: Both providers and patients need better digital skills.
- **Adaptability**: Agility in healthcare tech is crucial.
- **Human-Centric Care**: Technology should not replace empathy and relationships.

Call to action: Amplify patient voices

To create a patient-centric digital health ecosystem, consider:

- **Patient-Centered Design**: Involve patients in design processes.
- **Advisory Boards**: Use these for ongoing feedback.
- **Education**: Boost digital health literacy among patients.
- **Patient-Reported Outcomes**: Use these as metrics for evaluation.
- **Advocacy**: Encourage patient groups to support digital health.
- **Diverse Research**: Include all patient demographics in studies.
- **Data Transparency**: Keep patients informed about data usage.
- **Cocreation**: Make resources with patient input.
- **Accessible Design**: Ensure usability for those with disabilities.
- **Feedback Loops**: Use patient feedback for continuous improvement.
- **Ethical Focus**: Prioritize data privacy, security, and consent.

By taking these steps, we can make digital health more relevant, inclusive, and effective, improving healthcare outcomes and experiences.

A hopeful future through patient perspectives

Embracing patient input in digital health is crucial for:

- **Patient-Centered Care**: Tailored solutions improve health outcomes.
- **Improved Access**: Inclusive tech can overcome healthcare barriers.
- **Patient Engagement**: Being heard promotes adherence and healthier living.
- **Tech Adoption**: User-friendly designs increase tech use.
- **Cost Reduction**: Efficiency cuts costs for providers and patients.
- **Ethical Innovation**: Patient input ensures data privacy and ethical design.
- **Real-World Validity**: Patient experiences target real-world challenges.
- **Trust Building**: Including patient perspectives fosters public trust.
- **Collaboration**: Encourages partnerships among stakeholders.
- **Social Responsibility**: Reflects a commitment to community well-being.

In summary, prioritizing patient voices is essential for a more equitable and efficient healthcare system. It advances better health outcomes and inclusivity for all.

Final thoughts

As society ages and healthcare demands increase, it is crucial to ensure inclusive medical systems for all individuals. This includes the elderly, people with disabilities, diverse cultural backgrounds, and underserved regions. Inclusive medical systems bridge health disparities, offer remote access, respect privacy, and prioritize user-centered design.

In conclusion, as the demand for healthcare continues to grow with an aging population and evolving healthcare needs, society must prioritize creating medical systems that work for all people.

Index

Note: "Page numbers followed by *f* indicate figures and *t* indicate tables."

Q

R

S

Made in the USA
Monee, IL
14 September 2026

63198312R00304